THE CONTINENTAL PHILOSOPHY READER

'An impressive array of introductory texts.'
                                    Paul Patton, *University of Sydney*

'The editors' introductions to the readings are outstanding as background and orientation to the selected authors' philosophical contribution and to the specific work chosen.'
                        Patrick L. Bourgeois, *Loyola University*, *New Orleans*

'A well balanced and judicious selection.'
                        Richard Beardsworth, *American University of Paris*

The Continental Philosophy Reader is the first comprehensive anthology of the classic statements of the major figures in twentieth-century European thought.

Continental European thinkers have produced some of the most revolutionary work in our century. Heidegger and Sartre, Habermas and Arendt, Gramsci, Foucault and Derrida – to name but a few of the theorists covered by this collection – continue to exert an influence that goes well beyond the discipline of philosophy. This reader features the key thinkers with their most widely read and representative statements, covering philosophical movements from the turn of the century to the present.

Each selection is introduced and placed in its historical and philosophical context by the editors, and the book's chronology usefully relates the European philosophical tradition to other aspects of twentieth-century thought and culture.

Ideal for introductory courses in Continental philosophy and contemporary European thought, *The Continental Philosophy Reader* provides a powerful introduction to some of our century's most influential intellectual movements.

Richard Kearney is Professor of Philosophy at University College Dublin and Visiting Professor at Boston College. He is the author of many books on European thought and culture including *Poetics of Imagining: From Husserl to Lyotard*, *The Wake of Imagination* and *Continental Philosophy in the Twentieth Century* (volume 8 in the Routledge History of Philosophy series), all of which are published by Routledge. He has also written a number of books on Ireland and its culture, and has published a novel, *Sam's Fall*. **Mara Rainwater** is Lecturer in Philosophy at University College Dublin. She is a contributor to the Routledge History of Philosophy series and has published in academic and professional journals.

Related titles from Routledge

THE CULTURAL STUDIES READER
Edited by Simon During

THE LESBIAN AND GAY STUDIES READER
Edited by Henry Abelove, Michèle Aina Barale, and David Halperin

THE NEW HISTORICISM READER
Edited by Harold Veeser

The
CONTINENTAL
PHILOSOPHY READER

Edited by

Richard Kearney and
Mara Rainwater

London and New York

For the little ones –
Simone, Sarah and Elijah

First published 1996
by Routledge
11 New Fetter Lane, London EC4P 4EE

Simultaneously published in the USA and Canada
by Routledge
29 West 35th Street, New York, NY 10001

Reprinted 1998

Selection and editorial matter
© 1996 Richard Kearney and Mara Rainwater

Typeset in Sabon by Florencetype Ltd,
Stoodleigh, Devon
Printed and bound in Great Britain by
Redwood Books, Trowbridge, Wiltshire

British Library Cataloguing in Publication Data
A catalogue record for this book is available from the British Library.

Library of Congress Cataloguing in Publication Data
A catalogue record for this book has been requested.

ISBN 0–415–09525–5 (hbk)
ISBN 0–415–09526–3 (pbk)

Contents

CONTENTS

CONTENTS

Acknowledgements

Many of the essays in this collection have been edited both for reasons of space and to make them more accessible for readers new to Continental philosophy. Permission given by the following copyright holders and authors is gratefully acknowledged.

Edmund Husserl, 'The Vienna Lecture', extracted from *The Crisis of European Sciences and Transcendental Philosophy: An Introduction to Phenomenological Philosophy* (Evanston, Ill.: Northwestern University Press, 1970). © 1970 Northwestern University Press.

Edmund Husserl, extracts from the entry on 'Phenomenology' in the *Encyclopaedia Britannica* of 1929, reprinted in *Journal of the British Society for Phenomenology* 2 (1971).

Martin Heidegger, extracts from the introduction to *Being and Time* and §40 on 'Anxiety', from *Being and Time*, trans. J. Macquarrie and E. Robinson (Oxford: Blackwell, 1967). © 1927 Hans Niemeyer Verlag © 1967 Blackwell Publishers.

Karl Jaspers, extracts from the introduction to *Philosophy of Existence* (Philadelphia, Pa.: University of Pennsylvania Press, 1971). © 1971 in the English translation by the Trustees of the University of Pennsylvania. English translation by Richard F. Grabau © 1971 Blackwell Publishers.

Jean-Paul Sartre, extracts from *Existentialism and Humanism*, trans. Philip Mairet (London: Methuen, 1948). © 1948 Methuen & Co.

Maurice Merleau-Ponty, extracts from the preface to *Phenomenology of Perception*, trans. Colin Smith (London: Routledge & Kegan Paul, 1962). © 1962 Routledge & Kegan Paul.

Simone de Beauvoir, extracts from the introduction to *The Second Sex*, trans. Deirdre Bair (London: Jonathan Cape, 1953) © 1953 Jonathan Cape.

ACKNOWLEDGEMENTS

Reprinted from Simone de Beauvoir, *The Second Sex* (Washington, DC: Smithsonian Institution Press), pages 13–29, by permission of the publisher. Copyright © 1949 Smithsonian Institution Press.

Hans-Georg Gadamer, 'The Universality of the Hermeneutical Problem', extracted from *Philosophical Hermeneutics*, trans. and ed. David E. Linge (Berkeley, University of California Press, 1976). © 1976 The Regents of the University of California.

Emmanuel Levinas, 'Ethics as First Philosophy', extracted from *The Levinas Reader*, ed. Sean Hand (Oxford: Blackwell, 1989). © 1989 Blackwell Publishers.

Paul Ricoeur, 'On Interpretation', from *Philosophy in France Today*, ed. Alan Montefiore (Cambridge: Cambridge University Press, 1983). © 1983 Cambridge University Press.

Rosa Luxemburg, 'Leninism or Marxism?', extracted from *'The Russian Revolution' and 'Leninism or Marxism?'* (Ann Arbor: University of Michigan Press, 1961). This material is in the public domain.

Georg Lukács, 'Reification and the Consciousness of the Proletariat', extracted from *History and Class Consciousness*, trans. Rodney Livingstone (London: Merlin Press, 1971). © 1971 Merlin Press.

Antonio Gramsci, 'The Intellectuals', extracted from *Selections from the Prison Notebooks of Antonio Gramsci*, ed. Quintin Hoare and Geoffrey Nowell-Smith (London: Lawrence & Wishart, 1971). © 1971 Lawrence & Wishart Ltd.

Max Horkheimer and Theodor W. Adorno, 'The Concept of Enlightenment', extracted from *Dialectic of Enlightenment*, trans. John Cumming (London: Verso/New Left Books, 1979). © 1979 Verso.

Walter Benjamin, 'Theses on the Philosophy of History', from *Illuminations* by Walter Benjamin, English translation by Harry Zohn, copyright © 1955 by Suhrkamp Verlag, Frankfurt a.M., English translation copyright © 1968 by Harcourt, Brace & Company, reprinted by permission of Harcourt, Brace and Company. 'Theses on the Philosophy of History' will be included in the forthcoming collected works of Walter Benjamin to be published by Harvard University Press.

Herbert Marcuse, 'Political Preface to *Eros and Civilization*', from *Eros and Civilization* by Herbert Marcuse, copyright © 1955, 1966 by Beacon Press. Reprinted by permission of Beacon Press © 1955 Routledge & Kegan Paul.

ACKNOWLEDGEMENTS

Jürgen Habermas, 'Philosophy as Stand-in and Interpreter', *from Moral Consciousness and Communicative Action*, trans. C. Lenhardt and S. Weber Nicholsen (Cambridge, Mass.: MIT Press, 1990) © 1990 MIT Press. *Moral Consciousness and Communicative Action*, trans. C. Lenhardt and S. Weber Nicholsen (Oxford: Polity, 1990) © 1990 Blackwell Publishers.

Louis Althusser, 'From *Capital* to Marx's Philosophy', extracted from *Reading Capital* by Louis Althusser and Etienne Balibar, trans. Ben Brewster (London: Verso/New Left Books, 1970) © Verso 1970.

'Preface: The Gap Between Past and Future', from *Between Past and Future* by Hannah Arendt. Copyright © 1954, 1956, 1957, 1958, 1960, 1961 by Hannah Arendt. Used by permission of Viking Penguin, a division of Penguin Books USA Inc.

Ferdinand de Saussure, extracts from the *Course in General Linguistics* (London: Duckworth, 1983) © 1983 Duckworth.

Claude Lévi-Strauss, 'The Structural Study of Myth', extracted from *Structural Anthropology*, trans. Claire Jacobson and Brooke Grundfest Schoepf (Allen Lane The Penguin Press, 1968), copyright © 1963 Basic Books, Inc. Selected excerpts from pages 206–230 from *Structural Anthropology* by Claude Lévi-Strauss. Copyright ©1963 by Basic Books, Inc. Copyright renewed. Reprinted by permission of BasicBooks, a division of HarperCollins Publishers, Inc.

Jacques Lacan, 'The Mirror Stage as Formative of the Function of the I as Revealed in Psychoanalytic Experience', from *Ecrits: A Selection*, trans. Alan Sheridan Smith (London: Tavistock, 1977) © Methuen & Co.

Michel Foucault, 'The Discourse on Language', reprinted from Michel Foucault, 'The Discourse on Language', *Social Science Information* (April 1971), pp. 7–30 © 1971 Sage Publications, by permission of Sage Publications Ltd.

Roland Barthes, 'Inaugural Lecture at the Collège de France, 7 January 1977', reprinted from *Oxford Literary Review* 4 (1) 1979. 'Inaugural Lecture, Collège de France', from *A Barthes Reader* by Roland Barthes. Translation by Richard Howard © 1979 by Hill and Wang, a division of Farrar, Straus and Giroux, Inc.

Julia Kristeva, 'Women's Time', reprinted from *Signs* 7 (1) (Autumn 1981), pp. 13–55, by permission of the University of Chicago © 1981 University of Chicago.

ACKNOWLEDGEMENTS

Gilles Deleuze, extracts from the 'Introduction to *What is Philosophy*', reprinted from *Critical Inquiry* 17 (Spring 1991) by permission of the University of Chicago © 1991 University of Chicago.

Luce Irigaray, 'The Power of Discourse and the Subordination of the Feminine', reprinted from *This Sex Which Is Not One* by Luce Irigaray, trans. Catherine Porter with Carolyn Burke, copyright © 1985 Cornell University. Used by permission of Cornell University Press. Originally published in French under the title *Ce Sex qui n'en est pas un* © 1977 Editions de Minuit.

Jean-François Lyotard, 'Answering the Question: What is Postmodernism?', reprinted from *The Postmodern Condition*, trans. Geoff Bennington and Brian Massumi (Manchester: Manchester University Press, 1984) © 1984 Manchester University Press. Jean-François Lyotard, *The Postmodern Condition*, trans. Geoff Bennington and Brian Massumi (Minneapolis, Minn.: University of Minnesota Press, 1984), pp. 71–82 © 1984 University of Minnesota Press.

Jacques Derrida, 'Différance', reprinted from *Speech and Phenomena, and Other Essays on Husserl's Theory of Signs*, trans. David B. Allison (Evanston, Ill.: Northwestern University Press, 1973) © Northwestern University Press.

Introduction

There has long been a need, we believe, for a *Reader* in twentieth-century Continental philosophy. It is hoped that a volume of this kind will prove helpful to a wide variety of readers, whether they be students in an academic environment or those with a more general interest in modern thought.

Our aim is to render more available the texts of Continental European thinkers who have produced some of the most revolutionary work in our century, in such areas as ontology, political theory, philosophy of history, epistemology, aesthetics and ethics. The enormous range and diversity of Continental philosophy has led to a demand for such an anthology of accessible sources. We hope our selection responds to that demand.

A number of reasons are often cited to account for the difficulties experienced by those seeking to familiarize themselves with the work of Continental thinkers. Certainly, language itself poses a problem for the English-speaker, since most of the original sources are non-anglophone. And even where a translation is available, the distinctive stylistic character of many of these philosophers often presents an additional challenge. Although some fine commentaries exist in English on particular Continental movements and philosophers, the need for direct contact with a primary source cannot be met by commentary alone. There comes a time to move beyond the discourse of the secondary – exegesis, interpretation, exposition, criticism – and return to the texts themselves!

We have tried to assemble representative samples of 'classic' statements by these philosophers. Hence, our inclusion, where possible, of keynote addresses (Barthes, Derrida, Lacan, Foucault, Husserl); seminal introductions (Heidegger, Jaspers, Merleau-Ponty, Arendt, Marcuse, de Beauvoir); and retrospective summaries (Ricoeur, Sartre, Luxemburg, Deleuze, Lyotard). In each of these, the philosophers offer self-presentations of their own thought.

A few words are also in order regarding the generic divisions, titles and selections that have been chosen in organizing this volume. Clearly, the three divisions are not mutually exclusive, and, in some cases, the inclusion of a particular thinker in one section rather than another could have been decided differently. For example, Althusser's reading of Marx could have been considered under 'Structuralism' or 'Marxism'. Certain texts of Sartre or Merleau-Ponty could have been included under the rubric of 'Critical Theory' as easily as 'Phenomenology'. And while much of the early Derrida might be perceived as belonging to the margins of phenomenology, he features here along with other postmodern and poststructuralist thinkers.

We have had to remind ourselves more than once of Spinoza's observation that *omnis determinatio est negatio*. We have faced the difficult task of limiting our number of selections in order to offer sufficiently substantial readings for those chosen. The optimal inclusions in our ideal list would, needless to say, have expanded this volume into a prohibitively large tome. Constraints of focus and space necessitated the omission of many significant thinkers – Marcel, Weil, Dufrenne, Camus, Breton, Ingarden, Patočka, Bloch, Baudrillard, Eco, Greimas, Vattimo, Le Doeuff and others. Our choices throughout have been influenced by a determination to conform to our main, though by no means exclusive, rubrics of selection: Phenomenology, Existentialism, Hermeneutics, Marxism, Critical Theory, Structuralism, Poststructuralism, Postmodernism and Deconstruction.

The short introductions provided at the beginning of our selections should help to contextualize the work within the more global designs of each thinker. Bibliographies of primary sources available in English follow each of these introductions, and we would also recommend the fuller commentaries and secondary bibliographies contained in the companion volume to this book, the *Routledge History of Philosophy, Vol. 8: Continental Philosophy in the Twentieth Century.*

Continental thought continues to attract new readers who seek political, moral, aesthetic and ontological relevance in philosophy. At times controversial, at times difficult, Continental thinkers remain at the centre of ardent contemporary debate. We have witnessed a growing demand for this *Reader* in our own seminars, and we hope that others will find it both useful and engaging.

Richard Kearney and Mara Rainwater
University College Dublin

PART I

From Phenomenology to Hermeneutics

1

Edmund Husserl

(1859–1938)

The year 1900 ushered in the twentieth century with the publication of two momentous volumes. The first of these, Freud's *The Interpretation of Dreams*, announced the birth of psychoanalysis as a discipline. The second, Edmund Husserl's *Logical Investigations*, heralded the beginning of the phenomenological movement that would radically transform and revitalize Continental philosophy for the next hundred years. Husserl's thought has influenced the work of such diverse figures as Heidegger, Sartre, Merleau-Ponty and Derrida, all of whom would recognize Husserl as the rock upon which modern phenomenology was initially founded.

Ironically, Husserl did not begin his academic career as a philosopher. He studied mathematics at Leipzig, Berlin and Vienna, finishing his doctorate in 1882 at the University of Vienna with a thesis entitled 'Contributions to the theory of the calculus of variations'. He then returned to Berlin in 1883 to work as the private assistant to Carl Weierstrass, an esteemed mentor whose work had originally interested Husserl in seeking the radical ground of mathematics. However, by 1884 Husserl had already made the decision to intensify his study of consciousness with Franz Brentano in Vienna. Brentano's seminars, which attracted the young Freud and Meinong as well as Husserl, were based on his *Psychology from an Empirical Standpoint* (1874), part of an extended project in 'descriptive psychology' that aimed at a clarification of 'mental phenomena' such as time-consciousness, intuitional presentations, 'intentionality' and judgements. It is important to note that the budding field of psychology was being formed at this time in a crucible of interdisciplinary studies that still included metaphysics and philosophy of mind. In fact, Husserl's casual exposure to philosophy at Leipzig had been guided by Wilhelm Wundt, then a professor of philosophy, who today is acknowledged as a founder of what has become the separate and autonomous discipline of psychology. As we shall see, Husserl developed and changed many of Brentano's key concepts, particularly 'intentionality', and brought them to bear on his own project.

With encouragement from Brentano, in 1886 Husserl continued his studies with Carl Stumpf at the University of Halle, submitting 'On the concept of number: psychological analyses' as his thesis for teaching certification (*Habilitationsschrift*) in 1887. This was later incorporated into a more comprehensive work, *Philosophy of Arithmetic* (1891), which was attacked by the logician Gottlob Frege for its 'psychologism'. In order to clarify his own position and defend himself against Frege's accusations, Husserl wrote *Logical Investigations* (1900–1), which appeared in two volumes. There Husserl presented a lengthy 'Prolegomena' to the work that rejected any notion of logical rationality that could be explained by individual, contingently subjective processes, a view which he asserted should rightly be censured as blatant 'psychologism'. Instead, he presented an account of logic and reason that championed its *a priori* validity, but nevertheless required an investigation into the operations of consciousness that made such validity possible in the first place. Husserl accepted neither the extreme 'idealist' position that mind totally creates world, nor the extreme 'empiricist' position that worldly 'impressions' are arbitrarily associated as mere contents filling a passive theatre of mind.

Husserl wanted to forge a middle path, a path that would reliably ground and confirm the objectivity of human consciousness as it relates to the one world we all share. He agreed with Kant that we *actively* engage our world in consciousness, but importantly disagreed with Kant's two-world metaphysics that banished 'true' reality to some unknowable, 'noumenal' realm beyond the reach of human consciousness. For Husserl, subjectivity and objectivity exist only in relation to one another, and he explicated the nature of this relationship as manifest in the 'intentionality' of consciousness directed toward its intentional object. This 'mode of intentionality' may vary and overlap considerably, in so far as I may perceive a tiger, imagine a tiger, remember a tiger, and so forth. In short, consciousness is always consciousness *of something*. Yet, Husserl must not be seen as endorsing an agenda of naive phenomenological realism that makes an ontological commitment equating an intentional object with some actually existing entity. *Logical Investigations* might have left room for doubt regarding his stance on this issue, but he unreservedly emphasized in *Ideas I: General Introduction to Pure Phenomenology* (1913) that his problematic arose in the domain of transcendental consciousness. Thus, he insisted that the task of phenomenology would be to describe the activity of intending consciousness (*noesis*), as well as the 'intentional correlate' or thing intended (*noema*) and found in consciousness. But how was this to be done?

The first requirement for any productive phenomenological inquiry, according to Husserl, is the 'bracketing' (*epoche*) of the 'natural attitude' we usually maintain towards the world around us. This natural attitude takes for granted that the objects of our attention actually exist in a world that extends beyond our immediate focus towards the periphery of a 'misty horizon' providing the continuous background environment we experience less attentively. As Husserl says in *Ideas* (§ 27), the world is *'for me simply there'*. A phenomenological *epoche* or 'reduction' must lead us back to a neutral stance, whereby we neither affirm nor deny the existential status or empirical facts about entities, including oneself, in the world. Only then can consciousness be explored without prejudice. In this way, Husserl hoped to reveal the truly 'eidetic' or universal structures of consciousness that guarantee the certainty required for scientific research of all kinds. He thus saw his goals as strongly epistemological, an orientation that he expressed in his famous article for the journal *Logos*, 'Philosophy as a rigorous science' (1910).

Husserl readily agreed that he had invested in a 'transcendental' philosophy that postulated a rule-governed structure of mind, organizing and limiting the possible ways we can humanly experience the world. However, he denied that this model was solipsistic or isolated, a critique of the sort that could be levelled at Descartes' *cogito*. In his later writings, such as *Formal and Transcendental Logic* (1929), *Cartesian Meditations* (1931) and *The Crisis of European Sciences and Transcendental Phenomenology* (1938), Husserl especially emphasized the intersubjectivity rooted in the 'life-world'. He also moved from a relatively static to a more 'genetic' theory of constitution which acknowledged the role of sedimentation in active and passive syntheses. That is to say, our intentional activity is far from eternally virginal consciousness, somehow untouched by memory of prior experience. On the contrary, we remain always indebted to temporal horizons that precede and inform all intentional activities of consciousness whatsoever. Human history thereby acquires a significance in the later Husserl that cannot be circumvented, even by science.

Husserl's academic career was long and fruitful. He taught at the University of Halle (1887–1901), Göttingen University (1901–16) and Freiburg University (1916–28), where he remained Emeritus Professor after his retirement (1928–38). Although Husserl published many significant works during his life, a vast amount of material (40,000 pages) still remained unpublished in manuscript format at the time of his death. Indeed, it was highly probable that Hitler's National Socialists would use Husserl's Jewish heritage as an excuse to destroy the material he would leave behind as his *Nachlass*. Fortunately, H. L. Van Breda, a Belgian priest, recognized the danger and transported these manuscripts to the University of Louvain in Belgium, today the site of the Husserl Archives. A vibrant tradition of Husserl scholarship continues at Louvain, where the critical edition of *Husserliana* increases each year.

Of the two selections presented here, *Phenomenology* is drawn from Husserl's article for the *Encyclopaedia Britannica*, obviously an attempt to distil, in his own words, what he had been trying to accomplish for over twenty-five years. The other selection is from the first Appendix to *The Crisis of European Sciences and Transcendental Phenomenology*, first published posthumously in 1938, which sets forth the views of the later

Husserl as Europe prepared for its own destruction. Husserl did not survive to see the worst. He died on 27 April 1938.

SELECT BIBLIOGRAPHY OF HUSSERL'S WORKS IN ENGLISH

'Phenomenology', *Encyclopaedia Britannica*, vol. 17, 1929.

Cartesian Meditations, The Hague: Nijhoff, 1960.

Ideas: General Introduction in Pure Phenomenology, New York: Collier, 1962.

The Phenomenology of Internal Time Consciousness, The Hague: Nijhoff, 1964.

Phenomenology and the Crisis of Philosophy (*Philosophy as a Rigorous Science* and *Philosophy and the Crisis of European Man*), New York: Harper & Row, 1965.

Formal and Transcendental Logic, The Hague: Nijhoff, 1969.

The Crisis of European Sciences and Transcendental Phenomenology (includes Appendix with 'The origin of geometry'), Evanston, Ill.: Northwestern University Press, 1970.

Logical Investigations, Atlantic Highlands, N.J.: Humanities Press, 1970.

Experience and Judgement, Evanston, Ill.: Northwestern University Press, 1973.

The Idea of Phenomenology, The Hague: Nijhoff, 1973.

The Vienna Lecture

IN THIS LECTURE I shall venture the attempt to find new interest in the frequently treated theme of the European crisis by developing the philosophical-historical idea (or the teleological sense) of European humanity. As I exhibit, in the process, the essential function that philosophy and its branches, our sciences, have to exercise within that sense, the European crisis will also receive a new elucidation. . . .

I am certain that the European crisis has its roots in a misguided rationalism. But we must not take this to mean that rationality as such is evil or that it is of only subordinate significance for mankind's existence as a whole. Rationality, in that high and genuine sense of which alone we are speaking, the primordial Greek sense which in the classical period of Greek philosophy had become an ideal, still requires, to be sure, much clarification through self-reflection; but it is called in its mature form to guide [our] development. On the other hand we readily admit (and German Idealism preceded us long ago in this insight) that the stage of development of *ratio* represented by the rationalism of the Age of Enlightenment was a mistake, though certainly an understandable one. . . .

[handwritten margin note: ratio `à la grèce]

[handwritten margin note: rationalism as a mistake]

We must certainly distinguish between philosophy as a historical fact at a given time and philosophy as idea, as the idea of an infinite task. Any philosophy that exists at a given historical time is a more or less successful attempt to realize the guiding idea of the infinity and at the same time even the totality of truths. Practical ideals – namely, ideals discerned as eternal poles of which one cannot lose sight throughout one's whole life without compunction, without being untrue to oneself and thus becoming unhappy – are by no means always clearly and determinately discerned; they are anticipated in ambiguous generality. Determinateness results only when one concretely sets to work and succeeds, at least in a relative way. There is the constant threat of succumbing to one-sidedness and to premature satisfaction, which take their revenge in subsequent contradictions. Hence the contrast between the great [common] claims of the philosophical systems [and the fact that] they are nevertheless incompatible with one another. Also, there is the necessity – and at the same time the danger – of specialization.

In this way, a one-sided rationality can certainly become an evil. One can also say: it belongs to the essence of reason that the philosophers at first understand and labor at their task in an absolutely necessary one-sided way. Actually there is nothing perverse in this; it is not an error;

A lecture presented before the Vienna Cultural Society on 7 May and 10 May 1935 (i.e. six months before the Prague lecture, on which the *Crisis* is based) with the original title 'Philosophy in the Crisis of European Mankind'. From *The Crisis of European Sciences and Transcendental Philosophy: An Introduction to Phenomenological Philosophy*, Evanston, Ill.: Northwestern University Press, 1970.

rather, as we said, the straight and necessary path they must take allows them to see only one side of the task, at first without noticing that the whole infinite task of theoretically knowing the totality of what is has other sides as well. If inadequacy announces itself through obscurities and contradictions, this motivates the beginning of a universal reflection. Thus the philosopher must always devote himself to mastering the true and full sense of philosophy, the totality of its horizons of infinity. No line of knowledge, no single truth may be absolutized and isolated. Only through this highest form of self-consciousness, which itself becomes one of the branches of the infinite task, can philosophy fulfill its function of putting itself, and thereby a genuine humanity, on the road [to realization]. [The awareness] that this is the case itself belongs to the domain of philosophical knowledge at the level of highest self-reflection. Only through this constant reflexivity is a philosophy universal knowledge.

I said that the way of philosophy passes through naïveté. This is the place for the criticism offered by the irrationalism that is so highly esteemed [today], or rather the place to unmask the naïveté of that rationalism which is taken for philosophical rationality as such, which is admittedly characteristic of the philosophy of the whole modern period since the Renaissance and which takes itself to be the true, i.e., universal, rationalism. In this naïveté, then, unavoidable as a beginning stage, are caught all the sciences whose beginnings were already developed in antiquity. To put it more precisely, the most general title for this naïveté is *objectivism*, taking the form of the various types of naturalism, of the naturalization of the spirit. Old and new philosophies were and remain naïvely objectivist. In fairness we must add, though, that the German Idealism proceeding from Kant was passionately concerned with overcoming this naïveté, which had already become very troublesome, though it was unable to attain the higher stage of reflexivity which is decisive for the new form of philosophy and of European humanity. . . .

Natural man (let us consider him as man in the prephilosophical period) is directed towards the world in all his concerns and activities. The field of his life and his work is the surrounding world spread out spatiotemporally around him, of which he counts himself a part. This remains the case [even] in the theoretical attitude, which at first can be nothing other than that of the nonparticipating spectator of the world, whereby the world loses its mythical character. Philosophy sees in the world the universe of what is, and the world becomes the objective world as opposed to representations of the world, those which vary according to nation or individual subject; thus truth becomes objective truth. In this way philosophy begins as cosmology; it is first – as it were, obviously – directed in its theoretical interest toward corporeal nature, since, after all, everything given in space-time has in any case, at least at its basis, the existential formula of corporeity. Men and animals are not merely bodies, but in the orientation toward the surrounding world they appear as something with bodily existence and thus as realities ordered within universal space-time. In this sense all psychic occurrences, those of the particular ego, such as experiencing, thinking, willing, have a certain objectivity. The life of the community, that of families, peoples, etc., then seems to be resolved into that of particular individuals as psychophysical objects; the spiritual interrelation of psychophysical causality lacks a purely spiritual continuity; physical nature is everywhere involved.

The historical course of development is prefigured in a determined way by this attitude toward the surrounding world. Even the most fleeting glance at the corporeity to be found in the surrounding world shows that nature is a homogeneous, totally interrelated whole, a world by itself, so to speak, encompassed by homogeneous space-time, divided into particular things, all being alike as *res extensae* and determining one another causally. Quite rapidly, a first and great step of discovery is taken, namely, the overcoming of the finitude of nature already conceived as an objective in-itself, a finitude in spite of its open endlessness. Infinity is discovered, first in the form of the idealization of magnitudes, of measures, of numbers, figures, straight lines, poles, surfaces, etc. Nature, space, time, become extendable *idealiter* to infinity and divisible *idealiter* to infinity. From the art of surveying comes geometry, from the art of numbers arithmetic, from everyday mechanics mathematical mechanics, etc. Now without its being advanced explicitly as a hypothesis, intuitively given nature and world are transformed into a mathematical world, the world of the mathematical natural sciences. Antiquity led the way: in its mathematics was accomplished the first discovery of both infinite ideals and infinite tasks. This becomes for all later times the guiding star of the sciences.

What effect did the intoxicating success of this discovery of physical infinity have on the scientific mastery of the spiritual sphere? In the attitude directed toward the surrounding world, the constantly objectivistic attitude, everything spiritual appeared as if it were [simply] spread over [the surface of] physical bodies. Thus the application [to it] of the natural-scientific way of thinking seemed the obvious thing to do. Hence we find at the very beginnings [of philosophy] the materialism and determinism of Democritus. But the greatest spirits have recoiled from this and also from any sort of psychophysics in the more modern style. Since Socrates, man has become a theme in his specifically human qualities, as a person, man within the spiritual life of the community. Man still has a place within the order of the objective world; but for Plato and Aristotle this world becomes a great theme [in its own right]. Here a remarkable split makes itself felt; the human belongs to the sphere of objective facts, but as persons, as egos, men have goals, ends, norms given by the tradition, norms of truth – eternal norms. Though the development weakened in antiquity, it was nevertheless not lost. Let us make the leap to the so-called modern period. With a burning enthusiasm the infinite task of a mathematical knowledge of nature and of knowledge of the world in general is taken up. The immense successes in the knowledge of nature are now supposed to be shared by the knowledge of the spirit. Reason has demonstrated its force in relation to nature. 'Just as the sun is the one all-illuminating and warming sun, so reason is also the one reason' (Descartes). The method of natural science must also disclose the secrets of the spirit. The spirit is real, objectively in the world, and is founded as such on the living body. Thus the world-view immediately and dominantly assumes the form of a dualistic, and specifically a psychophysical, world-view. One causality, simply split into two sectors, encompasses the one world; the sense of rational explanation is everywhere the same, yet in such a way that all explanation of the spirit, if it is to be the sole and thus universal philosophical explanation, leads back to the physical. There can be no pure and self-enclosed explanatory inquiry into the spirit, a psychology or theory of spirit turned inward, extending from the ego, the psychic sphere of self-experience, to the alien psyche; the external path, the path of physics and chemistry, must be taken. All the beloved expressions about the community spirit, the will of the people, the ideal and political goals of nations, etc., are so much romanticism and mythology, arising out of a transposition by analogy of concepts that have a genuine meaning only in the sphere of individual persons. Spiritual being is fragmentary. To the question concerning the source of all our difficulties we must now reply: this objectivism, or this psychophysical world-view, in spite of its apparent obviousness, is naïvely one-sided and has constantly failed to be understood as such. The reality of the spirit as a supposed real annex to bodies, its supposed spatiotemporal being within nature, is an absurdity.

What we must do, however, in connection with our problem of the crisis, is to show how it happens that the 'modern age', which has been so proud for centuries of its theoretical and practical successes, finally becomes involved in a growing dissatisfaction, indeed must view its situation as one of distress. In all the sciences distress is felt, ultimately as a distress concerning method. But our European distress, though it is not understood, concerns very many people.

These are, throughout, problems which arise from the naïveté through which objectivist science takes what it calls the objective world for the universe of all that is, without noticing that no objective science can do justice to the [very] subjectivity which accomplishes science. Someone who is raised on natural science takes it for granted that everything merely subjective must be excluded and that the natural-scientific method, exhibiting itself in subjective manners of representation, determines objectively. Thus he seeks what is objectively true even for the psychic. Here it is immediately assumed that the subjective that has been excluded by the physicist is to be investigated as the psychic in psychology, and then naturally in psychophysical psychology. But the researcher of nature does not make clear to himself that the constant fundament of his – after all subjective – work of thought is the surrounding life-world; it is always presupposed as the ground, as the field of work upon which alone his questions, his methods of thought, make sense. Where is that huge piece of method subjected to critique and clarification [– that method] that leads from the intuitively given surrounding world to the idealization of mathematics and to the interpretation of these idealizations as objective being? Einstein's revolutionary innovations concern the formulae through which the idealized and naïvely objectified *physis* is dealt with. But how formulae in general, how mathematical objectification in general, receive meaning on the foundation of life and the intuitively given surrounding world – of this we learn nothing; and thus Einstein does not reform the space and time in which our vital life runs its course.

Mathematical natural science is a wonderful technique for making inductions with an efficiency, a degree of probability, a precision, and a computability that were simply unimaginable in earlier times. As an accomplishment it is a triumph of the human spirit. As for the rationality of its methods and theories, however, it is a thoroughly relative one. It even presupposes a fundamental approach that is itself totally lacking in rationality. Since the intuitively given surrounding world, this merely subjective realm, is forgotten in scientific investigation, the working subject is himself forgotten; the scientist does not become a subject of investigation. (Accordingly, from this standpoint, the rationality of the exact sciences is of a piece with the rationality of the Egyptian pyramids.)

To be sure, since Kant we have an epistemology in its own right, and on the other hand there is psychology, which, with its claims to natural-scientific exactness, seeks to be the universal fundamental science of the spirit. But our hope for true rationality, i.e., for true insight, is disappointed here as elsewhere. The psychologists do not notice at all that even they do not approach, in their subject matter, themselves as accomplishing scientists and their surrounding life-world. They do not notice that they necessarily presuppose themselves in advance as communalized men in their surrounding world and their historical time, even by the very fact that they seek to attain truth-in-itself, as truth valid for anyone at all. Because of its objectivism psychology is completely unable to obtain as its subject matter the soul in its own essential sense, which is, after all, the ego that acts and suffers. It may objectify and deal inductively with valuative experience, willing experience, as connected with bodily life. But can it do this with ends, values, norms? Can it take reason as its subject matter, perhaps as a 'disposition'? What is completely overlooked is the fact that objectivism, as the genuine accomplishment of an investigator oriented toward true norms, presupposes precisely those norms and that objectivism thus is not meant to be based on facts, since facts are thereby already meant as truths rather than mere opinion. Of course, some sense the difficulties involved here; and so the battle over psychologism breaks out. But the repudiation of a psychological grounding of norms, especially of norms for truth-in-itself, accomplishes nothing. The need for a reform of the whole of modern psychology is felt more and more on all sides, but it is not yet understood that it has failed because of its objectivism, that it does not at all attain the proper essence of the spirit, that its isolation of the objectively conceived soul and its psychophysical reinterpretation of being-in-community are a mistake. To be sure, it has not been without results, and it has revealed many, even practically valuable, empirical rules. But it is not a true psychology, any more than statistics about morals, with their no less valuable knowledge, constitute a moral science.

But everywhere, in our time, the burning need for an understanding of the spirit announces itself; and lack of clarity about the methodical and material relation between the natural sciences and the humanistic disciplines has become almost unbearable. Dilthey, one of the greatest humanists, devoted the energies of his whole life to a clarification of the relation between nature and spirit, to a clarification of the accomplishment of psychophysical psychology, which, as he thought, needed to be complemented by a new descriptive, classifying psychology. Efforts by Windelband and Rickert have unfortunately not produced the desired insights. Like all the others, they remain caught up in objectivism; and this is especially true of the new reformers in psychology, who think that the fault lies entirely in the long-dominant prejudice of atomism and that a new era has dawned with holistic psychology. But the situation can never improve so long as the objectivism arising out of a natural attitude toward the surrounding world is not seen through in its naïveté and so long as the recognition has not emerged that the dualistic view of the world, in which nature and spirit are to count as realities in a similar sense, though one is built on the other causally, is a mistake. In all seriousness, I think that an objective science of the spirit, an objective theory of the soul – objective in the sense that it attributes to souls, to personal communities, inexistence in the forms of space-time – has never existed and will never exist.

The spirit, and indeed only the spirit, exists in itself and for itself, is self-sufficient; and in its self-sufficiency, and only in this way, it can be treated truly rationally, truly and from the ground up scientifically. As for nature, however, in its natural-scientific truth, it is only apparently self-sufficient and can only apparently be brought by itself to rational knowledge in the natural sciences. For true nature in the sense of natural science is a product of the spirit that investigates nature and thus presupposes the science of the spirit. The spirit is by its essence capable of practicing self-knowledge, and as scientific spirit it is capable of practicing scientific self-knowledge, and this in an iterative way. Only in the knowledge belonging purely to the science of the spirit is the scientist not open to the objection that his own accomplishment conceals itself. Accordingly, it is a mistake for the humanistic disciplines to struggle with the natural sciences for equal rights. As soon as they concede to the latter their objectivity as self-sufficiency, they themselves fall prey to objectivism. But as they are now developed in their manifold disciplines, they lack the ultimate, true rationality made possible by the spiritual world-view. Precisely this lack of a genuine rationality on all sides is the source of man's now unbearable lack of clarity about his own existence and his infinite tasks. These are inseparably united in one task: *Only when the spirit returns from its naïve external orientation to itself, and remains with itself and purely with itself, can it be sufficient unto itself.*

But how did a beginning of such self-reflection occur? A beginning was not possible so long as sensationalism, or better, data-psychologism, the psychology of the *tabula rasa*, commanded the field. Only when Brentano made the demand for psychology as a science of intentional experiences was an impulse given that could lead further, although Brentano himself had not yet overcome objectivism and psychological naturalism. The development of an actual method for grasping the fundamental essence of the spirit in its intentionalities, and for constructing from there an analysis of the spirit that is consistent *in infinitum*, led to transcendental phenomenology. It overcomes naturalistic objectivism and every sort of objectivism in the only possible way, namely, through the fact that he who philosophizes proceeds from his own ego, and this purely as the performer of all his validities, of which he becomes the purely theoretical spectator. In this attitude it is possible to construct an absolutely self-sufficient science of the spirit in the form of consistently coming to terms with oneself and with the world as spiritual accomplishment. Here the spirit is not in or alongside nature; rather, nature is itself drawn into the spiritual sphere. Also, the ego is then no longer an isolated thing alongside other such things in a pregiven world; in general, the serious mutual exteriority of ego-persons, their being alongside one another, ceases in favor of an inward being-for-one-another and mutual interpenetration. . . .

I hope to have shown. . . that the old rationalism, which was an absurd naturalism incapable of grasping at all the spiritual problems that immediately concern us, is not being revived here. The *ratio* presently under discussion is nothing other than the spirit's truly universal and truly radical coming to terms with itself in the form of universal, responsible science, in which a completely new mode of scientific discipline is set in motion where all conceivable questions – questions of being and questions of norm, questions of what is called 'existence' [*Existenz*] – find their place. It is my conviction that intentional phenomenology has made of the spirit *qua* spirit for the first time a field of systematic experience and science and has thus brought about the total reorientation of the task of knowledge. The universality of the absolute spirit surrounds everything that exists with an absolute historicity, to which nature is subordinated as a spiritual structure. Intentional phenomenology, and specifically transcendental phenomenology, was first to see the light through its point of departure and its methods. Only through it do we understand, and from the most profound reasons, what naturalistic objectivism is and understand in particular that psychology, because of its naturalism, had to miss entirely the accomplishment, the radical and genuine problem, of the life of the spirit. . . .

The 'crisis of European existence', talked about so much today and documented in innumerable symptoms of the breakdown of life, is not an obscure fate, an impenetrable destiny; rather, it becomes understandable and transparent against the background of the *teleology of European history* that can be discovered philosophically. The condition for this understanding, however, is that the phenomenon 'Europe' be grasped in its central, essential nucleus. In order to be able to comprehend the disarray of the present 'crisis', we had to work out the *concept of Europe as the historical teleology of the infinite goals of reason*; we had to show how the European 'world' was born out of ideas of reason, i.e., out of the spirit of philosophy. The 'crisis' could then become distinguishable as the *apparent failure of rationalism*. The reason for the failure of a rational culture, however, as we said, lies not in the essence of rationalism itself but solely in its being rendered superficial, in its entanglement in 'naturalism' and 'objectivism'.

There are only two escapes from the crisis of European existence: the downfall of Europe in its estrangement from its own rational sense of life, its fall into hostility toward the spirit and into barbarity; or the rebirth of Europe from the spirit of philosophy through a heroism of reason that overcomes naturalism once and for all. Europe's greatest danger is weariness. If we struggle against this greatest of all dangers as 'good Europeans' with the sort of courage that does not fear even an infinite struggle, then out of the destructive blaze of lack of faith, the smoldering fire of despair over the West's mission for humanity, the ashes of great weariness, will rise up the phoenix of a new life-inwardness and spiritualization as the pledge of a great and distant future for man: for the spirit alone is immortal.

Phenomenology

INTRODUCTION

THE TERM 'PHENOMENOLOGY' designates two things: a new kind of descriptive method which made a breakthrough in philosophy at the turn of the century, and an *a priori* science derived from it; a science which is intended to supply the basic instrument (*Organon*) for a rigorously scientific philosophy and, in its consequent application, to make possible a methodical reform of all the sciences.

The Purely Psychical in Self-experience and Community Experience. The Universal Description of Intentional Experiences

... The first thing that is necessary is a clarification of what is peculiar to experience, and especially to the pure experience of the psychical – and specifically the purely psychical that experience reveals, which is to become the theme of a pure psychology. It is natural and appropriate that precedence will be accorded to the most immediate types of experience, which in each case reveal to us our own psychic being.

Focusing our experiencing gaze on our own psychic life necessarily takes place as reflection, as a turning about of a glance which had previously been directed elsewhere. Every experience can be subject to such reflection, as can indeed every manner in which we occupy ourselves with any real or ideal objects – for instance, thinking, or in the modes of feeling and will, valuing and striving. So when we are fully engaged in conscious activity, we focus exclusively on the specific thing, thoughts, values, goals, or means involved, but not on the psychical experience as such, in which these things are known as such. Only reflection reveals this to us. Through reflection, instead of grasping simply the matter straight-out – the values, goals, and instrumentalities – we grasp the corresponding subjective experiences in which we become 'conscious' of them, in which (in the broadest sense) they 'appear'. For this reason, they are called 'phenomena', and their most general essential character is to exist as the 'consciousness-of' or 'appearance-of' the specific things, thoughts (judged states of affairs, grounds, conclusions), plans, decisions, hopes, and so forth. This relatedness [of the appearing to the object of appearance] resides in the meaning of all expressions in the vernacular languages which relate to psychic experience – for instance, perception *of* something, recalling *of* something, thinking *of* something, hoping *for* something, fearing something, striving *for* something, deciding on something, and so on. If this

From the *Encyclopaedia Britannica*, 1929.

realm of what we call 'phenomena' proves to be the possible field for a pure psychological discipline related exclusively to phenomena, we can understand the designation of it as *phenomenological psychology*. The terminological expression, deriving from Scholasticism, for designating the basic character of being as consciousness, as consciousness of something, is *intentionality*. In unreflective holding of some object or other in consciousness, we are turned or directed towards it: our *'intentio'* goes out towards it. The phenomenological reversal of our gaze shows that this 'being directed' [*Gerichtetsein*] is really an immanent essential feature of the respective experiences involved; they are 'intentional' experiences.

An extremely large and variegated number of kinds of special cases fall within the general scope of this concept. Consciousness of something is not an empty holding of something; every phenomenon has its own total form of intention [*intentionale Gesamtform*], but at the same time it has a structure, which in intentional analysis leads always again to components which are themselves also intentional. So for example in starting from a perception of something (for example, a die), phenomenological reflection leads to a multiple and yet synthetically unified intentionality. There are continually varying differences in the modes of appearing of objects, which are caused by the changing of 'orientation' – of right and left, nearness and farness, with the consequent differences in perspective involved. There are further differences in appearance between the 'actually seen front' and the 'unseeable' [*'unanschaulichen'*] and relatively 'undetermined' reverse side, which is nevertheless 'meant along with it'. Observing the flux of modes of appearing and the manner of their 'synthesis', one finds that every phase and portion [of the flux] is already in itself 'consciousness-of' – but in such a manner that there is formed within the constant emerging of new phases the synthetically unified awareness that this is one and the same object. The intentional structure of any process of perception has its fixed essential type [*seine feste Wesenstypik*], which must necessarily be realized in all its extraordinary complexity just in order for a physical body simply to be perceived as such. If this same thing is intuited in other modes – for example, in the modes of recollection, fantasy or pictorial representation – to some extent the whole intentional content of the perception comes back, but all aspects peculiarly transformed to correspond to that mode. This applies similarly for every other category of psychic process: the judging, valuing, striving consciousness is not an empty having knowledge of the specific judgments, values, goals, and means. Rather, these constitute themselves, with fixed essential forms corresponding to each process, in a flowing intentionality. For psychology, the universal task presents itself: to investigate systematically the elementary intentionalities, and from out of these [unfold] the typical forms of intentional processes, their possible variants, their syntheses to new forms, their structural composition, and from this advance towards a descriptive knowledge of the totality of mental process, towards a comprehensive type of a life of the psyche [*Gesamttypus eines Lebens der Seele*]. Clearly, the consistent carrying out of this task will produce knowledge which will have validity far beyond the psychologist's own particular psychic existence.

Psychic life *is* accessible to us not only through self-experience but also through experience of others. This novel source of experience offers us not only what matches our self-experience but also what is new, inasmuch as, in terms of consciousness and indeed as experience, it establishes the differences between own and other, as well as the properties peculiar to the life of a community. At just this point there arises the task of also making phenomenologically understandable the mental life of the community, with all the intentionalities that pertain to it.

The Self-contained Field of the Purely Psychical – Phenomenological Reduction and True Inner Experience

The idea of a phenomenological psychology encompasses the whole range of tasks arising out of the experience of self and the experience of the other founded on it. But it is not yet clear whether phenomenological experience, followed through in exclusiveness and consistency, really provides us with a kind of closed-off field of being, out of which a science can grow which is exclusively focused on it and completely free of everything psychophysical. Here [in fact] difficulties do exist, which have hidden from psychologists the possibility of such a purely phenomenological psychology even after Brentano's discovery of intentionality. They are relevant already to the construction of a really pure self-experience, and therewith of a really pure psychic datum. A particular method of access is required for the pure phenomenological field: the method of 'phenomenological reduction'. This *method of 'phenomenological reduction'* is thus the foundational method of pure psychology and the presupposition of all its specifically theoretical methods. Ultimately the great difficulty rests on the way that already the self-experience of the psychologist is everywhere intertwined with external experience, with that of extra-psychical real things. The experienced 'exterior' does not belong to one's intentional interiority, although certainly the experience itself belongs to it as experience – *of* the exterior. Exactly this same thing is true of every kind of awareness directed at something out there in the world. A consistent *epoche* of the phenomenologist is required, if he wishes to break through to his own consciousness as pure phenomenon or as the totality of his purely mental processes. That is to say, in the accomplishment of phenomenological reflection he must inhibit every co-accomplishment of objective positing produced in unreflective consciousness, and therewith [inhibit] every judgmental drawing-in of the world as it 'exists' for him straightforwardly. The specific experience of this house, this body, of a world as

17

such, is and remains, however, according to its own essential content and thus inseparably, experience 'of this house', this body, this world; this is so for every mode of consciousness which is directed towards an object. It is, after all, quite impossible to describe an intentional experience – even if illusionary, an invalid judgment, or the like – without at the same time describing the object of that consciousness *as* such. The universal *epoche* of the world as it becomes known in consciousness (the 'putting it in brackets') shuts out from the phenomenological field the world as it exists for the subject in simple absoluteness; its place, however, is taken by the world as given in *consciousness* (perceived, remembered, judged, thought, valued, etc.) – the world *as such*, the 'world in brackets', or in other words, the world, or rather individual things in the world as absolute, are replaced by the respective meaning of each in *consciousness* [*Bewusstseinssinn*] in its various modes (perceptual meaning, recollected meaning, and so on).

With this, we have clarified and supplemented our initial determination of the phenomenological experience and its sphere of being. In going back from the unities posited in the natural attitude to the manifold of modes of consciousness in which they appear, the unities, as inseparable from these multiplicities – but as 'bracketed' – are also to be reckoned among what is purely psychical, and always specifically in the appearance-character in which they present themselves. The method of phenomenological reduction (to the pure 'phenomenon', the purely psychical) accordingly consists (1) in the methodical and rigorously consistent *epoche* of every objective positing in the psychic sphere, both of the individual phenomenon and of the whole psychic field in general; and (2) in the methodically practiced seizing and describing of the multiple 'appearances' as appearances of their objective units and these units as units of component meanings accruing to them each time in their appearances. With this is shown a twofold direction – the *noetic* and *noematic* of phenomenological description. Phenomenological experience in the methodical form of the phenomenological reduction is the only genuine 'inner experience' in the sense meant by any well-grounded science of psychology. In its own nature lies manifest the possibility of being carried out continuously *in infinitum* with methodical preservation of purity. The reductive method is transferred from self-experience to the experience of others insofar as there can be applied to the envisaged [*vergegen-wärtigten*] mental life of the Other the corresponding bracketing and description according to the subjective 'How' of its appearance and what is appearing ('*noesis*' and '*noema*'). As a further consequence, the community that is experienced in community experience is reduced not only to the mentally particularized intentional fields but also to the unity of the community life that connects them all together, the community mental life in its phenomenological purity (intersubjective reduction). Thus results the perfect expansion of the genuine psychological concept of 'inner experience'.

To every mind there belongs not only the unity of its multiple *intentional life-process* [*intentionalen Lebens*] with all its inseparable unities of sense directed towards the 'object'. There is also, inseparable from this life-process, the experiencing *I-subject* as the identical *I-pole* giving a centre for all specific intentionalities, and as the carrier of all habitualities growing out of this life-process. Likewise, then, the reduced intersubjectivity, in pure form and concretely grasped, is a community of pure 'persons' acting in the intersubjective realm of the pure life of consciousness. . . .

Transcendental Phenomenology as Ontology

Remarkable consequences arise when one weighs the significance of transcendental phenomenology. In its systematic development, it brings to realization the Leibnizian idea of a universal ontology as the systematic unity of all conceivable *a priori* sciences, but on a new foundation which overcomes 'dogmatism' through the use of the transcendental phenomenological method. Phenomenology as the science of all conceivable transcendental phenomena and especially the synthetic total structures in which alone they are concretely possible – those of the transcendental single subjects bound to communities of subjects is *eo ipso* the *a priori* science of all conceivable beings. But [it is the science] then not merely of the Totality of objectively existing beings, and certainly not in an attitude of natural positivity; rather, in the full concretion of being in general which derives its sense of being and its validity from the correlative intentional constitution. This also comprises the being of transcendental subjectivity itself, whose nature it is demonstrably to be constituted transcendentally in and for itself. Accordingly, a phenomenology properly carried through is the truly universal ontology, as over against the only illusory all-embracing ontology in positivity – and precisely for this reason it overcomes the dogmatic one-sidedness and hence unintelligibility of the latter, while at the same time it comprises within itself the truly legitimate content [of an ontology in positivity] as grounded originally in intentional constitution.

Phenomenology and the Crisis in the Foundations of the Exact Sciences

If we consider the how of this inclusion, we find that what is meant is that every *a priori* is ultimately prescribed in its validity of being precisely *as* a transcendental achievement; i.e., it is together with the essential structures of its constitution, with the kinds and levels of its givenness and confirmation of itself, and with the appertaining habitualities. This implies that in and through the establishment of the *a priori* the subjective *method* of this establishing is itself made transparent, and that for the *a priori* disciplines which are founded within phenomenology (for example, as mathematical sciences) there can be no 'paradoxes' and no 'crises of the foundations'. The consequence that arises [from all this] with reference to the *a priori* sciences that have come into being historically and in transcendental naïveté is that only a radical, phenomenological grounding can transform them into true, methodical, fully self-justifying sciences. But precisely by this they will cease to be positive (dogmatic) sciences and become dependent branches of the one phenomenology as all-encompassing eidetic ontology. . . .

The 'Ultimate and Highest' Problems as Phenomenological

In phenomenology all rational problems have their place, and thus also those that traditionally are in some special sense or other philosophically significant. For out of the absolute sources of transcendental experience, or eidetic intuiting, they first [are able to] obtain their genuine formulation and feasible means for their solution. In its universal relatedness-back-to-itself, phenomenology recognizes its particular function within a possible life of mankind [*Menschheitsleben*] at the transcendental level. It recognizes the absolute norms which are to be picked out intuitively from it [life of mankind], and also its primordial teleo-logical-tendential structure in a directedness towards disclosure of these norms and their conscious practical operation. It recognizes itself as a function of the all-embracing reflective meditation of (transcendental) humanity, [a self-examination] in the service of an all-inclusive praxis of reason; that is, in the service of striving towards the universal ideal of absolute perfection which lies in infinity, [a striving] which becomes free through [the process of] disclosure. Or, in different words it is a striving in the direction of the idea (lying in infinity) of a humanness which in action and thought would live and move [be, exist] in truth and genuineness. It recognizes its self-reflective function [of self-examination] for the relative realization of the correlative practical idea of a genuine human life [*Menschheitsleben*] in the second sense (whose structural forms of being and whose practical norms it is to investigate), namely as one [that is] consciously and purposively directed towards this absolute idea. In short, the metaphysically teleological, the ethical, and the problems of philosophy of history, no less than, obviously, the problems of judging reason, lie within its boundary, no differently from all significant problems whatever, and all [of them] in their inmost synthetic unity and order as [being] of transcendental spirituality [*Geistigkeit*].

The Phenomenological Resolution of All Philosophical Antitheses

In the systematic work of phenomenology, which progresses from intu-itively given [concrete] data to heights of abstraction, the old traditional ambiguous antitheses of the philosophical standpoint are resolved – by themselves and without the arts of an argumentative dialectic, and without weak efforts and compromises: oppositions such as between rationalism (Platonism) and empiricism, relativism and absolutism, subjectivism and objectivism, ontologism and transcendentalism, psychologism and anti-psychologism, positivism and metaphysics, or the teleological versus the causal interpretation of the world. Throughout all of these, [one finds] justified motives, but throughout also half-truths or impermissible absol-utizing of only relatively and abstractively legitimate one-sidednesses.

Subjectivism can only be overcome by the most all-embracing and consistent subjectivism (the transcendental). In this [latter] form it is at the same time objectivism [of a deeper sort], in that it represents the claims of whatever objectivity is to be demonstrated through concordant experience, but admittedly [this is an objectivism which] also brings out its full and genuine sense, against which [sense] the supposedly realistic objectivism sins by its failure to understand transcendental constitution. *Relativism* can only be overcome through the most all-embracing rela-tivism, that of transcendental phenomenology, which makes intelligible the relativity of all 'objective' being [or existence] as transcendentally constituted; but at one with this [it makes intelligible] the most radical relativity, the relatedness of the transcendental subjectivity to itself. But just this [relatedness, subjectivity] proves its identity to be the only possible sense of [the term] 'absolute' being – over against all 'objective' being that is relative to it – namely, as the 'for-itself' – being of transcendental subjectivity. Likewise: *Empiricism* can only be overcome by the most universal and consistent empiricism, which puts in place of the restricted [term] 'experience' of the empiricists the necessarily broadened concept of experience [inclusive] of intuition which offers original data, an intu-ition which in all its forms (intuition of *eidos*, apodictic self-evidence, phenomenological intuition of essence, etc.) shows the manner and form of its legitimation through phenomenological clarification. Phenomenology as eidetic is, on the other hand, rationalistic: it overcomes restrictive and dogmatic rationalism, however, through the most universal rationalism of inquiry into essences, which is related uniformly to transcendental subjec-tivity, to the I, consciousness, and conscious objectivity. And it is the same in reference to the other antitheses bound up with them. The tracing back of all being to the transcendental subjectivity and its constitutive intentional functions leaves open, to mention one more thing, no other way of contemplating the world than the *teleological*. And yet phenom-enology also acknowledges a kernel of truth in naturalism (or rather sensa-tionism). That is, by revealing associations as intentional phenomena,

21

indeed as a whole basic typology of forms of passive intentional synthesis with transcendental and purely passive genesis based on essential laws, phenomenology shows Humean fictionalism to contain anticipatory discoveries; particularly in his doctrine of the origin of such fictions as thing, persisting existence, causality – anticipatory discoveries all shrouded in absurd theories.

Phenomenological philosophy regards itself in its whole method as a pure outcome of methodical intentions which already animated Greek philosophy from its beginnings; above all, however, [it continues] the still vital intentions which reach, in the two lines of rationalism and empiricism, from Descartes through Kant and German idealism into our confused present day. A pure outcome of methodical intentions means real method which allows the problems to be taken in hand and completed. In the way of true science this path is endless. Accordingly, phenomenology demands that the phenomenologist foreswear the ideal of a philosophic system and yet as a humble worker in community with others, live for a perennial philosophy [*philosophia perennis*].

2

Martin Heidegger

(1889–1976)

If there is such a thing as a 'contemporary classic', many would agree that Martin Heidegger's *Being and Time* fills that role for the twentieth century. In it we find the point of departure for both existential and hermeneutic phenomenology, as well as the critique of Western metaphysics that has figured so prominently in the philosophical agenda of such movements as poststructuralism and deconstruction. Heidegger resurrected the 'question of the meaning of Being' (*Seinsfrage*), an interrogation that continued throughout his life.

Born in 1889, Heidegger was a native of Messkirch in the agrarian Black Forest region of Germany. He studied theology, mathematics and philosophy at the University of Freiburg (1909–13), and during this time found himself drawn to the work of Husserl. His brief account of early influences in 'My Way to Phenomenology' reveals that 'both volumes of Husserl's *Logical Investigations* lay on my desk in the theological seminary ever since my first semester there'. He had also been given a copy of Brentano's dissertation 'On the manifold meaning of Being in Aristotle' (1862), and notes:

> From Husserl's *Logical Investigations*, I expected a decisive aid
> in the questions stimulated by Brentano's thesis. Yet my efforts
> were in vain because I was not searching in the right way. I
> realized this only very much later. Still, I remained so fascinated
> by Husserl's work that I read it again and again in the years to
> follow without gaining sufficient insight into what fascinated
> me.

Heidegger continued studying at Freiburg for his Ph.D., finishing 'The doctrine of judgement in psychologism' in 1914, as well as his *Habilitationsschrift*, 'The theory of categories and meaning in Duns Scotus', in 1916. Both of these drew extensively on Husserl's published work. After Husserl was appointed to the Chair of Philosophy at Freiburg in 1916, Heidegger finally had the opportunity to work as his assistant (1919–23).

Despite this early and profound interest in Husserl's work, Heidegger began to develop his own phenomenological project in a direction that ultimately rejected some of the basic tenets of Husserlian phenomenology. During his time at Marburg (1923–8), Heidegger delivered a lecture series, eventually published as *The History of the Concept of Time*, in which we find the first explicit critique of Husserl's reliance on absolute consciousness for his model of intentionality. In many ways, these lectures announced the highly original treatment and redefinition of the phenomenological field to be found in Heidegger's first major publication, *Being and Time* (1927), which was dedicated to Husserl and which earned him the Chair of Philosophy at Freiburg on Husserl's retirement (1928). However, *Being and Time* was most emphatically never intended by Heidegger to follow as a development of strictly Husserlian phenomenology.

From the outset, Heidegger defines his project in *Being and Time* as an attempt to revive the question of the meaning of Being, which has been concealed and ignored by the Western philosophical tradition as represented by Plato, Descartes, Kant and Husserl. The tradition has relied on an ontology privileging 'substance', which in turn has led to a 'metaphysics of presence' that, according to Heidegger, has resulted in an unfortunate mind/matter duality. He maintains that any efforts to understand 'reality' along that path are doomed from the start. He stresses the ontological difference between 'Being' and 'beings', the *Sein/Seiende* distinction which aims to avoid the reduction of ontology to the mere categorization of existent entities. For any study of 'Being-in-general' (*Seinüberhaupt*), Heidegger sees the need to establish a 'fundamental ontology' that elucidates the conditions of intelligibility required for things to 'be' or show up for us in any way at all. And he intends to do this by interrogating the constitutive features of 'the being for whom Being is an issue', the being he calls Dasein.

Using a word that originally simply meant 'existence' in German, Heidegger plays on the etymological root of *Da-sein*, or 'being-there', as the temporal horizon of intelligibility for Being-in-general. Heidegger claims that his focus on Dasein is a strategic move, designed only as a point of entry into his larger problematic, and not a philosophical anthropology on the nature of 'human being'. However, since only part of the projected treatise was ever completed, the 'existential analytic of Dasein' in Division I of *Being and Time* has become an almost legendary phenomenological analysis of 'average everydayness' and Dasein's 'being-in-the-world'.

For the early Heidegger, Being is accessible only through our practical engagement with a world already understood because of its relevance to our ongoing projects. He rejects as derivative the 'theoretical' view that we encounter objects 'out-there' that are somehow laundered in a subjective consciousness through neutral 'perception'. Such a scientifically objective attitude is already a specific and limited comportment, like 'staring' at something. Indeed, Heidegger replaces the word 'perception' with 'circumspection' to emphasize that we tend to take-in only what makes contextual sense in a given situation. He gives examples of tools we work with like hammers or turn-signals in a car that are 'ready-to-hand' (*Zuhandenheit*), used equipmentally. Only when they break-down in some way do we actually look at them as mere objects that are 'present-at-hand' (*Vorhandenheit*). Dasein itself becomes the condition of possibility for access to the 'world-hood-of-the-world'.

Since 'existence precedes essence' for Heidegger, he posits an *a priori* structure of 'existentialia' that is constitutive of Dasein. We are 'thrown' (*geworfen*) into the world without notice and carry the burden of a certain 'facticity', not of our choosing. We also find ourselves already disposed toward the world in particular ways (*Befindlichkeit*) that become manifest as moods or attunement (*Stimmung*). A mood of *Angst* or anxiety, for example, serves to authentically awaken us to the precariousness of our situation as 'beings-towards-death', alienating us from the 'inauthentic' conformity and security of the crowd. Our days are thus lived in an ecstatic unity of time that retrieves our facticity from the past, but even more importantly projects our possibilities ahead of us towards the future. Above all, we have a pre-reflective 'understanding' (*Verstehen*) of our world that need not be articulated or expressly laid-out (*Auslegung*) as 'interpretation'. We exist always in a hermeneutic circle that originates in such pre-reflective understanding of Being-in-general; otherwise we could not even formulate the question of the meaning of Being.

Although the greater part of this introduction has been written to contextualize the selection chosen from *Being and Time*, it must be noted that the later Heidegger does not privilege Dasein to the same degree. After his essay 'On the essence of truth' (1930), we find fundamental ontology dropped from his agenda and replaced by a history of Being that emphasizes the participation of human beings in the 'happening' of Being. Language, especially poetic language, emerges to play a crucial role as the 'house of Being'. Such works as *Introduction to Metaphysics* (1935), 'The origin of the work of art' (1935, 1950), 'Letter on humanism' (1946) and *On the Way to Language* (1957), to name a few, remain focused on the question of Being, but develop this thematic in a new way. In Heidegger we see the confluence of phenomenology, existentialism and hermeneutics that has made his impact particularly powerful.

SELECT BIBLIOGRAPHY OF HEIDEGGER'S WORKS IN ENGLISH

'What is Metaphysics?' in *Existence and Being*, Chicago: Regnery, 1949.
Introduction to Metaphysics, New Haven: Yale University Press, 1959.
Identity and Difference, New York: Harper & Row, 1960.
Being and Time, Oxford: Blackwell, 1967.
Kant and the Problem of Metaphysics, Bloomington: Indiana University Press, 1962.

What is Called Thinking? New York: Harper & Row, 1967.

What Is a Thing? South Bend, Ind.: Gateway Books, 1967.

The Essence of Reason, Evanston, Ill.: Northwestern University Press, 1969.

Discourse on Thinking, New York: Harper & Row, 1970.

On the Way to Language, New York: Harper & Row, 1971.

Poetry, Language, Thought, New York: Harper & Row, 1971.

On Time and Being, New York: Harper & Row, 1972.

The End of Philosophy, New York: Harper & Row, 1973.

Early Greek Thinking, New York: Harper & Row, 1975.

The Piety of Thinking, Bloomington: Indiana University Press, 1976.

Basic Writings, New York: Harper & Row, 1977.

The Question Concerning Technology, New York: Harper & Row, 1977.

Nietzsche, 4 vols, New York: Harper & Row, 1979.

The Basic Problems of Phenomenology, Bloomington: Indiana University Press, 1982.

The Metaphysical Foundations of Logic, Bloomington: Indiana University Press, 1984.

The History of the Concept of Time, Bloomington: Indiana University Press, 1985.

Hegel's Phenomenology of Spirit, Bloomington: Indiana University Press, 1988.

The Principle of Reason, Bloomington: Indiana University Press, 1991.

From the Introduction to *Being and Time*

§2 THE FORMAL STRUCTURE OF THE QUESTION OF BEING

THE QUESTION OF the meaning of Being must be *formulated*. If it is a fundamental question, or indeed *the* fundamental question, it must be made transparent, and in an appropriate way. We must therefore explain briefly what belongs to any question whatsoever, so that from this standpoint the question of Being can be made visible as a *very special* one with its own distinctive character.

Every inquiry is a seeking [Suchen]. . . . Inquiry, as a kind of seeking, must be guided beforehand by what is sought. So the meaning of Being must already be available to us in some way. As we have intimated, we always conduct our activities in an understanding of Being. Out of this understanding arise both the explicit question of the meaning of Being and the tendency that leads us towards its conception. We do not *know* what 'Being' means. But even if we ask, 'What *is* "Being"?', we keep within an understanding of the 'is', though we are unable to fix conceptionally what that 'is' signifies. We do not even know the horizon in terms of which that meaning is to be grasped and fixed. *But this vague average understanding of Being is still a Fact.*

However much this understanding of Being (an understanding which is already available to us) may fluctuate and grow dim, and border on mere acquaintance with a word, its very indefiniteness is itself a positive phenomenon which needs to be clarified. An investigation of the meaning of Being cannot be expected to give this clarification at the outset. If we are to obtain the clue we need for Interpreting this average understanding of Being, we must first develop the concept of Being. In the light of this concept and the ways in which it may be explicitly understood, we can make out what this obscured or still unillumined understanding of Being means, and what kinds of obscuration – or hindrance to an explicit illumination – of the meaning of Being are possible and even inevitable.

Further, this vague average understanding of Being may be so infiltrated with traditional theories and opinions about Being that these remain hidden as sources of the way in which it is prevalently understood. What we seek when we inquire into Being is not something entirely unfamiliar, even if proximally we cannot grasp it at all.

In the question which we are to work out, *what is asked about* is Being – that which determines entities as entities, that on the basis of which [*woraufhin*] entities are already understood, however we may discuss them in detail. The Being of entities 'is' not itself an entity. If we are to understand

From *Being and Time*, trans. J. Macquarrie and E. Robinson, Oxford: Blackwell, 1967.

the problem of Being, our first philosophical step consists in not μῦθόν τινα διηγεῖσθαι, in not 'telling a story' – that is to say, in not defining enti- ties as entities by tracing them back in their origin to some other entities, as if Being had the character of some possible entity. Hence Being, as that which is asked about, must be exhibited in a way of its own, essentially different from the way in which entities are discovered. Accordingly, *what is to be found out by the asking* – the meaning of Being – also demands that it be conceived in a way of its own, essentially contrasting with the concepts in which entities acquire their determinate signification.

In so far as Being constitutes what is asked about, and 'Being' means the Being of entities, then entities themselves turn out to be *what is inter- rogated*. These are, so to speak, questioned as regards their Being. But if the characteristics of their Being can be yielded without falsification, then these entities must, on their part, have become accessible as they are in themselves. When we come to what is to be interrogated, the question of Being requires that the right way of access to entities shall have been obtained and secured in advance. But there are many things which we designate as 'being' [*seiend*], and we do so in various senses. Everything we talk about, everything we have in view, everything towards which we comport ourselves in any way, is being; what we are is being, and so is how we are. Being lies in the fact that something is, and in its Being as it is; in Reality; in presence-at-hand; in subsistence; in validity; in Dasein; in the 'there is'. In *which* entities is the meaning of Being to be discerned? From which entities is the disclosure of Being to take its departure? Is the starting-point optional, or does some particular entity have priority when we come to work out the question of Being? Which entity shall we take for our example, and in what sense does it have priority?

If the question about Being is to be explicitly formulated and carried through in such a manner as to be completely transparent to itself, then any treatment of it in line with the elucidations we have given requires us to explain how Being is to be looked at, how its meaning is to be understood and conceptually grasped; it requires us to prepare the way for choosing the right entity for our example, and to work out the genuine way of access to it. Looking at something, understanding and conceiving it, choosing, access to it – all these ways of behaving are constitutive for our inquiry, and therefore are modes of Being for those particular entities which we, the inquirers, are ourselves. Thus to work out the ques- tion of Being adequately, we must make an entity – the inquirer – trans- parent in his own Being. The very asking of this question is an entity's mode of *Being*; and as such it gets its essential character from what is inquired about – namely, Being. This entity which each of us is himself and which includes inquiring as one of the possibilities of its Being, we shall denote by the term '*Dasein*'. If we are to formulate our question explicitly and transparently, we must first give a proper explication of an entity (Dasein), with regard to its Being.

Is there not, however, a manifest circularity in such an undertaking? If we must first define an entity *in its Being*, and if we want to formulate the question of Being only on this basis, what is this but going in a circle? In working out our question, have we not 'presupposed' something which only the answer can bring? Formal objections such as the argument about 'circular reasoning', which can easily be cited at any time in the study of first principles, are always sterile when one is considering concrete ways of investigating. When it comes to understanding the matter at hand, they carry no weight and keep us from penetrating into the field of study.

But factically there is no circle at all in formulating our question as we have described. One can determine the nature of entities in their Being without necessarily having the explicit concept of the meaning of Being at one's disposal. Otherwise there could have been no ontological knowledge heretofore. One would hardly deny that factically there has been such knowledge. Of course 'Being' has been presupposed in all ontology up till now, but not as a *concept* at one's disposal – not as the sort of thing we are seeking. This 'presupposing' of Being has rather the character of taking a look at it beforehand, so that in the light of it the entities presented to us get provisionally Articulated in their Being. This guiding activity of taking a look at Being arises from the average understanding of Being in which we always operate and *which in the end belongs to the essential constitution of Dasein itself*. Such 'presupposing' has nothing to do with laying down an axiom from which a sequence of propositions is deductively derived. It is quite impossible for there to be any 'circular argument' in formulating the question about the meaning of Being; for in answering this question, the issue is not one of grounding something by such a derivation; it is rather one of laying bare the grounds for it and exhibiting them.

In the question of the meaning of Being there is no 'circular reasoning' but rather a remarkable 'relatedness backward or forward' which what we are asking about (Being) bears to the inquiry itself as a mode of Being of an entity. Here what is asked about has an essential pertinence to the inquiry itself, and this belongs to the ownmost meaning [*eigensten Sinn*] of the question of Being. This only means, however, that there is a way – perhaps even a very special one – in which entities with the character of Dasein are related to the question of Being. But have we not thus demonstrated that a certain kind of entity has a priority with regard to its Being? And have we not thus presented that entity which shall serve as the primary example to be *interrogated* in the question of Being? So far our discussion has not demonstrated Dasein's priority, nor has it shown decisively whether Dasein may possibly or even necessarily serve as the primary entity to be interrogated. But indeed something like a priority of Dasein has announced itself.

29

§3 THE ONTOLOGICAL PRIORITY OF THE QUESTION OF BEING

When we pointed out the characteristics of the question of Being, taking as our clue the formal structure of the question as such, we made it clear that this question is a peculiar one, in that a series of fundamental considerations is required for working it out, not to mention for solving it. But its distinctive features will come fully to light only when we have delimited it adequately with regard to its function, its aim, and its motives.

Hitherto our arguments for showing that the question must be restated have been motivated in part by its venerable origin but chiefly by the lack of a definite answer and even by the absence of any satisfactory formulation of the question itself. One may, however, ask what purpose this question is supposed to serve. Does it simply remain – or *is* it at all – a mere matter for soaring speculation about the most general of generalities, *or is it rather, of all questions, both the most basic and the most concrete?*

Being is always the Being of an entity. The totality of entities can, in accordance with its various domains, become a field for laying bare and delimiting certain definite areas of subject-matter. These areas, on their part (for instance, history, Nature, space, life, Dasein, language, and the like), can serve as objects which corresponding scientific investigations may take as their respective themes. Scientific research accomplishes, roughly and naïvely, the demarcation and initial fixing of the areas of subject-matter. The basic structures of any such area have already been worked out after a fashion in our pre-scientific ways of experiencing and interpreting that domain of Being in which the area of subject-matter is itself confined. The 'basic concepts' which thus arise remain our proximal clues for disclosing this area concretely for the first time. And although research may always lean towards this positive approach, its real progress comes not so much from collecting results and storing them away in 'manuals' as from inquiring into the ways in which each particular area is basically constituted [*Grundverfassungen*] – an inquiry to which we have been driven mostly by reacting against just such an increase in information.

The real 'movement' of the sciences takes place when their basic concepts undergo a more or less radical revision which is transparent to itself. The level which a science has reached is determined by how far it is *capable* of a crisis in its basic concepts. In such immanent crises the very relationship between positively investigative inquiry and those things themselves that are under interrogation comes to a point where it begins to totter. Among the various disciplines everywhere today there are freshly awakened tendencies to put research on new foundations.

Mathematics, which is seemingly the most rigorous and most firmly constructed of the sciences, has reached a crisis in its 'foundations'. In the controversy between the formalists and the intuitionists, the issue is one of obtaining and securing the primary way of access to what are supposedly the objects of this science. The relativity theory of *physics* arises from the tendency to exhibit the interconnectedness of Nature as it is 'in itself'. As a theory of the conditions under which we have access to Nature itself, it seeks to preserve the changelessness of the laws of motion by ascertaining all relativities, and thus comes up against the question of the structure of its own given area of study – the problem of matter. In *biology* there is an awakening tendency to inquire beyond the definitions which mechanism and vitalism have given for 'life' and 'organism', and to define anew the kind of Being which belongs to the living as such. In those *humane sciences which are historiological in character*, the urge towards historical actuality itself has been strengthened in the course of time by tradition and by the way tradition has been presented and handed down: the history of literature is to become the history of problems. *Theology* is seeking a more primordial interpretation of man's Being towards God, prescribed by the meaning of faith itself and remaining within it. It is slowly beginning to understand once more Luther's insight that the 'foundation' on which its system of dogma rests has not arisen from an inquiry in which faith is primary, and that conceptually this 'foundation' not only is inadequate for the problematic of theology, but conceals and distorts it.

Basic concepts determine the way in which we get an understanding beforehand of the area of subject-matter underlying all the objects a science takes as its theme, and all positive investigation is guided by this understanding. Only after the area itself has been explored beforehand in a corresponding manner do these concepts become genuinely demonstrated and 'grounded'. But since every such area is itself obtained from the domain of entities themselves, this preliminary research, from which the basic concepts are drawn, signifies nothing else than an interpretation of those entities with regard to their basic state of Being. Such research must run ahead of the positive sciences, and it *can*. Here the work of Plato and Aristotle is evidence enough. Laying the foundations for the sciences in this way is different in principle from the kind of 'logic' which limps along after, investigating the status of some science as it chances to find it, in order to discover its 'method'. Laying the foundations, as we have described it, is rather a productive logic – in the sense that it leaps ahead, as it were, into some area of Being, discloses it for the first time in the constitution of its Being, and, after thus arriving at the structures within it, makes these available to the positive sciences as transparent assignments for their inquiry. To give an example, what is philosophically primary is neither a theory of the concept-formation of historiology nor the theory of historiological knowledge, nor yet the theory of history as the Object of historiology; what is primary is rather the Interpretation of authentically historical entities as regards their historicality. Similarly the positive outcome of Kant's *Critique of Pure Reason* lies in what it has contributed towards the working out of what belongs to any Nature what-soever, not in a 'theory' of knowledge. His transcendental logic is an *a priori* logic for the subject-matter of that area of Being called 'Nature'.

But such an inquiry itself – ontology taken in the widest sense without favouring any particular ontological directions or tendencies – requires a further clue. Ontological inquiry is indeed more primordial, as over against the ontical inquiry of the positive sciences. But it remains itself naïve and opaque if in its researches into the Being of entities it fails to discuss the meaning of Being in general. And even the ontological task of constructing a non-deductive genealogy of the different possible ways of Being requires that we first come to an understanding of 'what we really mean by this expression "Being"'.

The question of Being aims therefore at ascertaining the *a priori* conditions not only for the possibility of the sciences which examine entities as entities of such and such a type, and, in so doing, already operate with an understanding of Being, but also for the possibility of those ontologies themselves which are prior to the ontical sciences and which provide their foundations. *Basically, all ontology, no matter how rich and firmly compacted a system of categories it has at its disposal, remains blind and perverted from its ownmost aim, if it has not first adequately clarified the meaning of Being, and conceived this clarification as its fundamental task.*

Ontological research itself, when properly understood, gives to the question of Being an ontological priority which goes beyond mere resumption of a venerable tradition and advancement with a problem that has hitherto been opaque. But this objectively scientific priority is not the only one.

§4 THE ONTICAL PRIORITY OF THE QUESTION OF BEING

Science in general may be defined as the totality established through an interconnection of true propositions. This definition is not complete, nor does it reach the meaning of science. As ways in which man behaves, sciences have the manner of Being which this entity – man himself – possesses. This entity we denote by the term '*Dasein*'. Scientific research is not the only manner of Being which this entity can have, nor is it the one which lies closest. Moreover, Dasein itself has a special distinctiveness as compared with other entities, and it is worth our while to bring this to view in a provisional way. Here our discussion must anticipate later analyses, in which our results will be authentically exhibited for the first time.

Dasein is an entity which does not just occur among other entities. Rather it is ontically distinguished by the fact that, in its very Being, that Being is an *issue* for it. But in that case, this is a constitutive state of

Dasein's Being, and this implies that Dasein, in its Being, has a relationship towards that Being – a relationship which itself is one of Being. And this means further that there is some way in which Dasein understands itself in its Being, and that to some degree it does so explicitly. It is peculiar to this entity that with and through its Being, this Being is disclosed to it. *Understanding of Being is itself a definite characteristic of Dasein's Being*. Dasein is ontically distinctive in that it *is* ontological.

Here 'Being-ontological' is not yet tantamount to 'developing an ontology'. So if we should reserve the term 'ontology' for that theoretical inquiry which is explicitly devoted to the meaning of entities, then what we have had in mind in speaking of Dasein's 'Being-ontological' is to be designated as something 'pre-ontological'. It does not signify simply 'being-ontical', however, but rather 'being in such a way that one has an understanding of Being'.

That kind of Being towards which Dasein can comport itself in one way or another, and always does comport itself somehow, we call '*existence*' [*Existenz*]. And because we cannot define Dasein's essence by citing a 'what' of the kind that pertains to a subject-matter [*eines sachhaltigen Was*], and because its essence lies rather in the fact that in each case it has its Being to be, and has it as its own, we have chosen to designate this entity as 'Dasein', a term which is purely an expression of its Being [*als reiner Seinsausdruck*].

Dasein always understands itself in terms of its existence – in terms of a possibility of itself: to be itself or not itself. Dasein has either chosen these possibilities itself, or got itself into them, or grown up in them already. Only the particular Dasein decides its existence, whether it does so by taking hold or by neglecting. The question of existence never gets straightened out except through existing itself. The understanding of oneself which leads *along this way* we call '*existentiell*'. The question of existence is one of Dasein's ontical 'affairs'. This does not require that the ontological structure of existence should be theoretically transparent. The question about that structure aims at the analysis [*Auseinanderlegung*] of what constitutes existence. The context [*Zusammenhang*] of such structures we call '*existentiality*'. Its analytic has the character of an understanding which is not existentiell, but rather *existential*. The task of an existential analytic of Dasein has been delineated in advance, as regards both its possibility and its necessity, in Dasein's ontical constitution.

So far as existence is the determining character of Dasein, the ontological analytic of this entity always requires that existentiality be considered beforehand. By 'existentiality' we understand the state of Being that is constitutive for those entities that exist. But in the idea of such a constitutive state of Being, the idea of Being is already included. And thus even the possibility of carrying through the analytic of Dasein depends on working out beforehand the question about the meaning of Being in general.

Sciences are ways of Being in which Dasein comports itself towards entities which it need not be itself. But to Dasein, Being in a world is something that belongs essentially. Thus Dasein's understanding of Being pertains with equal primordiality both to an understanding of something like a 'world', and to the understanding of the Being of those entities which become accessible within the world. So whenever an ontology takes for its theme entities whose character of Being is other than that of Dasein, it has its own foundation and motivation in Dasein's own ontical structure, in which a pre-ontological understanding of Being is comprised as a definite characteristic.

Therefore *fundamental ontology*, from which alone all other ontologies can take their rise, must be sought in the *existential analytic of Dasein*.

Dasein accordingly takes priority over all other entities in several ways. The first priority is an *ontical* one: Dasein is an entity whose Being has the determinate character of existence. The second priority is an *ontological* one: Dasein is in itself 'ontological', because existence is thus determinative for it. But with equal primordiality Dasein also possesses – as constitutive for its understanding of existence – an understanding of the Being of all entities of a character other than its own. Dasein has therefore a third priority as providing the ontico-ontological condition for the possibility of any ontologies. Thus Dasein has turned out to be, more than any other entity, the one which must first be interrogated ontologically.

But the roots of the existential analytic, on its part, are ultimately *existentiell*, that is, *ontical*. Only if the inquiry of philosophical research is itself seized upon in an existentiell manner as a possibility of the Being of each existing Dasein, does it become at all possible to disclose the existentiality of existence and to undertake an adequately founded ontological problematic. But with this, the ontical priority of the question of being has also become plain.

Dasein's ontico-ontological priority was seen quite early, though Dasein itself was not grasped in its genuine ontological structure, and did not even become a problem in which this structure was sought. Aristotle says: ἡ ψυχὴ τὰ ὄντα πώς ἐστιν. 'Man's soul is, in a certain way, entities'. The 'soul' which makes up the Being of man has αἴσθησις and νόησις among its ways of Being, and in these it discovers all entities, both in the fact that they are, and in their Being as they are – that is, always in their Being. Aristotle's principle, which points back to the ontological thesis of Parmenides, is one which Thomas Aquinas has taken up in a characteristic discussion. Thomas is engaged in the task of deriving the '*transcendentia*' – those characters of Being which lie beyond every possible way in which an entity may be classified as coming under some generic kind of subject-matter (every *modus specialis entis*), and which belong necessarily to anything, whatever it may be. Thomas has to demonstrate that the *verum* is such a *transcendens*. He does this by invoking an entity which, in accordance with its very manner of Being, is properly suited to 'come together with' entities of any sort whatever. This distinctive entity, the *ens quod natum est convenire cum omni ente*, is the soul (*anima*). Here the priority of 'Dasein' over all other entities emerges, although it has not been ontologically clarified. This priority has obviously nothing in common with a vicious subjectivizing of the totality of entities.

By indicating Dasein's ontico-ontological priority in this provisional manner, we have grounded our demonstration that the question of Being is ontico-ontologically distinctive. But when we analysed the structure of this question as such (Section 2), we came up against a distinctive way in which this entity functions in the very formulation of that question. Dasein then revealed itself as that entity which must first be worked out in an ontologically adequate manner, if the inquiry is to become a transparent one. But now it has been shown that the ontological analytic of Dasein in general is what makes up fundamental ontology, so that Dasein functions as that entity which in principle is to be *interrogated* beforehand as to its Being.

If to Interpret the meaning of Being becomes our task, Dasein is not only the primary entity to be interrogated; it is also that entity which already comports itself, in its Being, towards what we are asking about when we ask this question. But in that case the question of Being is nothing other than the radicalization of an essential tendency-of-Being which belongs to Dasein itself – the pre-ontological understanding of Being. . . .

§5 THE ONTOLOGICAL ANALYTIC OF DASEIN AS LAYING BARE THE HORIZON FOR AN INTERPRETATION OF THE MEANING OF BEING IN GENERAL

In designating the tasks of 'formulating' the question of Being, we have shown not only that we must establish which entity is to serve as our primary object of interrogation, but also that the right way of access to this entity is one which we must explicitly make our own and hold secure. We have already discussed which entity takes over the principal role within the question of Being. But how are we, as it were, to set our sights towards this entity, Dasein, both as something accessible to us and as something to be understood and interpreted?

In demonstrating that Dasein is ontico-ontologically prior, we may have misled the reader into supposing that this entity must also be what is given as ontico-ontologically primary not only in the sense that it can itself be grasped 'immediately', but also in that the kind of Being which it possesses is presented just as 'immediately'. Ontically, of course, Dasein is not only close to us – even that which is closest: we *are* it, each of us, we ourselves. In spite of this, or rather for just this reason, it is ontologically that which is farthest. To be sure, its ownmost Being is such that it has an understanding of that Being, and already maintains itself in each case as if its Being has been interpreted in some manner. But we are certainly not saying that when Dasein's own Being is thus interpreted pre-ontologically in the way which lies closest, this interpretation can be taken over as an appropriate clue, as if this way of understanding Being is what must emerge when one's ownmost state of Being is considered as an onto-logical theme. The kind of Being which belongs to Dasein is rather such that, in understanding its own Being, it has a tendency to do so in terms of that entity towards which it comports itself proximally and in a way which is essentially constant – in terms of the 'world'. In Dasein itself, and therefore in its own understanding of Being, the way the world is understood is, as we shall show, reflected back ontologically upon the way in which Dasein itself gets interpreted.

Thus because Dasein is ontico-ontologically prior, its own specific state of Being (if we understand this in the sense of Dasein's 'categorial structure') remains concealed from it. Dasein is ontically 'closest' to itself and ontologically farthest; but pre-ontologically it is surely not a stranger.

Here we have merely indicated provisionally that an Interpretation of this entity is confronted with peculiar difficulties grounded in the kind of Being which belongs to the object taken as our theme and to the very behaviour of so taking it. These difficulties are not grounded in any short-comings of the cognitive powers with which we are endowed, or in the lack of a suitable way of conceiving – a lack which seemingly would not be hard to remedy.

Not only, however, does an understanding of Being belong to Dasein, but this understanding develops or decays along with whatever kind of Being Dasein may possess at the time; accordingly there are many ways in which it has been interpreted, and these are all at Dasein's disposal. Dasein's ways of behaviour, its capacities, powers, possibilities, and vicis-situdes, have been studied with varying extent in philosophical psychology, in anthropology, ethics, and 'political science', in poetry, biography, and the writing of history, each in a different fashion. But the question remains whether these interpretations of Dasein have been carried through with a primordial existentiality comparable to whatever existentiell primor-diality they may have possessed. Neither of these excludes the other but they do not necessarily go together. Existentiell interpretation can demand an existential analytic, if indeed we conceive of philosophical cognition as something possible and necessary. Only when the basic structures of Dasein have been adequately worked out with explicit orientation towards the problem of Being itself, will what we have hitherto gained in inter-preting Dasein get its existential justification.

Thus an analytic of Dasein must remain our first requirement in the question of Being. But in that case the problem of obtaining and securing the kind of access which will lead to Dasein, becomes even more a burning one. To put it negatively, we have no right to resort to dogmatic constructions and to apply just any idea of Being and actuality to this entity, no matter how 'self-evident' that idea may be; nor may any of the 'categories' which such an idea prescribes be forced upon Dasein without proper ontological consideration. We must rather choose such a way of access and such a kind of interpretation that this entity can show itself in itself and from itself [*an ihm selbst von ihm selbst her*]. And this means that it is to be shown as it is *proximally and for the most part* – in its average *everydayness*. In this everydayness there are certain structures which we shall exhibit – not just any accidental structures, but essential ones which, in every kind of Being that factical Dasein may possess, persist as determinative for the character of its Being. Thus by having regard for the basic state of Dasein's everydayness, we shall bring out the Being of this entity in a preparatory fashion.

When taken in this way, the analytic of Dasein remains wholly oriented towards the guiding task of working out the question of Being. Its limits are thus determined. It cannot attempt to provide a complete ontology of Dasein, which assuredly must be constructed if anything like a 'philosophical' anthropology is to have a philosophically adequate basis.

If our purpose is to make such an anthropology possible, or to lay its ontological foundations, our Interpretation will provide only some of the 'pieces', even though they are by no means inessential ones. Our analysis of Dasein, however, is not only incomplete; it is also, in the first instance, *provisional*. It merely brings out the Being of this entity, without Interpreting its meaning. It is rather a preparatory procedure by which the horizon for the most primordial way of interpreting Being may be laid bare. Once we have arrived at that horizon, this preparatory analytic of Dasein will have to be repeated on a higher and authentically onto-logical basis.

We shall point to *temporality* as the meaning of the Being of that entity which we call 'Dasein'. If this is to be demonstrated, those structures of Dasein which we shall provisionally exhibit must be Interpreted over again as modes of temporality. In thus interpreting Dasein as temporality, however, we shall not give the answer to our leading question as to the meaning of Being in general. But the ground will have been prepared for obtaining such an answer.

We have already intimated that Dasein has a pre-ontological Being as its ontically constitutive state. Dasein *is* in such a way as to be something which understands something like Being. Keeping this inter-connection firmly in mind, we shall show that whenever Dasein tacitly understands and interprets something like Being, it does so with *time* as its standpoint. Time must be brought to light – and genuinely conceived – as the horizon for all understanding of Being and for any way of inter-preting it. In order for us to discern this, *time* needs to be *explicated primordially as the horizon for the understanding of Being, and in terms of temporality as the Being of Dasein, which understands Being*. This task as a whole requires that the conception of time thus obtained shall be distinguished from the way in which it is ordinarily understood. This ordinary way of understanding it has become explicit in an interpretation precipitated in the traditional concept of time, which has persisted from Aristotle to Bergson and even later. Here we must make clear that this conception of time and, in general, the ordinary way of understanding it, have sprung from temporality, and we must show how this has come about. We shall thereby restore to the ordinary conception the autonomy which is its rightful due, as against Bergson's thesis that the time one has in mind in this conception is space.

'Time' has long functioned as an ontological – or rather an ontical – criterion for naïvely discriminating various realms of entities. A distinction has been made between 'temporal' entities (natural processes and historical happenings) and 'non-temporal' entities (spatial and numerical relationships). We are accustomed to contrasting the 'timeless' meaning of propositions with the 'temporal' course of propositional assertions. It is also held that there is a 'cleavage' between 'temporal' entities and the 'supra-temporal' eternal, and efforts are made to bridge this over. Here 'temporal' always means simply being [*seiend*] 'in time' – a designation which, admittedly, is still pretty obscure. The fact remains that time, in the sense of 'being [*sein*] in time', functions as a criterion for distinguishing realms of Being. Hitherto no one has asked or troubled to investigate how time has come to have this distinctive ontological function, or with what right anything like time functions as such a criterion; nor has anyone asked whether the authentic ontological relevance which is possible for it, gets expressed when 'time' is used in so naïvely ontological a manner. 'Time' has acquired this 'self-evident' ontological function 'of its own accord', so to speak; indeed it has done so within the horizon of the way it is ordinarily understood. And it has maintained itself in this function to this day.

In contrast to all this, our treatment of the question of the meaning of Being must enable us to show that *the central problematic of all ontology is rooted in the phenomenon of time, if rightly seen and rightly explained*, and we must show *how* this is the case.

If Being is to be conceived in terms of time, and if, indeed, its various modes and derivatives are to become intelligible in their respective modifications and derivations by taking time into consideration, then Being itself (and not merely entities, let us say, as entities 'in time') is thus made visible in its 'temporal' character. But in that case, 'temporal' can no longer mean simply 'being in time'. Even the 'non-temporal' and the 'supra-temporal' are 'temporal' with regard to their Being, and not just privatively by contrast with something 'temporal' as an entity 'in time', but in a *positive* sense, though it is one which we must first explain. In both pre-philosophical and philosophical usage the expression 'temporal' has been pre-empted by the signification we have cited; in the following investigations, however, we shall employ it for another signification. Thus the way in which Being and its modes and characteristics have their meaning determined primordially in terms of time, is what we shall call its '*Temporal*' determinateness. Thus the fundamental ontological task of Interpreting Being as such includes working out the *Temporality of Being*. In the exposition of the problematic of Temporality the question of the meaning of Being will first be concretely answered.

Because Being cannot be grasped except by taking time into consideration, the answer to the question of Being cannot lie in any proposition that is blind and isolated. The answer is not properly conceived if what it asserts propositionally is just passed along, especially if it gets circulated as a free-floating result, so that we merely get informed about a 'standpoint' which may perhaps differ from the way this has hitherto been treated. Whether the answer is a 'new' one remains quite superficial and is of no importance. Its positive character must lie in its being *ancient* enough for us to learn to conceive the possibilities which the 'Ancients' have made ready for us. In its ownmost meaning this answer tells us that concrete ontological research must begin with an investigative inquiry which keeps within the horizon we have laid bare; and this is all that it tells us.

If, then, the answer to the question of Being is to provide the clues for our research, it cannot be adequate until it brings us the insight that the specific kind of Being of ontology hitherto, and the vicissitudes of its inquiries, its findings, and its failures, have been necessitated in the very character of Dasein.

§6 THE TASK OF DESTROYING THE HISTORY OF ONTOLOGY

All research – and not least that which operates within the range of the central question of Being – is an ontical possibility of Dasein. Dasein's Being finds its meaning in temporality. But temporality is also the condition which makes historicality possible as a temporal kind of Being which Dasein itself possesses, regardless of whether or how Dasein is an entity 'in time'. Historicality, as a determinate character, is prior to what is called 'history' (world-historical historizing).

'Historicality' stands for the state of Being that is constitutive for Dasein's 'historizing' as such; only on the basis of such 'historizing' is anything like 'world-history' possible or can anything belong historically to world-history. In its factical Being, any Dasein is as it already was, and it is 'what' it already was. It *is* its past, whether explicitly or not. And this is so not only in that its past is, as it were, pushing itself along 'behind' it, and that Dasein possesses what is past as a property which is still present-at-hand and which sometimes has after-effects upon it: Dasein 'is' its past in the way of *its* own Being, which, to put it roughly, 'historizes' out of its future on each occasion. Whatever the way of being it may have at the time, and thus with whatever understanding of Being it may possess, Dasein has grown up both into and in a traditional way of interpreting itself: in terms of this it understands itself proximally and, within a certain range, constantly. By this understanding, the possibilities of its Being are disclosed and regulated. Its own past – and this always means the past of its 'generation' – is not something which *follows along after* Dasein, but something which already goes ahead of it.

This elemental historicality of Dasein may remain hidden from Dasein itself. But there is a way by which it can be discovered and given proper attention. Dasein can discover tradition, preserve it, and study it explicitly. The discovery of tradition and the disclosure of what it 'transmits' and how this is transmitted, can be taken hold of as a task in its own right. In this way Dasein brings itself into the kind of Being which consists in historiological inquiry and research. But historiology – or more precisely historicity – is possible as a kind of Being which the inquiring Dasein may possess, only because historicality is a determining characteristic for Dasein in the very basis of its Being. If this historicality remains hidden from Dasein, and as long as it so remains, Dasein is also denied the possibility of historiological inquiry or the discovery of history. If historiology is wanting, this is not evidence *against* Dasein's historicality; on the contrary, as a deficient mode of this state of Being, it is evidence for it. Only because it is 'historical' can an era be unhistoriological.

On the other hand, if Dasein has seized upon its latent possibility not only of making its own existence transparent to itself but also of inquiring into the meaning of existentiality itself (that is to say, of previously inquiring into the meaning of Being in general), and if by such inquiry its eyes have been opened to its own essential historicality, then one cannot fail to see that the inquiry into Being (the ontico-ontological necessity of which we have already indicated) is itself characterized by historicality. The ownmost meaning of Being which belongs to the inquiry into Being as an historical inquiry, gives us the assignment [*Anweisung*] of inquiring into the history of that inquiry itself, that is, of becoming historiological. In working out the question of Being, we must heed this assignment, so that by positively making the past our own, we may bring ourselves into full possession of the ownmost possibilities of such inquiry. The question of the meaning of Being must be carried through by explicating Dasein beforehand in its temporality and historicality; the question thus brings itself to the point where it understands itself as historiological.

Our preparatory Interpretation of the fundamental structures of Dasein with regard to the average kind of Being which is closest to it (a kind of Being in which it is therefore proximally historical as well), will make manifest, however, not only that Dasein is inclined to fall back upon its world (the world in which it is) and to interpret itself in terms of that world by its reflected light, but also that Dasein simultaneously falls prey to the tradition of which it has more or less explicitly taken hold. This tradition keeps it from providing its own guidance, whether in inquiring or in choosing. This holds true – and by no means least – for that understanding which is rooted in Dasein's ownmost Being, and for the possibility of developing it – namely, for ontological understanding.

When tradition thus becomes master, it does so in such a way that what it 'transmits' is made so inaccessible, proximally and for the most part, that it rather becomes concealed. Tradition takes what has come down to us and delivers it over to self-evidence; it blocks our access to those primordial 'sources' from which the categories and concepts handed down to us have been in part quite genuinely drawn. Indeed it makes us forget that they have had such an origin, and makes us suppose that the necessity of going back to these sources is something which we need not even understand. Dasein has had its historicality so throughly uprooted by tradition that it confines its interest to the multiformity of possible types, directions, and standpoints of philosophical activity in the most exotic and alien of cultures; and by this very interest it seeks to veil the fact that it has no ground of its own to stand on. Consequently, despite all its historiological interests and all its zeal for an Interpretation which is philologically 'objective' ['*sachliche*'], Dasein no longer understands the most elementary conditions which would alone enable it to go back to the past in a positive manner and make it productively its own.

We have shown at the outset (Section I) not only that the question of the meaning of Being is one that has not been attended to and one that has been inadequately formulated, but that it has become quite forgotten in spite of all our interest in 'metaphysics'. Greek ontology and its history – which, in their numerous filiations and distortions, determine the conceptual character of philosophy even today – prove that when Dasein understands either itself or Being in general, it does so in terms of the 'world', and that the ontology which has thus arisen has deteriorated [*verfällt*] to a tradition in which it gets reduced to something self-evident – merely material for reworking, as it was for Hegel. In the Middle Ages this uprooted Greek ontology became a fixed body of doctrine. Its systematics, however, is by no means a mere joining together of traditional pieces into a single edifice. Though its basic conceptions of Being have been taken over dogmatically from the Greeks, a great deal of unpretentious work has been carried on further within these limits. With the peculiar character which the Scholastics gave it, Greek ontology has, in its essentials, travelled the path that leads through the *Disputationes metaphysicae* of Suarez to the 'metaphysics' and transcendental philosophy of modern times, determining even the foundations and the aims of Hegel's 'logic'. In the course of this history certain distinctive domains of Being have come into view and have served as the primary guides for subsequent problematics: the *ego cogito* of Descartes, the subject, the 'I', reason, spirit, person. But these all remain uninterrogated as to their Being and its structure, in accordance with the thoroughgoing way in which the question of Being has been neglected. It is rather the case that the categorial content of the traditional ontology has been carried over to these entities with corresponding formalizations and purely negative restrictions, or else dialectic has been called in for the purpose of Interpreting the substantiality of the subject ontologically.

If the question of Being is to have its own history made transparent, then this hardened tradition must be loosened up, and the concealments which it has brought about must be dissolved. We understand this task as one in which by taking *the question of Being as our clue*, we are to *destroy* the traditional content of ancient ontology until we arrive at those primordial experiences in which we achieved our first ways of determining the nature of Being – the ways which have guided us ever since.

In thus demonstrating the origin of our basic ontological concepts by an investigation in which their 'birth certificate' is displayed, we have nothing to do with a vicious relativizing of ontological standpoints. But this destruction is just as far from having the *negative* sense of shaking off the ontological tradition. We must, on the contrary, stake out the positive possibilities of that tradition, and this always means keeping it within its *limits*; these in turn are given factically in the way the question is formulated at the time, and in the way the possible field for investigation is thus bounded off. On its negative side, this destruction does not relate itself towards the past; its criticism is aimed at 'today' and at the prevalent way of treating the history of ontology, whether it is headed towards doxography, towards intellectual history, or towards a history of problems. But to bury the past in nullity [*Nichtigkeit*] is not the purpose of this destruction; its aim is *positive* . . .

§7 THE PHENOMENOLOGICAL METHOD OF INVESTIGATION

In provisionally characterizing the object which serves as the theme of our investigation (the Being of entities, or the meaning of Being in general), it seems that we have also delineated the method to be employed. The task of ontology is to explain Being itself and to make the Being of entities stand out in full relief. And the method of ontology remains questionable in the highest degree as long as we merely consult those ontologies which have come down to us historically, or other essays of that character. Since the term 'ontology' is used in this investigation in a sense which is formally broad, any attempt to clarify the method of ontology by tracing its history is automatically ruled out.

When, moreover, we use the term 'ontology', we are not talking about some definite philosophical discipline standing in interconnection with the others. Here one does not have to measure up to the tasks of some discipline that has been presented beforehand; on the contrary, only in terms of the objective necessities of definite questions and the kind of treatment which the 'things themselves' require, can one develop such a discipline.

With the question of the meaning of Being, our investigation comes up against the fundamental question of philosophy. This is one that must be treated *phenomenologically*. Thus our treatise does not subscribe to a 'stand-point' or represent any special 'direction'; for phenomenology is nothing of either sort, nor can it become so as long as it understands itself. The expression 'phenomenology' signifies primarily a *methodological conception*. This expression does not characterize the what of the objects of philosophical research as subject-matter, but rather the *how* of that research. The more genuinely a methodological concept is worked out and the more comprehensively it determines the principles on which a science is to be conducted, all the more primordially is it rooted in the way we come to terms with the things themselves, and the farther is it removed from what we call 'technical devices', though there are many such devices even in the theoretical disciplines.

Thus the term 'phenomenology' expresses a maxim which can be formulated as 'To the things themselves!' It is opposed to all free-floating constructions and accidental findings; it is opposed to taking over any conceptions which only seem to have been demonstrated; it is opposed to those pseudo-questions which parade themselves as 'problems', often for generations at a time. Yet this maxim, one may rejoin, is abundantly self-evident, and it expresses, moreover, the underlying principle of any scientific knowledge whatsoever. Why should anything so self-evident be taken up explicitly in giving a title to a branch of research? In point of fact, the issue here is a kind of 'self-evidence' which we should like to bring closer to us, so far as it is important to do so in casting light upon the procedure of our treatise. We shall expound only the preliminary conception [*Vorbegriff*] of phenomenology. . . .

The Preliminary Conception of Phenomenology

. . . 'Phenomenology' means ἀποφαίνεσθαι τὰ φαινόμενα – to let that which shows itself be seen from itself in the very way in which it shows itself from itself. This is the formal meaning of that branch of research which calls itself 'phenomenology'. But here we are expressing nothing else than the maxim formulated above: 'To the things themselves!'

Thus the term 'phenomenology' is quite different in its meaning from expressions such as 'theology' and the like. Those terms designate the objects of their respective sciences according to the subject-matter which they comprise at the time [*in ihrer jeweiligen Sachhaltigkeit*]. 'Phenomenology' neither designates the object of its researches, nor characterizes the subject-matter thus comprised. The word merely informs us of the *'how'* with which *what* is to be treated in this science gets exhibited and handled. To have a science 'of' phenomena means to grasp its objects *in such a way* that everything about them which is up for discussion must be treated by exhibiting it directly and demonstrating it directly. The expression 'descriptive phenomenology', which is at bottom tautological, has the same meaning. Here 'description' does not signify such a proce-dure as we find, let us say, in botanical morphology; the term has rather the sense of a prohibition – the avoidance of characterizing anything without such demonstration. The character of this description itself, the specific meaning of the λóγος, can be established first of all in terms of the 'thinghood' ['*Sachheit*'] of what is to be 'described' – that is to say, of what is to be given scientific definiteness as we encounter it phenom-enally. The signification of 'phenomenon', as conceived both formally and in the ordinary manner, is such that any exhibiting of an entity as it shows itself in itself, may be called 'phenomenology' with formal justification.

Now what must be taken into account if the formal conception of phenomenon is to be deformalized into the phenomenological one, and how is this latter to be distinguished from the ordinary conception? What is it that phenomenology is to 'let us see'? What is it that must be called a 'phenomenon' in a distinctive sense? What is it that by its very essence is *necessarily* the theme whenever we exhibit something *explicitly*? Manifestly, it is something that proximally and for the most part does *not* show itself at all: it is something that lies *hidden*, in contrast to that which proximally and for the most part does show itself; but at the same time it is something that belongs to what thus shows itself, and it belongs to it so essentially as to constitute its meaning and its ground.

Yet that which remains *hidden* in an egregious sense, or which relapses and gets *covered up* again, or which shows itself only '*in disguise*', is not just this entity or that, but rather the *Being* of entities, as our previous observations have shown. This Being can be covered up so extensively that it becomes forgotten and no question arises about it or about its meaning. Thus that which demands that it become a phenomenon, and which demands this in a distinctive sense and in terms of its ownmost content as a thing, is what phenomenology has taken into its grasp themat-ically as its object.

Phenomenology is our way of access to what is to be the theme of ontology, and it is our way of giving it demonstrative precision. *Only as phenomenology, is ontology possible.* In the phenomenological conception of 'phenomenon' what one has in mind as that which shows itself is the Being of entities, its meaning, its modifications and derivatives. And this showing-itself is not just any showing-itself, nor is it some such thing as appearing. Least of all can the Being of entities ever be anything such that 'behind it' stands something else 'which does not appear'.

'Behind' the phenomena of phenomenology there is essentially nothing else; on the other hand, what is to become a phenomenon can be hidden. And just because the phenomena are proximally and for the most part *not* given, there is need for phenomenology. Covered-up-ness is the counter-concept to 'phenomenon'.

There are various ways in which phenomena can be covered up. In the first place, a phenomenon can be covered up in the sense that it is still quite *undiscovered*. It is neither known nor unknown. Moreover, a phenomenon can be *buried over* [*verschüttet*]. This means that it has at some time been discovered but has deteriorated [*verfiel*] to the point of getting covered up again. This covering-up can become complete; or rather – and as a rule – what has been discovered earlier may still be visible, though only as a semblance. Yet so much semblance, so much 'Being'. This covering-up as a 'disguising' is both the most frequent and the most dangerous, for here the possibilities of deceiving and misleading are especially stubborn. Within a 'system', perhaps, those structures of Being – and their concepts – which are still available but veiled in their indigenous character, may claim their rights. For when they have been bound together constructively in a system, they present themselves as something 'clear', requiring no further justification, and thus can serve as the point of departure for a process of deduction.

The covering-up itself, whether in the sense of hiddenness, burying-over, or disguise, has in turn two possibilities. There are coverings-up which are accidental; there are also some which are necessary, grounded in what the thing discovered consists in [*der Bestandart des Entdeckten*]. Whenever a phenomenological concept is drawn from primordial sources, there is a possibility that it may degenerate if communicated in the form of an assertion. It gets understood in an empty way and is thus passed on, losing its indigenous character, and becoming a free-floating thesis. Even in the concrete work of phenomenology itself there lurks the possibility that what has been primordially 'within our grasp' may become hardened so that we can no longer grasp it. And the difficulty of this kind of research lies in making it self-critical in a positive sense.

The way in which Being and its structures are encountered in the mode of phenomenon is one which must first of all be *wrested* from the objects of phenomenology. Thus the very *point of departure* [*Ausgang*] for our analysis requires that it be secured by the proper method, just as much as does our *access* [*Zugang*] to the phenomenon, or our *passage* [*Durchgang*] through whatever is prevalently covering it up. The idea of grasping and explicating phenomena in a way which is 'original' and 'intuitive' [*'originären' und 'intuitiven'*] is directly opposed to the *naïveté* of a haphazard, 'immediate', and unreflective 'beholding' [*'Schauen'*].

Now that we have delimited our preliminary conception of phenomenology, the terms *'phenomenal'* and *'phenomenological'* can also be fixed in their signification. That which is given and explicable in the way the phenomenon is encountered is called 'phenomenal'; this is what we have in mind when we talk about 'phenomenal structures'. Everything which belongs to the species of exhibiting and explicating and which goes to make up the way of conceiving demanded by this research, is called 'phenomenological'.

Because phenomena, as understood phenomenologically, are never anything but what goes to make up Being, while Being is in every case the Being of some entity, we must first bring forward the entities themselves if it is our aim that Being should be laid bare; and we must do this in the right way. These entities must likewise show themselves with the kind of access which genuinely belongs to them. And in this way the ordinary conception of phenomenon becomes phenomenologically relevant. If our analysis is to be authentic, its aim is such that the prior task of assuring ourselves 'phenomenologically' of that entity which is to serve as our example, has already been prescribed as our point of departure.

With regard to its subject-matter, phenomenology is the science of the Being of entities – ontology. In explaining the tasks of ontology we found it necessary that there should be a fundamental ontology taking as its theme that entity which is ontologico-ontically distinctive, Dasein, in order to confront the cardinal problem – the question of the meaning of Being in general. Our investigation itself will show that the meaning of phenomenological description as a method lies in *interpretation*. The λόγος of the phenomenology of Dasein has the character of a ἑρμηνεύειν, through which the authentic meaning of Being, and also those basic structures of Being which Dasein itself possesses, are *made known* to Dasein's understanding of Being. The phenomenology of Dasein is a *hermeneutic* in the primordial signification of this word, where it designates this business of interpreting. But to the extent that by uncovering the meaning of Being and the basic structures of Dasein in general we may exhibit the horizon for any further ontological study of those entities which do not have the character of Dasein, this hermeneutic also becomes a 'hermeneutic' in the sense of working out the conditions on which the possibility of any ontological investigation depends. And finally, to the extent that Dasein, as an entity with the possibility of existence, has ontological priority over every other entity, 'hermeneutic', as an interpretation of Dasein's Being, has the third and specific sense of an analytic of the existentiality of existence; and this is the sense which is philosophically *primary*. Then so far as this hermeneutic works out Dasein's historicality ontologically as the ontical condition for the possibility of historiology, it contains the roots of what can be called 'hermeneutic' only in a derivative sense: the methodology of those humane sciences which are historiological in character.

Being, as the basic theme of philosophy, is no class or genus of entities; yet it pertains to every entity. Its 'universality' is to be sought higher up. Being and the structure of Being lie beyond every entity and every possible character which an entity may possess. *Being is the transcendens pure and simple.* And the transcendence of Dasein's Being is distinctive in that it implies the possibility and the necessity of the most radical *individuation.* Every disclosure of Being as the *transcendens* is *transcendental* knowledge. *Phenomenological truth (the disclosedness of Being) is veritas transcendentalis.*

Ontology and phenomenology are not two distinct philosophical disciplines among others. These terms characterize philosophy itself with regard to its object and its way of treating that object. Philosophy is universal phenomenological ontology, and takes its departure from the hermeneutic of Dasein, which, as an analytic of *existence*, has made fast the guiding-line for all philosophical inquiry at the point where it *arises* and to which it *returns*.

The following investigation would not have been possible if the ground had not been prepared by Edmund Husserl, with whose *Logische Untersuchungen* phenomenology first emerged. Our comments on the preliminary conception of phenomenology have shown that what is essential in it does not lie in its *actuality* as a philosophical 'movement' ['*Richtung*']. Higher than actuality stands *possibility.* . . .

MARTIN HEIDEGGER

Anxiety (*Being and Time*, §40)

... WE SHALL TRY to proceed towards the phenomenon of anxiety step by step.

Dasein's falling into the 'they' and the 'world' of its concern, is what we have called a 'fleeing' in the face of itself. But one is not necessarily fleeing whenever one shrinks back in the face of something or turns away from it. Shrinking back in the face of what fear discloses – in the face of something threatening – is founded upon fear; and this shrinking back has the character of fleeing. Our Interpretation of fear as a state-of-mind has shown that in each case that in the face of which we fear is a detrimental entity within-the-world which comes from some definite region but is close by and is bringing itself close, and yet might stay away. In falling, Dasein turns away from itself. That in the face of which it thus shrinks back must, in any case, be an entity with the character of threatening; yet this entity has the same kind of Being as the one that shrinks back: it is Dasein itself. That in the face of which it thus shrinks back cannot be taken as something 'fearsome', for anything 'fearsome' is always encountered as an entity within-the-world. The only threatening which can be 'fearsome' and which gets discovered in fear, always comes from entities within-the-world.

Thus the turning-away of falling is not a fleeing that is founded upon a fear of entities within-the-world. Fleeing that is so grounded is still less a character of this turning-away, when what this turning-away does is precisely to *turn thither* towards entities within-the-world by absorbing itself in them. *The turning-away of falling is grounded rather in anxiety, which in turn is what first makes fear possible.*

To understand this talk about Dasein's fleeing in the face of itself in falling, we must recall that Being-in-the-world is a basic state of Dasein. *That in the face of which one has anxiety [das Wovor der Angst] is Being-in-the-world as such.* What is the difference phenomenally between that in the face of which anxiety is anxious [*sich ängstet*] and that in the face of which fear is afraid? That in the face of which one has anxiety is not an entity within-the-world. Thus it is essentially incapable of having an involvement. This threatening does not have the character of a definite detrimentality which reaches what is threatened, and which reaches it with definite regard to a special factical potentiality-for-Being. That in the face of which one is anxious is completely indefinite. Not only does this indefiniteness leave factically undecided which entity within-the-world is threatening us, but it also tells us that entities within-the-world are not 'relevant' at all. Nothing which is ready-to-hand or present-at-hand within

From *Being and Time*, trans. J. Macquarrie and E. Robinson, Oxford: Blackwell, 1967.

the world functions as that in the face of which anxiety is anxious. Here the totality of involvements of the ready-to-hand and the present-at-hand discovered within-the-world, is, as such, of no consequence; it collapses into itself; the world has the character of completely lacking significance. In anxiety one does not encounter this thing or that thing which, as something threatening, must have an involvement.

Accordingly, when something threatening brings itself close, anxiety does not 'see' any definite 'here' or 'yonder' from which it comes. That in the face of which one has anxiety is characterized by the fact that what threatens is *nowhere*. Anxiety 'does not know' what that in the face of which it is anxious is. 'Nowhere', however, does not signify nothing: this is where any region lies, and there too lies any disclosedness of the world for essentially spatial Being-in. Therefore that which threatens cannot bring itself close from a definite direction within what is close by; it is already 'there', and yet nowhere; it is so close that it is oppressive and stifles one's breath, and yet it is nowhere.

In that in the face of which one has anxiety, the 'It is nothing and nowhere' becomes manifest. The obstinacy of the 'nothing and nowhere within-the-world' means as a phenomenon that *the world as such is that in the face of which one has anxiety*. The utter insignificance which makes itself known in the 'nothing and nowhere', does not signify that the world is absent, but tells us that entities within-the-world are of so little importance in themselves that on the basis of this *insignificance* of what is within-the-world, the world in its worldhood is all that still obtrudes itself.

What oppresses us is not this or that, nor is it the summation of everything present-at-hand; it is rather the *possibility* of the ready-to-hand in general; that is to say, it is the world itself. When anxiety has subsided, then in our everyday way of talking we are accustomed to say that 'it was really nothing'. And *what* it was, indeed, does get reached ontically by such a way of talking. Everyday discourse tends towards concerning itself with the ready-to-hand and talking about it. That in the face of which anxiety is anxious is nothing ready-to-hand within-the-world. But this 'nothing ready-to-hand', which only our everyday circumspective discourse understands, is not totally nothing. The 'nothing' of readiness-to-hand is grounded in the most primordial 'something' – in the *world*. Ontologically, however, the world belongs essentially to Dasein's Being as Being-in-the-world. So if the 'nothing' – that is, the world as such – exhibits itself as that in the face of which one has anxiety, this means that *Being-in-the-world itself is that in the face of which anxiety is anxious*.

Being-anxious discloses, primordially and directly, the world as world. It is not the case, say, that the world first gets thought of by deliberating about it, just by itself, without regard for the entities within-the-world, and that, in the face of this world, anxiety then arises; what is rather the case is that the *world as world* is disclosed first and foremost by anxiety, as a mode of state-of-mind. This does not signify, however, that in anxiety the worldhood of the world gets conceptualized.

Anxiety is not only anxiety in the face of something, but, as a state-of-mind, it is also *anxiety about* something. That which anxiety is profoundly anxious [*sich abängstet*] about is not a *definite* kind of Being for Dasein or a *definite* possibility for it. Indeed the threat itself is indefinite, and therefore cannot penetrate threateningly to this or that factically concrete potentiality-for-Being. That which anxiety is anxious about is Being-in-the-world itself. In anxiety what is environmentally ready-to-hand sinks away, and so, in general, do entities within-the-world. The 'world' can offer nothing more, and neither can the Dasein-with of Others. Anxiety thus takes away from Dasein the possibility of understanding itself, as it falls, in terms of the 'world' and the way things have been publicly interpreted. Anxiety throws Dasein back upon that which it is anxious about – its authentic potentiality-for-Being-in-the-world. Anxiety individualizes Dasein for its ownmost Being-in-the-world, which as something that understands, projects itself essentially upon possibilities. Therefore, with that which it is anxious about, anxiety discloses Dasein *as Being-possible*, and indeed as the only kind of thing which it can be of its own accord as something individualized in individualization [*vereinzeltes in der Vereinzelung*].

Anxiety makes manifest in Dasein its *Being towards* its ownmost potentiality-for-Being – that is, its *Being-free for* the freedom of choosing itself and taking hold of itself. Anxiety brings Dasein face to face with its *Being-free for* (*propensio in* . . .) the authenticity of its Being, and for this authenticity as a possibility which it always is. But at the same time, this is the Being to which Dasein as Being-in-the-world has been delivered over.

That *about which* anxiety is anxious reveals itself as that *in the face of which* it is anxious – namely, Being-in-the-world. The selfsameness of that in the face of which and that about which one has anxiety, extends even to anxiousness [*Sichängsten*] itself. For, as a state-of-mind, anxiousness is a basic kind of Being-in-the-world. *Here the disclosure and the disclosed are existentially selfsame in such a way that in the latter the world has been disclosed as world, and Being-in has been disclosed as a potentiality-for-Being which is individualized, pure, and thrown; this makes it plain that with the phenomenon of anxiety a distinctive state-of-mind has become a theme for Interpretation.* Anxiety individualizes Dasein and thus discloses it as '*solus ipse*'. But this existential 'solipsism' is so far from the displacement of putting an isolated subject-Thing into the innocuous emptiness of a worldless occurring, that in an extreme sense what it does is precisely to bring Dasein face to face with its world as world, and thus bring it face to face with itself as Being-in-the-world.

Again everyday discourse and the everyday interpretation of Dasein furnish our most unbiased evidence that anxiety as a basic state-of-mind is disclosive in the manner we have shown. As we have said earlier, a state-of-mind makes manifest 'how one is'. In anxiety one feels *'uncanny'*. Here the peculiar indefiniteness of that which Dasein finds itself alongside in anxiety, comes proximally to expression: the 'nothing and nowhere'. But here 'uncanniness' also means 'not-being-at-home' [*das Nichtzuhause-sein*]. In our first indication of the phenomenal character of Dasein's basic state and in our clarification of the existential meaning of 'Being-in' as distinguished from the categorial signification of 'insideness', Being-in was defined as 'residing alongside . . .', 'Being-familiar with . . .'. This character of Being-in was then brought to view more concretely through the everyday publicness of the 'they', which brings tranquillized self-assurance – 'Being-at-home', with all its obviousness – into the average everydayness of Dasein. On the other hand, as Dasein falls, anxiety brings it back from its absorption in the 'world'. Everyday familiarity collapses. Dasein has been individualized, but individualized *as* Being-in-the-world. Being-in enters into the existential 'mode' of the *'not-at-home'*. Nothing else is meant by our talk about 'uncanniness'.

By this time we can see phenomenally what falling, as fleeing, flees in the face of. It does not flee *in the face of* entities within-the-world; these are precisely what it flees *towards* – as entities alongside which our concern, lost in the 'they', can dwell in tranquillized familiarity. When in falling we flee *into* the 'at-home' of publicness, we flee *in the face of* the 'not-at-home'; that is, we flee in the face of the uncanniness which lies in Dasein – in Dasein as thrown Being-in-the-world, which has been delivered over to itself in its Being. This uncanniness pursues Dasein constantly, and is a threat to its everyday lostness in the 'they', though not explicitly. This threat can go together factically with complete assurance and self-sufficiency in one's everyday concern. Anxiety can arise in the most innocuous Situations. Nor does it have any need for darkness, in which it is commonly easier for one to feel uncanny. In the dark there is emphatically 'nothing' to see, though the very world itself is *still* 'there', and 'there' *more obtrusively*.

If we Interpret Dasein's uncanniness from an existential-ontological point of view as a threat which reaches Dasein itself and which comes from Dasein itself, we are not contending that in factical anxiety too it has always been understood in this sense. When Dasein 'understands' uncanniness in the everyday manner, it does so by turning away from it in falling; in this turning-away, the 'not-at-home' gets 'dimmed down'. Yet the everydayness of this fleeing shows phenomenally that anxiety, as a basic state-of-mind, belongs to Dasein's essential state of Being-in-the-world, which, as one that is existential, is never present-at-hand but is itself always in a mode of factical Being-there – that is, in the mode of a state-of-mind. That kind of Being-in-the-world which is tranquillized and familiar is a mode of Dasein's uncanniness, not the reverse. *From an existential-ontological point of view, the 'not-at-home' must be conceived as the more primordial phenomenon.*

And only because anxiety is always latent in Being-in-the-world, can such Being-in-the-world, as Being which is alongside the 'world' and which is concernful in its state-of-mind, ever be afraid. Fear is anxiety, fallen into the 'world', inauthentic, and, as such, hidden from itself.

After all, the mood of uncanniness remains, factically, something for which we mostly have no existentiell understanding. Moreover, under the ascendancy of falling and publicness, 'real' anxiety is rare. Anxiety is often conditioned by 'physiological' factors. This fact, in its facticity, is a problem *ontologically*, not merely with regard to its ontical causation and course of development. Only because Dasein is anxious in the very depths of its Being, does it become possible for anxiety to be elicited physiologically.

Even rarer than the existentiell Fact of 'real' anxiety are attempts to Interpret this phenomenon according to the principles of its existential-ontological Constitution and function. The reasons for this lie partly in the general neglect of the existential analytic of Dasein, but more particularly in a failure to recognize the phenomenon of state-of-mind. Yet the factical rarity of anxiety as a phenomenon cannot deprive it of its fitness to take over a methodological function *in principle* for the existential analytic. On the contrary, the rarity of the phenomenon is an index that Dasein, which for the most part remains concealed from itself in its authenticity because of the way in which things have been publicly interpreted by the 'they', becomes disclosable in a primordial sense in this basic state-of-mind.

Of course it is essential to every state-of-mind that in each case Being-in-the-world should be fully disclosed in all those items which are constitutive for it – world, Being-in, Self. But in anxiety there lies the possibility of a disclosure which is quite distinctive; for anxiety individualizes. This individualization brings Dasein back from its falling, and makes manifest to it that authenticity and inauthenticity are possibilities of its Being . . .

3

Karl Jaspers

(1883–1969)

The German philosopher Karl Jaspers turned his attention to many of the existentialist themes explored in the work of such thinkers as Heidegger and Sartre, but with a decisively different emphasis. For Jaspers, the existentialist project remained consistent and continuous with the historical practice of 'philosophizing' that has always shown a special affinity for the domains of science and religion. Although philosophizing itself cannot be reductively assimilated into a purely scientific or religious orientation, both of these spheres contribute greatly to the 'one, primordial philosophy' that guides our interrogations. Thus, Jaspers' specific privileging of *Existenz* did not fall outside 'philosophizing' as already understood within the Western philosophical tradition.

In taking this stance, Jaspers clearly separated himself from any overall critique of 'science-as-positivism' (such as we find in Heidegger or Adorno) that would condemn the scientific attitude *tout court*. He valued the procedural constraints of scientific method and consensus, affirming their role in the quest for reliable knowledge. Like Kant, he preferred to limit philosophy's claims to 'knowledge', thereby highlighting the danger of invoking an unrestrained speculative apparatus in this arena. However, he also cautioned against the opposite peril of equating science with philosophy, thus ignoring the possibility of transcendence that, according to Jaspers, especially marks our human condition in the world. Reason figures importantly in dealing with the problem of *Existenz*, but we inevitably face the dilemma of our own finitude and its transcendence that defines us as more than just objects of scientific observation.

Jaspers introduces the idea of 'the encompassing' (*das Umgreifende*) which provides an expanded horizon for contextualizing our complex experience of being situated in the world. In its subjective modes, 'the encompassing' grounds not only the practical concerns of our individual and communal existence, but also our more abstract intellectual and conceptual achievements as well. Above all, Jaspers designates the ultimate source and possibility of our freedom as *Existenz*, a transcendence which exceeds any particular or concrete actualization, but remains an open horizon for all individuals. This same freedom and openness also provides the occasion for our failure and guilt, the possibility of what Jaspers calls 'shipwreck' (*Schiffbruch*) or 'foundering' (*Scheitern*). Indeed, drawing on Kierkegaard's insight, Jaspers notes that such 'foundering' is significant because it spurs and deepens our human capacity for transcendence.

The questions which we must ultimately ask regarding 'boundary situations' (*Grenzsituationen*), such as the meaning of death, cannot be fully answered by appeals to the rational objectivity of scientific knowledge. Neither can we rely entirely on religious revelation to adequately address these uncomfortable but inevitable boundary questions. For Jaspers, the philosophical tradition is the one domain of inquiry that has attempted to explore such issues by recognizing our potential for *both* transcendence and rationality. In fact, Jaspers' great respect for the value of this philosophical tradition sets him apart from the mainstream of twentieth-century thought that has rejected this tradition and indicted it as the source of philosophical confusion that needs to be interrogated. Jaspers stands against Heidegger in this regard, despite the apparent similarity in their claims prioritizing existence over essence. Subsequent philosophical developments have undoubtedly taken their cue from Heidegger, particularly his critique of Cartesian subjectivity, while Jaspers' work has remained rather more unfashionably on the sidelines. However, Jaspers distinguishes himself by reminding us that the challenge and the burden of 'philosophical thinking' has a history, and we are but the most recent manifestations of that history.

The selection chosen is taken from the last public lecture that Jaspers was permitted to give in 1937, before being silenced for the remainder of the Nazi regime.

SELECT BIBLIOGRAPHY OF JASPERS' WORKS IN ENGLISH

The Question of German Guilt, New York: Dial Press, 1947.
The Perennial Scope of Philosophy, New York: Philosophical Library, 1949.
The Origin and Goal of History, New Haven: Yale University Press, 1953.
Truth and Symbol, London: Vision Press, 1959.
The Great Philosophers: The Foundations, New York: Harcourt, Brace & World, 1962.
General Psychopathology, Chicago: University of Chicago Press, 1963.
The Great Philosophers: The Original Thinkers, New York: Harcourt, Brace & World, 1966.
Philosophical Faith and Revelation, Chicago: University of Chicago Press, 1967.
Philosophy, 3 vols, Chicago: University of Chicago Press, 1969–71.
Philosophy of Existence, Philadelphia, Pa.: University of Pennsylvania Press, 1971.

Introduction to *Philosophy of Existence*

I HAVE BEEN invited to speak about the philosophy of existence. Part of philosophy today goes by this name. The distinguishing term 'existence' is meant to emphasize that it is of the present.

What is called philosophy of existence is really only a form of the one, primordial philosophy. It is no accident, however, that for the moment the word 'existence' became the distinguishing term. It emphasized the task of philosophy that for a time had been almost forgotten: *to catch sight of reality at its origin and to grasp it through the way in which I, in thought, deal with myself – in inner action.* From mere knowledge of something, from ways of speaking, from conventions and role-playing – from all kinds of foreground phenomena – philosophizing wanted to find its way back to reality. *Existenz* is one of the words for reality, with the accent Kierkegaard gave it: everything essentially real is for me only by virtue of the fact that I am I myself. We do not merely exist; rather, our existence is entrusted to us as the arena and the body for the realization of our origin.

Already in the nineteenth century, movements with this turn of mind kept recurring. People wanted 'life', wanted 'really to live'. They demanded 'realism'. Instead of wanting merely to know, they wanted to experience for themselves. Everywhere, they wanted the 'genuine', searched for 'origins', and wanted to press on to *man* himself. Superior men became more clearly visible; at the same time, it became possible to discover the true and the real in the smallest particle.

If for a century now the tenor of the age has been entirely different – namely, one of leveling, mechanization, the development of a mass mentality and universal interchangeability of everything and everyone where no one seemed to exist any longer as himself, it was also a stimulating background. Men who could be themselves woke up in this pitiless atmosphere in which every individual was sacrificed as individual. They wanted to take themselves seriously; they searched for the hidden reality; they wanted to know what was knowable; and they thought that by understanding themselves they could arrive at the foundation of their being.

But even this thinking frequently degenerated into the frivolous veiling of reality that is characteristic of the leveling process, by perversion into a tumultuous and pathetic philosophy of feeling and life. The will to experience being for oneself could be perverted into a contentment with the merely vital; the will to find the origin into a mania for primitivism; the sense of rank into a betrayal of the genuine orders of value.

From *Philosophy of Existence*, Philadelphia, Pa.: University of Pennsylvania Press, 1971.

We do not propose to consider in its totality this loss of reality in an age of apparently heightened realism – an age out of whose growing awareness developed the soul's distress, and philosophizing. Instead, we shall attempt to recall by an historical account the tortuous route taken by this return to reality – a return that took many shapes – using as an example *our relation to the sciences*, an example that is inherently essential to our theme.

At the turn of the century, philosophy was for the most part conceived as one science among others. It was a field of academic study, and was approached by young people as an educational possibility. Sparkling lectures offered vast surveys of its history, its doctrines, problems and systems. Vague feelings of a freedom and truth often devoid of content (because rarely effective in actual life) combined with a faith in the progress of philosophical knowledge. The thinker 'advanced further' and was convinced that with each step he stood at the summit of knowledge attained up to that time.

This philosophy, however, seemed to lack self-confidence. The boundless respect of the age for the exact empirical sciences made them the great exemplar. Philosophy wanted to regain its lost reputation before the judgment seat of the sciences by means of equal exactness. To be sure, all objects of inquiry had been parcelled out to the special sciences. But philosophy wanted to legitimize itself alongside of them by making the whole into a scientific object; the whole of knowledge, for example, by means of epistemology (since the fact of science in general was after all not the object of any particular science); the whole of the universe by means of a metaphysics constructed by analogy with scientific theories, and with their aid; the totality of human ideals by means of a doctrine of universally valid values. These seemed to be objects that did not belong to any special science and yet ought to be open to investigation by scientific methods. Nevertheless, the basic tenor of all this thinking was ambiguous. For it was at once scientific-objective and moral-normative. Men could think they were establishing a harmonious union between the 'needs of the mind' and the 'results of the sciences'. Finally, they could say that they merely wanted objectively to understand the possible world-views and values, and yet again could claim at the same time to be giving the one true world-view: the scientific.

Young people in those days were bound to experience a deep disillusionment. This was not what they had thought philosophy was all about. The passion for a life-grounding philosophy made them reject this scientific philosophy which was impressive in its methodological rigor and its demands for arduous thought, and thus at least of educational value, but was basically too innocuous, too easily satisfied, too blind to reality. Demanding reality, they rejected empty abstractions that, for all their systematic orderliness yet seemed like children's games; they rejected proofs that proved nothing despite great ostentation. There were some who took the hint implicit in the hidden self-condemnation of this philosophy which took its own measure from the empirical sciences; they pursued the empirical sciences themselves; they abandoned this philosophy, perhaps believing in another philosophy that they did not yet know.

What enthusiasm gripped those students at that time who left philosophy after a few semesters and went into the natural sciences, history and the other research sciences! Here were realities. Here the will to know could find satisfaction: what startling, alarming and yet again hope-inspiring facts of nature, of human existence, of society, and of historical events! What Liebig had written in 1840 about the study of philosophy was still true: 'I too have lived through this period, so rich in words and ideas and so poor in true knowledge and genuine research, and it has cost me two precious years of my life.'

But when the sciences were taken up as though they themselves already contained true philosophy, that is, when they were supposed to give what had been sought to no avail in philosophy, typical errors became possible. Men wanted a science that would tell them what goals to pursue in life – an evaluating science. They deduced from science the right ways of conduct, and pretended to know by means of science what in fact were articles of faith – albeit about things immanent in this world. Or, conversely, they despaired of science because it did not yield what is important in life and, worse, because scientific reflection seemed to paralyze life. Thus attitudes wavered between a superstitious faith in science that makes an absolute starting point out of presumed results, and an antagonism to science that rejects it as meaningless and attacks it as destructive. But these aberrations were only incidental. In fact, powers arose in the sciences themselves that defeated both aberrations, in that knowledge, as knowledge purified itself.

For, when in the sciences too much was asserted for which there was no proof, when comprehensive theories were all too confidently put forward as absolute knowledge of reality, when too much was accepted as self-evident without examination (for example, the basic idea of nature as a mechanism, or many question-begging theories such as the doctrine that the necessity of historical events can be known, and so on), bad philosophy reappeared in the sciences in even worse form. But – and this was magnificent and exalting – *criticism* still existed and was still at work in science itself: not the endless round of philosophical polemic that never leads to any agreement, but the effective, step-by-step criticism that determines the truth for everyone. This criticism destroyed illusions in order to grasp the really knowable in greater purity.

Also, there were great *scientific events* that broke through all dogmatism. At the turn of the century, with the discovery of radioactivity and the beginnings of quantum theory, began the intellectual relativizing of the rigid shell of the mechanistic view of nature. There began the development which has continued to this day, of ideas of discovery that no longer led into the cul-de-sac of a nature existing and known in itself. The earlier alternative, of either assuming that we know the reality of nature in itself, or else believing that we operate with mere fictions in order to be able to describe natural phenomena in the simplest way, collapsed. Precisely by breaking through every absolute, one was in touch with every reality open to investigation.

Analogous though less magnificent phenomena occurred everywhere in the special sciences. Every *absolute pre-supposition collapsed*. For example, the nineteenth-century dogma of psychiatry that diseases of the mind are diseases of the brain, was called into question. With the surrender of this confining dogma, the expansion of *factual* knowledge replaced an almost mythological construing of mental disturbances in terms of entirely unknown brain-changes. Researchers endeavored to discover *to what extent* mental illnesses are diseases of the brain, and learned to abstain from anticipatory general judgments: while they enormously extended the realistic knowledge of man, they still did not capture man.

Great, awe-inspiring investigators emerged – figures as merciless in their self-criticism as they were fertile in their discoveries.

Max Weber exposed the error in the assumption that science – e.g. economics and sociology – could discover and prove what ought to be done. The scientific method discloses facts and possibilities. To know them objectively and truly, the scientist must suspend his own value judgments in the cognitive act itself, particularly his wishes, sympathies and antipathies, although these provide fruitful stimuli and sharpen our vision on the way to cognition. Only in this way can he cancel out the obfuscation and onesidedness caused by his value judgments. Science has integrity only as *value-free science*. But, as Max Weber showed, this value-free science is in its turn always guided in its selection of problems and objects by valuations which it, science itself, is capable of recognizing. The passion for evaluation, predominant for life and indeed the basic reason why science should exist at all, and the self-conquest it takes to suspend value-judgments in the pursuit of knowledge, together comprise the power of scientific inquiry.

Such scientific experiences demonstrated the possibility of possessing a wholly determined and concrete knowledge at any given time, as well as the impossibility of finding in science what had been expected in vain from the philosophy of that time. Those who had searched in science for the basis of their own lives, for a guide to their actions, or for being itself, were bound to be disappointed.

The way *to philosophy* had to be found once again.

Our contemporary philosophizing is conditioned by this experience with science. The route from the disillusionment with *decayed philosophy* to the *real sciences*, and from these again to *authentic philosophy*, is such that it must have a decisive role in shaping the kind of philosophizing that is possible today. Therefore, before giving a rough sketch of the way back to philosophy, we must define the far from unambiguous relation between present-day philosophizing and science.

First, the *limits of science* become clear. They may be briefly indicated:

(a) Scientific *cognition of things* is not *cognition of being*. Scientific cognition is particular, concerned with determinate objects, not with being itself. The philosophical relevance of science, therefore, is that, precisely by means of knowledge, it produces the most decisive knowledge of our lack of knowledge, namely our lack of knowledge of what being itself is.

(b) Scientific cognition can provide *no goals whatever* for life. It establishes no valid values. Therefore it cannot lead. By its clarity and decisiveness it points to another source of our lives.

(c) Science can give no answer to the question of its *own meaning*. The existence of science rests upon impulses for which there is no scientific proof that they are true and legitimate.

At the same time as the limits of science became clear, the positive significance and *indispensability of science for philosophy* also became clear.

First, science, having in recent centuries achieved methodological and critical purification (although this had rarely been fully realized by scientists), offered for the first time, by its *contrast* with philosophy, the possibility of recognizing and overcoming the muddy *confusion* of philosophy and science.

The road of science is indispensable for philosophy, since only a knowledge of that road prevents philosophizing from again making unsound and subjective claims to factual knowledge that really belongs to methodologically exact research.

Conversely, philosophical clarity is indispensable to the life and purity of genuine science. Without philosophy, science does not understand itself, and even scientific investigators, though for a time capable of extending specialized knowledge by building on foundations laid by the great scientists, abandon science completely as soon as they are without the counsel of philosophy.

If on the one hand philosophy and science are impossible without each other, and on the other hand the muddy confusion can no longer endure, the present task is to establish their true unity following their separation. Philosophizing can neither be identical with nor opposed to scientific thought.

Second, only the sciences, which engage in research and thereby produce compelling knowledge of objects, bring us face to face with the factual content of appearances. Only the sciences teach me to know clearly the *way things are*. If the philosopher had no current knowledge of the sciences, he would remain without clear knowledge of the world, like a blind man.

Third, philosophizing that is a pursuit of truth rather than enthusiasm must incorporate the *scientific attitude* or *approach*. The scientific attitude is characterized by a continual discrimination of its compelling knowledge – between knowledge accompanied on the one hand by knowledge of the methods that have led to it, and, on the other hand, knowledge accompanied by knowledge of the limits of its validity. The scientific attitude further requires that the scientist be prepared to entertain every criticism of his assertions. For the scientist, criticism is a vital necessity. He cannot be questioned enough in order to test his insights. The genuine scientist profits even from unjustified criticism. If he shrinks from criticism he has no genuine will to know. Loss of the scientific attitude and approach is loss also of truthfulness in philosophizing.

Everything works together *to bind philosophy to science*. Philosophy deals with the sciences in such a way that their own meaning is brought out and set forth. By remaining in living touch with the sciences philosophy dissolves the dogmatism (that unclear pseudo-philosophy) which tends to spring up in them again and again. Above all, however, philosophy becomes the conscious witness for the scientific endeavor against the enemies of science. To live philosophically is inseparable from the attitude of mind that will affirm science without reservations.

Together with this clarification of the limits and the meaning of science, there emerged the *independence of philosophy's origin*. Only as each premature assertion was exposed to the sharp light of criticism in the bright realm of science, did men become aware of that independence, and the *one primordial philosophy* begin to speak again through its great representatives. It was as if long familiar texts had returned from oblivion to the light of day, and as if men learned only now to read them truly, with new eyes. Kant, Hegel, Schelling, Nicolas of Cusa, Anselm, Plotinus, Plato, and a few others became so freshly relevant that one experienced the truth of Schelling's remark that philosophy is an 'open secret'. One may *know* texts, and be able to trace their thought constructions with precision – and yet not *understand* them.

From this origin we may learn something no science teaches us. For philosophy cannot arise from scientific ways of thinking and scientific knowledge alone. Philosophy demands a *different thinking*, a thinking that, in knowing, reminds me, awakens me, brings me to myself, transforms me.

But the new discovery of philosophy's origin in the old tradition immediately demonstrated the *impossibility of finding the true philosophy ready-made in the past*. The old philosophy in its past forms cannot be ours.

Although we see the historical starting point of our philosophizing in the old philosophy, and develop our own thinking by studying it because only in dialogue with it can we gain clarity, philosophical thinking is nevertheless *always original* and must express itself historically under new conditions in every age.

Most striking among the new conditions is the development of the pure sciences we have just discussed. Philosophy can *no longer be both naive* and truthful. The naive union of philosophy and science was an incomparably forceful and in its cultural situation true cipher. But today such a union is possible only as a muddy confusion that must be radically overcome. As both science and philosophy come to understand themselves, awareness is enhanced. Philosophy, together with science, must create the philosophical thinking that stems from an origin other than science.

Present-day philosophy may, therefore, understand the sublime greatness of the pre-Socratics, but while it derives irreplaceable incentives from them, it cannot follow them. Nor can it any longer remain in the deep naïveté of the questions of its childhood. In order to preserve the depth which children for the most part likewise lose as they mature, philosophy must find paths of inquiry and verification that lie within reality as it is conceived today in all its manifestations. This reality, however, can in no instance be genuine and wholly present without science.

Although the origin speaks to us from the ancient texts, we cannot simply adopt their doctrines. Historical understanding of past doctrines must be distinguished from the appropriation of what is present in all philosophy at all times. For only this appropriation becomes in turn the ground of the possibility of an historical understanding of the distant and the strange.

4

Jean-Paul Sartre

(1905–1980)

The death of Jean-Paul Sartre on 15 April 1980, marked the occasion of one of the largest public funerals Parisians had ever witnessed. This open display of respect and affection in the streets of Paris bore witness to Sartre's powerful presence on the French philosophical scene for over fifty years. During this time, he championed a philosophy of freedom, imagination and ethical responsibility under the rubric of 'existentialism' that became almost synonymous with his name.

Sartre was born in 1905 in the village of Thiviers, located in the Dordogne region of France, but he moved to Paris with his widowed mother while still a child. Always precocious, he attended the prestigious Henri IV Lycée, and proceeded to university at the Ecole Normale Supérieure. There he studied philosophy, taking first place, in the company of such contemporaries as Simone de Beauvoir and Maurice Merleau-Ponty. Although Sartre did teach philosophy briefly, he made the decision to give up academic life, focusing his efforts instead on writing and criticism. Sartre is justly celebrated for his important philosophical contributions to phenomenology and existentialism in such works as *Psychology of Imagination* (1933), *Transcendence of the Ego* (1936), *Sketch for a Theory of Emotions* (1939), *Being and Nothingness* (1943), *Existentialism and Humanism* (1946) and *The Critique of Dialectical Reason* (1960). He also inscribed these philosophical themes in a 'literature of commitment' (*littérature engagée*), exemplified by such fictional and dramatic works as *Nausea, Roads to Freedom* and *No Exit*. His treatise *What is Literature?* (1947) further clarified his stance on the close connection between literary and political activity. As co-editor of the leftist journal *Les Temps modernes*, with Merleau-Ponty and Simone de Beauvoir, Sartre often found himself embroiled in controversy. Awarded the Nobel Prize for Literature in 1962, Sartre characteristically refused to accept.

In 1933, Sartre travelled to Berlin, where he did further research on the phenomenological projects of both Husserl and Heidegger. However, unlike Heidegger, who claimed his 'existential analytic of Dasein' in *Being and*

Time was merely propaedeutic to a deeper investigation of Being-in-general, Sartre embraced the study of 'human being' as the quintessential provenance of existential philosophy. In this regard, Sartre's focus is unashamedly 'anthropological', and the issue of 'authenticity' acquires an ethical imperative not found in Heidegger's treatment of the same thematic. For Sartre, especially in the early formulations of his philosophy of existence, our freedom to choose is unconditional. He rejects the notion that our actions can be 'determined' in any way by such factors as sociological background or psychological tendencies. We are always free to go beyond these limitations and begin anew; even refusing to choose is itself a choice for which we bear responsibility. However, it is also important to note that Sartre's commitment to Marxism is reflected in his later philosophy, which does acknowledge the explanatory force of historical materialism and socio-economic pressures.

Like many of his contemporaries in the 1930s, Sartre was greatly influenced by Kojève's lectures on Hegel's *Phenomenology of Spirit*, particularly the 'master-slave dialectic'. We see this residue surface in his analysis of human relationships in *Being and Nothingness*, where the primary feature of human consciousness as 'being-for-itself' (*être-pour-soi*) is, for Sartre, the only mode of 'authentic' being-in-the-world. That is to say, we are free to transcend and imaginatively negate the world of brute 'being-in-itself' (*être-en-soi*), a world of 'things' marked by necessity. In our encounters with others, he suggests that the desire to live authentically as 'being-for-itself' inevitably presents a scenario of conflict with others who then must be dominated as if they were mere 'things'. None of the possible responses and adaptations, such as sadism, masochism or indifference, ever resolve this problem. If we are to avoid 'bad faith' (*mauvaise foi*) and inauthenticity, we must resist being willingly transformed into objects by exercising our unconditional freedom.

In the selection from *Existentialism and Humanism* (1946) which follows, Sartre responds to critics who levelled charges of nihilism and excessive individualism at the existentialist project. Sartre stresses that when I do choose, I choose for all humanity. There is no human 'essence' emanating from God or society that alleviates the need to shape our lives in the heat of existence itself. This is the ethical challenge to which Sartre devoted most of his life.

SELECT BIBLIOGRAPHY OF SARTRE'S WORKS IN ENGLISH

Anti-Semite and Jew, New York: Schocken, 1948.
Existentialism and Humanism, London: Methuen, 1948.
The Psychology of Imagination, New York: Philosophical Library, 1948.
Being and Nothingness, New York: Philosophical Library, 1956.
The Transcendence of the Ego, New York: Noonday Press, 1957.

Imagination: A Psychological Critique, Ann Arbor: University of Michigan Press, 1962.

Literary and Philosophical Essays, New York: Collier Books, 1962.

Saint Genet, Actor and Martyr, New York: Braziller, 1963.

The Words, New York: Braziller, 1964.

Essays in Aesthetics, New York: Washington Square Press, 1966.

On Genocide, Boston: Beacon Press, 1968.

Search for a Method, New York: Vintage Books, 1968.

Between Existentialism and Marxism, New York: William Morrow, 1974.

Critique of Dialectical Reason, London: New Left Books, 1976.

Life/Situations, New York: Pantheon Books, 1977.

The Family Idiot, 4 vols, Chicago: University of Chicago Press, 1981–91.

What is Literature? and Other Essays, Cambridge, Mass.: Harvard University Press, 1988.

Notebooks for an Ethics, Chicago: University of Chicago Press, 1992.

Truth and Existence, Chicago: University of Chicago Press, 1992.

Existentialism and Humanism

MY PURPOSE HERE is to offer a defence of existentialism against several reproaches that have been laid against it.

First, it has been reproached as an invitation to people to dwell in quietism of despair. For if every way to a solution is barred, one would have to regard any action in this world as entirely ineffective, and one would arrive finally at a contemplative philosophy. Moreover, since contemplation is a luxury, this would be only another bourgeois philosophy. This is, especially, the reproach made by the Communists.

From another quarter we are reproached for having underlined all that is ignominious in the human situation, for depicting what is mean, sordid or base to the neglect of certain things that possess charm and beauty and belong to the brighter side of human nature: for example, according to the Catholic critic, Mlle Mercier, we forget how an infant smiles. Both from this side and from the other we are also reproached for leaving out of account the solidarity of mankind and considering man in isolation. And this, say the Communists, is because we base our doctrine upon pure subjectivity – upon the Cartesian, 'I think': which is the moment in which solitary man attains to himself; a position from which it is impossible to regain solidarity with other men who exist outside of the self. The *ego* cannot reach them through the *cogito*.

From the Christian side, we are reproached as people who deny the reality and seriousness of human affairs. For since we ignore the commandments of God and all values prescribed as eternal, nothing remains but what is strictly voluntary. Everyone can do what he likes, and will be incapable, from such a point of view, of condemning either the point of view or the action of anyone else.

It is to these various reproaches that I shall endeavour to reply today; that is why I have entitled this brief exposition 'Existentialism and Humanism'. Many may be surprised at the mention of humanism in this connection, but we shall try to see in what sense we understand it. In any case, we can begin by saying that existentialism, in our sense of the word, is a doctrine that does render human life possible; a doctrine, also, which affirms that every truth and every action imply both an environment and a human subjectivity. The essential charge laid against us is, of course, that of overemphasis upon the evil side of human life. I have lately been told of a lady who, whenever she lets slip a vulgar expression in a moment of nervousness, excuses herself by exclaiming, 'I believe I am becoming an existentialist'. So it appears that ugliness is being identified with existentialism. That is why some people say we are 'naturalistic', and if we are, it is strange to see how much we scandalize and horrify them, for no one

From *Existentialism and Humanism*, London: Methuen, 1948.

seems to be much frightened or humiliated nowadays by what is properly called naturalism. Those who can quite well keep down a novel by Zola such as *La Terre* are sickened as soon as they read an existentialist novel. Those who appeal to the wisdom of the people – which is a sad wisdom – find ours sadder still. And yet, what could be more disillusioned than such sayings as 'Charity begins at home' or 'Promote a rogue and he'll sue you for damage, knock him down and he'll do you homage'? We all know how many common sayings can be quoted to this effect, and they all mean much the same – that you must not oppose the powers-that-be; that you must not fight against superior force; must not meddle in matters that are above your station. Or that any action not in accordance with some tradition is mere romanticism; or that any undertaking which has not the support of proven experience is foredoomed to frustration; and that since experience has shown men to be invariably inclined to evil, there must be firm rules to restrain them, otherwise we shall have anarchy. It is, however, the people who are forever mouthing these dismal proverbs and, whenever they are told of some more or less repulsive action, say 'How like human nature!' – it is these very people, always harping upon realism, who complain that existentialism is too gloomy a view of things. Indeed their excessive protests make me suspect that what is annoying them is not so much our pessimism, but, much more likely, our optimism. For at bottom, what is alarming in the doctrine that I am about to try to explain to you is – is it not? – that *it confronts man with a possibility of choice*. To verify this, let us review the whole question upon the strictly philosophic level. What, then, is this that we call existentialism?

Most of those who are making use of this word would be highly confused if required to explain its meaning. For since it has become fashionable, people cheerfully declare that this musician or that painter is 'existentialist'. A columnist in *Clartés* signs himself 'The Existentialist', and, indeed, the word is now so loosely applied to so many things that it no longer means anything at all. It would appear that, for the lack of any novel doctrine such as that of surrealism, all those who are eager to join in the latest scandal or movement now seize upon this philosophy in which, however, they can find nothing to their purpose. For in truth this is of all teachings the least scandalous and the most austere: it is intended strictly for technicians and philosophers. All the same, it can easily be defined.

The question is only complicated because there are two kinds of existentialists. There are, on the one hand, the Christians, amongst whom I shall name Jaspers and Gabriel Marcel, both professed Catholics; and on the other the existential atheists, amongst whom we must place Heidegger as well as the French existentialists and myself. What they have in common is simply the fact that they believe that *existence* comes before *essence* – or, if you will, that we must begin from the subjective. What exactly do we mean by that?

If one considers an article of manufacture – as, for example, a book or a paper-knife – one sees that it has been made by an artisan who had a conception of it; and he has paid attention, equally, to the conception of a paper-knife and to the pre-existent technique of production which is a part of that conception and is, at bottom, a formula. Thus the paper-knife is at the same time an article producible in a certain manner and one which, on the other hand, serves a definite purpose, for one cannot suppose that a man would produce a paper-knife without knowing what it was for. Let us say, then, of the paper-knife that its essence – that is to say the sum of the formulae and the qualities which made its production and its definition possible – precedes its existence. The presence of such-and-such a paper-knife or book is thus determined before my eyes. Here, then, we are viewing the world from a technical standpoint, and we can say that production precedes existence.

When we think of God as the creator, we are thinking of him, most of the time, as a supernal artisan. Whatever doctrine we may be considering, whether it be a doctrine like that of Descartes, or of Leibniz himself, we always imply that the will follows, more or less, from the understanding or at least accompanies it, so that when God creates he knows precisely what he is creating. Thus, the conception of man in the mind of God is comparable to that of the paper-knife in the mind of the artisan: God makes man according to a procedure and a conception, exactly as the artisan manufactures a paper-knife, following a definition and a formula. Thus each individual man is the realization of a certain conception which dwells in the divine understanding. In the philosophic atheism of the eighteenth century, the notion of God is suppressed, but not, for all that, the idea that essence is prior to existence; something of that idea we still find everywhere, in Diderot, in Voltaire and even in Kant. Man possesses a human nature; that 'human nature', which is the conception of human being, is found in every man; which means that each man is a particular example of a universal conception, the conception of Man. In Kant, this universality goes so far that the wild man of the woods, man in the state of nature and the bourgeois are all contained in the same definition and have the same fundamental qualities. Here again, the essence of man precedes that historic existence which we confront in experience.

Atheistic existentialism, of which I am a representative, declares with greater consistency that if God does not exist there is at least one being whose existence comes before its essence, a being which exists before it can be defined by any conception of it. That being is man or, as Heidegger has it, the human reality. What do we mean by saying that existence precedes essence? We mean that man first of all exists, encounters himself, surges up in the world – and defines himself afterwards. If man as the existentialist sees him is not definable, it is because to begin with he is nothing. He will not be anything until later, and then he will be what he makes of himself. Thus, there is no human nature, because there is no

God to have a conception of it. Man simply is. Not that he is simply what he conceives himself to be, but he is what he wills, and as he conceives himself after already existing – as he wills to be after that leap towards existence. Man is nothing else but that which he makes of himself. That is the first principle of existentialism. And this is what people call its 'subjectivity', using the word as a reproach against us. But what do we mean to say by this, but that man is of a greater dignity than a stone or a table? For we mean to say that man primarily exists – that man is, before all else, something which propels itself towards a future and is aware that it is doing so. Man is, indeed, a project which possesses a subjective life, instead of being a kind of moss, or a fungus or a cauli-flower. Before that projection of the self nothing exists; not even in the heaven of intelligence: man will only attain existence when he is what he purposes to be. Not, however, what he may wish to be. For what we usually understand by wishing or willing is a conscious decision taken – much more often than not – after we have made ourselves what we are. I may wish to join a party, to write a book or to marry – but in such a case what is usually called my will is probably a manifestation of a prior and more spontaneous decision. If, however, it is true that existence is prior to essence, man is responsible for what he is. Thus, the first effect of existentialism is that it puts every man in possession of himself as he is, and places the entire responsibility for his existence squarely upon his own shoulders. And, when we say that man is responsible for himself, we do not mean that he is responsible only for his own individuality, but that he is responsible for all men. The word 'subjectivism' is to be under-stood in two senses, and our adversaries play upon only one of them. Subjectivism means, on the one hand, the freedom of the individual subject and, on the other, that man cannot pass beyond human subjectivity. It is the latter which is the deeper meaning of existentialism. When we say that man chooses himself, we do mean that every one of us must choose himself; but by that we also mean that in choosing for himself he chooses for all men. For in effect, of all the actions a man may take in order to create himself as he wills to be, there is not one which is not creative, at the same time, of an image of man such as he believes he ought to be. To choose between this or that is at the same time to affirm the value of that which is chosen; for we are unable ever to choose the worse. What we choose is always the better; and nothing can be better for us unless it is better for all. If, moreover, existence precedes essence and we will to exist at the same time as we fashion our image, that image is valid for all and for the entire epoch in which we find ourselves. Our responsi-bility is thus much greater than we had supposed, for it concerns mankind as a whole. If I am a worker, for instance, I may choose to join a Christian rather than a Communist trade union. And if, by that membership, I choose to signify that resignation is, after all, the attitude that best becomes a man, that man's kingdom is not upon this earth, I do not commit myself alone to that view. Resignation is my will for everyone, and my action is, in consequence, a commitment on behalf of all mankind. Or if, to take a more personal case, I decide to marry and to have children, even though this decision proceeds simply from my situation, from my passion or my desire, I am thereby committing not only myself, but humanity as a whole, to the practice of monogamy. I am thus responsible for myself and for all men, and I am creating a certain image of man as I would have him to be. In fashioning myself I fashion man.

This may enable us to understand what is meant by such terms – perhaps a little grandiloquent – as anguish, abandonment and despair. As you will soon see, it is very simple. First, what do we mean by anguish? The existentialist frankly states that man is in anguish. His meaning is as follows – When a man commits himself to anything, fully realizing that he is not only choosing what he will be, but is thereby at the same time a legislator deciding for the whole of mankind – in such a moment a man cannot escape from the sense of complete and profound responsibility. There are many, indeed, who show no such anxiety. But we affirm that they are merely disguising their anguish or are in flight from it. Certainly, many people think that in what they are doing they commit no one but themselves to anything: and if you ask them, 'What would happen if everyone did so?' they shrug their shoulders and reply, 'Everyone does not do so'. But in truth, one ought always to ask oneself what would happen if everyone did as one is doing; nor can one escape from that disturbing thought except by a kind of self-deception. The man who lies in self-excuse, by saying 'Everyone will not do it' must be ill at ease in his conscience, for the act of lying implies the universal value which it denies. By its very disguise his anguish reveals itself. This is the anguish that Kierkegaard called 'the anguish of Abraham'. You know the story: An angel commanded Abraham to sacrifice his son: and obedience was obligatory, if it really was an angel who had appeared and said, 'Thou, Abraham, shalt sacrifice thy son'. But anyone in such a case would wonder, first, whether it was indeed an angel and secondly, whether I am really Abraham. Where are the proofs? A certain mad woman who suffered from hallucinations said that people were telephoning to her, and giving her orders. The doctor asked, 'But who is it that speaks to you?' She replied: 'He says it is God'. And what, indeed, could prove to her that it was God? If an angel appears to me, what is the proof that it is an angel; or, if I hear voices, who can prove that they proceed from heaven and not from hell, or from my own subconsciousness or some pathological condition? Who can prove that they are really addressed to me?

Who, then, can prove that I am the proper person to impose, by my own choice, my conception of man upon mankind? I shall never find any proof whatever; there will be no sign to convince me of it. If a voice speaks to me, it is still I myself who must decide whether the voice is or is not that of an angel. If I regard a certain course of action as good, it is only I who choose to say that it is good and not bad. There is nothing to show that I am Abraham: nevertheless I also am obliged at every instant to perform actions which are examples. Everything happens to every man as though the whole human race had its eyes fixed upon what he is doing and regulated its conduct accordingly. So every man ought to say, 'Am I really a man who has the right to act in such a manner that humanity regulates itself by what I do?' If a man does not say that, he is dissembling his anguish. Clearly, the anguish with which we are concerned here is not one that could lead to quietism or inaction. It is anguish pure and simple, of the kind well known to all those who have borne responsibilities. When, for instance, a military leader takes upon himself the responsibility for an attack and sends a number of men to their death, he chooses to do it and at bottom he alone chooses. No doubt he acts under a higher command, but its orders, which are more general, require interpretation by him and upon that interpretation depends the life of ten, fourteen or twenty men. In making the decision, he cannot but feel a certain anguish. All leaders know that anguish. It does not prevent their acting, on the contrary it is the very condition of their action, for the action presupposes that there is a plurality of possibilities, and in choosing one of these, they realize that it has value only because it is chosen. Now it is anguish of that kind which existentialism describes, and moreover, as we shall see, makes explicit through direct responsibility towards other men who are concerned. Far from being a screen which could separate us from action, it is a condition of action itself.

And when we speak of 'abandonment' – a favourite word of Heidegger – we only mean to say that God does not exist, and that it is necessary to draw the consequences of his absence right to the end. The existentialist is strongly opposed to a certain type of secular moralism which seeks to suppress God at the least possible expense. Towards 1880, when the French professors endeavoured to formulate a secular morality, they said something like this: – God is a useless and costly hypothesis, so we will do without it. However, if we are to have morality, a society and a law-abiding world, it is essential that certain values should be taken seriously; they must have an *a priori* existence ascribed to them. It must be considered obligatory *a priori* to be honest, not to lie, not to beat one's wife, to bring up children and so forth; so we are going to do a little work on this subject, which will enable us to show that these values exist all the same, inscribed in an intelligible heaven although, of course, there is no God. In other words – and this is, I believe, the purport of all that we in France call radicalism – nothing will be changed if God does not exist; we shall re-discover the same norms of honesty, progress and humanity, and we shall have disposed of God as an out-of-date hypothesis which will die away quietly of itself. The existentialist, on the contrary, finds it extremely embarrassing that God does not exist, for there disappears with Him all possibility of finding values in an intelligible heaven. There can no longer be any good *a priori*, since there is no infinite and perfect consciousness to think it. It is nowhere written that 'the good' exists, that one must be honest or must not lie, since we are now upon the plane where there are only men. Dostoievsky once wrote 'If God did not exist, everything would be permitted'; and that, for existentialism, is the starting point. Everything is indeed permitted if God does not exist, and man is in consequence forlorn, for he cannot find anything to depend upon either within or outside himself. He discovers forthwith, that he is without excuse. For if indeed existence precedes essence, one will never be able to explain one's action by reference to a given and specific human nature; in other words, there is no determinism – man is free, man *is* freedom. Nor, on the other hand, if God does not exist, are we provided with any values or commands that could legitimize our behaviour. Thus we have neither behind us, nor before us in a luminous realm of values, any means of justification or excuse. We are left alone, without excuse. That is what I mean when I say that man is condemned to be free. Condemned, because he did not create himself, yet is nevertheless at liberty, and from the moment that he is thrown into this world he is responsible for everything he does. The existentialist does not believe in the power of passion. He will never regard a grand passion as a destructive torrent upon which a man is swept into certain actions as by fate, and which, therefore, is an excuse for them. He thinks that man is responsible for his passion. Neither will an existentialist think that a man can find help through some sign being vouchsafed upon earth for his orientation: for he thinks that the man himself interprets the sign as he chooses. He thinks that every man, without any support or help whatever, is condemned at every instant to invent man. As Ponge has written in a very fine article, 'Man is the future of man'. That is exactly true. Only, if one took this to mean that the future is laid up in Heaven, that God knows what it is, it would be false, for then it would no longer even be a future. If, however, it means that, whatever man may now appear to be, there is a future to be fashioned, a virgin future that awaits him – then it is a true saying. But in the present one is forsaken.

As an example by which you may the better understand this state of abandonment, I will refer to the case of a pupil of mine, who sought me out in the following circumstances. His father was quarrelling with his mother and was also inclined to be a 'collaborator'; his elder brother had been killed in the German offensive of 1940 and this young man, with a sentiment somewhat primitive but generous, burned to avenge him. His mother was living alone with him, deeply afflicted by the semi-treason of his father and by the death of her eldest son, and her one consolation was in this young man. But he, at this moment, had the choice between going to England to join the Free French Forces or of staying near his mother and helping her to live. He fully realized that this woman lived only for him and that his disappearance – or perhaps his death – would plunge her into despair. He also realized that, concretely and in fact, every action he performed on his mother's behalf would be sure of effect in the sense of aiding her to live, where as anything he did in order to go and fight would be an ambiguous action which might vanish like water into sand and serve no purpose. For instance, to set out for England he would have to wait indefinitely in a Spanish camp on the way through Spain; or, on arriving in England or in Algiers he might be put into an office to fill up forms. Consequently, he found himself confronted by two very different modes of action; the one concrete, immediate, but directed towards only one individual; and the other an action addressed to an end infinitely greater, a national collectivity, but for that very reason ambiguous – and it might be frustrated on the way. At the same time, he was hesitating between two kinds of morality; on the one side the morality of sympathy, of personal devotion and, on the other side, a morality of wider scope but of more debatable validity. He had to choose between those two. What could help him to choose? Could the Christian doctrine? No. Christian doctrine says: Act with charity, love your neighbour, deny yourself for others, choose the way which is hardest, and so forth. But which is the harder road? To whom does one owe the more brotherly love, the patriot or the mother? Which is the more useful aim, the general one of fighting in and for the whole community, or the precise aim of helping one particular person to live? Who can give an answer to that *a priori*? No one. Nor is it given in any ethical scripture. The Kantian ethic says, Never regard another as a means, but always as an end. Very well; if I remain with my mother, I shall be regarding her as the end and not as a means: but by the same token I am in danger of treating as means those who are fighting on my behalf; and the converse is also true, that if I go to the aid of the combatants I shall be treating them as the end at the risk of treating my mother as a means.

If values are uncertain, if they are still too abstract to determine the particular, concrete case under consideration, nothing remains but to trust in our instincts. That is what this young man tried to do; and when I saw him he said, 'In the end, it is feeling that counts; the direction in which it is really pushing me is the one I ought to choose. If I feel that I love my mother enough to sacrifice everything else for her – my will to be avenged, all my longings for action and adventure – then I stay with her. If, on the contrary, I feel that my love for her is not enough, I go.' But how does one estimate the strength of a feeling? The value of his feeling for his mother was determined precisely by the fact that he was standing by her. I may say that I love a certain friend enough to sacrifice such or such a sum of money for him, but I cannot prove that unless I have done it. I may say, 'I love my mother enough to remain with her', if actually I have remained with her. I can only estimate the strength of this affection if I have performed an action by which it is defined and ratified. But if I then appeal to this affection to justify my action, I find myself drawn into a vicious circle.

Moreover, as Gide has very well said, a sentiment which is play-acting and one which is vital are two things that are hardly distinguishable one from another. To decide that I love my mother by staying beside her, and to play a comedy the upshot of which is that I do so – these are nearly the same thing. In other words feeling is formed by the deeds that one does; therefore I cannot consult it as a guide to action. And that is to say that I can neither seek within myself for an authentic impulse to action, nor can I expect, from some ethic, formulae that will enable me to act. You may say that the youth did, at least, go to a professor to ask for advice. But if you seek counsel – from a priest, for example – you have selected that priest; and at bottom you already knew, more or less, what he would advise. In other words, to choose an adviser is nevertheless to commit oneself by that choice. If you are a Christian, you will say, Consult a priest; but there are collaborationists, priests who are resisters and priests who wait for the tide to turn: which will you choose? Had this young man chosen a priest of the resistance, or one of the collaboration, he would have decided beforehand the kind of advice he was to receive. Similarly, in coming to me, he knew what advice I should give him, and I had but one reply to make. You are free, therefore choose – that is to say, invent. No rule of general morality can show you what you ought to do: no signs are vouchsafed in this world. The Catholics will reply, 'Oh, but they are!' Very well; still, it is I myself, in every case, who have to interpret the signs. Whilst I was imprisoned, I made the acquaintance of a somewhat remarkable man, a Jesuit, who had become a member of that order in the following manner. In his life he had suffered a succession of rather severe setbacks. His father had died when he was a child, leaving him in poverty, and he had been awarded a free scholarship in a religious institution, where he had been made continually to feel that he was accepted for charity's sake, and, in consequence, he had been denied several of those distinctions and honours which gratify children. Later, about the age of eighteen, he came to grief in a sentimental affair; and finally, at twenty-two – this was a trifle in itself, but it was the last drop that overflowed his cup – he failed in his military examination. This young man, then, could regard himself as a total failure: it was a sign – but a sign of what? He might have taken refuge in bitterness or despair. But he took it – very cleverly for him – as a sign that he was not intended for secular successes, and that only the attainments of religion, those of sanctity and of faith, were accessible to him. He interpreted his record as a message from God, and became a member of the Order. Who can doubt but that this decision as to the meaning of the sign was his, and his alone? One could have drawn quite different conclusions from such a series of reverses – as, for example, that he had better become a carpenter or a revolutionary. For the decipherment of the sign, however, he bears the entire responsibility. That is what 'abandonment' implies, that we ourselves decide our being. And with this abandonment goes anguish.

As for 'despair', the meaning of this expression is extremely simple. It merely means that we limit ourselves to a reliance upon that which is within our wills, or within the sum of the probabilities which render our action feasible. Whenever one wills anything, there are always these elements of probability. If I am counting upon a visit from a friend, who may be coming by train or by tram, I presuppose that the train will arrive at the appointed time, or that the tram will not be derailed. I remain in the realm of possibilities; but one does not rely upon any possibilities beyond those that are strictly concerned in one's action. Beyond the point at which the possibilities under consideration cease to affect my action, I ought to disinterest myself. For there is no God and no prevenient design, which can adapt the world and all its possibilities to my will. When Descartes said, 'Conquer yourself rather than the world', what he meant was, at bottom, the same – that we should act without hope.

Marxists, to whom I have said this, have answered: 'Your action is limited, obviously, by your death; but you can rely upon the help of others. That is, you can count both upon what the others are doing to help you elsewhere, as in China and in Russia, and upon what they will do later, after your death, to take up your action and carry it forward to its final accomplishment which will be the revolution. Moreover you must rely upon this; not to do so is immoral.' To this I rejoin, first, that I shall always count upon my comrades-in-arms in the struggle, in so far as they are committed, as I am, to a definite, common cause; and in the unity of a party or a group which I can more or less control – that is, in which I am enrolled as a militant and whose movements at every moment are known to me. In that respect, to rely upon the unity and the will of the party is exactly like my reckoning that the train will run to time or that the tram will not be derailed. But I cannot count upon men whom I do not know, I cannot base my confidence upon human goodness or upon man's interest in the good of society, seeing that man is free and that there is no human nature which I can take as foundational. I do not know whither the Russian revolution will lead. I can admire it and take it as an example in so far as it is evident, today, that the proletariat plays a part in Russia which it has attained in no other nation. But I cannot affirm that this will necessarily lead to the triumph of the proletariat: I must confine myself to what I can see. Nor can I be sure that comrades-in-arms will take up my work after my death and carry it to the maximum perfection, seeing that those men are free agents and will freely decide, tomorrow, what man is then to be. Tomorrow, after my death, some men may decide to establish Fascism, and the others may be so cowardly or so slack as to let them do so. If so, Fascism will then be the truth of man, and so much the worse for us. In reality, things will be such as men have decided they shall be. Does that mean that I should abandon myself to quietism? No. First I ought to commit myself and then act my commitment, according to the time-honoured formula that 'one need not hope in order to undertake one's work'. Nor does this mean that I should not belong to a party, but only that I should be without illusion and that I should do what I can. For instance, if I ask myself 'Will the social ideal as such, ever become a reality?' I cannot tell, I only know that whatever may be in my power to make it so, I shall do; beyond that, I can count upon nothing.

Quietism is the attitude of people who say, 'let others do what I cannot do'. The doctrine I am presenting before you is precisely the opposite of this, since it declares that there is no reality except in action. It goes further, indeed, and adds, 'Man is nothing else but what he purposes, he exists only in so far as he realizes himself, he is therefore nothing else but the sum of his actions, nothing else but what his life is.' Hence we can well understand why some people are horrified by our teaching. For many have but one resource to sustain them in their misery, and that is to think, 'Circumstances have been against me, I was worthy to be something much better than I have been. I admit I have never had a great love or a great friendship; but that is because I never met a man or a woman who were worthy of it; if I have not written any very good books, it is because I had not the leisure to do so; or, if I have had no children to whom I could devote myself it is because I did not find the man I could have lived with. So there remains within me a wide range of abilities, inclinations and potentialities, unused but perfectly viable, which endow me with a worthiness that could never be inferred from the mere history of my actions.' But in reality and for the existentialist, there is no love apart from the deeds of love; no potentiality of love other than that which is manifested in loving; there is no genius other than that which is expressed in works of art. The genius of Proust is the totality of the works of Proust; the genius of Racine is the series of his tragedies, outside of which there is nothing. Why should we attribute to Racine the capacity to write yet another tragedy when that is precisely what he did not write? In life, a man commits himself, draws his own portrait and there is nothing but that portrait. No doubt this thought may seem comfortless to one who has not made a success of his life. On the other hand, it puts everyone in a position to understand that reality alone is reliable; that dreams, expectations and hopes serve to define a man only as deceptive dreams, abortive hopes, expectations unfulfilled; that is to say, they define him negatively, not positively. Nevertheless, when one says, 'You are nothing else but what you live', it does not imply that an artist is to be judged solely by his works of art, for a thousand other things contribute no less to his definition as a man. What we mean to say is that a man is no other than a series of undertakings, that he is the sum, the organization, the set of relations that constitute these undertakings.

In the light of all this, what people reproach us with is not, after all, our pessimism, but the sternness of our optimism. If people condemn our works of fiction, in which we describe characters that are base, weak, cowardly and sometimes even frankly evil, it is not only because those characters are base, weak, cowardly or evil. For suppose that, like Zola, we showed that the behaviour of these characters was caused by their heredity, or by the action of their environment upon them, or by determining factors, psychic or organic. People would be reassured, they would say, 'You see, that is what we are like, no one can do anything about it'. But the existentialist, when he portrays a coward, shows him as responsible for his cowardice. He is not like that on account of a cowardly heart or lungs or cerebrum, he has not become like that through his physiological organism; he is like that because he has made himself into a coward by his actions. There is no such thing as a cowardly temperament. There are nervous temperaments; there is what is called impoverished blood, and there are also rich temperaments. But the man whose blood is poor is not a coward for all that, for what produces cowardice is the act of giving up or giving way; and a temperament is not an action. A coward is defined by the deed that he has done. What people feel obscurely, and with horror, is that the coward as we present him is guilty of being a coward. What people would prefer would be to be born either a coward or a hero. One of the charges most often laid against the *Chemins de la Liberté* is something like this – 'But, after all, these people being so base, how can you make them into heroes?' That objection is really rather comic, for it implies that people are born heroes: and that is, at bottom, what such people would like to think. If you are born cowards, you can be quite content, you can do nothing about it and you will be cowards all your lives whatever you do; and if you are born heroes you can again be quite content; you will be heroes all your lives, eating and drinking heroically. Whereas the existentialist says that the coward makes himself cowardly, the hero makes himself heroic; and that there is always a possibility for the coward to give up cowardice and for the hero to stop being a hero. What counts is the total commitment . . .

5

Maurice Merleau-Ponty
(1908–1961)

Born in France in 1908, Maurice Merleau-Ponty began his philosophical studies in Paris when he entered the Ecole Normale Supérieure in 1926. There he encountered such promising contemporaries as Sartre and de Beauvoir, both of whom later joined him after the war in founding the anti-colonialist journal, *Les Temps modernes*. The publication in 1945 of Merleau-Ponty's major doctoral thesis, *Phenomenology of Perception*, in addition to his collected essays in *Sense and Non-Sense* (1948), signalled a new direction for phenomenology and earned him an appointment to the prestigious Chair of Philosophy at the Collège de France in 1952. Despite many fundamental differences with Sartre in his approach to existential phenomenology and the role of the Communist party in France, Merleau-Ponty remained highly influential until his untimely death in 1961 at the age of fifty-three. Among other works that have secured his legacy are *The Structure of Behaviour* (1942), *Adventures of the Dialectic* (1955) and *Signs* (1960), as well as posthumously published works, such as *Eye and Mind* (1964) and *The Visible and the Invisible* (1964).

The philosophical project of Merleau-Ponty may be seen as a constant effort to remind us of the insoluble link between consciousness and world. His 'ontology of the flesh' provided a new phenomenological focus on the body-subject, a focus implied – but never fully developed – in the work of Husserl and Heidegger. Merleau-Ponty had attended Husserl's lectures in Paris in 1929, which were later published as *Cartesian Meditations*. He was also the first visitor to utilize the Husserl Archives at Louvain in 1939, devoting his research particularly to Husserlian works dealing with the life-world, especially *Ideas II* and *The Crisis of European Sciences and Transcendental Phenomenology*. However, for Merleau-Ponty consciousness could never be fully explained as some autonomously innate or *a priori* condition for abstract cognition. To ignore the complex 'intertwining' (*chiasme*) between pre-theoretical, lived experience and conceptual judgment would always lead to the inevitable cul-de-sac of mind-body opposition. In his view, such dualism had plagued traditional philosophy at least

77

since the time of Descartes, and was still weaving its spell on Husserl and Sartre. Merleau-Ponty expanded on Heidegger's insight that 'being-in-the-world' was marked by existential temporality, a 'living-through' that can never be distilled with apodictic certainty. Ambiguity is endemic to the phenomenological attitude.

Thus, Merleau-Ponty maintains that consciousness is always 'embodied' consciousness, just as perception is already interpreted or 'stylized' by a horizon of human projects that elicits meaning. This pre-reflective experience is guided by a more fundamental and radical intentional stance, an 'operative intentionality' that prioritizes gesture, sexuality and even silence. Moreover, with his emphasis on temporalized or 'genetic' constitution of meaning, Merleau-Ponty pays special attention to the process of sedimentation that inevitably links perception and imagination. Cultural phenomena, art and literature all become accessible to phenomenological investigation as historically situated manifestations of a dialectic between self and world. Yet, Merleau-Ponty's 'hyperdialectic' offers no ultimate synthesis or recuperation of Being, the seductive lure of plenitude that falsely denies the plurality and intersubjectivity of a human life in progress. We remain always more than mere 'objects' in the world.

SELECT BIBLIOGRAPHY OF MERLEAU-PONTY'S WORKS IN ENGLISH

Phenomenology of Perception, London: Routledge & Kegan Paul, 1962.
In Praise of Philosophy, Evanston, Ill.: Northwestern University Press, 1963.
The Structure of Behavior, Boston: Beacon Press, 1963.
The Primacy of Perception, Evanston, Ill.: Northwestern University Press, 1964.
Sense and Non-Sense, Evanston, Ill.: Northwestern University Press, 1964.
Signs, Evanston, Ill.: Northwestern University Press, 1964.
The Visible and the Invisible, Evanston, Ill.: Northwestern University Press, 1968.
Humanism and Terror, Boston: Beacon Press, 1969.
Themes from the Lectures at the Collège de France 1952–60, Evanston, Ill.: Northwestern University Press, 1970.
Adventures in the Dialectic, Evanston, Ill.: Northwestern University Press, 1973.
Consciousness and the Acquisition of Language, Evanston, Ill.: Northwestern University Press, 1973.
The Prose of the World, Evanston, Ill.: Northwestern University Press, 1973.
Phenomenology, Language and Sociology: Selected Essays of Maurice Merleau-Ponty, London: Heinemann, 1974.

Preface to *Phenomenology of Perception*

WHAT IS PHENOMENOLOGY? It may seem strange that this question has still to be asked half a century after the first works of Husserl. The fact remains that it has by no means been answered. Phenomenology is the study of essences; and according to it, all problems amount to finding definitions of essences: the essence of perception, or the essence of consciousness, for example. But phenomenology is also a philosophy which puts essences back into existence, and does not expect to arrive at an understanding of man and the world from any starting point other than that of their 'facticity'. It is a transcendental philosophy which places in abeyance the assertions arising out of the natural attitude, the better to understand them; but it is also a philosophy for which the world is always 'already there' before reflection begins – as an inalienable presence; and all its efforts are concentrated upon re-achieving a direct and primitive contact with the world, and endowing that contact with a philosophical status. It is the search for a philosophy which shall be a 'rigorous science', but it also offers an account of space, time and the world as we 'live' them. It tries to give a direct description of our experience as it is, without taking account of its psychological origin and the causal explanations which the scientist, the historian or the sociologist may be able to provide. Yet Husserl in his last works mentions a 'genetic phenomenology',[1] and even a 'constructive phenomenology'.[2] One may try to do away with these contradictions by making a distinction between Husserl's and Heidegger's phenomenologies; yet the whole of *Sein und Zeit* springs from an indication given by Husserl and amounts to no more than an explicit account of the 'natürlicher Weltbegriff' or the 'Lebenswelt' which Husserl, towards the end of his life, identified as the central theme of phenomenology, with the result that the contradiction reappears in Husserl's own philosophy. The reader pressed for time will be inclined to give up the idea of covering a doctrine which says everything, and will wonder whether a philosophy which cannot define its scope deserves all the discussion which has gone on around it, and whether he is not faced rather by a myth or a fashion.

Even if this were the case, there would still be a need to understand the prestige of the myth and the origin of the fashion, and the opinion of the responsible philosopher must be that *phenomenology can be practised and identified as a manner or style of thinking, that it existed as a movement before arriving at complete awareness of itself as a philosophy.* It has been long on the way, and its adherents have discovered it in every quarter, certainly in Hegel and Kierkegaard, but equally in Marx, Nietzsche and Freud. A purely linguistic examination of the texts in question would yield no proof; we find in texts only what we put into them,

From *Phenomenology of Perception*, London: Routledge & Kegan Paul, 1962.

and if ever any kind of history has suggested the interpretations which should be put on it, it is the history of philosophy. We shall find in ourselves, and nowhere else, the unity and true meaning of phenomenology. It is less a question of counting up quotations than of determining and expressing in concrete form this *phenomenology for ourselves* which has given a number of present day readers the impression, on reading Husserl or Heidegger, not so much of encountering a new philosophy as of recognizing what they had been waiting for. Phenomenology is accessible only through a phenomenological method. Let us, therefore, try systematically to bring together the celebrated phenomenological themes as they have grown spontaneously together in life. Perhaps we shall then understand why phenomenology has for so long remained at an initial stage, as a problem to be solved and a hope to be realized.

It is a matter of describing, not of explaining or analysing. Husserl's first directive to phenomenology, in its early stages, to be a 'descriptive psychology', or to return to the 'things themselves', is from the start a rejection of science. I am not the outcome or the meeting-point of numerous causal agencies which determine my bodily or psychological make-up. I cannot conceive myself as nothing but a bit of the world, a mere object of biological, psychological or sociological investigation. I cannot shut myself up within the realm of science. All my knowledge of the world, even my scientific knowledge, is gained from my own particular point of view, or from some experience of the world without which the symbols of science would be meaningless. The whole universe of science is built upon the world as directly experienced, and if we want to subject science itself to rigorous scrutiny and arrive at a precise assessment of its meaning and scope, we must begin by reawakening the basic experience of the world of which science is the second-order expression. Science has not and never will have, by its nature, the same significance *qua* form of being as the world which we perceive, for the simple reason that it is a rationale or explanation of that world. I am, not a 'living creature' nor even a 'man', nor again even 'a consciousness' endowed with all the characteristics which zoology, social anatomy or inductive psychology recognize in these various products of the natural or historical process – I am the absolute source, my existence does not stem from my antecedents, from my physical and social environment; instead it moves out towards them and sustains them, for I alone bring into being for myself (and therefore into being in the only sense that the word can have for me) the tradition which I elect to carry on, or the horizon whose distance from me would be abolished – since that distance is not one of its properties – if I were not there to scan it with my gaze. Scientific points of view, according to which my existence is a moment of the world's, are always both naïve and at the same time dishonest, because they take for granted, without explicitly mentioning it, the other point of view, namely that of consciousness, through which from the outset a world forms itself round me and begins to exist for me. To return to things themselves is to return to that world which precedes knowledge, of which knowledge always *speaks,* and in relation to which every scientific schematization is an abstract and derivative sign-language, as is geography in relation to the countryside in which we have learnt beforehand what a forest, a prairie or a river is.

This move is absolutely distinct from the idealist return to consciousness, and the demand for a pure description excludes equally the procedure of analytical reflection on the one hand, and that of scientific explanation on the other. Descartes and particularly Kant *detached* the subject, or consciousness, by showing that I could not possibly apprehend anything as existing unless I first of all experienced myself as existing in the act of apprehending it. They presented consciousness, the absolute certainty of my existence for myself, as the condition of there being anything at all; and the act of relating as the basis of relatedness. It is true that the act of relating is nothing if divorced from the spectacle of the world in which relations are found; the unity of consciousness in Kant is achieved simultaneously with that of the world. And in Descartes methodical doubt does not deprive us of anything, since the whole world, at least in so far as we experience it, is reinstated in the *Cogito,* enjoying equal certainty, and simply labelled 'thought of . . .'. But the relations between subject and world are not strictly bilateral: if they were, the certainty of the world would, in Descartes, be immediately given with that of the *Cogito,* and Kant would not have talked about his 'Copernican revolution'. Analytical reflection starts from our experience of the world and goes back to the subject as to a condition of possibility distinct from that experience, revealing the all-embracing synthesis as that without which there would be no world. To this extent it ceases to remain part of our experience and offers, in place of an account, a reconstruction. It is understandable, in view of this, that Husserl, having accused Kant of adopting a 'faculty psychologism',[3] should have urged, in place of a noetic analysis which bases the world on the synthesizing activity of the subject, his own '*noematic reflection*' which remains within the object and, instead of begetting it, brings to light its fundamental unity.

The world is there before any possible analysis of mine, and it would be artificial to make it the outcome of a series of syntheses which link, in the first place sensations, then aspects of the object corresponding to different perspectives, when both are nothing but products of analysis, with no sort of prior reality. Analytical reflection believes that it can trace back the course followed by a prior constituting act and arrive, in the 'inner man' – to use Saint Augustine's expression – at a constituting power which has always been identical with that inner self. Thus reflection is carried away by itself and installs itself in an impregnable subjectivity, as yet untouched by being and time. But this is very ingenuous, or at least it is an incomplete form of reflection which loses sight of its own beginning. When I begin to reflect my reflection bears upon an unreflective

81

experience; moreover my reflection cannot be unaware of itself as an event, and so it appears to itself in the light of a truly creative act, of a changed structure of consciousness, and yet it has to recognize, as having priority over its own operations, the world which is given to the subject because the subject is given to himself. The real has to be described, not constructed or formed. Which means that I cannot put perception into the same category as the syntheses represented by judgements, acts or predications. My field of perception is constantly filled with a play of colours, noises and fleeting tactile sensations which I cannot relate precisely to the context of my clearly perceived world, yet which I nevertheless immediately 'place' in the world, without ever confusing them with my daydreams. Equally constantly I weave dreams round things. I imagine people and things whose presence is not incompatible with the context, yet who are not in fact involved in it: they are ahead of reality, in the realm of the imaginary. If the reality of my perception were based solely on the intrinsic coherence of 'representations', it ought to be for ever hesitant and, being wrapped up in my conjectures on probabilities, I ought to be ceaselessly taking apart misleading syntheses, and reinstating in reality stray phenomena which I had excluded in the first place. But this does not happen. The real is a closely woven fabric. It does not await our judgement before incorporating the most surprising phenomena, or before rejecting the most plausible figments of our imagination. Perception is not a science of the world, it is not even an act, a deliberate taking up of a position; it is the background from which all acts stand out, and is presupposed by them. The world is not an object such that I have in my possession the law of its making; it is the natural setting of, and field for, all my thoughts and all my explicit perceptions. Truth does not 'inhabit' only 'the inner man'[4] or more accurately, there is no inner man, man is in the world, and only in the world does he know himself. When I return to myself from an excursion into the realm of dogmatic common sense or of science, I find, not a source of intrinsic truth, but a subject destined to the world.

All of which reveals the true meaning of the famous phenomenological reduction. There is probably no question over which Husserl spent more time – or to which he more often returned, since the 'problematic of reduction' occupies an important place in his unpublished work. For a long time, and even in recent texts, the reduction is presented as the return to a transcendental consciousness before which the world is spread out and completely transparent, quickened through and through by a series of apperceptions which it is the philosopher's task to reconstitute on the basis of their outcome. Thus my sensation of redness is *perceived as* the manifestation of a certain redness experienced, this in turn as the manifestation of a red surface, which is the manifestation of a piece of red cardboard, and this finally is the manifestation or outline of a red thing, namely this book. We are to understand, then, that it is the apprehension of a certain *hylè*, as indicating a phenomenon of a higher degree, the *Sinngebung*, or active meaning-giving operation which may be said to define consciousness, so that the world is nothing but 'world-as-meaning', and the phenomenological reduction is idealistic, in the sense that there is here a transcendental idealism which treats the world as an indivisible unity of value shared by Peter and Paul, in which their perspectives blend. 'Peter's consciousness' and 'Paul's consciousness' are in communication, the perception of the world 'by Peter' is not Peter's doing any more than its perception 'by Paul' is Paul's doing; in each case it is the doing of pre-personal forms of consciousness, whose communication raises no problem, since it is demanded by the very definition of consciousness, meaning or truth. In so far as I am a consciousness, that is, in so far as something has meaning for me, I am neither here nor there, neither Peter nor Paul; I am in no way distinguishable from an 'other' consciousness, since we are immediately in touch with the world and since the world is, by definition, unique, being the system in which all truths cohere. A logically consistent transcendental idealism rids the world of its opacity and its transcendence. The world is precisely that thing of which we form a representation, not as men or as empirical subjects, but in so far as we are all one light and participate in the One without destroying its unity. Analytical reflection knows nothing of the problem of other minds, or of that of the world, because it insists that with the first glimmer of consciousness there appears in me theoretically the power of reaching some universal truth, and that the other person, being equally without thisness, location or body, the Alter and the Ego are one and the same in the true world which is the unifier of minds. There is no difficulty in understanding how *I* can conceive the Other, because the I and consequently the Other are not conceived as part of the woven stuff of phenomena; they have validity rather than existence. There is nothing hidden behind these faces and gestures, no domain to which I have no access, merely a little shadow which owes its very existence to the light. For Husserl, on the contrary, it is well known that there is a problem of other people, and the *alter ego* is a paradox. If the other is truly for himself alone, beyond his being for me, and if we are for each other and not both for God, we must necessarily have some appearance for each other. He must and I must have an outer appearance, and there must be, besides the perspective of the For Oneself – my view of myself and the other's of himself – a perspective of For Others – my view of others and theirs of me. Of course, these two perspectives, in each one of us, cannot be simply juxtaposed, *for in that case it is not I that the other would see, nor he that I should see*. I must be the exterior that I present to others, and the body of the other must be the other himself. This paradox and the dialectic of the Ego and the Alter are possible only provided that the Ego and the Alter Ego are defined by their situation and are not freed from all inherence; that is, provided that philosophy does not culminate in a return to the self, and that I discover by reflection not only my presence to myself, but also the possibility of an 'outside spectator'; that is, again, provided that at the very moment when I experience my existence – at the ultimate extremity of reflection – I fall short of the ultimate density which would place me outside time, and that I discover within myself a kind of internal weakness standing in the way of my being totally individualized: a weakness which exposes me to the gaze of others as a man among men or at least as a consciousness among consciousnesses. Hitherto the *Cogito* depreciated the perception of others, teaching me as it did that the I is accessible only to itself, since it defined *me* as the thought which I have of myself, and which clearly I am alone in having, at least in this ultimate sense. For the 'other' to be more than an empty word, it is necessary that my existence should never be reduced to my bare awareness of existing, but that it should take in also the awareness that *one* may have of it, and thus include my incarnation in some nature and the possibility, at least, of a historical situation. The *Cogito* must reveal me in a situation, and it is on this condition alone that transcendental subjectivity can, as Husserl puts it,[5] *be* an intersubjectivity. As a meditating Ego, I can clearly distinguish from myself the world and things, since I certainly do not exist in the way in which things exist. I must even set aside from myself my body understood as a thing among things, as a collection of physico-chemical processes. But even if the *cogitatio*, which I thus discover, is without location in objective time and space, it is not without place in the phenomenological world. The world, which I distinguished from myself as the totality of things or of processes linked by causal relationships, I rediscover 'in me' as the permanent horizon of all my *cogitationes* and as a dimension in relation to which I am constantly situating myself. The true *Cogito* does not define the subject's existence in terms of the thought he has of existing, and furthermore does not convert the indubitability of the world into the indubitability of thought about the world, nor finally does it replace the world itself by the world as meaning. On the contrary it recognizes my thought itself as an inalienable fact, and does away with any kind of idealism in revealing me as 'being-in-the-world'.

It is because we are through and through compounded of relationships with the world that for us the only way to become aware of the fact is to suspend the resultant activity, to refuse it our complicity (to look at it *ohne mitzumachen*, as Husserl often says), or yet again, to put it 'out of play'. Not because we reject the certainties of common sense and a natural attitude to things – they are, on the contrary, the constant theme of philosophy – but because, being the presupposed basis of any thought, they are taken for granted, and go unnoticed, and because in order to arouse them and bring them to view, we have to suspend for a moment our recognition of them. The best formulation of the reduction is probably that given by Eugen Fink, Husserl's assistant, when he spoke of 'wonder' in the face of the world.[6] Reflection does not withdraw from the world towards the unity of consciousness as the world's basis; it steps back to watch the forms of transcendence fly up like sparks from a fire; it slackens the intentional threads which attach us to the world and thus brings them to our notice; it alone is consciousness of the world because it reveals that world as strange and paradoxical. Husserl's transcendental is not Kant's and Husserl accuses Kant's philosophy of being 'worldly', because it *makes use* of our relation to the world, which is the motive force of the transcendental deduction, and makes the world immanent in the subject, instead of *being filled with wonder* at it and conceiving the subject as a process of transcendence towards the world. All the misunderstandings with his interpreters, with the existentialist 'dissidents' and finally with himself, have arisen from the fact that in order to see the world and grasp it as paradoxical, we must break with our familiar acceptance of it and, also, from the fact that from this break we can learn nothing but the unmotivated upsurge of the world. The most important lesson which the reduction teaches us is the impossibility of a complete reduction. This is why Husserl is constantly re-examining the possibility of the reduction. If we were absolute mind, the reduction would present no problem. But since, on the contrary, we are in the world, since indeed our reflections are carried out in the temporal flux on to which we are trying to seize (since they *sich einströmen*, as Husserl says), there is no thought which embraces all our thought. The philosopher, as the unpublished works declare, is a perpetual beginner, which means that he takes for granted nothing that men, learned or otherwise, believe they know. It means also that philosophy itself must not take itself for granted, in so far as it may have managed to say something true; that it is an ever-renewed experiment in making its own beginning; that it consists wholly in the description of this beginning, and finally, that radical reflection amounts to a consciousness of its own dependence on an unreflective life which is its initial situation, unchanging, given once and for all. Far from being, as has been thought, a procedure of idealistic philosophy, phenomenological reduction belongs to existential philosophy: Heidegger's 'being-in-the-world' appears only against the background of the phenomenological reduction.

A misunderstanding of a similar kind confuses the notion of the 'essences' in Husserl. Every reduction, says Husserl, as well as being transcendental is necessarily eidetic. That means that we cannot subject our perception of the world to philosophical scrutiny without ceasing to be identified with that act of positing the world, with that interest in it which delimits us, without drawing back from our commitment which is itself thus made to appear as a spectacle, without passing from the *fact* of our existence to its *nature*, from the Dasein to the Wesen. But it is clear that the essence is here not the end, but a means, that our effective involvement in the world is precisely what has to be understood and made amenable to conceptualization, for it is what polarizes all our conceptual particularizations. The need to proceed by way of essences does not mean that philosophy takes them as its object, but, on the contrary, that our existence is too tightly held in the world to be able to know itself as such at the moment of its involvement, and that it requires the field of ideality in order to become acquainted with and to prevail over its facticity. The Vienna Circle, as is well known, lays it down categorically that we can enter into relations only with meanings. For example, 'consciousness' is not for the Vienna Circle identifiable with what we are. It is a complex meaning which has developed late in time, which should be handled with care, and only after the many meanings which have contributed, throughout the word's semantic development, to the formation of its present one have been made explicit. Logical positivism of this kind is the antithesis of Husserl's thought. Whatever the subtle changes of meaning which have ultimately brought us, as a linguistic acquisition, the word and concept of consciousness, we enjoy direct access to what it designates. For we have the experience of ourselves, of that consciousness which we are, and it is on the basis of this experience that all linguistic connotations are assessed, and precisely through it that language comes to have any meaning at all for us. 'It is that as yet dumb experience . . . which we are concerned to lead to the pure expression of its own meaning.'[7] Husserl's essences are destined to bring back all the living relationships of experience, as the fisherman's net draws up from the depths of the ocean quivering fish and seaweed. Jean Wahl is therefore wrong in saying that 'Husserl separates essences from existence'.[8] The separated essences are those of language. It is the office of language to cause essences to exist in a state of separation which is in fact merely apparent, since through language they still rest upon the ante-predicative life of consciousness. In the silence of primary consciousness can be seen appearing not only what words mean, but also what things mean: the core of primary meaning round which the acts of naming and expression take shape.

Seeking the essence of consciousness will therefore not consist in developing the *Wortbedeutung* of consciousness and escaping from existence into the universe of things said; it will consist in rediscovering my actual presence to myself, the fact of my consciousness which is in the last resort what the word and the concept of consciousness mean. Looking for the world's essence is not looking for what it is as an idea once it has been reduced to a theme of discourse; it is looking for what it is as a fact for us, before any thematization. Sensationalism 'reduces' the world by noticing that after all we never experience anything but states of ourselves. Transcendental idealism too 'reduces' the world since, in so far as it guarantees the world, it does so by regarding it as thought or consciousness of the world, and as the mere correlative of our knowledge, with the result that it becomes immanent in consciousness and the aseity of things is thereby done away with. The eidetic reduction is, on the other hand, the determination to bring the world to light as it is before any falling back on ourselves has occurred; it is the ambition to make reflection emulate the unreflective life of consciousness. I aim at and perceive a world. If I said, as do the sensationalists, that we have here only 'states of consciousness', and if I tried to distinguish my perceptions from my dreams with the aid of 'criteria', I should overlook the phenomenon of the world. For if I am able to talk about 'dreams' and 'reality', to bother my head about the distinction between imaginary and real, and cast doubt upon the 'real', it is because this distinction is already made by me before any analysis; it is because I have an experience of the real as of the imaginary, and the problem then becomes one not of asking how critical thought can provide for itself secondary equivalents of this distinction, but of making explicit our primordial knowledge of the 'real', of describing our perception of the world as that upon which our idea of truth is forever based. We must not, therefore, wonder whether we really perceive a world, we must instead say: the world is what we perceive. In more general terms we must not wonder whether our self-evident truths are real truths, or whether, through some perversity inherent in our minds, that which is self-evident for us might not be illusory in relation to some truth in itself. For in so far as we talk about illusion, it is because we have identified illusions, and done so solely in the light of some perception which at the same time gave assurance of its own truth. It follows that doubt, or the fear of being mistaken, testifies as soon as it arises to our power of unmasking error, and that it could never finally tear us away from truth. We are in the realm of truth and it is 'the experience of truth' which is self-evident.[9] To seek the essence of perception is to declare that perception is, not presumed true, but defined as access to truth. So, if I now wanted, according to idealistic principles, to base this *de facto* self-evident truth, this irresistible belief, on some absolute self-evident truth, that is, on the absolute clarity which my thoughts have for me; if I tried to find in myself a creative thought which bodied forth the framework of the world or illumined it through and through, I should once more prove unfaithful to my experience of the world, and should be looking for what makes that experience possible instead of looking for what it is. The self-evidence of perception is not adequate thought or apodeictic self-evidence.[10] The world is not what I think, but what I live through. I am open to the world, I have no doubt that I am in communication with it, but I do not possess it; it is inexhaustible. 'There is a world', or rather: 'There is the world'; I can never completely account for this ever-reiterated assertion in my life. This facticity of the world is what constitutes the *Weltlichkeit der Welt*, what causes the world to be the world; just as the facticity of the *Cogito* is not an imperfection in itself, but rather what assures me of my existence. The eidetic method is the method of a phenomenological positivism which bases the possible on the real.

We can now consider the notion of intentionality, too often cited as the main discovery of phenomenology, whereas it is understandable only through the reduction. 'All consciousness is consciousness of something'; there is nothing new in that. Kant showed, in the *Refutation of Idealism*, that inner perception is impossible without outer perception, that the world, as a collection of connected phenomena, is anticipated in the consciousness of my unity, and is the means whereby I come into being as a consciousness. What distinguishes intentionality from the Kantian relation to a possible object is that the unity of the world, before being posited by knowledge in a specific act of identification, is 'lived' as ready-made or already there. Kant himself shows in the *Critique of Judgement* that there exists a unity of the imagination and the understanding and a unity of subjects *before the object*, and that, in experiencing the beautiful, for example, I am aware of a harmony between sensation and concept, between myself and others, which is itself without any concept. Here the subject is no longer the universal thinker of a system of objects rigorously interrelated, the positing power who subjects the manifold to the law of the understanding, in so far as he is to be able to put together a world – he discovers and enjoys his own nature as spontaneously in harmony with the law of the understanding. But if the subject has a nature, then the hidden art of the imagination must condition the categorial activity. It is no longer merely the aesthetic judgement, but knowledge too which rests upon this art, an art which forms the basis of the unity of consciousness and of consciousnesses.

Husserl takes up again the *Critique of Judgement* when he talks about a teleology of consciousness. It is not a matter of duplicating human consciousness with some absolute thought which, from outside, is imagined as assigning to it its aims. It is a question of recognizing consciousness itself as a project of the world, meant for a world which it neither embraces nor possesses, but towards which it is perpetually directed – and the world as this pre-objective individual whose imperious unity decrees what knowledge shall take as its goal. This is why Husserl distinguishes between intentionally of act, which is that of our judgements and of those occasions when we voluntarily take up a position – the only intentionality discussed in the *Critique of Pure Reason* – and operative intentionality (*fungierende Intentionalität*), or that which produces the natural and antepredicative unity of the world and of our life, being apparent in our desires, our evaluations and in the landscape we see, more clearly than in objective knowledge, and furnishing the text which our knowledge tries to translate into precise language. Our relationship to the world, as it is untiringly enunciated within us, is not a thing which can be any further clarified by analysis; philosophy can only place it once more before our eyes and present it for our ratification.

Through this broadened notion of intentionality, phenomenological 'comprehension' is distinguished from traditional 'intellection', which is confined to 'true and immutable natures', and so phenomenology can become a phenomenology of origins. Whether we are concerned with a thing perceived, a historical event or a doctrine, to 'understand' is to take in the total intention – not only what these things are for representation (the 'properties' of the thing perceived, the mass of 'historical facts', the 'ideas' introduced by the doctrine) – but the unique mode of existing expressed in the properties of the pebble, the glass or the piece of wax, in all the events of a revolution, in all the thoughts of a philosopher. It is a matter, in the case of each civilization, of finding the Idea in the Hegelian sense, that is, not a law of the physico-mathematical type, discoverable by objective thought, but that formula which sums up some unique manner of behaviour towards others, towards Nature, time and death: a certain way of patterning the world which the historian should be capable of seizing upon and making his own. These are the *dimensions* of history. In this context there is not a human word, not a gesture, even one which is the outcome of habit or absent-mindedness, which has not some meaning. For example, I may have been under the impression that I lapsed into silence through weariness, or some minister may have thought he had uttered merely an appropriate platitude, yet my silence or his words immediately take on a significance, because my fatigue or his falling back upon a ready-made formula are not accidental, for they express a certain lack of interest, and hence some degree of adoption of a definite position in relation to the situation.

When an event is considered at close quarters, at the moment when it is lived through, everything seems subject to chance: one man's ambition, some lucky encounter, some local circumstance or other appears to have been decisive. But chance happenings offset each other, and facts in their multiplicity coalesce and show up a certain way of taking a stand in relation to the human situation, reveal in fact an *event* which has its definite outline and about which we can talk. Should the starting-point for the understanding of history be ideology, or politics, or religion, or economics? Should we try to understand a doctrine from its overt content, or from the psychological make-up and the biography of its author? We must seek an understanding from all these angles simultaneously, everything has meaning, and we shall find this same structure of being underlying all relationships. All these views are true provided that they are not isolated, that we delve deeply into history and reach the unique core of existential meaning which emerges in each perspective. It is true, as Marx says, that history does not walk on its head, but it is also true that it does not think with its feet. Or one should say rather that it is neither its 'head' not its 'feet' that we have to worry about, but its body. All economic and psychological explanations of a doctrine are true, since the thinker never thinks from any starting-point but the one constituted by what he is. Reflection even on a doctrine will be complete only if it succeeds in linking up with the doctrine's history and the extraneous explanations of it, and in putting back the causes and meaning of the doctrine in an existential structure. There is, as Husserl says, a 'genesis of meaning' (*Sinngenesis*),[11] which alone, in the last resort, teaches us what the doctrine 'means'. Like understanding, criticism must be pursued at all levels, and naturally, it will be insufficient, for the refutation of a doctrine, to relate it to some accidental event in the author's life: its significance goes beyond, and there is no pure accident in existence or in co-existence, since both absorb random events and transmute them into the rational.

Finally, as it is indivisible in the present, history is equally so in its sequences. Considered in the light of its fundamental dimensions, all periods of history appear as manifestations of a single existence, or as episodes in a single drama – without our knowing whether it has an ending. Because we are in the world, we are *condemned to meaning*, and we cannot do or say anything without its acquiring a name in history.

Probably the chief gain from phenomenology is to have united extreme subjectivism and extreme objectivism in its notion of the world or of rationality. Rationality is precisely measured by the experiences in which it is disclosed. To say that there exists rationality is to say that perspectives blend, perceptions confirm each other, a meaning emerges. But it should not be set in a realm apart, transposed into absolute Spirit, or into a world in the realist sense. The phenomenological world is not pure being, but the sense which is revealed where the paths of my various experiences intersect, and also where my own and other people's intersect and engage each other like gears. It is thus inseparable from subjectivity and intersubjectivity, which find their unity when I either take up my past experiences in those of the present, or other people's in my own. For the first time the philosopher's thinking is sufficiently conscious not to anticipate itself and endow its own results with reified form in the world. The philosopher tries to conceive the world, others and himself and their interrelations. But the meditating Ego, the 'impartial spectator' (*uninteressierter Zuschauer*)[12] do not rediscover an already given rationality, they 'establish themselves',[13] and establish it, by an act of initiative which has no guarantee in being, its justification resting entirely on the effective power which it confers on us of taking our own history upon ourselves.

The phenomenological world is not the bringing to explicit expression of a pre-existing being, but the laying down of being. Philosophy is not the reflection of a pre-existing truth, but, like art, the act of bringing truth into being. One may well ask how this creation is *possible*, and if it does not recapture in things a pre-existing Reason. The answer is that the only pre-existent Logos is the world itself, and that the philosophy which brings it into visible existence does not begin by being *possible*; it is actual or real like the world of which it is a part, and no explanatory hypothesis is clearer than the act whereby we take up this unfinished world in an effort to complete and conceive it. Rationality is not a *problem*. There is behind it no unknown quantity which has to be determined by deduction, or, beginning with it, demonstrated inductively. We witness every minute the miracle of related experiences, and yet nobody knows better than we do how this miracle is worked, for we are ourselves this network of relationships. The world and reason are not problematical. We may say, if we wish, that they are mysterious, but their mystery defines them: there can be no question of dispelling it by some 'solution', it is on the hither side of all solutions. True philosophy consists in relearning to look at the world, and in this sense a historical account can give meaning to the world quite as 'deeply' as a philosophical treatise. We take our fate in our hands, we become responsible for our history through reflection, but equally by a decision on which we stake our life, and in both cases what is involved is a violent act which is validated by being performed.

Phenomenology, as a disclosure of the world, rests on itself, or rather provides its own foundation.[14] All knowledge is sustained by a 'ground' of postulates and finally by our communication with the world as primary embodiment of rationality. Philosophy, as radical reflection, dispenses in principle with this resource. As, however, it too is in history, it too exploits the world and constituted reason. It must therefore put to itself the question which it puts to all branches of knowledge, and so duplicate itself infinitely, being, as Husserl says, a dialogue or infinite meditation, and, in so far as it remains faithful to its intention, never knowing where it is going. The unfinished nature of phenomenology and the inchoative atmosphere which has surrounded it are not to be taken as a sign of failure, they were inevitable because phenomenology's task was to reveal the mystery of the world and of reason.[15] If phenomenology was a movement before becoming a doctrine or a philosophical system, this was attributable neither to accident, nor to fraudulent intent. It is as painstaking as the works of Balzac, Proust, Valéry or Cézanne – by reason of the same kind of attentiveness and wonder, the same demand for awareness, the same will to seize the meaning of the world or of history as that meaning comes into being. In this way it merges into the general effort of modern thought.

NOTES

1 *Méditations cartésiennes*, pp. 120ff.
2 See the unpublished *6th Méditation cartésienne*, edited by Eugen Fink, to which G. Berger has kindly referred us.
3 *Logische Untersuchungen, Prolegomena zur reinen Logik*, p. 93.
4 In te redi; in interiore homine habitat veritas (Saint Augustine).
5 *Die Krisis der europäischen Wissenschaften und die transzendentale Phänomenologie*, III (unpublished).

6 *Die phänomenologische Philosophie Edmund Husserls in der gegenwärtigen Kritik*, pp. 331 and ff.

7 *Méditations cartésiennes*, p. 33.

8 *Réalisme, dialectique et mystère*, l'Arbalète, Autumn, 1942, unpaginated.

9 *Das Erlebnis der Wahrheit (Logische Untersuchungen, Prolegomena zur reinen Logik)* p. 190.

10 There is no apodeictic self-evidence, the *Formale und transzendentale Logik* (p. 142) says in effect.

11 The usual term in the unpublished writings. The idea is already to be found in the *Formale und transzendentale Logik*, pp. 184 and ff.

12 *6th Méditation cartésienne* (unpublished).

13 Ibid.

14 'Rückbeziehung der Phänomenologie auf sich selbst', say the unpublished writings.

15 We are indebted for this last expression to G. Gusdorf, who may well have used it in another sense.

6

Simone de Beauvoir
(1908–1986)

Nearly half a century after the publication of *The Second Sex* in 1949, Simone de Beauvoir is still recognized as the first philosophical thinker to have systematically raised the issue of 'sexual difference'. Her work has inspired many subsequent developments in feminist theory, as well as shaping the gender critique within the discipline of philosophy itself. While it is true that de Beauvoir's position has often been criticized for some of its existentialist assumptions, it is equally true that even her most trenchant critics credit her with having the courage and tenacity to scrutinize a topic ignored by Western philosophy for over two millennia.

Born in 1908 in Paris, Simone de Beauvoir studied philosophy at the Ecole Normale Supérieure with both Sartre and Merleau-Ponty, colleagues with whom she also edited *Les Temps modernes* after the Second World War. Indeed, she became one of the leading exponents of a 'philosophy of existence' that privileged freedom, transcendence and authenticity. During this time, however, de Beauvoir also became increasingly convinced that the ideal of freedom, as expressed by 'being-for-itself', could be seriously impeded by the socio-cultural structures and institutions limiting individual development. For de Beauvoir, the oppression of women throughout history represented the paradigm case of this constraint. She maintained that 'man' had consistently defined himself as pure 'being-for-itself', leaving only the role of an inessential and objectified 'other' for 'woman' to fill. Moreover, this attitude had been internalized by women themselves, thereby reinforcing the invisibility of this oppression. In *The Second Sex* de Beauvoir sought to unpack the genealogy of women's peripheral status, as well as to suggest how this status could be actively and historically changed.

De Beauvoir vigorously rejected as too simplistic the commonly accepted biological, psychological and economic explanations for women's marginal condition. While she acknowledged that the reproductive facts of sexual difference did perhaps burden women more than men, she claimed that the context of social values and attitudes counted far more than the physical facts themselves. Thus, it was not the reality of bearing children that isolated women, but rather the dominant institutions of wifehood and motherhood that left them without access to socially shared means of nurturing children. Likewise, she questioned the Freudian rationalization that women's 'castration complex' forced them to complete themselves by identifying with the male figure who possessed the penis they lacked. Would it not be more reasonable to examine the features of social privilege and power that accompanied 'the prestige of the penis', rather than the bare 'gonadology' itself? De Beauvoir also remained sceptical of the prevailing Marxist attitude synthesizing women's oppression and 'class oppression' under capitalism. She wagered that nothing would change for women, even in a socialist environment, until they became fully aware of the ontological feature of human consciousness that manifested itself as a will to dominate and objectify 'the other'.

In brief, de Beauvoir located the site of women's continuing oppression in patriarchal institutions and myths, both invented and sustained by men, much to their immediate advantage. The 'essential feminine' qualities of self-sacrifice and narcissism promoted by these myths were targeted by de Beauvoir as particularly detrimental to women's identity. All of women's efforts towards freedom and transcendence would face insurmountable odds as long as they remained passive and accommodating in their social roles. She suggested that women seek their economic independence through work outside the home, while simultaneously challenging themselves intellectually to understand their own history and prospects for the future.

In addition to *The Second Sex*, de Beauvoir wrote a treatise exploring the project of existentialist ethics entitled *The Ethics of Ambiguity* (1948), as well as numerous philosophical essays. Sharing the view of 'committed literature' held by compatriots like Sartre and Camus, she also thematized her philosophical insights in novels and memoires that were meant to reach far beyond the halls of academia, such as *The Mandarins* (1954) and *Memoires of a Dutiful Daughter* (1958). Despite the success of a long and wide-ranging philosophical career, Simone de Beauvoir will be remembered and celebrated most for her canonical achievement in *The Second Sex*, boldly confronting the issue of sexual difference for generations of women yet to be born.

SELECT BIBLIOGRAPHY OF DE BEAUVOIR'S WORKS IN ENGLISH

The Second Sex, London: Cape, 1953.
Memoires of a Dutiful Daughter, London: Deutsch, 1959.
The Ethics of Ambiguity, Secaucus: Citadel Press, 1980.
All Said and Done, Harmondsworth: Penguin, 1990.
Old Age, Harmondsworth: Penguin, 1990.
Letters to Sartre, London: Radius, 1991.

Introduction to *The Second Sex*

FOR A LONG time I have hesitated to write a book on woman. The subject is irritating, especially to women; and it is not new. Enough ink has been spilled in quarrelling over feminism, and perhaps we should say no more about it. It is still talked about, however, for the voluminous nonsense uttered during the last century seems to have done little to illuminate the problem. After all, is there a problem? And if so, what is it? Are there women, really? Most assuredly the theory of the eternal feminine still has its adherents who will whisper in your ear: 'Even in Russia women still are *women*'; and other erudite persons – sometimes the very same – say with a sigh: 'Woman is losing her way, woman is lost'. One wonders if women still exist, if they will always exist, whether or not it is desirable that they should, what place they occupy in this world, what their place should be. 'What has become of women?' was asked recently in an ephemeral magazine.

But first we must ask: what is a woman? '*Tota mulier in utero*', says one, 'woman is a womb'. But in speaking of certain women, connoisseurs declare that they are not women, although they are equipped with a uterus like the rest. All agree in recognizing the fact that females exist in the human species; today as always they make up about one half of humanity. And yet we are told that femininity is in danger; we are exhorted to be women, remain women, become women. It would appear, then, that every female human being is not necessarily a woman; to be so considered she must share in that mysterious and threatened reality known as femininity. Is this attribute something secreted by the ovaries? Or is it a Platonic essence, a product of the philosophic imagination? Is a rustling petticoat enough to bring it down to earth? Although some women try zealously to incarnate this essence, it is hardly patentable. It is frequently described in vague and dazzling terms that seem to have been borrowed from the vocabulary of the seers, and indeed in the times of St Thomas it was considered an essence as certainly defined as the somniferous virtue of the poppy.

But conceptualism has lost ground. The biological and social sciences no longer admit the existence of unchangeably fixed entities that determine given characteristics, such as those ascribed to woman, the Jew, or the Negro. Science regards any characteristic as a reaction dependent in part upon a *situation*. If today femininity no longer exists, then it never existed. But does the word *woman*, then, have no specific content? This is stoutly affirmed by those who hold to the philosophy of the enlightenment, of rationalism, of nominalism; women, to them, are merely the human beings arbitrarily designated by the word *woman*. Many American

From *The Second Sex*, trans. D. Bair, ed. H. M. Parshley, London: Cape, 1953.

women particularly are prepared to think that there is no longer any place for woman as such; if a backward individual still takes herself for a woman, her friends advise her to be psychoanalysed and thus get rid of this obsession. In regard to a work, *Modern Woman: The Lost Sex*, which in other respects has its irritating features, Dorothy Parker has written: 'I cannot be just to books which treat of woman as woman . . . My idea is that all of us, men as well as women, should be regarded as human beings'. But nominalism is a rather inadequate doctrine, and the anti-feminists have had no trouble in showing that women simply *are not* men. Surely woman is, like man, a human being; but such a declaration is abstract. The fact is that every concrete human being is always a singular, separate individual. To decline to accept such notions as the eternal feminine, the black soul, the Jewish character, is not to deny that Jews, Negroes, women exist today – this denial does not represent a liberation for those concerned, but rather a flight from reality. Some years ago a well-known woman writer refused to permit her portrait to appear in a series of photographs especially devoted to women writers; she wished to be counted among the men. But in order to gain this privilege she made use of her husband's influence! Women who assert that they are men lay claim none the less to masculine consideration and respect. I recall also a young Trotskyite standing on a platform at a boisterous meeting and getting ready to use her fists, in spite of her evident fragility. She was denying her feminine weakness; but it was for love of a militant male whose equal she wished to be. The attitude of defiance of many American women proves that they are haunted by a sense of their femininity. In truth, to go for a walk with one's eyes open is enough to demonstrate that humanity is divided into two classes of individuals whose clothes, faces, bodies, smiles, gaits, interests, and occupations are manifestly different. Perhaps these differences are superficial, perhaps they are destined to disappear. What is certain is that they do most obviously exist.

If her functioning as a female is not enough to define woman, if we decline also to explain her through 'the eternal feminine', and if nevertheless we admit, provisionally, that women do exist, then we must face the question: what is a woman?

To state the question is, to me, to suggest, at once, a preliminary answer. The fact that I ask it is in itself significant. A man would never set out to write a book on the peculiar situation of the human male. But if I wish to define myself, I must first of all say: 'I am a woman'; on this truth must be based all further discussion. A man never begins by presenting himself as an individual of a certain sex; it goes without saying that he is a man. The terms *masculine* and *feminine* are used symmetrically only as a matter of form, as on legal papers. In actuality the relation of the two sexes is not quite like that of two electrical poles, for man represents both the positive and the neutral, as is indicated by the common use of *man* to designate human beings in general; whereas woman represents only the negative, defined by limiting criteria, without recip-rocity. In the midst of an abstract discussion it is vexing to hear a man say: 'You think thus and so because you are a woman'; but I know that my only defence is to reply: 'I think thus and so because it is true', thereby removing my subjective self from the argument. It would be out of the question to reply: 'And you think the contrary because you are a man', for it is understood that the fact of being a man is no peculiarity. A man is in the right in being a man; it is the woman who is in the wrong. It amounts to this: just as for the ancients there was an absolute vertical with reference to which the oblique was defined, so there is an absolute human type, the masculine. Woman has ovaries, a uterus: these peculiar-ities imprison her in her subjectivity, circumscribe her within the limits of her own nature. It is often said that she thinks with her glands. Man superbly ignores the fact that his anatomy also includes glands, such as the testicles, and that they secrete hormones. He thinks of his body as a direct and normal connection with the world, which he believes he appre-hends objectively, whereas he regards the body of woman as a hindrance, a prison, weighed down by everything peculiar to it. 'The female is a female by virtue of a certain *lack* of qualities', said Aristotle; 'we should regard the female nature as afflicted with a natural defectiveness'. And St Thomas for his part pronounced woman to be an 'imperfect man', an 'incidental' being. This is symbolized in Genesis where Eve is depicted as made from what Bossuet called 'a supernumerary bone' of Adam.

Thus humanity is male and man defines woman not in herself but as relative to him; she is not regarded as an autonomous being. Michelet writes: 'Woman, the relative being . . .' And Benda is most positive in his *Rapport d'Uriel*: 'The body of man makes sense in itself quite apart from that of woman, whereas the latter seems wanting in significance by itself . . . Man can think of himself without woman. She cannot think of herself without man'. And she is simply what man decrees; thus she is called 'the sex', by which is meant that she appears essentially to the male as a sexual being. For him she is sex – absolute sex, no less. She is defined and differ-entiated with reference to man and not he with reference to her; she is the incidental, the inessential as opposed to the essential. He is the Subject, he is the Absolute – she is the Other.[1]

The category of the *Other* is as primordial as consciousness itself. In the most primitive societies, in the most ancient mythologies, one finds the expression of a duality – that of the Self and the Other. This duality was not originally attached to the division of the sexes; it was not dependent upon any empirical facts. It is revealed in such works as that of Granet on Chinese thought and those of Dumézil on the East Indies and Rome. The feminine element was at first no more involved in such pairs as Varuna–Mitra, Uranus–Zeus, Sun–Moon, and Day–Night than it was in the con-trasts between Good and Evil, lucky and unlucky auspices, right and left, God and Lucifer. Otherness is a fundamental category of human thought.

Thus it is that no group ever sets itself up as the One without at once setting up the Other over against itself. If three travellers chance to occupy the same compartment, that is enough to make vaguely hostile 'others' out of all the rest of the passengers on the train. In small-town eyes all persons not belonging to the village are 'strangers' and suspect; to the native of a country all who inhabit other countries are 'foreigners'; Jews are 'different' for the anti-Semite, Negroes are 'inferior' for American racists, aborigines are 'natives' for colonists, proletarians are the 'lower class' for the privileged.

Lévi-Strauss, at the end of a profound work on the various forms of primitive societies, reaches the following conclusion: 'Passage from the state of Nature to the state of Culture is marked by man's ability to view biological relations as a series of contrasts; duality, alternation, opposition, and symmetry, whether under definite or vague forms, constitute not so much phenomena to be explained as fundamental and immediately given data of social reality'. These phenomena would be incomprehensible if in fact human society were simply a *Mitsein* or fellowship based on solidarity and friendliness. Things become clear, on the contrary, if, following Hegel, we find in consciousness itself a fundamental hostility towards every other consciousness; the subject can be posed only in being opposed – he sets himself up as the essential, as opposed to the other, the inessential, the object.

But the other consciousness, the other ego, sets up a reciprocal claim. The native travelling abroad is shocked to find himself in turn regarded as a 'stranger' by the natives of neighbouring countries. As a matter of fact, wars, festivals, trading, treaties, and contests among tribes, nations, and classes tend to deprive the concept *Other* of its absolute sense and to make manifest its relativity; willy-nilly, individuals and groups are forced to realize the reciprocity of their relations. How is it, then, that this reciprocity has not been recognized between the sexes, that one of the contrasting terms is set up as the sole essential, denying any relativity in regard to its correlative and defining the latter as pure otherness? Why is it that women do not dispute male sovereignty? No subject will readily volunteer to become the object, the inessential; it is not the Other who, in defining himself as the Other, establishes the One. The Other is posed as such by the One in defining himself as the One. But if the Other is not to regain the status of being the One, he must be submissive enough to accept this alien point of view. Whence comes this submission in the case of woman?

There are, to be sure, other cases in which a certain category has been able to dominate another completely for a time. Very often this privilege depends upon inequality of numbers – the majority imposes its rule upon the minority or persecutes it. But women are not a minority, like the American Negroes or the Jews; there are as many women as men on earth. Again, the two groups concerned have often been originally independent; they may have been formerly unaware of each other's existence, or perhaps they recognized each other's autonomy. But a historical event has resulted in the subjugation of the weaker by the stronger. The scattering of the Jews, the introduction of slavery into America, the conquests of imperialism are examples in point. In these cases the oppressed retained at least the memory of former days; they possessed in common a past, a tradition, sometimes a religion or a culture.

The parallel drawn by Bebel between women and the proletariat is valid in that neither ever formed a minority or a separate collective unit of mankind. And instead of a single historical event it is in both cases a historical development that explains their status as a class and accounts for the membership of *particular individuals* in that class. But proletarians have not always existed, whereas there have always been women. They are women in virtue of their anatomy and physiology. Throughout history they have always been subordinated to men, and hence their dependency is not the result of a historical event or a social change – it was not something that *occurred*. The reason why otherness in this case seems to be an absolute is in part that it lacks the contingent or incidental nature of historical facts. A condition brought about at a certain time can be abolished at some other time, as the Negroes of Haiti and others have proved; but it might seem that a natural condition is beyond the possibility of change. In truth, however, the nature of things is no more immutably given, once for all, than is historical reality. If woman seems to be the inessential which never becomes the essential, it is because she herself fails to bring about this change. Proletarians say 'We'; Negroes also. Regarding themselves as subjects, they transform the bourgeois, the whites, into 'others'. But women do not say 'We', except at some congress of feminists or similar formal demonstration; men say 'women', and women use the same word in referring to themselves. They do not authentically assume a subjective attitude. The proletarians have accomplished the revolution in Russia, the Negroes in Haiti, the Indo-Chinese are battling for it in Indo-China; but the women's effort has never been anything more than a symbolic agitation. They have gained only what men have been willing to grant; they have taken nothing, they have only received.

The reason for this is that women lack concrete means for organizing themselves into a unit which can stand face to face with the correlative unit. They have no past, no history, no religion of their own; and they have no such solidarity of work and interest as that of the proletariat. They are not even promiscuously herded together in the way that creates community feeling among the American Negroes, the ghetto Jews, the workers of Saint-Denis, or the factory hands of Renault. They live dispersed among the males, attached through residence, housework, economic condition, and social standing to certain men – fathers or husbands – more firmly than they are to other women. If they belong to

the bourgeoisie, they feel solidarity with men of that class, not with proletarian women; if they are white, their allegiance is to white men, not to
Negro women. The proletariat can propose to massacre the ruling class,
and a sufficiently fanatical Jew or Negro might dream of getting sole
possession of the atomic bomb and making humanity wholly Jewish or
black; but woman cannot even dream of exterminating the males. The
bond that unites her to her oppressors is not comparable to any other.
The division of the sexes is a biological fact, not an event in human
history. Male and female stand opposed within a primordial *Mitsein*, and
woman has not broken it. The couple is a fundamental unity with its two
halves riveted together, and the cleavage of society along the line of sex
is impossible. Here is to be found the basic trait of woman: she is the
Other in a totality of which the two components are necessary to one
another.

One could suppose that this reciprocity might have facilitated the
liberation of woman. When Hercules sat at the feet of Omphale and
helped with her spinning, his desire for her held him captive; but why
did she fail to gain a lasting power? To revenge herself on Jason, Medea
killed their children; and this grim legend would seem to suggest that she
might have obtained a formidable influence over him through his love for
his offspring. In *Lysistrata* Aristophanes gaily depicts a band of women
who joined forces to gain social ends through the sexual needs of their
men; but this is only a play. In the legend of the Sabine women, the latter
soon abandoned their plan of remaining sterile to punish their ravishers.
In truth woman has not been socially emancipated through man's need –
sexual desire and the desire for offspring – which makes the male dependent for satisfaction upon the female.

Master and slave, also, are united by a reciprocal need, in this case
economic, which does not liberate the slave. In the relation of master to
slave the master does not make a point of the need that he has for the
other; he has in his grasp the power of satisfying this need through his
own action; whereas the slave, in his dependent condition, his hope and
fear, is quite conscious of the need he has for his master. Even if the need
is at bottom equally urgent for both, it always works in favour of the
oppressor and against the oppressed. That is why the liberation of
the working class, for example, has been slow.

Now, woman has always been man's dependant, if not his slave; the
two sexes have never shared the world in equality. And even today woman
is heavily handicapped, though her situation is beginning to change.
Almost nowhere is her legal status the same as man's, and frequently it
is much to her disadvantage. Even when her rights are legally recognized
in the abstract, long-standing custom prevents their full expression in the
mores. In the economic sphere men and women can almost be said to
make up two castes; other things being equal, the former hold the better
jobs, get higher wages, and have more opportunity for success than their

new competitors. In industry and politics men have a great many more positions and they monopolize the most important posts. In addition to all this, they enjoy a traditional prestige that the education of children tends in every way to support, for the present enshrines the past – and in the past all history has been made by men. At the present time, when women are beginning to take part in the affairs of the world, it is still a world that belongs to men – they have no doubt of it at all and women have scarcely any. To decline to be the Other, to refuse to be a party to the deal – this would be for women to renounce all the advantages conferred upon them by their alliance with the superior caste. Man-the-sovereign will provide woman-the-liege with material protection and will undertake the moral justification of her existence; thus she can evade at once both economic risk and the metaphysical risk of a liberty in which ends and aims must be contrived without assistance. Indeed, along with the ethical urge of each individual to affirm his subjective existence, there is also the temptation to forgo liberty and become a thing. This is an inauspicious road, for he who takes it – passive, lost, ruined – becomes henceforth the creature of another's will, frustrated in his transcendence and deprived of every value. But it is an easy road; on it one avoids the strain involved in undertaking an authentic existence. When man makes of woman the *Other*, he may, then, expect to manifest deep-seated tendencies towards complicity. Thus, woman may fail to lay claim to the status of subject because she lacks definite resources, because she feels the necessary bond that ties her to man regardless of reciprocity, and because she is often very well pleased with her role as the *Other*.

But it will be asked at once: how did all this begin? It is easy to see that the duality of the sexes, like any duality, gives rise to conflict. And doubtless the winner will assume the status of absolute. But why should man have won from the start? It seems possible that women could have won the victory; or that the outcome of the conflict might never have been decided. How is it that this world has always belonged to the men and that things have begun to change only recently? Is this change a good thing? Will it bring about an equal sharing of the world between men and women?

These questions are not new, and they have often been answered. But the very fact that woman is the *Other* tends to cast suspicion upon all the justifications that men have ever been able to provide for it. These have all too evidently been dictated by men's interest. A little-known feminist of the seventeenth century, Poulain de la Barre, put it this way: 'All that has been written about women by men should be suspect, for the men are at once judge and party to the lawsuit'. Everywhere, at all times, the males have displayed their satisfaction in feeling that they are the lords of creation. 'Blessed be God . . . that He did not make me a woman', say the Jews in their morning prayers, while their wives pray on a note of resignation: 'Blessed be the Lord, who created me according to His will'. The first among the blessings for which Plato thanked the gods was that he had been created free, not enslaved; the second, a man, not a woman. But the males could not enjoy this privilege fully unless they believed it to be founded on the absolute and the eternal; they sought to make the fact of their supremacy into a right. 'Being men, those who have made and compiled the laws have favoured their own sex, and jurists have elevated these laws into principles', to quote Poulain de la Barre once more.

Legislators, priests, philosophers, writers, and scientists have striven to show that the subordinate position of woman is willed in heaven and advantageous on earth. The religions invented by men reflect this wish for domination. In the legends of Eve and Pandora men have taken up arms against women. They have made use of philosophy and theology, as the quotations from Aristotle and St Thomas have shown. Since ancient times satirists and moralists have delighted in showing up the weaknesses of women. We are familiar with the savage indictments hurled against women throughout French literature. Montherlant, for example, follows the tradition of Jean de Meung, though with less gusto. This hostility may at times be well founded, often it is gratuitous; but in truth it more or less successfully conceals a desire for self-justification. As Montaigne says, 'It is easier to accuse one sex than to excuse the other'. Sometimes what is going on is clear enough. For instance, the Roman law limiting the rights of woman cited 'the imbecility, the instability of the sex' just when the weakening of family ties seemed to threaten the interests of male heirs. And in the effort to keep the married woman under guardianship, appeal was made in the sixteenth century to the authority of St Augustine, who declared that 'woman is a creature neither decisive nor constant', at a time when the single woman was thought capable of managing her property. Montaigne understood clearly how arbitrary and unjust was woman's appointed lot: 'Women are not in the wrong when they decline to accept the rules laid down for them, since the men make these rules without consulting them. No wonder intrigue and strife abound.' But he did not go so far as to champion their cause.

It was only later, in the eighteenth century, that genuinely democratic men began to view the matter objectively. Diderot, among others, strove to show that woman is, like man, a human being. Later John Stuart Mill came fervently to her defence. But these philosophers displayed unusual impartiality. In the nineteenth century the feminist quarrel became again a quarrel of partisans. One of the consequences of the industrial revolution was the entrance of women into productive labour, and it was just here that the claims of the feminists emerged from the realm of theory and acquired an economic basis, while their opponents became the more aggressive. Although landed property lost power to some extent, the bourgeoisie clung to the old morality that found the guarantee of private property in the solidity of the family. Woman was ordered back into the home the more harshly as her emancipation became a real menace. Even within the working class the men endeavoured to restrain woman's liberation, because they began to see the women as dangerous competitors – the more so because they were accustomed to work for lower wages.

In proving woman's inferiority, the anti-feminists then began to draw not only upon religion, philosophy, and theology, as before, but also upon science – biology, experimental psychology, etc. At most they were willing to grant 'equality in difference' to the *other* sex. That profitable formula is most significant; it is precisely like the 'equal but separate' formula of the Jim Crow laws aimed at the North American Negroes. As is well known, this so-called equalitarian segregation has resulted only in the most extreme discrimination. The similarity just noted is in no way due to chance, for whether it is a race, a caste, a class, or a sex that is reduced to a position of inferiority, the methods of justification are the same. 'The eternal feminine' corresponds to 'the black soul' and to 'the Jewish character'. True, the Jewish problem is on the whole very different from the other two – to the anti-Semite the Jew is not so much an inferior as he is an enemy for whom there is to be granted no place on earth, for whom annihilation is the fate desired. But there are deep similarities between the situation of woman and that of the Negro. Both are being emancipated today from a like paternalism, and the former master class wishes to 'keep them in their place' – that is, the place chosen for them. In both cases the former masters lavish more or less sincere eulogies, either on the virtues of 'the good Negro' with his dormant, childish, merry soul – the submissive Negro – or on the merits of the woman who is 'truly feminine' – that is, frivolous, infantile, irresponsible – the submissive woman. In both cases the dominant class bases its argument on a state of affairs that it has itself created. As George Bernard Shaw puts it, in substance. 'The American white relegates the black to the rank of shoeshine boy; and he concludes from this that the black is good for nothing but shining shoes.' This vicious circle is met with in all analogous circumstances; when an individual (or a group of individuals) is kept in a situation of inferiority, the fact is that he *is* inferior. But the significance of the verb to *be* must be rightly understood here; it is in bad faith to give it a static value when it really has the dynamic Hegelian sense of 'to have become'. Yes, women on the whole *are* today inferior to men; that is, their situation affords them fewer possibilities. The question is: should that state of affairs continue?

Many men hope that it will continue; not all have given up the battle. The conservative bourgeoisie still see in the emancipation of women a menace to their morality and their interests. Some men dread feminine competition. Recently a male student wrote in the *Hebdo-Latin*: 'Every woman student who goes into medicine or law robs us of a job.' He never questioned his rights in this world. And economic interests are not the only ones concerned. One of the benefits that oppression confers upon the oppressors is that the most humble among them is made to *feel* superior; thus, a 'poor white' in the South can console himself with the thought that he is not a 'dirty nigger' – and the more prosperous whites cleverly exploit this pride.

Similarly, the most mediocre of males feels himself a demigod as compared with women. It was much easier for M. de Montherlant to think himself a hero when he faced women (and women chosen for his purpose) than when he was obliged to act the man among men – something many women have done better than he, for that matter. And in September 1948, in one of his articles in the *Figaro littéraire*, Claude Mauriac – whose great originality is admired by all – could[2] write regarding woman: '*We* listen on a tone [*sic!*] of polite indifference . . . to the most brilliant among them, well knowing that her wit reflects more or less luminously ideas that come from *us*'. Evidently the speaker referred to is not reflecting the ideas of Mauriac himself, for no one knows of his having any. It may be that she reflects ideas originating with men, but then, even among men there are those who have been known to appropriate ideas not their own; and one can well ask whether Claude Mauriac might not find more interesting a conversation reflecting Descartes, Marx, or Gide rather than himself. What is really remarkable is that by using the questionable *we* he identifies himself with St Paul, Hegel, Lenin, and Nietzsche, and from the lofty eminence of their grandeur looks down disdainfully upon the bevy of women who make bold to converse with him on a footing of equality. In truth, I know of more than one woman who would refuse to suffer with patience Mauriac's 'tone of polite indifference'.

I have lingered on this example because the masculine attitude is here displayed with disarming ingenuousness. But men profit in many more subtle ways from the otherness, the alterity of woman. Here is a miraculous balm for those afflicted with an inferiority complex, and indeed no one is more arrogant towards women, more aggressive or scornful, than the man who is anxious about his virility. Those who are not fear-ridden in the presence of their fellow men are much more disposed to recognize a fellow creature in woman; but even to these the myth of Woman, the Other, is precious for many reasons.[3] They cannot be blamed for not cheerfully relinquishing all the benefits they derive from the myth, for they realize what they would lose in relinquishing woman as they fancy her to be, while they fail to realize what they have to gain from the woman of tomorrow. Refusal to pose oneself as the Subject, unique and absolute, requires great self-denial. Furthermore, the vast majority of men make no such claim explicitly. They do not *postulate* woman as inferior, for today they are too thoroughly imbued with the ideal of democracy not to recognize all human beings as equals.

In the bosom of the family, woman seems in the eyes of childhood and youth to be clothed in the same social dignity as the adult males. Later on, the young man, desiring and loving, experiences the resistance, the independence of the woman desired and loved; in marriage, he respects woman as wife and mother, and in the concrete events of conjugal life she stands there before him as a free being. He can therefore feel that social subordination as between the sexes no longer exists and that on the whole, in spite of differences, woman is an equal. As, however, he observes some points of inferiority – the most important being unfitness for the professions – he attributes these to natural causes. When he is in a co-operative and benevolent relation with woman, his theme is the principle of abstract equality, and he does not base his attitude upon such inequality as may exist. But when he is in conflict with her, the situation is reversed: his theme will be the existing inequality, and he will even take it as justification for denying abstract equality.

So it is that many men will affirm as if in good faith that women *are* the equals of man and that they have nothing to clamour for, while *at the same time* they will say that women can never be the equals of man and that their demands are in vain. It is, in point of fact, a difficult matter for man to realize the extreme importance of social discriminations which seem outwardly insignificant but which produce in woman moral and intellectual effects so profound that they appear to spring from her original nature. The most sympathetic of men never fully comprehend woman's concrete situation. And there is no reason to put much trust in the men when they rush to the defence of privileges whose full extent they can hardly measure. We shall not, then, permit ourselves to be intimidated by the number and violence of the attacks launched against women, nor to be entrapped by the self-seeking eulogies bestowed on the 'true woman', nor to profit by the enthusiasm for woman's destiny manifested by men who would not for the world have any part of it.

We should consider the arguments of the feminists with no less suspicion, however, for very often their controversial aim deprives them of all real value. If the 'woman question' seems trivial, it is because masculine arrogance has made of it a 'quarrel'; and when quarrelling one no longer reasons well. People have tirelessly sought to prove that woman is superior, inferior, or equal to man. Some say that, having been created after Adam, she is evidently a secondary being; others say on the contrary that Adam was only a rough draft and that God succeeded in producing the human being in perfection when He created Eve. Woman's brain is smaller; yes, but it is relatively larger. Christ was made a man; yes, but perhaps for his greater humility. Each argument at once suggests its opposite, and both are often fallacious. If we are to gain understanding, we must get out of these ruts; we must discard the vague notions of superiority, inferiority, equality which have hitherto corrupted every discussion of the subject and start afresh.

Very well, but just how shall we pose the question? And, to begin with, who are we to propound it at all? Man is at once judge and party to the case; but so is woman. What we need is an angel – neither man nor woman – but where shall we find one? Still, the angel would be poorly qualified to speak, for an angel is ignorant of all the basic facts involved in the problem. With a hermaphrodite we should be no better off, for here the situation is most peculiar; the hermaphrodite is not really the combination of a whole man and a whole woman, but consists of parts of each and thus is neither. It looks to me as if there are, after all, certain women who are best qualified to elucidate the situation of woman. Let us not be misled by the sophism that because Epimenides was a Cretan he was necessarily a liar; it is not a mysterious essence that compels men and women to act in good or in bad faith, it is their situation that inclines them more or less towards the search for truth. Many of today's women, fortunate in the restoration of all the privileges pertaining to the estate of the human being, can afford the luxury of impartiality – we even recognize its necessity. We are no longer like our partisan elders; by and large we have won the game. In recent debates on the status of women the United Nations has persistently maintained that the equality of the sexes is now becoming a reality, and already some of us have never had to sense in our femininity an inconvenience or an obstacle. Many problems appear to us to be more pressing than those which concern us in particular, and this detachment even allows us to hope that our attitude will be objective. Still, we know the feminine world more intimately than do the men because we have our roots in it, we grasp more immediately than do men what it means to a human being to be feminine; and we are more concerned with such knowledge. I have said that there are more pressing problems, but this does not prevent us from seeing some importance in asking how the fact of being women will affect our lives. What opportunities precisely have been given us and what withheld? What fate awaits our younger sisters, and what directions should they take? It is significant that books by women on women are in general animated in our day less by a wish to demand our rights than by an effort towards clarity and understanding. As we emerge from an era of excessive controversy, this book is offered as one attempt among others to confirm that statement.

But it is doubtless impossible to approach any human problem with a mind free from bias. The way in which questions are put, the points of view assumed, presuppose a relativity of interest; all characteristics imply values, and every objective description, so called, implies an ethical background. Rather than attempt to conceal principles more or less definitely implied, it is better to state them openly, at the beginning. This will make it unnecessary to specify on every page in just what sense one uses such words as *superior, inferior, better, worse, progress, reaction*, and the like. If we survey some of the works on woman, we note that one of the points of view most frequently adopted is that of the public good, the general interest; and one always means by this the benefit of society as one wishes it to be maintained or established. For our part, we hold that the only public good is that which assures the private good of the citizens; we shall pass judgement on institutions according to their effectiveness in giving concrete opportunities to individuals. But we do not confuse the idea of private interest with that of happiness, although that is another common point of view. Are not women of the harem more happy than women voters? Is not the housekeeper happier than the working-woman? It is not too clear just what the word *happy* really means and still less what true values it may mask. There is no possibility of measuring the happiness of others, and it is always easy to describe as happy the situation in which one wishes to place them.

In particular those who are condemned to stagnation are often pronounced happy on the pretext that happiness consists in being at rest. This notion we reject, for our perspective is that of existentialist ethics. Every subject plays his part as such specifically through exploits or projects that serve as a mode of transcendence; he achieves liberty only through a continual reaching out towards other liberties. There is no justification for present existence other than its expansion into an indefinitely open future. Every time transcendence falls back into immanence, stagnation, there is a degradation of existence into the '*en-soi*' the brutish life of subjection to given conditions – and of liberty into constraint and contingence. This downfall represents a moral fault if the subject consents to it; if it is inflicted upon him, it spells frustration and oppression. In both cases it is an absolute evil. Every individual concerned to justify his existence feels that his existence involves an undefined need to transcend himself, to engage in freely chosen projects.

Now, what peculiarly signalizes the situation of woman is that she – a free and autonomous being like all human creatures – nevertheless finds herself living in a world where men compel her to assume the status of the Other. They propose to stabilize her as object and to doom her to immanence since her transcendence is to be overshadowed and for ever transcended by another ego (*conscience*) which is essential and sovereign. The drama of woman lies in this conflict between the fundamental aspirations of every subject (ego) – who always regards the self as the essential – and the compulsions of a situation in which she is the inessential. How can a human being in woman's situation attain fulfilment? What roads are open to her? Which are blocked? How can independence be recovered in a state of dependency? What circumstances limit woman's liberty and how can they be overcome? These are the fundamental questions on which I would fain throw some light. This means that I am interested in the fortunes of the individual as defined not in terms of happiness but in terms of liberty.

Quite evidently this problem would be without significance if we were to believe that woman's destiny is inevitably determined by physiological, psychological, or economic forces. Hence I shall discuss first of all the light in which woman is viewed by biology, psychoanalysis, and historical materialism. Next I shall try to show exactly how the concept of the

SIMONE DE BEAUVOIR

'truly feminine' has been fashioned – why woman has been defined as the Other – and what have been the consequences from man's point of view. Then from woman's point of view I shall describe the world in which women must live; and thus we shall be able to envisage the difficulties in their way as, endeavouring to make their escape from the sphere hitherto assigned them, they aspire to full membership in the human race.

NOTES

1 E. Lévinas expresses this idea most explicitly in his essay *Temps et l'Autre*. 'Is there not a case in which otherness, alterity [*altérité*], unquestionably marks the nature of a being, as its essence, an instance of otherness not consisting purely and simply in the opposition of two species of the same genus? I think that the feminine represents the contrary in its absolute sense, this contrariness being in no wise affected by any relation between it and its correlative and thus remaining absolutely other. Sex is not a certain specific difference . . . no more is the sexual difference a mere contradiction . . . Nor does this difference lie in the duality of two complementary terms, for two complementary terms imply a pre-existing whole . . . Otherness reaches its full flowering in the feminine, a term of the same rank as consciousness but of opposite meaning'.

I suppose that Lévinas does not forget that woman, too, is aware of her own consciousness, or ego. But it is striking that he deliberately takes a man's point of view, disregarding the reciprocity of subject and object. When he writes that woman is mystery, he implies that she is mystery for man. Thus his description, which is intended to be objective, is in fact an assertion of masculine privilege.

2 Or at least he thought he could.

3 A significant article on this theme by Michel Carrouges appeared in No. 292 of the *Cahiers du Sud*. He writes indignantly: 'Would that there were no woman-myth at all but only a cohort of cooks, matrons, prostitutes, and blue-stockings serving functions of pleasure or usefulness!' That is to say, in his view woman has no existence in and for herself; he thinks only of her *function* in the male world. Her reason for existence lies in man. But then, in fact, her poetic 'function' as a myth might be more valued than any other. The real problem is precisely to find out why woman should be defined with relation to man.

7

Hans-Georg Gadamer
(b. 1900)

Hans-Georg Gadamer is acknowledged to be one of the most prominent hermeneutic thinkers to emerge in the twentieth century. Born in Marburg, Germany in 1900, he remained there to pursue his education in philosophy and classical philology, studying with such renowned thinkers as Paul Natorp, Martin Heidegger and Paul Friedländer. Gadamer finished his doctorate on Plato in 1922, and held university posts in Marburg (1929–37), Leipzig (1938–47), Frankfurt (1947–9) and Heidelberg (1949–68) until his retirement. Many of the essays written on philosophical hermeneutics and language throughout his fruitful academic life were first gathered together as *Kleine Schriften* (4 vols, Tübingen: Mohr, 1967–79), and later translated for numerous anthologies in English, as cited in our select bibliography. At present, Gadamer's collected works (*Gesammelte Werke*) are projected to fill ten volumes, nine of which have already appeared.

We shall see that a main theme reverberating throughout Gadamer's hermeneutic philosophy is that 'understanding' (*Verstehen*) must be historically and linguistically mediated. There is always some pre-understanding or prejudice (*Vorurteil*) that makes our encounter with tradition possible at all. In other words, both the tradition and those who attempt to interpret it constitute part of a historical continuum that cannot be artificially separated or segregated. According to Gadamer, the error of the Enlightenment was its 'prejudice against prejudice', i.e. the refusal to recognize the significance of our own insertion in a tradition that, at some level, we already understand. Thus, he emphasizes the importance of the 'effective history' (*Wirkungsgeschichte*) that underlies any potential 'fusion of horizons' (*Horizontsverschmelzung*) that we could hope to achieve.

Equally dangerous, in Gadamer's view, is the romantic or psychologistic approach of classical hermeneutics, particularly Schleiermacher, who sought to collapse historical distance by fostering 'empathy' with the mental attitude, dispositions and worlds of those who created the traditional texts we interpret. For Gadamer, this merely presents the mirror-image of the Enlightenment's ideal of a detached and privileged 'reason', by substituting the Romantic ideal of an ancient, primeval wisdom that could somehow be recuperated. While less critical, in this regard, of a hermeneutic predecessor such as Dilthey, Gadamer also rejects Dilthey's suggestion that the historical or human sciences (*Geisteswissenschaften*) can be studied by applying the same methodology as that applied to the natural sciences. The transmission of culture, as well as the understanding of ourselves as human beings, can never be reduced to what Gadamer considered the often positivistic methodologies of natural scientists. Gadamer examined these and related issues in great detail in his enormously influential work *Truth and Method* (*Wahrheit und Methode*, 1960). He defended his claim that tradition already constitutes part of our historical horizon in his extended debate with Habermas in the early 1960s. There Gadamer argued that even the philosophy of 'critique' has its roots in the Enlightenment, burdened by all of the assumptions that tradition entails.

In his attempt to broaden the significance of a truly 'philosophical hermeneutics', Gadamer stresses the dominant role of language (*Sprachlichkeit*) and the linguistic resources that mediate both our encounters with tradition and with each other. We are always partners in dialogue, whether it be with 'eminent texts' or with one another in conversation. Thus, the path to understanding can only be traversed through language, as he emphasizes repeatedly in the selection which follows.

SELECT BIBLIOGRAPHY OF GADAMER'S WORKS IN ENGLISH

Truth and Method, New York: Seabury Press, 1975.

Philosophical Hermeneutics, ed. David E. Linge, Berkeley: University of California Press, 1976.

Dialogue and Dialectic: Eight Hermeneutical Studies on Plato, New Haven: Yale University Press, 1980.

Reason in the Age of Science, Cambridge, Mass.: MIT Press, 1981.

Hegel's Dialectic: Five Hermeneutical Studies, New Haven: Yale University Press, 1982.

Philosophical Apprenticeships, Cambridge, Mass.: MIT Press, 1985.

The Idea of the Good in Platonic–Aristotelian Philosophy, New Haven: Yale University Press, 1986.

The Relevance of the Beautiful and Other Essays, ed. Robert Bernasconi, Cambridge: Cambridge University Press, 1986.

'Reply to Jacques Derrida', in Diane P. Michelfelder and Richard E. Palmer (eds), *Dialogue and Deconstruction: The Gadamer–Derrida Encounter*, Albany: State University of New York Press, 1989.

Plato's Dialectical Ethics: Phenomenological Interpretations Relating to the Philebus, New Haven: Yale University Press, 1991.

Heidegger's Ways, Albany: State University of New York Press, 1994.

Literature and Philosophy in Dialogue, Albany: State University of New York Press, 1994.

The Universality of the Hermeneutical Problem

WHY HAS THE problem of language come to occupy the same central position in current philosophical discussions that the concept of thought, or 'thought thinking itself', held in philosophy a century and a half ago? By answering this question, I shall try to give an answer indirectly to the central question of the modern age – a question posed for us by the existence of modern science. It is the question of how our natural view of the world – the experience of the world that we have as we simply live out our lives – is related to the unassailable and anonymous authority that confronts us in the pronouncements of science. Since the seventeenth century, the real task of philosophy has been to mediate this new employment of man's cognitive and constructive capacities with the totality of our experience of life. This task has found expression in a variety of ways, including our own generation's attempt to bring the topic of language to the center of philosophical concern. Language is the fundamental mode of operation of our being-in-the-world and the all-embracing form of the constitution of the world. Hence we always have in view the pronouncements of the sciences, which are fixed in nonverbal signs. And our task is to reconnect the objective world of technology, which the sciences place at our disposal and discretion, with those fundamental orders of our being that are neither arbitrary nor manipulable by us, but rather simply demand our respect.

I want to elucidate several phenomena in which the universality of this question becomes evident. I have called the point of view involved in this theme 'hermeneutical', a term developed by Heidegger. Heidegger was continuing a perspective stemming originally from Protestant theology and transmitted into our own century by Wilhelm Dilthey.

What is hermeneutics? I would like to start from two experiences of alienation that we encounter in our concrete existence: the experience of alienation of the aesthetic consciousness and the experience of alienation of the historical consciousness. In both cases what I mean can be stated in a few words. The aesthetic consciousness realizes a possibility that as such we can neither deny nor diminish in its value, namely, that we relate ourselves, either negatively or affirmatively, to the quality of an artistic form. This statement means we are related in such a way that the judgment we make decides in the end regarding the expressive power and validity of what we judge. What we reject has nothing to say to us – or we reject it because it has nothing to say to us. This characterizes our relation to art in the broadest sense of the word, a sense that, as Hegel has shown, includes the entire religious world of the ancient Greeks, whose religion of beauty experienced the divine in concrete works of art that

From *Philosophical Hermeneutics*, Berkeley: University of California Press, 1976.

111

man creates in response to the gods. When it loses its original and unquestioned authority, this whole world of experience becomes alienated into
an object of aesthetic judgment. At the same time, however, we must
admit that the world of artistic tradition – the splendid contemporane-
ousness that we gain through art with so many human worlds – is more
than a mere object of our free acceptance or rejection. Is it not true that
when a work of art has seized us it no longer leaves us the freedom to
push it away from us once again and to accept or reject it on our own
terms? And is it not also true that these artistic creations, which come
down through the millennia, were not created for such aesthetic acceptance or rejection? No artist of the religiously vital cultures of the past
ever produced his work of art with any other intention than that his
creation should be received in terms of what it says and presents and that
it should have its place in the world where men live together. The
consciousness of art – the aesthetic consciousness – is always secondary
to the immediate truth-claim that proceeds from the work of art itself.
To this extent, when we judge a work of art on the basis of its aesthetic
quality, something that is really much more intimately familiar to us is
alienated. This alienation into aesthetic judgment always takes place when
we have withdrawn ourselves and are no longer open to the immediate
claim of that which grasps us. Thus one point of departure for my reflections in *Truth and Method* was that the aesthetic sovereignty that claims
its rights in the experience of art represents an alienation when compared
to the authentic experience that confronts us in the form of art itself.

About thirty years ago, this problem cropped up in a particularly
distorted form when National Socialist politics of art, as a means to its
own ends, tried to criticize formalism by arguing that art is bound to a
people. Despite its misuse by the National Socialists, we cannot deny that
the idea of art being bound to a people involves a real insight. A genuine
artistic creation stands within a particular community, and such a community is always distinguishable from the cultured society that is informed
and terrorized by art criticism.

The second mode of the experience of alienation is the historical
consciousness – the noble and slowly perfected art of holding ourselves
at a critical distance in dealing with witnesses to past life. Ranke's celebrated description of this idea as the extinguishing of the individual
provided a popular formula for the ideal of historical thinking: the historical consciousness has the task of understanding all the witnesses of
a past time out of the spirit of that time, of extricating them from the
preoccupations of our own present life, and of knowing, without moral
smugness, the past as a human phenomenon. In his well-known essay *The
Use and Abuse of History*, Nietzsche formulated the contradiction between
this historical distancing and the immediate will to shape things that
always cleaves to the present. And at the same time he exposed many of
the consequences of what he called the 'Alexandrian', weakened form

of the will, which is found in modern historical science. We might recall his indictment of the weakness of evaluation that has befallen the modern mind because it has become so accustomed to considering things in ever different and changing lights that it is blinded and incapable of arriving at an opinion of its own regarding the objects it studies. It is unable to determine its own position *vis-à-vis* what confronts it. Nietzsche traces the value-blindness of historical objectivism back to the conflict between the alienated historical world and the life-powers of the present.

To be sure, Nietzsche is an ecstatic witness. But our actual experience of the historical consciousness in the last one hundred years has taught us most emphatically that there are serious difficulties involved in its claim to historical objectivity. Even in those masterworks of historical scholarship that seem to be the very consummation of the extinguishing of the individual demanded by Ranke, it is still an unquestioned principle of our scientific experience that we can classify these works with unfailing accuracy in terms of the political tendencies of the time in which they were written. When we read Mommsen's *History of Rome*, we know who alone could have written it, that is, we can identify the political situation in which this historian organized the voices of the past in a meaningful way. We know it too in the case of Treitschke or of Sybel, to choose only a few prominent names from Prussian historiography. This clearly means, first of all, that the whole reality of historical experience does not find expression in the mastery of historical method. No one disputes the fact that controlling the prejudices of our own present to such an extent that we do not misunderstand the witnesses of the past is a valid aim, but obviously such control does not completely fulfill the task of understanding the past and its transmissions. Indeed, it could very well be that only *insignificant* things in historical scholarship permit us to approximate this ideal of totally extinguishing individuality, while the great productive achievements of scholarship always preserve something of the splendid magic of immediately mirroring the present in the past and the past in the present. Historical science, the second experience from which I begin, expresses only one part of our actual experience – our actual encounter with historical tradition – and it knows only an alienated form of this historical tradition.

We can contrast the hermeneutical consciousness with these examples of alienation as a more comprehensive possibility that we must develop. But, in the case of this hermeneutical consciousness also, our initial task must be to overcome the epistemological truncation by which the traditional 'science of hermeneutics' has been absorbed into the idea of modern science. If we consider Schleiermacher's hermeneutics, for instance, we find his view of this discipline peculiarly restricted by the modern idea of science. Schleiermacher's hermeneutics shows him to be a leading voice of historical romanticism. But at the same time, he kept the concern of the Christian theologian clearly in mind, intending his hermeneutics, as a general doctrine of the art of understanding, to be of value in the special work of interpreting Scripture. Schleiermacher defined hermeneutics as the art of avoiding misunderstanding. To exclude by controlled, methodical consideration whatever is alien and leads to misunderstanding – misunderstanding suggested to us by distance in time, change in linguistic usages, or in the meanings of words and modes of thinking – that is certainly far from an absurd description of the hermeneutical endeavor. But the question also arises as to whether the phenomenon of understanding is defined appropriately when we say that to understand is to avoid misunderstanding. It is not, in fact, the case that every misunderstanding presupposes a 'deep common accord'?

I am trying to call attention here to a common experience. We say, for instance, that understanding and misunderstanding take place between I and thou. But the formulation 'I and thou' already betrays an enormous alienation. There is nothing like an 'I and thou' at all – there is neither the I nor the thou as isolated, substantial realities. I may say 'thou' and I may refer to myself over against a thou, but a common understanding [*Verständigung*] always precedes these situations. We all know that to say 'thou' to someone presupposes a deep common accord [*tiefes Einverständnis*]. Something enduring is already present when this word is spoken. When we try to reach agreement on a matter on which we have different opinions, this deeper factor always comes into play, even if we are seldom aware of it. Now the science of hermeneutics would have us believe that the opinion we have to understand is something alien that seeks to lure us into misunderstanding, and our task is to exclude every element through which a misunderstanding can creep in. We accomplish this task by a controlled procedure of historical training, by historical criticism, and by a controllable method in connection with powers of psychological empathy. It seems to me that this description is valid in one respect, but yet it is only a partial description of a comprehensive life-phenomenon that constitutes the 'we' that we all are. Our task, it seems to me, is to transcend the prejudices that underlie the aesthetic consciousness, the historical consciousness, and the hermeneutical consciousness that has been restricted to a technique for avoiding misunderstandings and to overcome the alienations present in them all.

What is it, then, in these three experiences that seemed to us to have been left out, and what makes us so sensitive to the distinctiveness of these experiences? What is the *aesthetic* consciousness when compared to the fullness of what has already addressed us – what we call 'classical' in art? Is it not always already determined in this way what will be expressive for us and what we will find significant? Whenever we say with an instinctive, even if perhaps erroneous, certainty (but a certainty that is initially valid for our consciousness) 'this is classical; it will endure', what we are speaking of has already preformed our possibility for aesthetic judgment. There are no purely formal criteria that can claim to judge and sanction the formative level simply on the basis of its artistic virtuosity. Rather, our sensitive-spiritual existence is an aesthetic resonance chamber that resonates with the voices that are constantly reaching us, preceding all explicit aesthetic judgment.

The situation is similar with the historical consciousness. Here, too, we must certainly admit that there are innumerable tasks of historical scholarship that have no relation to our own present and to the depths of its historical consciousness. But it seems to me there can be no doubt that the great horizon of the past, out of which our culture and our present live, influences us in everything we want, hope for, or fear in the future. History is only present to us in light of our futurity. Here we have all learned from Heidegger, for he exhibited precisely the primacy of futurity for our possible recollection and retention, and for the whole of our history.

Heidegger worked out this primacy in his doctrine of the productivity of the hermeneutical circle. I have given the following formulation to this insight: It is not so much our judgments as it is our prejudices that constitute our being. This is a provocative formulation, for I am using it to restore to its rightful place a positive concept of prejudice that was driven out of our linguistic usage by the French and the English Enlightenment. It can be shown that the concept of prejudice did not originally have the meaning we have attached to it. Prejudices are not necessarily unjustified and erroneous, so that they inevitably distort the truth. In fact, the historicity of our existence entails that prejudices, in the literal sense of the word, constitute the initial directedness of our whole ability to experience. Prejudices are biases of our openness to the world. They are simply conditions whereby we experience something – whereby what we encounter says something to us. This formulation certainly does not mean that we are enclosed within a wall of prejudices and only let through the narrow portals those things that can produce a pass saying, 'Nothing new will be said here'. Instead we welcome just that guest who promises something new to our curiosity. But how do we know the guest whom we admit is one who has something *new* to say to us? Is not our expectation and our readiness to hear the new also necessarily determined by the old that has already taken possession of us? The concept of prejudice is closely connected to the concept of authority, and the above image makes it clear that it is in need of hermeneutical rehabilitation. Like every image, however, this one too is misleading. The nature of the hermeneutical experience is not that something is outside and desires admission. Rather, we are possessed by something and precisely by means of it we are opened up for the new, the different, the true. Plato made this clear in his beautiful comparison of bodily foods with spiritual nourishment: while we can refuse the former (e.g. on the advice of a physician), we have always taken the latter into ourselves already.

115

But now the question arises as to how we can legitimate this hermeneutical conditionedness of our being in the face of modern science, which stands or falls with the principle of being unbiased and prejudiceless. We will certainly not accomplish this legitimation by making prescriptions for science and recommending that it toe the line – quite aside from the fact that such pronouncements always have something comical about them. Science will not do us this favor. It will continue along its own path with an inner necessity beyond its control, and it will produce more and more breathtaking knowledge and controlling power. It can be no other way. It is senseless, for instance, to hinder a genetic researcher because such research threatens to breed a superman. Hence the problem cannot appear as one in which our human consciousness ranges itself over against the world of science and presumes to develop a kind of antiscience. Nevertheless, we cannot avoid the question of whether what we are aware of in such apparently harmless examples as the aesthetic consciousness and the historical consciousness does not represent a problem that is also present in modern natural science and our technological attitude toward the world. If modern science enables us to erect a new world of technological purposes that transforms everything around us, we are not thereby suggesting that the researcher who gained the knowledge decisive for this state of affairs even considered technical applications. The genuine researcher is motivated by a desire for knowledge and by nothing else. And yet, over against the whole of our civilization that is founded on modern science, we must ask repeatedly if something has not been omitted. If the presuppositions of these possibilities for knowing and making remain half in the dark, cannot the result be that the hand applying this knowledge will be destructive?

The problem is really universal. The hermeneutical question, as I have characterized it, is not restricted to the areas from which I began in my own investigations. My only concern there was to secure a theoretical basis that would enable us to deal with the basic factor of contemporary culture, namely, science and its industrial, technological utilization. Statistics provide us with a useful example of how the hermeneutical dimension encompasses the entire procedure of science. It is an extreme example, but it shows us that science always stands under definite conditions of methodological abstraction and that the successes of modern sciences rest on the fact that other possibilities for questioning are concealed by abstraction. This fact comes out clearly in the case of statistics, for the anticipatory character of the questions statistics answer make it particularly suitable for propaganda purposes. Indeed, effective propaganda must always try to influence initially the judgment of the person addressed and to restrict his possibilities of judgment. Thus what is established by statistics seems to be a language of facts, but which questions these facts answer and which facts would begin to speak if other questions were asked are hermeneutical questions. Only a hermeneutical inquiry would legitimate the meaning of these facts and thus the consequences that follow from them.

But I am anticipating, and have inadvertently used the phrase, 'which answers to which questions fit the facts'. This phrase is in fact the hermeneutical *Urphänomen*: No assertion is possible that cannot be understood as an answer to a question, and assertions can only be understood in this way. It does not impair the impressive methodology of modern science in the least. Whoever wants to learn a science has to learn to master its methodology. But we also know that methodology as such does not guarantee in any way the productivity of its application. Any experience of life can confirm the fact that there is such a thing as methodological sterility, that is, the application of a method to something not really worth knowing, to something that has not been made an object of investigation on the basis of a genuine question.

The methodological self-consciousness of modern science certainly stands in opposition to this argument. A historian, for example, will say in reply: It is all very nice to talk about the historical tradition in which alone the voices of the past gain their meaning and through which the prejudices that determine the present are inspired. But the situation is completely different in questions of serious historical research. How could one seriously mean, for example, that the clarification of the taxation practices of fifteenth-century cities or of the marital customs of Eskimos somehow first receive their meaning from the consciousness of the present and its anticipations? These are questions of historical knowledge that we take up as tasks quite independently of any relation to the present.

In answering this objection, one can say that the extremity of this point of view would be similar to what we find in certain large industrial research facilities, above all in America and Russia. I mean the so-called random experiment in which one simply covers the material without concern for waste or cost, taking the chance that some day one measurement among the thousands of measurements will finally yield an interesting finding; that is, it will turn out to be the answer to a question from which someone can progress. No doubt modern research in the humanities also works this way to some extent. One thinks, for instance, of the great editions and especially of the ever more perfect indexes. It must remain an open question, of course, whether by such procedures modern historical research increases the chances of actually noticing the interesting fact and thus gaining from it the corresponding enrichment of our knowledge. But even if they do, one might ask: Is this an ideal, that countless research projects (i.e. determinations of the connection of facts) are extracted from a thousand historians, so that the 1,001st historian can find something interesting? Of course I am drawing a caricature of genuine scholarship. But in every caricature there is an element of truth, and this one contains an indirect answer to the question of what it is that really makes the productive scholar. That he has learned the methods? The person who never produces anything new has also done that. It is imagination [*Phantasie*] that is the decisive function of the scholar. Imagination naturally has a hermeneutical function and serves the sense for what is questionable. It serves the ability to expose real, productive questions, something in which, generally speaking, only he who masters all the methods of his science succeeds.

As a student of Plato, I particularly love those scenes in which Socrates gets into a dispute with the Sophist virtuosi and drives them to despair by his questions. Eventually they can endure his questions no longer and claim for themselves the apparently preferable role of the questioner. And what happens? They can think of nothing at all to ask. Nothing at all occurs to them that is worth while going into and trying to answer.

I draw the following inference from this observation. The real power of hermeneutical consciousness is our ability to see what is questionable. Now if what we have before our eyes is not only the artistic tradition of a people, or historical tradition, or the principle of modern science in its hermeneutical preconditions but rather the whole of our experience, then we have succeeded, I think, in joining the experience of science to our own universal and human experience of life. For we have now reached the fundamental level that we can call (with Johannes Lohmann) the 'linguistic constitution of the world'.[1] It presents itself as the consciousness that is effected by history [*wirkungsgeschichtliches Bewusstsein*] and that provides an initial schematization for all our possibilities of knowing. I leave out of account the fact that the scholar – even the natural scientist – is perhaps not completely free of custom and society and from all possible factors in his environment. What I mean is that precisely *within* his scientific experience it is not so much the 'laws of ironclad inference' (Helmholz) that present fruitful ideas to him, but rather unforseen constellations that kindle the spark of scientific inspiration (e.g. Newton's falling apple or some other incidental observation).

The consciousness that is effected by history has its fulfillment in what is linguistic. We can learn from the sensitive student of language that language, in its life and occurrence, must not be thought of as merely changing, but rather as something that has a teleology operating within it. This means that the words that are formed, the means of expression that appear in a language in order to say certain things, are not accidentally fixed, since they do not once again fall altogether into disuse. Instead, a definite articulation of the world is built up – a process that works as if guided and one that we can always observe in children who are learning to speak.

We can illustrate this by considering a passage in Aristotle's *Posterior Analytics* that ingeniously describes one definite aspect of language formation.[2] The passage treats what Aristotle calls the *epagoge*, that is, the formation of the universal. How does one arrive at a universal? In philosophy we say: how do we arrive at a general concept, but even words in this sense are obviously general. How does it happen that they are 'words', that is, that they have a general meaning? In his first apperception, a sensuously equipped being finds himself in a surging sea of stimuli, and finally one day he begins, as we say, to know something. Clearly we do not mean that he was previously blind. Rather, when we say 'to know' [erkennen] we mean 'to recognize' [wiedererkennen], that is, to pick something out [herauserkennen] of the stream of images flowing past as being identical. What is picked out in this fashion is clearly retained. But how? When does a child know its mother for the first time? When it sees her for the first time? No. Then when? How does it take place? Can we really say at all that there is a single event in which a first knowing extricates the child from the darkness of not knowing? It seems obvious to me that we cannot. Aristotle has described this wonderfully. He says it is the same as when an army is in flight, driven by panic, until at last someone stops and looks around to see whether the foe is still dangerously close behind. We cannot say that the army stops when one soldier has stopped. But then another stops. The army does not stop by virtue of the fact that two soldiers stop. When does it actually stop, then? Suddenly it stands its ground again. Suddenly it obeys the command once again. A subtle pun is involved in Aristotle's description, for in Greek 'command' means arche, that is, principium. When is the principle present as a principle? Through what capacity? This question is in fact the question of the occurrence of the universal.

If I have not misunderstood Johannes Lohmann's exposition, precisely this same teleology operates constantly in the life of language. When Lohmann speaks of linguistic tendencies as the real agents of history in which specific forms expand, he knows of course that it occurs in these forms of realization, of 'coming to a stand' [Zum-Stehen-Kommen], as the beautiful German word says. What is manifest here, I contend, is the real mode of operation of our whole human experience of the world. Learning to speak is surely a phase of special productivity, and in the course of time we have all transformed the genius of the three-year-old into a poor and meager talent. But in the utilization of the linguistic interpretation of the world that finally comes about, something of the productivity of our beginnings remains alive. We are all acquainted with this, for instance, in the attempt to translate, in practical life or in literature or wherever; that is, we are familiar with the strange, uncomfortable, and tortuous feeling we have as long as we do not have the right word. When we have found the right expression (it need not always be one word), when we are certain that we have it, then it 'stands', then something has come to a 'stand'. Once again we have a halt in the midst of the rush of the foreign language, whose endless variation makes us lose our orientation. What I am describing is the mode of the whole human experience of the world. I call this experience hermeneutical, for the process we are describing is repeated continually throughout our familiar experience.

There is always a world already interpreted, already organized in its basic relations, into which experience steps as something new, upsetting what has led our expectations and undergoing reorganization itself in the upheaval. Misunderstanding and strangeness are not the first factors, so that avoiding misunderstanding can be regarded as the specific task of hermeneutics. Just the reverse is the case. Only the support of familiar and common understanding makes possible the venture into the alien, the lifting up of something out of the alien, and thus the broadening and enrichment of our own experience of the world.

This discussion shows how the claim to universality that is appropriate to the hermeneutical dimension is to be understood. Understanding is language-bound. But this assertion does not lead us into any kind of linguistic relativism. It is indeed true that we live within a language, but language is not a system of signals that we send off with the aid of a telegraphic key when we enter the office or transmission station. That is not speaking, for it does not have the infinity of the act that is linguistically creative and world experiencing. While we live wholly within a language, the fact that we do so does not constitute linguistic relativism because there is absolutely no captivity within a language – not even within our native language. We all experience this when we learn a foreign language, especially on journeys insofar as we master the foreign language to some extent. To master the foreign language means precisely that when we engage in speaking it in the foreign land, we do not constantly consult inwardly our own world and its vocabulary. The better we know the language, the less such a side glance at our native language is perceptible, and only because we never know foreign languages well enough do we always have something of this feeling. But it is nevertheless already speaking, even if perhaps a stammering speaking, for stammering is the obstruction of a desire to speak and is thus opened into the infinite realm of possible expression. Any language in which we live is infinite in this sense, and it is completely mistaken to infer that reason is fragmented because there are various languages. Just the opposite is the case. Precisely through our finitude, the particularity of our being, which is evident even in the variety of languages, the infinite dialogue is opened in the direction of the truth that we are.

If this is correct, then the relation of our modern industrial world, founded by science, which we described at the outset, is mirrored above all on the level of language. We live in an epoch in which an increasing leveling of all life-forms is taking place – that is the rationally necessary requirement for maintaining life on our planet. The food problem of mankind, for example, can only be overcome by the surrender of the lavish wastefulness that has covered the earth. Unavoidably, the mechanical, industrial world is expanding within the life of the individual as a sort of sphere of technical perfection. When we hear modern lovers talking to each other, we often wonder if they are communicating with words or with advertising labels and technical terms from the sign language of the modern industrial world. It is inevitable that the leveled life-forms of the industrial age also affect language, and in fact the impoverishment of the vocabulary of language is making enormous progress, thus bringing about an approximation of language to a technical sign-system. Leveling tendencies of this kind are irresistible. Yet in spite of them the simultaneous building up of our own world in language still persists whenever we want to say something to each other. The result is the actual relationship of men to each other. Each one is at first a kind of linguistic circle, and these linguistic circles come into contact with each other, merging more and more. Language occurs once again, in vocabulary and grammar as always, and never without the inner infinity of the dialogue that is in progress between every speaker and his partner. That is the fundamental dimension of hermeneutics. Genuine speaking, which has something to say and hence does not give prearranged signals, but rather seeks words through which one reaches the other person, is the universal human task – but it is a special task for the theologian, to whom is commissioned the saying-further (*Weitersagen*) of a message that stands written.

NOTES

1 Cf. Johannes Lohmann, *Philosophie und Sprachwissenschaft* (Berlin: Duncker & Humbolt, 1963).
2 Aristotle, *Posterior Analytics*, 100a 11–13.

8

Emmanuel Levinas
(b. 1906)

One of the most significant ethical thinkers of the twentieth century, Emmanuel Levinas has expanded the domain of phenomenology beyond the projects initiated by Husserl and Heidegger. For Levinas, the crucial focus and central concern of his own work is the priority of 'otherness', a radical alterity that demands our ethical response.

Born in Kaunas, Lithuania in 1906, Levinas was deeply influenced by his family's Judaic heritage, as well as by his early exposure to Russian language and literature. The family moved to the Russian Ukraine while Levinas was still a child, and he later witnessed the events of the 1917 Revolution. In 1923, Levinas went to France as a student enrolled in the University of Strasbourg, where he encountered prominent figures such as Blondel, Blanchot and Héring. His initial encounter with phenomenology grounded further studies with Husserl and Heidegger in Germany at the University of Freiburg in 1928, just one year after the momentous publication of *Being and Time*. Levinas returned to France, becoming a French citizen in 1930. Remarkably, the sequence of this global itinerary had all occurred by the time Levinas reached the age of twenty-four.

Levinas made an immediate impact on the growing circle of French existentialists with his first publication in 1930, *The Theory of Intuition in Husserl's Phenomenology*. Both de Beauvoir and Sartre acknowledged the importance and inspiration of this work for their early study of phenomenology. Levinas recognized the priority of intentionality in Husserl's project of examining lived experience without presuppositions. However, he realized that Heidegger's critical insight in *Being and Time* was to highlight our being-in-the-world as manifested by moods and attunement (*Stimmung*), thus avoiding the inevitable idealism of Husserl's transcendental ego. Hence, it is 'existence', rather than the 'whatness' or *quiddity* of beings that demands our phenomenological attention.

For Levinas, this ontology remains captive to its concern with 'mineness' (*Jemeinigkeit*) and the anxiety of confronting one's *own* death. By contrast, the turn to ethics as first philosophy privileges the death of the other and our responsibility for it. In *Totality and Infinity* Levinas speaks of the encounter with the 'face' of the other as the ultimate summons to validate the existence of another human being who cannot be totalized or recuperated into one's self. This radical alterity is the call of the Infinite, a transcendence that already inhabits all human encounters. Levinas thus rejects the purely 'ontological' relationship with the world that philosophy has traditionally prioritized with its exclusive concern for Being-as-totality, with human being as merely one cog in that machine. Levinas believes that only the primacy of ethical philosophy can reveal and foster the infinite transcendence of our relation to the other.

Levinas has remained in France for most of his life becoming Director of the Ecole Normale Israélite Orientale in Paris after the Second World War. He has also lectured at the Collège Philosophique, the University of Poitiers, Paris-Nanterre and the Sorbonne.

SELECT BIBLIOGRAPHY OF LEVINAS' WORKS IN ENGLISH

Totality and Infinity, Pittsburgh: Duquesne University Press, 1969.
The Theory of Intuition in Husserl's Phenomenology, Evanston, III.: Northwestern University Press, 1973.
Existence and Existents, The Hague: Nijhoff, 1978.
Otherwise than Being or Beyond Essence, The Hague: Nijhoff, 1981.
'Ethics of the Infinite' in R. Kearney, *Dialogues with Contemporary Continental Thinkers*, Manchester: Manchester University Press, 1984.
Ethics and Infinity. Pittsburgh: Duquesne University Press, 1985.
Face to Face with Levinas, ed. R. Cohen, Albany: State University of New York Press, 1986.
Collected Philosophical Papers, ed. A. Lingis, Dordrecht: Nijhoff, 1987.
Time and the Other, Pittsburgh: Duquesne University Press, 1987.
The Levinas Reader, ed. Sean Hand, Oxford: Blackwell, 1989.
Difficult Freedom, London: Athlone, 1990.
Nine Talmudic Readings, Bloomington: Indiana University Press, 1990.

EMMANUEL LEVINAS

Ethics as First Philosophy

I

THE CORRELATION BETWEEN *knowledge*, understood as disinterested contemplation, and *being*, is, according to our philosophical tradition, the very site of intelligibility, the occurrence of meaning (*sens*). The comprehension of being – the semantics of this verb – would thus be the very possibility of or the occasion for wisdom and the wise and, as such, is *first philosophy*. The intellectual, and even spiritual life, of the West, through the priority it gives to knowledge identified with Spirit, demonstrates its fidelity to the first philosophy of Aristotle, whether one interprets the latter according to the ontology of book F of the *Metaphysics* or according to the theology or onto-theology of book A where the ultimate explanation of intelligibility in terms of the primary casuality of God is a reference to a God defined by being *qua* being.

The correlation between knowledge and being, or the thematics of contemplation, indicates both a difference and a difference that is *overcome* in the *true*. Here the known is understood and so *appropriated* by knowledge, and as it were *freed* of its otherness. In the realm of truth, being, as the *other* of thought becomes the characteristic *property* of thought as knowledge. The ideal of rationality or of sense (*sens*) begins already to appear as the immanence of the real to reason; just as, in being, a privilege is granted to the *present*, which is presence to thought, of which the future and the past are modalities or modifications: re-presentations.

But in knowledge there also appears the notion of an intellectual activity or of a reasoning will – a way of doing something which consists precisely of thinking through knowing, of seizing something and making it one's own, of reducing to presence and representing the difference of being, an activity which *appropriates* and *grasps* the otherness of the known. A certain grasp: as an entity, being becomes the characteristic property of thought, as it is grasped by it and becomes known. Knowledge as perception, concept, comprehension, refers back to an act of grasping. The metaphor should be taken literally: even before any technical application of knowledge, it expresses the principle rather than the result of the future technological and industrial order of which every civilization bears at least the seed. The immanence of the known to the act of knowing is already the embodiment of seizure. This is not something applied like a form of magic to the 'impotent spirituality' of thinking, nor is it the guarantee of certain psycho-physiological conditions, but rather belongs to that unit of knowledge in which *Auffassen* (*understanding*) is also, and always has been, a *Fassen* (*gripping*). The mode of thought known as

From *The Levinas Reader*, ed. Sean Hand, Oxford: Blackwell, 1989.

knowledge involves man's concrete existence in the world he inhabits, in which he moves and works and possesses. The most abstract lessons of science – as Husserl showed in his *The Crisis of European Sciences and Transcendental Phenomenology* – have their beginnings in the 'world of life' and refer to things within hand's reach. It is to this hand that the idea of a 'given world' concretely refers. Things contain the promise of satisfaction – their concreteness puts them on a scale fit for a knowing form of thought. Thought as knowledge is already the labour of thought. A thought that assesses what is equal and adequate, and can give satisfaction. The rationality of beings stems from their presence and adequation. The operations of knowledge reestablish rationality behind the diachrony of *becoming* in which presence occurs or is foreseen. Knowledge is re-presentation, a return to presence, and nothing may remain *other* to it.

Thought is an activity, where something is appropriated by a knowledge that is independent, of course, of any finality exterior to it, an activity which is disinterested and self-sufficient and whose self-sufficiency, sovereignty, *bonne conscience*[1] and happy solitude are asserted by Aristotle. 'The wise man can practise contemplation by himself' says Book Ten of the *Nicomachean Ethics*.[2] This is a regal and as it were unconditioned activity, a sovereignty which is possible only as solitude, an unconditioned activity, even if limited for man by biological needs and by death. But it is a notion that allows a second one to be sustained, the notion of the pure *theoretic*, of its freedom, of the equivalence between wisdom and freedom, of that partial coincidence of the human domain with the divine life of which Aristotle speaks at the end of the seventh section of Book Ten of the *Ethics*. Here already the strange and contradictory concept of a *finite freedom* begins to take shape.

Throughout the whole history of Western philosophy, *contemplation* or *knowledge* and the *freedom of knowledge* are inspiration for the mind (*l'esprit*). Knowing is the psyche or pneumatic force of thought, even in the act of *feeling* or *willing*. It is to be found in the concept of *consciousness* at the dawn of the modern age with the interpretation of the concept of *cogito* given by Descartes in his Second Meditation. Husserl, returning to a medieval tradition, then, describes it as intentionality, which is understood as 'consciousness of something', and so is inseparable from its 'intentional object'. This structure has a noetic-noematic composition in which representation or objectivization is the incontestable model. The whole of human lived experience, in the period up to and above all including the present, has been expressed in terms of experience, that is, has been converted into accepted doctrine, teachings, sciences. Relationships with neighbours, with social groups, with God equally represent collective and religious *experiences*.

Modernity will subsequently be distinguished by the attempt to develop from the identification and appropriation of being *by* knowledge toward the identification of being *and* knowledge. The passage from the *cogito* to the *sum* leads to that point where the free activity of knowledge, an activity alien to any external goal, will also find itself on the side of what is known. This free activity of knowledge will also come to constitute the mystery of being *qua* being, whatever is known by knowledge (*le connu du savoir*). The *Wisdom of first philosophy* is reduced to self-consciousness. Identical and non-identical are identified. The labour of thought wins out over the otherness of things and men. Since Hegel, any goal considered alien to the disinterested acquisition of knowledge has been subordinated to the freedom of knowledge as a science (*savoir*); and within this freedom, *being* itself is from that point understood as *the active affirming of that same being*, as *the strength and strain of being*. Modern man persists in his being as a sovereign who is merely concerned to maintain the *powers of his sovereignty*. Everything that is possible is permitted. In this way the experience of Nature and Society would gradually get the better of any exteriority. A miracle of modern Western freedom unhindered by any memory or remorse, and opening onto a 'glittering future' where everything can be rectified. Only by death is this freedom thwarted. The obstacle of death is insurmountable, inexorable and fundamentally incomprehensible. The recognition of finitude will of course characterize a new test for ontology. But finitude and death will not have called into question the *bonne conscience* with which the freedom of knowledge operates. They will simply have put a check on its powers.

II

In this essay we wish to ask whether thought understood as knowledge, since the ontology of the first philosophy, has exhausted the possible modes of meaning for thought, and whether, beyond knowledge and its hold on being, a more urgent form does not emerge, that of wisdom. We propose to begin with the notion of intentionality, as it figures in Husserlian phenomenology, which is one of the culminating points in Western philosophy. The equivalence of thought and knowledge in relation to being is here formulated by Husserl in the most direct manner. Whilst successfully isolating the idea of an originary, non-theoretical intentionality from the active emotional life of consciousness, he continues to base his theory on *representation*, the objectivizing act, adopting Brentano's thesis at this point, in spite of all the precautions he takes in his new formulation of this thesis. Now, within consciousness – which is consciousness of something – knowledge is, by the same token, a relation to an *other* of consciousness and almost the aim or the will of that other which is an *object*. Husserl, inviting us to question the intentionality of consciousness, wants us also to ask 'worauf sie eigentlich hinauswill' (*What are you getting at?*), an intention or wish which, incidentally, would justify calling the units of consciousness acts. At the same time, knowledge, within the intuition of truth, is described as a 'filling out' that gratifies a longing for the being as object, given and received in the original, *present* in a representation. It is a hold on being which equals a constitution of that being. This Transcendental Reduction suspends all independence in the world other than that of consciousness itself, and causes the world to be rediscovered as *noema*. As a result, it leads – or ought to lead – to full self-consciousness affirming itself as absolute being, and confirming itself as an *I* that, through all possible 'differences', is identified as master of its own nature as well as of the universe and able to illuminate the darkest recesses of resistance to its powers. As Merleau-Ponty in particular has shown, the I that constitutes the world comes up against a sphere in which it is by its very flesh implicated; it is implicated in what it otherwise would have constituted and so is implicated in the world. But it is present in the world as it is present in its own body, an intimate incarnation which no longer purely and simply displays the exteriority of an object.[3]

But this reduced consciousness – which, in reflecting upon itself, rediscovers and masters its own acts of perception and science as objects in the world, thereby affirming itself as self-consciousness and absolute being – also remains a non-intentional consciousness of itself, as though it were a surplus somehow devoid of any wilful aim. A non-intentional conciousness operating, if one may put it like this, unknowingly as knowledge, as a non-objectivizing knowledge. As such it accompanies all the intentional processes of consciousness and of the *ego* (*moi*) which, in that consciousness, 'acts' and 'wills' and has 'intentions'. Consciousness of consciousness, indirect, implicit and aimless, without any initiative that might refer back to an ego; passive like time passing and ageing me without my intervening (*sans moi*). A 'non-intentional' consciousness to be distinguished from philosophical reflection, or the internal perception to which, indeed, non-intentional consciousness might easily offer itself as an internal object and for which it might substitute itself by making explicit the implicit messages it bears. The intentional consciousness of reflection, in taking as its object the transcendental ego, along with its mental acts and states, may also thematize and grasp supposedly implicit modes of non-intentional lived experience. It is invited to do this by philosophy in its fundamental project which consists in enlightening the inevitable transcendental naivety of a consciousness forgetful of its horizon, of its implicit content and even of the time it lives through.

Consequently one is forced, no doubt too quickly, to consider in philosophy all this immediate consciousness merely as a still confused representation to be duly brought to 'light'. The obscure context of whatever is thematized is converted by reflection, or intentional consciousness, into clear and distinct data, like those which present the perceived world or a transcendental reduced consciousness.

One may ask, however, whether, beneath the gaze of reflected consciousness taken as self-consciousness, the non-intentional, experienced as the counterpoint to the intentional, does not conserve and free its true meaning. The critique of introspection as traditionally practised has always been suspicious of a modification that a supposedly spontaneous consciousness might undergo beneath the scrutinizing, thematizing, objectivizing and indiscreet gaze of reflection, and has seen this as a violation or distortion of some sort of secret. This is a critique which is always refuted only to be reborn.

The question is what exactly happens, then, in this non-reflective consciousness considered merely to be pre-reflective and the implicit partner of an intentional consciousness which, in reflection, intentionally aims for the thinking self (*soi*), as if the thinking ego (*moi*) appeared in the world and belonged to it? What might this supposed confusion or implication really mean? One cannot simply refer to the formal notion of potentiality. Might there not be grounds for distinguishing between the envelopment of the particular in the conceptual, the implicit understanding of the presupposition in a notion, the potentiality of what is considered possible within the horizon, on the one hand, and, on the other hand, the intimacy of the non-intentional within what is known as pre-reflective consciousness and which is duration itself?

III

Does the 'knowledge' of pre-reflective self-consciousness really know? As a confused, implicit consciousness preceding all intentions – or as duration freed of all intentions – it is less an act than a pure passivity. This is not only due to its being-without-having-chosen-to-be or its fall into a confused world of possibilities already realized even before any choice might be made, as in Heidegger's *Geworfenheit*. It is a 'consciousness' that signifies not so much a knowledge of oneself as something that effaces presence or makes it discreet. Phenomenological analysis, of course, describes such a pure duration of the time within reflection, as being intentionally structured by a play of retentions and protentions which, in the very duration of time, at least remain non-explicit and suppose, in that they represent a flow, another sort of time. This duration remains free from the sway of the will, absolutely outside all activity of the ego, and exactly like the ageing process which is probably the perfect model of passive synthesis, a lapse of time no act of remembrance, reconstructing the past, could possibly reverse. Does not the temporality of implicit time, like the implication of the implicit, here signify otherwise than as knowledge taken on the run, otherwise than a way of representing presence or the non-presence of the future and the past? Duration as pure duration, non-intervention as being without insistence, as being that dare not speak its name, being that dare not be; the agency of the instant without the insistence of the ego, which is already a lapse in time, which is 'over before it's begun'! This implication of the non-intentional is a form of *mauvaise conscience*: it has no intentions, or aims, and cannot avail itself of the protective mask of a character contemplating in the mirror of the world a reassured and self-positing portrait. It has no name, no situation, no status. It has a presence afraid of presence, afraid of the insistence of the identical ego, stripped of all qualities. In its non-intentionality, not yet at the stage of willing, and prior to any fault, in its non-intentional identification, identity recoils before its affirmation. It dreads the insistence in the return to self that is a necessary part of identification. This is either *mauvaise conscience* or timidity; it is not guilty, but accused; and responsible for its very presence. It has not yet been invested with any attributes or justified in any way. This creates the reserve of the stranger or 'sojourner on earth', as it says in the Psalms, the countryless or 'homeless' person who dare not enter in. Perhaps the interiority of the mental is originally an insufficient courage to assert oneself in one's being or in body or flesh. One comes not into the world but into question. By way of reference to this, or in 'memory' of this, the ego (*moi*) which is already declaring and affirming itself (*s'affirme*) – or making itself firm (*s'affermit*) – itself in being, still remains ambiguous or enigmatic enough to recognize itself as hateful, to use Pascal's term, in this very manifestation of its emphatic identity of its ipseity, in the 'saying I'. The superb priority of $A = A$, the principle of intelligibility and meaning,[4] this sovereignty, or freedom within the human ego, is also, as it were, the moment when humility occurs. This questions the affirmation and strengthening of being found in the famous and facilely rhetorical quest for the meaning of life, which suggests that the absolute ego, already endowed with meaning by its vital, psychic and social forces, or its transcendental sovereignty, then returned to its *mauvaise conscience*.

Pre-reflective, non-intentional consciousness would never be able to return to a moral realization of this passivity, as if, in that form of consciousness, one could already see a subject postulating itself in the 'indeclinable nominative', assured of its right to be and 'dominating' the timidity of the non-intentional like a spiritual infancy that is outgrown, or an attack of weakness that becomes an impassive psyche. The non-intentional is from the start passivity, and the accusative in some way its 'first case'. (Actually, this passivity, which does not correlate to any activity, is not so much something that describes the *mauvaise conscience* of the non-intentional [as] something that is described by it.) This *mauvaise conscience* is not the finitude of existence signalled by anguish. My death, which is always going to be premature, does perhaps put a check on being which, *qua* being, perseveres in being, but in anguish this scandal fails to shake the *bonne conscience* of being, or the morality founded upon the inalienable right of the *conatus* which is also the right and the *bonne conscience* of freedom. However, it is in the passivity of the non-intentional, in the way it is spontaneous and precedes the formation of any metaphysical ideas on the subject, that the very justice of the position within being is questioned, a position which asserts itself with intentional thought, knowledge and a grasp of the here and now. What one sees in this questioning is being as *mauvaise conscience*; to be open to question, but also to questioning, to have to respond. Language is born in responsibility. One has to speak, to say *I*, to be in the first person, precisely to be me (*moi*). But, from that point, in affirming this *me* being, one has to respond to one's right to be. It is necessary to think through to this point Pascal's phrase, 'the I (*mon*) is hateful'.

IV

One has to respond to one's right to be, not by referring to some abstract and anonymous law, or judicial entity, but because of one's fear for the Other. My being-in-the-world or my 'place in the sun',[5] my being at home,[6] have these not also been the usurpation of spaces belonging to the other man whom I have already oppressed or starved, or driven out into a third world; are they not acts of repulsing, excluding, exiling, stripping, killing? Pascal's 'my place in the sun' marks the beginning of the image of the usurpation of the whole earth. A fear for all the violence and murder my existing might generate, in spite of its conscious and intentional innocence. A fear which reaches back past my 'self-consciousness' in spite of whatever moves are made towards a *bonne conscience* by a pure perseverance in being. It is the fear of occupying someone else's place with the *Da* of my *Dasein*; it is the inability to occupy a place, a profound utopia.

In my philosophical essays, I have spoken a lot about the face of the Other as being the original site of the sensible. May I now briefly take up again the description, as I now see it, of the irruption of the face into the phenomenal order of appearances?

The proximity of the other is the face's meaning, and it means from the very start in a way that goes beyond those plastic forms which forever try to cover the face like a mask of their presence to perception. But always the face shows through these forms. Prior to any particular expression and beneath all particular expressions, which cover over and protect with an immediately adopted face or countenance, there is the nakedness and destitution of the expression as such, that is to say extreme exposure, defencelessness, vulnerability itself. This extreme exposure – prior to any human aim – is like a shot 'at point blank range'. Whatever has been invested is extradited, but it is a hunt that occurs prior to anything being actually tracked down and beaten out into the open. From the beginning there is a face to face steadfast in its exposure to invisible death, to a mysterious forsakenness. Beyond the visibility of whatever is unveiled, and prior to any knowledge about death, mortality lies in the Other.

Does not expression resemble more closely this extreme exposure than it does some supposed recourse to a code? True *self*-expression stresses the nakedness and defencelessness that encourages and directs the violence of the first crime: the goal of a murderous uprightness is especially well-suited to exposing or expressing the face. The first murderer probably does not realize the result of the blow he is about to deliver, but his violent design helps him to find the line with which death may give an air of unimpeachable rectitude to the face of the neighbour; the line is traced like the trajectory of the blow that is dealt and the arrow that kills.

But, in its expression, in its mortality, the face before me summons me, calls for me, begs for me, as if the invisible death that must be faced by the Other, pure otherness, separated, in some way, from any whole, were my business. It is as if that invisible death, ignored by the Other, whom already it concerns by the nakedness of its face, were already 'regarding' me prior to confronting me, and becoming the death that stares me in the face. The other man's death calls me into question, as if, by my possible future indifference, I had become the accomplice of the death to which the other, who cannot see it, is exposed; and as if, even before vowing myself to him, I had to answer for this death of the other, and to accompany the Other in his mortal solitude. The Other becomes my neighbour precisely through the way the face summons me, calls for me, begs for me, and in so doing recalls my responsibility, and calls me into question.

Responsibility for the Other, for the naked face of the first individual to come along. A responsibility that goes beyond what I may or may not have done to the Other or whatever acts I may or may not have committed, as if I were devoted to the other man before being devoted to myself. Or more exactly, as if I had to answer for the other's death even before *being*. A guiltless responsibility, whereby I am none the less open to an accusation of which no alibi, spatial or temporal, could clear me. It is as if the other established a relationship or a relationship were established whose whole intensity consists in not presupposing the idea of community. A responsibility stemming from a time before my freedom – before my (*moi*) beginning, before any present. A fraternity existing in extreme separation. *Before*, but in what past? Not in the time preceding the present, in which I might have contracted any commitments. Responsibility for my neighbour dates from before my freedom in an immemorial past, an unrepresentable past that was never present and is more ancient than consciousness of. . . . A responsibility for my neighbour, for the other man, for the stranger or sojourner, to which nothing in the rigorously ontological order binds me – nothing in the order of the thing, of the something, of number or causality.

It is the responsibility of a hostage which can be carried to the point of being substituted for the other person and demands an infinite subjection of subjectivity. Unless this anarchic responsibility, which summons me from nowhere into a present time, is perhaps the measure or the manner or the system of an immemorial freedom that is even older than being, or decisions, or deeds.

V

This summons to responsibility destroys the formulas of generality by which my knowledge (*savoir*) or acquaintance (*connaissance*) of the other man re-presents him to me as my fellow man. In the face of the other man I am inescapably responsible and consequently the unique and chosen one. By this freedom, humanity in me (*moi*) – that is, humanity as me – signifies, in spite of its ontological contingence of finitude and mortality, the anteriority and uniqueness of the non-*interchangeable*.

This is the anteriority and chosen nature of an excellence that cannot be reduced to the features distinguishing or constituting individual beings in the order of their world or people, in the role they play on history's social stage, as characters, that is, in the mirror of reflection or in self-consciousness.

Fear for the Other, fear for the other man's death, is *my* fear, but is in no way an *individual's* taking fright. It thus stands out against the admirable phenomenological analysis of *Befindlichkeit*[7] found in *Sein und Zeit*: a reflective structure expressed by a pronominal verb, in which emotion is always emotion for something moving you, but also emotion for oneself. Emotion therefore consists in being moved – being scared by something, overjoyed by something, saddened by something, but also in feeling joy or sadness for oneself. All affectivity therefore has repercussions for my being-for-death. There is a double intentionality in the *by* and the *for* and so there is a turning back on oneself and a return to anguish for oneself, for one's finitude: in the fear inspired *by* the wolf, an anguish *for* my death. Fear for the other man's death does not turn back into anguish for my death. It extends beyond the ontology of the Heideggerian *Dasein* and the *bonne conscience* of being in the sight of that being itself. There is ethical awareness and vigilance in this emotional unease. Certainly, Heidegger's being-for-death marks, for the being (*étant*), the end of his being-in-the-sight-of-that-being as well as the scandal provoked by that ending, but in that ending no scruple of being (*être*) is awakened.

This is the hidden human face behind perseverance in being! Hidden behind the affirmation of being persisting analytically – or animally – in its being, and in which the ideal vigour of identity identifying and affirming and strengthening itself in the life of human individuals and in their struggle for vital existence, whether conscious or unconscious or rational, the miracle of the ego vindicated in the eyes of the neighbour – or the miracle of the ego (*moi*) which has got rid of self (*soi*) and instead fears for the Other – is thus like the suspension, or epochè, of the eternal and irreversible return of the identical to itself and of the intangible nature of its logical and ontological privilege. What is suspended is its ideal priority, which wipes out all otherness by murder or by all-encompassing and totalizing thought; or war and politics which pass themselves off as the relation of the Same to the Other (*l'Autre*). It is in the laying down by the ego of its sovereignty (in its 'hateful' modality), that we find ethics and also probably the very spirituality of the soul, but most certainly the question of the meaning of being, that is, its appeal for justification. This first philosophy shows through the ambiguity of the identical, an identical which declares itself to be *I* at the height of its unconditional and even logically indiscernable identity, an autonomy above all criteria, but which precisely at the height of this unconditional identity confesses that it is hateful.

The ego is the very crisis of the being of a being (*de l'être de l'étant*) in the human domain. A crisis of being, not because the sense of this verb might still need to be understood in its semantic secret and might call on the powers of ontology, but because I begin to ask myself if my being is justified, if the *Da* of my *Dasein* is not already the usurpation of somebody else's place.

This question has no need of a theoretical reply in the form of new information. Rather it appeals to responsibility, which is not a practical stopgap measure designed to console knowledge in its failure to match being. This responsibility does not deny knowledge the ability to comprehend and grasp; instead, it is the excellence of ethical proximity in its sociality, in its love without concupiscence. The human is the return to the interiority of non-intentional consciousness, to *mauvaise conscience*, to its capacity to fear injustice more than death, to prefer to suffer than to commit injustice, and to prefer that which justifies being over that which assures it.

VI

To be or not to be – is that the question? Is it the first and final question? Does being human consist in forcing oneself to be and does the understanding of the meaning of being – the semantics of the verb to be – represent the first philosophy required by a consciousness which from the first would be knowledge and representation conserving its assurance in being-for-death, asserting itself as the lucidity of a thought thinking itself right through, even unto death and which, even in its finitude – already or still an unquestioned *mauvaise conscience* as regards its right to be – is either anguished or heroic in the precariousness of its finitude? Or does the first question arise rather in the *mauvaise conscience*, an instability which is different from that threatened by my death and my suffering? It poses the question of my right to be which is already my responsibility for the death of the Other, interrupting the carefree spontaneity of my naive perseverance. The right to be and the legitimacy of this right are not finally referred to the abstraction of the universal rules of the Law – but in the last resort are referred, like that law itself and justice – or for the other of my non-indifference, to death, to which the face of the Other – beyond my ending – in its very rectitude is exposed. Whether he regards me or not, he 'regards' me. In this question being and life are awakened to the human dimension. This is the question of the meaning of being: not the ontology of the understanding of that extra-ordinary verb, but the ethics of its justice. The question *par excellence* or the question of philosophy. Not 'Why being rather than nothing?', but how being justifies itself.

NOTES

1 We have decided to leave the phrases *bonne conscience* and *mauvaise conscience* in the original French. This is because, in addition to suggesting a good and a bad conscience (which is how they are translated in *Time and the Other*, for example) or a clear and a guilty conscience, they also carry the connotation of consciousness and *unhappy consciousness*. For Hegel, unhappy consciousness (*das unglückliches Bewusstsein*) is an inwardly disrupted one, with a dual and essentially contradictory nature. It is there-fore 'the gazing of one self-consciousness into another, and itself *is* both' (*Phenomenology of Spirit*). It is the coexistence of master and slave, eternal and mortal, 'the Unchangeable' and the 'changeable'. Critics are divided, however, over whether or not this duality is a sincerely felt representation of Christianity.

2 Aristotle, *The Nicomachean Ethics* (Harmondsworth: Penguin, 1955, 1981).

3 A reference to Merleau-Ponty's 'body intentionality'. See the *Phenomen-ology of Perception*, part 1. In addition, see *Totality and Infinity*.

4 Hegel characterizes the Absolute as *A=A* in the Preface to the *Phenomen-ology of Spirit*. The equation is in turn a reference to Leibniz, who calls *A=A* 'the law of identity', arguing ultimately that no distinctions are real, and that identity with itself is the only ultimate equivalence.

5 A reference to Pascal's *Pensées*.

6 Levinas is alluding here to Heidegger's sense of *bei sich*, the real and originary sense in which the existent comes to exist 'for itself'. The meaning of '*bei*' is close to that of 'at' in 'at home' or '*chez*' in '*chez moi*'. Cf. *Being and Time*, H.54: 'The expression "*bin*" is connected with "*bei*", and so "*ich bin*" (I am) means in its turn "I reside" or "dwell alongside" the world, as that which is familiar to me in such and such a way. "Being" (*Sein*), as the infinitive of "*ich bin*" (that is to say, when it is understood as an *existen-tiale*), signifies "to reside alongside . . .", "to be familiar with . . .". "*Being-in*" is thus the formal existential expression for the Being of Dasein, which has Being-in-the-world as its essential state.'

7   *Befindlichkeit* has always been translated into English as 'state-of-mind', an
    expression also used for '*befinden*' and '*befindlich*'. More literally, it means
    'the state in which one may be found', which is the sense it carries here in
    Levinas. As such, Heidegger's translators make it clear that 'the "of-mind"
    belongs to English idiom, has no literal counterpart in the structure of the
    German word, and fails to bring out the important connotation of finding
    oneself' (*Being and Time*, footnote to H.134).

9

Paul Ricoeur

(b. 1913)

Paul Ricoeur's philosophical concerns in hermeneutics have been deeply influenced and moulded by his encounter with both phenomenological and existential thought. Born in Valence, France in 1913, Ricoeur's interest in the question of subjectivity led him to read the work of both Husserl and Heidegger while he was a prisoner of war in Germany. Indeed, his publication of *Husserl: An Analysis of his Phenomenology* (1950) still remains one of the clearest explications of Husserl's *Ideas*. Ricoeur also explored a more specifically existentialist domain in such early works as *Karl Jaspers and the Philosophy of Existence* (1947) and *Gabriel Marcel and Karl Jaspers* (1948). He has held positions as Professor of the History of Philosophy at the University of Strasbourg (1948–57) and Professor of Metaphysics at the Sorbonne (1957–66) and Nanterre (1966–80). He has also continued an affiliation with the University of Chicago where he has held a post as John Nuveen Professor since 1960.

Ricoeur began to interrogate Husserl's notion of the transcendental ego more vigorously as he worked on his three-volume 'philosophy of will': *The Voluntary and the Involuntary* (1950), *Fallible Man* (1960) and *The Symbolism of Evil* (1960). During the decade over which these works appeared, Ricoeur became committed to a hermeneutic phenomenology that rejected the transparency of a self-reflective *cogito*, seeking instead to examine the process of mediation found in myth, religion, and, above all, in language. Since no meanings are immediately given to us, we must make a hermeneutic detour through the symbolic apparatus of culture. In *Freud and Philosophy: An Essay on Interpretation* (1965), Ricoeur extended his project to the field of psychoanalysis, suggesting that Freud must also be seen as a master of 'the hermeneutics of suspicion', in the company of Nietzsche and Marx. Thus, ideology itself requires a critical hermeneutics that unmasks the repressed, distorted and hidden meanings that lie dormant below a commonly accepted, but superficial, 'truth of the matter'. There is no master discourse that settles our quest for univocal meaning once and for all. Instead, as Ricoeur posited in *The Conflict of Inter-*

pretations, we must accord diverse paths to understanding their due, for each contributes in its own way. The explanatory procedures of the human sciences do perform a hermeneutic function, but literature and the arts offer a different avenue of approach that must be equally valued for their potential to mediate self and world.

Ricoeur's later work, such as *The Rule of Metaphor* (1975), the three-volume *Time and Narrative* (1984–7) and *Oneself as Another* (1992) confront the complex interaction of discursivity and temporality as inherently creative features of language. Our attempt to structure time through our use of language, in history as well as in fiction, fulfills a narrative function that ultimately leads back to the question of the self. In some ways, Ricoeur has returned to his initial problematics of subjectivity, will and action, but he has changed his focus to include the mediation of culture and narrative. Briefly, the transparent *cogito* has been superseded by narrative identity. In the essay which follows, Ricoeur clarifies this project of hermeneutic phenomenology.

SELECT BIBLIOGRAPHY OF RICOEUR'S WORKS IN ENGLISH

Fallible Man, Chicago: Regnery, 1965.

History and Truth, Evanston, Ill.: Northwestern University Press, 1965.

Freedom and Nature: The Voluntary and the Involuntary, Evanston, Ill.: Northwestern University Press, 1966.

Husserl: An Analysis of his Phenomenology, Evanston, Ill.: Northwestern University Press, 1967.

The Symbolism of Evil, New York: Harper & Row, 1967.

Freud and Philosophy: An Essay on Interpretation, New Haven: Yale University Press, 1970.

The Conflict of Interpretations: Essays in Hermeneutics, Evanston, Ill.: Northwestern University Press, 1974.

Political and Social Essays, ed. D. Stewart and J. Bien, Athens, Ohio: Ohio University Press, 1974.

Interpretation Theory: Discourse and the Surplus of Meaning, Fort Worth: Texas Christian University Press, 1976.

The Philosophy of Paul Ricoeur: An Anthology of his Work, ed. C. Regan and D. Stewart, Boston: Beacon Press, 1978.

The Rule of Metaphor: Multi-disciplinary Studies of the Creation of Meaning in Language, Toronto: University of Toronto Press, 1978.

Hermeneutics and the Human Sciences, ed. J.B. Thompson, Cambridge: Cambridge University Press, 1981.

'On interpretation', in A. Montefiore (ed.), *Philosophy in France Today*, Cambridge: Cambridge University Press, 1983.

Time and Narrative, 3 vols, Chicago: University of Chicago Press, 1984–7.

Lectures on Ideology and Utopia, New York: Columbia University Press, 1986.

From Text to Action: Essays in Hermeneutics II, London: Athlone Press, 1991.

Oneself as Another, Chicago: University of Chicago Press, 1992.

PAUL RICOEUR

On Interpretation

THE MOST APPROPRIATE way of giving an idea of the problems which have occupied me over the past thirty years and of the tradition to which my way of dealing with these problems belongs is, it seems to me, to start with my current work on narrative function, going on from there to show the relationship between this study and my earlier studies of metaphor, psychoanalysis, symbolism and other related problems, in order, finally, to work back from these partial investigations towards the presuppositions, both theoretical and methodological, upon which the whole of my research is based. This backwards movement into my own work allows me to leave until the end my discussion of the presuppositions of the phenomenological and hermeneutical tradition to which I belong, by showing in what way my analyses at one and the same time continue and correct this tradition and, on occasion, bring it into question.

I

I shall begin, then, by saying something about my work in progress on narrative function.

Three major preoccupations are apparent here. This inquiry into the act of storytelling responds first of all to a very general concern, one which I have previously discussed in the first chapter of my book *Freud and Philosophy* – that of preserving the fullness, the diversity and the irreducibility of the various *uses* of language. It can thus be seen that from the start I have affiliated myself with those analytical philosophers who resist the sort of reductionism according to which 'well-formed languages' are alone capable of evaluating the meaning-claims and truth-claims of all non-'logical' uses of language.

A second concern completes and, in a certain sense, tempers the first: that of *gathering together* the diverse forms and modes of the game of storytelling. Indeed, throughout the development of the cultures to which we are the heirs, the act of storytelling has never ceased to ramify into increasingly well-determined literary genres. This fragmentation presents a major problem for philosophers by virtue of the major dichotomy which divides the narrative field and which produces a thorough-going opposition between, on the one hand, narratives which have a truth-claim comparable to that of the descriptive forms of discourse to be found in the sciences – let us say history and the related literary genres of biography and autobiography – and, on the other hand, fictional narratives

From *Philosophy in France Today*, ed. A. Montefiore, Cambridge: Cambridge University Press, 1983.

such as epics, dramas, short stories and novels, to say nothing of narrative modes that use a medium other than language: films, for example, and possibly painting and other plastic arts.

In opposition to this endless fragmentation, I acknowledge the existence of a *functional* unity among the multiple narrative modes and genres. My basic hypothesis, in this regard, is the following: the common feature of human experience, that which is marked, organized and clarified by the fact of storytelling in all its forms, is its *temporal character*. Everything that is recounted occurs in time, takes time, unfolds temporally; and what unfolds in time can be recounted. Perhaps, indeed, every temporal process is recognized as such only to the extent that it can, in one way or another, be recounted. This reciprocity which is assumed to exist between narrativity and temporality is the theme of my present research. Limited as this problem may be compared to the vast scope of all the real and potential uses of language, it is actually immense. Under a single heading, it groups together a number of problems that are usually treated under different rubrics: the epistemology of historical knowledge, literary criticism applied to works of fiction, theories of time (which are themselves scattered among cosmology, physics, biology, psychology and sociology). By treating the temporal quality of experience as the common reference of both history and fiction, I make of fiction, history and time one single problem.

It is here that a third concern comes in, one which offers the possibility of making the problematic of temporality and narrativity easier to work with: namely, the testing of the selective and organizational capacity of language itself when it is ordered into those units of discourse longer than the sentence which we can call *texts*. If, indeed, narrativity is to mark, organize and clarify temporal experience – to repeat the three verbs employed above – we must seek in language use a standard of measurement which satisfies this need for delimiting, ordering and making explicit. That the text is the linguistic unit we are looking for and that it constitutes the appropriate medium between temporal experience and the narrative act can be briefly outlined in the following manner. As a linguistic unit, a text is, on the one hand, an expansion of the first unit of present meaning which is the sentence. On the other hand, it contributes a principle of transsentential organization that is exploited by the act of storytelling in all its forms.

We can term *poetics* – after Aristotle – that discipline which deals with the laws of composition that are added to discourse as such in order to form of it a text which can stand as a narrative, a poem or an essay.

The question then arises of identifying the major characteristic of the act of story-making. I shall once again follow Aristotle in his designation of the sort of verbal *composition* which constitutes a text as a narrative. Aristotle designates this verbal composition by use of the term *muthos*, a term that has been translated by 'fable' or 'plot'. He speaks of 'the combination [*sunthesis*, or, in another context, *sustasis*] of incidents or the fable' (*Poetics* 1450 A5 and I5). By this, Aristotle means more than a structure in the static sense of the word, but rather an operation (as indicated by the ending -*sis* as in *poiesis, sunthesis, sustasis*), namely the structuring that makes us speak of putting-into-the-form-of-a-plot (*emplotment*) rather than of *plot*. The emplotment consists mainly in the selection and arrangement of the events and the actions recounted, which make of the fable a story that is 'complete and entire' (*Poetics* 1450 B25) with a beginning, middle and end. Let us understand by this that no action is a beginning except in a story that it inaugurates; that no action constitutes a middle unless it instigates a change of fortune in the story told, an 'intrigue' to be sorted out, a surprising 'turn of events', a series of 'pitiful' or 'terrifying' incidents; finally, no action, taken in itself, constitutes an end except insofar as it concludes a course of action in the story told, unravels an intrigue, explains the surprising turn of fortune or seals the hero's fate by a final event which clarifies the whole action and produces in the listener the catharsis of pity and terror.

It is this notion of plot that I take as a guideline for my entire investigation, in the area of the history of historians (or historiography) as well as in that of fiction (from epics and folk tales to the modern novel). I shall limit myself here to stressing the feature which, to my mind, makes the notion of plot so fruitful, namely its *intelligibility*. The intelligible character of plot can be brought out in the following way: the plot is the set of combinations by which events are made *into* a story or – correlatively – a story is made *out of* events. The plot mediates between the event and the story. This means that nothing is an event unless it contributes to the progress of a story. An event is not only an occurrence, something that happens, but a narrative component. Broadening the scope of the plot even more in order to escape the opposition, associated with the aesthetics of Henry James, between plot and characters, I shall say that the plot is the intelligible unit that holds together circumstances, ends and means, initiatives and unwanted consequences. According to an expression borrowed from Louis Mink, it is the act of 'taking together' – of com-posing – those ingredients of human action which, in ordinary experience, remain dissimilar and discordant.

From this intelligible character of the plot, it follows that the ability to follow a story constitutes a very sophisticated form of *understanding*.

I shall now say a few words about the problems posed by an extension of the Aristotelian notion of plot to historiography. I shall cite two.

The first concerns historiography. It would appear, indeed, to be arguing a lost cause to claim that modern history has preserved the narrative character to be found in earlier chronicles and which has continued up to our own days in the accounts given by political, diplomatic or ecclesiastical history of battles, treaties, parcelling and, in general, of the changes of fortune which affect the exercise of power by given individuals. (1) It seems, in the first place, that, as history moves away not only from the ancient form of the chronicle, but also from the political model and becomes social, economic, cultural and spiritual history, it no longer has as its fundamental referent individual action, as it generates datable events. It therefore no longer proposes to tie together events with a chronological and causal thread; and it ceases, thus, to tell stories. (2) Moreover, in changing its themes history changes its method. It seeks to move closer to the model of the nomological sciences which explain the events of nature by combining general laws with the description of the initial conditions. (3) Finally, whereas narrative is assumed to be subject to the uncritical perspective of agents plunged into the confusion of their present experience, history is an inquiry independent of the immediate comprehension of events by those who make or undergo them.

My thesis is that the tie between history and narrative cannot be broken without history losing its specificity among the human sciences.

To take these three arguments in reverse order, I shall assert first of all that the basic error comes from the failure to recognize the intelligible character conferred upon the narrative by the plot, a character that Aristotle was the first to emphasize. A naive notion of narrative, considered as a disconnected series of events, is always to be found behind the critique of the narrative character of history. Its episodic character alone is seen, while its configurational character, which is the basis of its intelligibility, is forgotten. At the same time the distance introduced by narrative between itself and lived experience is overlooked. Between living and recounting, a gap – however small it may be – is opened up. Life is lived, history is recounted.

Secondly, in overlooking narrative's basic intelligibility, one overlooks the possibility that historical explanation may be grafted onto narrative comprehension, in the sense that, in explaining more, one recounts better. The error of the proponents of nomological models is not so much that they are mistaken about the nature of the laws that the historian may borrow from other and most advanced social sciences – demography, economics, linguistics, sociology, etc. – but about how these laws work. They fail to see that these laws take on an historical meaning to the extent that they are grafted onto a prior narrative organization which has already characterized events as contributing to the development of a plot.

Thirdly, in turning away from the history of events (*histoire événementielle*), and in particular from political history, historiography has moved less from narrative history than historians might claim. Even when history as social, economic or cultural history becomes the history of long time-spans, it is still tied to time and still accounts for the changes that link a terminal to an initial situation. The rapidity of the change makes no difference here. In remaining bound to time and to change, history remains tied to human action, which, in Marx's words, makes history in circumstances it has not made. Directly or indirectly, history is always the history of men who are the bearers, the agents and the victims of the currents, institutions, functions and structures in which they find themselves placed. Ultimately, history cannot make a complete break with narrative because it cannot break with action, which itself implies agents, aims, circumstances, interactions and results both intended and unintended. But the plot is the basic narrative unity which organizes these heterogeneous ingredients into an intelligible totality.

The second problem I should like to touch on concerns the reference, *common* to both history and fiction, to the temporal background of human experience.

This problem is of considerable difficulty. On the one hand, indeed, only history seems to refer to reality, even if this reality is a past one. It alone seems to claim to speak of events that have really occurred. The novelist can disregard the burden of material proof related to the contraints imposed by documents and archives. An irreducible asymmetry seems to oppose historical reality to fictional reality.

There is no question of denying this asymmetry. On the contrary, it must be recognized in order to perceive the overlap, the figure of the chiasmus formed by the criss-crossing, referential modes characteristic of fiction and history: the historian speaking of the absent past in terms of fiction, the novelist speaking of what is irreal as if it had really taken place. On the one hand, we must not say that fiction has no reference. On the other hand, we must not say that history refers to the historical past in the same way as empirical descriptions refer to present reality. To say that fiction does not lack a reference is to reject an overly narrow conception of reference, which would relegate fiction to a purely emotional role. In one way or another, all symbol systems contribute to *shaping* reality. More particularly, the plots that we invent help us to shape our confused, formless and in the last resort mute temporal experience. 'What is time?' Augustine asked. 'If no one asks me, I know what it is, if someone asks me, I no longer know.' The plot's referential function lies in the capacity of fiction to shape this mute temporal experience. We are here brought back to the link between *muthos* and *mimesis* in Aristotle's *Poetics*: 'the fable', he says, '[is] an imitation of an action' (1450 A2).

This is why suspending the reference can only be an intermediary moment between the pre-understanding of the world of action and the transfiguration of daily reality brought about by fiction itself. Indeed, the models *of* actions elaborated by narrative fiction are models *for* redescribing the practical field in accordance with the narrative typology resulting from the work of the productive imagination. Because it is a world, the world of the text necessarily collides with the real world in order to 're-make' it, either by confirming it or by denying it. However, even the most ironic relation between art and reality would be incomprehensible if art did not both disturb and rearrange our relation to reality. If the world of the text were without any assignable relation to the real world, then language would not be 'dangerous', in the sense in which Hölderlin called it so before both Nietzsche and Walter Benjamin.

So much for this brief sketch of the paradoxical problematic of 'productive' reference, characteristic of narrative fiction. I confess to have drawn in here only the outlines of the problem, not those of its solution.

A parallel approach to history is called for. Just as narrative fiction does not lack reference, the reference proper to history is not unrelated to the 'productive' reference of fictional narrative. Not that the past is unreal: but past reality is, in the strict sense of the word, unverifiable. Insofar as it no longer exists, the discourse of history can seek to grasp it only *indirectly*. It is here that the relationship with fiction shows itself as crucial. The reconstruction of the past, as Collingwood maintained so forcefully, is the work of the imagination. The historian, too, by virtue of the links mentioned earlier between history and narrative, shapes the plots which the documents may authorize or forbid but which they never contain in themselves. History, in this sense, combines narrative coherence with conformity to the documents. This complex tie characterizes the status of history as interpretation. The way is thus open for a positive investigation of all the interrelations between the asymmetrical, but also the indirect and mediate, referential modalities of fiction and of history. It is due to this complex interplay between the indirect reference to the past and the productive reference of fiction that human experience in its profound temporal dimension never ceases to be shaped.

I can only indicate here the threshold of this investigation, which is my current object of research.

II

I now propose to place my current investigation of narrative function within the broader framework of my earlier work, before attempting to bring to light the theoretical and epistemological presuppositions that have continued to grow stronger and more precise in the course of time.

I shall divide my remarks into two groups. The first concerns the structure or, better, the 'sense' immanent in the statements themselves, whether they be narrative or metaphorical. The second concerns the extralinguistic 'reference' of the statements and, hence, the truth claims of both sorts of statements.

A.   Let us restrict ourselves in the first instance to the level of 'sense'.

(a) Between the narrative as a literary 'genre' and the metaphorical 'trope', the most basic link, on the level of sense, is constituted by the fact that both belong to discourse, that is to say to uses of language involving units as long as or longer than the sentence.

One of the first results that contemporary research on metaphor seems to me to have attained is, indeed, to have shifted the focus of analysis from the sphere of the *word* to that of the *sentence*. According to the definitions of classical rhetoric, stemming from Aristotle's *Poetics*, metaphor is the transfer of the everyday name of one thing to another in virtue of their resemblance. This definition, however, says nothing about the operation which results in this 'transfer' of sense. To understand the operation that generates such an extension, we must step outside the framework of the word to move up to the level of the sentence and speak of a metaphorical statement rather than of a word-metaphor. It then appears that metaphor constitutes a work on language consisting in the attribution to logical subjects of predicates that are incompossible with them. By this should be understood that, before being a deviant naming, metaphor is a peculiar predication, an attribution which destroys the consistency or, as has been said, the semantic relevance of the sentence as it is established by the ordinary, that is the lexical, meanings of the terms employed.

(b) This analysis of metaphor in terms of the sentence rather than the word or, more precisely, in terms of peculiar predication rather than deviant naming, prepares the way for a comparison between the theory of narrative and theory of metaphor. Both indeed have to do with the phenomenon of *semantic innovation*. This phenomenon constitutes the most fundamental problem that metaphor and narrative have in common on the level of sense. In both cases, the novel – the not-yet-said, the unheard-of – suddenly arises in language: here, *living* metaphor, that is to say a *new* relevance in predication, there, wholly *invented* plot, that is to say a *new* congruence in the emplotment. On both sides, however, human creativity is to be discerned and to be circumscribed within forms that make it accessible to analysis.

(c) If we now ask about the reasons behind the privileged role played by metaphor and emplotment, we must turn towards the functioning of the *productive imagination* and of the *schematism* which constitutes its intelligible matrix. Indeed, in both cases innovation is produced in the milieu of language and reveals something about what an imagination that produces in accordance with rules might be. This rule-generated production is expressed in the construction of plots by way of a continual interchange between the invention of particular plots and the constitution by sedimentation of a narrative typology. A dialectic is at work in the production of new plots in the interplay between conformity and deviance in relation to the norms inherent in every narrative typology.

Now this dialectic has its counterpart in the birth of a new semantic relevance in new metaphors. Aristotle said that 'to be happy in the use of metaphors' consists in the 'discernment of resemblances' (*Poetics*, 1459 A4–8). But what is it to discern resemblances? If the establishment of a new semantic relevance is that in virtue of which the statement 'makes sense' as a whole, resemblance consists in the *rapprochement*, the bringing closer together of terms which, previously 'remote', suddenly appear 'close'. Resemblance thus consists in a change of distance in logical space. It is nothing other than this emergence of a new generic kinship between heterogeneous ideas.

It is here that the productive imagination comes into play as the schematization of this synthetic operation of bringing closer together. It is the 'seeing' – the sudden insight – inherent to discourse itself, which brings about the change in logical distance, the bringing-closer-together itself. This productive character of insight may be called *predicative assimilation*. The imagination can justly be termed productive because, by an extension of polysemy, it makes terms, previously heterogeneous, *resemble* one another, and thus homogeneous. The imagination, consequently, is this competence, this capacity for producing new logical kinds by means of predicative assimilation and for producing them in spite of . . . and thanks to . . . the initial difference between the terms which resist assimilation.

(d) If, now, we put the stress on the *intelligible* character of semantic innovation, a new parallelism may be seen between the domain of the narrative and that of metaphor. We insisted above on the very particular mode of *understanding* involved in the activity of following a story and we spoke in this regard of narrative understanding. And we have maintained the thesis that historical *explanation* in terms of laws, regular causes, functions and structures is grafted onto this narrative understanding.

This same relation between understanding and explanation is to be observed in the domain of poetics. The act of understanding which would correspond in this domain to the ability to follow a story consists in grasping the semantic dynamism by virtue of which, in a metaphorical statement, a new semantic relevance emerges from the ruins of the semantic non-relevance as this appears in a literal reading of the sentence. To understand is thus to perform or to repeat the discursive operation by which the semantic innovation is conveyed. Now, upon this understanding by which the author or reader '*makes*' the metaphor is superimposed a scholarly explanation which, for its part, takes a completely different starting point than that of the dynamism of the sentence and which will not admit the units of discourse to be irreducible to the signs belonging to the language system. Positing the principle of the structure homology of all levels of language, from the phoneme to the text, the explanation of metaphor is thus included within a general semiotics which takes the sign as its basic unit. My thesis here, just as in the case of the narrative function, is that explanation is not primary but secondary in relation to understanding. Explanation, conceived as a combinatory system of signs, hence as a semiotics, is built up on the basis of a

145

first-order understanding bearing on discourse as an act that is both indivisible and capable of innovation. Just as the narrative structures brought out by explanation presuppose an understanding of the structuring act by which plot is produced, so the structures brought out by structural semiotics are based upon the structuring of discourse, whose dynamism and power of innovation are revealed by metaphor.

In the third part of this essay we shall say in what way this twofold approach to the relation between explanation and understanding contributes to the contemporary development of hermeneutics. We shall say beforehand how the theory of metaphor conspires with the theory of narrative in the elucidation of the problem of reference.

B. In the preceding discussion, we have purposely isolated the 'sense' of the metaphorical statement, that is to say its internal predicative structure, from its 'reference', that is to say its claim to reach an extra-linguistic reality, hence its claim to say something true.

Now, the study of the narrative function has already confronted us with the problem of poetic reference in the discussion of the relation between *muthos* and *mimesis* in Aristotle's *Poetics*. Narrative fiction, we said, 'imitates' human action, not only in that, before referring to the text, it refers to our own pre-understanding of the meaningful structures of action and of its temporal dimensions, but also in that it contributes, beyond the text, to reshaping these structures and dimensions in accordance with the imaginary configuration of the plot. Fiction has the power to 'remake' reality and, within the framework of narrative fiction in particular, to remake real praxis to the extent that the text intentionally aims at a horizon of new reality which we may call a world. It is this world of the text which intervenes in the world of action in order to give it a new configuration or, as we might say, in order to transfigure it.

The study of metaphor enables us to penetrate farther into the mechanism of this operation of transfiguration and to extend it to the whole set of imaginative productions which we designate by the general term of fiction. What metaphor alone permits us to perceive is the conjunction between the two constitutive moments of poetic reference.

The first of these moments is the easiest to identify. Language takes on a poetic function whenever it redirects our attention away from the reference and towards the message itself. In Roman Jakobson's terms, the poetic function stresses the message *for its own sake* at the expense of the referential function which, on the contrary, is dominant in descriptive language. One might say that a centripetal movement of language towards itself takes the place of the centrifugal movement of the referential function. Language glorifies itself in the play of sound and sense.

However, the suspension of the referential function implied by the stress laid on the message *for its own sake* is only the reverse side, or the negative condition, of a more concealed referential function of discourse, one which is, as it were, set free when the descriptive value of statements is suspended. It is in this way that poetic discourse brings to language aspects, qualities and values of reality which do not have access to directly descriptive language and which can be said only thanks to the complex play of the metaphorical utterance and of the ordered transgression of the ordinary meaning of our words. In my work, *The Rule of Metaphor*, I compared this indirect functioning of metaphorical reference to that of models used in the physical sciences, when these are more than aids to discovery or teaching but are incorporated into the very meaning of theories and into their truth claims. These models then have the heuristic power of 're-describing' a reality inaccessible to direct description. In the same way, one may say that poetic language re-describes the world thanks to the suspension of direct description by way of objective language.

This notion of metaphorical re-description exactly parallels the mimetic function that we earlier assigned to narrative fiction. The latter operates typically in the field of action and its temporal values, while metaphorical re-description reigns rather in the field of sensory, affective, aesthetic and axiological values which make the world one that can be *inhabited*.

What is beginning to take shape in this way is the outline of a vast poetic sphere that includes both metaphorical statement and narrative discourse.

The philosophical implications of this theory of indirect reference are as considerable as those of the dialectic between explanation and understanding. Let us now set them within the field of philosophical hermeneutics. Let us say, provisionally, that the function of the transfiguration of reality which we have attributed to poetic fiction implies that we cease to identify reality with empirical reality or, what amounts to the same thing, that we cease to identify experience with empirical experience. Poetic language draws its prestige from its capacity for bringing to language certain aspects of what Husserl called the *Lebenswelt* and Heidegger *In-der-Welt-Sein*. By this very fact, we find ourselves forced to rework our conventional concept of truth, that is to say to cease to limit this concept to logical coherence and empirical verification alone, so that the truth claim related to the transfiguring action of fiction can be taken into account. No more can be said about reality and truth – and no doubt about Being as well – until we have first attempted to make explicit the philosophical presuppositions of the entire enterprise.

III

A Hermeneutical Philosophy

I wish now to attempt to reply to two questions which the preceding analyses cannot have failed to provoke in the minds of readers who have been brought up in a different philosophical tradition from my own. What are the presuppositions that characterize the philosophical tradition to which I recognize myself as belonging? How do the preceding analyses fit into this tradition?

As to the first question, I should like to characterize this philosophical tradition by three features: it stands in the line of a *reflexive*[1] philosophy; it remains within the sphere of Husserlian *phenomenology*; it strives to be a *hermeneutical* variation of this phenomenology.

By reflexive philosophy, I mean broadly speaking the mode of thought stemming from the Cartesian *cogito* and handed down by way of Kant and French post-Kantian philosophy, a philosophy which is little known abroad and which, for me at least, was most striking represented by Jean Nabert. A reflexive philosophy considers the most radical philosophical problems to be those which concern the possibility of *self-understanding* as the subject of the operations of knowing, willing, evaluating, etc. Reflexion is that act of turning back upon itself by which a subject grasps, in a moment of intellectual clarity and moral responsibility, the unifying principle of the operations among which it is dispersed and forgets itself as subject. 'The "I think"', says Kant, 'must be able to accompany all my representations.' All reflexive philosophers would recognize themselves in this formula.

But how can the 'I think' know or recognize itself? It is here that phenomenology – and more especially hermeneutics – represent both a realization and a radical transformation of the very programme of reflexive philosophy. Indeed, the idea of reflexion carries with it the desire for absolute transparence, a perfect coincidence of the self with itself, which would make consciousness of self indubitable knowledge and, as such, more fundamental than all forms of positive knowledge. It is this fundamental demand that phenomenology first of all, and then hermeneutics, continue to project onto an ever more distant horizon as philosophy goes on providing itself with the instruments of thought capable of satisfying it.

Thus Husserl, in those of his theoretical texts most evidently marked by an idealism reminiscent of Fichte, conceives of phenomenology not only as a method of description in terms of their essences of the fundamental modes of organizing experience (perceptive, imaginative, intellectual, volitional, axiological, etc.), but also as a radical self-grounding in the most complex intellectual clarity. In the reduction – or *epoche* – applied to the natural attitude, he then sees the conquest of an empire of sense from which any question concerning things-in-themselves is excluded by being put into brackets. It is this empire of sense, thus freed from any matter-of-fact question, which constitutes the privileged field of phenomenological experience, the domain of intuition *par excellence*. Returning, beyond Kant, to Descartes, he holds that every apprehension of transcendence is open to doubt but that self-immanence is indubitable. It is in virtue of this assertion that phenomenology remains a reflexive philosophy.

And yet, whatever the theory it applies to itself and to its ultimate claims, in its effective practice phenomenology already displays its distance from rather than its realization of the dream of such a radical grounding in the transparence of the subject to itself. The great discovery of phenomenology, within the limits of the phenomenological reduction itself, remains intentionality, that is to say, in its least technical sense, the priority of the consciousness *of something* over self-consciousness. This definition of intentionality, however, is still trivial. In its rigorous sense, intentionality signifies that the *act* of intending something is accomplished only through the identifiable and reidentifiable unity of intended *sense* – what Husserl calls the 'noema' or the 'intentional correlate of the noetic intention'. Moreover, upon this noema are superimposed the various layers which result from the synthetic activities that Husserl terms 'constitution' (constitution of things, constitution of space, constitution of time, etc.). Now the concrete work of phenomenology, in particular in the studies devoted to the constitution of 'things', reveals, by way of regression, levels, always more and more fundamental, at which the active syntheses continually refer to ever more radical passive syntheses. Phenomenology is thus caught up in an infinite movement of 'backwards questioning' in which its project of radical self-grounding fades away. Even the last works devoted to the *life-world* designate by this term an horizon of immediateness that is forever out of reach. The *Lebenswelt* is never actually given but always presupposed. It is phenomenology's paradise lost. It is in this sense that phenomenology has undermined its own guiding idea in the very attempt to realize it. It is this that gives to Husserl's work its tragic grandeur.

It is with this paradoxical result in mind that we can understand how hermeneutics has been able to graft itself onto phenomenology and to maintain with respect to the latter the same twofold relation as that which phenomenology maintains with its Cartesian and Fichtean ideal. The antecedents of hermeneutics seem at first to set it apart from the reflexive tradition and from the phenomenological project. Hermeneutics, in fact, was born – or rather revived – at the time of Schleiermacher and of the fusion of biblical exegesis, classical philology and jurisprudence. This fusion of several different disciplines was made possible thanks to a Copernican reversal which gave priority to the question of *what it is to understand* over that of the sense of this or that text or of this or that category of texts (sacred or profane, poetical or juridical). It is this investigation of *Verstehen* which, a century later, was to come across the phenomenological question *par excellence*, namely the investigation of the intentional sense of noetic acts. It is true that hermeneutics continued to embody concerns different from those of concrete phenomenology. Whereas the latter tended to raise the question of sense in the dimensions of cognition and perception, hermeneutics, since Dilthey, has raised it rather in those of history and the human sciences. But on both sides the fundamental question was the same, namely that of the relation between *sense* and *self*, between the *intelligibility* of the first and the *reflexive* nature of the second.

The phenomenological rooting of hermeneutics is not limited to this very general kinship between the understanding of texts and the intentional relation of a consciousness to a sense with which it finds itself faced. The theme of the *Lebenswelt*, a theme which phenomenology came up against in spite of itself, one might say, is adopted by post-Heideggerian hermeneutics no longer as something left over, but as a prior condition. It is because we find ourselves first of all in a world to which we belong and in which we cannot help but participate, that we are then able, in a second movement, to set up objects in opposition to ourselves, objects that we claim to constitute and to master intellectually. *Verstehen* for Heidegger has an ontological signification. It is the response of a being thrown into the world who finds his way about it by projecting onto it his ownmost possibilities. Interpretation, in the technical sense of the interpretation of texts, is but the development, the making explicit of this ontological understanding, an understanding always inseparable from a being that has initially been thrown into the world. The subject–object relation – on which Husserl continues to depend – is thus subordinated to the testimony of an ontological link more basic than any relation of knowledge.

This subversion of phenomenology by hermeneutics calls for another such action: the famous 'reduction' by which Husserl separates the 'sense' from the background of existence in which natural consciousness is initially immersed can no longer be considered a primary philosophical move. Henceforth it takes on a derived epistemological meaning: it is a move of distantiation that comes second – and, in this sense, a move by which the primary rootedness of understanding is forgotten, a move which calls for all the objectivizing operations characteristic both of common and of scientific knowledge. This distantiation, however, presupposes the involvement as participant thanks to which we actually belong to the world before we are subjects capable of setting up objects in opposition to ourselves in order to judge them and to submit them to our intellectual and technical mastery. In this way, Heideggerian and post-Heideggerian hermeneutics, though they are indeed heirs to Husserlian phenomenology, constitute in the end the reversal of this phenomenology to the very extent indeed that they also constitute its realization.

The philosophical consequences of this reversal are considerable. They are not apparent, however, if we limit ourselves to emphasizing the finite character of Being which renders null and void the ideal of the self-transparence of a fundamental subject. The idea of the finite is in itself banal, even trivial. At best, it simply embodies in negative terms the renouncement of all *hybris* on the part of reflection, of any claim that the subject may make to found itself on itself. The discovery of the precedence of Being-in-the-world in relation to any foundational project and to any attempt at ultimate justification takes on its full force when we draw the positive conclusions of the new ontology of understanding for epistemology. It is in drawing these epistemological consequences that I shall bring my answers to the first question raised at the start of the third part of this essay to bear on the second question. I can sum up these epistemological consequences in the following way: there is no self-understanding which is not *mediated* by signs, symbols and texts; in the last resort understanding coincides with the interpretation given to these mediating terms. In passing from one to the other, hermeneutics gradually frees itself from the idealism with which Husserl had tried to identify phenomenology. Let us now follow the stages of this emancipation.

Mediation by *signs*: that is to say that it is *language* that is the primary condition of all human experience. Perception is articulated, desire is articulated; this is something that Hegel had already shown in the *Phenomenology of Mind*. Freud drew another consequence from this, namely that there is no emotional experience so deeply buried, so concealed or so distorted that it cannot be brought up to the clarity of language and so revealed in its own proper sense, thanks to desire's access to the sphere of language. Psychoanalysis, as a *talk-cure*, is based on this very hypothesis, that of the primary proximity between desire and speech. And since speech is heard before it is uttered, the shortest path from the self to itself lies in the speech of the other which leads me across the open space of signs.

Mediation by *symbols*: by this term I mean those expressions carrying a double sense which traditional cultures have grafted onto the naming of the 'elements' of the cosmos (fire, water, wind, earth, etc.), of its 'dimensions' (height and depth, etc.). These double-sense expressions are themselves hierarchically ordered into the most universal symbols, then those that belong to one particular culture, and, finally, those that are the creation of a particular thinker, even of just one work. In this last case, the symbol merges into living metaphor. However, there is, on the other hand, perhaps no symbolic creation which is not in the final analysis rooted in the common symbolical ground of humanity. I myself once sketched out a *Symbolism of Evil* based entirely on this mediating role of certain double-sense expressions, such as stain, fall, deviation, in reflections on ill will. At that time, I even went so far as to reduce hermeneutics to the interpretation of symbols, that is to say to the making explicit of the second – and often hidden – sense of these double-sense expressions.

Today this definition of hermeneutics in terms of symbolic interpretation appears to me too narrow. And this for two reasons, which will lead us from mediation by symbols to mediation by texts. First of all I came to realize that no symbolism, whether traditional or private, can display its resources of *multiple meaning (multivocité)* outside appropriate contexts, that is to say, within the framework of an entire text, of a poem, for example. Next, the same symbolism can give rise to competitive – even diametrically opposed – interpretations, depending on whether the interpretation aims at reducing the symbolism to its literal basis, to its unconscious sources or its social motivations, or at amplifying it in accordance with its highest power of multiple meaning. In the one case, hermeneutics aims at demystifying a symbolism by unmasking the unavowed forces that are concealed within it; in the other case, it aims at a re-collection of meaning in its richest, its most elevated, most spiritual diversity. But this conflict of interpretations is also to be found at the level of texts.

It follows that hermeneutics can no longer be defined simply in terms of the interpretation of symbols. Nevertheless, this definition should be preserved at least as a stage separating the very general recognition of the linguistic character of experience and the more technical definition of hermeneutics in terms of textual interpretation. What is more, this intermediary definition helps to dissipate the illusion of an intuitive self-knowledge by forcing self-understanding to take the roundabout path of the whole treasury of symbols transmitted by the cultures within which we have come, at one and the same time, into both existence and speech.

Finally, mediation by *texts*: at first sight this mediation seems more limited than the mediation by signs and by symbols, which can be simply oral and even non-verbal. Mediation by texts seems to restrict the sphere of interpretation to writing and to literature to the detriment of oral cultures. This is true. But what the definition loses in extension, it gains in intensity. Indeed, writing opens up new and original resources for discourse. Thanks to writing, discourse acquires a threefold semantic autonomy: in relation to the speaker's intention, to its reception by its original audience, and to the economic, social and cultural circumstances of its production. It is in this sense that writing tears itself free of the limits of face-to-face dialogue and becomes the condition for discourse itself *becoming-text*. It is to hermeneutics that falls the task of exploring the implications of this *becoming-text* for the work of interpretation.

The most important consequence of all this is that an end is put once and for all to the Cartesian and Fichtean – and to an extent Husserlian – ideal of the subject's transparence to itself. To understand oneself is to understand oneself as one confronts the text and to receive from it the conditions for a self other than that which first undertakes the reading. Neither of the two subjectivities, neither that of the author nor that of the reader, is thus primary in the sense of an originary presence of the self to itself.

Once it is freed from the primacy of subjectivity, what may be the first task of hermeneutics? It is, in my opinion, to seek in the text itself, on the one hand, the internal dynamic which governs the structuring of the work and, on the other hand, the power that the work possesses to project itself outside itself and to give birth to a world which would truly be the 'thing' referred to by the text. This internal dynamic and external projection constitute what I call the work of the text. It is the task of hermeneutics to reconstruct this twofold work.

We can look back on the path that has led us from the first presupposition, that of philosophy as reflexivity, by way of the second, that of philosophy as phenomenology, right up to the third, that of the mediation first by signs, then by symbols and, finally, by texts.

A hermeneutical philosophy is a philosophy which accepts all the demands of this long detour and which gives up the dream of a total mediation, at the end of which reflection would once again amount to intellectual intuition in the transparence to itself of an absolute subject.

I can now, in conclusion, attempt to reply to the second question raised at the start of the third part of this essay. If such are the presuppositions characteristic of the tradition to which my works belong, what, in my opinion, is their place in the development of this tradition?

In order to reply to this question, I have only to relate the last definition I have just given of the task of hermeneutics to the conclusions reached at the end of the two sections of part II.

The task of hermeneutics, we have just said, is twofold: to reconstruct the internal dynamic of the text, and to restore to the work its ability to project itself outside itself in the representation of a world that I could inhabit.

It seems to me that all of my analyses aimed at the interrelation of understanding and explanation, at the level of what I have called the 'sense' of the work, are related to the first task. In my analyses of narrative as well as in those of metaphor, I am fighting on two fronts: on the one hand, I cannot accept the irrationalism of immediate understanding, conceived as an extension to the domain of texts of the empathy by which a subject puts himself in the place of a foreign consciousness in a situation of face-to-face intensity. This undue extension maintains the romantic illusion of a direct link of congeniality between the two subjectivities implied by the work, that of the author and that of the reader. However, I am equally unable to accept a rationalistic explanation which would extend to the text the structural analysis of sign systems that are characteristic not of discourse but of language as such. This equally undue extension gives rise to the positivist illusion of a textual objectivity closed in upon itself and wholly independent of the subjectivity of both author and reader. To these two one-sided attitudes, I have opposed the dialectic of understanding and explanation. By understanding I mean the ability to take up again within oneself the work of structuring that is performed by the text, and by explanation the second-order operation grafted onto this understanding which consists in bringing to light the codes underlying this work of structuring that is carried through in company with the reader. This combat on two separate fronts against a reduction of understanding to empathy and a reduction of explanation to an abstract combinatory system, leads me to define interpretation by this very dialectic of understanding and explanation at the level of the 'sense' immanent to the text. This specific manner of responding to the first task of hermeneutics offers the signal advantage, in my opinion, of preserving the dialogue between philosophy and the human sciences, a dialogue that is interrupted by the two counterfeit forms of understanding and explanation which I reject. This would be my first contribution to the hermeneutical philosophy from out of which I am working.

In what I have written above, I have tried to set my analyses of the 'sense' of metaphorical statements and of that of narrative plots against the background of the theory of *Verstehen*, limited to its epistemological usage, in the tradition of Dilthey and Max Weber. The distinction between 'sense' and 'reference', applied to these statements and to these plots, gives me the right to limit myself provisionally to what has thus been established by hermeneutical philosophy, which seems to me to remain unaffected by its later development in Heidegger and Gadamer, in the sense of a subordination of the epistemological to the ontological theory of *Verstehen*. I want neither to ignore the epistemological phase, which involves philosophy's dialogue with the human sciences, nor to neglect this shift in the hermeneutical problematic, which henceforth emphasizes Being-in-the-world and the participatory belonging which precedes any relation of a subject to an object which confronts him.

It is against this background of the new hermeneutical ontology that I should like to set my analyses of the 'reference' of metaphorical statements and of narrative plots. I confess willingly that these analyses continually *presuppose* the conviction that discourse never exists *for its own sake*, for its own glory, but that in all of its uses it seeks to bring into language an experience, a way of living in and of Being-in-the-world which precedes it and which demands to be said. It is this conviction that there is always a *Being-demanding-to-be-said* (*un être-à-dire*) which precedes our actual saying, which explains my obstinacy in trying to discover in the poetic uses of language the referential mode appropriate to them and through which discourse continues to 'say' Being even when it appears to have withdrawn into itself for the sake of self-celebration. This vehement insistence on preventing language from closing up on itself I have inherited from Heidegger's *Sein und Zeit* and from Gadamer's *Wahrheit und Methode*. In return, however, I should like to believe that the description I propose of the reference of metaphorical and of narrative statements contributes to this ontological vehemence an analytical precision which it would otherwise lack.

On the one hand, indeed, it is what I have just called ontological vehemence in the theory of language that leads me to attempt to give an ontological dimension to the referential claim of metaphorical statements: in this way, I venture to say that to see something as ... is to make manifest the *being-as* of that thing. I place the 'as' in the position of the exponent of the verb 'to be' and I make 'being-as' the ultimate referent of the metaphorical statement. This thesis undeniably bears the imprint of post-Heideggerian ontology. But, on the other hand, the testimony to *being-as* . . . cannot, in my opinion, be separated from a detailed study of the referential modes of discourse and requires a properly analytical treatment of indirect reference, on the basis of the concept of 'split reference' taken from Roman Jakobson. My thesis concerning the *mimesis* of the narrative work and my distinction between the three stages of *mimesis* – prefiguration, configuration and transfiguration of the world of action by the poem – express one and the same concern to combine analytical precision with ontological testimony.

The concern I have just expressed brings me back to that other concern, which I mentioned above, not to oppose understanding and explanation on the level of the dynamic immanent to poetic utterances. Taken together, these two concerns mark my hope that in working for the progress of hermeneutical philosophy, I contribute, in however small a way, to arousing an interest in this philosophy on the part of analytical philosophers.

NOTE

1   *Translator's Note:* In French, the adjective 'réflexive' incorporates two meanings which are distinguished in English by *reflective* and *reflexive*. On the advice of the author we have chosen to retain the latter in order to emphasize that this philosophy is subject-oriented; it is reflexive in the subject's act of turning back upon itself. The other possible meaning should, however, also be kept in mind.

PART II

From Marxism to Critical Theory

10

Rosa Luxemburg

(1870–1919)

Rosa Luxemburg achieved notoriety as a Marxist agitator and revolutionary. Born in Zamosc, Poland to a Jewish family in 1870, she fled to Switzerland at the age of nineteen to avoid arrest for political activities. Though she entered the University of Zurich as a refugee, she managed to earn two doctorate degrees, one in law and another in philosophy. Eventually, Luxemburg settled in Germany because the largest enclave of active socialists resided there.

Rosa Luxemburg was murdered by Prussian soldiers in 1919 after the failure of the workers' uprising led by the 'Spartacists' in Berlin. Her body was thrown into a canal where it lay rotting, undiscovered for five months. She left few written works, held no scholarly academic posts, was sporadically jailed, and received more opprobrium than honours during her life. Yet, the collapse of the Soviet Marxist regime in less than eighty years and, more importantly, its totalitarian nature, lead us to look with renewed interest at Luxemburg's essay 'Leninism or Marxism?'

Originally written in 1904 with the title 'Organizational questions of the Russian social democracy', Luxemburg's essay appeared in the socialist journal *Neue Zeit*. We should note that the 'October Revolution' of 1917 is at this time still thirteen years in the future. Luxemburg confronts Lenin, questioning the necessity for a political party of guardians, an elite that understands working-class needs better than the proletariat itself. In this early piece, Luxemburg challenges Lenin on his centralist aspirations and his implicit contempt for the working class. From our perspective nearly a century later, she is interesting because she mounts this interrogation in a pre-Bolshevik environment not yet dominated by the canonical Leninist view.

It seems likely that some of the problems faced by Soviet Marxism lay in the very organizational structure posited by Lenin himself: a mammoth machine controlled by an elite, a scenario ultimately rife with potential for totalitarian abuse. This is not to say that Luxemburg's 'spontaneity' solution left orthodox Marxism with better prospects. Her own 'Spartacist' wing acted spontaneously in bringing revolution to the streets of Berlin, but they assumed mass support for their action where none existed. Their defeat was permanent; they had no second chance.

In many ways Luxemburg represents the quintessential Marxist at the turn of the century. If one can paradoxically speak of 'halcyon days' for a Marxist revolutionary, these were the days before anyone had actually noticed that capitalism itself was changing, accommodating tensions and contradictions that Marx had predicted would apocalyptically devour it. When an early 'revisionist', Eduard Bernstein, returned from exile in London, he brought the unwelcome news that economic crisis seemed unlikely, and that the bourgeoisie was growing more numerous and content. He suggested that reform rather than revolution might be a superior strategy. With dogmatic orthodoxy, Luxemburg wrote 'Social reform or revolution', refusing to consider such transformational powers in capitalism's repertoire.

In a sense, the murder of Rosa Luxemburg created an icon and a legend whose power far surpassed that of the woman herself while she lived. She left a legacy that proclaimed the worldwide solidarity of the oppressed beyond all national boundaries. And she fought for their right to speak in their own name, unfettered by the organizational chains of party hierarchies. It is little wonder that long after Rosa Luxemburg was dead, the spirit of freedom she represented made dictators like Hitler and Stalin still fear her name.

SELECT BIBLIOGRAPHY OF LUXEMBURG'S WORKS IN ENGLISH

The Accumulation of Capital, London: Routledge & Kegan Paul, 1951.
'The Russian Revolution' and 'Leninism or Marxism?', Ann Arbor: University of Michigan Press, 1961.
The Mass Strike, the Political Party, and the Trade Unions, Colombo, 1964.
The Junius Pamphlet – The Crisis in the German Social Democracy, London: Merlin Press, 1967.
Selected Political Writings of Rosa Luxemburg, ed. Dick Howard, New York, London: Monthly Review Press, 1971.
Selected Political Writings of Rosa Luxemburg, ed. Robert Looker, London: Jonathan Cape, 1972.

Leninism or Marxism?

I

AN UNPRECEDENTED TASK in the history of the socialist movement has fallen to the lot of the Russian Social Democracy. It is the task of deciding on what is the best socialist tactical policy in a country where absolute monarchy is still dominant. It is a mistake to draw a rigid parallel between the present Russian situation and that which existed in Germany during the years 1878–90, when Bismarck's antisocialist laws were in force. The two have one thing in common – police rule. Otherwise, they are in no way comparable.

The obstacles offered to the socialist movement by the absence of democratic liberties are of relatively secondary importance. Even in Russia, the people's movement has succeeded in overcoming the barriers set up by the state. The people have found themselves a 'constitution' (though a rather precarious one) in street disorders. Persevering in this course, the Russian people will in time attain complete victory over the autocracy.

The principal difficulty faced by socialist activity in Russia results from the fact that in that country the domination of the bourgeoisie is veiled by absolutist force. This gives socialist propaganda an abstract character, while immediate political agitation takes on a democratic-revolutionary guise.

Bismarck's antisocialist laws put our movement out of constitutional bounds in a highly developed bourgeois society, where class antagonisms had already reached their full bloom in parliamentary contests. (Here, by the way, lay the absurdity of Bismarck's scheme.) The situation is quite different in Russia. The problem there is how to create a Social Democratic movement at a time when the state is not yet in the hands of the bourgeoisie.

This circumstance has an influence on agitation, on the manner of transplanting socialist doctrine to Russian soil. It also bears in a peculiar and direct way on the question of *party organization*.

Under ordinary conditions – that is, where the political domination of the bourgeoisie has preceded the socialist movement – the bourgeoisie itself instills in the working class the rudiments of political solidarity. At this stage, declares the Communist Manifesto, the unification of the workers is not yet the result of their own aspiration to unity but comes as a result of the activity of the bourgeoisie, 'which, in order to attain its own political ends, is compelled to set the proletariat in motion. . . .'

In Russia, however, the Social Democracy must make up by its own efforts an entire historic period. It must lead the Russian proletarians

From 'The Russian Revolution' and 'Leninism or Marxism?', Ann Arbor: University of Michigan Press, 1961.

161

from their present 'atomized' condition, which prolongs the autocratic regime, to a class organization that would help them to become aware of their historic objectives and prepare them to struggle to achieve those objectives.

The Russian socialists are obliged to undertake the building of such an organization without the benefit of the formal guarantees commonly found under a bourgeois-democratic setup. They do not dispose of the political raw material that in other countries is supplied by bourgeois society itself. Like God Almighty they must have this organization arise out of the void, so to speak.

How to effect a transition from the type of organization characteristic of the preparatory stage of the socialist movement – usually featured by disconnected local groups and clubs, with propaganda as a principal activity – to the unity of a large, national body, suitable for concerted political action over the entire vast territory ruled by the Russian state? That is the specific problem which the Russian Social Democracy has mulled over for some time.

Autonomy and isolation are the most pronounced characteristics of the old organizational type. It is, therefore, understandable why the slogan of the persons who want to see an inclusive national organization should be 'Centralism!'

Centralism was the theme of the campaign that has been carried on by the *Iskra* group for the last three years. This campaign has produced the Congress of August 1903, which has been described as the second congress of the Russian Social Democratic Party but was, in fact, its constituent assembly.

At the Party Congress, it became evident that the term 'centralism' does not completely cover the question of organization for the Russian Social Democracy. Once again we have learned that no rigid formula can furnish the solution of any problem in the socialist movement.

One Step Forward, Two Steps Backward, written by Lenin, an outstanding member of the *Iskra* group, is a methodical exposition of the ideas of the ultra-centralist tendency in the Russian movement. The viewpoint presented with incomparable vigor and logic in this book, is that of pitiless centralism. Laid down as principles are: (1) The necessity of selecting, and constituting as a separate corps, all the active revolutionists, as distinguished from the unorganized, though revolutionary, mass surrounding this elite.

Lenin's thesis is that the party Central Committee should have the privilege of naming all the local committees of the party. It should have the right to appoint the effective organs of all local bodies from Geneva to Liège, from Tomsk to Irkutsk. It should also have the right to impose on all of them its own ready-made rules of party conduct. It should have the right to rule without appeal on such questions as the dissolution and reconstitution of local organizations. This way, the Central Committee

162

could determine, to suit itself, the composition of the highest party organs as well as of the party congress. The Central Committee would be the only thinking element in the party. All other groupings would be its executive limbs.

Lenin reasons that the combination of the socialist mass movement with such a rigorously centralized type of organization is a specific principle of revolutionary Marxism. To support this thesis, he advances a series of arguments, with which we shall deal below.

Generally speaking it is undeniable that a strong tendency toward centralization is inherent in the Social Democratic movement. This tendency springs from the economic makeup of capitalism which is essentially a centralizing factor. The Social Democratic movement carries on its activity inside the large bourgeois city. Its mission is to represent, within the boundaries of the national state, the class interests of the proletariat, and to oppose those common interests to all local and group interests.

Therefore, the Social Democracy is, as a rule, hostile to any manifestations of localism or federalism. It strives to unite all workers and all worker organizations in a single party, no matter what national, religious, or occupational differences may exist among them. The Social Democracy abandons this principle and gives way to federalism only under exceptional conditions, as in the case of the Austro-Hungarian Empire.

It is clear that the Russian Social Democracy should not organize itself as a federative conglomerate of many national groups. It must rather become a single party for the entire empire. However, that is not really the question considered here. What we are considering is the degree of centralization necessary inside the unified, single Russian party in view of the peculiar conditions under which it has to function.

Looking at the matter from the angle of the formal tasks of the Social Democracy in its capacity as a party of class struggle, it appears at first that the power and energy of the party are directly dependent on the possibility of centralizing the party. However, these formal tasks apply to all active parties. In the case of the Social Democracy, they are less important than is the influence of historic conditions.

The Social Democratic movement is the first in the history of class societies which reckons, in all its phases and through its entire course, on the organization and the direct, independent action of the masses.

Because of this, the Social Democracy creates an organizational type that is entirely different from those common to earlier revolutionary movements, such as those of the Jacobins and the adherents of Blanqui.

Lenin seems to slight this fact when he presents in his book the opinion that the revolutionary Social Democrat is nothing else than a 'Jacobin indissolubly joined to the organization of the proletariat, which has become conscious of its class interests'.

For Lenin, the difference between the Social Democracy and Blanquism is reduced to the observation that in place of a handful of conspirators we have a class-conscious proletariat. He forgets that this difference implies a complete revision of our ideas on organization and, therefore, an entirely different conception of centralism and the relations existing between the party and the struggle itself.

Blanquism did not count on the direct action of the working class. It, therefore, did not need to organize the people for the revolution. The people were expected to play their part only at the moment of revolution. Preparation for the revolution concerned only the little group of revolutionists armed for the coup. Indeed, to assure the success of the revolutionary conspiracy, it was considered wiser to keep the mass at some distance from the conspirators. Such a relationship could be conceived by the Blanquists only because there was no close contact between the conspiratorial activity of their organization and the daily struggle of the popular masses.

The tactics and concrete tasks of the Blanquist revolutionists had little connection with the elementary class struggle. They were freely improvised. They could, therefore, be decided on in advance and took the form of a ready-made plan. In consequence of this, ordinary members of the organization became simple executive organs, carrying out the orders of a will fixed beforehand, and outside of their particular sphere of activity. They became the instruments of a Central Committee. Here we have the second peculiarity of conspiratorial centralism – the absolute and blind submission of the party sections to the will of the center, and the extension of this authority to all parts of the organization.

However, Social Democratic activity is carried on under radically different conditions. It arises historically out of the elementary class struggle. It spreads and develops in accordance with the following dialectical contradiction. The proletarian army is recruited and becomes aware of its objectives in the course of the struggle itself. The activity of the party organization, the growth of the proletarians' awareness of the objectives of the struggle and the struggle itself, are not different things separated chronologically and mechanically. They are only different aspects of the same process. Except for the general principles of the struggle, there do not exist for the Social Democracy detailed sets of tactics which a Central Committee can teach the party membership in the same way as troops are instructed in their training camps. Furthermore, the range of influence of the socialist party is constantly fluctuating with the ups and downs of the struggle in the course of which the organization is created and grows.

For this reason Social Democratic centralism cannot be based on the mechanical subordination and blind obedience of the party membership to the leading party center. For this reason, the Social Democratic movement cannot allow the erection of an air-tight partition between the class-conscious nucleus of the proletariat already in the party and its immediate popular environment, the nonparty sections of the proletariat.

Now the two principles on which Lenin's centralism rests are precisely these: (1) The blind subordination, in the smallest detail, of all party organs, to the party center, which alone thinks, guides, and decides for all. (2) The rigorous separation of the organized nucleus of revolutionaries from its social-revolutionary surroundings.

Such centralism is a mechanical transposition of the organizational principles of Blanquism into the mass movement of the socialist working class.

In accordance with this view, Lenin defines his 'revolutionary Social Democrat' as a 'Jacobin joined to the organization of the proletariat, which has become conscious of its class interests'.

The fact is that the Social Democracy is not *joined* to the organization of the proletariat. It is itself the proletariat. And because of this, Social Democratic centralism is essentially different from Blanquist centralism. It can only be the concentrated will of the individuals and groups representative of the most class-conscious, militant, advanced sections of the working class. It is, so to speak, the 'self-centralism' of the advanced sectors of the proletariat. It is the rule of the majority within its own party.

The indispensable conditions for the realization of Social-Democratic centralism are: (1) The existence of a large contingent of workers educated in the political struggle. (2) The possibility for the workers to develop their own political activity through direct influence on public life, in a party press, and public congresses, etc.

These conditions are not yet fully formed in Russia. The first – a proletarian vanguard, conscious of its class interests and capable of self-direction in political activity – is only now emerging in Russia. All efforts of socialist agitation and organization should aim to hasten the formation of such a vanguard. The second condition can be had only under a regime of political liberty.

With these conclusions, Lenin disagrees violently. He is convinced that all the conditions necessary for the formation of a powerful and centralized party already exist in Russia. He declares that 'it is no longer the proletarians but certain intellectuals in our party who need to be educated in the matters of organization and discipline'. He glorifies the educative influence of the factory, which, he says, accustoms the proletariat to 'discipline and organization'.

Saying all this, Lenin seems to demonstrate again that his conception of socialist organization is quite mechanistic. The discipline Lenin has in mind is being implanted in the working class not only by the factory but also by the military and the existing state bureaucracy – by the entire mechanism of the centralized bourgeois state.

We misuse words and we practice self-deception when we apply the same term – discipline – to such dissimilar notions as: (1) the absence of thought and will in a body with a thousand automatically moving hands and legs, and (2) the spontaneous co-ordination of the conscious, political acts of a body of men. What is there in common between the regulated docility of an oppressed class and the self-discipline and organization of a class struggling for its emancipation?

The self-discipline of the Social Democracy is not merely the replacement of the authority of the bourgeois rulers with the authority of a socialist central committee. The working class will acquire the sense of the new discipline, the freely assumed self-discipline of the Social Democracy, not as a result of the discipline imposed on it by the capitalist state, but by extirpating, to the last root, its old habits of obedience and servility.

Centralism in the socialist sense is not an absolute thing applicable to any phase whatsoever of the labor movement. It is a *tendency*, which becomes real in proportion to the development and political training acquired by the working masses in the course of their struggle.

No doubt, the absence of the conditions necessary for the complete realization of this kind of centralism in the Russian movement presents a formidable obstacle.

It is a mistake to believe that it is possible to substitute 'provisionally' the absolute power of a Central Committee (acting somehow by 'tacit delegation') for the yet unrealizable rule of the majority of conscious workers in the party, and in this way replace the open control of the working masses over the party organs with the reverse control by the Central Committee over the revolutionary proletariat.

The history of the Russian labor movement suggests the doubtful value of such centralism. An all-powerful center, invested, as Lenin would have it, with the unlimited right to control and intervene, would be an absurdity if its authority applied only to technical questions, such as the administration of funds, the distribution of tasks among propagandists and agitators, the transportation and circulation of printed matter. The political purpose of an organ having such great powers is understandable only if those powers apply to the elaboration of a uniform plan of action, if the central organ assumes the initiative of a vast revolutionary act.

But what has been the experience of the Russian socialist movement up to now? The most important and most fruitful changes in its tactical policy during the last ten years have not been the inventions of several leaders and even less so of any central organizational organs. They have always been the spontaneous product of the movement in ferment. This was true during the first stage of the proletarian movement in Russia, which began with the spontaneous general strike of St Petersburg in 1896, an event that marks the inception of an epoch of economic struggle by the Russian working people. It was no less true during the following period, introduced by the spontaneous street demonstrations of St Petersburg students in March 1901. The general strike of Rostov-on-Don, in 1903, marking the next great tactical turn in the Russian proletarian movement, was also a spontaneous act. 'All by itself', the strike expanded into political demonstrations, street agitation, great outdoor meetings, which the most optimistic revolutionist would not have dreamed of several years before.

Our cause made great gains in these events. However, the initiative and conscious leadership of the Social Democratic organizations played an insignificant role in this development. It is true that these organizations were not specifically prepared for such happenings. However, the unimportant part played by the revolutionists cannot be explained by this fact. Neither can it be attributed to the absence of an all-powerful central party apparatus similar to what is asked for by Lenin. The existence of such a guiding center would have probably increased the disorder of the local committees by emphasizing the difference between the eager attack of the mass and the prudent position of the Social Democracy. The same phenomenon – the insignificant part played by the initiative of central party organs in the elaboration of actual tactical policy – can be observed today in Germany and other countries. In general, the tactical policy of the Social Democracy is not something that may be 'invented'. It is the product of a series of great creative acts of the often spontaneous class struggle seeking its way forward.

The unconscious comes before the conscious. The logic of the historic process comes before the subjective logic of the human beings who participate in the historic process. The tendency is for the directing organs of the socialist party to play a conservative role. Experience shows that every time the labor movement wins new terrain those organs work it to the utmost. They transform it at the same time into a kind of bastion, which holds up advance on a wider scale.

The present tactical policy of the German Social Democracy has won universal esteem because it is supple as well as firm. This is a sign of the fine adaptation of the party, in the smallest detail of its everyday activity, to the conditions of a parliamentary regime. The party has made a methodical study of all the resources of this terrain. It knows how to utilize them without modifying its principles.

However, the very perfection of this adaptation is already closing vaster horizons to our party. There is a tendency in the party to regard parliamentary tactics as the immutable and specific tactics of socialist activity. People refuse, for example, to consider the possibility (posed by Parvus) of changing our tactical policy in case general suffrage is abolished in Germany, an eventuality not considered entirely improbable by the leaders of the German Social Democracy.

Such inertia is due, in a large degree, to the fact that it is very inconvenient to define, within the vacuum of abstract hypotheses, the lines and forms of still nonexistent political situations. Evidently, the important thing for the Social Democracy is not the preparation of a set of directives all ready for future policy. It is important: (1) to encourage a correct historic

167

appreciation of the forms of struggle corresponding to the given situations, and (2) to maintain an understanding of the relativity of the current phase and the inevitable increase of revolutionary tension as the final goal of the class struggle is approached.

Granting, as Lenin wants, such absolute powers of a negative character to the top organ of the party, we strengthen, to a dangerous extent, the conservatism inherent in such an organ. If the tactics of the socialist party are not to be the creation of a Central Committee but of the whole party, or, still better, of the whole labor movement, then it is clear that the party sections and federations need the liberty of action which alone will permit them to develop their revolutionary initiative and to utilize all the resources of a situation. The ultra-centralism asked by Lenin is full of the sterile spirit of the overseer. It is not a positive and creative spirit. *Lenin's concern is not so much to make the activity of the party more fruitful as to control the party – to narrow the movement rather than to develop it, to bind rather than to unify it.*

In the present situation, such an experiment would be doubly dangerous to the Russian Social Democracy. It stands on the eve of decisive battles against tsarism. It is about to enter, or has already entered, on a period of intensified creative activity, during which it will broaden (as is usual in a revolutionary period) its sphere of influence and will advance spontaneously by leaps and bounds. To attempt to bind the initiative of the party at this moment, to surround it with a network of barbed wire, is to render it incapable of accomplishing the tremendous tasks of the hour.

The general ideas we have presented on the question of socialist centralism are not by themselves sufficient for the formulation of a constitutional plan suiting the Russian party. In the final instance, a statute of this kind can only be determined by the conditions under which the activity of the organization takes place in a given epoch. The question of the moment in Russia is how to set in motion a large proletarian organization. No constitutional project can claim infallibility. It must prove itself in fire. . . .

11

Georg Lukács
(1885–1971)

Acknowledged to be one of the most significant critical and cultural theorists of our time, Georg (György) Lukács was born in 1885 to an affluent Jewish family in Budapest, which was then still part of the Austro-Hungarian empire. Throughout his life he remained committed to the belief that collective human consciousness can change historical circumstances. Lukács' formative influences combined diverse currents in modern European thought, both 'East' and 'West', which were creatively synthesized in his own philosophical project.

Educated at universities in Germany and Hungary, Lukács was equally fluent in German and his native Hungarian. He submitted a doctoral thesis on aesthetic theory to the University of Budapest in 1906, and continued to explore the philosophical terrain of such German thinkers as Kant, Hegel, Husserl, Weber, Dilthey and Marx. As a young man, Lukács published *The History of the Evolution of the Modern Drama* (1911) and *Soul and Form* (1911) in Hungarian, but all of his subsequent work was written in German, thereby attracting a wider audience. Some of these works include *The Theory of the Novel* (1920), *History and Class Consciousness* (1923), *The Historical Novel* (1936) and *The Meaning of Contemporary Realism* (1958).

Always a Hegelian-Marxist, Lukács claimed that Marx had managed to retrieve the active dialectical element in Hegel's philosophy, augmenting it with a concrete awareness of historical materialism. It is important to realize that Lukács anticipated this Hegelian and humanist strain in Marxist thought long before the 1931 rediscovery of Marx's early *Paris Manuscripts* that confirmed his insights. Lukács offered an alternative, pre-Bolshevik interpretation of Marx that rejected the deterministic and 'scientistic' excesses of Stalinist dogma. In fact, despite his own political commitment to communism, Lukács was denounced as a 'revisionist' by Stalin and spent much of his life under constant threat of being purged from the Communist party by orthodox Soviet authorities.

In his *History and Class Consciousness* (1923), Lukács presented a collection of essays that emphasized Marx's transformation of Hegelian concepts, leading to a new theoretical stance towards alienation and labour. In the fourth essay entitled 'Reification and the consciousness of the proletariat', Lukács turns to an analysis of the complementary relationship between 'commodity fetishism' and the 'reification' of human beings. Marx had already pointed to the centrality of commodity exchange and its fundamental importance for the functioning of capitalist economies. All activity becomes measurable in terms of quantifiable exchange, thus diminishing the value accorded to human labour. Lukács recognized that such 'commodity fetishism' infiltrated all aspects of life and consciousness under capitalism, eventually leading to the debasement of human beings as calculable objects to be regarded as mere things. This reification of human relationships engenders profound alienation that, according to Lukács, can only be remedied by the social praxis of a collective proletarian consciousness engaged in the qualitative transformation of concrete historical reality.

Lukács also made significant contributions to aesthetic theory, claiming that art has the power to project a utopian vision, thereby transforming our fragmented experience of social alienation. In brief, for Lukács, the work of art dialectically mediates 'subjective consciousness' and 'objective reality'. Affirming his own commitment to Marxism and the ideals of Communism, he valorized 'social realism' in art forms such as the novel. Lukács remained unreceptive to what, on his account, he saw as the bourgeois decadence of certain 'modernist' works that celebrated their own textuality as an end in itself. He focused instead on the 'quest motivation' of fictional characters whose actions testify to the creative human potential for liberation and genuinely 'dereified' human relations.

Always engaged in political praxis himself, Lukács spent much of his life in exile from his native Hungary. He was forced to flee Budapest for the first time in 1919 after the collapse of Béla Kun's short-lived socialist government. He opposed Soviet imperialism in eastern Europe, and was ultimately expelled from the Communist party for supporting the Hungarian revolt in 1956. Exiled again, Lukács lived in Romania until he was finally permitted to return home to his beloved Budapest just before his death in 1971.

SELECT BIBLIOGRAPHY OF LUKÁCS' WORKS IN ENGLISH

The Historical Novel, London: Merlin Press, 1962.
The Meaning of Contemporary Realism, London: Merlin Press, 1962.
Essays on Thomas Mann, New York: Grosset & Dunlop, 1965.
Goethe and His Age, London: Merlin Press, 1968.
Lenin: A Study on the Unity of His Thought, London: New Left Books, 1970.
Writer and Critic and Other Essays, London: Merlin Press, 1970.
History and Class Consciousness, London: Merlin Press, 1971.
Theory of the Novel: A Historico-Philosophical Essay on the Forms of Great Literature, Cambridge, Mass.: MIT Press, 1971.

Marxism and Human Liberation: Essays on History, Culture and Revolution, New York: Delta Books, 1973.

The Ontology of Social Being, 3 vols, London: Merlin Press, 1978–80.

The Destruction of Reason, London: Merlin Press, 1979.

GEORG LUKÁCS

Reification and the Consciousness of the Proletariat

> To be radical is to go to the root of the matter. For man,
> however, the root is man himself.
>
> (Marx: *Critique of Hegel's Philosophy of Right*)

IT IS NO accident that Marx should have begun with an analysis of
commodities when, in the two great works of his mature period, he set
out to portray capitalist society in its totality and to lay bare its fundamental nature. For at this stage in the history of mankind there is no
problem that does not ultimately lead back to that question and there is
no solution that could not be found in the solution to the riddle of
commodity-*structure*. Of course the problem can only be discussed with
this degree of generality if it achieves the depth and breath to be found
in Marx's own analyses. That is to say, the problem of commodities must
not be considered in isolation or even regarded as the central problem in
economics, but as the central, structural problem of capitalist society
in all its aspects. Only in this case can the structure of commodity-
relations be made to yield a model of all the objective forms of bourgeois
society together with all the subjective forms corresponding to them.

I

THE PHENOMENON OF REIFICATION

1

The essence of commodity-structure has often been pointed out. Its basis
is that a relation between people takes on the character of a thing and
thus acquires a 'phantom objectivity', an autonomy that seems so strictly
rational and all-embracing as to conceal every trace of its fundamental
nature: the relation between people. It is beyond the scope of this essay to
discuss the central importance of this problem for economics itself. Nor
shall we consider its implications for the economic doctrines of the vulgar
Marxists which follow from their abandonment of this starting-point.

Our intention here is to *base* ourselves on Marx's economic analyses
and to proceed from there to a discussion of the problems growing out
of the fetish character of commodities, both as an objective form and also
as a subjective stance corresponding to it. Only by understanding this can
we obtain a clear insight into the ideological problems of capitalism and
its downfall.

From *History and Class Consciousness: Studies in Marxist Dialectics*, London:
Merlin Press, 1971.

Before tackling the problem itself we must be quite clear in our minds that commodity fetishism is a *specific* problem of our age, the age of modern capitalism. Commodity exchange and the corresponding subjective and objective commodity relations existed, as we know, when society was still very primitive. What is at issue *here*, however, is the question: how far is commodity exchange together with its structural consequences able to influence the *total* outer and inner life of society? Thus the extent to which such exchange is the dominant form of metabolic change in a society cannot simply be treated in quantitative terms – as would harmonize with the modern modes of thought already eroded by the reifying effects of the dominant commodity form. The distinction between a society where this form is dominant, permeating every expression of life, and a society where it only makes an episodic appearance is essentially one of quality. For depending on which is the case, all the subjective and objective phenomena in the societies concerned are objectified in qualitatively different ways.

Marx lays great stress on the essentially episodic appearance of the commodity form in primitive societies:

> Direct barter, the original natural form of exchange, represents rather the beginning of the transformation of use-values into commodities, than that of commodities into money. Exchange value has as yet no form of its own, but is still directly bound up with use-value. This is manifested in two ways. Production, in its entire organisation, aims at the creation of use-values and not of exchange values, and it is only when their supply exceeds the measure of consumption that use-values cease to be use-values, and become means of exchange, i.e. commodities. At the same time, they become commodities only within the limits of being direct use-values distributed at opposite poles, so that the commodities to be exchanged by their possessors must be use-values to both – each commodity to its non-possessor. As a matter of fact, the exchange of commodities originates not within the primitive communities, but where they end, on their borders at the few points where they come in contact with other communities. That is where barter begins, and from here it strikes back into the interior of the community, decomposing it.[1]

We note that the observation about the disintegrating effect of a commodity exchange directed in upon itself clearly shows the qualitative change engendered by the dominance of commodities.

However, even when commodities have this impact on the internal structure of a society, this does not suffice to make them constitutive of that society. To achieve that it would be necessary – as we emphasized above – for the commodity structure to penetrate society in all its aspects and to remould it in its own image. It is not enough merely to establish an external link with independent processes concerned with the production of exchange values. The qualitative difference between the commodity as one form among many regulating the metabolism of human society and the commodity as the universal structuring principle has effects over and above the fact that the commodity relation as an isolated phenomenon exerts a negative influence at best on the structure and organization of society. The distinction also has repercussions upon the nature and validity of the category itself. Where the commodity is universal it manifests itself differently from the commodity as a particular, isolated, non-dominant phenomenon.

The fact that the boundaries lack sharp definition must not be allowed to blur the qualitative nature of the decisive distinction. The situation where commodity exchange is not dominant has been defined by Marx as follows:

> The quantitative ratio in which products are exchanged is at first quite arbitrary. They assume the form of commodities inasmuch as they are exchangeables, i.e. expressions of one and the same third. Continued exchange and more regular reproduction for exchange reduces this arbitrariness more and more. But at first not for the producer and consumer, but for their go-between, the merchant, who compares money-prices and pockets the difference. It is through his own movements that he establishes equivalence. Merchant's capital is originally merely the intervening movement between extremes which it does not control and between premises which it does not create.[2]

And *this* development of the commodity to the point where it becomes the dominant form in society did not take place until the advent of modern capitalism. Hence it is not to be wondered at that the personal nature of economic relations was still understood clearly on occasion at the start of capitalist development, but that as the process advanced and forms became more complex and less direct, it became increasingly difficult and rare to find anyone penetrating the veil of reification. Marx sees the matter in this way:

> In preceding forms of society this economic mystification arose principally with respect to money and interest-bearing capital. In the nature of things it is excluded, in the first place, where production for the use-value, for immediate personal requirements, predominates; and secondly, where slavery or serfdom form the broad foundation of social production, as in antiquity and during the Middle Ages. Here, the domination of the producers by the conditions of production is concealed by the relations of dominion and servitude which appear and are evident as the direct motive power of the process of production.[3]

The commodity can only be understood in its undistorted essence when it becomes the universal category of society as a whole. Only in this context does the reification produced by commodity relations assume decisive importance both for the objective evolution of society and for the stance adopted by men towards it. Only then does the commodity become crucial for the subjugation of men's consciousness to the forms in which this reification finds expression and for their attempts to comprehend the process or to rebel against its disastrous effects and liberate themselves from servitude to the 'second nature' so created.

Marx describes the basic phenomenon of reification as follows:

> A commodity is therefore a mysterious thing, simply because in it the social character of men's labour appears to them as an objective character stamped upon the product of that labour; because the relation of the producers to the sum total of their own labour is presented to them as a social relation, existing not between themselves, but between the products of their labour. This is the reason why the products of labour become commodities, social things whose qualities are at the same time perceptible and imperceptible by the senses. ... It is only a definite social relation between men that assumes, in their eyes, the fantastic form of a relation between things.[4]

What is of central importance here is that because of this situation a man's own activity, his own labour becomes something objective and independent of him, something that controls him by virtue of an autonomy alien to man. There is both an objective and a subjective side to this phenomenon. *Objectively* a world of objects and relations between things springs into being (the world of commodities and their movements on the market). The laws governing these objects are indeed gradually discovered by man, but even so they confront him as invisible forces that generate their own power. The individual can use his knowledge of these laws to his own advantage, but he is not able to modify the process by his own activity. *Subjectively* – where the market economy has been fully developed – a man's activity becomes estranged from himself, it turns into a commodity which, subject to the non-human objectivity of the natural laws of society, must go its own way independently of man just like any consumer article. 'What is characteristic of the capitalist age,' says Marx, 'is that in the eyes of the labourer himself labour-power assumes the form of a commodity belonging to him. On the other hand it is only at this moment that the commodity form of the products of labour becomes general.'[5]

Thus the universality of the commodity form is responsible both objectively and subjectively for the abstraction of the human labour incorporated in commodities. (On the other hand, this universality becomes historically possible because this process of abstraction has been completed.) *Objectively*, in so far as the commodity form facilitates the equal exchange of qualitatively different objects, it can only exist if that formal equality is in fact recognized – at any rate in *this* relation, which indeed confers upon them their commodity nature. *Subjectively*, this formal equality of human labour in the abstract is not only the common

175

factor to which the various commodities are reduced; it also becomes the real principle governing the actual production of commodities.

Clearly, it cannot be our aim here to describe even in outline the growth of the modern process of labour, of the isolated, 'free' labourer and of the division of labour. Here we need only establish that labour, abstract, equal, comparable labour, measurable with increasing precision according to the time socially necessary for its accomplishment, the labour of the capitalist division of labour existing both as the presupposition and the product of capitalist production, is born only in the course of the development of the capitalist system. Only then does it become a category of society influencing decisively the objective form of things and people in the society thus emerging, their relation to nature and the possible relations of men to each other.

If we follow the path taken by labour in its development from the handicraft via co-operation and manufacture to machine industry we can see a continuous trend towards greater rationalization, the progressive elimination of the qualitative, human and individual attributes of the worker. On the one hand, the process of labour is progressively broken down into abstract, rational, specialized operations so that the worker loses contact with the finished product and his work is reduced to the mechanical repetition of a specialized set of actions. On the other hand, the period of time necessary for work to be accomplished (which forms the basis of rational calculation) is converted, as mechanization and rationalization are intensified, from a merely empirical average figure to an objectively calculable work-stint that confronts the worker as a fixed and established reality. With the modern 'psychological' analysis of the work-process (in Taylorism) this rational mechanization extends right into the worker's 'soul': even his psychological attributes are separated from his total personality and placed in opposition to it so as to facilitate their integration into specialized rational systems and their reduction to statistically viable concepts.[6]

We are concerned above all with the *principle* at work here: the principle of rationalization based on what is and *can be calculated*. The chief changes undergone by the subject and object of the economic process are as follows: (1) in the first place, the mathematical analysis of work-processes denotes a break with the organic, irrational and qualitatively determined unity of the product. Rationalization in the sense of being able to predict with ever greater precision all the results to be achieved is only to be acquired by the exact breakdown of every complex into its elements and by the study of the special laws governing production. Accordingly it must declare war on the organic manufacture of whole products based on the *traditional amalgam of empirical experiences of work*: rationalization is unthinkable without specialization.[7]

The finished article ceases to be the object of the work-process. The latter turns into the objective synthesis of rationalized special systems whose unity is determined by pure calculation and which must therefore seem to be arbitrarily connected with each other. This destroys the organic necessity with which interrelated special operations are unified in the end-product. The unity of a product as a *commodity* no longer coincides with its unity as a use-value: as society becomes more radically capitalistic the increasing technical autonomy of the special operations involved in production is expressed also, as an economic autonomy, as the growing relativization of the commodity character of a product at the various stages of production.[8] It is thus possible to separate forcibly the production of a use-value in time and space. This goes hand in hand with the union in time and space of special operations that are related to a set of heterogeneous use-values.

(2) In the second place, this fragmentation of the object of production necessarily entails the fragmentation of its subject. In consequence of the rationalization of the work-process the human qualities and idiosyncrasies of the worker appear increasingly as *mere sources of error* when contrasted with these abstract special laws functioning according to rational predictions. Neither objectively nor in his relation to his work does man appear as the authentic master of the process; on the contrary, he is a mechanical part incorporated into a mechanical system. He finds it already pre-existing and self-sufficient, it functions independently of him and he has to conform to its laws whether he likes it or not.[9] As labour is progressively rationalized and mechanized his lack of will is reinforced by the way in which his activity becomes less and less active and more and more *contemplative*.[10] The contemplative stance adopted towards a process mechanically conforming to fixed laws and enacted independently of man's consciousness and impervious to human intervention, i.e. a perfectly closed system, must likewise transform the basic categories of man's immediate attitude to the world: it reduces space and time to a common denominator and degrades time to the dimension of space.

Marx puts it thus:

> Through the subordination of man to the machine the situation arises in which men are effaced by their labour; in which the pendulum of the clock has become as accurate a measure of the relative activity of two workers as it is of the speed of two locomotives. Therefore, we should not say that one man's hour is worth another man's hour, but rather that one man during an hour is worth just as much as another man during an hour. Time is everything, man is nothing; he is at the most the incarnation of time. Quality no longer matters. Quantity alone decides everything: hour for hour, day for day.[11]

Thus time sheds its qualitative, variable, flowing nature; it freezes into an exactly delimited, quantifiable continuum filled with quantifiable 'things' (the reified, mechanically objectified 'performance' of the worker, wholly separated from his total human personality): in short, it becomes space.[12]

In this environment where time is transformed into abstract, exactly measurable, physical space, an environment at once the cause and effect of the scientifically and mechanically fragmented and specialized production of the object of labour, the subjects of labour must likewise be rationally fragmented. On the one hand, the objectification of their labour-power into something opposed to their total personality (a process already accomplished with the sale of that labour-power as a commodity) is now made into the permanent ineluctable reality of their daily life. Here, too, the personality can do no more than look on helplessly while its own existence is reduced to an isolated particle and fed into an alien system. On the other hand, the mechanical disintegration of the process of production into its components also destroys those bonds that had bound individuals to a community in the days when production was still 'organic'. In this respect, too, mechanization makes of them isolated abstract atoms whose work no longer brings them together directly and organically; it becomes mediated to an increasing extent exclusively by the abstract laws of the mechanism which imprisons them.

The internal organization of a factory could not possibly have such an effect – even within the factory itself – were it not for the fact that it contained in concentrated form the whole structure of capitalist society. Oppression and an exploitation that knows no bounds and scorns every human dignity were known even to pre-capitalist ages. So too was mass production with mechanical, standardized labour, as we can see, for instance, with canal construction in Egypt and Asia Minor and the mines in Rome.[13] But mass projects of this type could never be *rationally mechanized*; they remained isolated phenomena within a community that organized its production on a different ('natural') basis and which therefore lived a different life. The slaves subjected to this exploitation, therefore, stood outside what was thought of as 'human' society and even the greatest and noblest thinkers of the time were unable to consider their fate as that of human beings.

As the commodity becomes universally dominant, this situation changes radically and qualitatively. The fate of the worker becomes the fate of society as a whole; indeed, this fate must become universal as otherwise industrialization could not develop in this direction. For it depends on the emergence of the 'free' worker who is freely able to take his labour-power to market and offer it for sale as a commodity 'belonging' to him, a thing that he 'possesses'.

While this process is still incomplete the methods used to extract surplus labour are, it is true, more obviously brutal than in the later, more highly developed phase, but the process of reification of work and hence also of the consciousness of the worker is much less advanced. Reification requires that a society should learn to satisfy all its needs in terms of commodity exchange. The separation of the producer from his means of production, the dissolution and destruction of all 'natural' production units, etc., and all the social and economic conditions necessary for the emergence of modern capitalism tend to replace 'natural' relations which exhibit human relations more plainly by rationally reified relations. 'The social relations between individuals in the performance of their labour', Marx observes with reference to pre-capitalist societies, 'appear at all events as their own personal relations, and are not disguised under the shape of social relations between the products of labour.'[14]

But this implies that the principle of rational mechanization and calculability must embrace every aspect of life. Consumer articles no longer appear as the products of an organic process within a community (as for example in a village community). They now appear, on the one hand, as abstract members of a species identical by definition with its other members and, on the other hand, as isolated objects the possession or non-possession of which depends on rational calculations. Only when the whole life of society is thus fragmented into the isolated acts of commodity exchange can the 'free' worker come into being; at the same time his fate becomes the typical fate of the whole society.

Of course, this isolation and fragmentation is only apparent. The movement of commodities on the market, the birth of their value, in a word, the real framework of every rational calculation is not merely subject to strict laws but also presupposes the strict ordering of all that happens. The atomization of the individual is, then, only the reflex in consciousness of the fact that the 'natural laws' of capitalist production have been extended to cover every manifestation of life in society; that – for the first time in history – the whole of society is subjected, or tends to be subjected, to a unified economic process, and that the fate of every member of society is determined by unified laws. (By contrast, the organic unities of pre-capitalist societies organized their metabolism largely in independence of each other.)

However, if this atomization is only an illusion it is a necessary one. That is to say, the immediate, practical as well as intellectual confrontation of the individual with society, the immediate production and reproduction of life – in which for the individual the commodity structure of all 'things' and their obedience to 'natural laws' is found to exist already in a finished form, as something immutably given – could only take place in the form of rational and isolated acts of exchange between isolated commodity owners. As emphasized above, the worker, too, must present himself as the 'owner' of his labour-power, as if it were a commodity. His specific situation is defined by the fact that his labour-power is his only possession. His fate is typical of society as a whole in that this self-objectification, this transformation of a human function into a commodity reveals in all its starkness the dehumanized and dehumanizing function of the commodity relation. . . .

NOTES

1 *A Contribution to the Critique of Political Economy.*
2 *Capital* III.
3 *Capital* III.
4 *Capital* I. On this antagonism cf. the purely economic distinction between the exchange of goods in terms of their value and the exchange in terms of their cost of production, *Capital* III.
5 *Capital* I.
6 This whole process is described systematically and historically in *Capital* I. The facts themselves can also be found in the writings of bourgeois economists like Bücher, Sombart, A. Weber and Gottl among others – although for the most part they are not seen in connection with the problem of reification.
7 *Capital* I.
8 *Capital* I.
9 That this should appear so is fully justified from the point of view of the *individual* consciousness. As far as class is concerned we would point out that this subjugation is the product of a lengthy struggle which enters upon a new stage with the organization of the proletariat into a class – but on a higher plane and with different weapons.
10 *Capital* I. It goes without saying that this 'contemplation' can be more demanding and demoralizing than 'active' labour. But we cannot discuss this further here.
11 *The Poverty of Philosophy.*
12 *Capital* I.
13 Cf. Gottl, *Wirtschaft und Technik*, Grundriss der Sozialökonomik II.
14 *Capital* I.

12

Antonio Gramsci

(1891–1937)

Antonio Gramsci presented one of the earliest revisions of Marxist theory under the changing conditions of advanced capitalism in the twentieth century. A strong critic of 'scientistic' Marxism, Gramsci was born in Sardinia to a working-class family in 1891. As a young man, he was greatly influenced by Benedetto Croce's philosophical idealism in the Hegelian tradition. Gramsci committed himself to the belief that human beings can alter their historical circumstances when consciousness and praxis interact. He himself took part in the Turin factory strikes between 1916 and 1919, as well as being a founder of the Italian Communist Party and editor of its journal, *Ordine Nuovo*. His bitter experiences with the defeated workers in Turin made him reassess the theoretical framework of the Marxist movement.

Despite his election to the Italian parliament in 1924, he was incarcerated by Mussolini in 1926 for the last eleven years of his life. During that time, Gramsci filled thirty-two notebooks with his reflections on the battle for revolutionary consciousness. These *Prison Notebooks*, as they have come to be known, encouraged the growth of European Marxism by recognizing the vital connection between a given power structure and the cultural–ideological superstructure that supports it. Gramsci called this relationship 'ideological hegemony', claiming that one must look beyond the economic base to see how power is legitimated by the willing consensus of those who are most exploited. In other words, he asks how the ruling bourgeoisie actually achieves ideological control and, thereby, stability. Gramsci points out that the use of physical force and military intervention to maintain an authoritarian regime can only be a short-term solution for a ruling class. Popular consensus is thus essential for continued survival. This requires the diffusion throughout society of bourgeois values, beliefs and morality, a task which is accomplished through institutions such as those that control education, religion, government bureaucracy and media. Ultimately, the prevailing consciousness seems to be a world-view that is natural, unquestioned and accepted by everyone, even those who have most to lose.

Gramsci emphasizes that this world-view must not only be passively accepted by the masses, it must also be actively promoted by the intellectuals who supervise the institutions and agencies of socialization. The diffusion and circulation of appropriate knowledge, ideas, attitudes, symbols and prejudices depend on these intellectuals whose role is to organize all sectors – cultural, political and economic. However, Gramsci makes a distinction between 'traditional' intellectuals who seem to be removed from social struggles or class interests, and 'organic' intellectuals who identify with the social group from which they emerge, share their political and economic interests, and are aware of their own functions in the system. Gramsci notes that it is not simply a matter of dealing with 'cognitive' issues that defines intellectuals as a group:

> The most widespread error of method seems to me that of having looked for this criterion of distinction in the intrinsic nature of intellectual activities, rather than in the ensemble of the system of relations in which these activities (and therefore the intellectual groups who personify them) have their place within the general complex of social relations.
>
> (*Selections from the Prison Notebooks*, p. 8)

Even the category of supposedly neutral 'traditional' intellectuals found, for example, in academic institutions, contributes to the overall maintenance of system dynamics. Generally identified as individuals with an impartial expertise in a given area, these intellectuals still serve the functions of defining canonical texts, preserving disciplinary boundaries, excluding and labelling students through examination procedures, and validating certain ideological constructs as universally sound. All of these activities must appear equitable and unbiased in their application, while simultaneously reinforcing a hegemonic agenda of class interests.

Thus, for Gramsci, the primary focus for organic intellectuals emerging from the working class should be a long-term 'war of position' that attempts to foster a discerning political consciousness towards existing social arrangements. He stressed that the relatively brief and infrequent crises involving a direct confrontation, or 'war of movement', would be stillborn if Marxists continued to ignore the critical significance of winning 'the hearts and minds' of the oppressed to do battle for their own cause.

SELECT BIBLIOGRAPHY OF GRAMSCI'S WORKS IN ENGLISH

The Modern Prince and Other Writings, New York: International Publishers, 1957.

Selections from the Prison Notebooks, London: Lawrence & Wishart, 1971.

Letters from Prison, New York: Harper & Row, 1973.

Selections from Political Writings, 1910–1920, London: Lawrence & Wishart, 1977.
Selections from Political Writings, 1921–1926, London: Lawrence & Wishart, 1978.

ANTONIO GRAMSCI

The Intellectuals

THE FORMATION OF THE INTELLECTUALS

ARE INTELLECTUALS AN autonomous and independent social group, or does every social group have its own particular specialized category of intellectuals? The problem is a complex one, because of the variety of forms assumed to date by the real historical process of formation of the different categories of intellectuals.

The most important of these forms are two:

(1) Every social group, coming into existence on the original terrain of an essential function in the world of economic production, creates together with itself, organically, one or more strata[1] of intellectuals which give it homogeneity and an awareness of its own function not only in the economic but also in the social and political fields. The capitalist entrepreneur creates alongside himself the industrial technician, the specialist in political economy, the organizers of a new culture, of a new legal system, etc. It should be noted that the entrepreneur himself represents a higher level of social elaboration, already characterized by a certain directive [*dirigente*] and technical (i.e. intellectual) capacity: he must have a certain technical capacity, not only in the limited sphere of his activity and initiative but in other spheres as well, at least in those which are closest to economic production. He must be an organizer of masses of men; he must be an organizer of the 'confidence' of investors in his business, of the customers for his product, etc.

If not all entrepreneurs, at least an *élite* amongst them must have the capacity to be an organizer of society in general, including all its complex organism of services, right up to the state organism, because of the need to create the conditions most favourable to the expansion of their own class; or at the least they must possess the capacity to choose the deputies (specialized employees) to whom to entrust this activity of organizing the general system of relationships external to the business itself. It can be observed that the 'organic' intellectuals which every new class creates alongside itself and elaborates in the course of its development, are for the most part 'specializations' of partial aspects of the primitive activity of the new social type which the new class has brought into prominence.*

From *Selections from the Prison Notebooks of Antonio Gramsci*, ed. Quintin Hoare and Geoffrey Nowell Smith, London: Lawrence & Wishart, 1971.

* Mosca's *Elementi di Scienza Politica* (new expanded edition, 1923) are worth looking at in this connection. Mosca's so-called 'political class'[2] is nothing other than the intellectual category of the dominant social group. Mosca's concept of 'political class' can be connected with Pareto's concept of the *élite*, which is another attempt to interpret the historical phenomenon of the intellectuals and their

Even feudal lords were possessors of a particular technical capacity, military capacity, and it is precisely from the moment at which the aristocracy loses its monopoly of technico–military capacity that the crisis of feudalism begins. But the formation of intellectuals in the feudal world and in the preceding classical world is a question to be examined separately: this formation and elaboration follows ways and means which must be studied concretely. Thus it is to be noted that the mass of the peasantry, although it performs an essential function in the world of production, does not elaborate its own 'organic' intellectuals, nor does it 'assimilate' any stratum of 'traditional' intellectuals, although it is from the peasantry that other social groups draw many of their intellectuals and a high proportion of traditional intellectuals are of peasant origin.[3]

(2)   However, every 'essential' social group which emerges into history out of the preceding economic structure, and as an expression of a development of this structure, has found (at least in all of history up to the present) categories of intellectuals already in existence and which seemed indeed to represent an historical continuity uninterrupted even by the most complicated and radical changes in political and social forms.

The most typical of these categories of intellectuals is that of the ecclesiastics, who for a long time (for a whole phase of history, which is partly characterized by this very monopoly) held a monopoly of a number of important services: religious ideology, that is the philosophy and science of the age, together with schools, education, morality, justice, charity, good works, etc. The category of ecclesiastics can be considered the category of intellectuals organically bound to the landed aristocracy. It had equal status juridically with the aristocracy, with which it shared the exercise of feudal ownership of land, and the use of state privileges connected with property.[†] But the monopoly held by the ecclesiastics in

function in the life of the state and of society. Mosca's book is an enormous hotch-potch, of a sociological and positivistic character, plus the tendentiousness of immediate politics which makes it less indigestible and livelier from a literary point of view.

† For one category of these intellectuals, possibly the most important after the ecclesiastical for its prestige and the social function it performed in primitive societies, the category of *medical men* in the wide sense, that is all those who 'struggle' or seem to struggle against death and disease, compare the *Storia della medicina* of Arturo Castiglioni. Note that there has been a connection between religion and medicine, and in certain areas there still is: hospitals in the hands of religious orders for certain organizational functions, apart from the fact that wherever the doctor appears, so does the priest (exorcism, various forms of assistance, etc.). Many great religious figures were and are conceived of as great 'healers': the idea of miracles, up to the resurrection of the dead. Even in the case of kings the belief long survived that they could heal with the laying on of hands, etc.

the superstructural field‡ was not exercised without a struggle or without limitations, and hence there took place the birth, in various forms (to be gone into and studied concretely), of other categories, favoured and enabled to expand by the growing strength of the central power of the monarch, right up to absolutism. Thus we find the formation of the *noblesse de robe*, with its own privileges, a stratum of administrators, etc., scholars and scientists, theorists, non-ecclesiastical philosophers, etc.

Since these various categories of traditional intellectuals experience through an '*esprit de corps*' their uninterrupted historical continuity and their special qualification, they thus put themselves forward as autonomous and independent of the dominant social group. This self-assessment is not without consequences in the ideological and political field, consequences of wide-ranging import. The whole of idealist philosophy can easily be connected with this position assumed by the social complex of intellectuals and can be defined as the expression of that social utopia by which the intellectuals think of themselves as 'independent', autonomous, endowed with a character of their own, etc.

One should note however that if the Pope and the leading hierarchy of the Church consider themselves more linked to Christ and to the apostles than they are to senators Agnelli and Benni,[4] the same does not hold for Gentile and Croce, for example: Croce in particular feels himself closely linked to Aristotle and Plato, but he does not conceal, on the other hand, his links with senators Agnelli and Benni, and it is precisely here that one can discern the most significant character of Croce's philosophy.

What are the 'maximum' limits of acceptance of the term 'intellectual'? Can one find a unitary criterion to characterize equally all the diverse and disparate activities of intellectuals and to distinguish these at the same time and in an essential way from the activities of other social groupings? The most widespread error of method seems to me that of having looked for this criterion of distinction in the intrinsic nature of intellectual activities, rather than in the ensemble of the system of relations in which these activities (and therefore the intellectual groups who personify them) have their place within the general complex of social relations. Indeed the worker or proletarian, for example, is not specifically characterized by his manual or instrumental work, but by performing this work in specific conditions and in specific social relations (apart from the consideration that purely physical labour does not exist and that even Taylor's phrase of 'trained gorilla'[5] is a metaphor to indicate a limit in a certain direction: in any physical work, even the most degraded and mechanical, there exists a minimum of technical qualification, that is, a

‡ From this has come the general sense of 'intellectual' or 'specialist' of the word '*chierico*' (clerk, cleric) in many languages of romance origin or heavily influenced, through church Latin, by the romance languages, together with its correlative '*laico*' (lay, layman) in the sense of profane, non-specialist.

minimum of creative intellectual activity). And we have already observed that the entrepreneur, by virtue of his very function, must have to some degree a certain number of qualifications of an intellectual nature although his part in society is determined not by these, but by the general social relations which specifically characterize the position of the entrepreneur within industry.

All men are intellectuals, one could therefore say: but not all men have in society the function of intellectuals.*

When one distinguishes between intellectuals and non-intellectuals, one is referring in reality only to the immediate social function of the professional category of the intellectuals, that is, one has in mind the direction in which their specific professional activity is weighted, whether towards intellectual elaboration or towards muscular–nervous effort. This means that, although one can speak of intellectuals, one cannot speak of non-intellectuals, because non-intellectuals do not exist. But even the relationship between efforts of intellectual–cerebral elaboration and muscular–nervous effort is not always the same, so that there are varying degrees of specific intellectual activity. There is no human activity from which every form of intellectual participation can be excluded: *homo faber* cannot be separated from *homo sapiens*.[6] Each man, finally, outside his professional activity, carries on some form of intellectual activity, that is, he is a 'philosopher', an artist, a man of taste, he participates in a particular conception of the world, has a conscious line of moral conduct, and therefore contributes to sustain a conception of the world or to modify it, that is, to bring into being new modes of thought.

The problem of creating a new stratum of intellectuals consists therefore in the critical elaboration of the intellectual activity that exists in everyone at a certain degree of development, modifying its relationship with the muscular–nervous effort towards a new equilibrium, and ensuring that the muscular–nervous effort itself, in so far as it is an element of a general practical activity, which is perpetually innovating the physical and social world, becomes the foundation of a new and integral conception of the world. The traditional and vulgarized type of the intellectual is given by the man of letters, the philosopher, the artist. Therefore journalists, who claim to be men of letters, philosophers, artists, also regard themselves as the 'true' intellectuals. In the modern world, technical education, closely bound to industrial labour even at the most primitive and unqualified level, must form the basis of the new type of intellectual.

On this basis the weekly *Ordine Nuovo*[7] worked to develop certain forms of new intellectualism and to determine its new concepts, and this

* Thus, because it can happen that everyone at some time fries a couple of eggs or sews up a tear in a jacket, we do not necessarily say that everyone is a cook or a tailor.

was not the least of the reasons for its success, since such a conception corresponded to latent aspirations and conformed to the development of the real forms of life. The mode of being of the new intellectual can no longer consist in eloquence, which is an exterior and momentary mover of feelings and passions, but in active participation in practical life, as constructor, organizer, 'permanent persuader' and not just a simple orator (but superior at the same time to the abstract mathematical spirit); from technique-as-work one proceeds to technique-as-science and to the humanistic conception of history, without which one remains 'specialized' and does not become 'directive'[8] (specialized and political).

Thus there are historically formed specialized categories for the exercise of the intellectual function. They are formed in connection with all social groups, but especially in connection with the more important, and they undergo more extensive and complex elaboration in connection with the dominant social group. One of the most important characteristics of any group that is developing towards dominance is its struggle to assimilate and to conquer 'ideologically' the traditional intellectuals, but this assimilation and conquest is made quicker and more efficacious the more the group in question succeeds in simultaneously elaborating its own organic intellectuals.

The enormous development of activity and organization of education in the broad sense in the societies that emerged from the medieval world is an index of the importance assumed in the modern world by intellectual functions and categories. Parallel with the attempt to deepen and to broaden the 'intellectuality' of each individual, there has also been an attempt to multiply and narrow the various specializations. This can be seen from educational institutions at all levels, up to and including the organisms that exist to promote so-called 'high culture' in all fields of science and technology.

School is the instrument through which intellectuals of various levels are elaborated. The complexity of the intellectual function in different states can be measured objectively by the number and gradation of specialized schools: the more extensive the 'area' covered by education and the more numerous the 'vertical' 'levels' of schooling, the more complex is the cultural world, the civilization, of a particular state. A point of comparison can be found in the sphere of industrial technology: the industrialization of a country can be measured by how well equipped it is in the production of machines with which to produce machines, and in the manufacture of ever more accurate instruments for making both machines and further instruments for making machines, etc. The country which is best equipped in the construction of instruments for experimental scientific laboratories and in the construction of instruments with which to test the first instruments, can be regarded as the most complex in the technical–industrial field, with the highest level of civilization, etc. The same applies to the preparation of intellectuals and to the schools dedicated to this preparation; schools and institutes of high culture can be assimilated to each other. In this field also, quantity cannot be separated from quality. To the most refined technical–cultural specialization there cannot but correspond the maximum possible diffusion of primary education and the maximum care taken to expand the middle grades numerically as much as possible. Naturally this need to provide the widest base possible for the selection and elaboration of the top intellectual qualifications – i.e. to give a democratic structure to high culture and top-level technology – is not without its disadvantages: it creates the possibility of vast crises of unemployment for the middle intellectual strata, and in all modern societies this actually takes place.

It is worth noting that the elaboration of intellectual strata in concrete reality does not take place on the terrain of abstract democracy but in accordance with very concrete traditional historical processes. Strata have grown up which traditionally 'produce' intellectuals and these strata coincide with those which have specialized in 'saving', i.e. the petty and middle landed bourgeoisie and certain strata of the petty and middle urban bourgeoisie. The varying distribution of different types of school (classical and professional)[9] over the 'economic' territory and the varying aspirations of different categories within these strata determine, or give form to, the production of various branches of intellectual specialization. Thus in Italy the rural bourgeoisie produces in particular state functionaries and professional people, whereas the urban bourgeoisie produces technicians for industry. Consequently it is largely northern Italy which produces technicians and the South which produces functionaries and professional men.

The relationship between the intellectuals and the world of production is not as direct as it is with the fundamental social groups but is, in varying degrees, 'mediated' by the whole fabric of society and by the complex of superstructures, of which the intellectuals are, precisely, the 'functionaries'. It should be possible both to measure the 'organic quality' [*organicità*] of the various intellectual strata and their degree of connection with a fundamental social group, and to establish a gradation of their functions and of the superstructures from the bottom to the top (from the structural base upwards). What we can do, for the moment, is to fix two major superstructural 'levels': the one that can be called 'civil society', that is the ensemble of organisms commonly called 'private', and that of 'political society' or 'the State'. These two levels correspond on the one hand to the function of 'hegemony' which the dominant group exercises throughout society and on the other hand to that of 'direct domination' or command exercised through the State and 'juridical' government. The functions in question are precisely organizational and connective. The intellectuals are the dominant group's 'deputies' exercising the subaltern functions of social hegemony and political government. These comprise:

1 The 'spontaneous' consent given by the great masses of the population to the general direction imposed on social life by the dominant
fundamental group; this consent is 'historically' caused by the prestige
(and consequent confidence) which the dominant group enjoys because
of its position and function in the world of production.

2 The apparatus of state coercive power which 'legally' enforces discipline on those groups who do not 'consent' either actively or passively.
This apparatus is, however, constituted for the whole of society in
anticipation of moments of crisis of command and direction when
spontaneous consent has failed.

This way of posing the problem has as a result a considerable extension
of the concept of intellectual, but it is the only way which enables one
to reach a concrete approximation of reality. It also clashes with precon-
ceptions of caste. The function of organizing social hegemony and state
domination certainly gives rise to a particular division of labour and
therefore to a whole hierarchy of qualifications in some of which there
is no apparent attribution of directive or organizational functions.
For example, in the apparatus of social and state direction there exist
a whole series of jobs of a manual and instrumental character (non-
executive work, agents rather than officials or functionaries).[10] It is
obvious that such a distinction has to be made just as it is obvious that
other distinctions have to be made as well. Indeed, intellectual activity
must also be distinguished in terms of its intrinsic characteristics, according
to levels which in moments of extreme opposition represent a real
qualitative difference – at the highest level would be the creators of the
various sciences, philosophy, art, etc., at the lowest the most humble
'administrators' and divulgators of pre-existing, traditional, accumulated
intellectual wealth.*

In the modern world the category of intellectuals, understood in this
sense, has undergone an unprecedented expansion. The democratic–
bureaucratic system has given rise to a great mass of functions which are
not all justified by the social necessities of production, though they are
justified by the political necessities of the dominant fundamental group.
Hence Loria's[12] conception of the unproductive 'worker' (but unproductive in relation to whom and to what mode of production?), a conception which could in part be justified if one takes account of the fact that
these masses exploit their position to take for themselves a large cut out
of the national income. Mass formation has standardized individuals both

---

* Here again military organization offers a model of complex gradations between
subaltern officers, senior officers and general staff, not to mention the NCOs,
whose importance is greater than is generally admitted. It is worth observing that
all these parts feel a solidarity and indeed that it is the lower strata that display
the most blatant *esprit de corps*, from which they derive a certain 'conceit'[11] which
is apt to lay them open to jokes and witticisms.

190

psychologically and in terms of individual qualification and has produced the same phenomena as with other standardized masses: competition which makes necessary organizations for the defence of professions, unemployment, over-production in the schools, emigration, etc. . . .

Intellectuals of the urban type have grown up along with industry and are linked to its fortunes. Their function can be compared to that of subaltern officers in the army. They have no autonomous initiative in elaborating plans for construction. Their job is to articulate the relationship between the entrepreneur and the instrumental mass and to carry out the immediate execution of the production plan decided by the industrial general staff, controlling the elementary stages of work. On the whole the average urban intellectuals are very standardized, while the top urban intellectuals are more and more identified with the industrial general staff itself.

Intellectuals of the rural type are for the most part 'traditional', that is they are linked to the social mass of country people and the town (particularly small-town) petite bourgeoisie, not as yet elaborated and set in motion by the capitalist system. This type of intellectual brings into contact the peasant masses with the local and state administration (lawyers, notaries, etc.). Because of this activity they have an important politico-social function, since professional mediation is difficult to separate from political. Furthermore: in the countryside the intellectual (priest, lawyer, notary, teacher, doctor, etc.), has on the whole a higher or at least a different living standard from that of the average peasant and consequently represents a social model for the peasant to look to in his aspiration to escape from or improve his condition. The peasant always thinks that at least one of his sons could become an intellectual (especially a priest), thus becoming a gentleman and raising the social level of the family by facilitating its economic life through the connections which he is bound to acquire with the rest of the gentry. The peasant's attitude towards the intellectual is double and appears contradictory. He respects the social position of the intellectuals and in general that of state employees, but sometimes affects contempt for it, which means that his admiration is mingled with instinctive elements of envy and impassioned anger. One can understand nothing of the collective life of the peasantry and of the germs and ferments of development which exist within it, if one does not take into consideration and examine concretely and in depth this effective subordination to the intellectuals. Every organic development of the peasant masses, up to a certain point, is linked to and depends on movements among the intellectuals.

With the urban intellectuals it is another matter. Factory technicians do not exercise any political function over the instrumental masses, or at least this is a phase that has been superseded. Sometimes, rather, the contrary takes place, and the instrumental masses, at least in the person of their own organic intellectuals, exercise a political influence on the technicians.

The central point of the question remains the distinction between intellectuals as an organic category of every fundamental social group and intellectuals as a traditional category. From this distinction there flow a whole series of problems and possible questions for historical research.

NOTES

1   The Italian word here is '*ceti*' which does not carry quite the same connotations as 'strata', but which we have been forced to translate in that way for lack of alternatives. It should be noted that Gramsci tends, for reasons of censorship, to avoid using the word 'class' in contexts where its Marxist overtones would be apparent, preferring (as for example in this sentence) the more neutral 'social group'. The word 'group' however, is not always a euphemism for 'class', and to avoid ambiguity Gramsci uses the phrase 'fundamental social group' when he wishes to emphasize the fact that he is referring to one or other of the major social classes (bourgeoisie, proletariat) defined in strict Marxist terms by its position in the fundamental relations of production. Class groupings which do not have this fundamental role are often described as 'castes' (aristocracy, etc.). The word 'category', on the other hand, which also occurs on this page, Gramsci tends to use in the standard Italian sense of members of a trade or profession, though also more generally. Throughout, we have rendered Gramsci's usage as literally as possible.

2   Usually translated in English as 'ruling class', which is also the title of the English version of Mosca's *Elementi* (G. Mosca, *The Ruling Class*, New York 1939). Gaetano Mosca (1858–1941) was, together with Pareto and Michels, one of the major early Italian exponents of the theory of political *élites*. Although sympathetic to fascism, Mosca was basically a conservative, who saw the *élite* in rather more static terms than did some of his fellows.

3   Notably in Southern Italy. Gramsci's general argument, here as elsewhere in the *Quaderni*, is that the person of peasant origin who becomes an 'intellectual' (priest, lawyer, etc.) generally thereby ceases to be organically linked to his class of origin. One of the essential differences between, say, the Catholic Church and the revolutionary party of the working class lies in the fact that, ideally, the proletariat should be able to generate its own 'organic' intellectuals within the class and who remain intellectuals *of* their class.

4   Heads of FIAT and Montecatini (Chemicals) respectively.

5   For Frederick Taylor and his notion of the manual worker as a 'trained gorilla', see Gramsci's essay *Americanism and Fordism*.

6   i.e. Man the maker (or tool-bearer) and Man the thinker.

7   The *Ordine Nuovo*, the magazine edited by Gramsci during his days as a militant in Turin, ran as a 'weekly review of Socialist culture' in 1919 and 1920.

8   '*Dirigente.*' This extremely condensed and elliptical sentence contains a number of key Gramscian ideas: on the possibility of proletarian cultural hegemony through domination of the work process, on the distinction

between organic intellectuals of the working class and traditional intellectuals from outside, on the unity of theory and practice as a basic Marxist postulate, etc.

9 The Italian school system above compulsory level is based on a division between academic ('classical' and 'scientific') education and vocational training for professional purposes. Technical and, at the academic level, 'scientific' colleges tend to be concentrated in the Northern industrial areas.

10 '*funzionari*': in Italian usage the word is applied to the middle and higher echelons of the bureaucracy. Conversely 'administrators' ('*amministratori*') is used here (end of paragraph) to mean people who merely 'administer' the decisions of others. The phrase 'non-executive work' is a translation of '[*impiego] di ordine e non di concetto*' which refers to distinctions within clerical work.

11 '*boria*'. This is a reference to an idea of Vico.

12 The notion of the 'unproductive labourer' is not in fact an invention of Loria's but has its origins in Marx's definitions of productive and unproductive labour in *Capital*, which Loria, in his characteristic way, both vulgarized and claimed as his own discovery.

13

Max Horkheimer
(1895–1971)

and Theodor W. Adorno
(1903–1969)

MAX HORKHEIMER

Born in 1895 to an affluent Jewish family, Max Horkheimer became one of the earliest members of the Institute of Social Research. He was appointed its second Director in 1931, and, after the Nazi rise to power in 1933, he remained its leader during the period of exile in Geneva and America. When the Institute finally returned to Frankfurt in 1950, Horkheimer continued to serve as Director until his retirement in 1959.

Although he was trained commercially during his formative years and encouraged to join his father's successful manufacturing business, Horkheimer decided to pursue academic studies in psychology and philosophy, writing his doctorate in 1922 while studying under Husserl and Heidegger at the University of Freiburg. In 1925, he submitted a *Habilitationsschrift* to the University of Frankfurt entitled 'Kant's *Critique of Judgment* as a bridge between theoretical and practical philosophy', thematically claiming a unifying function for Teleological Reason as set forth in the Third Critique. On the strength of this thesis, Horkheimer was invited to lecture as *Privatdozent* at the university and in 1929 was appointed to the Chair of social philosophy. During this period, however, he was also involved in the activities being undertaken by the Institute of Social Research under its first Director, the Marxist economist, Carl Grünberg. Many of Horkheimer's important essays were first published as articles in the Institute's journal (*Zeitschrift für Sozialforschung*), and his collected works in German fill eighteen volumes. Works published in English include *Dialectic of Enlightenment* (1947, with Adorno), *Eclipse of Reason* (1947), *Critique of Instrumental Reason* (1967) and *Critical Theory: Selected Essays* (1968).

The Institute of Social Research (*Institut für Sozialforschung*) was first established in 1923, funded by an endowment from Felix Weil, the son of a wealthy manufacturer. Under Grünberg's leadership, the Institute

194

produced strongly empirical Marxist studies, such as Wittfogel's *Economy and Society in China*, Pollock's *Experiments in Economic Planning in the Soviet Union, 1917–1927* and Grossman's *The Law of Accumulation and Collapse in the Capitalist System*. Upon the retirement of Grünberg in 1929, this empiricist and Marxist orientation changed considerably.

Under the new leadership of Max Horkheimer in 1931, joined by Marcuse, Fromm, Benjamin and Adorno, a new emphasis was placed on the philosophical ground and dialectical constitution of social reality. The discovery of Marx's early 'humanist' *Paris Manuscripts* in 1931, the exposure of members to phenomenology via Husserl and Heidegger, and an interest in Freudian psychoanalysis, all influenced the development of what has come to be known as 'The Frankfurt School' of critical theory. Taking the form of *Kulturkritik*, a cultural criticism emerged that no longer particularly concerned itself with the kinds of economic and historical Marxist studies that had marked the output of the early Institute during the 1920s.

Horkheimer's classic essay, 'Traditional and critical theory' (1937) reinforced what is perhaps the best definition of what should constitute 'critical theory', formulated by Karl Marx in 1843 as 'the self-clarification of the struggles and wishes of the age'. Horkheimer emphasized that the traditional view of the researcher or social philosopher as a detached observer and commentator clarifying 'objective facts' had to be reassessed. Critical theorists recognize the inevitably historical nature of such inquiry, a stance that acknowledges the potential for ideological critique leading to social and political change. The rejection of static 'traditional' methods and explanations in the face of changing socio-historical contexts, Horkheimer insisted, demands a new commitment to research in a critical mode.

It is important to note at this juncture that, although the Hegelian and Freudian influences within the Institute at this stage of its development are quite evident, the Neo-Kantian commitments of its members go largely unrecognized. Horkheimer and Adorno had studied philosophy with Hans Cornelius, a Neo-Kantian well known for his Spenglerian pessimism; and both had written a *Habilitationsschrift* on a Kantian theme. The other powerful influence on the Institute was the social theory of Max Weber. Weber distanced himself from the Durkheimian position that a theory of society dealt purely with anonymous 'social facts'. He maintained, on the contrary, that it was only by mapping the motivations of *individual* social actors that a theory of social action could actually be formulated. Weber also followed the lead of the early Baden Neo-Kantians like Rickert in separating the appropriate methodologies for the natural sciences, which could be purely empirical, from the methods to be followed in the social sciences (the *Kulturwissenschaften*), taking a strong anti-positivist stance.

Yet there was also an aspect of Weberian social theory that reinforced strains of pessimism ultimately to be found in Horkheimer and Adorno's 1947 *Dialectic of Enlightenment* (*Dialektik der Aufklärung*), which documented the tendency of enlightened reason to self-destruct. For Weber, all social action shared the feature of 'instrumental rationality' (*Zweckrationalität*), that is, goal-oriented, strategic action. And it was this instrumental rationality that led to modernity's 'disenchantment' (*Entzauberung*) of the world, and our consequent incarceration in the 'iron cage' of bureaucratic rationalization and technological domination. It is this deformation of the Enlightenment's faith in rationality that strikes the keynote of our selection from *Dialectic of Enlightenment*. The initially optimistic appraisal of reason's power to liberate humanity from prejudice and authority is pessimistically revealed to be just another myth, but a myth that hides its agenda of repression and domination.

Select Bibliography of Horkheimer's Works in English

'Schopenhauer today' in K. H. Wolff and B. Moore Jr (eds), *The Critical Spirit: Essays in Honor of Herbert Marcuse*, Boston: Beacon Press, 1967.
Critical Theory: Selected Essays, New York: Seabury, 1972.
Dialectic of Enlightenment (with Adorno), London: Verso, 1979.
Critique of Instrumental Reason, New York: Seabury, 1974.
Eclipse of Reason, New York: Seabury, 1974.
Dawn and Decline, New York: Seabury, 1978.

THEODOR W. ADORNO

Horkheimer's collaborator in writing *Dialectic of Enlightenment* was Frankfurt-born Theodor Wiesengrund Adorno, who chose to use his maternal surname throughout his professional life. Adorno spent his formative years studying philosophy, music, psychology and sociology at the University of Frankfurt. After receiving a doctorate in philosophy there in 1924, he moved to Vienna in order to study musical composition with Alban Berg and affiliate himself with the avant-garde Schönberg circle. He published a number of articles on Schönberg's music and edited a journal of music criticism while in Vienna.

Adorno subsequently returned to Frankfurt to complete a *Habilitationsschrift* in 1927, 'The concept of the unconscious in the transcendental theory of mind'. More familiarly known as the 'Kant–Freud' thesis, it was rejected by the predominantly Neo-Kantian faculty. Undeterred, he began work on another thesis, *Kierkegaard: The Construction of the Aesthetic*, which was ultimately accepted by the University in 1931 and published in 1933. By this time, however, Adorno had become far more interested in his informal involvement with the Institute of Social Research under Horkheimer's leadership. And although he did not officially become a member of the Institute until 1938, Adorno participated extensively in the evolving project of Frankfurt School critical theory. In addition to *Dialectic of Enlightenment* (1947), some of his most renowned works include *Philosophy of Modern Music* (1949), *Minima Moralia* (1951), *Against Epistemology* (1956), *The Jargon of Authenticity* (1964), *Negative Dialectics* (1966), *Aesthetic Theory* (1970) and a collection of essays in cultural criticism, *Prisms* (1955).

Sharing the same fate as other Jewish members of the Institute who were forced to flee Nazi Germany, Adorno spent four years at Oxford's Merton College (1934–8), and then joined Horkheimer in the United States, remaining there until 1953. During this time, as well as continuing his own work and collaborating with Horkheimer, he participated in a project of collective research on authoritarianism and prejudice which was published in 1950 as *The Authoritarian Personality*. The Institute returned to Frankfurt after the war, once again under the leadership of Horkheimer, and Adorno was invited to become Assistant Director. Upon the retirement of Horkheimer in 1959, Adorno assumed the directorship of the Institute which he held until his death in 1969.

Adorno's published work provides many examples of cultural criticism (*Kulturkritik*) exposing the existence of a 'culture industry' that permeates all aspects of our lives. He points to the pivotal role of mass media, such as television and radio, in distributing and promoting entertainment that numbs the consumer into a lethargic acceptance of whatever is on offer. The result of such cultural impoverishment is an atrophy of critical ability that extends to political and economic issues as well. It should be noted that Adorno himself has often been accused of a certain elitism in his wholesale rejection of all forms of 'popular culture', even jazz, espousing instead an aesthetics of the avant-garde. However, for Adorno, only those artistic efforts that are 'autonomous' enough to clash with bourgeois norms can inspire change.

Throughout his life, Adorno rejected positivistic thinking, which, he claimed, was synonymous with unified science that proceeds by verification, quantification and abstraction. According to Adorno, positivism refuses to negotiate the question of individuality and, more importantly, it impedes an ethical awareness of the particular. Although some critics have claimed that Adorno uses the term 'positivism' rather indiscriminately, he would have responded that positivism is the dominant paradigm of our culture, a paradigm that we have internalized even in our encounters with other human beings. Adorno prefers to engage reality with dialectical thinking, but not along the Hegelian model of a totalization that prioritizes subjectivity. Adorno's negative dialectics supports a theory of 'non-identity thinking' that stresses the resistance to recuperation of that which cannot be simply conceptualized. The unique and material ground of aesthetic experience is paradigmatically non-identical for Adorno. Thus, the category of the subject is never privileged at the expense of otherness and particularity.

Adorno died in 1969 in the midst of finishing what some consider to be his most important work, *Aesthetic Theory*.

MAX HORKHEIMER AND THEODOR W. ADORNO

Select Bibliography of Adorno's Works in English

Prisms, London: Neville Spearman, 1967.

Dialectic of Enlightenment (with Horkheimer), London: Verso, 1979.

The Jargon of Authenticity, London: Routledge & Kegan Paul, 1973.

Negative Dialectics, New York: Seabury, 1973.

Philosophy of Modern Music, London, Sheed & Ward, 1973.

Minima Moralia: Reflections from Damaged Life, London: New Left Books, 1974.

Introduction to the Sociology of Music, New York: Seabury, 1976.

In Search of Wagner, London: New Left Books, 1981.

Against Epistemology: A Metacritique, Cambridge, Mass.: MIT Press, 1982.

Aesthetic Theory, London: Routledge & Kegan Paul, 1984.

Notes to Literature, 2 vols, New York: Columbia University Press, 1992.

The Concept of Enlightenment

IN THE MOST general sense of progressive thought, the Enlightenment has always aimed at liberating men from fear and establishing their sovereignty. Yet the fully enlightened earth radiates disaster triumphant. The program of the Enlightenment was the disenchantment of the world; the dissolution of myths and the substitution of knowledge for fancy. Bacon, the 'father of experimental philosophy',[1] had defined its motives. . . .

Despite his lack of mathematics, Bacon's view was appropriate to the scientific attitude that prevailed after him. The concordance between the mind of man and the nature of things that he had in mind is patriarchal: the human mind, which overcomes superstition, is to hold sway over a disenchanted nature. Knowledge, which is power, knows no obstacles: neither in the enslavement of men nor in compliance with the world's rulers. As with all the ends of bourgeois economy in the factory and on the battlefield, origin is no bar to the dictates of the entrepreneurs: kings, no less directly than businessmen, control technology; it is as democratic as the economic system with which it is bound up. Technology is the essence of this knowledge. It does not work by concepts and images, by the fortunate insight, but refers to method, the exploitation of others' work, and capital. The 'many things' which, according to Bacon, 'are reserved', are themselves no more than instrumental: the radio as a sublimated printing press, the dive bomber as a more effective form of artillery, radio control as a more reliable compass. What men want to learn from nature is how to use it in order wholly to dominate it and other men. That is the only aim. Ruthlessly, in despite of itself, the Enlightenment has extinguished any trace of its own self-consciousness. The only kind of thinking that is sufficiently hard to shatter myths is ultimately self-destructive. In face of the present triumph of the factual mentality, even Bacon's nominalist credo would be suspected of a metaphysical bias and come under the same verdict of vanity that he pronounced on scholastic philosophy. Power and knowledge are synonymous. . . .[2]

For the Enlightenment, whatever does not conform to the rule of computation and utility is suspect. So long as it can develop undisturbed by any outward repression, there is no holding it. In the process, it treats its own ideas of human rights exactly as it does the older universals. Every spiritual resistance it encounters serves merely to increase its strength.[3] Which means that Enlightenment still recognizes itself even in myths. Whatever myths the resistance may appeal to, by virtue of the very fact that they become arguments in the process of opposition, they acknowledge the principle of dissolvent rationality for which they reproach the Enlightenment. Enlightenment is totalitarian.

From *Dialectic of Enlightenment*, London: Verso, 1979.

Enlightenment has always taken the basic principle of myth to be anthropomorphism, the projection onto nature of the subjective.[4] In this view, the supernatural, spirits and demons, are mirror images of men who allow themselves to be frightened by natural phenomena. Consequently the many mythic figures can all be brought to a common denominator, and reduced to the human subject. Oedipus' answer to the Sphinx's riddle: 'It is man!' is the Enlightenment stereotype repeatedly offered as information, irrespective of whether it is faced with a piece of objective intelligence, a bare schematization, fear of evil powers, or hope of redemption. In advance, the Enlightenment recognizes as being and occurrence only what can be apprehended in unity: its ideal is the system from which all and everything follows. Its rationalist and empiricist versions do not part company on that point. Even though the individual schools may interpret the axioms differently, the structure of scientific unity has always been the same. Bacon's postulate of *una scientia universalis*,[5] whatever the number of fields of research, is as inimical to the unassignable as Leibniz's *mathesis universalis* is to discontinuity. The multiplicity of forms is reduced to position and arrangement, history to fact, things to matter. According to Bacon, too, degrees of universality provide an unequivocal logical connection between first principles and observational judgments. De Maistre mocks him for harboring *'une idole d'échelle'*.[6] Formal logic was the major school of unified science. It provided the Enlightenment thinkers with the schema of the calculability of the world. The mythologizing equation of Ideas with numbers in Plato's last writings expresses the longing of all demythologization: number became the canon of the Enlightenment. The same equations dominate bourgeois justice and commodity exchange. 'Is not the rule, *"Si inaequalibus aequalia addas, omnia erunt inaequalia,"* an axiom of justice as well as of the mathematics? And is there not a true coincidence between commutative and distributive justice, and arithmetical and geometrical proportion?'[7] Bourgeois society is ruled by equivalence. It makes the dissimilar comparable by reducing it to abstract quantities. To the Enlightenment, that which does not reduce to numbers, and ultimately to the one, becomes illusion; modern positivism writes it off as literature. Unity is the slogan from Parmenides to Russell. The destruction of gods and qualities alike is insisted upon....

Myth turns into enlightenment, and nature into mere objectivity. Men pay for the increase of their power with alienation from that over which they exercise their power. Enlightenment behaves toward things as a dictator toward men. He knows them in so far as he can manipulate them. The man of science knows things in so far as he can make them. In this way their potentiality is turned to his own ends. In the metamorphosis the nature of things, as a substratum of domination, is revealed as always the same. This identity constitutes the unity of nature....

The principle of immanence, the explanation of every event as repetition, that the Enlightenment upholds against mythic imagination, is the principle of myth itself. That arid wisdom that holds there is nothing new under the sun, because all the pieces in the meaningless game have been played, and all the great thoughts have already been thought, and because all possible discoveries can be construed in advance and all men are decided on adaptation as the means to self-preservation – that dry sagacity merely reproduces the fantastic wisdom that it supposedly rejects: the sanction of fate that in retribution relentlessly remakes what has already been. What was different is equalized. That is the verdict which critically determines the limits of possible experience. . . .

Abstraction, the tool of enlightenment, treats its objects as did fate, the notion of which it rejects: it liquidates them. Under the leveling domination of abstraction (which makes everything in nature repeatable), and of industry (for which abstraction ordains repetition), the freedom themselves finally came to form that 'herd' which Hegel[8] has declared to be the result of the Enlightenment. . . .

Man imagines himself free from fear when there is no longer anything unknown. That determines the course of demythologization, of enlightenment, which compounds the animate with the inanimate just as myth compounds the inanimate with the animate. Enlightenment is mythic fear turned radical. The pure immanence of positivism, its ultimate product, is no more than a so-to-speak universal taboo. Nothing at all may remain outside, because the mere idea of outsideness is the very source of fear. . . .

For science the word is a sign: as sound, image, and word proper it is distributed among the different arts, and is not permitted to reconstitute itself by their addition, by synesthesia, or in the composition of the *Gesamtkunstwerk*. As a system of signs, language is required to resign itself to calculation in order to know nature, and must discard the claim to be like her. As image, it is required to resign itself to mirror-imagery in order to be nature entire, and must discard the claim to know her. With the progress of enlightenment, only authentic works of art were able to avoid the mere imitation of that which already is. The practicable antithesis of art and science, which tears them apart as separate areas of culture in order to make them both manageable as areas of culture ultimately allows them, by dint of their own tendencies, to blend with one another even as exact contraries. In its neo-positivist version, science becomes aestheticism, a system of detached signs devoid of any intention that would transcend the system: it becomes the game which mathematicians have for long proudly asserted is their concern. But the art of integral representability, even in its techniques, subscribed to positive science, and in fact adapts to the world yet again, becoming ideological duplication, partisan reproduction. The separation of sign and image is irremediable. Should unconscious self-satisfaction cause it once again to become hypostatized, then each of the two isolated principles tends toward the destruction of truth.

In the relationship of intuition (i.e. direct perception) and concept, philosophy already discerned the gulf which opened with that separation, and again tries in vain to close it: philosophy, indeed, is defined by this very attempt. For the most part it has stood on the side from which it derives its name. Plato banned poetry with the same gesture that positivism used against the theory of ideas (*Ideenlehre*). With his much-renowned art, Homer carried out no public or private reforms, and neither won a war nor made any discovery. We know of no multitude of followers who might have honored or adored him. Art must first prove its utility.[9] For art, as for the Jews, imitation is proscribed. Reason and religion deprecate and condemn the principle of magic enchantment. Even in resigned self-distancing from real existence, as art, it remains dishonest; its practitioners become travelers, latterday nomads who find no abiding home under the established what-has-come-to-be. Nature must no longer be influenced by approximation, but mastered by labor. The work of art still has something in common with enchantment: it posits its own, self-enclosed area, which is withdrawn from the context of profane existence, and in which special laws apply. Just as in the ceremony the magician first of all marked out the limits of the area where the sacred powers were to come into play, so every work of art describes its own circumference which closes it off from actuality. This very renunciation of influence, which distinguishes art from magical sympathy, retains the magic heritage all the more surely. It places the pure image in contrast to animate existence, the elements of which it absorbs. It is in the nature of the work of art, or aesthetic semblance, to be what the new, terrifying occurrence became in the primitive's magic: the appearance of the whole in the particular. In the work of art that duplication still occurs by which the thing appeared as spiritual, as the expression of *mana*. This constitutes its aura. As an expression of totality art lays claim to the dignity of the absolute. This sometimes causes philosophy to allow it precedence to conceptual knowledge. According to Schelling, art comes into play where knowledge forsakes mankind. For him it is 'the prototype of science, and only where there is art may science enter in.'[10] In his theory, the separation of image and sign is 'wholly canceled by every single artistic representation.'[11] The bourgeois world was but rarely open to such confidence in art. Where it restricted knowledge, it usually did so not for the sake of art, but in order to make room for faith. Through faith the militant religiousness of the new age hoped to reconcile Torquemada, Luther, Mohammed, spirit and real life. But faith is a privative concept: it is destroyed as faith if it does not continually display its contradistinction to, or conformity with, knowledge. Since it is always set upon the restriction of knowledge, it is itself restricted. The attempt of Protestant faith to find, as in prehistory, the transcendental principle of truth (without which belief cannot exist) directly in the word itself, and to reinvest this with symbolic power, has been paid for with obedience to the word, and not to the sacred. As long as faith remains unhesitatingly tied – as friend or foe – to knowledge, it perpetuates the separation in the very course of the struggle to overcome it: its fanaticism is the occasion of its untruth, the objective admission that he who only has faith, for that very reason no longer has it. Bad conscience is its second nature. In the secret consciousness of the deficiency – necessarily inherent in faith – of its immanent contradiction in making reconciliation a vocation, lies the reason why the integrity of all believers has always been a sensitive and dangerous thing. The atrocities of fire and sword, counter-Reformation and Reformation, have occurred not as exaggerations but as realizations of the principle of faith itself. Faith constantly reveals itself to be of the same cut as the world-history which it would dictate to – in modern times, indeed, it becomes its favorite instrument, its particular stratagem. It is not merely the Enlightenment of the eighteenth century that, as Hegel confirmed, is relentless but – as no one knew better than he – the advance of thought itself. The lowest and the highest insight alike manifest that distance from truth which makes apologists liars. The paradoxical nature of faith ultimately degenerates into a swindle, and becomes the myth of the twentieth century; and its irrationality turns it into an instrument of rational administration by the wholly enlightened as they steer society toward barbarism. . . .

Domination lends increased consistency and force to the social whole in which it establishes itself. The division of labor to which domination tends serves the dominated whole for the end of self-preservation. But then the whole as whole, the manifestation of its immanent reason, necessarily leads to the execution of the particular. To the individual, domination appears to be the universal: reason in actuality. Through the division of labor imposed on them, the power of all the members of society – for whom as such there is no other course – amounts over and over again to the realization of the whole, whose rationality is reproduced in this way. What is done to all by the few, always occurs as the subjection of individuals by the many: social repression always exhibits the masks of repression by a collective. It is this unity of the collectivity and domination, and not direct social universality, solidarity, which is expressed in thought forms. By virtue of the claim to universal validity, the philosophic concepts with which Plato and Aristotle represented the world, elevated the conditions they were used to substantiate to the level of true reality. These concepts originated, as Vico puts it,[12] in the market-place of Athens; they reflected with equal clarity the laws of physics, the equality of full citizens and the inferiority of women, children and slaves. Language itself gave what was asserted, the conditions of domination, the universality that they had assumed as the means of intercourse of a bourgeois society. The metaphysical emphasis, and sanction by means of ideas and norms, were no more than a hypostatization of the rigidity and exclusiveness which concepts were generally compelled to assume wherever language united the community of rulers with the giving of orders. As a mere means of reinforcing the social power of language, ideas became all the more superfluous as this power grew, and the language of science prepared the way for their ultimate desuetude. The suggestion of something still akin to the terror of the fetish did not inhere in conscious justification; instead the unity of collectivity and domination is revealed in the universality necessarily assumed by the bad content of language, both metaphysical and scientific. Metaphysical apology betrayed the injustice of the status quo least of all in the incongruence of concept and actuality. In the impartiality of scientific language, that which is powerless has wholly lost any means of expression, and only the given finds its neutral sign. This kind of neutrality is more metaphysical than metaphysics. Ultimately, the Enlightenment consumed not just the symbols but their successors, universal concepts, and spared no remnant of metaphysics apart from the abstract fear of the collective from which it arose. The situation of concepts in the face of the Enlightenment is like that of men of private means in regard to industrial trusts: none can feel safe. . . .

For enlightenment is as totalitarian as any system. Its untruth does not consist in what its romantic enemies have always reproached it for: analytical method, return to elements, dissolution through reflective thought; but instead in the fact that for enlightenment the process is always decided from the start. When in mathematical procedure the unknown becomes the unknown quantity of an equation, this marks it as the well-known even before any value is inserted. Nature, before and after the quantum theory, is that which is to be comprehended mathematically; even what cannot be made to agree, indissolubility and irrationality, is converted by means of mathematical theorems. In the anticipatory identification of the wholly conceived and mathematized world with truth, enlightenment intends to secure itself against the return of the mythic. It confounds thought and mathematics. In this way the latter is, so to speak, released and made into an absolute instance.

> An infinite world, in this case a world of idealities, is conceived as one whose objects do not accede singly, imperfectly, and as if by chance to our cognition, but are attained by a rational, systematically unified method – in a process of infinite progression – so that each object is ultimately apparent according to its full inherent being . . . In the Galilean mathematization of the world, however, *this self-ness* is idealized under the guidance of the new mathematics: in modern terms, it becomes itself a mathematical multiplicity.[13]

Thinking objectifies itself to become an automatic, self-activating process; an impersonation of the machine that it produces itself so that ultimately the machine can replace it. Enlightenment[14] has put aside the classic requirement of thinking about thought – Fichte is its extreme manifestation – because it wants to avoid the precept of dictating practice that Fichte himself wished to obey. Mathematical procedure became, so to speak, the ritual of thinking. In spite of the axiomatic self-restriction, it establishes itself as necessary and objective: it turns thought into a thing, an instrument – which is its own term for it. But this kind of mimesis, in which universal thought is equalized, so turns the actual into the unique, that even atheism itself is subjected to the ban on metaphysics. For positivism, which represents the court of judgment of enlightened reason, to digress into intelligible worlds is no longer merely forbidden, but meaningless prattle. It does not need – fortunately – to be atheistic, because objectified thinking cannot even raise the problem. The positivist censor lets the established cult escape as willingly as art – as a cognition-free special area of social activity; but he will never permit that denial of it which itself claims to be knowledge. For the scientific mind, the separation of thought from business for the purpose of adjusting actuality, departure from the privileged area of real existence, is as insane and self-destructive as the primitive magician would consider stepping out of the magic circle he has prepared for his invocation; in both cases the offense against the taboo will actually result in the malefactor's ruin. The mastery of nature draws the circle into which the criticism of pure reason banished thought. Kant joined the theory of its unceasingly laborious advance into infinity with an insistence on its deficiency and everlasting limitation. His judgment is an oracle. There is no form of being in the world that science could not penetrate, but what can be penetrated by science is not being. According to Kant, philosophic judgment aims at the new; and yet it recognizes nothing new, since it always merely recalls what reason has always deposited in the object. But there is a reckoning for this form of thinking that considers itself secure in the various departments of science – secure from the dreams of a ghost-seer: world domination over nature turns against the thinking subject himself; nothing is left of him but that eternally same *I think* that must accompany all my ideas. Subject and object are both rendered ineffectual. The abstract self, which justifies record-making and systematization, has nothing set over against it but the abstract material which possesses no other quality than to be a substrate of such possession. The equation of spirit and world arises eventually, but only with a mutual restriction of both sides. The reduction of thought to a mathematical apparatus conceals the sanction of the world as its own yardstick. What appears to be the triumph of subjective rationality, the subjection of all reality to logical formalism, is paid for by the obedient subjection of reason to what is directly given. What is abandoned is the whole claim and approach of knowledge: to comprehend the given as such; not merely to determine the abstract spatiotemporal relations of the facts which allow them just to be grasped, but on the contrary to conceive them as the superficies, as mediated conceptual moments which come to fulfillment only in the development of their social, historical, and human significance. The task of cognition does not consist in mere apprehension, classification, and calculation, but in the determinate negation of each immediacy. Mathematical formalism, however, whose medium is number, the most abstract form of the immediate, instead holds thinking firmly to mere immediacy. Factuality wins the day; cognition is restricted to its repetition; and thought becomes mere tautology. The more the machinery of thought subjects existence to itself, the more blind its resignation in reproducing existence. Hence enlightenment returns to mythology, which it never really knew how to elude. . . .

The social work of every individual in bourgeois society is mediated through the principle of self; for one, labor will bring an increased return on capital; for others, the energy for extra labor. But the more the process of self-preservation is effected by the bourgeois division of labor, the more it requires the self-alienation of the individuals who must model their body and soul according to the technical apparatus. This again is taken into account by enlightened thought: in the end the transcendental subject of cognition is apparently abandoned as the last reminiscence of subjectivity and replaced by the much smoother work of automatic control mechanisms. Subjectivity has given way to the logic of the allegedly indifferent rules of the game, in order to dictate all the more unrestrainedly. Positivism, which finally did not spare thought itself, the chimera in a cerebral form, has removed the very last insulating instance between individual behavior and the social norm. The technical process, into which the subject has objectified itself after being removed from the consciousness, is free of the ambiguity of mythic thought as of all meaning altogether, because reason itself has become the mere instrument of the all-inclusive economic apparatus. It serves as a general tool, useful for the manufacture of all other tools, firmly directed toward its end, as fateful as the precisely calculated movement of material production, whose result for mankind is beyond all calculation. At last its old ambition, to be a pure organ of ends, has been realized. The exclusiveness of logical laws originates in this unique functional significance, and ultimately in the compulsive nature of self-preservation. And self-preservation repeatedly culminates in the choice between survival and destruction, apparent again in the principle that of two contradictory propositions only one can be true and only one false. The formalism of this principle, and of the entire logic in which form it is established, derives from the opacity and complexity of interests in a society in which the maintenance of forms and the preservation of individuals coincide only by chance. The derivation of thought from logic ratifies in the lecture room the reification of man in the factory and the office. In this way the taboo encroaches upon the anathematizing power, and enlightenment upon the spirit which it itself comprises. Then, however, nature as true self-preservation is released by the very process which promised to extirpate it, in the individual as in the collective destiny of crisis and armed conflict. If the only norm that remains for theory is the ideal of unified science, practice must be subjected to the irrepressible process of world history. The self that is wholly comprehended by civilization resolves itself in an element of the inhumanity which from the beginning has aspired to evade civilization. The primordial fear of losing one's own name is realized. . . .

The curse of irresistible progress is irresistible regression. This regression is not restricted to the experience of the sensuous world bound up with the circumambient animate, but at the same time affects the self-dominant intellect, which separates from sensuous experience in order to subjugate it. The unification of intellectual functions by means of which domination over the senses is achieved, the resignation of thought to the rise of unanimity, means the impoverishment of thought and of experience: the separation of both areas leaves both impaired. The restriction of thought to organization and administration, practiced by rulers from the cunning Odysseus to the naïve managing directors of today, necessarily implies the restriction which comes upon the great as soon as it is no longer merely a question of manipulating the small. Hence the spirit becomes the very apparatus of domination and self-domination which bourgeois thought has always mistakenly supposed it to be. The stopped ears which the pliable proletarians have retained ever since the time of myth have no advantage over the immobility of the master. The over-maturity of society lives by the immaturity of the dominated. The more complicated and precise the social, economic, and scientific apparatus with whose service the production system has long harmonized the body, the more impoverished the experiences which it can offer. The elimination of qualities, their conversion into functions, is translated from science by means of rationalized modes of labor to the experiential world of nations, and tends to approximate it once more to that of the amphibians. The regression of the masses today is their inability to hear the unheard-of with their own ears, to touch the unapprehended with their own hands – the new form of delusion which deposes every conquered mythic form. Through the mediation of the total society which embraces all relations and emotions, men are once again made to be that against which the evolutionary law of society, the principle of self, had turned: mere species beings, exactly like one another through isolation in the forcibly united collectivity. The oarsmen, who cannot speak to one another, are each of them yoked in the same rhythm as the modern worker in the factory, movie theater, and collective. The actual working conditions in society compel conformism – not the conscious influences which also made the suppressed men dumb and separated them from truth. The impotence of the worker is not merely a stratagem of the rulers, but the logical consequence of the industrial society into which the ancient Fate – in the very course of the effort to escape it – has finally changed.

But this logical necessity is not conclusive. It remains tied to domination, as both its reflection and its tool. Therefore its truth is no less questionable than its evidence is irrefutable. Of course thought has always sufficed concretely to characterize its own equivocation. It is the servant that the master cannot check as he wishes. Domination, ever since men settled down, and later in the commodity society, has become objectified as law and organization and must therefore restrict itself. The instrument achieves independence: the mediating instance of the spirit, independently of the will of the master, modifies the directness of economic injustice. The instruments of domination, which would encompass all – language, weapons, and finally machines – must allow themselves to be encompassed by all. Hence in domination the aspect of rationality prevails as one that is also different from it. The 'objectivity' of the means, which makes it universally available, already implies the criticism of that domination as whose means thought arose. On the way from mythology to logistics, thought has lost the element of self-reflection, and today machinery disables men even as it nurtures them. But in the form of machines the alienated *ratio* moves toward a society which reconciles thought in its fixed form as a material and intellectual apparatus with free, live, thought, and refers to society itself as the real subject of thought. The specific origin of thought and its universal perspective have always been inseparable. Today, with the transformation of the world into industry, the perspective of universality, the social realization of thought, extends so far that in its behalf the rulers themselves disavow thought as mere ideology. The bad conscience of cliques which ultimately embody economic necessity is betrayed in that its revelations, from the intuitions of the Leader to the dynamic *Weltanschauung*, no longer recognize (in marked contrast to earlier bourgeois apologetics) their own misdeeds as necessary consequences of statutory contexts. The mythological lies of mission and destiny which they use as substitutes never declare the whole truth: gone are the objective laws of the market which ruled in the actions of the entrepreneurs and tended toward catastrophe. Instead the conscious decision of the managing directors executes as results (which are more obligatory than the blindest price-mechanisms) the old law of value and hence the destiny of capitalism. The rulers themselves do not believe in any objective necessity, even though they sometimes describe their concoctions thus. They declare themselves to be the engineers of world history. Only the ruled accept as unquestionable necessity the course of development that with every decreed rise in the standard of living makes them so much more powerless. When the standard of living of those who are still employed to service the machines can be assured with a minimal part of the working time available to the rulers of society, the superfluous remainder, the vast mass of the population, is drilled as yet another battalion – additional material to serve the present and future great plans of the system. The masses are fed and quartered as the army of the unemployed. In their eyes, their reduction to mere objects of the administered life, which preforms every sector of modern existence including language and perception, represents objective necessity, against which they believe there is nothing they can do. Misery as the antithesis of power and powerlessness grows immeasurably, together with the capacity to remove all misery permanently. Each individual is unable to penetrate the forest of cliques and institutions which, from the highest levels of command to the last professional rackets, ensure the boundless persistence of status. For the union boss, let alone the director, the proletarian (should he ever come face to face with him) is nothing but a supernumerary example of the mass, while the boss in his turn has to tremble at the thought of his own liquidation.

The absurdity of a state of affairs in which the enforced power of the system over men grows with every step that takes it out of the power of nature, denounces the rationality of the rational society as obsolete. Its necessity is illusive, no less than the freedom of the entrepreneurs who ultimately reveal their compulsive nature in their inevitable wars and contracts. This illusion, in which a wholly enlightened mankind has lost itself, cannot be dissolved by a philosophy which, as the organ of domination, has to choose between command and obedience. Without being able to escape the confusion which still ensnares it in prehistory, it is nevertheless able to recognize the logic of either-or, of consequence and antimony, with which it radically emancipated itself from nature, as this very nature, unredeemed and self-alienated. Thinking, in whose mechanism of compulsion nature is reflected and persists, inescapably reflects its very own self as its own forgotten nature – as a mechanism of compulsion. Ideation is only an instrument. In thought, men distance themselves from nature in order thus imaginatively to present it to themselves – but only in order to determine how it is to be dominated. Like the thing, the material tool, which is held on to in different situations as the same thing, and hence divides the world as the chaotic, manysided, and disparate from the known, one, and identical, the concept is the ideal tool, fit to do service for everything, wherever it can be applied. And so thought becomes illusionary whenever it seeks to deny the divisive function, distancing and objectification. All mystic unification remains deception, the impotently inward trace of the absolved revolution. But while enlightenment maintains its justness against any hypostatization of utopia and unfailingly proclaims domination to be disunion, the dichotomy between subject and object that it will not allow to be obscured becomes the index of the untruth of that dichotomy and of truth. The proscription of superstition has always signified not only the progress of domination but its compromise. Enlightenment is more than enlightenment – the distinct representation of nature in its alienation. In the self-cognition of the spirit as nature in disunion with itself, as in prehistory, nature calls itself to account; no longer directly, as *mana* – that is, with the alias that signifies omnipotence – but as blind and lame. The decline, the forfeiture, of nature consists in the subjugation of nature without which spirit does not exist. Through the decision in which spirit acknowledges itself to be domination and retreats into nature, it abandons the claim to domination which makes it a vassal of nature. Even though in the flight from necessity, in progress and civilization, mankind cannot hold the course without abandoning knowledge itself, at least it no longer mistakes the ramparts that it erects against necessity (the institutions and practices of subjection that have always redounded on society from the subjugation of nature) for guarantees of the freedom to come. Every progress made by civilization has renewed together with domination that prospect of its removal. Whereas, however, real history is woven out of a real suffering that is not lessened in proportion to the growth of means for its abrogation, the realization of the prospect is referred to the notion, the concept. For it does not merely, as science, distance men from nature, but, as the self-consideration of thought that in the form of science remains tied to blind economic tendency, allows the distance perpetuating injustice to be measured. . . .

But to recognize domination, even in thought itself, as unreconciled nature, would mean a slackening of the necessity whose perpetuity socialism itself prematurely confirmed as a concession to reactionary common sense. By elevating necessity to the status of the basis for all time to come, and by idealistically degrading the spirit for ever to the very apex, socialism held on all too surely to the legacy of bourgeois philosophy. Hence the relation of necessity to the realm of freedom would remain merely quantitative and mechanical, and nature, posited as wholly alien – just as in the earliest mythology – would become totalitarian and absorb freedom together with socialism. With the abandonment of thought, which in its reified form of mathematics, machine, and organization avenges itself on the men who have forgotten it, enlightenment has relinquished its own realization. By taking everything unique and individual under its tutelage, it left the uncomprehended whole the freedom, as domination, to strike back at human existence and consciousness by way of things. But true revolutionary practice depends on the intransigence of theory in the face of the insensibility with which society allows thought to ossify. It is not the material prerequisites of fulfillment – liberated technology as such – which jeopardize fulfillment. That is asserted by those sociologists who are again searching for an antidote, and – should it be a collectivist measure – to master the antidote.[15] Guilt is a context of social delusion. The mythic scientific respect of the peoples of the earth for the status quo that they themselves unceasingly produce, itself finally becomes positive fact: the oppressor's fortress in regard to which even revolutionary imagination despises itself as utopism and decays to the condition of pliable trust in the objective tendency of history. As the organ of this kind of adaptation, as a mere construction of means, the Enlightenment is as destructive as its romantic enemies accuse it of being. It comes into its own only when it surrenders the last remaining concordance with the latter and dares to transcend the false absolute, the principle of blind domination. . . .

Today, when Bacon's utopian vision that we should 'command nature by action' – that is, in practice – has been realized on a tellurian scale, the nature of the thralldom that he ascribed to unsubjected nature is clear. It was domination itself. And knowledge, in which Bacon was certain the 'sovereignty of man lieth hid', can now become the dissolution of domination. But in the face of such a possibility, and in the service of the present age, enlightenment becomes wholesale deception of the masses.

NOTES

1 Voltaire, *Lettres Philosophiques, XII, Œuvres Complètes* (Garnier: Paris 1879), Vol. XXII, p. 118.
2 Cf. Bacon, *Novum Organum, Works*, vol. XIV, p. 31.
3 Cf. Hegel, *Phänomenologie des Geistes* (*The Phenomenology of Spirit*), *Werke*, vol. II, pp. 410ff.
4 Xenophanes, Montaigne, Hume, Feuerbach, and Salomon Reinach are at one here. See, for Reinach: *Orpheus*, trans. F. Simmons (London & New York, 1909), pp. 9ff.
5 Bacon, *De Augmentis Scientiarum, Works*, vol. VIII, p. 152.
6 *Les Soirées de Saint-Pétersbourg* (5ième entretien), *Œuvres Complètes* (Lyon, 1891), vol. IV, p. 256.
7 Bacon, *Advancement of Learning, Works*, vol. II, p. 126.
8 *Phänomenologie des Geistes*, p. 424.
9 Cf. Plato, *Republic*, book X.
10 *Erster Entwurf eines Systems der Naturphilosophie*, S. 5, *Werke*, Abt. 1, vol. II p. 623.
11 Ibid., p. 626.
12 Giambattista Vico, *Scienza Nuova (Principles of a New Science of the Common Nature of Nations).*
13 Edmund Husserl, '*Die Krisis der europäischen Wissenschaften und die transzendentale Phänomenologie*', in *Philosophia* (Belgrade, 1936), pp. 95ff.
14 Cf. Schopenhauer, *Parerga und Paralipomena*, vol. II, S. 356; *Werke*, ed. Deussen, vol. V, p. 671.
15 'The supreme question which confronts our generation today – the question to which all other problems are merely corollaries – is whether technology can be brought under control ... Nobody can be sure of the formula by which this end can be achieved ... We must draw on all the resources to which access can be had ...' (*The Rockefeller Foundation. A Review for 1943* [New York, 1944], pp. 33ff.)

14

Walter Benjamin

(1892–1940)

An elusive figure whose works defy facile categorization, Walter Benjamin has become increasingly recognized as a major critical thinker unappreciated during his own lifetime. The son of a Jewish art dealer, he was born in Berlin in 1892. Benjamin was deeply influenced by Gershom Scholem, a brilliant Talmudic scholar and Zionist, as well as by Marxists like Lukács and Brecht. Although Benjamin studied philosophy and literature in Freiburg and Berlin, he never secured an academic post that would have provided him with a dependable income. He submitted his *Habilitationsschrift* to the University of Frankfurt in 1925, 'The origin of German tragic drama', only to have it rejected as too unconventional.

Benjamin, nevertheless, survived as a *flâneur* himself, a wanderer without means who continued to write on topics as diverse as Jewish mysticism and Marxism, in styles as diverse as prose, aphorisms and fragments. He explored surrealism, interrogated Kafka's 'allegories' and completed part of a complex study of Baudelaire and nineteenth-century Paris ('The Arcades Project'). His collected works in German comprise six volumes, while a selection of his shorter works introduced by Hannah Arendt (*Illuminations*), has highlighted Benjamin's importance to contemporary philosophical debates.

In one of his most prophetic essays, 'The work of art in the age of mechanical reproduction' (1936), he makes a distinction between traditional 'auratic' art and 'mechanical' art. According to Benjamin, the 'aura' of authenticity surrounding a work of art that cannot be mechanically reproduced leads to a meditative experience of spiritual integration. A work received in this way maintains the continuity of traditional wisdom in a community by drawing deeply on archetypal, unconscious images that affect the collective psyche. By comparison, 'mechanical' art is atomized into the discrete and fragmented presentations of immediate moments. Electronic mass media can only be experienced in a constantly changing flow of simulated presence that precludes any kind of contemplative activity. There is, therefore, an inevitable loss of 'aura' surrounding original works of art as traditionally encountered. The aesthetic quality surrounding the authentic version of a work evaporates when the technology of photography or filmic image makes multiple copies easily accessible.

Although he remains sympathetic to the value of auratic art, Benjamin also notes the positive effects of enabling a mass audience to encounter such works for the first time in any medium at all, as well as the creative potential for design offered by the new medium of reproduction. In an era when aesthetics serves a political function, as evidenced by the cultic rituals of fascism, tradition becomes a conservative and repressive force. By recognizing, even if not particularly welcoming, the contemporary politicization of art, Benjamin creates a space for revolutionary praxis. Strongly influenced by Brecht's more populist brand of Marxism, Benjamin did not wholly agree with the general disdain of Frankfurt theorists for mass culture. The ritual of traditional aesthetic experience may well be irrevocably altered, but another experience, as yet undefined, must arise in its place.

Benjamin's 'Theses on the philosophy of history' attest to the need for an interpretive strategy that 'brushes history against the grain'. His enigmatic parables and images resist the temptation to view history as a neutral and seamless web, progressing inexorably through 'empty time', yielding a continuous narrative whole. On the contrary, what has been forgotten lies scattered anonymously, crying out for renewed efforts to reveal the truth suppressed by officially legitimated sources. In his words, 'there is no cultural document that is not at the same time a record of barbarism'. Each 'now' (*Jetztzeit*) bears a Messianic potential for revolutionary change that denies the purported homogeneity of historical experience. Benjamin is equally critical of dogmatic Marxism that traces a single line of economic inquiry to arrive at a reductionist account of historical determinism. He counters with a kabbalistic insight that offers forty-nine levels of meaning for every interpretation actually excavated, thus insuring an openness to history that promises redemption rather than closure. Benjamin creates a portrait of the 'angel of history' propelled toward the future by the storm of progress, but still left facing the past, watching the catastrophic 'wreckage upon wreckage' left at its feet. Diving into the wreckage for clues remains our only choice.

Benjamin died fleeing from the Nazis as he attempted to leave France. Stopped at the Spanish border, he took his own life on 25 September 1940.

SELECT BIBLIOGRAPHY OF BENJAMIN'S WORKS IN ENGLISH

Charles Baudelaire: A Lyric Poet in the Era of High Capitalism, London: New Left Books, 1973.

Illuminations, with an introduction by Hannah Arendt, London: Fontana, 1973.

Understanding Brecht, London: New Left Books, 1973.

WALTER BENJAMIN

The Origins of German Tragic Drama, London: New Left Books, 1977.
One Way Street, London: New Left Books, 1979.
Reflections, Essays, Aphorisms, Autobiographical Writings, New York: Schocken Books, 1986.
The Correspondence of Walter Benjamin and Gershom Scholem, 1932–1940, New York: Schocken Books, 1989.

Theses on the Philosophy of History

I

THE STORY IS told of an automaton constructed in such a way that it could play a winning game of chess, answering each move of an opponent with a countermove. A puppet in Turkish attire and with a hookah in its mouth sat before a chessboard placed on a large table. A system of mirrors created the illusion that this table was transparent from all sides. Actually, a little hunchback who was an expert chess player sat inside and guided the puppet's hand by means of strings. One can imagine a philosophical counterpart to this device. The puppet called 'historical materialism' is to win all the time. It can easily be a match for anyone if it enlists the services of theology, which today, as we know, is wizened and has to keep out of sight.

II

'One of the most remarkable characteristics of human nature,' writes Lotze, 'is, alongside so much selfishness in specific instances, the freedom from envy which the present displays toward the future.' Reflection shows us that our image of happiness is thoroughly colored by the time to which the course of our own existence has assigned us. The kind of happiness that could arouse envy in us exists only in the air we have breathed, among people we could have talked to, women who could have given themselves to us. In other words, our image of happiness is indissolubly bound up with the image of redemption. The same applies to our view of the past, which is the concern of history. The past carries with it a temporal index by which it is referred to redemption. There is a secret agreement between past generations and the present one. Our coming was expected on earth. Like every generation that preceded us, we have been endowed with a *weak* Messianic power, a power to which the past has a claim. That claim cannot be settled cheaply. Historical materialists are aware of that.

III

A chronicler who recites events without distinguishing between major and minor ones acts in accordance with the following truth: nothing that has ever happened should be regarded as lost for history. To be sure, only a redeemed mankind receives the fullness of its past – which is to say, only

From *Illuminations*, London: Fontana, 1973.

for a redeemed mankind has its past become citable in all its moments. Each moment it has lived becomes a *citation à l'ordre du jour* – and that day is Judgment Day.

IV

> Seek for food and clothing first, then the Kingdom of God shall be added unto you.
>
> (Hegel, 1807)

The class struggle, which is always present to a historian influenced by Marx, is a fight for the crude and material things without which no refined and spiritual things could exist. Nevertheless, it is not in the form of the spoils which fall to the victor that the latter make their presence felt in the class struggle. They manifest themselves in this struggle as courage, humor, cunning, and fortitude. They have retroactive force and will constantly call in question every victory, past and present, of the rulers. As flowers turn toward the sun, by dint of a secret heliotropism the past strives to turn toward that sun which is rising in the sky of history. A historical materialist must be aware of this most inconspicuous of all transformations.

V

The true picture of the past flits by. The past can be seized only as an image which flashes up at the instant when it can be recognized and is never seen again. 'The truth will not run away from us': in the historical outlook of historicism these words of Gottfried Keller mark the exact point where historical materialism cuts through historicism. For every image of the past that is not recognized by the present as one of its own concerns threatens to disappear irretrievably. (The good tidings which the historian of the past brings with throbbing heart may be lost in a void the very moment he opens his mouth.)

VI

To articulate the past historically does not mean to recognize it 'the way it really was' (Ranke). It means to seize hold of a memory as it flashes up at a moment of danger. Historical materialism wishes to retain that image of the past which unexpectedly appears to man singled out by history at a moment of danger. The danger affects both the content of the tradition and its receivers. The same threat hangs over both: that of becoming a tool of the ruling classes. In every era the attempt must be made anew to wrest tradition away from a conformism that is about to overpower it. The Messiah comes not only as the redeemer, he comes as the subduer of Antichrist. Only that historian will have the gift of fanning the spark of hope in the past who is firmly convinced that *even the dead* will not be safe from the enemy if he wins. And this enemy has not ceased to be victorious.

VII

> Consider the darkness and the great cold
> In this vale which resounds with mysery.
> (Brecht, *The Threepenny Opera*)

To historians who wish to relive an era, Fustel de Coulanges recommends that they blot out everything they know about the later course of history. There is no better way of characterizing the method with which historical materialism has broken. It is a process of empathy whose origin is the indolence of the heart, *acedia*, which despairs of grasping and holding the genuine historical image as it flares up briefly. Among medieval theologians it was regarded as the root cause of sadness. Flaubert, who was familiar with it, wrote: '*Peu de gens devineront combien il a fallu être triste pour ressusciter Carthage.*'[1] The nature of this sadness stands out more clearly if one asks with whom the adherents of historicism actually empathize. The answer is inevitable: with the victor. And all rulers are the heirs of those who conquered before them. Hence, empathy with the victor invariably benefits the rulers. Historical materialists know what that means. Whoever has emerged victorious participates to this day in the triumphal procession in which the present rulers step over those who are lying prostrate. According to traditional practice, the spoils are carried along in the procession. They are called cultural treasures, and a historical materialist views them with cautious detachment. For without exception the cultural treasures he surveys have an origin which he cannot contemplate without horror. They owe their existence not only to the efforts of the great minds and talents who have created them, but also to the anonymous toil of their contemporaries. There is no document of civilization which is not at the same time a document of barbarism. And just as such a document is not free of barbarism, barbarism taints also the manner in which it was transmitted from one owner to another. A historical materialist therefore dissociates himself from it as far as possible. He regards it as his task to brush history against the grain.

VIII

The tradition of the oppressed teaches us that the 'state of emergency' in which we live is not the exception but the rule. We must attain to a conception of history that is in keeping with this insight. Then we shall clearly realize that it is our task to bring about a real state of emergency, and this will improve our position in the struggle against Fascism. One reason why Fascism has a chance is that in the name of progress its opponents treat it as a historical norm. The current amazement that the things we are experiencing are 'still' possible in the twentieth century is *not* philosophical. This amazement is not the beginning of knowledge – unless it is the knowledge that the view of history which gives rise to it is untenable.

IX

Mein Flügel ist zum Schwung bereit,
ich kehrte gern zurück,
denn blieb ich auch lebendige Zeit,
ich hätte wenig Glück.

(Gerhard Scholem, 'Gruss vom Angelus')[2]

A Klee painting named 'Angelus Novus' shows an angel looking as though he is about to move away from something he is fixedly contemplating. His eyes are staring, his mouth is open, his wings are spread. This is how one pictures the angel of history. His face is turned toward the past. Where we perceive a chain of events, he sees one single catastrophe which keeps piling wreckage upon wreckage and hurls it in front of his feet. The angel would like to stay, awaken the dead, and make whole what has been smashed. But a storm is blowing from Paradise; it has got caught in his wings with such violence that the angel can no longer close them. This storm irresistibly propels him into the future to which his back is turned, while the pile of debris before him grows skyward. This storm is what we call progress.

X

The themes which monastic discipline assigned to friars for meditation were designed to turn them away from the world and its affairs. The thoughts which we are developing here originate from similar considerations. At a moment when the politicians in whom the opponents of Fascism had placed their hopes are prostrate and confirm their defeat by betraying their own cause, these observations are intended to disentangle the political worldlings from the snares in which the traitors have entrapped them. Our consideration proceeds from the insight that the politicians' stubborn faith in progress, their confidence in their 'mass basis', and, finally, their servile integration in an uncontrollable apparatus have been three aspects of the same thing. It seeks to convey an idea of the high price our accustomed thinking will have to pay for a conception of history that avoids any complicity with the thinking to which these politicians continue to adhere.

XI

The conformism which has been part and parcel of Social Democracy from the beginning attaches not only to its political tactics but to its economic views as well. It is one reason for its later breakdown. Nothing has corrupted the German working class so much as the notion that it was moving with the current. It regarded technological developments as the fall of the stream with which it thought it was moving. From there it was but a step to the illusion that the factory work which was supposed to tend toward technological progress constituted a political achievement. The old Protestant ethics of work was resurrected among German workers in secularized form. The Gotha Program[3] already bears traces of this confusion, defining labor as 'the source of all wealth and all culture'. Smelling a rat, Marx countered that '... the man who possesses no other property than his labor power' must of necessity become 'the slave of other men who have made themselves the owners. ...' However, the confusion spread, and soon thereafter Josef Dietzgen proclaimed: 'The savior of modern times is called work. The ... improvement ... of labor constitutes the wealth which is now able to accomplish what no redeemer has ever been able to do.' This vulgar-Marxist conception of the nature of labor bypasses the question of how its products might benefit the workers while still not being at their disposal. It recognizes only the progress in the mastery of nature, not the retrogression of society; it already displays the technocratic features later encountered in Fascism. Among these is a conception of nature which differs ominously from the one in the Socialist utopias before the 1848 revolution. The new conception of labor amounts to the exploitation of nature, which with naïve complacency is contrasted with the exploitation of the proletariat. Compared with this positivistic conception, Fourier's fantasies, which have so often been ridiculed, prove to be surprisingly sound. According to Fourier, as a result of efficient co-operative labor, four moons would illuminate the earthly night, the ice would recede from the poles, sea water would no longer taste salty, and beasts of prey would do man's bidding. All this illustrates a kind of labor which, far from exploiting nature, is capable of delivering her of the creations which lie dormant in her womb as potentials. Nature, which, as Dietzgen puts it, 'exists gratis', is a complement to the corrupted conception of labor.

XII

> We need history, but not the way a spoiled loafer in the garden
> of knowledge needs it.
> > (Nietzsche, *Of The Use and Abuse of History*)

Not man or men but the struggling, oppressed class itself is the depository of historical knowledge. In Marx it appears as the last enslaved class, as the avenger that completes the task of liberation in the name of generations of the downtrodden. This conviction, which had a brief resurgence in the Spartacist group,[4] has always been objectionable to Social Democrats. Within three decades they managed virtually to erase the name of Blanqui, though it had been the rallying sound that had reverberated through the preceding century. Social Democracy thought fit to assign to the working class the role of the redeemer of future generations, in this way cutting the sinews of its greatest strength. This training made the working class forget both its hatred and its spirit of sacrifice, for both are nourished by the image of enslaved ancestors rather than that of liberated grandchildren.

XIII

> Every day our cause becomes clearer and people get smarter.
> > (Wilhelm Dietzgen, *Die Religion der Sozialdemokratie*)

Social Democratic theory, and even more its practice, have been formed by a conception of progress which did not adhere to reality but made dogmatic claims. Progress as pictured in the minds of Social Democrats was, first of all, the progress of mankind itself (and not just advances in men's ability and knowledge). Secondly, it was something boundless, in keeping with the infinite perfectibility of mankind. Thirdly, progress was regarded as irresistible, something that automatically pursued a straight or spiral course. Each of these predicates is controversial and open to criticism. However, when the chips are down, criticism must penetrate beyond these predicates and focus on something that they have in common. The concept of the historical progress of mankind cannot be sundered from the concept of its progression through a homogeneous, empty time. A critique of the concept of such a progression must be the basis of any criticism of the concept of progress itself.

XIV

Origin is the goal.

(Karl Kraus, Worte in Versen, Vol. 1)

History is the subject of a structure whose site is not homogeneous, empty time, but time filled by the presence of the now [*Jetztzeit*].[5] Thus, to Robespierre ancient Rome was a past charged with the time of the now which he blasted out of the continuum of history. The French Revolution viewed itself as Rome reincarnate. It evoked ancient Rome the way fashion evokes costumes of the past. Fashion has a flair for the topical, no matter where it stirs in the thickets of long ago; it is a tiger's leap into the past. This jump, however, takes place in an arena where the ruling class gives the commands. The same leap in the open air of history is the dialectical one, which is how Marx understood the revolution.

XV

The awareness that they are about to make the continuum of history explode is characteristic of the revolutionary classes at the moment of their action. The great revolution introduced a new calendar. The initial day of a calendar serves as a historical time-lapse camera. And, basically, it is the same day that keeps recurring in the guise of holidays, which are days of remembrance. Thus the calendars do not measure time as clocks do; they are monuments of a historical consciousness of which not the slightest trace has been apparent in Europe in the past hundred years. In the July revolution an incident occurred which showed this consciousness still alive. On the first evening of fighting it turned out that the clocks in towers were being fired on simultaneously and independently from several places in Paris. An eye-witness, who may have owed his insight to the rhyme, wrote as follows:

> Qui le croirait! on dit, qu'irrités contre l'heure
> De nouveaux Josués au pied de chaque tour,
> Tiraient sur les cadrans pour arrêter le jour.[6]

XVI

A historical materialist cannot do without the notion of a present which is not a transition, but in which time stands still and has come to a stop. For this notion defines the present in which he himself is writing history. Historicism gives the 'eternal' image of the past; historical materialism supplies a unique experience with the past. The historical materialist leaves it to others to be drained by the whore called 'Once upon a time' in historicism's bordello. He remains in control of his powers, man enough to blast open the continuum of history.

XVII

Historicism rightly culminates in universal history. Materialistic historiography differs from it as to method more clearly than from any other kind. Universal history has no theoretical armature. Its method is additive; it musters a mass of data to fill the homogeneous, empty time. Materialistic historiography, on the other hand, is based on a constructive principle. Thinking involves not only the flow of thoughts, but their arrest as well. Where thinking suddenly stops in a configuration pregnant with tensions, it gives that configuration a shock, by which it crystallizes into a monad. A historical materialist approaches a historical subject only where he encounters it as a monad. In this structure he recognizes the sign of a Messianic cessation of happening, or, put differently, a revolutionary chance in the fight for the oppressed past. He takes cognizance of it in order to blast a specific era out of the homogeneous course of history – blasting a specific life out of the era or a specific work out of the lifework. As a result of this method the lifework is preserved in this work and at the same time canceled;[7] in the lifework, the era; and in the era, the entire course of history. The nourishing fruit of the historically understood contains time as a precious but tasteless seed.

XVIII

'In relation to the history of organic life on earth,' writes a modern biologist, 'the paltry fifty millennia of *homo sapiens* constitute something like two seconds at the close of a twenty-four-hour day. On this scale, the history of civilized mankind would fill one-fifth of the last second of the last hour.' The present, which, as a model of Messianic time, comprises the entire history of mankind in an enormous abridgment, coincides exactly with the stature which the history of mankind has in the universe.

A

Historicism contents itself with establishing a causal connection between various moments in history. But no fact that is a cause is for that very reason historical. It became historical posthumously, as it were, through events that may be separated from it by thousands of years. A historian who takes this as his point of departure stops telling the sequence of events like the beads of a rosary. Instead, he grasps the constellation which his own era has formed with a definite earlier one. Thus he establishes a conception of the present as the 'time of the now' which is shot through with chips of Messianic time.

B

The soothsayers who found out from time what it had in store certainly did not experience time as either homogeneous or empty. Anyone who keeps this in mind will perhaps get an idea of how past times were experienced in remembrance – namely, in just the same way. We know that the Jews were prohibited from investigating the future. The Torah and the prayers instruct them in remembrance, however. This stripped the future of its magic, to which all those succumb who turn to the soothsayers for enlightenment. This does not imply, however, that for the Jews the future turned into homogeneous, empty time. For every second of time was the strait gate through which the Messiah might enter.

NOTES

1 'Few will be able to guess how sad one had to be in order to resuscitate Carthage.'
2 My wing is ready for flight,
   I would like to turn back,
   If I stayed timeless time,
   I would have little luck.
3 The Gotha Congress of 1875 united the two German Socialist parties, one led by Ferdinand Lassalle, the other by Karl Marx and Wilhelm Liebknecht. The program, drafted by Liebknecht and Lassalle, was severely attacked by Marx in London. See his 'Critique of the Gotha Program'.
4 Leftist group, founded by Karl Liebknecht and Rosa Luxemburg at the beginning of World War I in opposition to the pro-war policies of the German Socialist party, later absorbed by the Communist party.
5 Benjamin says '*Jetztzeit*' and indicates by the quotation marks that he does not simply mean an equivalent to *Gegenwart*, that is, present. He clearly is thinking of the mystical *nunc stans*.
6 Who would have believed it! we are told that new Joshuas
   at the foot of every tower, as though irritated with
   time itself, fired at the dials in order to stop the day.
7 The Hegelian term *aufheben* in its threefold meaning: to preserve, to elevate, to cancel.

15

Herbert Marcuse

(1898–1979)

A critical theorist of international renown, Marcuse was born in Berlin to an assimilated Jewish family in 1898. At an early age he became politically involved with the Social Democratic Party, and was barely twenty-one years old in 1919 when the German revolution he ardently supported was crushed in the streets of Berlin. Thereafter, although still dedicated to political and social change, Marcuse chose to express this commitment by his prolific and wide-ranging contributions to philosophy, aesthetics and psychoanalytic theory. In his 1922 doctorate, 'The German artist-novel' (*Künstlerroman*), he explored a recurring thematic in his later work, i.e. the aesthetics of alienation that remind us of a utopian, 'anticipatory memory' of a better past.

He studied philosophy with both Husserl and Heidegger at the University of Freiburg, finishing the prototype of what was to become his first published work, entitled 'Contributions to a phenomenology of historical materialism' (1928). Throughout most of his life, Marcuse remained a Hegelian-Marxist, always recognizing the dialectical need for both critical negation and utopian affirmation. His works include *Hegel's Ontology* (1932), *Reason and Revolution: Hegel and the Rise of Social Theory* (1941), *Eros and Civilization: A Philosophical Inquiry into Freud* (1955), *One-Dimensional Man* (1964), *An Essay on Liberation* (1969), *Counterrevolution and Revolt* (1972) and *The Aesthetic Dimension: Toward a Critique of Marxist Aesthetics* (1978).

Marcuse became a member of the Institute of Social Research at the time of the Nazi rise to power in 1933, going into exile with other members of the Institute. He followed Horkheimer to Geneva and New York, and continued working with the Institute until 1940. During the ensuing decade, Marcuse's knowledge of Eastern European affairs proved invaluable for his work with the US State Department. He remained in the United States, teaching at Columbia University, Harvard University, Brandeis University in Boston (1954–67) and the University of California. In the midst of a positivistic milieu, Marcuse creatively deployed the Hegelian and Marxist dialectic of his own Continental tradition to address the crucial problems of racial and ethnic prejudice, fascism, alienation and mass culture in the context of advanced capitalism. He thereby became one of the most influential thinkers inspiring New Left politics during the turbulent 1960s and 1970s.

Marcuse's 'critical social theory' synthesized and related insights he had drawn from his diverse background in phenomenology, existentialism, humanist Marxism and Freudian psychoanalysis. He first attempted a 'dialectical phenomenology' that sought to combine the concrete analysis of human existence at the root of both the existentialist and Marxist impulse. Striking the keynotes of subjectivity and human consciousness, he emphasized the correlation between aesthetic expression and the project of liberation. Marcuse counselled 'The Great Refusal' of art which resisted the domination of a repressive social reality. He especially critiqued the homogeneity and reification fostered by unbalanced technological growth in contemporary industrial societies, an effect that inevitably produces 'one-dimensional' lives for those inhabiting these societies. Stereotyped values are accepted without question, and an inability to imagine alternative, utopian possibilities impoverishes the future as well as the present.

The prefatory remarks presented in our selection from *Eros and Civilization* exemplify Marcuse's revision of Freudian psychoanalytic theory. For Freud, the very existence of civilized society is founded upon the permanent repression of libidinal instincts that can potentially threaten social harmony and interaction. In the Freudian corpus, the gratification of erotic drives toward pleasure must be repressed and sacrificed to cultural development if civilization is to flourish. While Marcuse would agree with Freud that such a scenario could have pertained under conditions of scarcity and hardship, he rejects the need for the same kind of repressive social constraints under technologically advanced capitalism. Automation replaces the need for some of the most dehumanizing forms of 'alienated labour', thus freeing the body from its role as a mere instrument of production. Libidinal and erotic instincts can be channelled to support social activities that liberate rather than repress. We are presented, according to Marcuse, with 'reality and performance' principles in the guise of technical rationality already burdened by a 'surplus repression' beyond what is needed to support civilization. By suggesting a possible confluence of Freudian 'reality and pleasure' principles, Marcuse appeals to a potentially creative, dynamic and instinctual source of utopian change.

Perhaps Marcuse was disappointed by the short-lived resistance of 1960s radicalism, once so inspired by his celebration of eros. Before his death in 1979, he turned again to the 'estranging' power of 'the aesthetic dimension', where art transcends domination and beckons us to follow the promise of freedom.

SELECT BIBLIOGRAPHY OF MARCUSE'S WORKS IN ENGLISH

Reason and Revolution: Hegel and the Rise of Social Theory, Oxford: Oxford University Press, 1941.

Eros and Civilization: A Philosophical Inquiry into Freud, Boston: Beacon Press, 1955.

Soviet Marxism: A Critical Analysis, New York: Columbia University Press, 1958.

One-Dimensional Man: Studies in the Ideology of Advanced Industrial Society, Boston: Beacon Press, 1964.

Negations: Essays in Critical Theory, Boston: Beacon Press, 1968.

An Essay on Liberation, Boston: Beacon Press, 1969.

Five Lectures, Boston: Beacon Press, 1970.

Counterrevolution and Revolt, Boston: Beacon Press, 1972.

Studies in Critical Philosophy, Boston: Beacon Press, 1973.

Revolution or Reform: A Confrontation (with Karl Popper), ed. A. Ferguson, Chicago: Chicago University Press, 1976.

The Aesthetic Dimension: Toward a Critique of Marxist Aesthetics, Boston: Beacon Press, 1978.

Hegel's Ontology, Cambridge, Mass.: MIT Press, 1987.

Political Preface 1966 to *Eros and Civilization*

EROS AND CIVILIZATION: the title expressed an optimistic, euphemistic, even positive thought, namely, that the achievements of advanced industrial society would enable man to reverse the direction of progress, to break the fatal union of productivity and destruction, liberty and repression – in other words, to learn the gay science (*gaya sciencia*) of how to use the social wealth for shaping man's world in accordance with his Life Instincts, in the concerted struggle against the purveyors of Death. This optimism was based on the assumption that the rationale for the continued acceptance of domination no longer prevailed, that scarcity and the need for toil were only 'artificially' perpetuated – in the interest of preserving the system of domination. I neglected or minimized the fact that this 'obsolescent' rationale had been vastly strengthened (if not replaced) by even more efficient forms of social control. The very forces which rendered society capable of pacifying the struggle for existence served to repress in the individuals the need for such a liberation. Where the high standard of living does not suffice for reconciling the people with their life and their rulers, the 'social engineering' of the soul and the 'science of human relations' provide the necessary libidinal cathexis. In the affluent society, the authorities are hardly forced to justify their dominion. They deliver the goods; they satisfy the sexual and the aggressive energy of their subjects. Like the unconscious, the destructive power of which they so successfully represent, they are this side of good and evil, and the principle of contradiction has no place in their logic.

As the affluence of society depends increasingly on the uninterrupted production and consumption of waste, gadgets, planned obsolescence, and means of destruction, the individuals have to be adapted to these requirements in more than the traditional ways. The 'economic whip', even in its most refined forms, seems no longer adequate to insure the continuation of the struggle for existence in today's outdated organization, nor do the laws and patriotism seem adequate to insure active popular support for the ever more dangerous expansion of the system. Scientific management of instinctual needs has long since become a vital factor in the reproduction of the system: merchandise which has to be bought and used is made into objects of the libido; and the national Enemy who has to be fought and hated is distorted and inflated to such an extent that he can activate and satisfy aggressiveness in the depth dimension of the unconscious. Mass democracy provides the political paraphernalia for effectuating this introjection of the Reality Principle; it not only permits the people (up to a point) to choose their own masters and to participate

From *Eros and Civilization: A Philosophical Inquiry into Freud*, Boston: Beacon Press, 1966.

(up to a point) in the government which governs them – it also allows the masters to disappear behind the technological veil of the productive and destructive apparatus which they control, and it conceals the human (and material) costs of the benefits and comforts which it bestows upon those who collaborate. The people, efficiently manipulated and organized, are free; ignorance and impotence, introjected heteronomy, is the price of their freedom.

It makes no sense to talk about liberation to free men – and we are free if we do not belong to the oppressed minority. And it makes no sense to talk about surplus repression when men and women enjoy more sexual liberty than ever before. But the truth is that this freedom and satisfaction are transforming the earth into hell. The inferno is still concentrated in certain far away places: Vietnam, the Congo, South Africa, and in the ghettos of the 'affluent society': in Mississippi and Alabama, in Harlem. These infernal places illuminate the whole. It is easy and sensible to see in them only pockets of poverty and misery in a growing society capable of eliminating them gradually and without a catastrophe. This interpretation may even be realistic and correct. The question is: eliminated at what cost – not in dollars and cents, but in human lives and in human freedom?

I hesitate to use the word – freedom – because it is precisely in the name of freedom that crimes against humanity are being perpetrated. This situation is certainly not new in history: poverty and exploitation were products of economic freedom; time and again, people were liberated all over the globe by their lords and masters, and their new liberty turned out to be submission, not to the rule of law but to the rule of the law of the others. What started as subjection by force soon became 'voluntary servitude', collaboration in reproducing a society which made servitude increasingly rewarding and palatable. The reproduction, bigger and better, of the same ways of life came to mean, ever more clearly and consciously, the closing of those other possible ways of life which could do away with the serfs and the masters, with the productivity of repression.

Today, this union of freedom and servitude has become 'natural' and a vehicle of progress. Prosperity appears more and more as the prerequisite and by-product of a self-propelling productivity ever seeking new outlets for consumption and for destruction, in outer and inner space, while being restrained from 'overflowing' into the areas of misery – at home and abroad. As against this amalgam of liberty and aggression, production and destruction, the image of human freedom is dislocated: it becomes the project of the *subversion of this sort of progress*. Liberation of the instinctual needs for peace and quiet, of the 'asocial' autonomous Eros presupposes liberation from repressive affluence: a reversal in the direction of progress.

It was the thesis of *Eros and Civilization*, more fully developed in my *One Dimensional Man*, that man could avoid the fate of a Welfare-Through-Warfare State only by achieving a new starting point where he could reconstruct the productive apparatus without that 'innerworldly asceticism' which provided the mental basis for domination and exploration. This image of man was the determinate negation of Nietzsche's superman: man intelligent enough and healthy enough to dispense with all heroes and heroic virtues, man without the impulse to live dangerously, to meet the challenge; man with the good conscience to make life an end-in-itself, to live in joy a life without fear. 'Polymorphous sexuality' was the term which I used to indicate that the new direction of progress would depend completely on the opportunity to activate repressed or arrested *organic*, biological needs: to make the human body an instrument of pleasure rather than labor. The old formula, the development of prevailing needs and faculties, seemed to be inadequate; the emergence of new, qualitatively different needs and faculties seemed to be the prerequisite, the content of liberation.

The idea of such a new Reality Principle was based on the assumption that the material (technical) preconditions for its development were either established, or could be established in the advanced industrial societies of our time. It was self-understood that the translation of technical capabilities into reality would mean a revolution. But the very scope and effectiveness of the democratic introjection have suppressed the historical subject, the agent of revolution: free people are not in need of liberation, and the oppressed are not strong enough to liberate themselves. These conditions redefine the concept of Utopia: liberation is the most realistic, the most concrete of all historical possibilities and at the same time the most rationally and effectively repressed – the most abstract and remote possibility. No philosophy, no theory can undo the democratic introjection of the masters into their subjects. When, in the more or less affluent societies, productivity has reached a level at which the masses participate in its benefits, and at which the opposition is effectively and democratically 'contained', then the conflict between master and slave is also effectively contained. Or rather it has changed its social location. It exists, and explodes, in the revolt of the backward countries against the intolerable heritage of colonialism and its prolongation by neo-colonialism. The Marxian concept stipulated that only those who were free from the blessings of capitalism could possibly change it into a free society: those whose existence was the very negation of capitalist property could become the historical agents of liberation. In the international arena, the Marxian concept regains its full validity. To the degree to which the exploitative societies have become global powers, to the degree to which the new independent nations have become the battlefield of their interests, the 'external' forces of rebellion have ceased to be extraneous forces: they are the enemy within the system. This does not make these rebels the messengers of humanity. By themselves, they are not (as little as the Marxian proletariat was) the representatives of freedom. Here too, the Marxian concept applies according to which the international proletariat would get its intellectual armor from outside: the 'lightning of thought' would strike the '*naiven Volksboden.*' Grandiose ideas about the union of theory and practice do injustice to the feeble beginnings of such a union. Yet the revolt in the backward countries has found a response in the advanced countries where youth is in protest against repression in affluence and war abroad.

Revolt against the false fathers, teachers, and heroes – solidarity with the wretched of the earth: is there any 'organic' connection between the two facets of the protest? There seems to be an all but instinctual solidarity. The revolt at home against home seems largely impulsive, its targets hard to define: nausea caused by 'the way of life', revolt as a matter of physical and mental hygiene. The body against 'the machine' – not against the mechanism constructed to make life safer and milder, to attenuate the cruelty of nature, but against the machine which has taken over the mechanism: the political machine, the corporate machine, the cultural and educational machine which has welded blessing and curse into one rational whole. The whole has become too big, its cohesion too strong, its functioning too efficient – does the power of the negative concentrate in still partly unconquered, primitive, elemental forces? The body against the machine: men, women, and children fighting, with the most primitive tools, the most brutal and destructive machine of all times and keeping it in check – does guerrilla warfare define the revolution of our time?

Historical backwardness may again become the historical chance of turning the wheel of progress to another direction. Technical and scientific overdevelopment stands refuted when the radar-equipped bombers, the chemicals, and the 'special forces' of the affluent society are let loose on the poorest of the earth, on their shacks, hospitals, and rice fields. The 'accidents' reveal the substance: they tear the technological veil behind which the real powers are hiding. The capability to overkill and to overburn, and the mental behavior that goes with it are by-products of the development of the productive forces within a system of exploitation and repression; they seem to become more productive the more comfortable the system becomes to its privileged subjects. The affluent society has now demonstrated that it is a society at war; if its citizens have not noticed it, its victims certainly have.

The historical advantage of the late-comer, of technical backwardness, may be that of skipping the stage of the affluent society. Backward peoples by their poverty and weakness may be forced to forego the aggressive and wasteful use of science and technology, to keep the productive apparatus *à la mesure de l'homme*, under his control, for the satisfaction and development of vital individual and collective needs.

For the overdeveloped countries, this chance would be tantamount to the abolition of the conditions under which man's labor perpetuates, as self-propelling power, his subordination to the productive apparatus, and, with it, the obsolete forms of the struggle for existence. The abolition of these forms is, just as it has always been, the task of political action, but there is a decisive difference in the present situation. Whereas previous revolutions brought about a larger and more rational development of the productive forces, in the overdeveloped societies of today, revolution would mean reversal of this trend: elimination of overdevelopment, and of its repressive rationality. The rejection of affluent productivity, far from being a commitment to purity, simplicity, and 'nature', might be the token (and weapon) of a higher stage of human development, based on the achievements of the technological society. As the production of wasteful and destructive goods is discontinued (a stage which would mean the end of capitalism in all its forms) – the somatic and mental mutilations inflicted on man by this production may be undone. In other words, the shaping of the environment, the transformation of nature, may be propelled by the liberated rather than the repressed Life Instincts, and aggression would be subjected to their demands.

The historical chance of the backward countries is in the absence of conditions which make for repressive exploitative technology and industrialization for aggressive productivity. The very fact that the affluent warfare state unleashes its annihilating power on the backward countries illuminates the magnitude of the threat. In the revolt of the backward peoples, the rich societies meet, in an elemental and brutal form, not only a social revolt in the traditional sense, but also an instinctual revolt – biological hatred. The spread of guerrilla warfare at the height of the technological century is a symbolic event: the energy of the human body rebels against intolerable repression and throws itself against the engines of repression. Perhaps the rebels know nothing about the ways of organizing a society, of constructing a socialist society; perhaps they are terrorized by their own leaders who know something about it, but the rebels' frightful existence is in total need of liberation, and their freedom is the contradiction to the overdeveloped societies.

Western civilization has always glorified the hero, the sacrifice of life for the city, the state, the nation; it has rarely asked the question of whether the established city, state, nation were worth the sacrifice. The taboo on the unquestionable prerogative of the whole has always been maintained and enforced, and it has been maintained and enforced the more brutally the more the whole was supposed to consist of free individuals. The question is now being asked – asked from without – and it is taken up by those who refuse to play the game of the affluents – the question of whether the abolition of this whole is not the precondition for the emergence of a truly human city, state, nation.

The odds are overwhelmingly on the side of the powers that be. What is romantic is not the positive evaluation of the liberation movements in the backward countries, but the positive evaluation of their prospects. There is no reason why science, technology, and money should not again do the job of destruction, and then the job of reconstruction in their own image. The price of progress is frightfully high, but we shall overcome. Not only the deceived victims but also their chief of state have said so. And yet there are photographs that show a row of half naked corpses laid out for the victors in Vietnam: they resemble in all details the pictures of the starved, emasculated corpses of Auschwitz and Buchenwald. Nothing and nobody can ever overcome these deeds, nor the sense of guilt which reacts in further aggression. But aggression can be turned against the aggressor. The strange myth according to which the unhealing wound can only be healed by the weapon that afflicted the wound has not yet been validated in history: the violence which breaks the chain of violence may start a new chain. And yet, in and against this continuum, the fight will continue. It is not the struggle of Eros against Thanatos, because the established society too has its Eros: it protects, perpetuates, and enlarges life. And it is not a bad life for those who comply and repress. But in the balance, the general presumption is that aggressiveness in defense of life is less detrimental to the Life Instincts than aggressiveness in aggression.

In defense of life: the phrase has explosive meaning in the affluent society. It involves not only the protest against neo-colonial war and slaughter, the burning of draft cards at the risk of prison, the fight for civil rights, but also the refusal to speak the dead language of affluence, to wear the clean clothes, to enjoy the gadgets of affluence, to go through the education for affluence. The new bohème, the beatniks and hipsters, the peace creeps – all these 'decadents' now have become what decadence probably always was: poor refuge of defamed humanity.

Can we speak of a juncture between the erotic and political dimension?

In and against the deadly efficient organization of the affluent society, not only radical protest, but even the attempt to formulate, to articulate, to give word to protest assume a childlike, ridiculous immaturity. Thus it is ridiculous and perhaps 'logical' that the Free Speech Movement at Berkeley terminated in the row caused by the appearance of a sign with the four-letter word. It is perhaps equally ridiculous and right to see deeper significance in the buttons worn by some of the demonstrators (among them infants) against the slaughter in Vietnam: MAKE LOVE, NOT WAR. On the other side, against the new youth who refuse and rebel, are the representatives of the old order who can no longer protect its life without sacrificing it in the work of destruction and waste and pollution. They now include the representatives of organized labor – correctly so to the extent to which employment within the capitalist prosperity depends on the continued defense of the established social system.

Can the outcome, for the near future, be in doubt? The people, the majority of the people in the affluent society, are on the side of that which is – not that which can and ought to be. And the established order is strong enough and efficient enough to justify this adherence and to assure its continuation. However, the very strength and efficiency of this order may become factors of disintegration. Perpetuation of the obsolescent need for full-time labor (even in a very reduced form) will require the increasing waste of resources, the creation of ever more unnecessary jobs and services, and the growth of the military or destructive sector. Escalated wars, permanent preparation for war, and total administration may well suffice to keep the people under control, but at the cost of altering the morality on which the society still depends. Technical progress, itself a necessity for the maintenance of the established society, fosters needs and faculties which are antagonistic to the social organization of labor on which the system is built. In the course of automation, the value of the social product is to an increasingly smaller degree determined by the labor time necessary for its production. Consequently, the real social need for productive labor declines, and the vacuum must be filled with unproductive activities. An ever larger amount of the work actually performed becomes superfluous, expendable, meaningless. Although these activities can be sustained and even multiplied under total administration, there seems to exist an upper limit to their augmentation. This limit would be reached when the surplus value created by productive labor no longer suffices to pay for non-production work. A progressive reduction of labor seems to be inevitable, and for this eventuality, the system has to provide for occupation without work; it has to develop needs which transcend the market economy and may even be incompatible with it.

The affluent society is in its own way preparing for this eventuality by organizing 'the desire for beauty and the hunger for community', the renewal of the 'contact with nature', the enrichment of the mind, and honors for 'creation for its own sake'. The false ring of such proclamations is indicative of the fact that, within the established system, these aspirations are translated into administered cultural activities, sponsored by the government and the big corporations – an extension of their executive arm into the soul of the masses. It is all but impossible to recognize in the aspirations thus defined those of Eros and its autonomous transformation of a repressive environment and a repressive existence. If these goals are to be satisfied without an irreconcilable conflict with the requirements of the market economy, they must be satisfied within the framework of commerce and profit. But this sort of satisfaction would be tantamount to denial, for the erotic energy of the Life Instincts cannot be freed under the dehumanizing conditions of profitable affluence. To be sure, the conflict between the necessary development of noneconomic needs which would validate the idea of the abolition of labor (life as an end in itself) on the one hand, and the necessity for maintaining the need for earning a living on the other is quite manageable (especially as long as the Enemy within and without can serve as propelling force behind the defense of the status quo). However, the conflict may become explosive if it is accompanied and aggravated by the prospective changes at the very base of advanced industrial society, namely, the gradual under-mining of capitalist enterprise in the course of automation.

In the meantime, there are things to be done. The system has its weakest point where it shows its most brutal strength: in the escalation of its military potential (which seems to press for periodic actualization with ever shorter interruptions of peace and preparedness). This tendency seems reversible only under strongest pressure, and its reversal would open the danger spots in the social structure: its conversion into a 'normal' capitalist system is hardly imaginable without a serious crisis and sweeping economic and political changes. Today, the opposition to war and mili-tary intervention strikes at the roots: it rebels against those whose economic and political dominion depends on the continued (and enlarged) reproduction of the military establishment, its 'multipliers', and the poli-cies which necessitate this reproduction. These interests are not hard to identify, and the war against them does not require missiles, bombs, and napalm. But it does require something that is much harder to produce – the spread of uncensored and unmanipulated knowledge, consciousness, and above all, the organized refusal to continue work on the material and *intellectual* instruments which are now being used against man – for the defense of the liberty and prosperity of those who dominate the rest.

To the degree to which organized labor operates in defense of the status quo, and to the degree to which the share of labor in the material process of production declines, *intellectual* skills and capabilities become social and political factors. Today, the organized refusal to cooperate of the scientists, mathematicians, technicians, industrial psychologists and public opinion pollsters may well accomplish what a strike, even a large-scale strike, can no longer accomplish but once accomplished, namely, the beginning of the reversal, the preparation of the ground for political action. That the idea appears utterly unrealistic does not reduce the polit-ical responsibility involved in the position and function of the intellectual in contemporary industrial society. The intellectual refusal may find support in another catalyst, the instinctual refusal among the youth in protest. It is their lives which are at stake, and if not their lives, their mental health and their capacity to function as unmutilated humans. Their protest will continue because it is a biological necessity. 'By nature', the young are in the forefront of those who live and fight for Eros against Death, and against a civilization which strives to shorten the 'detour to death' while controlling the means for lengthening the detour. But in the administered society, the biological necessity does not immediately issue in action; organization demands counter-organization. Today the fight for life, the fight for Eros, is the *political* fight.

16

Jürgen Habermas

(b. 1929)

One of the most prolific 'second-generation' Frankfurt School theorists, Jürgen Habermas was born in Düsseldorf in 1929. He attended the universities of Göttingen, Bonn and Zurich, completing his doctorate on Schelling in 1954. Habermas assisted Adorno for three years (1956–9) at the Institute of Social Research, taught philosophy at Heidelberg, and was awarded Horkheimer's Chair of Philosophy and Sociology at the University of Frankfurt in the early 1960s. He served as Director of the Max Planck Institute in Starnberg between 1971 and 1983, and since that time has held the position of Professor of Philosophy at the University of Frankfurt. Some of the works and collections of essays that have earned Habermas wide recognition as critical theory's leading contemporary thinker include the following: *Theory and Practice, Knowledge and Human Interests, The Logic of the Social Sciences, Towards a Rational Society, Legitimation Crisis, The Theory of Communicative Action*, (2 vols), *The Philosophical Discourse of Modernity, Postmetaphysical Thinking, Moral Consciousness and Communicative Action* and *Justification and Application*.

In his early work of the 1960s, such as *Knowledge and Human Interests* (1968), Habermas maintains an anti-positivist stance already characteristic of Frankfurt School theorists. He rejects the claim that knowledge in all domains must fit the model of knowledge as pursued in the natural sciences. This kind of 'scientism', he claims, leads to an inadequate and reductionist view of knowledge which in fact is constituted by interests other than the purely technical. He suggests that the historical–hermeneutical sciences are driven by a practical interest in achieving mutual understanding via social interaction, and therefore must be guided by their own methodologies. Finally, knowledge in the critical social sciences is constituted by an emancipatory interest in autonomy and justice that challenges and interrogates ideological assumptions of both 'objective' science and hermeneutic 'tradition'. Critical self-reflection reveals that *all* knowledge is guided by cognitive interests of some kind, interests that should be acknowledged rather than denied by the objective illusions of positivistic inquiry.

Thus, technical, practical and emancipatory interests must be granted their relevant domains.

Habermas continues his indictment of technocracy in *Legitimation Crisis* (1973), where he examines the systematic ideological distortions needed to legitimate the status quo under advanced capitalism. On the one hand, the operational requirements allowing the system to function actually demand exploitation, domination, class segregation and repression. Yet, the hegemonic requirements procuring voluntary consensus towards these conditions demand, at least superficially, a commitment to democratic processes, freedom and equal opportunity. This paradoxical tension provokes repeated 'motivational' crises that reveal the gap between un-fulfilled expectations that are part of a society's self-representation and the forces that prevent their realization. It is only by repeated adjustments and 'accommodations' that these crises can be temporarily evaded.

In his later work on communicative action, Habermas has developed the insights of Karl-Otto Apel on 'the *a priori* of communication' or 'transcen-dental pragmatics'. That is to say, the ultimate ground for consensus is sought in the 'conditions of possibility' already presupposed by the commu-nicative encounter. All participants in ideal practical discourses have the right to raise normative claims until 'the force of the better argument' leads to understanding and agreement. Needless to say, this emphasis on an 'ideal speech situation' has raised doubts about the critical potential of the Habermasian programme. Political theorists and feminists alike have challenged the transcendental hypothesis of any argumentative context that remains untouched by hierarchical relations of power. A critical pragmatics of speech events must, they claim, perform a deeper analysis that includes not only assertions, but also implicature, status, gesture, tone of voice, and even spatial proxemics to fully understand how consensus is achieved. While Habermas posits a 'lifeworld' that is a privileged zone for commu-nicative action, they counter that no such *cordon sanitaire* exists as a buffer against strategic action.

Habermas has also been criticized for adopting Kohlberg's framework of moral psychology that presents evolutionary stages in the development of 'moral consciousness' recognizing Kantian universal norms. Since the profiles of those who have supposedly reached the highest stages of moral development in Kohlberg's studies are largely white, male, middle class and college educated, Carol Gilligan has suggested that there are perhaps problematic assumptions in Kohlberg's research design that need to be questioned.

In the selection which follows, Habermas advocates a new role for philos-ophy as a discipline which interacts with 'reconstructive' human sciences. He encourages philosophy to serve an additional role as mediator between the 'tangled mobile' of these diverse spheres of expert knowledge and the lifeworld. Habermas has distinctly skewed the orientation of critical theory away from the rather pessimistic outlook of first-generation Frankfurt

School thinkers. Broadly speaking, his own project attempts to retrieve the emancipatory potential of Enlightenment 'reason', and to instantiate that retrieval at the core of communicative praxis. In contrast to the negative appraisal of rationality and progress as the covert domination set forth in *Dialectic of Enlightenment*, Habermas emphasizes a regulative ideal of reason that fosters moral-practical competencies in communicative action. He has produced a theoretically complex and extensive body of work that has had interdisciplinary reverberations.

SELECT BIBLIOGRAPHY OF HABERMAS' WORKS IN ENGLISH

Towards a Rational Society (including 'Technology and science as ideology'), Boston: Beacon Press, 1971.
Knowledge and Human Interests, Boston: Beacon Press, 1972.
Legitimation Crisis, Boston: Beacon Press, 1973.
Theory and Practice, Boston: Beacon Press, 1973.
Communication and the Evolution of Society, Boston: Beacon Press, 1979.
Theory of Communicative Action, 2 vols, Boston: Beacon Press, 1984, 1987.
Autonomy and Solidarity (interviews), London: Verso, 1986.
The Philosophical Discourse of Modernity, Cambridge, Mass.: MIT Press, 1987.
On the Logic of the Social Sciences, Cambridge, Mass.: MIT Press, 1988.
The New Conservativism, Cambridge, Mass.: MIT Press, 1989.
The Structural Transformation of the Public Sphere, Cambridge, Mass.: MIT Press, 1989.
Moral Consciousness and Communicative Action, Cambridge, Mass.: MIT Press, 1990.
Postmetaphysical Thinking, Cambridge, Mass.: MIT Press, 1992.
Justification and Application, Cambridge, Mass.: MIT Press, 1993.

JÜRGEN HABERMAS

Philosophy as Stand-in and Interpreter

MASTER THINKERS HAVE fallen on hard times. This has been true of Hegel ever since Popper unmasked him in the forties as an enemy of the open society. It has also been intermittently true of Marx. The last to denounce Marx as a false prophet were the New Philosophers in the seventies. Today even Kant is affected by this decline. If I am correct, he is being viewed for the first time as a *maître penseur*, that is, as the magician of a false paradigm from the intellectual constraints of which we have to escape. Though among a philosophical audience there may still be a majority of scholars whose image of Kant has stayed the same, in the world outside his reputation is being eclipsed, and not for the first time, by Nietzsche.

Historically, Kantian philosophy marks the birth of a new mode of justification. Kant felt that the physics of his time and the growth of knowledge brought by it were important developments to which the philosopher had to respond. For Kant, the new science represented not some philosophically indifferent fact of life but proof of man's capacity to know. Specifically, the challenge Newtonian physics posed for philosophy was to explain how empirical knowledge is at all possible, an explanation that could not itself be empirical but had to be transcendental. What Kant calls 'transcendental' is an inquiry into the a priori conditions of what makes experience possible. The specific upshot of Kant's transcendental inquiry is that those conditions are identical with the conditions of possible objects of experience. The first job for the philosopher, then, is to analyze the concepts of objects as we 'always already' intuitively use them. Transcendental analysis is a nonempirical reconstruction of the a priori achievements of the cognizing subject, achievements for which there is no alternative: No experience shall be thought possible under *different* conditions. Transcendental justification has nothing to do with deduction from first principles. Rather, the hallmark of the transcendental justifica-tion is the notion that we can prove the nonsubstitutability of certain mental operations that we always already (intuitively) perform in accor-dance with rules.

As a master thinker, Kant fell into disfavor because he used tran-scendental justification to found the new discipline of epistemology. In so doing, he redefined the task, or vocation if you like, of philosophy in a more demanding way. There are two principal reasons why the Kantian view of philosophy's vocation has a dubious ring today.

The first reason has directly to do with the foundationalism of epis-temology. In championing the idea of a cognition *before* cognition, Kantian philosophy sets up a domain between itself and the sciences, arrogating

From *Moral Consciousness and Communicative Action*, Cambridge, Mass.: MIT Press, 1990.

authority to itself. It wants to clarify the foundations of the sciences once and for all, defining the limits of what can and cannot be experienced. This is tantamount to an act of showing the sciences their proper place. I think philosophy cannot and should not try to play the role of usher.

The second reason lies in the fact that transcendental philosophy refuses to be confined to epistemology. Above and beyond analyzing the bases of cognition, the critique of pure reason is also supposed to enable us to criticize the abuses of this cognitive faculty, which is limited to phenomena. Kant replaces the substantive concept of reason found in traditional metaphysics with a concept of reason the moments of which have undergone differentiation to the point where their unity is merely formal. He sets up practical reason, judgment, and theoretical cognition in isolation from each other, giving each a foundation unto itself, with the result that philosophy is cast in the role of the highest arbiter for all matters, including culture as a whole. Kantian philosophy differentiates what Weber was to call the 'value spheres of culture' (science and technology, law and morality, art and art criticism), while at the same time legitimating them within their respective limits. Thus Kant's philosophy poses as the highest court of appeal *vis-à-vis* the sciences and culture as a whole.[1]

There is a necessary link between the Kantian foundationalism in epistemology, which nets philosophy the unenviable role of usher, and the ahistoricity of the conceptual system Kant superimposes on culture, which nets philosophy the equally undesirable role of a judge parceling out separate areas of jurisdiction to science, morality, and art.

> Without the Kantian assumption that the philosopher can decide *questiones juris* concerning the rest of culture, this self-image collapses. ... To drop the notion of the philosopher as knowing something about knowing which nobody else knows so well would be to drop the notion that his voice always has an overriding claim on the attention of the other participants in the conversation. It would also be to drop the notion that there is something called 'philosophical method' or 'philosophical technique' or 'the philosophical point of view' which enables the professional philosopher, *ex officio*, to have interesting views about, say, the respectability of psychoanalysis, the legitimacy of certain dubious laws, the resolution of moral dilemmas, the soundness of schools of historiography or literary criticism, and the like.[2]

Richard Rorty's impressive critique of philosophy assembles compelling metaphilosophical arguments in support of the view that the roles Kant the master thinker had envisaged for philosophy, namely those of usher and judge, are too big for it. While I find myself in agreement with much of what Rorty says, I have trouble accepting his conclusion, which is that if philosophy forswears these two roles, it must also surrender the function of being the 'guardian of rationality'. If I understand Rorty, he is saying that the new modesty of philosophy involves the abandonment of any claim to reason – the very claim that has marked philosophical thought since its inception. Rorty not only argues for the demise of philosophy; he also unflinchingly accepts the end of the belief that ideas like truth or the unconditional with their transcending power are a necessary condition of humane forms of collective life.

Implied by Kant's conception of formal, differentiated reason is a theory of modernity. Modernity is characterized by a rejection of the substantive rationality typical of religious and metaphysical worldviews and by a belief in procedural rationality and its ability to give credence to our views in the three areas of objective knowledge, moral-practical insight, and aesthetic judgment. What I am asking myself is this: Is it true that this (or a similar) concept of modernity becomes untenable when you dismiss the claims of a foundationalist theory of knowledge?

What follows is an attempt to narrate a story that might help put Rorty's criticism of philosophy in perspective. Granted, by going this route I cannot settle the controversy. What I can do is throw light on some of its presuppositions. At the outset (section 1 below) I will look at Hegel's critique of Kantian foundationalism and the substitution of a dialectical mode of justification for Kant's transcendental one. Next (section 2) I will retrace some of the lines of criticism and self-criticism that have emerged in the Kantian and Hegelian traditions. In section 3 I will dwell on a more radical form of criticism originating in pragmatist and hermeneuticist quarters, a form of attack that repudiates Kant and Hegel simultaneously. Section 4 deals with thinkers, respectable ones no less, who respond to this situation by annulling philosophy's long-standing claim to reason. In conclusion (section 5) I will argue that philosophy, while well advised to withdraw from the problematic roles of usher (*Platzanweiser*) and judge, can and ought to retain its claim to reason, provided it is content to play the more modest roles of stand-in (*Platzhalter*) and interpreter.

1

Hegel fashioned his dialectical mode of justification in deliberate opposition to the transcendental one of Kant. Hegel – and I can only hint at this here – agrees with those who charge that in the end Kant failed to justify or ground the pure concepts of the understanding, for he merely culled them from the table of forms of judgment, unaware of their historical specificity. Thus he failed, in Hegel's eyes, to prove that the *a priori* conditions of what makes experience possible are truly necessary. In his *Phenomenology of Spirit* Hegel proposes to correct this flaw by taking a genetic approach. What Kant regarded as a unique (Copernican) turn to transcendental reflection becomes in Hegel a general mechanism for turning consciousness back upon itself. This mechanism has been switched on and off time and time again in the development of spirit. As the subject becomes conscious of itself, it destroys one form of consciousness after another. This process epitomizes the subjective experience that what initially appears to the subject as a being in itself can become content only in the forms imparted to it by the subject. The transcendental philosopher's experience is thus, according to Hegel, reenacted naively whenever an in-itself becomes a for-the-subject. What Hegel calls 'dialectical' is the reconstruction of this recurrent experience and of its assimilation by the subject, which gives rise to ever more complex structures. Hegel goes beyond the particular manifestation of consciousness that Kant analyzed, attaining in the end knowledge that has become autonomous, that is, absolute knowledge. This highest vantage point enables Hegel, the phenomenologist, to witness the genesis of structures of consciousness that Kant had assumed to be timeless.

Hegel, it should be noted, exposes himself to a criticism similar to the one he levels against Kant. Reconstructing successive forms of consciousness is one thing. Proving the necessity of their succession is quite another. Hegel is not unaware of this gap, and he tries to close it by logical means, thereby laying the basis for a philosophical absolutism that claims an even grander role for philosophy than did Kant. In Hegel's *Logic* philosophy's role is to effect an encyclopedic conceptual synthesis of the diffuse chunks of content thrown up by the sciences. In addition, Hegel picks up Kant's latent theory of modernity, making it explicit and developing it into a critique of the diremptive, self-contradictory features of modernity. It is this peculiar twist that gave philosophy a new world-historical relevance in relation to culture as a whole. And this is the stuff of which the suspect image of Hegel as a master thinker is made.[3]

The metaphilosophical attack on the *maîtres penseurs*, whether its target be Hegel's absolutism or Kant's foundationalism, is a recent phenomenon. Antecedents of it can be found in the strands of self-criticism that have run through Kantianism and Hegelianism for quite some time. I shall comment briefly on two lines of self-criticism that I think complement each other in an interesting way.

2

In reference to Kant's transcendental philosophy there are today three distinct critical positions: the analytic one of Strawson, the constructivist one of Lorenzen, and the critical-rationalist one of Popper.

Analytic philosophy appropriates Kant by jettisoning any claim to ultimate justification (*Letztbegründung*). From the very outset it drops the objective Kant had in mind when he deduced the pure concepts of the understanding from the unity of self-consciousness. The analytic reception of Kant is confined to comprehending those concepts and rules that underlie experience insofar as it can be couched in elementary propositions. The analysis focuses on general, indispensable, conceptual preconditions that make experience possible. Unable to prove the objective validity of its basic concepts and presuppositions, this analysis nevertheless makes a universalistic claim. Redeeming it involves changing Kant's transcendental strategy of justification into a testing procedure. If the hypothetically reconstructed conceptual system underlying experience as such is valid, not a single intelligible alternative to it can possibly exist. This means any alternative proposal will be scrutinized with a view to proving its derivative character, that is, with a view to showing that the alleged alternative inevitably utilizes portions of the very hypothesis it seeks to supplant. A strategy of argumentation like this tries to prove that the concepts and presuppositions it singles out as fundamental cannot be dispensed with. Turned modest, the transcendental philosopher of the analytic variety takes on the role of the skeptic who keeps trying to find counterexamples that might invalidate his theories.[4] In short, he acts like a hypothesis-testing scientist.

The *constructivist position* tried to compensate for the justificatory shortfall that has now opened up from the perspective of transcendental philosophy in the following way. It concedes from the start that the basic conceptual organization of experience is conventional while at the same time putting a constructivist critique of language in the service of epistemology.[5] Those conventions are considered valid that are generated methodically and therefore transparently. It should be clear that this approach lays, rather than uncovers, the foundations of cognition.

On the face of it, the *critical-rationalist position* breaks completely with transcendentalism. It holds that the three horns of the 'Munchhausen trilemma' – logical circularity, infinite regress, and recourse to absolute certitude – can only be avoided if one gives up any hope of grounding or justifying whatsoever.[6] Here the notion of justification is being dislodged in favor of the concept of critical testing, which becomes the critical rationalist's equivalent for justification. In this connection I would argue that criticism is itself a procedure whose employment is never presuppositionless. That is why I think that critical rationalism, by clinging to the idea of irrefutable rules of criticism, allows a weak version of the Kantian justificatory mode to sneak into its inner precincts through the back door.[7]

Self-criticism in the Hegelian tradition has developed along lines parallel to the self-criticism among Kantians. Again, three distinct positions might be said to be represented by the young Lukács and his materialist critique of epistemology, which restricts the claim to justification of dialectics to the man-made world and excludes nature; by K. Korsch's and H. Freyer's practicism, wherein the classical relation of theory and practice is stood on its head and the 'interested' perspective of creating a society of the future informs the theoretical reconstruction of social development; and finally by the negativism of Adorno, who finds in comprehensive logic of

242

development only the proof that it is impossible to break the spell of an instrumental reason gone mad.

I cannot examine these positions here. All I shall do is to point out certain interesting parallels between the Hegelian and Kantian strands of self-criticism. The self-criticism that begins by doubting the Kantian transcendental deduction and the self-criticism that begins by doubting Hegel's passage to absolute knowledge have this in common: they reject the claim that the categorial makeup and the pattern of development of the human spirit can be proved to be necessary. With regard to constructivism and practicism a similar convergence occurs: both are involved in a shift from rational reconstruction to creative praxis, which is to make possible a theoretical recapitulation of this praxis. Critical rationalism and negativism, for their part, share something too, which is that they reject transcendental and dialectical means of cognition while at the same time using them in a paradoxical way. One may also view these two attempts at radical negation as showing that these two modes of justification cannot be abolished except on penalty of self-contradiction.

My comparison between parallel self-critical strategies to restrict the justificatory claims of transcendental and dialectical philosophies gives rise to the following question: Do these self-limiting tendencies merely reinforce each other, encouraging the skeptic to reject justification all the more roundly? Or does the retrenchment on either side to a position of diminished justificatory objectives and strategies represent a precondition for viewing them not as opposites but as supplementing each other? I think the second possibility deserves serious consideration. The genetic structuralism of Jean Piaget provides an instructive model along these lines, instructive for all philosophers, I think, but particularly those who want to remain philosophers. Piaget conceives 'reflective abstraction' as that learning mechanism which explains the transition between cognitive stages in ontogenetic development. The end point of this development is a decentered understanding of the world. Reflective abstraction is similar to transcendental reflection in that it brings out the formal elements hidden in the cognitive content, identifies them as the schemata that underlie the knowing subject's action, differentiates them, and reconstructs them at the next highest stage of reflection. Seen from a different perspective, the same learning mechanism has a function similar to Hegel's power of negation, which dialectically supersedes self-contradictory forms of consciousness.[8]

3

The aforementioned six positions in the tradition of Kant and Hegel stick to a claim to reason, however small in scope, however cautious in formulation. It is this final intention that sets off Popper and Lakatos from a

Feyerabend and Horkheimer and Adorno from a Foucault. They still say *something* about the indispensable conditions of claims to the validity of those beliefs we hold to be justified, claims that transcend all restrictions of time and place. Now any attack on the master thinkers questions this residual claim to reason and thus in essence makes a plea for the abolition of philosophy. I can explain this radical turn by talking briefly about a wholly different criticism, one that has been raised against both Kant *and* Hegel.

Its proponents can be found in *pragmatism* and *hermeneutic philosophy*. Their doubts concerning the justificatory and self-justificatory potential of philosophy operate at a more profound level than do the self-criticisms within the Kantian and Hegelian traditions. They step resolutely outside the parameters set by the philosophy of consciousness and its cognitive paradigm, which stresses the perception and representation of objects. Pragmatism and hermeneutics oust the traditional notion of the solitary subject that confronts objects and becomes reflective only by turning itself into an object. In its place they put an idea of cognition that is mediated by language and linked to action. Moreover, they emphasize the web of everyday life and communication surrounding 'our' cognitive achievements. The latter are intrinsically intersubjective and cooperative. It is unimportant just how this web is conceptualized, whether as 'form of life', 'lifeworld', 'practice', 'linguistically mediated interaction', a 'language game', 'convention', 'cultural background', a 'tradition', 'effective history', or what have you. The important thing is that these commonsensical ideas, though they may function quite differently, attain a status that used to be reserved for the basic concepts of epistemology. Pragmatism and hermeneutics, then, accord a higher position to acting and speaking than to knowing. But there is more to it than that. Purposive action and linguistic communication play a qualitatively different role from that of self-reflection in the philosophy of consciousness. They have no justificatory function any more save one: to expose the need for foundational knowledge as unjustified.

Charles S. Peirce doubted that radical doubt is possible. His intentions were the same as those of Dilthey, who doubted that neutrality in interpretive understanding is possible. For Peirce problems always arise in a specific situation. They come to us, as it were. We do not go to them, for we do not fully control the totality of our practical existence. In a similar vein Dilthey argues that we cannot grasp a symbolic expression unless we have an intuitive preunderstanding of its context, for we do not have unlimited freedom to convert the unproblematic background knowledge of our own culture into explicit knowledge. Every instance of problem solving and every interpretation depend on a web of myriad presuppositions. Since this web is holistic and particularistic at the same time, it can never be grasped by an abstract, general analysis. It is from this standpoint that the myth of the given – that is, the distinctions between sensibility and understanding, intuition and concept, form and content – can be debunked, along with the distinctions between analytic and synthetic judgments, between *a priori* and *a posteriori*. These Kantian dualisms are all being dissolved, a fact that is vaguely reminiscent of Hegel's metacritique. Of course, a full-fledged return to Hegel is made impossible by the contextualism and historicism to which the pragmatist and hermeneutic approaches subscribe.

There is no denying that pragmatism and hermeneutics represent a gain. Instead of focusing introspectively on consciousness, these two points of view look outside at objectifications of action and language. Gone is the fixation on the cognitive function of consciousness. Gone too is the emphasis on the representational function of language and the visual metaphor of the 'mirror of nature'. What takes their place is the notion of justified belief spanning the whole spectrum of what can be said – of what Wittgenstein and Austin call illocutionary force – rather than just the contents of fact-stating discourses. 'Saying things is not always saying how things are.'[9]

Do these considerations strengthen Rorty's interpretation of pragmatism and hermeneutics, which argues for the abnegation by philosophical thought of any claim to rationality and indeed for the abnegation of philosophy *per se*? Or do they mark the beginning of a new paradigm that, while discarding the mentalistic language game of the philosophy of consciousness, retains the justificatory modes of that philosophy in the modest, self-critical form in which I have presented them? I cannot answer this question directly for want of compelling and simple arguments. Once again, the answer I will give is a narrative one.

4

Marx wanted to supersede (*aufheben*) philosophy by realizing it – so convinced was he of the truth of Hegelian philosophy, whose only fault was that concept and reality cleaved unbearably, a fault that Hegel studiously overlooked. The corresponding, though fundamentally different, present-day attitude toward philosophy is the dismissive goodbye and good riddance. These farewells take many forms, three of which are currently in vogue. For simplicity's sake I will call them the therapeutic, the heroic, and the salvaging farewell.

Wittgenstein championed the notion of a *therapeutic* philosophy, therapeutic in the specific sense of self-healing, for philosophy was sick to the core. Wittgenstein's diagnosis was that philosophy had disarrayed language games that function perfectly well in everyday life. The weakness of this particular farewell to philosophy is that it leaves the world as it is. For the standards by which philosophy is being criticized are taken straight from the self-sufficient, routinized forms of life in which philosophy happens to survive for now. And what about possible successors? Field research in cultural anthropology seems to be the strongest candidate to succeed philosophy after its demise. Surely the history of philosophy will henceforth be interpreted as the unintelligible doings of some outlandish tribe that today is fortunately extinct. (Perhaps Rorty will one day be celebrated as the path-breaking Thucydides of this new approach, which incidentally could only get under way after Wittgenstein's medicine had proved effective.)

There is a sharp contrast between the soft-spoken farewell of the therapeutic philosopher and the noisy demolition undertaken by someone like Georges Bataille or Heidegger. Their goodbye is *heroic*. From their perspective too, false habits of living and thinking are concentrated in elevated forms of philosophical reflection. But instead of accusing philosophy of homely category mistakes or simple disruptions of everyday life, their deconstruction of metaphysics and objectivating thought has a more incisive, epochal quality. This more dramatic farewell to philosophy does not promise a cure. Rather, it resembles Hölderlin's pathos-laden idea of a rescue attempt *in extremis*. The devalued and discredited philosophical tradition, rather than being replaced by something even more valueless than itself, is supposed to give way to a *different* medium that makes possible a return to the immemorial – to Bataille's sovereignty or Heidegger's Being.

Least conspicuous, finally, is the *salvaging* type of farewell to philosophy. Contemporary neo-Aristotelians best exemplify this type insofar as they do exegeses that are informed by hermeneutics. Some of their work is unquestionably significant. But all too often it departs from pure interpretation in an effort to salvage some old truth or other. At any rate, this farewell to philosophy has a disingenuous ring: While the salvager keeps invoking the need to preserve philosophy, he wants to have nothing to do with its systematic claims. He does not try to make the ancients relevant to the discussion of some subject matter. Nor does he present the classics as a cultural treasure prepared by philosophy and history. What he does is to appropriate by assimilation texts that were once thought to embody knowledge, treating them instead as sources of illumination and edification.

Let us return for a moment to the critique of Kant, the master thinker, and in particular to his foundationalism in epistemology. Clearly, present-day philosophies of the sort just described wisely sidestep the Kantian trap. The last thing they think they can do is show the natural sciences to their proper place. Contemporary poststructuralist, late-pragmatist, and neohistoricist tendencies share a narrow objectivistic conception of science. Over against scientific cognition they carve out a sphere where thought can be illuminating or awakening instead of being objective. These tendencies prefer to sever all links with general, criticizable claims to validity. They would rather make do without notions like consensus, incontrovertible results, and justified beliefs. Paradoxically enough, whereas they make these (unnecessary) sacrifices, they somehow keep believing in the authority and superiority of philosophical insights: their own. In terms of their views on science, the philosophers of the definitive farewell agree with the existentialist proposal (Jaspers, Sartre, Kolakowski) for a division of labor that puts science on one side and philosophical faith, life, existential freedom, myth, cultivation, or what have you, on the other. All these juxtapositions are identical in structure. Where they differ is in their assessment of what Max Weber termed the cultural relevance of science, which may range from negative to neutral to positive. As is well known, Continental philosophy has a penchant for dramatizing the dangers of objectivism and instrumental reason, whereas Anglo-American philosophy takes a more relaxed view of them.

With his distinction between normal and abnormal discourse, Richard Rorty has come up with an interesting variation on the above theme. In times of widely acknowledged theoretical progress, normality takes hold of the established sciences. This means methods become available that make problem solving and dispute settling possible. What Rorty calls commensurable discourses are those discourses that operate with reliable criteria of consensus building. In contrast, discourses are incommensurable or abnormal when basic orientations are contested. Generally, abnormal conversations tend to pass over into normal ones, their ultimate purpose being to annul themselves and to bring about universal agreement. Occasionally, however, abnormal discourses stop short of taking this self-transcending step and are content with 'interesting and fruitful disagreement'. That is, they become *sufficient unto themselves*. It is at this point that abnormal discourses take on the quality that Rorty calls 'edifying'. According to him, philosophy as a whole verges on edifying conversation once it has sloughed off all pretensions to problem solving. Such philosophical edification enjoys the benefits of all three types of farewell: therapeutic relief, heroic overcoming, and hermeneutic reawaking. It combines the inconspicuously subversive force of leisure with an elitist notion of creative linguistic imagination and with the wisdom of the ages. The desire for edification, however, works to the detriment of the desire for truth: 'Edifying philosophers can never end philosophy, but they can help prevent it from attaining the secure path of a science'.[10]

I am partly sympathetic to Rorty's allocation of roles, for I agree that philosophy has no business playing the part of the highest arbiter in matters of science and culture. I find his argument unconvincing all the same. For even a philosophy that has been taught its limits by pragmatism and hermeneuticism will not be able to find a resting place in edifying conservation *outside* the sciences without immediately being drawn back into argumentation, that is, justificatory discourse.

The existentialist or, if you like, exclusive division of labor between philosophy and science is untenable. This is borne out by the particular version of discourse theory Rorty proposes. Ultimately, there is only one criterion by which beliefs can be judged valid, and that is that they are based on agreement reached by argumentation. This means that *everything* whose validity is at all disputable rests on shaky foundations. It matters little if the ground underfoot shakes a bit less for those who debate problems of physics than for those who debate problems of morals and aesthetics. The difference is a matter of degree only, as the post-empiricist philosophy of science has shown. Normalization of discourse is not a sufficiently trenchant criterion for distinguishing science from edifying philosophical conversation.

5

To those who advocate a cut-and-dried division of labor, research traditions representing a blend of philosophy and science have always been particularly offensive. Marxism and psychoanalysis are cases in point. They cannot, on this view, help being pseudosciences because they straddle normal and abnormal discourse, refusing to fall on either side of the dividing line. On this point Rorty speaks the same language as Jaspers. What I know about the history of the social sciences and psychology leads me to believe that hybrid discourses such as Marxism and psychoanalysis are by no means atypical. To the contrary, they may well stand for a type of approach that marks the beginning of new research traditions.

What holds for Freud applies to all seminal theories in these disciplines, for instance, those of Durkheim, Mead, Max Weber, Piaget, and Chomsky. Each inserted a genuinely philosophical idea like a detonator into a particular context of research. Symptom formation through repression, the creation of solidarity through the sacred, the identity-forming function of role taking, modernization as rationalization of society, decentration as an outgrowth of reflective abstraction from action, language acquisition as an activity of hypothesis testing – these key phrases stand for so many paradigms in which a philosophical idea is present in embryo while at the same time empirical, yet universal, questions are being posed. It is no coincidence that theoretical approaches of this kind are the favorite target of empiricist counterattacks. Such cyclical movements in the history of science, incidentally, do not point to a convergence of these disciplines in one unified science. It makes better sense to view them as stages on the road to the philosophization of the sciences of man (*Philosophischwerden der Humanwissenschaften*) than as stages in the triumphal march toward objectivist approaches, such as neurophysiology, that quaint favorite child of the analytic philosophers.

What I have said lies mainly in the realm of speculative conjecture. But unless I am completely mistaken, it makes sense to suggest that philosophy, instead of just dropping the usher role and being left with nothing, ought to exchange it for the part of stand-in (*Platzhalter*). Whose seat would philosophy be keeping; what would it be standing in for? Empirical theories with strong universalistic claims. As I have indicated, there have surfaced and will continue to surface in nonphilosophical disciplines fertile minds who will give such theories a try. The chance for their emergence is greatest in the reconstructive sciences. Starting primarily from the intuitive knowledge of competent subjects – competent in terms of judgment, action, and language – and secondarily from systematic knowledge handed down by culture, the reconstructive sciences explain the presumably universal bases of rational experience and judgment, as well as of action and linguistic communication. Marked down in price, the venerable transcendental and dialectical modes of justification may still come in handy. All they can fairly be expected to furnish, however, is reconstructive hypotheses for use in empirical settings. Telling examples of a successful cooperative integration of philosophy and science can be seen in the development of a theory of rationality. This is an area where philosophers work as suppliers of ideas without raising foundationalist or absolutist claims à la Kant or Hegel. Fallibilistic in orientation, they reject the dubious faith in philosophy's ability to do things single-handedly, hoping instead that the success that has for so long eluded it might come from an auspicious matching of different theoretical fragments. From the vantage point of my own research interests, I see such a cooperation taking shape between philosophy of science and history of science, between speech act theory and empirical approaches to pragmatics of language, between a theory of informal argumentation and empirical approaches to natural argumentation, between cognitivist ethics and a psychology of moral development, between philosophical theories of action and the ontogenetic study of action competences.

If it is true that philosophy has entered upon a phase of cooperation with the human sciences, does it not run the risk of losing its identity? There is some justification in Spaemann's warning 'that every philosophy makes a practical and a theoretical claim to totality and that not to make such a twofold claim is to be doing something which does not qualify as philosophy'.[11] In defense, one might argue that a philosophy that contributes something important to an analysis of the rational foundations of knowing, acting, and speaking does retain at least a thematic connection with the whole. But is this enough? What becomes of the theory of modernity, what of the window on the totality of culture that Kant and Hegel opened with their foundational and hypostatizing concepts of reason? Down to Husserl's *Crisis of the European Sciences*, philosophy not only usurped the part of supreme judge, it also played a directing role. Again, what happens when it surrenders the role of judge in matters of science as well as culture? Does this mean philosophy's relation to the totality is severed? Does this mean it can no longer be the guardian of rationality?

The situation of culture as a whole is no different from the situation of science as a whole. As totalities, neither needs to be grounded or justified or given a place by philosophy. Since the dawn of modernity in the eighteenth century, culture has generated those structures of rationality that Max Weber and Emil Lask conceptualized as cultural value spheres. Their existence calls for description and analysis, not philosophical justification.

Reason has split into three moments – modern science, positive law and posttraditional ethics, and autonomous art and institutionalized art criticism – but philosophy had precious little to do with this disjunction. Ignorant of sophisticated critiques of reason, the sons and daughters of modernity have progressively learned to differentiate their cultural tradition in terms of these three aspects of rationality such that they deal with issues of truth, justice, and taste discretely rather than simultaneously. At a different level, this shift toward differentiation produces the following phenomena: (1) The sciences disgorge more and more elements of religion, thus renouncing their former claim to being able to interpret nature and history as one whole. (2) Cognitivist moral theories disgorge issues of the good life, focusing instead strictly on deontological, generalizable aspects of ethics, so that all that remains of 'the good'is the just. (3) With art it is likewise. Since the turn to autonomy, art has striven mightily to mirror one basic aesthetic experience, the increasing decentration of subjectivity. It occurs as the subject leaves the spatiotemporal structures of everyday life behind, freeing itself from the conventions of everyday perception, of purposive behavior, and of the imperatives of work and utility.

I repeat, these eminent trends toward compartmentalization, constituting as they do the hallmark of modernity, can do very well without philosophical justification. But they do pose problems of mediation. First, how can reason, once it has been thus sundered, go on being a unity on the level of culture? And second, how can expert cultures, which are being pushed more and more to the level of rarefied, esoteric forms, be made to stay in touch with everyday communication? To the extent to which philosophy keeps at least one eye trained on the topic of rationality, that is, to the extent to which it keeps inquiring into the conditions of the unconditional, to that extent it will not dodge the demand for these two kinds of efforts at mediation.

The first type of problem of mediation arises within the spheres of science, morals, and art. In this area we witness the rise of countermovements. For example, in human sciences nonobjectivist approaches bring moral and aesthetic criticism into play without undermining the primacy of issues of truth. Another example is the way in which the discussion of ethics of responsibility and ethics of conviction and the expanded role of utilitarian considerations within universalist ethics have brought the calculation of consequences and the interpretation of needs into play – and these are perspectives situated rather in the domains of the cognitive and the expressive. Let us finally look at postmodern art as the third example. It is characterized by a strange simultaneity of realistic, politically committed schools on the one hand and authentic followers of the classical modernism to which we owe the crystallization of the specific meaning of the aesthetic on the other. In realistic and politically committed art, elements of the cognitive and the moral-practical come into play once again, but at the level of the wealth of forms unloosed by the avant-garde. To that extent they act as agents of mediation. Counterdevelopments like these, it seems, mitigate the radical differentiation of reason and point to its unity. Everyday life, however, is a more promising medium for regaining the lost unity of reason than are today's expert cultures or yesteryear's classical philosophy of reason.

In everyday communication, cognitive interpretations, moral expectations, expressions, and evaluations cannot help overlapping and interpenetrating. Reaching understanding in the lifeworld requires a cultural tradition that ranges across *the whole spectrum*, not just the fruits of science and technology. As far as philosophy is concerned, it might do well to refurbish its link with the totality by taking on the role of interpreter on behalf of the lifeworld. It might then be able to help set in motion the interplay between the cognitive-instrumental, moral-practical, and aesthetic-expressive dimensions that has come to a standstill today like a tangled mobile.[12] This simile at least helps identify the issue philosophy will face when it stops playing the part of the arbiter that inspects culture and instead starts playing the part of a mediating interpreter. That issue is how to overcome the isolation of science, morals, and art and their respective expert cultures. How can they be joined to the impoverished traditions of the lifeworld, and how can this be done without detriment to their regional rationality? How can a new balance between the separated moments of reason be established in communicative everyday life?

The critic of the master thinkers will likely express his alarm one more time. What in the world, he will ask, gives the philosopher the right to offer his services as a translator mediating between the everyday world and cultural modernity with its autonomous sectors when he is already more than busy trying to hold open a place for ambitious theoretical strategies within the system of the sciences? I think pragmatism and hermeneutics have joined forces to answer this question by attributing epistemic authority to the community of those who cooperate and speak with one another. Everyday communication makes possible a kind of understanding that is based on claims to validity and then furnishes the only real alternative to exerting influence on one another in more or less coercive ways. The validity claims that we raise in conversation – that is, when we say something with conviction – transcend this specific conversational context, pointing to something beyond the spatiotemporal ambit of the occasion. Every agreement, whether produced for the first time or reaffirmed, is based on (controvertible) grounds or reasons. Grounds have a special property: they force us into yes or no positions. Thus, built into the structure of action oriented toward reaching understanding is an element of unconditionality. And it is this unconditional element that makes the validity (*Gültigkeit*) that we claim for our views different from the mere de facto acceptance (*Geltung*) of habitual practices.[13] From the perspective of first persons, what we consider justified is not a function of custom but a question of justification or grounding. That is why philosophy is 'rooted in the urge to see social practices of justification as more than just such practices'.[14] The same urge is at work when people like me stubbornly cling to the notion that philosophy is the guardian of rationality.

NOTES

1 'The critique . . . arriving at all its decisions in the light of fundamental principles of its own institution, the authority of which no one can question, secures to us the peace of a legal order, in which our disputes have to be conducted solely by the recognized methods of legal action.' I. Kant, *Critique of Pure Reason*, trans. N. Kemp Smith, p. 601.

2 Richard Rorty, *Philosophy and the Mirror of Nature* (Princeton, 1979), pp. 392ff.

3 Rorty approvingly paraphrases a dictum by Eduard Zeller: 'Hegelianism produced an image of philosophy as a discipline which somehow both completed and swallowed up the other disciplines, rather than *grounding* them. It also made philosophy too popular, too interesting, too important, to be properly professional; it challenged philosophy professors to embody the World-Spirit, rather than simply getting on with their *Fach*.' Rorty (1979), p. 135.

4 G. Schönrich, *Kategorien und transzendentale Argumentation* (Frankfurt, 1981), ch. 4, pp. 182ff; R. Bittner, 'Transzendental', in *Handbuch philosophischer Grundbegriffe*, vol. 5 (Munich 1974), pp. 1524ff.

5 C. F. Gethmann and R. Hegselmann, 'Das Problem der Begründung zwischen Dezisionismus und Fundamentalismus', *Zeitschrift für allegemeine Wissenschaftstheorie* 8 (1977): 432ff.

6 H. Albert, *Treatise on Critical Reason* (Princeton, 1985).

7 H. Lenk, 'Philosophische Logikbegründung und rationaler Kritizismus', *Zeitschrift für philosophische Forschung* 24 (1970): 183ff.

8 T. Kesselring, *Entwicklung und Widerspruch – Ein Vergleich zwischen Piagets genetischer Erkenntnistheorie und Hegels Dialektik* (Frankfurt, 1981).

9 Rorty (1979), p. 371.

10 Rorty (1979), p. 372.

11 R. Spaemann, 'Der Streit der Philosophen', in H. Lübbe, ed., *Wozu Philosophie?* (Berlin, 1978), p. 96.

12 J. Habermas, 'Modernity versus Postmodernity', *New German Critique* 22 (1981): 3–14.
13 See J. Habermas, *Theory of Communicative Action* (Boston, 1984), vol. 1, pp. 114ff.
14 Rorty (1979), p. 390.

17

Louis Althusser

(1918–1990)

Usually classified as a 'structuralist' thinker, Louis Althusser provides an interesting counterpoint to the primarily 'humanist' Marxist thinkers we have already encountered. Born in Algeria in 1918, he came to Paris in 1939 to study for his *agrégation* at the Ecole Normale Supérieure. Delayed by the Second World War, during which he was taken prisoner by the Germans, he did not finish until 1948. For the rest of his professional career he taught at the Ecole Normale, mentoring such students as Foucault and Derrida. Althusser's work came to prominence largely in the 1960s with the publication of *For Marx* (1965), *Reading Capital* (with Balibar, 1968) and *Lenin and Philosophy and Other Essays* (1969). He specifically aimed to reappropriate canonical Marxist texts as an epistemological project of scientific practice, a task which also led him to indict as 'ideological' all other Marxist philosophies that privileged a unified, autonomous subject of consciousness.

Althusser rejects the 'myth' of what he claims is the typically idealist view of social relations constituted by the interactions of individual human subjects who atomistically intervene to shape the historical landscape. According to him, the philosophies that promote this scenario – phenomenology, existentialism, Frankfurt School critical theory – remain too indebted to Hegel and the early Marx of the *Paris Manuscripts* (1844) to yield a 'scientific' approach to Marxist theory. By contrast, he consults the later Marx of *Capital* (1867) for a structural understanding of a social order grounded in the mode of production. We should note that Althusser did not see his own project as being motivated by the French structuralist movement of the 1950s and 1960s. The structural priority of system over individual is already inherent in Marx's theoretical analysis, and it is in this sense that Althusser's interrogation of whole–part relations proceeds in Marx's footsteps, not Saussure's. What is revealed by structural analysis is a complex set of relatively autonomous cultural, political and economic 'fields' that operate under the systemic pressures of a 'dominating structure'. While the economic 'field' is significant, it alone does not determine the activities within other fields, as a simple economic determinism of 'base–superstructure' would have it. In order to avoid such a reductionist 'empirical' reading of Marx, Althusser reads *Capital* 'symptomatically' between the lines, reconstructing what he considers the genuine problematic of the text. He maintains that effects are 'overdetermined' rather than simply 'determined', in that contradictions within any one sphere will resonate with hidden effects throughout the structure.

Althusser's emphasis on the structuralist paradigm for Marxist theory relegated 'ideological critique' to an uncertain status. He addressed this issue in his essay 'Ideology and ideological state apparatuses' in 1970. He asks, 'What, then, is *the reproduction of the conditions of production*?' He first distinguishes between 'repressive' state apparatuses, such as the army and police, and 'ideological' state apparatuses, such as churches, media, schools and legal institutions. In a manner somewhat reminiscent of Gramsci's analysis of 'ideological hegemony', Althusser focuses on the power of ideology to reproduce the status quo by obscuring the relationship of individuals to 'the relations of production' and 'the relations that derive from them'. Ideology provides the ritual practices in which we are all instantiated, by which we are labelled, and to which we aspire in transparent fashion. Subjects are formed by and through their nexus of 'imaginary' relations within these institutions and practices, all of which seems quite natural because they are embedded everywhere in every sphere. We decide to take up certain options only because we already have passed through certain rituals that lead us to the next step. Nobody, according to Althusser, escapes ideological formation, which operates invisibly to maintain a given social order.

What remains problematical in Althusser's project is the cul-de-sac after epistemological clarity is gained through a 'scientific' praxis that reveals the beast, but offers no motivational plan of action to change the beast. The knowledge we have as a result of his nuanced analyses leaves us better informed about how we are constructed as de-centred subjects caught in a complex web of structural forces beyond our control. But is Marxism thus relegated to an 'armchair discipline' limited to interrogation? One is reminded of the graffiti scrawled throughout Paris during the tumultuous uprising of May 1968, when Althusser was nowhere to be found: *'Althusser – où est-il maintenant?'*

SELECT BIBLIOGRAPHY OF ALTHUSSER'S WORKS IN ENGLISH

Reading Capital (with Etienne Balibar), London: New Left Books, 1970.
Lenin and Philosophy and Other Essays, London: New Left Books, 1971.
Politics and History, London: New Left Books, 1972.
Essays in Self-Criticism, London: New Left Books, 1976.
Essays on Ideology, London: Verso, 1984.

LOUIS ALTHUSSER

Philosophy and the Spontaneous Philosophy of the Scientists, London: Verso, 1985.

For Marx, London: Verso, 1990.

The Future Lasts a Long Time, London: Chatto & Windus, 1993.

From *Capital* to Marx's Philosophy

1

OF COURSE, WE have all read, and all do read *Capital*. For almost a century, we have been able to read it every day, transparently, in the dramas and dreams of our history, in its disputes and conflicts, in the defeats and victories of the workers' movement which is our only hope and our destiny. Since we 'came into the world', we have read *Capital* constantly in the writings and speeches of those who have read it for us, well or ill, both the dead and the living, Engels, Kautsky, Plekhanov, Lenin, Rosa Luxemburg, Trotsky, Stalin, Gramsci, the leaders of the workers' organizations, their supporters and opponents: philosophers, economists, politicians. We have read bits of it, the 'fragments' which the conjuncture had 'selected' for us. We have even all, more or less, read Volume One, from 'commodities' to the 'expropriation of the expropriators'.

But some day it is essential to read *Capital* to the letter. To read the text itself, complete, all four volumes, line by line, to return ten times to the first chapters, or to the schemes of simple reproduction and reproduction on an enlarged scale, before coming down from the arid table-lands and plateaus of Volume Two into the promised land of profit, interest and rent. And it is essential to read *Capital* not only in its French translation (even Volume One in Roy's translation, which Marx revised, or rather, rewrote), but also in the German original, at least for the fundamental theoretical chapters and all the passages where Marx's key concepts come to the surface.

That is how we decided to read *Capital*. The studies that emerged from this project are no more than the various individual protocols of this reading: each having cut the peculiar oblique path that suited him through the immense forest of this Book. And we present them in their immediate form without making any alterations so that all the risks and advantages of this adventure are reproduced; so that the reader will be able to find in them new-born the experience of a reading; and so that he in turn will be dragged in the wake of this first reading into a second one which will take us still further.

2

But as there is no such thing as an innocent reading, we must say what reading we are guilty of.

We were all philosophers. We did not read *Capital* as economists, as

From *Reading Capital*, London: New Left Books, 1970.

historians or as philologists. We did not pose *Capital* the question of its economic or historical content, nor of its mere internal 'logic'. We read *Capital* as philosophers, and therefore posed it a different question. To go straight to the point, let us admit: we posed it the question of its *relation to its object*, hence both the question of the specificity of its *object*, and the question of the specificity of its *relation* to that object, i.e. the question of the nature of the type of discourse set to work to handle this object, the question of scientific discourse. And since there can never be a definition without a difference, we posed *Capital* the question of the specific difference both of its object and of its discourse – asking ourselves at each step in our reading, what distinguishes the object of *Capital* not only from the object of classical (and even modern) political economy, but also from the object of Marx's Early Works, in particular from the object of the *1844 Manuscripts*; and hence what distinguishes the discourse of *Capital* not only from the discourse of classical economics, but also from the philosophical (ideological) discourse of the Young Marx.

To have read *Capital* as economists would have meant reading it while posing the question of the economic content and value of its analyses and schemes, hence comparing its discourse with an object already defined outside it, without questioning that object itself. To have read *Capital* as historians would have meant reading it while posing the question of the relation between its historical analyses and a historical object already defined outside it, without questioning that object itself. To have read *Capital* as logicians would have meant posing it the question of its methods of exposition and proof, but in the abstract, once again without questioning the object to which the methods of this discourse relate.

To read *Capital* as philosophers is precisely to question the specific object of a specific discourse, and the specific relationship between this discourse and its object; it is therefore to put to the *discourse–object* unity the question of the epistemological status which distinguishes this particular unity from other forms of discourse–object unity. Only this reading can determine the answer to a question that concerns the place *Capital* occupies in the history of knowledge. This question can be crystallized as follows: is *Capital* merely one ideological product among others, classical economics given a Hegelian form, the imposition of anthropological categories defined in the philosophical Early Works on the domain of economic reality; the 'realization' of the idealist aspirations of the *Jewish Question* and the *1844 Manuscripts*? Is *Capital* merely a continuation or even culmination of classical political economy, from which Marx inherited both object and concepts? And is *Capital* distinguished from classical economics not by its object, but only by its *method*, the dialectic he borrowed from Hegel? Or, on the contrary, does *Capital* constitute a real epistemological mutation of its object, theory and method? Does *Capital* represent the founding moment of a new discipline, the founding moment of a science – and hence a real event, a theoretical revolution, simultaneously rejecting

the classical political economy and the Hegelian and Feuerbachian ideologies of its prehistory – the absolute beginning of the history of a science?
And if this new science is the theory of *history* will it not make possible
in return a knowledge of its own *prehistory* – and hence a clear view of
both classical economics and the philosophical works of Marx's Youth?
Such are the implications of the epistemological question posed to *Capital*
by a philosophical reading of it.

Hence a philosophical reading of *Capital* is quite the opposite of an
innocent reading. It is a guilty reading, but not one that absolves its crime
on confessing it. On the contrary, it takes the responsibility for its crime as
a 'justified crime' and defends it by proving its necessity. It is therefore a
special reading which exculpates itself as a reading by posing every guilty
reading the very question that unmasks its innocence, the mere question of
its innocence: *what is it to read?*

3

However paradoxical it may seem, I venture to suggest that our age
threatens one day to appear in the history of human culture as marked
by the most dramatic and difficult trial of all, the discovery of and training
in the meaning of the 'simplest' acts of existence: seeing, listening,
speaking, reading – the acts which relate men to their works, and to
those works thrown in their faces, their 'absences of works'. And
contrary to all today's reigning appearances, we do not owe these
staggering knowledges to psychology, which is built on the absence of
a concept of them, but to a few men: Marx, Nietzsche and Freud.
Only since Freud have we begun to suspect what listening, and hence
what speaking (and keeping silent), *means* (*veut dire*); that this
'*meaning*' (*vouloir dire*) of speaking and listening reveals beneath the
innocence of speech and hearing the culpable depth of a second,
quite different discourse, the discourse of the unconscious.[1] I dare
maintain that only since Marx have we had to begin to suspect what,
in theory at least, *reading* and hence writing *means* (*veut dire*). It is
certainly no accident that we have been able to reduce all the ideological
pretensions which reigned on high over the *1844 Manuscripts*, and
still craftily haunt the temptations to historicist backsliding in *Capital*,
to the explicit innocence of a *reading*. For the Young Marx, to know
the essence of things, the essence of the historical human world, of its
economic, political, aesthetic and religious productions, was simply to
read (*lesen, herauslesen*) in black and white the presence of the 'abstract'
essence in the transparency of its 'concrete' existence. This immediate
reading of essence in existence expresses the religious model of
Hegel's Absolute Knowledge, that End of History in which the concept
at last becomes fully visible, present among us in person, tangible in its

259

sensory existence – in which *this* bread, *this* body, *this* face and *this* man are the Spirit itself. This sets us on the road to understanding that the yearning for a reading *at sight*, for Galileo's '*Great Book of the World*' itself, is older than all science, that it is still silently pondering the religious fantasies of epiphany and parousia, and the fascinating myth of the Scriptures, in which the body of truth, dressed in its words, is the Book: the Bible. This makes us suspect that to treat nature or reality as a Book, in which, according to Galileo, is spoken the silent discourse of a language whose 'characters are triangles, circles and other geometrical figures', it was necessary to have a certain idea of *reading* which makes a written discourse the immediate transparency of the true, and the real the discourse of a voice.

The first man ever to have posed the problem of *reading*, and in consequence, of *writing*, was Spinoza, and he was also the first man in the world to have proposed both a theory of history and a philosophy of the opacity of the immediate. With him, for the first time ever, a man linked together in this way the essence of reading and the essence of history in a theory of the difference between the imaginary and the true. This explains to us why Marx could not possibly have become Marx except by founding a theory of history and a philosophy of the historical distinction between ideology and science, and why in the last analysis this foundation was consummated in the dissipation of the religious myth of *reading*. The Young Marx of the *1844 Manuscripts* read the human essence at sight, immediately, in the transparency of its alienation. *Capital*, on the contrary, exactly measures a distance and an internal dislocation (*décalage*) in the real, inscribed in its *structure*, a distance and a dislocation such as to make their own effects themselves illegible, and the illusion of an immediate reading of them the ultimate apex of their effects: *fetishism*. It was essential to turn to history to track down this myth of reading to its lair, for it was from the history in which they offered it the cult of their religions and philosophies that men had projected it onto nature, so as not to perish in the daring project of knowing it. Only from history in thought, the theory of history, was it possible to account for the historical religion of reading: by discovering that the truth of history cannot be read in its manifest discourse, because the text of history is not a text in which a voice (the Logos) speaks, but the inaudible and illegible notation of the effects of a structure of structures. A reading of some of our expositions will show that, far from making metaphorical suggestions, I take the terms I am using literally. To break with the religious myth of reading: with Marx this theoretical necessity took precisely the form of a rupture with the Hegelian conception of the whole as a 'spiritual' totality, to be precise, as an *expressive* totality. It is no accident that when we turn the thin sheet of the theory of reading, we discover beneath it a theory of *expression*, and that we discover this theory of the expressive totality (in which each part is *pars totalis*, immediately expressing the whole that it inhabits in person) to be the theory which, in Hegel, for the last time and on the terrain of history itself, assembled all the complementary religious myths of the voice (the Logos) speaking in the sequences of a discourse; of the Truth that inhabits its Scripture; – and of the ear that hears or the eye that reads this discourse, in order to discover in it (if they are pure) the speech of the Truth which inhabits each of its Words in person. Need I add that once we have broken with the religious complicity between Logos and Being; between the Great Book that was, in its very being, the World, and the discourse of the knowledge of the world; between the essence of things and its reading; – once we have broken those tacit pacts in which the men of a still fragile age secured themselves with magical alliances against the precariousness of history and the trembling of their own daring – need I add that, once we have broken these ties, a new conception of *discourse* at last becomes possible?

4

Returning to Marx, we note that not only in what he says but in what he does we can grasp the transition from an earlier idea and practice of reading to a new practice of reading, and to a theory of history capable of providing us with a new theory of *reading*.

When we read Marx, we immediately find a *reader* who *reads* to us, and out loud. The fact that Marx was a prodigious reader is much less important for us than the fact that Marx felt the need to fill out his text by reading out loud, not only for the pleasure of quotation, or through scrupulousness in his references (his accuracy in this was fanatical, as his opponents learnt to their cost), not only because of the intellectual honesty which made him always and generously recognize his debts (alas, *he* knew what a debt was), but for reasons deeply rooted in the theoretical conditions of his work of discovery. So Marx reads out loud to us, not only in the *Theories of Surplus Value*[2] (a book which remains essentially in note form), but also in *Capital*: he reads Quesnay, he reads Smith, he reads Ricardo, etc. He reads them in what seems a perfectly lucid way: in order to support himself with what is correct in what they say, and in order to criticize what is false in what they say – in sum, to *situate* himself with respect to the acknowledged masters of Political Economy. However, the reading Marx makes of Smith and Ricardo is only lucid for a certain reading of this reading: for an immediate reading that does not question what it reads, but takes the obvious in the text read for hard cash. In reality, Marx's reading of Smith–Ricardo (they will be my example here) is, on *looking* at it closely, a rather special one. It is a double reading – or rather a reading which involves two radically different reading principles.

261

In the *first reading*, Marx reads his predecessor's discourse (Smith's for instance) through his own discourse. The result of this reading through a grid, in which Smith's text is seen through Marx's, projected onto it as a measure of it, is merely a summary of concordances and discordances, the balance of what Smith discovered and what he missed, of his merits and failings, of his presences and absences. In fact, this reading is a retrospective theoretical reading, in which what Smith could not see or understand appears only as a radical omission. Certain of these omissions do refer to others, and the latter to a primary omission – but even this reduction restricts us to the observation of presences and absences. As for the omissions themselves, this reading does not provide reasons for them, since the observation of them destroys them: the continuity of Marx's discourse shows the lacunae in Smith's discourse which are invisible (to Smith) beneath the apparent continuity of his discourse. Marx very often explains these omissions by Smith's distractions, or in the strict sense, his *absences*: he did not *see* what was, however, staring him in the face, he did not grasp what was, however, in his hands. 'Oversights' (*bévues*) all more or less related to the '*enormous oversight*', the confusion of constant capital and variable capital which dominates all classical economics with its 'incredible' aberration. This reduces every weakness in the system of concepts that makes up knowledge to a psychological weakness of 'vision'. And if it is absences of *vision* that explain these *oversights*, in the same way and by the same necessity, it is the presence and acuteness of 'vision' that will explain these '*sightings*' (*vues*): all the knowledges recognized.

This single logic of sighting and oversight thus reveals itself to us as what it is: the logic of a conception of knowledge in which all the work of knowledge is reduced in principle to the recognition of the mere relation of *vision*; in which the whole nature of its object is reduced to the mere condition of a *given*. What Smith did not see, through a weakness of vision, Marx sees: what Smith did not see was perfectly visible, and it was because it was visible that Smith could fail to see it while Marx could see it. We are in a circle – we have relapsed into the mirror myth of knowledge as the vision of a given object or the reading of an established text, neither of which is ever anything but transparency itself – the sin of blindness belonging by right to vision as much as the virtue of clear-sightedness – to the eye of man. But as one is always treated as one treats others, this reduces Marx to Smith minus the myopia – it reduces to nothing the whole gigantic effort by which Marx *tore* himself from Smith's supposed myopia; it reduces to a mere difference of *vision* this day in which all cats are no longer grey; it reduces to nothing the historical distance and theoretical dislocation (*décalage*) in which Marx thinks the theoretical difference that nevertheless separates him from Smith for ever. And finally, we too are condemned to the same fate of vision – condemned to see in Marx only what he *saw*.

But there is in Marx a *second quite different reading*, with nothing in common with the first. The latter, which is only sustained by the dual and conjoint observation of presences and absences, of sights and over-sights, can itself be blamed for a remarkable oversight: it does not *see* that the combined existence of sightings and oversights in an author poses a problem, the problem of their *combination*. It does not see this problem, precisely because this problem is only visible insofar as it is invisible, because this problem concerns something quite different from given objects that can be seen so long as one's eyes are clear: a necessary invisible connexion between the field of the visible and the field of the invisible, a connexion which defines the necessity of the obscure field of the invisible, as a necessary effect of the structure of the visible field.

But in order to make what I mean by this more comprehensible, I shall leave this abrupt posing of the question in suspense for the moment, and make a detour back to it through an analysis of the *second kind of reading* we find in Marx. I only need one example: the admirable Chapter XIX of *Capital*, on wages (T.II, pp. 206ff.; vol. I, pp. 535ff.),[3] secretly reflected backstage in Engels's extraordinary theoretical remarks in his Preface to Volume Two (pp. 14–19).

I therefore quote Marx, *reader* of the classical economists:

> Classical political economy naively borrowed from everyday life the category 'price of labour' without any prior verification, and then asked the question, how is this price determined? It soon recognized that the relations of demand and supply explained, in regard to the price of labour, as of all other commodities, nothing but the oscilla-tions of the market-price above or below a certain figure. If demand and supply balance, the variation in prices they produce ceases, but then the effect of demand and supply ceases, too. At the moment when demand and supply are in equilibrium, the price of labour no longer depends on their action and must be determined as if they did not exist. This price, the centre of gravity of the market prices, thus emerged as the true object of scientific analysis.
>
> The same result was obtained by taking a period of several years and calculating the averages to which the alternative rising and falling movements could be reduced by continuous compensations. This left an average price, a relatively constant magnitude, which predomi-nates over the oscillations in the market prices and regulates them internally. This average price, the Physiocrats' 'necessary price' – Adam Smith's 'natural-price' – can, with labour, as with all other commodities, be nothing else than its *value* expressed in money. 'The commodity,' says Smith, 'is then sold for precisely *what it is worth*.'
>
> In this way, classical political economy believed it had ascended from the accidental prices of labour to the real value of labour. It then determined this value by the value of the subsistence goods

necessary for the maintenance and reproduction of the labourer. *It thus unwittingly changed terrain* by substituting for the value of labour, up to this point, *the apparent object of its investigations*, the value of labour power, a power which only exists in the personality of the labourer, and is as different from its function, labour, as a machine is from its performance. Hence the course of the analysis had led them forcibly not only from the market prices of labour to its necessary price and its value, but had led to their resolution of the so-called value of labour into the value of labour power, so that from then on the former should have been treated merely as a phenomenal form of the latter. The result the analysis led to, therefore, was *not a resolution of the problem as it emerged at the beginning, but a complete change in the terms of that problem.*

Classical economy never arrived at an awareness of this substitution, exclusively preoccupied as it was with the difference between the current prices of labour and its value, with the relation of this value to the values of commodities, to the rate of profit, etc. The deeper it went into the analysis of value in general, the more the so-called value of labour led it into inextricable contradictions ...

(T.II, pp. 208–9; vol. I, pp. 537–8)

I take this astonishing text for what it is: a protocol of Marx's *reading* of classical economics. Here again it is tempting to believe that we are destined to a conception of reading which adds up the balance of sightings and oversights. Classical political economy certainly saw that ... but it did not see that ... it 'never arrived at' a sight of ... Here again, it seems as if this balance of sights and oversights is found beneath a grid, the classical absences revealed by the Marxist presences. But there is one small, one very small difference, which, I warn the reader straight away, we have no intention of *not seeing*! It is this: what classical political economy does not see, is not what it does not see, it is *what it sees*; it is not what it lacks, on the contrary, it is *what it does not lack*; it is not what it misses, on the contrary, it is *what it does not miss*. The oversight, then, is not to see what one sees, the oversight no longer concerns the object, but *the sight* itself. The oversight is an oversight that concerns *vision*: non-vision is therefore inside vision, it is a form of vision and hence has a necessary relationship with vision.

We have reached our real problem, the problem that exists *in* and is posed *by* the actual identity of this organic confusion of non-vision in vision. Or rather, in this observation of non-vision, or of oversight, we are no longer dealing with a reading of classical economics through the grid of Marx's theory alone, with a comparison between classical theory and Marxist theory, the latter providing the standard – for we never compare classical theory with anything *except itself*, its non-vision with its vision. We are therefore dealing with our problem in its pure state, defined in a single domain, without any regression to infinity. To understand this necessary and paradoxical identity of non-vision and vision within vision itself is very exactly to pose our problem (the problem of the necessary connexion which unites the visible and the invisible), and to pose it properly is to give ourselves a chance of solving it.

6

How, therefore, is this identity of non-vision and vision in vision possible? Let us reread our text carefully. In the course of the questions classical economics asked about the 'value of labour' something very special has happened. Classical political economy has *'produced'* (just as Engels will say, in the Preface to Volume Two, that phlogistic chemistry 'produced' oxygen and classical economics 'produced' surplus value) a correct answer: the value of 'labour' is equal to the value of the subsistence goods necessary for the reproduction of 'labour'. A correct answer is a correct answer. Any reader in the 'first manner' will give Smith and Ricardo a good mark and pass on to other observations. Not Marx. For what we shall call his eye has been attracted by a remarkable property of this answer; *it is the correct answer to a question that has just one failing: it was never posed.*

The original question as the classical economic text formulated it was: what is the value of *labour*? Reduced to the content that can be rigorously defended in the text where classical economics produced it, the answer should be written as follows: *'The value of* labour (   ) *is equal to the value of the subsistence goods necessary for the maintenance and reproduction of labour (   )'*. There are two *blanks*, two absences in the text of the answer. Thus Marx makes us *see* blanks in the text of classical economics' answer; but that is merely to make us see what the classical text itself says while not saying it, does not say while saying it. Hence it is not Marx who says what the classical text does not say, it is not Marx who intervenes to impose from without on the classical text a discourse which reveals its silence – *it is the classical text itself which tells us that it is silent*: its silence is *its own words*. In fact, if we suppress our 'slots', our blanks, we still have the same discourse, the same apparently 'full' sentence: *'the value of labour is equal to the value of the subsistence goods necessary for the maintenance and reproduction of labour.'* But this sentence means nothing: what is the maintenance of 'labour'? What is the reproduction of 'labour'? The substitution of one word for another at the end of the answer: 'labourer' for 'labour', might seem to settle the question. *'The value of labour is equal to the value of the subsistence goods necessary for the maintenance and reproduction of the labourer.'* But as the labourer is not the labour the term at the end of the sentence now clashes with the term at the beginning: they do not have the same content and the equation cannot be made, for it is not the labourer who is bought for the wages, but his 'labour'. And how are we to situate the first labour in the second term: 'labourer'? In even uttering this sentence, therefore, precisely at the level of the term '*labour*', at the beginning and end of the answer, there is something lacking, and this lack is strictly designated by the function of the terms themselves in the whole sentence. If we suppress our slots – our blanks – we are merely reconstituting a sentence which, if it is taken literally, itself designates in itself these *points of emptiness*, restores these slots as the marks of an omission produced by the 'fullness' of the utterance itself.

This omission, located *by the answer* in the answer itself immediately next to the word '*labour*', is no more than the presence in the answer of the absence of its question, the omission of *its question*. For the question posed does not seem to contain anything by which to *locate* in it this omission. '*What is the value of labour?*' is a sentence identical to a concept, it is a concept-sentence which is content to *utter* the concept 'value of labour', an utterance-sentence which does not designate any omission in itself, unless it is itself as a whole, as a concept, a question *manqué*, a concept *manqué*, the omission (*manque*) of a concept. It is the answer that answers us about the question, since the question's only space is this very concept of 'labour' which is designated by the answer as *the site of the omission*. It is the answer that tells us that the question is *its own omission*, and nothing else.

If the answer, including its omissions, is correct, and if *its* question is merely the omission of its concept, it is because the answer is the answer to *a different question*, which is peculiar in one respect, it has not been uttered in the classical economic text, but is uttered as slots in its answer, precisely *in the slots in its answer*. That is why Marx can write:

> The result the analysis led to, therefore, was not a resolution of the problem as it emerged at the beginning, but a complete change in the terms of the problem.

That is why Marx can pose the unuttered *question*, simply by uttering the concept present in an unuttered form in the emptinesses in the *answer*, sufficiently present in this answer to produce and reveal these emptinesses as the emptinesses of a presence. Marx re-establishes the continuity of the utterance by introducing/re-establishing in the utterance the concept of *labour power*, present in the emptinesses in the utterance of classical political economy's answer – and at the same time as establishing/re-establishing the continuity of the answer, by the utterance of the concept of labour power, he produces the as yet unposed question, which the as yet un-asked-for answer answered.

The answer then becomes: '*The value of labour-power is equal to the value of the subsistence goods necessary for the maintenance and reproduction of labour power*' – and *its* question is produced as follows: '*what is the value of labour power?*'

This restoration of an utterance containing emptinesses and this production of *its* question out of the answer enable us to bring to light the reasons why classical economics was blind to what it nevertheless saw, and thus to explain the non-vision inside its vision. Moreover, it is clear that the mechanism whereby Marx is able to see what classical economics did not see while seeing it, is identical with the mechanism whereby Marx saw what classical economics did not see at all – and also, at least in principle, identical with the mechanism whereby we are at this moment reflecting this operation of the sighting of a non-sight of the seen, by *reading* a text by Marx which is itself a *reading* of a text of classical economics.

7

We have now reached the point we had to reach in order to discover from it the reason for this *oversight* where a *sighting* is concerned: we must completely reorganize the idea we have of knowledge, we must abandon the mirror myths of immediate vision and reading, and conceive knowledge as a production.

What made the mistake of political economy possible does indeed affect the *transformation of the object* of its oversight. What political economy does not see is not a pre-existing object which it could have seen but did not see – but an object which it produced itself in its oper- ation of knowledge and which did not pre-exist it: precisely the produc- tion itself, which is identical with the object. What political economy does not see is what it *does*: its production of a new answer without a ques- tion, and simultaneously the production of a new latent question contained by default in this new answer. Through the lacunary terms of its new answer political economy produced a new question, but '*unwittingly*'. It made '*a complete change in the terms of the*' original '*problem*', and thereby produced a new problem, but without knowing it. Far from knowing it, it remained convinced that it was still on the terrain of the old problem, whereas it has '*unwittingly changed terrain*'. Its blindness and its 'oversight' lie in this misunderstanding, between what it produces and what it sees, in this '*substitution*', which Marx elsewhere calls a '*play on words*' (*Wortspiel*) that is necessarily impenetrable for its author.

Why is political economy necessarily blind to what it produces and to its work of production? Because its eyes are still fixed on *the old ques- tion*, and it continues to relate its new answer to its old question; because it is still concentrating on the old '*horizon*' (*Capital*, T.II, p. 210) within which the new problem '*is not visible*' (ibid.). Thus the metaphors in which Marx thinks this necessary 'substitution' suggest the image of a change of terrain and a corresponding change of horizon. They raise a crucial point which enables us to escape from the psychological reduc- tion of the 'oversight' or 'unwittingness'. In fact, what is at stake in the production of this new problem contained *unwittingly* in the new answer is not a particular new object which has emerged among other, already identified objects, like an unexpected guest at a family reunion; on the contrary, what has happened involves a transformation of the *entire* terrain and its *entire* horizon, which are the background against which the new problem is produced. The emergence of this new critical problem is merely a particular index of a possible critical transformation and of a possible latent mutation which affect the reality of this terrain throughout its extent, including the extreme limits of its 'horizon'. Putting this fact in a language I have already used,[4] the production of a new problem endowed with this *critical* character (critical in the sense of a critical situation) is the unstable index of the possible production of a new theoretical *problematic*, of which this problem is only one symptomatic mode. Engels says this luminously in his Preface to Volume Two of *Capital*: the mere 'production' of oxygen by phlogistic chemistry, or of surplus value by classical economics, contains the wherewithal not only to modify the old theory *at one point*, but also to 'revolutionize *all* economics' or *all* chemistry (Vol. II, p. 15). Hence what is in balance in this unstable and apparently local event is the possibility of a revolution in the old theory and hence in the old problematic *as a totality*. This introduces us to a fact peculiar to the very existence of science: it can only pose problems on the terrain and within the horizon of a definite theoretical structure, its problematic, which constitutes its absolute and definite condition of possibility, and hence the absolute determination of *the forms in which all problems must be posed*, at any given moment in the science.[5]

This opens the way to an understanding of the determination of the *visible* as visible, and conjointly, of the invisible as invisible, and of the organic link binding the invisible to the visible. Any object or problem situated on the terrain and within the horizon, i.e. in the definite structured field of the theoretical problematic of a given theoretical discipline, is visible. We must take these words literally. The sighting is thus no longer the act of an individual subject, endowed with the faculty of 'vision' which he exercises either attentively or distractedly; the sighting is the act of its structural conditions, it is the relation of immanent reflection[6] between the field of the problematic and *its* objects and *its* problems. Vision then loses the religious privileges of divine reading: it is no more than a reflection of the immanent necessity that ties an object or problem to its conditions of existence, which lie in the conditions of its production. It is literally no longer the eye (the mind's eye) of a subject which *sees* what exists in the field defined by a theoretical problematic: it is this field itself which *sees itself* in the objects or problems it defines – sighting being merely the necessary reflection of the field on its objects. (This no doubt explains a 'substitution' in the classical philosophies of vision, which are very embarrassed by *having* to say *both* that the light of vision comes from the eye, *and* that it comes from the object.)

The same connexion that defines the visible also defines the invisible as its shadowy obverse. It is the field of the problematic that defines and structures the invisible as the defined excluded, *excluded* from the field of visibility and *defined* as excluded by the existence and peculiar structure of the field of the problematic; as what forbids and represses the reflection of the field on its object, i.e. the necessary and immanent interrelationship of the problematic and one of its objects. This is the case with oxygen in the phlogistic theory of chemistry, or with surplus value and the definition of the 'value of labour' in classical economics. These new objects and problems are necessarily *invisible* in the field of the existing theory, because they are not objects of this theory, because they are *forbidden* by it – they are objects and problems necessarily without any necessary relations with the field of the visible as defined by this problematic. They are invisible because they are rejected in principle, repressed from the field of the visible: and that is why their fleeting presence in the field when it does occur (in very peculiar and symptomatic circumstances) *goes unperceived*, and becomes literally an undivulgeable absence – since the whole function of the field is not to see them, to forbid any sighting of them. Here again, the invisible is no more a function of *a subject's sighting* than is the visible: the invisible is the theoretical problematic's non-vision of its non-objects, the invisible is the darkness, the blinded eye of the theoretical problematic's self-reflection when it scans its non-objects, its non-problems without seeing them, *in order not to look at them*.

And since, to use terms adopted from some very remarkable passages in the preface to Michel Foucault's *Histoire de la Folie*,[7] we have evoked the conditions of possibility of the visible and the invisible, of the inside and the outside of the theoretical field that defines the visible – perhaps we can go one step further and show that *a certain relation of necessity* may exist between the visible and the invisible thus defined. In the development of a theory, the invisible of a visible field is not generally *anything whatever* outside and foreign to the visible defined by that field. The invisible is defined by the visible as *its* invisible, *its* forbidden vision: the invisible is not therefore simply what is outside the visible (to return to the spatial metaphor), the outer darkness of exclusion – but the *inner darkness of exclusion*, inside the visible itself because defined by its structure. In other words, the seductive metaphors of the terrain, the horizon and hence the limits of a visible field defined by a given problematic threaten to induce a false idea of the nature of this field, if we think this field literally according to the spatial metaphor[8] as a space limited by *another space outside it*. This other space is also in the first space which contains it as its own denegation; this other space is the first space in person, which is only defined by the denegation of what it excludes from its own limits. In other words, all its limits are *internal*, it carries its outside inside it. Hence, if we wish to preserve the spatial metaphor, the paradox of the theoretical field is that it is an *infinite* because *definite* space, i.e. it has no limits, no external frontiers separating it from nothing, precisely because it is *defined* and limited within itself, carrying in itself the finitude of its definition, which, by excluding what it is not, makes it what it is. Its *definition* (a scientific operation *par excellence*), then is what makes it both *infinite in its kind*, and marked inside itself, in all its determinations, by what is excluded from it *in it* by its very definition. And when it happens that, in certain very special critical circumstances, the development of the questions produced by the problematic (in the present case, the development of the questions of political economy investigating the 'value of labour') leads to the *production* of the *fleeting presence of an aspect* of its invisible within the visible field of the existing problematic – this product can then only be *invisible*, since the light of the field scans it blindly without reflecting on it. This invisible thus disappears as a theoretical lapse, absence, lack of symptom. It manifests itself exactly as it is: invisible to theory – and that is why Smith made his 'oversight'.

To see this invisible, to see these 'oversights', to identify the lacunae in the fullness of this discourse, the blanks in the crowded text, we need something quite different from an acute or attentive gaze; we need an *informed* gaze, a new gaze, itself produced by a reflection of the 'change of terrain' on the exercise of vision, in which Marx pictures the transformation of the problematic. Here I take this transformation for a fact, without any claim to analyse the mechanism that unleashed it and completed it. The fact that this '*change of terrain*' which produces as its effect this metamorphosis in the gaze, was itself only produced in very specific, complex and often dramatic conditions; that it is absolutely irreducible to the idealist myth of a mental decision to change 'view-points'; that it brings into play a whole process that the subject's sighting, far from producing, merely reflects in its own place; that in this process of real transformation of the means of production of knowledge, the claims of a 'constitutive subject' are as vain as are the claims of the subject of vision in the production of the visible; that the whole process takes place in the dialectical crisis of the mutation of a theoretical structure in which the 'subject' plays, not the part it believes it is playing, but the part which is assigned to it by the mechanism of the process – all these are questions that cannot be studied here. It is enough to remember that the subject must have occupied its new place in the new terrain,[9] in other words that the subject must already, even partly unwittingly, have been installed in this new terrain, for it to be possible to apply to the old invisible the informed gaze that will make that invisible visible. Marx can see what escaped Smith's gaze because he has already occupied this new terrain which, in what new answers it had produced, had nevertheless been produced though unwittingly, by the old problematic.

8

Such is Marx's second reading: a reading which might well be called '*symptomatic*' (*symptomale*), insofar as it divulges the undivulged event in the text it reads, and in the same movement relates it to *a different text*, present as a necessary absence in the first. Like his first reading, Marx's second reading presupposes the existence of *two texts*, and the measurement of the first against the second. But what distinguishes this new reading from the old one is the fact that in the new one the *second text* is articulated with the lapses in the first text. Here again, at least in the way peculiar to theoretical texts (the only ones whose analysis is at issue here), we find the necessity and possibility of one reading on two bearings simultaneously.

In the papers you are about to *read*, and which do not escape the law I have pronounced – assuming that they have some claim to be treated, for the time being at least, as discourses with a theoretical meaning – we have simply tried to apply to Marx's reading the *'symptomatic' reading* with which Marx managed to read the illegible in Smith, by measuring the problematic initially visible in his writings against the invisible problematic contained in the paradox of *an answer which does not correspond to any question posed*. You will also find that the infinite distance which separates Marx from Smith and in consequence our relation to Marx from Marx's relation to Smith, is the following radical difference: whereas in his text Smith produces an answer which not only does not answer any of the immediately preceding questions, but does not even answer *any* other question he ever posed anywhere in his work; with Marx, on the contrary, when he does happen to formulate *an answer without a question*, with a little patience and perspicacity we can find the *question* itself *elsewhere*, twenty or one hundred pages further on, with respect to some other object, enveloped in some other matter, or, on occasion, in Engel's immediate comments on Marx, for Engels has flashes of profound inspiration.[10] And if, as I have dared suggest, there is undoubtedly in Marx an important *answer* to a *question that is nowhere posed*, an answer which Marx only succeeds in formulating on condition of multiplying the images required to render it, the answer of the *'Darstellung'* and its avatars, it is surely because the age Marx lived in did not provide him, and he could not acquire in his lifetime, an adequate concept with which to think what he produced: *the concept of the effectivity of a structure on its elements*. It will no doubt be said that this is merely a word, and that only the word is missing, since the *object* of the word is there complete. Certainly, but this word is a *concept*, and the repercussions of the structural lack of this concept can be found in certain precise theoretical effects on certain assignable *forms* of Marx's discourse, and in certain of his identifiable *formulations* which are not without their consequences. Which may help to illuminate, but this time *from within*, i.e. not as a relic of a past, a survival, a raffish 'flirtation' (the famous *'kokettieren'*), or a trap for fools (the advantage of my dialectic is that I say things little by little – and when they think I have finished, and rush to refute me, they merely make an untimely manifestation of their asininity!

271

– Letter to Engels, 27 June 1867), the *real presence* of certain Hegelian forms and references in the discourse of *Capital*. *From within*, as the exact measurement of a disconcerting but inevitable absence, the absence of the concept (and of all the sub-concepts) *of the effectivity of a structure on its elements* which is the visible/invisible, absent/present keystone of his whole work. Perhaps therefore it is not impermissible to think that if Marx does 'play' so much with Hegelian formulae in certain passages, the game is not just raffishness or sarcasm, but *the action of a real drama*, in which old concepts desperately play the part of something absent *which is nameless*, in order to call it onto the stage in person – whereas they only 'produce' its presence in their failures, in the dislocation between the characters and their roles.

If it is true that the identification and location of this omission, which is a *philosophical* omission, can also lead us to the threshold of Marx's philosophy, we can hope for other gains from it in the theory of history itself. A conceptual omission that has not been divulged, but on the contrary, consecrated as a non-omission, and proclaimed as a fullness, may, in certain circumstances, seriously hinder the development of a science or of certain of its branches. To be convinced of this we need only note that a science only progresses, i.e. *lives*, by the extreme attention it pays to the points where it is theoretically fragile. By these standards, it depends less for its life on what it knows than on what it *does not know*: its absolute precondition is to focus on this unknown, and to pose it in the rigour of a problem. But the unknown of a science is not what empiricist ideology thinks: its 'residue', what it leaves out, what it cannot conceive or resolve; but *par excellence* what it contains that is fragile despite its apparently unquestionable 'obviousness', certain silences in its discourse, certain conceptual omissions and lapses in its rigour, in brief, everything in it that 'sounds hollow' to an attentive ear, despite its fullness.[11] If it is true that a science progresses and lives by knowing how to hear what 'sounds hollow' in it, some part of the life of the Marxist theory of history perhaps depends on this precise point where Marx shows us in a thousand ways the presence of a concept essential to his thought, but absent from his discourse.

NOTES

1 We owe this result, which has revolutionized our *reading* of Freud to Jacques Lacan's intransigent and lucid – and for many years isolated – theoretical effort. At a time when the radical novelty of what Jacques Lacan has given us is beginning to pass into the public domain, where everyone can make use of it and profit by it in his own way, I feel bound to acknowledge my debt to an exemplary reading lesson which, as we shall see, goes beyond its object of origin in some of its effects. I feel bound to acknowledge this

publicly, so that 'the tailor's labour (does not) disappear . . . into the coat' (Marx), even into my coat. Just as I feel bound to acknowledge the obvious or concealed debts which bind us to our masters in reading learned works, once Gaston Bachelard and Jean Cavaillès and now Georges Canguilhem and Michel Foucault.

2 Two volumes out of three translated into English and published by Lawrence & Wishart.

3 References to *Capital* Volume One are given first to Roy's French translation in the three volumes of the Éditions Sociales version (T.I, T.II, T.III) and then to the English translation of Moore and Aveling in one volume published by Lawrence & Wishart (vol. I). References to Volumes Two and Three are given to the English translation only (vol. II, vol. III).

4 *For Marx*, Allen Lane, London 1969, pp. 46, 66–70, etc.

5 Auguste Comte often came very close to this idea.

6 'Relation of immanent reflection': this 'reflection' itself poses a theoretical problem which I cannot deal with here.

7 Plon, Paris 1961; abridged translation, *Madness and Civilization*, Tavistock Press, London 1967.

8 The recourse made in this text to spatial metaphors (field, terrain, space, site, situation, position, etc.) poses a theoretical problem: the problem of the validity of its *claim* to existence in a discourse with scientific pretensions. The problem may be formulated as follows: *why* does a certain form of scientific discourse necessarily need the use of metaphors borrowed from non-scientific disciplines?

9 I retain the spatial metaphor. But the change of terrain takes place *on the spot*: in all strictness, we should speak of the mutation of the *mode* of theoretical production and of the change of function of the subject induced by this change of mode.

10 If I may invoke my personal experience, I should like to give two precise examples of this presence *elsewhere* in Marx or in Engels of the question absent from its answer. At the cost of a decidedly laborious investigation, the text of which (*For Marx*, pp. 89ff) bears the mark of these difficulties, I succeeded in identifying a pertinent absence in the idea of the 'inversion' of the Hegelian dialectic by Marx: the absence of its concept, and therefore of its question. I managed to reconstruct this *question* laboriously, by showing that the 'inversion' Marx mentions had as its effective content a revolution in the problematic. But later, reading Engels's Preface to Volume Two of *Capital*, I was stupefied to find that the question I had had such trouble in formulating was there in black and white! Engels expressly identifies the 'inversion', the 'setting right side up again' of the chemistry and political economy which had been standing on their heads, with a change in their 'theory', and therefore in their problematic. Or again: in one of my first essays, I had suggested that Marx's theoretical revolution lay not in his change of the answers, but in his change of the questions, and that therefore Marx's revolution in the theory of history consisted of a *'change of elements'* by which he moved from the terrain of ideology to the terrain of science (*For Marx*, p. 47). But recently, reading the chapter of *Capital* on wages, I was stupefied to see that Marx used the very expression *'change of terrain'* to express this change of theoretical problematic. Here again, the

question (or its concept) which I had laboriously reconstituted out of its *absence* in one precise point of Marx's, Marx himself gave in black and white *somewhere else* in his work.

11 Pierre Macherey: 'A propos de la rupture', *La Nouvelle critique*, Paris, May 1965, p. 139.

18

Hannah Arendt

(1906–1975)

An original and unorthodox thinker, Hannah Arendt is not easily classified by labels and categories. The diverse strands of her thought have inspired others across a wide variety of disciplines, including philosophy, feminism and political theory. With hindsight, we can see that Arendt also anticipated critical theory's current attention to communicative ethics, evidenced by her unwavering commitment to the public sphere as the realm of action where freedom can be realized. If we add to this portrait a background enriched by classical philosophy, phenomenology, Kant and the German philosophical tradition, we begin to understand why she eludes easy definition. Her major works include *The Origins of Totalitarianism* (1951), *The Human Condition* (1958), *Rahel Varnhagen: The Life of a Jewish Woman* (1958), *Between Past and Future: Eight Exercises in Political Thought* (1961), *Eichmann in Jerusalem: A Report on the Banality of Evil* (1963), *On Revolution* (1963), *On Violence* (1970), *The Life of the Mind* (1978) and *Lectures on Kant's Political Philosophy* (1982).

Arendt was born in Hanover, Germany in 1906 to Jewish parents, but the family relocated to Königsberg when she was still quite young. Although her father died by the time she was seven, Arendt was encouraged by her widowed mother to follow the complex and controversial political events occurring in Germany after the First World War, including the fate of Rosa Luxemburg and the Sparticist revolt. Arendt continued her education at the University of Marburg in 1924, where she studied phenomenology with Martin Heidegger and *Existenz* philosophy with Karl Jaspers. In 1929 she completed a doctorate under Jaspers' supervision entitled 'The concept of love in Augustine'. When the Nazis rose to power in 1933, she and her husband were forced to flee Germany. Arendt encountered other Jewish exiles in Paris, in particular Walter Benjamin, but again she and her husband were barely ahead of the Nazi *Wehrmacht* when they left for New York in 1940 with the fall of France. At this point Arendt began to teach at the New School for Social Research in New York, an affiliation that lasted thirty-five years until her death in 1975.

Her analysis of totalitarianism in *The Origins of Totalitarianism* (1951) focuses on the plight of those who become stateless nomads, deprived of legal protection and freedom by a bureaucratic efficiency that scapegoats human beings mechanically and procedurally. Certainly, the victims of the Holocaust were Arendt's immediately apparent topic in that volume, but the power of her analysis lies in its generality and applicability to all cases where human beings are forced to live outside of law. Such victims suffer not only the loss of legal protection, but the loss of participatory action as well. Their removal from the public sphere, according to Arendt, assures their potential annihilation just as much as their physical incarceration in a labour camp. Arendt returns to this theme of community and action in *The Human Condition*, arguing for an understanding of action as a political and public expression of freedom. While she is often criticized for nostalgically assuming the idealized Greek *polis* to be a politically adequate model for our own era, detractors forget the motivation for her theme. Without a public sphere that enables us to take responsibility or demand justice, we must abandon ourselves to a mute acceptance of fate.

Arendt's coverage of the Eichmann trial in 1963 for the *New Yorker* (*Eichmann in Jerusalem*) is the occasion for revealing to us 'the banality of evil', even in one accountable for so many deaths. Surprisingly, where we expect to discover in Eichmann the epitome of moral depravity and psychopathic tendencies, she perceives the most frightening truth: he saw himself as a small man 'just doing his job'. The bureaucratic machine in which he operated demanded nothing more than systematic efficiency, accuracy and complete obedience. Of course, the horror she reports is that of actually recognizing a 'typical' human being, exactly like millions of others, with no sense of agency or conscience.

For Arendt, the ultimate indictment of mechanistic totalitarian rule, whether Nazi or Stalinist, rests on the evidence of the dehumanized individuals it creates to carry out its banal tasks of carnage and elimination.

SELECT BIBLIOGRAPHY OF ARENDT'S WORKS IN ENGLISH

The Human Condition, Chicago: University of Chicago Press, 1958.
Between Past and Future: Eight Exercises in Political Thought, New York: Viking, 1961.
Eichmann in Jerusalem: A Report on the Banality of Evil, London: Faber & Faber, 1963.
The Origins of Totalitarianism, 3rd edn, London: Allen & Unwin, 1967.
Men in Dark Times, London: Cape, 1970.
On Violence, London: Allen Lane, 1970.
Crises of the Republic, New York: Harcourt Brace Jovanovich, 1972.
On Revolution, Harmondsworth: Penguin, 1973.
The Jew as Pariah: Jewish Identity and Politics in the Modern Age, ed. R. Feldman, New York: Grove Press, 1978.

The Life of the Mind, vol. I: *Thinking*; vol. II: *Willing*, New York: Harcourt Brace Jovanovich, 1978.

Lectures on Kant's Political Philosophy, ed. R. Beiner, Chicago: University of Chicago Press, 1982.

HANNAH ARENDT

Preface to *Between Past and Future*

THE GAP BETWEEN PAST AND FUTURE

NOTRE HÉRITAGE N'EST *précédé d'aucun testament* – 'our inheritance
was left to us by no testament' – this is perhaps the strangest of the
strangely abrupt aphorisms into which René Char, French poet and writer,
compressed the gist of what four years in the *résistance* had come to mean
to a whole generation of European writers and men of letters. The collapse
of France, to them a totally unexpected event, had emptied, from one day
to the next, the political scene of their country, leaving it to the puppet-
like antics of knaves or fools, and they who as a matter of course had
never participated in the official business of the Third Republic were
sucked into politics as though with the force of a vacuum. Thus, without
premonition and probably against their conscious inclinations, they had
come to constitute willy-nilly a public realm where – without the paraphernalia of officialdom and hidden from the eyes of friend and foe – all
relevant business in the affairs of the country was transacted in deed and
word.

It did not last long. After a few short years they were liberated from
what they originally had thought to be a 'burden' and thrown back into
what they now knew to be the weightless irrelevance of their personal
affairs, once more separated from 'the world of reality' by an *épaisseur
triste*, the 'sad opaqueness' of a private life centered about nothing but
itself. And if they refused 'to go back to [their] very beginnings, to [their]
most indigent behavior', they could only return to the old empty strife of
conflicting ideologies which after the defeat of the common enemy once
more occupied the political arena to split the former comrades-in-arms
into innumerable cliques which were not even factions and to engage them
in the endless polemics and intrigues of a paper war. What Char had foreseen, clearly anticipated, while the real fight was still on – 'If I survive,
I know that I shall have to break with the aroma of these essential years,
silently reject (not repress) my treasure' – had happened. They had lost
their treasure.

What was this treasure? As they themselves understood it, it seems
to have consisted, as it were, of two interconnected parts: they had discovered that he who 'joined the Resistance, *found* himself', that he ceased
to be 'in quest of [himself] without mastery, in naked unsatisfaction', that
he no longer suspected himself of 'insincerity', of being 'a carping, suspicious actor of life', that he could afford 'to go naked'. In this nakedness,
stripped of all masks – of those which society assigns to its members as

From *Between Past and Future: Eight Exercises in Political Thought*, New York:
Viking, 1961.

well as those which the individual fabricates for himself in his psychological reactions against society – they had been visited for the first time
in their lives by an apparition of freedom, not, to be sure, because they
acted against tyranny and things worse than tyranny – this was true
for every soldier in the Allied armies – but because they had become
'challengers', had taken the initiative upon themselves and therefore,
without knowing or even noticing it, had begun to create that public space
between themselves where freedom could appear. 'At every meal that we
eat together, freedom is invited to sit down. The chair remains vacant,
but the place is set.'

The men of the European Resistance were neither the first nor the
last to lose their treasure. The history of revolutions – from the summer
of 1776 in Philadelphia and the summer of 1789 in Paris to the autumn
of 1956 in Budapest – which politically spells out the innermost story of
the modern age, could be told in parable form as the tale of an age-old
treasure which, under the most varied circumstances, appears abruptly,
unexpectedly, and disappears again, under different mysterious conditions,
as though it were a *fata Morgana*. There exist, indeed, many good reasons
to believe that the treasure was never a reality but a mirage, that we deal
here not with anything substantial but with an apparition, and the best
of these reasons is that the treasure thus far has remained nameless. Does
something exist, not in outer space but in the world and the affairs of
men on earth, which has not even a name? Unicorns and fairy queens
seem to possess more reality than the lost treasure of the revolutions. And
yet, if we turn our eyes to the beginnings of this era, and especially to
the decades preceding it, we may discover to our surprise that the eighteenth century on both sides of the Atlantic possessed a name for this
treasure, a name long since forgotten and lost – one is tempted to say –
even before the treasure itself disappeared. The name in America was
'public happiness', which, with its overtones of 'virtue' and 'glory', we
understand hardly better than its French counterpart, 'public freedom';
the difficulty for us is that in both instances the emphasis was on 'public'.

However that may be, it is the namelessness of the lost treasure to
which the poet alludes when he says that our inheritance was left us by
no testament. The testament, telling the heir what will rightfully be his,
wills past possessions for a future. Without testament or, to resolve the
metaphor, without tradition – which selects and names, which hands down
and preserves, which indicates where the treasures are and what their
worth is – there seems to be no willed continuity in time and hence,
humanly speaking, neither past nor future, only sempiternal change of the
world and the biological cycle of living creatures in it. Thus the treasure
was lost not because of historical circumstances and the adversity of reality
but because no tradition had foreseen its appearance or its reality, because
no testament had willed it for the future. The loss, at any rate, perhaps
inevitable in terms of political reality, was consummated by oblivion, by

279

a failure of memory, which befell not only the heirs but, as it were, the actors, the witnesses, those who for a fleeting moment had held the treasure in the palms of their hands, in short, the living themselves. For remembrance, which is only one, though one of the most important, modes of thought, is helpless outside a pre-established framework of reference, and the human mind is only on the rarest occasions capable of retaining something which is altogether unconnected. Thus the first who failed to remember what the treasure was like were precisely those who had possessed it and found it so strange that they did not even know how to name it. At the time this did not bother them; if they did not know their treasure, they knew well enough the meaning of what they did and that it was beyond victory and defeat: 'Action that has a meaning for the living has value only for the dead, completion only in the minds that inherit and question it'. The tragedy began not when the liberation of the country as a whole ruined, almost automatically, the small hidden islands of freedom that were doomed anyhow, but when it turned out that there was no mind to inherit and to question, to think about and to remember. The point of the matter is that the 'completion', which indeed every enacted event must have in the minds of those who then are to tell the story and to convey its meaning, eluded them; and without this thinking completion after the act, without the articulation accomplished by remembrance, there simply was no story left that could be told.

There is nothing in this situation that is altogether new. We are only too familiar with the recurring outbursts of passionate exasperation with reason, thought, and rational discourse which are the natural reactions of men who know from their own experiences that thought and reality have parted company, that reality has become opaque for the light of thought and that thought, no longer bound to incident as the circle remains bound to its focus, is liable either to become altogether meaningless or to rehash old verities which have lost all concrete relevance. Even the anticipating recognition of the predicament has by now become familiar. When Tocqueville returned from the New World, which he so superbly knew how to describe and to analyze that his work has remained a classic and survived more than a century of radical change, he was well aware of the fact that what Char called the 'completion' of act and event had still eluded him; and Char's 'Our inheritance was left to us by no testament' sounds like a variation of Tocqueville's 'Since the past has ceased to throw its light upon the future, the mind of man wanders in obscurity'. Yet the only exact description of this predicament is to be found, as far as I know, in one of those parables of Franz Kafka which, unique perhaps in this respect in literature, are real παραβολαί, thrown alongside and around the incident like rays of light which, however, do not illuminate its outward appearance but possess the power of X-rays to lay bare its inner structure that, in our case, consists of the hidden processes of the mind.

Kafka's parable reads as follows:

> He has two antagonists: the first presses him from behind, from the origin. The second blocks the road ahead. He gives battle to both. To be sure, the first supports him in his fight with the second, for he wants to push him forward, and in the same way the second supports him in his fight with the first, since he drives him back. But it is only theoretically so. For it is not only the two antagonists who are there, but he himself as well, and who really knows his intentions? His dream, though, is that some time in an unguarded moment – and this would require a night darker than any night has ever been yet – he will jump out of the fighting line and be promoted, on account of his experience in fighting, to the position of umpire over his antagonists in their fight with each other.

The incident which this parable relates and penetrates follows, in the inner logic of the matter, upon the events whose gist we found contained in René Char's aphorism. It begins, in fact, at precisely the point where our opening aphorism left the sequence of events hanging, as it were, in mid-air. Kafka's fight begins when the course of action has run its course and when the story which was its outcome waits to be completed 'in the minds that inherit and question it'. The task of the mind is to understand what happened, and this understanding, according to Hegel, is man's way of reconciling himself with reality; its actual end is to be at peace with the world. The trouble is that if the mind is unable to bring peace and to induce reconciliation, it finds itself immediately engaged in its own kind of warfare.

However, historically speaking, this stage in the development of the modern mind was preceded, at least in the twentieth century, by two, rather than one, previous acts. Before the generation of René Char, whom we have chosen here as its representative, found itself thrown out of literary pursuits into the commitments of action, another generation, only slightly older, had turned to politics for the solution of philosophic perplexities and had tried to escape from thought into action. It was this older generation which then became the spokesmen and creators of what they themselves called existentialism; for existentialism, at least in its French version, is primarily an escape from the perplexities of modern philosophy into the unquestioning commitment of action. And since, under the circumstances of the twentieth century, the so-called intellectuals – writers, thinkers, artists, men of letters, and the like – could find access to the public realm only in time of revolution, the revolution came to play, as Malraux once noticed (in *Man's Fate*), 'the role which once was played by eternal life': it 'saves those that make it'. Existentialism, the rebellion of the philosopher against philosophy, did not arise when philosophy turned out to be unable to apply its own rules to the realm of political affairs; this failure of political philosophy as Plato would have understood it is almost as old as the history of Western philosophy and metaphysics; and it did not even arise when it turned out that philosophy was equally unable to perform the task assigned to it by Hegel and the philosophy of history, that is, to understand and grasp conceptually histor-ical reality and the events that made the modern world what it is. The situation, however, became desperate when the old metaphysical questions were shown to be meaningless; that is, when it began to dawn upon modern man that he had come to live in a world in which his mind and his tradition of thought were not even capable of asking adequate, mean-ingful questions, let alone of giving answers to its own perplexities. In this predicament action, with its involvement and commitment, its being *engagée*, seemed to hold out the hope, not of solving any problems, but of making it possible to live with them without becoming, as Sartre once put it, a *salaud*, a hypocrite.

The discovery that the human mind had ceased, for some mysterious reasons, to function properly forms, so to speak, the first act of the story with which we are concerned here. I mentioned it here, however briefly, because without it the peculiar irony of what was to follow would be lost on us. René Char, writing during the last months of the Resistance, when liberation – which in our context meant liberation from action – loomed large, concluded his reflections with an appeal to thought for the prospective survivors no less urgent and no less passionate than the appeal to action of those who preceded him. If one were to write the intellec-tual history of our century, not in the form of successive generations, where the historian must be literally true to the sequence of theories and attitudes, but in the form of the biography of a single person, aiming at no more than a metaphorical approximation to what actually happened in the minds of men, this person's mind would stand revealed as having been forced to turn full circle not once but twice, first when he escaped from thought into action, and then again when action, or rather having acted, forced him back into thought. Whereby it would be of some rele-vance to notice that the appeal to thought arose in the odd in-between period which sometimes inserts itself into historical time when not only the later historians but the actors and witnesses, the living themselves, become aware of an interval in time which is altogether determined by things that are no longer and by things that are not yet. In history, these intervals have shown more than once that they may contain the moment of truth.

We now may return to Kafka, who in the logic of these matters, though not in their chronology, occupies the last and, as it were, the most advanced position. (The riddle of Kafka, who in more than thirty-five years of growing posthumous fame has established himself as one of the foremost writers' writers, is still unsolved; it consists primarily in a kind of breath-taking reversal of the established relationship between expe-rience and thought. While we find it a matter of course to associate rich-ness of concrete detail and dramatic action with the experience of a given reality and to ascribe to mental processes abstract pallor as the price exacted for their order and precision, Kafka, by sheer force of intelligence and spiritual imagination, created out of a bare, 'abstract' minimum of experience a kind of thought-landscape which, without losing in precision, harbors all the riches, varieties, and dramatic elements characteristic of 'real' life. Because thinking to him was the most vital and the liveliest part of reality, he developed this uncanny gift of anticipation which even today, after almost forty years full of unprecedented and unforeseeable events, does not cease to amaze us.) The story in its utter simplicity and brevity records a mental phenomenon, something which one may call a thought-event. The scene is a battleground on which the forces of the past and the future clash with each other; between them we find the man whom Kafka calls 'he', who, if he wants to stand his ground at all, must give battle to both forces. Hence, there are two or even three fights going on simultaneously: the fight between 'his' antagonists and the fight of the man in between with each of them. However, the fact that there is a fight at all seems due exclusively to the presence of the man, without whom the forces of the past and of the future, one suspects, would have neutralized or destroyed each other long ago.

The first thing to be noticed is that not only the future – 'the wave of the future' – but also the past is seen as a force, and not, as in nearly all our metaphors, as a burden man has to shoulder and of whose dead weight the living can or even must get rid in their march into the future. In the words of Faulkner, 'the past is never dead, it is not even past'. This past, moreover, reaching all the way back into the origin, does not pull back but presses forward, and it is, contrary to what one would expect, the future which drives us back into the past. Seen from the viewpoint of man, who always lives in the interval between past and future, time is not a continuum, a flow of uninterrupted succession; it is broken in the middle, at the point where 'he' stands; and 'his' standpoint is not the present as we usually understand it but rather a gap in time which 'his' constant fighting, 'his' making a stand against past and future, keeps in existence. Only because man is inserted into time and only to the extent that he stands his ground does the flow of indifferent time break up into tenses; it is this insertion – the beginning of a beginning, to put it into Augustinian terms – which splits up the time continuum into forces which then, because they are focused on the particle or body that gives them their direction, begin fighting with each other and acting upon man in the way Kafka describes.

Without distorting Kafka's meaning, I think one may go a step further. Kafka describes how the insertion of man breaks up the unidirectional flow of time but, strangely enough, he does not change the traditional image according to which we think of time as moving in a straight line. Since Kafka retains the traditional metaphor of a rectilinear temporal movement, 'he' has barely enough room to stand and whenever 'he' thinks of striking out on 'his' own 'he' falls into the dream of a region over and above the fighting-line – and what else is this dream and this region but the old dream which Western metaphysics has dreamed from Parmenides to Hegel of a timeless, spaceless, suprasensuous realm as the proper region of thought? Obviously what is missing in Kafka's description of a thought-event is a spatial dimension where thinking could exert itself without being forced to jump out of human time altogether. The trouble with Kafka's story in all its magnificence is that it is hardly possible to retain the notion of a rectilinear temporal movement if its unidirectional flow is broken up into antagonistic forces being directed toward and acting upon man. The insertion of man, as he breaks up the continuum, cannot but cause the forces to deflect, however lightly, from their original direction, and if this were the case, they would no longer clash head on but meet at an angle. In other words, the gap where 'he' stands is, potentially at least, no simple interval but resembles what the physicists call a parallelogram of forces.

Ideally, the action of the two forces which form the parallelogram of forces where Kafka's 'he' has found his battlefield should result in a third force, the resultant diagonal whose origin would be the point at which the forces clash and upon which they act. This diagonal force would in one respect differ from the two forces whose result it is. The two antagonistic forces are both unlimited as to their origins, the one coming from an infinite past and the other from an infinite future; but though they have no known beginning, they have a terminal ending, the point at which they clash. The diagonal force, on the contrary, would be limited as to its origin, its starting-point being the clash of the antagonistic forces, but it would be infinite with respect to its ending by virtue of having resulted from the concerted action of two forces whose origin is infinity. This diagonal force, whose origin is known, whose direction is determined by past and future, but whose eventual end lies in infinity, is the perfect metaphor for the activity of thought. If Kafka's 'he' were able to exert his forces along this diagonal, in perfect equidistance from past and future, walking along this diagonal line, as it were, forward and backward with the slow, ordered movements which are the proper motion for trains of thought, he would not have jumped out of the fighting-line and be above the mêlée as the parable demands, for this diagonal, though pointing toward the infinite, remains bound to and is rooted in the present; but he would have discovered – pressed as he was by his antagonists into the only direction from which he could properly see and survey what was most his own, what had come into being only with his own, self-inserting appearance – the enormous, ever-changing time-space which is created and limited by the forces of past and future; he would have found the place in time which is sufficiently removed from past and future to offer 'the umpire' a position from which to judge the forces fighting with each other with an impartial eye.

But, one is tempted to add, this is 'only theoretically so'. What is much more likely to happen – and what Kafka in other stories and parables has often described – is that the 'he', unable to find the diagonal which would lead him out of the fighting-line and into the space ideally constituted by the parallelogram of forces, will 'die of exhaustion', worn out under the pressure of constant fighting, oblivious of his original intentions, and aware only of the existence of this gap in time which, as long as he lives, is the ground on which he must stand, though it seems to be a battlefield and not a home.

To avoid misunderstandings: the imagery I am using here to indicate metaphorically and tentatively the contemporary conditions of thought can be valid only within the realm of mental phenomena. Applied to historical or biographical time, none of these metaphors can possibly make sense because gaps in time do not occur there. Only insofar as he thinks, and that is insofar as he is ageless – a 'he' as Kafka so rightly calls him, and not a 'somebody' – does man in the full actuality of his concrete being live in this gap of time between past and future. The gap, I suspect, is not modern phenomenon, it is perhaps not even a historical datum but is coeval with the existence of man on earth. It may well be the region of the spirit or, rather, the path paved by thinking, this small track of non-time which the activity of thought beats within the time-space of mortal men and into which the trains of thought, of remembrance and anticipation, save whatever they touch from the ruin of historical and biographical time. This small non-time-space in the very heart of time, unlike the world and the culture into which we are born, can only be indicated, but cannot be inherited and handed down from the past; each new generation, indeed every new human being as he inserts himself between an infinite past and an infinite future, must discover and ploddingly pave it anew.

The trouble, however, is that we seem to be neither equipped nor prepared for this activity of thinking, of settling down in the gap between past and future. For very long times in our history, actually throughout the thousands of years that followed upon the foundation of Rome and were determined by Roman concepts, this gap was bridged over by what, since the Romans, we have called tradition. That this tradition has worn thinner and thinner as the modern age progressed is a secret to nobody. When the thread of tradition finally broke, the gap between past and future ceased to be a condition peculiar only to the activity of thought and restricted as an experience to those few who made thinking their primary business. It became a tangible reality and perplexity for all; that is, it became a fact of political relevance. . . .

PART III

From Structuralism to Deconstruction

19

Ferdinand de Saussure

(1857–1913)

The philosophical movement known as 'structuralism' owes its methodological genesis to the work of Ferdinand de Saussure, a Swiss linguist
who was the first to emphasize the priority of linguistic structure in the
scientific study of language.

Saussure's focus differed considerably from the traditional approach to
linguistics prevalent at the beginning of the twentieth century. At that time,
philology and linguistics still privileged the historical (diachronic) and referential features of language, an approach which resulted in the empirical
accumulation of concrete linguistic data for analysis and classification. The
massive volume of random 'facts' generated in this way led Saussure to
seek a more foundational organizing principle for linguistics as a human
science. In brief, we can say that Saussure provided the revolutionary
insight that language must also be viewed as a system of structural
relations that precedes and is presupposed by any given utterance.

Saussure called his new theory of language 'semiology', or the 'science
of signs', as he developed it during his lectures on linguistics in Paris and
Geneva. Most remarkably, it was not until three years after his death in
1913 that notes from these seminal lectures were finally collated and
published as the *Cours de linguistique générale* (1916). This work was still
not available in English for over forty years until translated and published
as the *Course in General Linguistics* in 1959. Thus, Saussure's semiology
was already influencing French philosophical thought by mid-century, and
it was in this milieu that the structuralist paradigm first flourished. Although
Saussure primarily explicated the technical aspects of his theory pertaining
specifically to linguistics, he also recognized the potential for extending
'semiology' as a discipline to all cultural systems of signification. He effectively anticipated the work of such thinkers as Lévi-Strauss, Barthes, Lacan,
Foucault and Kristeva, all of whom viewed language as a critical fulcrum
in a wider cultural domain.

Saussure's own expertise in phonology led him to observe that the
acoustic aspect of language provides us with an internally related system

of sound-differences, or 'binary oppositions', which make 'meaning' possible in the first place. For example, the smallest units of acoustic contrast, which he called 'phonemes', allow us to distinguish between such words as *bat, hat, cat, sat* and so forth. Our ability to articulate such phonemes when we speak – and to discern them when we listen – provides a clue to the constitution of meaning within the self-regulating system of language. This linguistic feature of phonemic opposition or difference enables us to exclude all possibilities that have *not* been selected, or we might say, possibilities which are conspicuous by their absence. For Saussure, neither an emphasis on semantics, nor an ontological commitment towards a purported 'word–thing' correspondence gives us adequate insight into the autonomy of language.

Among the most significant distinctions noted by Saussure is that between 'language' and 'speech' (*langue* and *parole*), a distinction which strikes the keynote of structuralist analysis. *Langue* may be seen as the totality of a rule-governed, abstract system of language already embracing individual utterance or *parole*. Language is thus a *social* phenomenon, not merely an expression of ideal essence or speculative grammar made manifest in the consciousness of an isolated *cogito*. Language is 'always there' for us in advance; we never invent language, but rather participate in it. These relations between part and whole, according to Saussure, are best interrogated by examining structural form rather than referential content. Saussure also reminds us that linguistic signs are *arbitrary*. The pairing of an acoustic 'signifier' with a concept thereby 'signified' is simply a matter of convention that differs between one natural language and another. The use of '*horse*' or '*cheval*' or '*caballo*' as acoustic 'signifiers' is an arbitrary feature fixed only by the sedimented usage of our own linguistic communities.

In the few selections from Saussure's *Course in General Linguistics* which follow, it is naturally impossible to cover all aspects of the structuralist paradigm generated by his work. However, whether we find ourselves attempting to understand the social semiotics of Barthes or Derridean '*différance*', the enduring importance of Saussure's impact on twentieth-century Continental thought must be emphatically recognized.

BIBLIOGRAPHY OF SAUSSURE'S WORKS IN ENGLISH

Course in General Linguistics, London: Duckworth, 1983.

Selections from the *Course in General Linguistics*

THE OBJECT OF STUDY

§1 On Defining a Language

WHAT IS IT that linguistics sets out to analyse? What is the actual object of study in its entirety? The question is a particularly difficult one. We shall see why later. First, let us simply try to grasp the nature of the difficulty.

Other sciences are provided with objects of study given in advance, which are then examined from different points of view. Nothing like that is the case in linguistics. Suppose someone pronounces the French word *nu* ('naked'). At first sight, one might think this would be an example of an independently given linguistic object. But more careful consideration reveals a series of three or four quite different things, depending on the viewpoint adopted. There is a sound, there is the expression of an idea, there is a derivative of Latin *nūdum*, and so on. The object is not given in advance of the viewpoint: far from it. Rather, one might say that it is the viewpoint adopted which creates the object. Furthermore, there is nothing to tell us in advance whether one of these ways of looking at it is prior to or superior to any of the others.

Whichever viewpoint is adopted, moreover, linguistic phenomena always present two complementary facets, each depending on the other. For example:

1 The ear perceives articulated syllables as auditory impressions. But the sounds in question would not exist without the vocal organs. There would be no *n*, for instance, without these two complementary aspects to it. So one cannot equate the language simply with what the ear hears. One cannot divorce what is heard from oral articulation. Nor, on the other hand, can one specify the relevant movements of the vocal organs without reference to the corresponding auditory impression.

2 But even if we ignored this phonetic duality, would language then be reducible to phonetic facts? No. Speech sounds are only the instrument of thought, and have no independent existence. Here another complementarity emerges, and one of great importance. A sound, itself a complex auditory–articulatory unit, in turn combines with an idea to form another complex unit, both physiologically and psychologically. Nor is this all.

3 Language has an individual aspect and a social aspect. One is not conceivable without the other. Furthermore:

From *Course in General Linguistics*, London: Duckworth, 1983.

4   Language at any given time involves an established system and an evolution. At any given time, it is an institution in the present and a product of the past. At first sight, it looks very easy to distinguish between the system and its history, between what it is and what it was. In reality, the connexion between the two is so close that it is hard to separate them. Would matters be simplified if one considered the ontogenesis of linguistic phenomena, beginning with a study of children's language, for example? No. It is quite illusory to believe that where language is concerned the problem of origins is any different from the problem of permanent conditions. There is no way out of the circle.

So however we approach the question, no one object of linguistic study emerges of its own accord. Whichever way we turn, the same dilemma confronts us. Either we tackle each problem on one front only, and risk failing to take into account the dualities mentioned above: or else we seem committed to trying to study language in several ways simultaneously, in which case the object of study becomes a muddle of disparate, unconnected things. By proceeding thus one opens the door to various sciences – psychology, anthropology, prescriptive grammar, philology, and so on – which are to be distinguished from linguistics. These sciences could lay claim to language as falling in their domain; but their methods are not the ones that are needed.

One solution only, in our view, resolves all these difficulties. *The linguist must take the study of linguistic structure as his primary concern, and relate all other manifestations of language to it.* Indeed, amid so many dualities, linguistic structure seems to be the one thing that is independently definable and provides something our minds can satisfactorily grasp.

What, then, is linguistic structure? It is not, in our opinion, simply the same thing as language. Linguistic structure is only one part of language, even though it is an essential part. The structure of a language is a social product of our language faculty. At the same time, it is also a body of necessary conventions adopted by society to enable members of society to use their language faculty. Language in its entirety has many different and disparate aspects. It lies astride the boundaries separating various domains. It is at the same time physical, physiological and psychological. It belongs both to the individual and to society. No classification of human phenomena provides any single place for it, because language as such has no discernible unity.

A language as a structured system, on the contrary, is both a self-contained whole and a principle of classification. As soon as we give linguistic structure pride of place among the facts of language, we introduce a natural order into an aggregate which lends itself to no other classification.

It might be objected to this principle of classification that our use of language depends on a faculty endowed by nature: whereas language systems are acquired and conventional, and so ought to be subordinated to – instead of being given priority over – our natural ability.

To this objection one might reply as follows.

First, it has not been established that the function of language, as manifested in speech, is entirely natural: that is to say, it is not clear that our vocal apparatus is made for speaking as our legs for walking. Linguists are by no means in agreement on this issue. Whitney, for instance, who regards languages as social institutions on exactly the same footing as all other social institutions, holds it to be a matter of chance or mere convenience that it is our vocal apparatus we use for linguistic purposes. Man, in his view, might well have chosen to use gestures, thus substituting visual images for sound patterns. Whitney's is doubtless too extreme a position. For languages are not in all respects similar to other social institutions. Moreover, Whitney goes too far when he says that the selection of the vocal apparatus for language was accidental. For it was in some measure imposed upon us by Nature. But the American linguist is right about the essential point: the language we use is a convention, and it makes no difference what exactly the nature of the agreed sign is. The question of the vocal apparatus is thus a secondary one as far as the problem of language is concerned.

This idea gains support from the notion of *language articulation*. In Latin, the word *articulus* means 'member, part, subdivision in a sequence of things'. As regards language, articulation may refer to the division of the chain of speech into syllables, or to the division of the chain of meanings into meaningful units. It is in this sense that one speaks in German of *gegliederte Sprache*. On the basis of this second interpretation, one may say that it is not spoken language which is natural to man, but the faculty of constructing a language, i.e. a system of distinct signs corresponding to distinct ideas.

Broca discovered that the faculty of speech is localized in the third frontal convolution of the left hemisphere of the brain. This fact has been seized upon to justify regarding language as a natural endowment. But the same localization is known to hold for *everything* connected with language, including writing. Thus what seems to be indicated, when we take into consideration also the evidence from various forms of aphasia due to lesions in the centres of localization is: (1) that the various disorders which affect spoken language are interconnected in many ways with disorders affecting written language, and (2) that in all cases of aphasia or agraphia what is affected is not so much the ability to utter or inscribe this or that, but the ability to produce in any given mode signs corresponding to normal language. All this leads us to believe that, over and above the functioning of the various organs, there exists a more general faculty governing signs, which may be regarded as the linguistic faculty *par excellence*. So by a different route we are once again led to the same conclusion.

Finally, in support of giving linguistic structure pride of place in our study of language, there is this argument: that, whether natural or not, the faculty of articulating words is put to use only by means of the linguistic instrument created and provided by society. Therefore it is no absurdity to say that it is linguistic structure which gives language what unity it has.

§2 Linguistic Structure: Its Place Among the Facts of Language

In order to identify what role linguistic structure plays within the totality of language, we must consider the individual act of speech and trace what takes place in the speech circuit. This act requires at least two individuals: without this minimum the circuit would not be complete. Suppose, then, we have two people, *A* and *B*, talking to each other:

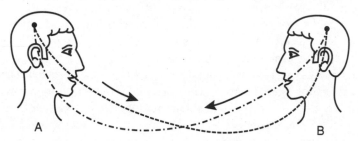

The starting point of the circuit is in the brain of one individual, for instance *A*, where facts of consciousness which we shall call concepts are associated with representations of linguistic signs or sound patterns by means of which they may be a expressed. Let us suppose that a given concept triggers in the brain a corresponding sound pattern. This is an entirely *psychological* phenomenon, followed in turn by a *physiological* process: the brain transmits to the organs of phonation an impulse corresponding to the pattern. Then sound waves are sent from *A*'s mouth to *B*'s ear: a purely *physical* process. Next, the circuit continues in *B* in the opposite order: from ear to brain, the physiological transmission of the sound pattern; in the brain, the psychological association of this pattern with the corresponding concept. If *B* speaks in turn, this new act will pursue – from his brain to *A*'s – exactly the same course as the first, passing through the same successive phases, which we may represent as follows:

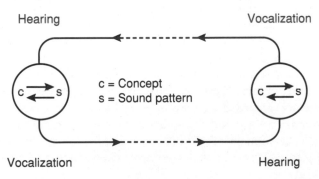

Hearing   Vocalization

c = Concept
s = Sound pattern

Vocalization   Hearing

This analysis makes no claim to be complete. One could go on to distinguish the auditory sensation itself, the identification of that sensation with the latent sound pattern, the patterns of muscular movement associated with phonation, and so on. We have included only those elements considered essential; but our schematization enables us straight away to separate the parts which are physical (sound waves) from those which are physiological (phonation and hearing) and those which are psychological (the sound patterns of words and the concepts). It is particularly important to note that the sound patterns of the words are not to be confused with actual sounds. The word patterns are psychological, just as the concepts associated with them are.

The circuit as here represented may be further divided:

(a) into an external part (sound vibrations passing from mouth to ear) and an internal part (comprising all the rest);

(b) into a psychological and a non-psychological part, the latter comprising both the physiological facts localized in the organs and the physical facts external to the individual; and

(c) into an active part and a passive part, the former comprising everything which goes from the association centre of one individual to the ear of the other, and the latter comprising everything which goes from an individual's ear to his own association centre.

Finally, in the psychological part localized in the brain, one may call everything which is active 'executive' ($c \rightarrow s$), and everything which is passive 'receptive' ($s \rightarrow c$).

In addition, one must allow for a faculty of association and co-ordination which comes into operation as soon as one goes beyond individual signs in isolation. It is this faculty which plays the major role in the organization of the language as a system.

But in order to understand this role, one must leave the individual act, which is merely language in embryo, and proceed to consider the social phenomenon.

All the individuals linguistically linked in this manner will establish among themselves a kind of mean; all of them will reproduce – doubtless not exactly, but approximately – the same signs linked to the same concepts.

What is the origin of this social crystallization? Which of the parts of the circuit is involved? For it is very probable that not all of them are equally relevant.

The physical part of the circuit can be dismissed from consideration straight away. When we hear a language we do not know being spoken, we hear the sounds but we cannot enter into the social reality of what is happening, because of our failure to comprehend.

The psychological part of the circuit is not involved in its entirety either. The executive side of it plays no part, for execution is never carried out by the collectivity: it is always individual, and the individual is always master of it. This is what we shall designate by the term *speech*.

The individual's receptive and co-ordinating faculties build up a stock of imprints which turn out to be for all practical purposes the same as the next person's. How must we envisage this social product, so that the language itself can be seen to be clearly distinct from the rest? If we could collect the totality of word patterns stored in all those individuals, we should have the social bond which constitutes their language. It is a fund accumulated by the members of the community through the practice of speech, a grammatical system existing potentially in every brain, or more exactly in the brains of a group of individuals; for the language is never complete in any single individual, but exists perfectly only in the collectivity.

By distinguishing between the language itself and speech, we distinguish at the same time: (1) what is social from what is individual, and (2) what is essential from what is ancillary and more or less accidental.

The language itself is not a function of the speaker. It is the product passively registered by the individual. It never requires premeditation, and reflexion enters into it only for the activity of classifying to be discussed below.

Speech, on the contrary, is an individual act of the will and the intelligence, in which one must distinguish: (1) the combinations through which the speaker uses the code provided by the language in order to express his own thought, and (2) the psycho-physical mechanism which enables him to externalize these combinations.

It should be noted that we have defined things, not words. Consequently the distinctions established are not affected by the fact that certain ambiguous terms have no exact equivalents in other languages. Thus in German the word *Sprache* covers individual languages as well as language in general, while *Rede* answers more or less to 'speech', but also has the special sense of 'discourse'. In Latin the word *sermo* covers language in general and also speech, while *lingua* is the word for 'a language'; and so on. No word corresponds precisely to any one of the notions we have tried to specify above. That is why all definitions based on words are vain. It is an error of method to proceed from words in order to give definitions of things.

To summarize then, a language as a structured system may be characterized as follows:

1   Amid the disparate mass of facts involved in language, it stands out as a well-defined entity. It can be localized in that particular section of the speech circuit where sound patterns are associated with concepts. It is the social part of language, external to the individual, who by himself is powerless either to create it or to modify it. It exists only in virtue of a kind of contract agreed between the members of a community. On the other hand, the individual needs an apprenticeship

in order to acquaint himself with its workings: as a child, he assimilates it only gradually. It is quite separate from speech: a man who loses the ability to speak none the less retains his grasp of the language system, provided he understands the vocal signs he hears.

2   A language system, as distinct from speech, is an object that may be studied independently. Dead languages are no longer spoken, but we can perfectly well acquaint ourselves with their linguistic structure. A science which studies linguistic structure is not only able to dispense with other elements of language, but is possible only if those other elements are kept separate.

3   While language in general is heterogeneous, a language system is homogeneous in nature. It is a system of signs in which the one essential is the union of sense and sound pattern, both parts of the sign being psychological.

4   Linguistic structure is no less real than speech, and no less amenable to study. Linguistic signs, although essentially psychological, are not abstractions. The associations, ratified by collective agreement, which go to make up the language are realities localized in the brain. Moreover, linguistic signs are, so to speak, tangible: writing can fix them in conventional images, whereas it would be impossible to photograph acts of speech in all their details. The utterance of a word, however small, involves an infinite number of muscular movements extremely difficult to examine and to represent. In linguistic structure, on the contrary, there is only the sound pattern, and this can be represented by one constant visual image. For if one leaves out of account that multitude of movements required to actualize it in speech, each sound pattern, as we shall see, is only the sum of a limited number of elements or speech sounds, and these can in turn be represented by a corresponding number of symbols in writing. Our ability to identify elements of linguistic structure in this way is what makes it possible for dictionaries and grammars to give us a faithful representation of a language. A language is a repository of sound patterns, and writing is their tangible form.

§3   Languages and their Place in Human Affairs. Semiology

The above characteristics lead us to realize another, which is more important. A language, defined in this way from among the totality of facts of language, has a particular place in the realm of human affairs, whereas language does not.

A language, as we have just seen, is a social institution. But it is in various respects distinct from political, juridical and other institutions. Its special nature emerges when we bring into consideration a different order of facts.

A language is a system of signs expressing ideas, and hence comparable to writing, the deaf-and-dumb alphabet, symbolic rites, forms of politeness, military signals, and so on. It is simply the most important of such systems.

It is therefore possible to conceive of a science *which studies the role of signs as part of social life*. It would form part of social psychology, and hence of general psychology. We shall call it *semiology* (from the Greek *sēmeîon* 'sign'). It would investigate the nature of signs and the laws governing them. Since it does not yet exist, one cannot say for certain that it will exist. But it has a right to exist, a place ready for it in advance. Linguistics is only one branch of this general science. The laws which semiology will discover will be laws applicable in linguistics, and linguistics will thus be assigned to a clearly defined place in the field of human knowledge.

It is for the psychologist to determine the exact place of semiology. The linguist's task is to define what makes languages a special type of system within the totality of semiological facts. The question will be taken up later on: here we shall make just one point, which is that if we have now for the first time succeeded in assigning linguistics its place among the sciences, that is because we have grouped it with semiology.

Why is it that semiology is not yet recognized as an autonomous science with its own object of study, like other sciences? The fact is that here we go round in a circle. On the one hand, nothing is more appropriate than the study of languages to bring out the nature of the semiological problem. But to formulate the problem suitably, it would be necessary to study what a language is in itself: whereas hitherto a language has usually been considered as a function of something else, from other points of view.

In the first place, there is the superficial view taken by the general public, which sees a language merely as a nomenclature. This is a view which stifles any inquiry into the true nature of linguistic structure.

Then there is the viewpoint of the psychologist, who studies the mechanism of the sign in the individual. This is the most straightforward approach, but it takes us no further than individual execution. It does not even take us as far as the linguistic sign itself, which is social by nature.

Even when due recognition is given to the fact that the sign must be studied as a social phenomenon, attention is restricted to those features of languages which they share with institutions mainly established by voluntary decision. In this way, the investigation is diverted from its goal. It neglects those characteristics which belong only to semiological systems in general, and to languages in particular. For the sign always to some extent eludes control by the will, whether of the individual or of society: that is its essential nature, even though it may be by no means obvious at first sight.

So this characteristic emerges clearly only in languages, but its manifestations appear in features to which least attention is paid. All of which contributes to a failure to appreciate either the necessity or the particular utility of a science of semiology. As far as we are concerned, on the other hand, the linguistic problem is first and foremost semiological. All our proposals derive their rationale from this basic fact. If one wishes to discover the true nature of language systems, one must first consider what they have in common with all other systems of the same kind. Linguistic factors which at first seem central (for example, the workings of the vocal apparatus) must be relegated to a place of secondary importance if it is found that they merely differentiate languages from other such systems. In this way, light will be thrown not only upon the linguistic problem. By considering rites, customs, etc., as signs, it will be possible, we believe, to see them in a new perspective. The need will be felt to consider them as semiological phenomena and to explain them in terms of the laws of semiology. . . .

NATURE OF THE LINGUISTIC SIGN

§1 Sign, Signification, Signal

For some people a language, reduced to its essentials, is a nomenclature a list of terms corresponding to a list of things. For example, Latin would be represented as:

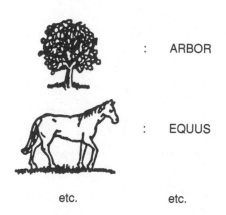

| : | ARBOR |
| : | EQUUS |

etc.   etc.

This conception is open to a number of objections. It assumes that ideas already exist independently of words. It does not clarify whether the name is a vocal or a psychological entity, for *ARBOR* might stand for either. Furthermore, it leads one to assume that the link between a name and a thing is something quite unproblematic, which is far from being the case. None the less, this naive view contains one element of truth, which is that linguistic units are dual in nature, comprising two elements.

As has already been noted in connexion with the speech circuit, the two elements involved in the linguistic sign are both psychological and are connected in the brain by an associative link. This is a point of major importance.

A linguistic sign is not a link between a thing and a name, but between a concept and a sound pattern. The sound pattern is not actually a sound; for a sound is something physical. A sound pattern is the hearer's psychological impression of a sound, as given to him by the evidence of his senses. This sound pattern may be called a 'material' element only in that it is the representation of our sensory impressions. The sound pattern may thus be distinguished from the other element associated with it in a linguistic sign. This other element is generally of a more abstract kind (the concept).

The psychological nature of our sound patterns becomes clear when we consider our own linguistic activity. Without moving either lips or tongue, we can talk to ourselves or recite silently a piece of verse. We grasp the words of a language as sound patterns. That is why it is best to avoid referring to them as composed of 'speech sounds'. Such a term, implying the activity of the vocal apparatus, is appropriate to the spoken word, to the actualization of the sound pattern in discourse. Speaking of the *sounds* and *syllables* of a word need not give rise to any misunderstanding, provided one always bears in mind that this refers to the sound pattern.

The linguistic sign is, then, a two-sided-psychological entity, which may be represented by the following diagram.

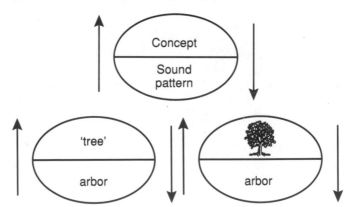

These two elements are intimately linked and each triggers the other. Whether we are seeking the meaning of the Latin word *arbor* or the word by which Latin designates the concept 'tree', it is clear that only the connexions institutionalized in the language appear to us as relevant. Any other connexions there may be we set on one side.

This definition raises an important question of terminology. In our terminology a *sign* is the combination of a concept and a sound pattern. But in current usage the term *sign* generally refers to the sound pattern alone, e.g. the word form *arbor*. It is forgotten that if *arbor* is called a sign, it is only because it carries with it the concept 'tree', so that the sensory part of the term implies reference to the whole.

The ambiguity would be removed if the three notions in question were designated by terms which are related but contrast. We propose to keep the term *sign* to designate the whole, but to replace *concept* and *sound pattern* respectively by *signification* and *signal*. The latter terms have the advantage of indicating the distinction which separates each from the other and both from the whole of which they are part. We retain the term *sign*, because current usage suggests no alternative by which it might be replaced.

The linguistic sign thus defined has two fundamental characteristics. In specifying them, we shall lay down the principles governing all studies in this domain.

§2 First Principle: The Sign is Arbitrary

The link between signal and signification is arbitrary. Since we are treating a sign as the combination in which a signal is associated with a signification, we can express this more simply as: *the linguistic sign is arbitrary*.

There is no internal connexion, for example, between the idea 'sister' and the French sequence of sounds *s-ö-r* which acts as its signal. The same idea might as well be represented by any other sequences of sounds. This is demonstrated by differences between languages, and even by the existence of different languages. The signification 'ox' has as its signal *b-ö-f* on one side of the frontier, but *o-k-s* (*Ochs*) on the other side.

No one disputes the fact that linguistic signs are arbitrary. But it is often easier to discover a truth than to assign it to its correct place. The principle stated above is the organizing principle for the whole of linguistics, considered as a science of language structure. The consequences which flow from this principle are innumerable. It is true that they do not all appear at first sight equally evident. One discovers them after many circuitous deviations, and so realizes the fundamental importance of the principle.

It may be noted in passing that when semiology is established one of the questions that must be asked is whether modes of expression which rely upon signs that are entirely natural (mime, for example) fall within the province of semiology. If they do, the main object of study in semiology will none the less be the class of systems based upon the arbitrary nature of the sign. For any means of expression accepted in a society rests in principle upon a collective habit, or on convention, which comes to the same thing. Signs of politeness, for instance, although often endowed with a certain natural expressiveness (prostrating oneself nine times on the ground is the way to greet an emperor in China) are none the less fixed

301

by rule. It is this rule which renders them obligatory, not their intrinsic value. We may therefore say that signs which are entirely arbitrary convey better than others the ideal semiological process. That is why the most complex and the most widespread of all systems of expression, which is the one we find in human languages, is also the most characteristic of all. In this sense, linguistics serves as a model for the whole of semiology, even though languages represent only one type of semiological system.

The word *symbol* is sometimes used to designate the linguistic sign, or more exactly that part of the linguistic sign which we are calling the signal. This use of the word *symbol* is awkward, for reasons connected with our first principle. For it is characteristic of symbols that they are never entirely arbitrary. They are not empty configurations. They show at least a vestige of natural connexion between the signal and its signification. For instance, our symbol of justice, the scales, could hardly be replaced by a chariot.

The word *arbitrary* also calls for comment. It must not be taken to imply that a signal depends on the free choice of the speaker. (We shall see later that the individual has no power to alter a sign in any respect once it has become established in a linguistic community.) The term implies simply that the signal is *unmotivated*: that is to say arbitrary in relation to its signification, with which it has no natural connexion in reality.

In conclusion, two objections may be mentioned which might be brought against the principle that linguistic signs are arbitrary.

1 *Onomatopoeic* words might be held to show that a choice of signal is not always arbitrary. But such words are never organic elements of a linguistic system. Moreover, they are far fewer than is generally believed. French words like *fouet* ('whip') or *glas* ('knell') may strike the ear as having a certain suggestive sonority. But to see that this is in no way intrinsic to the words themselves, it suffices to look at their Latin origins. *Fouet* comes from Latin *fāgus* ('beech tree') and *glas* from Latin *classicum* ('trumpet call'). The suggestive quality of the modern pronunciation of these words is a fortuitous result of phonetic evolution.

As for genuine onomatopoeia (e.g. French *glou-glou* ('gurgle'), *tic-tac* 'ticking (of a clock)'), not only is it rare but its use is already to a certain extent arbitrary. For onomatopoeia is only the approximate imitation, already partly conventionalized, of certain sounds. This is evident if we compare a French dog's *ouaoua* and a German dog's *wauwau*. In any case, once introduced into the language, onomatopoeic words are subjected to the same phonetic and morphological evolution as other words. The French word *pigeon* ('pigeon') comes from Vulgar Latin *pīpiō*, itself of onomatopoeic origin, which clearly proves that onomatopoeic words themselves may lose their original character and take on that of the linguistic sign in general, which is unmotivated.

2 Similar considerations apply to *exclamations*. These are not unlike

onomatopoeic words, and they do not undermine the validity of our thesis. People are tempted to regard exclamations as spontaneous expressions called forth, as it were, by nature. But in most cases it is difficult to accept that there is a necessary link between the exclamatory signal and its signification. Again, it suffices to compare two languages in this respect to see how much exclamations vary. For example, the French exclamation *aïe!* corresponds to the German *au!* Moreover, it is known that many exclamations were originally meaningful words (e.g. *diable!* 'devil', *mordieu!* 'God's death').

In short, onomatopoeic and exclamatory words are rather marginal phenomena, and their symbolic origin is to some extent disputable.

§3   Second Principle: Linear Character of the Signal

The linguistic signal, being auditory in nature, has a temporal aspect, and hence certain temporal characteristics: (a) *it occupies a certain temporal space*, and (b) *this space is measured in just one dimension: it is a line.*

This principle is obvious, but it seems never to be stated, doubtless because it is considered too elementary. However, it is a fundamental principle and its consequences are incalculable. Its importance equals that of the first law. The whole mechanism of linguistic structure depends upon it. Unlike visual signals (e.g. ships' flags) which can exploit more than one dimension simultaneously, auditory signals have available to them only the linearity of time. The elements of such signals are presented one after another: they form a chain. This feature appears immediately when they are represented in writing, and a spatial line of graphic signs is substituted for a succession of sounds in time.

In certain cases, this may not be easy to appreciate. For example, if I stress a certain syllable, it may seem that I am presenting a number of significant features simultaneously. But that is an illusion. The syllable and its accentuation constitute a single act of phonation. There is no duality within this act, although there are various contrasts with what precedes and follows.

INVARIABILITY AND VARIABILITY OF THE SIGN ...

§5   Synchronic and Diachronic Linguistics: Their Methods and Principles Contrasted

Diachronic and synchronic studies contrast in every way.

For example, to begin with the most obvious fact, they are not of equal importance. It is clear that the synchronic point of view takes precedence over the diachronic, since for the community of language users that is the one and only reality. The same is true for the linguist. If he takes a diachronic point of view, he is no longer examining the language, but a series of events which modify it. It is often claimed that there is nothing more important than knowing how a given state originated. In a certain sense, that is true. The conditions which gave rise to the state throw light upon its true nature and prevent us from entertaining certain misconceptions. But what that proves is that diachrony has no end in itself. One might say, as has been said of journalism as a career, that it leads nowhere until you leave it behind.

Their methods are also different in two respects:

(a) Synchrony has only one perspective, that of the language users; and its whole method consists of collecting evidence from them. In order to determine to what extent something is a reality, it is necessary and also sufficient to find out to what extent it exists as far as the language users are concerned. Diachronic linguistics, however, needs to distinguish two perspectives. One will be *prospective*, following the course of time, and the other *retrospective*, going in the opposite direction. It follows that two diachronic methods are required ...

(b) A second difference derives from the different areas covered by the two disciplines. The object of synchronic study does not comprise everything which is simultaneous, but only the set of facts corresponding to any particular language. In this, it will take into account where necessary a division into dialects and sub-dialects. The term *synchronic*, in fact, is not sufficiently precise. *Idiosynchronic* would be a better term, even though it is somewhat cumbersome. Diachronic linguistics, on the contrary, needs no such particularization, and indeed rejects it. The items diachronic linguistics deals with do not necessarily belong to a single language. (Compare Proto-Indo-European *ésti*, Greek *ésti*, German *ist*, French *est*.) It is precisely the succession of diachronic facts and their proliferation in space which gives rise to the diversity of languages. In order to justify comparing two forms, it is sufficient that there should be some historical connexion between them, however indirect.

These are not the most striking contrasts, nor the most profound. The consequences of the radical difference between facts of evolution and static facts is that all notions pertinent to the former and all notions pertinent to the latter are mutually irreducible. Any of the notions in question may be used to demonstrate this truth. No synchronic phenomenon has anything in common with any diachronic phenomenon. One is a relationship between simultaneous elements, and the other a substitution of one element for another in time, that is to say an event. We shall also see that diachronic identities and synchronic identities are two very different things. Historically, the French negative particle *pas* is the same as the noun *pas* ('pace'), whereas in modern French these two units are entirely separate. Realizing these facts should be sufficient to bring home the necessity of not confusing the two points of view.

20

Claude Lévi-Strauss

(b. 1908)

Born in Belgium in 1908, Claude Lévi-Strauss radically changed the field of social anthropology by applying the tools of structuralist analysis first developed by Saussure to the domain of cultural relations. While teaching at the New School for Social Research in the 1940s, he was introduced to Saussure's work by the renowned formalist Roman Jakobson. Lévi-Strauss recognized the significance of semiology for cultural analysis and attempted to explore the coded relations governing social interactions in a number of highly influential works, such as *The Elementary Structures of Kinship* (1949), *Tristes Tropiques* (1955), *Structural Anthropology* (1958), *The Savage Mind* (1962), *Mythologiques* (4 vols, 1964–72), *The Raw and the Cooked* (1970), to name just a few of the most celebrated. In addition to the New School, he taught at the University of Sao Paolo in Brazil, the University of Paris and the Collège de France in Paris.

Lévi-Strauss asserted that language preconditioned human culture, as reflected in the 'symbolic order' of aesthetic, religious and social life. He maintained that all cultural patterning depended on the vast reservoir of unconscious and universal structures of mind. These deep structures underlying the surface manifestations of cultural signification could be analysed, as Saussure had suggested, by identifying the synchronic, timeless relations presupposed by diachronic, historical change. The totality of abstract possible relations in human culture served as the analogous equivalent of Saussure's '*langue*', while the actual relations concretized within a particular culture were analogous to '*parole*'. In place of Saussure's 'phonemes', Lévi-Strauss introduced such terminology as 'mythemes' for binary oppositions that combined to form one version of a myth, or 'gustemes' for oppositions that marked the symbolic distinctions of edible and inedible combinations. Lévi-Strauss stressed that the totality of unconscious possibilities governing even cultural practices and relations that, superficially at least, seemed to be non-linguistic were always imbued with the symbolizing power of language.

One of the most significant distinctions made by Lévi-Strauss in the course of his anthropological investigations was the difference between 'hot' and 'cold' societies. Cultures in Western Europe that changed rapidly and remained open to widely divergent influences he categorized as 'hot', whereas those cultures that changed very little over time were 'cold'. Lévi-Strauss found a prime example of 'cold' society in the Amazon Indians, whose culture he encountered while teaching in Brazil. His research there suggested a '*pensée sauvage*', or savage mind, which could be seen as prototypical for the universal structures of mind permeating human culture in both hot and cold societies. Although the synchronic structures under-lying historical change might be more evident in 'cold' cultures, such structures served as the foundation for cultural patterning in 'hot' cultures as well, albeit disguised by the frenzied pace of diachronic change.

For Lévi-Strauss, all aspects of culture – sexual taboos, kinship laws, marriage rites, cookery, social hierarchies, religious rituals, mythic systems, etc. – proved amenable to structural analysis. He called attention to the great surplus of symbolic signifiers over what is signified, i.e. manifold surface expressions pointing to the same deep and hidden structures. The many varieties of myth, such as the Oedipus myth analysed in the selec-tion which follows, might seem arbitrary and disparate, but all actually provide a logic of analogy that resolves fundamental contradictions in our lived experience, with certain topics and relations appearing again and again. Difference is always ordered under the principle of a rule.

The rise of the structuralist paradigm under Lévi-Strauss was also marked by his scathing critique of Sartre's existential consciousness which chooses freedom 'for-itself'. According to Lévi-Strauss, no such isolated conscious-ness could possibly escape the principles of universal mind structuring our experience of the lifeworld. The 'symbolic order' of culture must always remain a shared social order of structural relations.

SELECT BIBLIOGRAPHY OF LÉVI–STRAUSS' WORKS IN ENGLISH

Structural Anthropology, New York: Basic Books, 1963.
Totemism, Boston: Beacon Press, 1963.
Tristes Tropiques, New York: Basic Books, 1963.
The Savage Mind, Chicago: University of Chicago Press, 1966.
The Scope of Anthropology (Inauguration Lecture to the *Collège de France*, 1960), London: Cape, 1967.
The Elementary Structures of Kinship, London: Eyre & Spottiswoode, 1969.
From Honey to Ashes, London: Cape, 1970.
The Origin of Table Manners, London: Cape, 1973.
Myth and Meaning, London: Routledge & Kegan Paul, 1978.
The Naked Man, London: Cape, 1981.
Introduction to the World of Marcel Mauss, Routledge, 1987.
View from Afar, Penguin, 1987.
The Jealous Potter, University of Chicago Press, 1988.

The Structural Study of Myth

> It would seem that mythological worlds have been built up only to
> be shattered again, and that new worlds were built from the frag-
> ments.
>
> (Franz Boas)[1]

DESPITE SOME RECENT attempts to renew them, it seems that during the
past twenty years anthropology has increasingly turned from studies in
the field of religion. At the same time, and precisely because the interest
of professional anthropologists has withdrawn from primitive religion, all
kinds of amateurs who claim to belong to other disciplines have seized
this opportunity to move in, thereby turning into their private playground
what we had left as a wasteland. The prospects for the scientific study of
religion have thus been undermined in two ways.

The explanation for this situation lies to some extent in the fact that
the anthropological study of religion was started by men like Tylor, Frazer,
and Durkheim, who were psychologically oriented although not in a position to keep up with the progress of psychological research and theory.
Their interpretations, therefore, soon became vitiated by the outmoded
psychological approach which they used as their basis. Although they were
undoubtedly right in giving their attention to intellectual processes, the
way they handled these remained so crude that it discredited them altogether. This is much to be regretted, since, as Hocart so profoundly noted
in his introduction to a posthumous book recently published,[2] psychological interpretations were withdrawn from the intellectual field only to
be introduced again in the field of affectivity, thus adding to 'the inherent
defects of the psychological school ... the mistake of deriving clear-cut
ideas ... from vague emotions'. Instead of trying to enlarge the framework of our logic to include processes which, whatever their apparent
differences, belong to the same kind of intellectual operation, a naïve
attempt was made to reduce them to inarticulate emotional drives, which
resulted only in hampering our studies.

Of all the chapters of religious anthropology probably none has
tarried to the same extent as studies in the field of mythology. From a
theoretical point of view the situation remains very much the same as it
was fifty years ago, namely, chaotic. Myths are still widely interpreted in
conflicting ways: as collective dreams, as the outcome of a kind of esthetic
play, or as the basis of ritual. Mythological figures are considered as
personified abstractions, divinized heroes, or fallen gods. Whatever the
hypothesis, the choice amounts to reducing mythology either to idle play
or to a crude kind of philosophic speculation.

In order to understand what a myth really is, must we choose between

From *Structural Anthropology*, New York: Basic Books, 1963.

platitude and sophism? Some claim that human societies merely express, through their mythology, fundamental feelings common to the whole of mankind, such as love, hate, or revenge, or that they try to provide some kind of explanations for phenomena which they cannot otherwise understand – astronomical, meteorological, and the like. But why should these societies do it in such elaborate and devious ways, when all of them are also acquainted with empirical explanations? On the other hand, psychoanalysts and many anthropologists have shifted the problems away from the natural or cosmological toward the sociological and psychological fields. But then the interpretation becomes too easy: If a given mythology confers prominence on a certain figure, let us say an evil grandmother, it will be claimed that in such a society grandmothers are actually evil and that mythology reflects the social structure and the social relations; but should the actual data be conflicting, it would be as readily claimed that the purpose of mythology is to provide an outlet for repressed feelings. Whatever the situation, a clever dialectic will always find a way to pretend that a meaning has been found.

Mythology confronts the student with a situation which at first sight appears contradictory. On the one hand it would seem that in the course of a myth anything is likely to happen. There is no logic, no continuity. Any characteristic can be attributed to any subject; every conceivable relation can be found. With myth, everything becomes possible. But on the other hand, this apparent arbitrariness is belied by the astounding similarity between myths collected in widely different regions. Therefore the problem: If the content of a myth is contingent, how are we going to explain the fact that myths throughout the world are so similar?

It is precisely this awareness of a basic antinomy pertaining to the nature of myth that may lead us toward its solution. For the contradiction which we face is very similar to that which in earlier times brought considerable worry to the first philosophers concerned with linguistic problems; linguistics could only begin to evolve as a science after this contradiction had been overcome. Ancient philosophers reasoned about language the way we do about mythology. On the one hand, they did notice that in a given language certain sequences of sounds were associated with definite meanings, and they earnestly aimed at discovering a reason for the linkage between those *sounds* and that *meaning*. Their attempt, however, was thwarted from the very beginning by the fact that the same sounds were equally present in other languages although the meaning they conveyed was entirely different. The contradiction was surmounted only by the discovery that it is the combination of sounds, not the sounds themselves, which provides the significant data.

It is easy to see, moreover, that some of the more recent interpretations of mythological thought originated from the same kind of misconception under which those early linguists were laboring. Let us consider, for instance, Jung's idea that a given mythological pattern – the so-called archetype – possesses a certain meaning. This is comparable to the long-supported error that a sound may possess a certain affinity with a meaning: for instance the 'liquid' semi-vowels with water, the open vowels with things that are big, large, loud, or heavy, etc., a theory which still has its supporters.[3] Whatever emendations the original formulation may now call for,[4] everybody will agree that the Saussurean principle of the arbitrary character of linguistic signs was a prerequisite for the accession of linguistics to the scientific level.

To invite the mythologist to compare his precarious situation with that of the linguist in the prescientific stage is not enough. As a matter of fact we may thus be led only from one difficulty to another. There is a very good reason why myth cannot simply be treated as language if its specific problems are to be solved; myth *is* language: to be known, myth has to be told; it is a part of human speech. In order to preserve its specificity we must be able to show that it is both the same thing as language, and also something different from it. Here, too, the past experience of linguists may help us. For language itself can be analyzed into things which are at the same time similar and yet different. This is precisely what is expressed in Saussure's distinction between *langue* and *parole*, one being the structural side of language, the other the statistical aspect of it, *langue* belonging to a reversible time, *parole* being non-reversible. If those two levels already exist in language, then a third one can conceivably be isolated.

We have distinguished *langue* and *parole* by the different time referents which they use. Keeping this in mind, we may notice that myth uses a third referent which combines the properties of the first two. On the one hand, a myth always refers to events alleged to have taken place long ago. But what gives the myth an operational value is that the specific pattern described is timeless; it explains the present and the past as well as the future. This can be made clear through a comparison between myth and what appears to have largely replaced it in modern societies, namely, politics. When the historian refers to the French Revolution, it is always as a sequence of past happenings, a non-reversible series of events the remote consequences of which may still be felt at present. But to the French politician, as well as to his followers, the French Revolution is both a sequence belonging to the past – as to the historian – and a timeless pattern which can be detected in the contemporary French social structure and which provides a clue for its interpretation, a lead from which to infer future developments. Michelet, for instance, was a politically minded historian. He describes the French Revolution thus: 'That day ... everything was possible.... Future became present ... that is, no more time, a glimpse of eternity'.[5] It is that double structure, altogether historical and ahistorical, which explains how myth, while pertaining to the realm of *parole* and calling for an explanation as such, as well as to that of *langue* in which it is expressed, can also be an absolute entity on a third level which, though it remains linguistic by nature, is nevertheless distinct from the other two.

A remark can be introduced at this point which will help to show the originality of myth in relation to other linguistic phenomena. Myth is the part of language where the formula *traduttore, tradittore* reaches its lowest truth value. From that point of view it should be placed in the gamut of linguistic expressions at the end opposite to that of poetry, in spite of all the claims which have been made to prove the contrary. Poetry is a kind of speech which cannot be translated except at the cost of serious distortions; whereas the mythical value of the myth is preserved even through the worst translation. Whatever our ignorance of the language and the culture of the people where it originated, a myth is still felt as a myth by any reader anywhere in the world. Its substance does not lie in its style, its original music, or its syntax, but in the *story* which it tells. Myth is language, functioning on an especially high level where meaning succeeds practically at 'taking off' from the linguistic ground on which it keeps on rolling.

To sum up the discussion at this point, we have so far made the following claims: (1) If there is a meaning to be found in mythology, it cannot reside in the isolated elements which enter into the composition of a myth, but only in the way those elements are combined. (2) Although myth belongs to the same category as language, being, as a matter of fact, only part of it, language in myth exhibits specific properties. (3) Those properties are only to be found *above* the ordinary linguistic level, that is, they exhibit more complex features than those which are to be found in any other kind of linguistic expression.

If the above three points are granted, at least as a working hypothesis, two consequences will follow: (1) Myth, like the rest of language, is made up of constituent units. (2) These constituent units presuppose the constituent units present in language when analyzed on other levels – namely, phonemes, morphomes, and sememes – but they, nevertheless, differ from the latter in the same way as the latter differ among themselves; they belong to a higher and more complex order. For this reason, we shall call them *gross constituent units*.

How shall we proceed in order to identify and isolate these gross constituent units or mythemes? We know that they cannot be found among phonemes, morphemes, or sememes, but only on a higher level; otherwise myth would become confused with any other kind of speech. Therefore, we should look for them on the sentence level. The only method we can suggest at this stage is to proceed tentatively, by trial and error, using as a check the principles which serve as a basis for any kind of structural analysis: economy of explanation; unity of solution; and ability to reconstruct the whole from a fragment, as well as later stages from previous ones.

The technique which has been applied so far by this writer consists in analyzing each myth individually, breaking down its story into the shortest possible sentences, and writing each sentence on an index card bearing a number corresponding to the unfolding of the story.

Practically each card will thus show that a certain function is, at a given time, linked to a given subject. Or, to put it otherwise, each gross constituent unit will consist of a *relation*.

However, the above definition remains highly unsatisfactory for two different reasons. First, it is well known to structural linguists that constituent units on all levels are made up of relations, and the true difference between our *gross* units and the others remains unexplained; second, we still find ourselves in the realm of a non-reversible time, since the numbers of the cards correspond to the unfolding of the narrative. Thus the specific character of mythological time, which as we have seen is both reversible and non-reversible, synchronic and diachronic, remains unaccounted for. From this springs a new hypothesis, which constitutes the very core of our argument: The true constituent units of a myth are not the isolated relations but *bundles of such relations*, and it is only as bundles that these relations can be put to use and combined so as to produce a meaning. Relations pertaining to the same bundle may appear diachronically at remote intervals, but when we have succeeded in grouping them together we have reorganized our myth according to a time referent of a new nature, corresponding to the prerequisite of the initial hypothesis, namely a two-dimensional time referent which is simultaneously diachronic and synchronic, and which accordingly integrates the characteristics of *langue* on the one hand, and those of *parole* on the other. To put it in even more linguistic terms, it is as though a phoneme were always made up of all its variants.

Two comparisons may help to explain what we have in mind.

Let us first suppose that archaeologists of the future coming from another planet would one day, when all human life had disappeared from the earth, excavate one of our libraries. Even if they were at first ignorant of our writing, they might succeed in deciphering it – an undertaking which would require, at some early stage, the discovery that the alphabet, as we are in the habit of printing it, should be read from left to right and from top to bottom. However, they would soon discover that a whole category of books did not fit the usual pattern – these would be the orchestra scores on the shelves of the music division. But after trying, without success, to decipher staffs one after the other, from the upper down to the lower, they would probably notice that the same patterns of notes recurred at intervals, either in full or in part, or that some patterns were strongly reminiscent of earlier ones. Hence the hypothesis: What if patterns showing affinity, instead of being considered in succession, were to be treated as one complex pattern and read as a whole? By getting at what we call *harmony*, they would then see that an orchestra score, to be meaningful, must be read diachronically along one axis – that is, page after page, and from left to right – and synchronically along the other axis, all the notes written vertically making up one gross constituent unit, that is, one bundle of relations.

The other comparison is somewhat different. Let us take an observer ignorant of our playing cards, sitting for a long time with a fortune-teller. He would know something of the visitors: scx, age, physical appearance, social situation, etc., in the same way as we know something of the different cultures whose myths we try to study. He would also listen to the séances and record them so as to be able to go over them and make comparisons – as we do when we listen to myth-telling and record it. Mathematicians to whom I have put the problem agree that if the man is bright and if the material available to him is sufficient, he may be able to reconstruct the nature of the deck of cards being used, that is, fifty-two or thirty-two cards according to the case, made up of four homologous sets consisting of the same units (the individual cards) with only one varying feature, the suit.

Now for a concrete example of the method we propose. We shall use the Oedipus myth, which is well known to everyone. I am well aware that the Oedipus myth has only reached us under late forms and through literary transmutations concerned more with esthetic and moral preoccupations than with religious or ritual ones, whatever these may have been. But we shall not interpret the Oedipus myth in literal terms, much less offer an explanation acceptable to the specialist. We simply wish to illustrate – and without reaching any conclusions with respect to it – a certain technique, whose use is probably not legitimate in this particular instance, owing to the problematic elements indicated above. The 'demonstration' should therefore be conceived, not in terms of what the scientist means by this term, but at best in terms of what is meant by the street peddler, whose aim is not to achieve a concrete result, but to explain, as succinctly as possible, the functioning of the mechanical toy which he is trying to sell to the onlookers.

The myth will be treated as an orchestra score would be if it were unwittingly considered as a unilinear series; our task is to re-establish the correct arrangement. Say, for instance, we were confronted with a sequence of the type: 1,2,4,7,8,2,3,4,6,8,1,4,5,7,8,1,2,5,7,3,4,5,6,8 . . ., the assignment being to put all the 1's together, all the 2's, the 3's, etc.; the result is a chart:

1	2		4			7	8
	2	3	4		6		8
1			4	5		7	8
1	2			5		7	
		3	4	5	6		8

We shall attempt to perform the same kind of operation on the Oedipus myth, trying out several arrangements of the mythemes until we find one which is in harmony with the principles enumerated above. Let us suppose, for the sake of argument, that the best arrangement is the following (although it might certainly be improved with the help of a specialist in Greek mythology):

Cadmos seeks his sister Europa, ravished by Zeus			
		Cadmos kills the dragon	
	The Spartoi kill one another		
			Labdacos (Laios' father) = *lame* (?)
	Oedipus kills his father, Laios		Laios (Oedipus' father) = *left-sided* (?)
		Oedipus kills the Sphinx	
			Oedipus = *swollen-foot* (?)
Oedipus marries his mother, Jocasta			
	Eteocles kills his brother, Polynices		
Antigone buries her brother, Polynices, despite prohibition			

We thus find ourselves confronted with four vertical columns, each of which includes several relations belonging to the same bundle. Were we to *tell* the myth, we would disregard the columns and read the rows from left to right and from top to bottom. But if we want to *understand* the myth, then we will have to disregard one half of the diachronic dimension (top to bottom) and read from left to right, column after column, each one being considered as a unit.

All the relations belonging to the same column exhibit one common feature which it is our task to discover. For instance, all the events grouped in the first column on the left have something to do with blood relations which are overemphasized, that is, are more intimate than they should be. Let us say, then, that the first column has as its common feature the *overrating of blood relations*. It is obvious that the second column expresses the same thing, but inverted: *underrating of blood relations*.

The third column refers to monsters being slain. As to the fourth, a few words of clarification are needed. The remarkable connotation of the surnames in Oedipus' father-line has often been noticed. However, linguists usually disregard it, since to them the only way to define the meaning of a term is to investigate all the contexts in which it appears, and personal names, precisely because they are used as such, are not accompanied by any context. With the method we propose to follow the objection disappears, since the myth itself provides its own context. The significance is no longer to be sought in the eventual meaning of each name, but in the fact that all the names have a common feature: All the hypothetical meanings (which may well remain hypothetical) refer to *difficulties in walking straight and standing upright.*

What then is the relationship between the two columns on the right? Column three refers to monsters. The dragon is a chthonian being which has to be killed in order that mankind be born from the Earth; the Sphinx is a monster unwilling to permit men to live. The last unit reproduces the first one, which has to do with the *autochthonous origin* of mankind. Since the monsters are overcome by men, we may thus say that the common feature of the third column is *denial of the autochthonous origin of man.*[6]

This immediately helps us to understand the meaning of the fourth column. In mythology it is a universal characteristic of men born from the Earth that at the moment they emerge from the depth they either cannot walk or they walk clumsily. This is the case of the chthonian beings in the mythology of the Pueblo: Muyingwu, who leads the emergence, and the chthonian Shumaikoli are lame ('bleeding-foot', 'sore-foot'). The same happens to the Koskimo of the Kwakiutl after they have been swallowed by the chthonian monster, Tsiakish: When they returned to the surface of the earth 'they limped forward or tripped sideways'. Thus the common feature of the fourth column is *the persistence of the autochthonous origin of man.* It follows that column four is to column three as column one is to column two. The inability to connect two kinds of relationships is overcome (or rather replaced) by the assertion that contradictory relationships are identical inasmuch as they are both self-contradictory in a similar way. Although this is still a provisional formulation of the structure of mythical thought, it is sufficient at this stage.

Turning back to the Oedipus myth, we may now see what it means. The myth has to do with the inability, for a culture which holds the belief that mankind is autochthonous (see, for instance, Pausanias, VIII, xxix, 4: plants provide a *model* for humans), to find a satisfactory transition between this theory and the knowledge that human beings are actually born from the union of man and woman. Although the problem obviously cannot be solved, the Oedipus myth provides a kind of logical tool which relates the original problem – born from one or born from two? – to the derivative problem: born from different or born from same? By a correlation of this type, the overrating of blood relations is to the under-rating of blood relations as the attempt to escape autochthony is to the impossibility to succeed in it. Although experience contradicts theory, social life validates cosmology by its similarity of structure. Hence cosmology is true.

Two remarks should be made at this stage.

In order to interpret the myth, we left aside a point which has worried the specialists until now, namely, that in the earlier (Homeric) versions of the Oedipus myth, some basic elements are lacking, such as Jocasta killing herself and Oedipus piercing his own eyes. These events do not alter the substance of the myth although they can easily be integrated, the first one as a new case of autodestruction (column three) and the second as another case of crippledness (column four). At the same time there is something significant in these additions, since the shift from foot to head is to be correlated with the shift from autochthonous origin to self-destruction.

Our method thus eliminates a problem which has, so far, been one of the main obstacles to the process of mythological studies, namely, the quest for the *true* version, or the *earlier* one. On the contrary, we define the myth as consisting of all its versions; or to put it otherwise, a myth remains the same as long as it is felt as such. A striking example is offered by the fact that our interpretation may take into account the Freudian use of the Oedipus myth and is certainly applicable to it. Although the Freudian problem has ceased to be that of autochthony *versus* bisexual reproduction, it is still the problem of understanding how *one* can be born from *two*: How is it that we do not have only one procreator, but a mother plus a father? Therefore, not only Sophocles, but Freud himself, should be included among the recorded versions of the Oedipus myth on a par with earlier or seemingly more 'authentic' versions.

An important consequence follows. If a myth is made up of all its variants, structural analysis should take all of them into account. After analyzing all the known variants of the Theban version, we should thus treat the others in the same way: first, the tales about Labdacos' collateral line including Agave, Pentheus, and Jocasta herself; the Theban variant about Lycos with Amphion and Zetos as the city founders; more remote variants concerning Dionysus (Oedipus' matrilateral cousin); and Athenian legends where Cecrops takes the place of Cadmos, etc. For each of them a similar chart should be drawn and then compared and reorganized according to the findings: Cecrops killing the serpent with the parallel episode of Cadmos; abandonment of Dionysus with abandonment of Oedipus; 'Swollen Foot' with Dionysus' *loxias*, that is, walking obliquely; Europa's quest with Antiope's; the founding of Thebes by the Spartoi or by the brothers Amphion and Zetos; Zeus kidnapping Europa and Antiope and the same with Semele; the Theban Oedipus and the Argian Perseus, etc. We shall then have several two-dimensional charts, each dealing with a variant, to be organized in a three-dimensional order, as shown in the following figure, so that three different readings become possible: left to right, top to bottom, front to back (or vice versa). All of these charts cannot be expected to be identical; but experience shows that any difference to be observed may be correlated with other differences, so that a logical treatment of the whole will allow simplifications, the final outcome being the structural law of the myth.

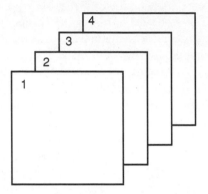

At this point the objection may be raised that the task is impossible to perform, since we can only work with known versions. Is it not possible that a new version might alter the picture? This is true enough if only one or two versions are available, but the objection becomes theoretical as soon as a reasonably large number have been recorded. Let us make this point clear by a comparison. If the furniture of a room and its arrangement were known to us only through its reflection in two mirrors placed on opposite walls, we should theoretically dispose of an almost infinite number of mirror images which would provide us with a complete knowledge. However, should the two mirrors be obliquely set, the number of mirror images would become very small; nevertheless, four or five such images would very likely give us, if not complete information, at least a sufficient coverage so that we would feel sure that no large piece of furniture is missing in our description.

On the other hand, it cannot be too strongly emphasized that all available variants should be taken into account. If Freudian comments on the Oedipus complex are a part of the Oedipus myth, then questions such as whether Cushing's version of the Zuni origin myth should be retained or discarded become irrelevant. There is no single 'true' version of which all the others are but copies or distortions. Every version belongs to the myth.

The reason for the discouraging results in works on general mythology can finally be understood. They stem from two causes. First, comparative mythologists have selected preferred versions instead of using them all. Second, we have seen that the structural analysis of *one* variant of *one* myth belonging to *one* tribe (in some cases, even *one* village) already requires two dimensions. When we use several variants of the same myth for the same tribe or village, the frame of reference becomes three-dimensional, and as soon as we try to enlarge the comparison, the number of dimensions required increases until it appears quite impossible to handle them intuitively. The confusions and platitudes which are the outcome of comparative mythology can be explained by the fact that multi-dimensional frames of reference are often ignored or are naïvely replaced by two- or three-dimensional ones. Indeed, progress in comparative mythology depends largely on the cooperation of mathematicians who would undertake to express in symbols multi-dimensional relations which cannot be handled otherwise.

To check this theory,[7] an attempt was made from 1952 to 1954 toward an exhaustive analysis of all the known versions of the Zuni origin and emergence myth: Cushing, 1883 and 1896; Stevenson, 1904; Parsons, 1923; Bunzel, 1932; Benedict, 1934. Furthermore, a preliminary attempt was made at a comparison of the results with similar myths in other Pueblo tribes, Western and Eastern. Finally, a test was undertaken with Plains mythology. In all cases, it was found that the theory was sound; light was thrown, not only on North American mythology, but also on a previously unnoticed kind of logical operation, or one known so far only in a wholly different context. The bulk of material which needs to be handled practically at the outset of the work makes it impossible to enter into details, and we shall have to limit ourselves here to a few illustrations.

A simplified chart of the Zuni emergence myth would read:

CHANGE			DEATH
mechanical value of plants (used as ladders to emerge from lower world)	emergence led by Beloved Twins	sibling incest (origin of water)	gods kill children of men (by drowning)
food values of wild plants	migration led by the two Newekwe (ceremonial clowns)		magical contest with People of the Dew (collecting wild food *versus* cultivation)
		brother and sister sacrificed (to gain victory)	
food value of cultivated plants			
		brother and sister adopted (in exchange for corn)	
DEATH			PERMANENCE

CHANGE			DEATH
periodical character of agricultural work			
			war against the Kyanakwe (gardeners *versus* hunters)
food value of game (hunting)			
	war led by the two War-Gods		
inevitability of warfare			salvation of the tribe (center of the World found)
	brother and sister sacrificed (to avoid the Flood)		
DEATH			PERMANENCE

As the chart indicates, the problem is the discovery of a life–death mediation. For the Pueblo, this is especially difficult; they understand the origin of human life in terms of the model of plant life (emergence from the earth). They share that belief with the ancient Greeks, and it is not without reason that we chose the Oedipus myth as our first example. But in the American Indian case, the highest form of plant life is to be found in agriculture which is periodical in nature, that is, which consists in an alternation between life and death. If this is disregarded, the contradiction appears elsewhere: Agriculture provides food, therefore life; but hunting provides food and is similar to warfare which means death. Hence there are three different ways of handling the problem. In the Cushing version, the difficulty revolves around an opposition between activities yielding an immediate result (collecting wild food) and activities yielding a delayed result – death has to become integrated so that agriculture can exist. Parsons' version shifts from hunting to agriculture, while Stevenson's version operates the other way around. It can be shown that all the differences between these versions can be rigorously correlated with these basic structures.

Thus the three versions describe the great war waged by the ancestors of the Zuni against a mythical population, the Kyanakwe, by introducing into the narrative significant variations which consist (1) in the friendship or hostility of the gods; (2) in the granting of final victory to one camp or the other; (3) in the attribution of the symbolic function to the Kyanakwe, described sometimes as hunters (whose bows are strung with animal sinews) and sometimes as gardeners (whose bows are strung with plant fibers).

CUSHING	PARSONS	STEVENSON
Gods, Kyanakwe } allied, use fiber string on their bows (gardeners)	Kyanakwe, alone, use fiber string	Gods, Men } allied, use fiber string

VICTORIOUS OVER	VICTORIOUS OVER	VICTORIOUS OVER
Men, alone, use sinew (until they shift to fiber)	Gods, Men } allied, use sinew string	Kyanakwe, alone, use sinew string

Since fiber string (agriculture) is always superior to sinew string (hunting), and since (to a lesser extent) the gods' alliance is preferable to their antagonism, it follows that in Cushing's version, men are seen as doubly under-privileged (hostile gods, sinew string); in the Stevenson version, doubly privileged (friendly gods, fiber string); while Parsons' version confronts us with an intermediary situation (friendly gods, but sinew strings, since men begin by being hunters). Hence:

OPPOSITIONS	CUSHING	PARSONS	STEVENSON
gods/men	–	+	+
fiber/sinew	–	–	+

Bunzel's version is of the same type as Cushing's from a structural point of view. However, it differs from both Cushing's and Stevenson's, inasmuch as the latter two explain the emergence as the result of man's need to evade his pitiful condition, while Bunzel's version makes it the consequence of a call from the higher powers – hence the inverted sequences of the means resorted to for the emergence: In both Cushing and Stevenson, they go from plants to animals; in Bunzel, from mammals to insects, and from insects to plants.

Among the Western Pueblo the logical approach always remains the same; the starting point and the point of arrival are simplest, whereas the intermediate stage is characterized by ambiguity:

LIFE (= INCREASE) (Mechanical) value of the plant kingdom, taking growth alone into account	ORIGINS
Food value of the plant kingdom, limited to wild plants	FOOD-GATHERING
Food value of the plant kingdom, including wild and cultivated plants	AGRICULTURE

Food value of the animal kingdom, limited to animals	(*but there is a contradiction here, owing to the negation of life = destruction, hence:*)	
Destruction of the animal kingdom, extended to human beings		HUNTING
DEATH (= DECREASE)		WARFARE

The fact that contradiction appears in the middle of the dialectical process results in a double set of dioscuric pairs, the purpose of which is to mediate between conflicting terms:

1. 2 divine messengers — 2 ceremonial clowns — 2 war-gods

2. homogeneous pair: dioscuri (2 brothers) — siblings (brother and sister) — couple (husband and wife) — heterogeneous pair: (grandmother and grandchild)

We have here combinational variants of the same function in different contexts (hence the war attribute of the clowns, which has given rise to so many queries).

The problem, often regarded as insoluble, vanishes when it is shown that the clowns – gluttons who may with impunity make excessive use of agricultural products – have the same function in relation to food production as the war-gods. (This function appears, in the dialectical process, as *overstepping the boundaries* of hunting, that is, hunting for men instead of for animals for human consumption.)

Some Central and Eastern Pueblos proceed the other way around. They begin by stating the identity of hunting and cultivation (first corn obtained by Game-Father sowing deer-dewclaws), and they try to derive both life and death from that central notion. Then, instead of extreme terms being simple and intermediary ones duplicated as among the Western groups, the extreme terms become duplicated (i.e. the two sisters of the Eastern Pueblo) while a simple mediating term comes to the foreground (for instance, the Poshaiyanne of the Zia), but endowed with equivocal attributes. Hence the attributes of this 'messiah' can be deduced from the place it occupies in the time sequence: good when at the beginning (Zuni, Cushing), equivocal in the middle (Central Pueblo), bad at the end (Zia), except in Bunzel's version, where the sequence is reversed as has been shown.

By systematically using this kind of structural analysis it becomes possible to organize all the known variants of a myth into a set forming a kind of permutation group, the two variants placed at the far ends being in a symmetrical, though inverted, relationship to each other.

Our method not only has the advantage of bringing some kind of order to what was previously chaos; it also enables us to perceive some basic logical processes which are at the root of mythical thought.[8] Three main processes should be distinguished.

The trickster of American mythology has remained so far a problematic figure. Why is it that throughout North America his role is assigned practically everywhere to either coyote or raven? If we keep in mind that mythical thought always progresses from the awareness of oppositions toward their resolution, the reason for these choices becomes clearer. We need only assume that two opposite terms with no intermediary always tend to be replaced by two equivalent terms which admit of a third one as a mediator; then one of the polar terms and the mediator become replaced by a new triad, and so on. Thus we have a mediating structure of the following type:

INITIAL PAIR	FIRST TRIAD	SECOND TRIAD
Life		
	Agriculture	
		Herbivorous animals
		Carrion-eating animals
		(raven; coyote)
	Hunting	
		Beasts of prey
	Warfare	
Death		

The unformulated argument is as follows: carrion-eating animals are like beasts of prey (they eat animal food), but they are also like food-plant producers (they do not kill what they eat). Or to put it otherwise, Pueblo style (for Pueblo agriculture is more 'meaningful' than hunting): ravens are to gardens as beasts of prey are to herbivorous animals. But it is also clear that herbivorous animals may be called first to act as mediators on the assumption that they are like collectors and gatherers (plant-food eaters), while they can be used as animal food though they are not themselves hunters. Thus we may have mediators of the first order, of the second order, and so on, where each term generates the next by a double process of opposition and correlation.

This kind of process can be followed in the mythology of the Plains, where we may order the data according to the set:

Unsuccessful mediator between Earth and Sky
(Star-Husband's wife)

Heterogeneous pair of mediators
(grandmother and grandchild)

Semi-homogeneous pair of mediators
(Lodge-Boy and Thrown-away)

While among the Pueblo (Zuni) we have the corresponding set:

Successful mediator between Earth and Sky
(Poshaiyanki)

Semi-homogeneous pair of mediators
(Uyuyewi and Matsailema)

Homogeneous pair of mediators
(the two Ahaiyuta)

On the other hand, correlations may appear on a horizontal axis (this is true even on the linguistic level; see the manifold connotation of the root *pose* in Tewa according to Parsons: coyote, mist, scalp, etc.). Coyote (a carrion-eater) is intermediary between herbivorous and carnivorous just as mist between Sky and Earth; as scalp between war and agriculture (scalp is a war crop); as corn smut between wild and cultivated plants; as garments between 'nature' and 'culture'; as refuse between village and outside; and as ashes (or soot) between roof (sky vault) and hearth (in the ground). This chain of mediators, if one may call them so, not only throws light on entire parts of North American mythology – why the Dew-God may be at the same time the Game-Master and the giver of raiments and be personified as an 'Ash-Boy'; or why scalps are mist-producing; or why the Game-Mother is associated with corn smut; etc. – but it also probably corresponds to a universal way of organizing daily experience. See, for instance, the French for plant smut (*nielle*, from Latin *nebula*); the luck-bringing power attributed in Europe to refuse (old shoe) and ashes (kissing chimney sweeps); and compare the American Ash-Boy cycle with the Indo-European Cinderella: Both are phallic figures (mediators between male and female); masters of the dew and the game; owners of fine raiments; and social mediators (low class marrying into high class); but they are impossible to interpret through recent diffusion, as has been contended, since Ash-Boy and Cinderella are symmetrical but inverted in every detail (while the borrowed Cinderella tale in America – Zuni Turkey-Girl – is parallel to the prototype). Hence the chart:

	EUROPE	AMERICA
Sex	female	male
Family status	double family (remarried father)	no family (orphan)
Appearance	pretty girl	ugly boy
Sentimental status	nobody likes her	unrequited love for girl
Transformation	luxuriously clothed with supernatural help	stripped of ugliness with supernatural help

Thus, like Ash-Boy and Cinderella, the trickster is a mediator. Since his mediating function occupies a position halfway between two polar terms,

322

he must retain something of that duality – namely an ambiguous and equivocal character. But the trickster figure is not the only conceivable form of mediation; some myths seem to be entirely devoted to the task of exhausting all the possible solutions to the problem of bridging the gap between *two* and *one*. For instance, a comparison between all the variants of the Zuni emergence myth provides us with a series of mediating devices each of which generates the next one by a process of opposition and correlation:

> messiah > dioscuri > trickster > bisexual being > sibling
> pair > married couple > grandmother-grandchild > four-term
> group > triad

In Cushing's version, this dialectic is associated with a change from a spatial dimension (mediation between Sky and Earth) to a temporal dimension (mediation between summer and winter, that is, between birth and death). But while the shift is being made from space to time, the final solution (triad) re-introduces space, since a triad consists of a dioscuric pair *plus* a messiah, present simultaneously; and while the point of departure was ostensibly formulated in terms of a space referent (Sky and Earth), this was nevertheless implicitly conceived in terms of a time referent (first the messiah calls, *then* the dioscuri descend). Therefore the logic of myth confronts us with a double, reciprocal exchange of functions to which we shall return shortly.

Not only can we account for the ambiguous character of the trickster, but we can also understand another property of mythical figures the world over, namely, that the same god is endowed with contradictory attributes – for instance, he may be *good* and *bad* at the same time. If we compare the variants of the *Hopi myth* of the origin of Shalako, we may order them in terms of the following structure:

$$(\text{Masauwu: } x) \simeq (\text{Muyingwu: Masauwu}) \simeq (\text{Shalako: Muyingwu}) \simeq (y: \text{Masauwu})$$

where x and y represent arbitrary values corresponding to the fact that in the two 'extreme' variants the god Masauwu, while appearing alone rather than associated with another god, as in variant two, or being absent, as in variant three, still retains intrinsically a relative value. In variant one, Masauwu (alone) is depicted as helpful to mankind (though not as helpful as he could be), and in version four, harmful to mankind (though not as harmful as he could be). His role is thus defined – at least implicitly – in contrast with another role which is possible but not specified and which is represented here by the values x and y. In version two, on the other hand, Muyingwu is relatively more helpful than Masauwu, and in version three, Shalako more helpful than Muyingwu. We find an identical series when ordering the Keresan variants:

(Poshaiyanki: x) $\simeq$ (Lea: Poshaiyanki) $\simeq$ (Poshaiyanki: Tiamoni) $\simeq$ (y: Poshaiyanki)

This logical framework is particularly interesting, since anthropologists are already acquainted with it on two other levels – first, in regard to the problem of the pecking order among hens, and second, to what this writer has called *generalized exchange* in the field of kinship. By recognizing it also on the level of mythical thought, we may find ourselves in a better position to appraise its basic importance in anthropological studies and to give it a more inclusive theoretical interpretation.

Finally, when we have succeeded in organizing a whole series of variants into a kind of permutation group, we are in a position to formulate the law of that group. Although it is not possible at the present stage to come closer than an approximate formulation which will certainly need to be refined in the future, it seems that every myth (considered as the aggregate of all its variants) corresponds to a formula of the following type:

$$F_x(a): F_y(b) \simeq F_x(b): F_{a-1}(y)$$

Here, with two terms, a and b, being given as well as two functions, x and y, of these terms, it is assumed that a relation of equivalence exists between two situations defined respectively by an inversion of *terms* and *relations*, under two conditions: (1) that one term be replaced by its opposite (in the above formula, a and a–1); (2) that an inversion be made between the *function value* and the *term value* of two elements (above, y and a).

This formula becomes highly significant when we recall that Freud considered that *two traumas* (and not one, as is so commonly said) are necessary in order to generate the individual myth in which a neurosis consists. By trying to apply the formula to the analysis of these traumas (and assuming that they correspond to conditions 1 and 2 respectively) we should not only be able to provide a more precise and rigorous formulation of the genetic law of the myth, but we would find ourselves in the much desired position of developing side by side the anthropological and the psychological aspects of the theory; we might also take it to the laboratory and subject it to experimental verification.

At this point it seems unfortunate that with the limited means at the disposal of French anthropological research no further advance can be made. It should be emphasized that the task of analyzing mythological literature, which is extremely bulky, and of breaking it down into its constituent units, requires team work and technical help. A variant of average length requires several hundred cards to be properly analyzed. To discover a suitable pattern of rows and columns for those cards, special devices are needed, consisting of vertical boards about six feet long and four and a half feet high, where cards can be pigeon-holed and moved at will. In order to build up three-dimensional models enabling one to compare the variants, several such boards are necessary, and this in turn requires a spacious workshop, a commodity particularly unavailable in Western Europe nowadays. Furthermore, as soon as the frame of reference becomes multi-dimensional (which occurs at an early stage, as has been shown above) the board system has to be replaced by perforated cards, which in turn require IBM equipment, etc.

Three final remarks may serve as conclusion.

First, the question has often been raised why myths, and more generally oral literature, are so much addicted to duplication, triplication, or quadruplication of the same sequence. If our hypotheses are accepted, the answer is obvious: The function of repetition is to render the structure of the myth apparent. For we have seen that the synchronic–diachronic structure of the myth permits us to organize it into diachronic sequences (the rows in our tables) which should be read synchronically (the columns). Thus, a myth exhibits a 'slated' structure, which comes to the surface, so to speak, through the process of repetition.

However, the slates are not absolutely identical. And since the purpose of myth is to provide a logical model capable of overcoming a contradiction (an impossible achievement if, as it happens, the contradiction is real), a theoretically infinite number of slates will be generated, each one slightly different from the others. Thus, myth grows spiral-wise until the intellectual impulse which has produced it is exhausted. Its *growth* is a continuous process, whereas its *structure* remains discontinuous. If this is the case, we should assume that it closely corresponds, in the realm of the spoken word, to a crystal in the realm of physical matter. This analogy may help us to better understand the relationship of myth to both *langue* on the one hand and *parole* on the other. Myth is an intermediary entity between a statistical aggregate of molecules and the molecular structure itself.

Prevalent attempts to explain alleged differences between the so-called primitive mind and scientific thought have resorted to qualitative differences between the working processes of the mind in both cases, while assuming that the entities which they were studying remained very much the same. If our interpretation is correct, we are led toward a completely different view – namely, that the kind of logic in mythical thought is as rigorous as that of modern science and that the difference lies, not in the quality of the intellectual process, but in the nature of the things to which it is applied. This is well in agreement with the situation known to prevail in the field of technology: What makes a steel ax superior to a stone ax is not that the first one is better made than the second. They are equally well made, but steel is quite different from stone. In the same way we may be able to show that the same logical processes operate in myth as in science, and that man has always been thinking equally well; the improvement lies, not in an alleged progress of man's mind, but in the discovery of new areas to which it may apply its unchanged and unchanging powers.

NOTES

1   In Boas' Introduction to James Teit, 'Traditions of the Thompson River Indians of British Columbia', *Memoirs of the American Folklore Society*, VI (1898), p. 18.

2   A. M. Hocart, *Social Origins* (London: 1954), p. 7.

3   See, for instance, Sir, R. A. Paget, 'The Origin of Language', *Journal of World History*, I, no. 2 (UNESCO, 1953).

4   See Emile Benveniste, 'Nature du signe linguistique', *Acta Linguistica*, I, no. I (1939).

5   Jules Michelet, *Histoire de la Révolution française*, IV, I. I took this quotation from M. Merleau-Ponty, *Les Aventures de la dialectique* (Paris: 1955), p. 273.

6   We are not trying to become involved with specialists in an argument; this would be presumptuous and even meaningless on our part. Since the Oedipus myth is taken here merely as an example treated in arbitrary fashion, the chthonian nature ascribed to the Sphinx might seem surprising; we shall refer to the testimony of Marie Delcourt: 'In the archaic legends, [she is] certainly born of the Earth itself' (*Oedipe ou la légende du conquérant* [Liège: 1944], p. 108). No matter how remote from Delcourt's our method may be (and our conclusions would be, no doubt, if we were competent to deal with the problem in depth), it seems to us that she has convincingly established the nature of the Sphinx in the archaic tradition, namely, that of a female monster who attacks and rapes young men; in other words, the personification of a female being with an inversion of the sign. This explains why, in the handsome iconography compiled by Delcourt at the end of her work, men and women are always found in an inverted 'sky/earth' relationship.

    As we shall point out below, we selected the Oedipus myth as our first example because of the striking analogies that seem to exist between certain aspects of archaic Greek thought and that of the Pueblo Indians, from whom we have borrowed the examples that follow. In this respect it should be noted that the figure of the Sphinx, as reconstructed by Delcourt, coincides with two figures of North American mythology (who probably merge into one). We are referring, on the one hand, to 'the old hag', a repulsive witch whose physical appearance presents a 'problem' to the young hero. If he 'solves' this problem – that is, if he responds to the advances of the abject creature – he will find in his bed, upon awakening, a beautiful young woman who will confer power upon him (this is also a Celtic theme). The Sphinx, on the other hand, recalls even more 'the child-protruding woman' of the Hopi Indians, that is, a phallic mother *par excellence*. This young woman was abandoned by her group in the course of a difficult migration, just as she was about to give birth. Henceforth she wanders in the desert as the 'Mother of Animals', which she withholds from hunters. He who meets her in her bloody clothes 'is so frightened that he has an erection', of which she takes advantage to rape him, after which she rewards him with unfailing success in hunting. See H. R. Voth, 'The Oraibi Summer Snake Ceremony', *Field Columbian Museum*, publication no. 83, Anthropological Series, vol. III, no. 4 (Chicago: 1903), pp. 352–3 and p. 353, n I.

7   See *Annuaire de l'Ecole pratique des Hautes Etudes*, Section des Sciences religieuses, 1952–1953, pp. 19–21, and 1953–1954, pp. 27–9. Thanks are due here to an unrequested but deeply appreciated grant from the Ford Foundation.

8   For another application of this method, see our study 'Four Winnebago Myths: A Structural Sketch', in Stanley Diamond (ed.), *Culture in History: Essays in Honor of Paul Radin* (New York: 1960), pp. 351–62.

21

Jacques Lacan

(1901–1981)

In the same way that Lévi-Strauss extended Saussure's structural model of linguistics to the realm of anthropology, Jacques Lacan adapted this model for a radical reinterpretation of Freudian psychoanalysis. This transformation began with a new perspective on the 'unconscious', no longer assumed to be the biologically determined field of libidinal instincts and drives postulated by Freud, but rather semiologically 'structured like a language' with its own logic of dream, fantasy and symptom. Analogously, the unconscious could be compared to Saussure's '*langue*' underlying the '*parole*' of consciousness.

Lacan's attempts to combine Saussurian and Freudian insights in psychoanalysis were almost all originally presented as spoken discourses at seminars or conferences. Starting in 1953, and for twenty years thereafter, Lacan's annual 'Seminars' were attended by some of the most illustrious French intellectuals, while his conference appearances often escalated into volatile, polemical events. A collection of his discourses was assembled as *Ecrits* for the first time in 1966, and some of his 'Seminars' were gradually edited for publication. Yet Lacan's impact on French philosophical circles and the larger psychoanalytic community was already becoming quite significant as early as 1953, when he delivered his famous – or infamous – *Rome Discourse* to the International Psychoanalytic Association. More specifically entitled 'The function and field of speech and language', this paper marked Lacan's initial break with classic psychoanalysis.

Lacan challenged the model of ego psychology which dominated Anglo-American psychoanalysis, and went even further to denounce the conformism and adaptation which seemed to be its goal. In particular, the work of Heinz Hartmann (*Ego Psychology and the Problem of Adaptation*) was rejected by Lacan as reductionistic and erroneous in its privileging of an autonomous and sovereign ego. Lacan offered an alternative model, which suggested that ego formation was inevitably rooted in the narcissism of an 'imaginary' order. The 'specular ego' develops during a 'mirror stage' that Lacan suggested occurred at six to eighteen months. At that time, the infant finds the means to escape its condition of fragmentation and 'lack' by identifying with what it sees reflected as its 'imago' in the maternal 'Other'.

In short, for Lacan there can never be a presumed authority of conscious ego, because the 'Imaginary I' always remains a split subject, a divided self, a reflection of others' desires. Lacan was also obviously influenced by Hegel's account of dialectically mediated self-consciousness in *The Phenomenology of Mind* (1807); again the desire of the 'other' must be confronted for an ego to become conscious of itself. Most importantly for Lacan, the conscious ego struggles continuously to maintain the illusion of its unity, but can only avoid recognizing its fragmentation by continued narcissism to keep this 'imaginary' ego intact. The entry into language marks the threshold of the (paternal) 'Symbolic Order' and the emergence of the Oedipal conflict. Simultaneously, entering the Symbolic also means separation from the mother and the dissolution of the imaginary ego. Only in this way is it possible for the symbolizing subject to emerge. Through language, the split subject confronts its own irreparable division and lack.

According to Lacan, as an ethical injunction, psychoanalysis should not dedicate its praxis to disguising, ignoring or concealing this lack, which he maintained was precisely the misguided project of ego psychology. Lacan's reliance on the *early* texts of Freud, such as *The Interpretation of Dreams* (1900) and *The Psychopathology of Everyday Life* (1901), always distinguished his approach from those psychoanalysts committed to the biologism of the later Freud. He deeply interrogated the fundamental praxis of psychoanalysis, which he claimed should avoid the illusion of a 'cure', or a belief in the supposed infallibility and authority of the analyst. A medical doctor himself, Lacan was firmly convinced that to understand the language of unconscious desire in dreams or symptoms, a psychoanalyst needed less science and more art.

SELECT BIBLIOGRAPHY OF LACAN'S WORKS IN ENGLISH

The Language of the Self: The Function of Language in Psychoanalysis, Baltimore: Johns Hopkins University Press, 1968.

Ecrits: A Selection, London: Tavistock, 1977.

The Four Fundamental Concepts of Psychoanalysis, Harmondsworth: Penguin, 1977.

Feminine Sexuality: Jacques Lacan and the 'Ecole Freudienne', ed. J. Mitchell and J. Rose, New York: Macmillan, 1982.

The Seminar, Book I: Freud's Papers on Technique (1953–1954), Cambridge: Cambridge University Press, 1987.

The Seminar, Book II: The Ego in Freud's Theory and in the Technique of Psychoanalysis (1954–1955), Cambridge: Cambridge University Press, 1988.

Seminar VII: The Ethics of Psychoanalysis (1959–1960), London: Routledge, 1992.

JACQUES LACAN

The Mirror Stage as Formative of the Function of the I as Revealed in Psychoanalytic Experience

THE CONCEPTION OF the mirror stage that I introduced at our last congress, thirteen years ago, has since become more or less established in the practice of the French group. However, I think it worthwhile to bring it again to your attention, especially today, for the light it sheds on the formation of the *I* as we experience it in psychoanalysis. It is an experience that leads us to oppose any philosophy directly issuing from the *Cogito*.

Some of you may recall that this conception originated in a feature of human behaviour illuminated by a fact of comparative psychology. The child, at an age when he is for a time, however short, outdone by the chimpanzee in instrumental intelligence, can nevertheless already recognize as such his own image in a mirror. This recognition is indicated in the illuminative mimicry of the *Aha-Erlebnis*, which Köhler sees as the expression of situational apperception, an essential stage of the act of intelligence.

This act, far from exhausting itself, as in the case of the monkey, once the image has been mastered and found empty, immediately rebounds in the case of the child in a series of gestures in which he experiences in play the relation between the movements assumed in the image and the reflected environment, and between this virtual complex and the reality it reduplicates – the child's own body, and the persons and things, around him.

This event can take place, as we have known since Baldwin, from the age of six months, and its repetition has often made me reflect upon the startling spectacle of the infant in front of the mirror. Unable as yet to walk, or even to stand up, and held tightly as he is by some support, human or artificial (what, in France, we call a '*trotte-bébé*'), he nevertheless overcomes, in a flutter of jubilant activity, the obstructions of his support and, fixing his attitude in a slightly leaning-forward position, in order to hold it in his gaze, brings back an instantaneous aspect of the image.

For me, this activity retains the meaning I have given it up to the age of eighteen months. This meaning discloses a libidinal dynamism, which has hitherto remained problematic, as well as an ontological structure of the human world that accords with my reflections on paranoiac knowledge.

We have only to understand the mirror stage *as an identification*, in the full sense that analysis gives to the term: namely, the transformation that takes place in the subject when he assumes an image – whose predes-

Delivered at the 16th International Congress of Psychoanalysis, Zürich, 17 July 1949. From *Ecrits: A Selection*, London: Tavistock, 1977.

tination to this phase-effect is sufficiently indicated by the use, in analytic theory, of the ancient term *imago*.

This jubilant assumption of his specular image by the child at the *infans* stage, still sunk in his motor incapacity and nursling dependence, would seem to exhibit in an exemplary situation the symbolic matrix in which the *I* is precipitated in a primordial form, before it is objectified in the dialectic of identification with the other, and before language restores to it, in the universal, its function as subject.

This form would have to be called the Ideal-I,[1] if we wished to incorporate it into our usual register, in the sense that it will also be the source of secondary identifications, under which term I would place the functions of libidinal normalization. But the important point is that this form situates the agency of the ego, before its social determination, in a fictional direction, which will always remain irreducible for the individual alone, or rather, which will only rejoin the coming-into-being (*le devenir*) of the subject asymptotically, whatever the success of the dialectical syntheses by which he must resolve as *I* his discordance with his own reality.

The fact is that the total form of the body by which the subject anticipates in a mirage the maturation of his power is given to him only as *Gestalt*, that is to say, in an exteriority in which this form is certainly more constituent than constituted, but in which it appears to him above all in a contrasting size (*un relief de stature*) that fixes it and in a symmetry that inverts it, in contrast with the turbulent movements that the subject feels are animating him. Thus, this *Gestalt* – whose pregnancy should be regarded as bound up with the species, though its motor style remains scarcely recognizable – by these two aspects of its appearance, symbolizes the mental permanence of the *I*, at the same time as it prefigures its alienating destination; it is still pregnant with the correspondences that unite the *I* with the statue in which man projects himself, with the phantoms that dominate him, or with the automation in which, in an ambiguous relation, the world of his own making tends to find completion.

Indeed, for the *imagos* – whose veiled faces it is our privilege to see in outline in our daily experience and in the penumbra of symbolic efficacity[2] – the mirror-image would seem to be the threshold of the visible world, if we go by the mirror disposition that the *imago of one's own body* presents in hallucinations or dreams, whether it concerns its individual features, or even its infirmities, or its object-projections; or if we observe the role of the mirror apparatus in the appearances of the *double*, in which psychical realities, however heterogeneous, are manifested.

That a *Gestalt* should be capable of formative effects in the organism is attested by a piece of biological experimentation that is itself so alien to the idea of psychical causality that it cannot bring itself to formulate its results in these terms. It nevertheless recognizes that it is a necessary condition for the maturation of the gonad of the female pigeon that it should see another member of its species, of either sex; so sufficient in itself is this condition that the desired effect may be obtained merely by placing the individual within reach of the field of reflection of a mirror. Similarly, in the case of the migratory locust, the transition within a generation from the solitary to the gregarious form can be obtained by exposing the individual, at a certain stage, to the exclusively visual action of a similar image, provided it is animated by movements of a style sufficiently close to that characteristic of the species. Such facts are inscribed in an order of homeomorphic identification that would itself fall within the larger question of the meaning of beauty as both formative and erogenic.

But the facts of mimicry are no less instructive when conceived as cases of heteromorphic identification, in as much as they raise the problem of the signification of space for the living organism – psychological concepts hardly seem less appropriate for shedding light on these matters than ridiculous attempts to reduce them to the supposedly supreme law of adaptation. We have only to recall how Roger Caillois (who was then very young, and still fresh from his breach with the sociological school in which he was trained) illuminated the subject by using the term 'legendary psychasthenia' to classify morphological mimicry as an obsession with space in its derealizing effect.

I have myself shown in the social dialectic that structures human knowledge as paranoiac[3] why human knowledge has greater autonomy than animal knowledge in relation to the field of force of desire, but also why human knowledge is determined in that 'little reality' (ce peu de réalité), which the Surrealists, in their restless way, saw as its limitation. These reflections lead me to recognize in the spatial captation manifested in the mirror-stage, even before the social dialectic, the effect in man of an organic insufficiency in his natural reality – in so far as any meaning can be given to the word 'nature'.

I am led, therefore, to regard the function of the mirror-stage as a particular case of the function of the imago, which is to establish a relation between the organism and its reality – or, as they say, between the Innenwelt and the Umwelt.

In man, however, this relation to nature is altered by a certain dehiscence at the heart of the organism, a primordial Discord betrayed by the signs of uneasiness and motor unco-ordination of the neo-natal months. The objective notion of the anatomical incompleteness of the pyramidal system and likewise the presence of certain humoral residues of the maternal organism confirm the view I have formulated as the fact of a real specific prematurity of birth in man.

It is worth noting, incidentally, that this is a fact recognized as such by embryologists, by the term foetalization, which determines the prevalence of the so-called superior apparatus of the neurax, and especially of the cortex, which psycho-surgical operations lead us to regard as the intra-organic mirror.

This development is experienced as a temporal dialectic that decisively projects the formation of the individual into history. The *mirror stage* is a drama whose internal thrust is precipitated from insufficiency to anticipation – and which manufactures for the subject, caught up in the lure of spatial identification, the succession of phantasies that extends from a fragmented body-image to a form of its totality that I shall call orthopaedic – and, lastly, to the assumption of the armour of an alienating identity, which will mark with its rigid structure the subject's entire mental development. Thus, to break out of the circle of the *Innenwelt* into the *Umwelt* generates the inexhaustible quadrature of the ego's verifications.

This fragmented body – which term I have also introduced into our system of theoretical references – usually manifests itself in dreams when the movement of the analysis encounters a certain level of aggressive disintegration in the individual. It then appears in the form of disjointed limbs, or of these organs represented in exoscopy, growing wings and taking up arms for intestinal persecutions – the very same that the visionary Hieronymus Bosch has fixed, for all time, in painting, in their ascent from the fifteenth century to the imaginary zenith of modern man. But this form is even tangibly revealed at the organic level, in the lines of 'fragilization' that define the anatomy of phantasy, as exhibited in the schizoid and spasmodic symptoms of hysteria.

Correlatively, the formation of the *I* is symbolized in dreams by a fortress, or a stadium – its inner arena and enclosure, surrounded by marshes and rubbish-tips, dividing it into two opposed fields of contest where the subject flounders in quest of the lofty, remote inner castle whose form (sometimes juxtaposed in the same scenario) symbolizes the id in a quite startling way. Similarly, on the mental plane, we find realized the structures of fortified works, the metaphor of which arises spontaneously, as if issuing from the symptoms themselves, to designate the mechanisms of obsessional neurosis – inversion, isolation, reduplication, cancellation and displacement.

But if we were to build on these subjective givens alone – however little we free them from the condition of experience that makes us see them as partaking of the nature of a linguistic technique – our theoretical attempts would remain exposed to the charge of projecting themselves into the unthinkable of an absolute subject. This is why I have sought in the present hypothesis, grounded in a conjunction of objective data, the guiding grid for a *method of symbolic reduction*.

It establishes in the *defences of the ego* a genetic order, in accordance with the wish formulated by Miss Anna Freud, in the first part of her great work, and situates (as against a frequently expressed prejudice) hysterical repression and its returns at a more archaic stage than obsessional inversion and its isolating processes, and the latter in turn as preliminary to paranoic alienation, which dates from the deflection of the specular *I* into the social *I*.

This moment in which the mirror-stage comes to an end inaugurates, by the identification with the *imago* of the counterpart and the drama of primordial jealousy (so well brought out by the school of Charlotte Bühler in the phenomenon of infantile *transitivism*), the dialectic that will henceforth link the *I* to socially elaborated situations.

It is this moment that decisively tips the whole of human knowledge into mediatization through the desire of the other, constitutes its objects in an abstract equivalence by the co-operation of others, and turns the *I* into that apparatus for which every instinctual thrust constitutes a danger, even though it should correspond to a natural maturation – the very normalization of this maturation being henceforth dependent, in man, on a cultural mediation as exemplified, in the case of the sexual object, by the Oedipus complex.

In the light of this conception, the term primary narcissism, by which analytic doctrine designates the libidinal investment characteristic of that moment, reveals in those who invented it the most profound awareness of semantic latencies. But it also throws light on the dynamic opposition between this libido and the sexual libido, which the first analysts tried to define when they invoked destructive and, indeed, death instincts, in order to explain the evident connection between the narcissistic libido and the alienating function of the *I*, the aggressivity it releases in any relation to the other, even in a relation involving the most Samaritan of aid.

In fact, they were encountering that existential negativity whose reality is so vigorously proclaimed by the contemporary philosophy of being and nothingness.

But unfortunately that philosophy grasps negativity only within the limits of a self-sufficiency of consciousness, which, as one of its premises, links to the *méconnaissances* that constitute the ego, the illusion of autonomy to which it entrusts itself. This flight of fancy, for all that it draws, to an unusual extent, on borrowings from psychoanalytic experience, culminates in the pretention of providing an existential psychoanalysis.

At the culmination of the historical effort of a society to refuse to recognize that it has any function other than the utilitarian one, and in the anxiety of the individual confronting the 'concentrational'[4] form of the social bond that seems to arise to crown this effort, existentialism must be judged by the explanations it gives of the subjective impasses that have indeed resulted from it; a freedom that is never more authentic than when it is within the walls of a prison; a demand for commitment, expressing the impotence of a pure consciousness to master any situation; a voyeuristic sadistic idealization of the sexual relation; a personality that realizes itself only in suicide; a consciousness of the other that can be satisfied only by Hegelian murder.

These propositions are opposed by all our experience, in so far as it teaches us not to regard the ego as centred on the *perception–consciousness*

334

system, or as organized by the 'reality principle' – a principle that is the expression of a scientific prejudice most hostile to the dialectic of knowledge. Our experience shows that we should start instead from the *function of méconnaissance* that characterizes the ego in all its structures, so markedly articulated by Miss Anna Freud. For, if the *Verneinung* represents the patent form of that function, its effects will, for the most part, remain latent, so long as they are not illuminated by some light reflected on to the level of fatality, which is where the id manifests itself.

We can thus understand the inertia characteristic of the formations of the *I,* and find there the most extensive definition of neurosis – just as the captation of the subject by the situation gives us the most general formula for madness, not only the madness that lies behind the walls of asylums, but also the madness that deafens the world with its sound and fury.

The sufferings of neurosis and psychosis are for us a schooling in the passions of the soul, just as the beam of the psychoanalytic scales, when we calculate the tilt of its threat to entire communities, provides us with an indication of the deadening of the passions in society.

At this junction of nature and culture, so persistently examined by modern anthropology, psychoanalysis alone recognizes this knot of imaginary servitude that love must always undo again, or sever.

For such a task, we place no trust in altruistic feeling, we who lay bare the aggressivity that underlies the activity of the philanthropist, the idealist, the pedagogue, and even the reformer.

In the recourse of subject to subject that we preserve, psychoanalysis may accompany the patient to the ecstatic limit of the *'Thou art that',* in which is revealed to him the cipher of his mortal destiny, but it is not in our mere power as practitioners to bring him to that point where the real journey begins.

NOTES

1   Throughout this article I leave in its peculiarity the translation I have adopted for Freud's *Ideal-Ich* [i.e. 'je-idéal'], without further comment, other than to say that I have not maintained it since.
2   Cf. Claude Lévi-Strauss, *Structural Anthropology,* chapter X.
3   Cf. 'Aggressivity in Psychoanalysis', p. 8 and *Ecrits,* p. 180.
4   'Concentrationnaire', an adjective coined after World War II (this article was written in 1949) to describe the life of the concentration-camp. In the hands of certain writers it became, by extension, applicable to many aspects of 'modern' life [Tr.].

22

Michel Foucault

(1926–1984)

Although the work of Michel Foucault gave widespread currency to structuralist methods of analysis, Foucault himself resisted any attempt to label him solely as a 'structuralist' thinker. At the Collège de France in Paris, where he taught for many years, he was 'Professor of the History and Systems of Thought', a title which credits the historical dimension of discursive practices so important to his project. While it is true that 'structuralism' might seem an appropriate methodological description for certain phases of his work, clearly he does not fit unproblematically with such purists of structural analysis as Lévi-Strauss or Saussure. For Foucault, no universal and timeless laws prevail over discourse that could sever it completely from the social practices in which it functions.

Looking at the larger canvas of Foucault's work, we see a consistency in his investigations focusing on the social and discursive practices that play a role in the formation of the human subject. In the selection which follows, Foucault claims that 'in appearance, speech may well be of little account, but the prohibitions surrounding it soon reveal its links with desire and power'. Throughout his philosophical career, he examined the means by which social and personal identity are generated and objectified. One of the most important of these strategies consists of dividing practices which categorize, label, isolate and exclude the subject from what is considered 'normal' social intercourse.

In *Madness and Civilization: A History of Insanity in the Age of Reason* (1961), Foucault researched historical records to foreground how these dividing practices operated in the case of those categorized as 'insane', and pointed out that the manipulative procedures used to implement dividing practices change over time. For example, at the end of the Middle Ages, the Ship of Fools travelling from port to port with its 'deviant' cargo was still a familiar sight. However, with the disappearance of leprosy, former leprosariums were turned into workhouses and by the seventeenth century were being used for the purpose of indiscriminately confining criminals, the unemployed and the insane. The classificatory schemes for excluding and labelling 'deviant' human beings soon became 'scientific' modes of inquiry that nurtured professional disciplines dedicated to further objectifying the human subject by their discourse. Foucault continued this geneaological investigation of the rules and norms generating dividing practices in *The Birth of the Clinic: An Archaeology of Medical Perception* (1963) and *Discipline and Punish: The Birth of the Prison* (1976).

Yet, there is another aspect to Foucault's work that highlights a more 'structuralist' perspective. His project in both *The Order of Things: An Archaeology of the Human Sciences* (1966) and *The Archaeology of Knowledge* (1969) focuses more specifically on the autonomous structures of knowledge which are presupposed in rational and scientific discourse. These self-regulating 'epistemes' underlie the dominant discourses of any historical era, but are only synchronic during that particular era. Radical disjunctions occur during which the dominant epistemic paradigm undergoes change and a new structure of knowledge emerges. Foucault suggests that by 'archeologically' uncovering these 'rules of formation', which have never been made explicit, such discourses become vulnerable to critique. In this way, he links the epistemic structure that legitimates certain kinds of knowledge with the interests of domination served by its subsequent diffusion throughout socially powerful institutions. Knowledge is thus always part of a cultural matrix of power relations.

In addition to his emphasis on the autonomy of epistemological structure, Foucault also took an anti-humanist stance in these works that heralded the 'death of man', the end of human subjectivity as we have tended to interpret it. The very idea 'Man' thereby becomes a surface manifestation of the modern episteme. In rejecting the humanist paradigm, Foucault sought to challenge the Cartesian model of the human subject as an isolated consciousness or disembedded *cogito*. Yet his three-volume *History of Sexuality* again returned to the complex issue of subjectivity by questioning how a human being actively participates in the process of becoming a subject, rather than merely suffering the effects of domination. In 'The Discourse on Language', which follows, Foucault stresses the crucial role played by language in accomplishing this transfomation.

SELECT BIBLIOGRAPHY OF FOUCAULT'S WORKS IN ENGLISH

Madness and Civilization: A History of Insanity in the Age of Reason, New York: Pantheon, 1965.
The Order of Things: An Archaeology of the Human Sciences, New York: Pantheon, 1970.
The Archaeology of Knowledge, New York: Pantheon, 1972.
The Birth of the Clinic: An Archaeology of Medical Perception, New York: Random House, 1975.
I, Pierre Rivière, New York: Pantheon, 1975.

MICHEL FOUCAULT

Language, Counter-Memory, Practice, Oxford: Blackwell, 1977.

The History of Sexuality, Volume 1: An Introduction, New York: Pantheon, 1978.

Discipline and Punish: The Birth of the Prison, New York: Random House, 1979.

Power/Knowledge: Selected Interviews and Other Writings 1972–1977, New York: Pantheon, 1980.

'The Subject and Power', afterword to *Michel Foucault: Beyond Structuralism and Hermeneutics*, H. Dreyfus and P. Rabinow, Chicago: University of Chicago Press, 1983.

The Foucault Reader, ed. P. Rabinow, New York: Pantheon, 1985.

The History of Sexuality, Volume 2: The Uses of Pleasure, New York: Pantheon, 1985.

Death and the Labyrinth: The World of Raymond Roussel, New York: Doubleday, 1986.

The History of Sexuality, Volume 3: The Care of the Self, New York: Pantheon, 1986.

Mental Illness and Psychology, Berkeley: University of California Press, 1987.

The Discourse on Language

I would really like to have slipped imperceptibly into this lecture, as into all the others I shall be delivering, perhaps over the years ahead. I would have preferred to be enveloped in words, borne way beyond all possible beginnings. At the moment of speaking, I would like to have perceived a nameless voice, long preceding me, leaving me merely to enmesh myself in it, taking up its cadence, and to lodge myself, when no one was looking, in its interstices as if it had paused an instant, in suspense, to beckon to me. There would have been no beginnings: instead, speech would proceed from me, while I stood in its path – a slender gap – the point of its possible disappearance.

Behind me, I should like to have heard (having been at it long enough already, repeating in advance what I am about to tell you) the voice of Molloy, beginning to speak thus: 'I must go on; I can't go on; I must go on; I must say words as long as there are words, I must say them until they find me, until they say me – heavy burden, heavy sin; I must go on; maybe it's been done already; maybe they've already said me; maybe they've already borne me to the threshold of my story, right to the door opening onto my story; I'd be surprised if it opened.'

A good many people, I imagine, harbour a similar desire to be freed from the obligation to begin, a similar desire to find themselves, right from the outside, on the other side of discourse, without having to stand outside it, pondering its particular, fearsome, and even devilish features. To this all too common feeling, institutions have an ironic reply, for they solemnise beginnings, surrounding them with a circle of silent attention; in order that they can be distinguished from far off, they impose ritual forms upon them.

Inclination speaks out: 'I don't want to have to enter this risky world of discourse; I want nothing to do with it insofar as it is decisive and final; I would like to feel it all around me, calm and transparent, profound, infinitely open, with others responding to my expectations, and truth emerging, one by one. All I want is to allow myself to be borne along, within it, and by it, a happy wreck.' Institutions reply: 'But you have nothing to fear from launching out; we're here to show you discourse is within the established order of things, that we've waited a long time for its arrival, that a place has been set aside for it – a place which both honours and disarms it; and if it should happen to have a certain power, then it is we, and we alone, who give it that power.'

This lecture was delivered in French at the Collège de France on December 2, 1970. The original French text has been published with the title *L'ordre du discours* (Paris, Gallimard, 1971). The English translation by Rupert Swyer was first published in *Social Science Information*, April 1971, pp. 7–30. Reprinted by permission of Sage Publications Ltd.

Yet, maybe this institution and this inclination are but two converse responses to the same anxiety: anxiety as to just what discourse is, when it is manifested materially, as a written or spoken object; but also, uncertainty faced with a transitory existence, destined for oblivion – at any rate, not belonging to us; uncertainty at the suggestion of barely imaginable powers and dangers behind this activity, however humdrum and grey it may seem; uncertainty when we suspect the conflicts, triumphs, injuries, dominations and enslavements that lie behind these words, even when long use has chipped away their rough edges.

What is so perilous, then, in the fact that people speak, and that their speech proliferates? Where is the danger in that?

Here then is the hypothesis I want to advance, tonight, in order to fix the terrain – or perhaps the very provisional theatre – within which I shall be working. I am supposing that in every society the production of discourse is at once controlled, selected, organised and redistributed according to a certain number of procedures, whose role is to avert its powers and its dangers, to cope with chance events, to evade its ponderous, awesome materiality.

In a society such as our own we all know the rules of *exclusion*. The most obvious and familiar of these concerns what is *prohibited*. We know perfectly well that we are not free to say just anything, that we cannot simply speak of anything, when we like or where we like; not just anyone, finally, may speak of just anything. We have three types of prohibition, covering objects, ritual with its surrounding circumstances, the privileged or exclusive right to speak of a particular subject; these prohibitions interrelate, reinforce and complement each other, forming a complex web, continually subject to modification. I will note simply that the areas where this web is most tightly woven today, where the danger spots are most numerous, are those dealing with politics and sexuality. It is as though discussion, far from being a transparent, neutral element, allowing us to disarm sexuality and to pacify politics, were one of those privileged areas in which they exercised some of their more awesome powers. In appearance, speech may well be of little account, but the prohibitions surrounding it soon reveal its links with desire and power. This should not be very surprising, for psychoanalysis has already shown us that speech is not merely the medium which manifests – or dissembles – desire; it is also the object of desire. Similarly, historians have constantly impressed upon us that speech is no mere verbalisation of conflicts and systems of domination, but that it is the very object of man's conflicts.

But our society possesses yet another principle of exclusion; not another prohibition, but a division and a rejection. I have in mind the opposition: reason and folly. From the depths of the Middle Ages, a man was mad if his speech could not be said to form part of the common discourse of men. His words were considered null and void, without truth or significance, worthless as evidence, inadmissible in the authentification

340

of acts or contracts, incapable even of bringing about transubstantiation
– the transformation of bread into flesh – at Mass. And yet, in contrast
to all others, his words were credited with strange powers, of revealing
some hidden truth, of predicting the future, of revealing, in all their
naiveté, what the wise were unable to perceive. It is curious to note that
for centuries, in Europe, the words of a madman were either totally
ignored or else were taken as words of truth. They either fell into a void
– rejected the moment they were proffered – or else men deciphered in
them a naive or cunning reason, rationality more rational than that of a
rational man. At all events, whether excluded or secretly invested with
reason, the madman's speech did not strictly exist. It was through his
words that one recognised the madness of the madman; but they were
certainly the medium within which this division became active; they
were neither heard nor remembered. No doctor before the end of the
eighteenth century had ever thought of listening to the content – how it
was said and why – of these words; and yet it was these which signalled
the difference between reason and madness. Whatever a madman said, it
was taken for mere noise; he was credited with words only in a symbolic
sense, in the theatre, in which he stepped forward, unarmed and reconciled, playing his role: that of masked truth.

Of course people are going to say all that is over and done with, or
that it is in the process of being finished with, today; that the madman's
words are no longer on the other side of this division; that they are no
longer null and void, that, on the contrary, they alert us to the need to
look for a sense behind them, for the attempt at, or the ruins of some
'œuvre'; we have even come to notice these words of madmen in our own
speech, in those tiny pauses when we forget what we are talking about.
But all this is no proof that the old vision is not just as active as before;
we have only to think of the systems by which we decipher this speech;
we have only to think of the network of institutions established to permit
doctors and psychoanalysts to listen to the mad and, at the same time,
enabling the mad to come and speak, or, in desperation, to withhold
their meagre words; we have only to bear all this in mind to suspect
that the old division is just as active as ever, even if it is proceeding
along different lines and, via new institutions, producing rather different
effects. Even when the role of the doctor consists of lending an ear to
this finally liberated speech, this procedure still takes place in the context
of a hiatus between listener and speaker. For he is listening to speech
invested with desire, crediting itself – for its greater exultation or for its
greater anguish – with terrible powers. If we truly require silence to cure
monsters, then it must be an attentive silence, and it is in this that the
division lingers.

It is perhaps a little risky to speak of the opposition between true
and false as a third system of exclusion, along with those I have mentioned
already. How could one reasonably compare the constraints of truth

341

with those other divisions, arbitrary in origin if not developing out of historical contingency – not merely modifiable but in a state of continual flux, supported by a system of institutions imposing and manipulating them, acting not without constraint, nor without an element, at least, of violence?

Certainly, as a proposition, the division between true and false is neither arbitrary, nor modifiable, nor institutional, nor violent. Putting the question in different terms, however – asking what has been, what still is, throughout our discourse, this will to truth which has survived throughout so many centuries of our history; or if we ask what is, in its very general form, the kind of division governing our will to knowledge – then we may well discern something like a system of exclusion (historical, modifiable, institutionally constraining) in the process of development.

It is, undoubtedly, a historically constituted division. For, even with the sixth-century Greek poets, true discourse – in the meaningful sense – inspiring respect and terror, to which all were obliged to submit, because it held sway over all and was pronounced by men who spoke as of right, according to ritual, meted out justice and attributed to each his rightful share; it prophesied the future, not merely announcing what was going to occur, but contributing to its actual event, carrying men along with it and thus weaving itself into the fabric of fate. And yet, a century later, the highest truth no longer resided in what discourse *was*, nor in what it *did*: it lay in what was *said*. They day dawned when truth moved over from the ritualised act – potent and just – of enunciation to settle on what was enunciated itself: its meaning, its form, its object and its relation to what it referred to. A division emerged between Hesiod and Plato, separating true discourse from false; it was a new division for, henceforth, true discourse was no longer considered precious and desirable, since it had ceased to be discourse linked to the exercise of power. And so the Sophists were routed.

This historical division has doubtless lent its general form to our will to knowledge. Yet it has never ceased shifting: the great mutations of science may well sometimes be seen to flow from some discovery, but they may equally be viewed as the appearance of new forms of the will to truth. In the nineteenth century there was undoubtedly a will to truth having nothing to do, in terms of the forms examined, of the fields to which it addressed itself, nor the techniques upon which it was based, with the will to knowledge which characterised classical culture. Going back a little in time, to the turn of the sixteenth and seventeenth centuries – and particularly in England – a will to knowledge emerged which, anticipating its present content, sketched out a schema of possible, observable, measurable and classifiable objects; a will to knowledge which imposed upon the knowing subject – in some ways taking precedence over all experience – a certain position, a certain viewpoint, and a certain function (look rather than read, verify rather than comment), a will to knowledge which prescribed (and, more generally speaking, all instruments determined) the technological level at which knowledge could be employed in order to be verifiable and useful (navigation, mining, pharmacopoeia). Everything seems to have occurred as though, from the time of the great Platonic division onwards, the will to truth had its own history, which is not at all that of the constraining truths: the history of a range of subjects to be learned, the history of the functions of the knowing subject, the history of material, technical and instrumental investment in knowledge.

But this will to truth, like the other systems of exclusion, relies on institutional support: it is both reinforced and accompanied by whole strata of practices such as pedagogy – naturally – the book-system, publishing, libraries, such as the learned societies in the past, and laboratories today. But it is probably even more profoundly accompanied by the manner in which knowledge is employed in a society, the way in which it is exploited, divided and, in some ways, attributed. It is worth recalling at this point, if only symbolically, the old Greek adage, that arithmetic should be taught in democracies, for it teaches relations of equality, but that geometry alone should be reserved for oligarchies, as it demonstrates the proportions within inequality.

Finally, I believe that this will to knowledge, thus reliant upon institutional support and distribution, tends to exercise a sort of pressure, a power of constraint upon other forms of discourse – I am speaking of our own society. I am thinking of the way Western literature has, for centuries, sought to base itself in nature, in the plausible, upon sincerity and science – in short, upon true discourse. I am thinking, too, of the way economic practices, codified into precepts and recipes – as morality, too – have sought since the eighteenth century, to found themselves, to rationalise and justify their currency, in a theory of wealth and production; I am thinking, again, of the manner in which such prescriptive ensembles as the Penal Code have sought their bases or justifications. For example, the Penal Code started out as a theory of Right; then, from the time of the nineteenth century, people looked for its validation in sociological, psychological, medical and psychiatric knowledge. It is as though the very words of the law had no authority in our society, except insofar as they are derived from true discourse. Of the three great systems of exclusion governing discourse – prohibited words, the division of madness and the will to truth – I have spoken at greatest length concerning the third. With good reason: for centuries, the former have continually tended towards the latter; because this last has, gradually, been attempting to assimilate the others in order both to modify them and to provide them with a firm foundation. Because, if the two former are continually growing more fragile and less certain to the extent that they are now invaded by the will to truth, the latter, in contrast, daily grows in strength, in depth and implacability.

And yet we speak of it least. As though the will to truth and its vicis-situdes were masked by truth itself and its necessary unfolding. The reason is perhaps this: if, since the time of the Greeks, true discourse no longer responds to desire or to that which exercises power in the will to truth, in the will to speak out in true discourse, what, then, is at work, if not desire and power? True discourse, liberated by the nature of its form from desire and power, is incapable of recognising the will to truth which pervades it; and the will to truth, having imposed itself upon us for so long, is such that the truth it seeks to reveal cannot fail to mask it.

Thus, only one truth appears before our eyes: wealth, fertility and sweet strength in all its insidious universality. In contrast, we are unaware of the prodigious machinery of the will to truth, with its vocation of exclusion. All those who, at one moment or another in our history, have attempted to remould this will to truth and to turn it against truth at that very point where truth undertakes to justify the taboo, and to define madness; all those, from Nietzsche to Artaud and Tabaille, must now stand as (probably haughty) signposts for all our future work.

There are, of course, many other systems for the control and delim-itation of discourse. Those I have spoken of up to now are, to some extent, active on the exterior; they function as systems of exclusion; they concern that part of discourse which deals with power and desire.

I believe we can isolate another group: internal rules, where discourse exercises its own control; rules concerned with the principles of classifi-cation, ordering and distribution. It is as though we were now involved in the mastery of another dimension of discourse: that of events and chance.

In the first place, commentary. I suppose, though I am not altogether sure, there is barely a society without its major narratives, told, retold and varied; formulae, texts, ritualised texts to be spoken in well-defined circumstances; things said once, and conserved because people suspect some hidden secret or wealth lies buried within. In short, I suspect one could find a kind of gradation between different types of discourse within most societies: discourse 'uttered' in the course of the day and in casual meetings, and which disappears with the very act which gave rise to it; and those forms of discourse that lie at the origins of a certain number of new verbal acts, which are reiterated, transformed or discussed; in short, discourse which *is spoken* and remains spoken, indefinitely, beyond its formulation, and which remains to be spoken. We know them in our own cultural system: religious or judicial texts, as well as some curious texts, from the point of view of their status, which we term 'literary'; to a certain extent, scientific texts also.

What is clear is that this gap is neither stable, nor constant, nor absolute. There is no question of there being one category, fixed for all time, reserved for fundamental or creative discourse, and another for those which reiterate, expound and comment. Not a few major texts become blurred and disappear, and commentaries sometimes come to occupy the former position. But while the details of application may well change, the function remains the same, and the principle of hierarchy remains at work. The radical denial of this gradation can never be anything but play, utopia or anguish. Play, as Borges uses the term, in the form of commentary that is nothing more than the reappearance, word for word (though this time it is solemn and anticipated) of the text commented on; or again, the play of a work of criticism talking endlessly about a work that does not exist. It is a lyrical dream of talk reborn, utterly afresh and innocent, at each point; continually reborn in all its vigour, stimulated by things, feelings or thoughts. Anguish, such as that of Janet when sick, for whom the least utterance sounded as the 'word of the Evangelist', concealing an inexhaustible wealth of meaning, worthy to be broadcast, rebegun, commented upon indefinitely: 'When I think', he said on reading or listening; 'When I think of this phrase, continuing its journey through eternity, while I, perhaps, have only incompletely understood it . . .'

But who can fail to see that this would be to annul one of the terms of the relationship each time, and not to suppress the relationship itself? A relationship in continual process of modification; a relationship taking multiple and diverse forms in a given epoch: juridical exegesis is very different – and has been for a long time – from religious commentary; a single work of literature can give rise, simultaneously, to several distinct types of discourse. The *Odyssey*, as a primary text, is repeated in the same epoch, in Berand's translation, in infinite textual explanations and in Joyce's *Ulysses*.

For the time being, I would like to limit myself to pointing out that, in what we generally refer to as commentary, the difference between primary text and secondary text plays two interdependent roles. On the one hand, it permits us to create new discourses ad infinitum: the top-heaviness of the original text, its permanence, its status as discourse ever capable of being brought up to date, the multiple or hidden meanings with which it is credited, the reticence and wealth it is believed to contain, all this creates an open possibility for discussion. On the other hand, whatever the techniques employed, commentary's only role is to say *finally*, what has silently been articulated *deep down*. It must – and the paradox is ever-changing yet inescapable – say, for the first time, what has already been said, and repeat tirelessly what was, nevertheless, never said. The infinite rippling of commentary is agitated from within by the dream of masked repetition: in the distance there is, perhaps, nothing other than what was there at the point of departure: simple recitation. Commentary averts the chance element of discourse by giving it its due: it gives us the opportunity to say something other than the text itself, but on condition that it is the text itself which is uttered and, in some ways, finalised. The open multiplicity, the fortuitousness, is transferred, by the principle of commentary, from what is liable to be said to the number, the form, the masks and the circumstances of repetition. The novelty lies no longer in what is said, but in its reappearance.

I believe there is another principle of rarefaction, complementary to the first: the author. Not, of course, the author in the sense of the individual who delivered the speech or wrote the text in question, but the author as the unifying principle in a particular group of writings or statements, lying at the origins of their significance, as the seat of their coherence. This principle is not constant at all times. All around us, there are sayings and texts whose meaning or effectiveness has nothing to do with any author to whom they might be attributed: mundane remarks, quickly forgotten; orders and contacts that are signed, but have no recognisable author; technical prescriptions anonymously transmitted. But even in those fields where it is normal to attribute a work to an author – literature, philosophy, science – the principle does not always play the same role; in the order of scientific discourse, it was, during the Middle Ages, indispensable that a scientific text be attributed to an author, for the author was the index of the work's truthfulness. A proposition was held to derive its scientific value from its author. But since the seventeenth century this function has been steadily declining; it barely survives now, save to give a name to a theorem, an effect, an example or a syndrome. In literature, however, and from about the same period, the author's function has become steadily more important. Now, we demand of all those narratives, poems, dramas and comedies which circulated relatively anonymously throughout the Middle Ages, whence they come, and we virtually insist they tell us who wrote them. We ask authors to answer for the unity of the works published in their names; we ask that they reveal, or at least display the hidden sense pervading their work; we ask them to reveal their personal lives, to account for their experiences and the real story that gave birth to their writings. The author is he who implants, into the troublesome language of fiction, its unities, its coherence, its links with reality.

I know what people are going to say: 'But there you are speaking of the author in the same way as the critic reinvents him after he is dead and buried, when we are left with no more than a tangled mass of scrawlings. Of course, then you have to put a little order into what is left, you have to imagine a structure, a cohesion, the sort of theme you might expect to arise out of an author's consciousness or his life, even if it is a little fictitious. But all that cannot get away from the fact that the author existed, irrupting into the midst of all the words employed, infusing them with his genius, or his chaos.'

Of course, it would be ridiculous to deny the existence of individuals who write, and invent. But I think that, for some time, at least, the individual who sits down to write a text, at the edge of which lurks a possible *œuvre*, resumes the functions of the author. What he writes and does not write, what he sketches out, even preliminary sketches for the work, and what he drops as simple mundane remarks, all this interplay of differences is prescribed by the author-function. It is from his new position, as an author, that he will fashion – from all he might have said, from all he says daily, at any time – the still shaky profile of his *œuvre*.

Commentary limited the hazards of discourse through the action of an *identity* taking the form of *repetition* and *sameness*. The author principle limits this same chance element through the action of an *identity* whose form is that of *individuality* and the *I*.

But we have to recognise another principle of limitation in what we call, not sciences, but 'disciplines'. Here is yet another relative, mobile principle, one which enables us to construct, but within a narrow framework.

The organisation of disciplines is just as much opposed to the commentary principle as it is to that of the author. Opposed to that of the author, because disciplines are defined by groups of objects, methods, their corpus of propositions considered to be true, the interplay of rules and definitions, of techniques and tools: all these constitute a sort of anonymous system, freely available to whoever wishes, or whoever is able to make use of them, without there being any question of their meaning or their validity being derived from whoever happened to invent them. But the principles involved in the formation of disciplines are equally opposed to that of commentary. In a discipline, unlike in commentary, what is supposed at the point of departure is not some meaning which must be rediscovered, nor an identity to be reiterated; it is that which is required for the construction of new statements. For a discipline to exist there must be the possibility of formulating – and of doing so ad infinitum – fresh propositions.

But there is more, and there is more, probably, in order that there may be less. A discipline is not the sum total of all the truths that may be uttered concerning something; it is not even the total of all that may be accepted, by virtue of some principle of coherence and systematisation, concerning some given fact or proposition. Medicine does not consist of all that may be truly said about disease; botany cannot be defined by the sum total of the truths one could say about plants. There are two reasons for this, the first being that botany and medicine, like other disciplines, consist of errors as well as truths, errors that are in no way residuals, or foreign bodies, but have their own positive functions and their own valid history, such that their roles are often indissociable from that of the truths. The other reason is that, for a proposition to belong to botany or pathology, it must fulfil certain conditions, in a stricter and more complex sense than that of pure and simple truth: at any rate, other conditions. The proposition must refer to a specific range of objects; from the end of the seventeenth century, for example, a proposition, to be 'botanical', had to be concerned with the visible structure of plants, with its system of close and not so close resemblances, or with the behaviour of its fluids; (but it could no longer retain, as had still been the case in the sixteenth century, references to its symbolic value or to the virtues and properties accorded it in antiquity). But without belonging to any discipline, a proposition is obliged to utilise conceptual instruments and techniques of a well-defined type; from the nineteenth century onwards, a proposition was no longer medical – it became 'non-medical', becoming more of an individual fantasy or item of popular imagery – if it employed metaphorical or qualitative terms or notions of essence (congestion, fermented liquids, dessicated solids); in return, it could – it had to – appeal to equally metaphorical notions, though constructed according to a different functional and physiological model (concerning irritation, inflammation or the decay of tissue). But there is more still, for in order to belong to a discipline, a proposition must fit into a certain type of theoretical field. Suffice it to recall that the quest for primitive language, a perfectly acceptable theme up to the eighteenth century, was enough, in the second half of the nineteenth century, to throw any discourse into, I hesitate to say error, but into a world of chimera and reverie – into pure and simple linguistic monstrosity.

Within its own limits, every discipline recognises true and false propositions, but it repulses a whole teratology of learning. The exterior of a science is both more, and less, populated than one might think: certainly, there is immediate experience, imaginary themes bearing on and continually accompanying immemorial beliefs; but perhaps there are no errors in the strict sense of the term, for error can only emerge and be identified within a well-defined process; there are monsters on the prowl, however, whose forms alter with the history of knowledge. In short, a proposition must fulfil some onerous and complex conditions before it can be admitted within a discipline; before it can be pronounced true or false it must be, as Monsieur Canguilhem might say, 'within the true'.

People have often wondered how on earth nineteenth-century botanists and biologists managed not to see the truth of Mendel's statements. But it was precisely because Mendel spoke of objects, employed methods and placed himself within a theoretical perspective totally alien to the biology of his time. But then, Naudin had suggested that hereditary traits constituted a separate element before him; and yet, however novel or unfamiliar the principle may have been, it was nevertheless reconcilable, if only as an enigma, with biological discourse. Mendel, on the other hand, announced that hereditary traits constituted an absolutely new biological object, thanks to a hitherto untried system of filtrage: he detached them from species, from the sex transmitting them, the field in which he observed being that infinitely open series of generations in which hereditary traits appear and disappear with statistical regularity. Here was a new object, calling for new conceptual tools, and for fresh theoretical foundations. Mendel spoke the truth, but he was not *dans le vrai* (within the true) of contemporary biological discourse: it simply was not along such lines that objects and biological concepts were formed. A whole change in scale, the deployment of a totally new range of objects in biology was required before Mendel could enter into the true and his propositions appear, for the mot part, exact. Mendel was a true monster, so much so that science could not even properly speak of him. And yet Schleiden, for example, thirty years earlier, denying, at the height of the nineteenth century, vegetable sexuality, was committing no more than a disciplined error.

It is always possible one could speak the truth in a void; one would only be in the true, however, if one obeyed the rules of some discursive 'policy' which would have to be reactivated every time one spoke.

Disciplines constitute a system of control in the production of discourse, fixing its limits through the action of an identity taking the form of a permanent reactivation of the rules.

We tend to see, in an author's fertility, in the multiplicity of commentaries and in the development of a discipline so many infinite resources available for the creation of discourse. Perhaps so, but they are nonetheless principles of constraint, and it is probably impossible to appreciate their positive, multiplicatory role without first taking into consideration their restrictive, constraining role.

There is, I believe, a third group of rules serving to control discourse. Here, we are no longer dealing with the mastery of the powers contained within discourse, nor with averting the hazards of its appearance; it is more a question of determining the conditions under which it may be employed, of imposing a certain number of rules upon those individuals who employ it, thus denying access to everyone else. This amounts to a rarefaction among speaking subjects: none may enter into discourse on a specific subject unless he has satisfied certain conditions or if he is not, from the outset, qualified to do so. More exactly, not all areas of discourse are equally open and penetrable; some are forbidden territory (differentiated and differentiating) while others are virtually open to the winds and stand, without any prior restrictions, open to all.

Here, I would like to recount a little story so beautiful I fear it may well be true. It encompasses all the constraints of discourse: those limiting its powers, those controlling its chance appearances and those which select from among speaking subjects. At the beginning of the seventeenth century, the Shogun heard tell of European superiority in navigation, commerce, politics and the military arts, and that this was due to their knowledge of mathematics. He wanted to obtain this precious knowledge. When someone told him of an English sailor possessed of this marvellous discourse, he summoned him to his palace and kept him there. The Shogun took lessons from the mariner in private and familiarised himself with mathematics, after which he retained power and lived to a very old age. It was not until the nineteenth century that there were *Japanese* mathematicians. But that is not the end of the anecdote, for it has its European aspect as well. The story has it that the English sailor, Will Adams, was a carpenter and an autodidact. Having worked in a shipyard he had learnt geometry. Can we see in this narrative the expression of one of the great myths of European culture? To the monopolistic, secret knowledge of oriental tyranny, Europe opposed the universal communication of knowledge and the infinitely free exchange of discourse.

This notion does not, in fact, stand up to close examination. Exchange and communication are positive forces at play within complex but restrictive systems; it is probable that they cannot operate independently of these. The most superficial and obvious of these restrictive systems is constituted by what we collectively refer to as ritual; ritual defines the qualifications required of the speaker (of who in dialogue, interrogation or recitation, should occupy which position and formulate which type of utterance); it lays down gestures to be made, behaviour, circumstances and the whole range of signs that must accompany discourse; finally, it lays down the supposed, or imposed significance of the words used, their effect upon those to whom they are addressed, the limitations of their constraining validity. Religious discourse, juridical and therapeutic as well as, in some ways, political discourse are all barely dissociable from the functioning of a ritual that determines the individual properties and agreed roles of the speakers.

A rather different function is filled by 'fellowships of discourse', whose function is to preserve or to reproduce discourse, but in order that it should circulate within a closed community, according to strict regulations, without those in possession being dispossessed by this very distribution. An archaic model of this would be those groups of Rhapsodists, possessing knowledge of poems to recite or, even, upon which to work variations and transformations. But though the ultimate object of this knowledge was ritual recitation, it was protected and preserved within a determinate group, by the, often extremely complex, exercises of memory implied by such a process. Apprenticeship gained access both to a group and to a secret which recitation made manifest, but did not divulge. The roles of speaking and listening were not interchangeable.

Few such 'fellowships of discourse' remain, with their ambiguous interplay of secrecy and disclosure. But do not be deceived; even in true discourse, even in the order of published discourse, free from all ritual, we still find secret-appropriation and non-interchangeability at work. It could even be that the act of writing, as it is institutionalised today, with its books, its publishing system and the personality of the writer, occurs within a diffuse, yet constraining, 'fellowship of discourse'. The separateness of the writer, continually opposed to the activity of all other writing and speaking subjects, the intransitive character he lends to his discourse, the fundamental singularity he has long accorded to 'writing', the affirmed dissymmetry between 'creation' and any use of linguistic systems – all this manifests in its formulation (and tends moreover to accompany the interplay of these factors in practice) the existence of a certain 'fellowship of discourse'. But there are many others, functioning according to entirely different schemas of exclusivity and disclosure: one has only to think of technical and scientific secrets, of the forms of diffusion and circulation in medical discourse, of those who have appropriated economic or political discourse.

At first sight, 'doctrine' (religious, political, philosophical) would seem to constitute the very reverse of a 'fellowship of discourse'; for among the latter, the number of speakers were, if not fixed, at least limited, and it was among this number that discourse was allowed to circulate and be transmitted. Doctrine, on the other hand, tends to diffusion: in the holding in common of a single ensemble of discourse that individuals, as many as you wish, could define their reciprocal allegiance. In appearance, the sole requisite is the recognition of the same truths and the acceptance of a certain rule – more or less flexible – of conformity with validated discourse. If it were a question of just that, doctrines would barely be any different from scientific disciplines, and discursive control would bear merely on the form or content of what was uttered, and not on the speaker. Doctrinal adherence, however, involves both speaker and the spoken, the one through the other. The speaking subject is involved through, and as a result of, the spoken, as is demonstrated by the rules of exclusion and the rejection mechanism brought into play when a speaker formulates one, or many, inassimilable utterances; questions of heresy and unorthodoxy in no way arise out of fanatical exaggeration of doctrinal mechanisms; they are a fundamental part of them. But conversely, doctrine involves the utterances of speakers in the sense that doctrine is, permanently, the sign, the manifestation and the instrument of a prior adherence – adherence to a class, to a social or racial status, to a nationality or an interest, to a struggle, a revolt, resistance or acceptance. Doctrine links individuals to certain types of utterance while consequently barring them from all others. Doctrine effects a dual subjection, that of speaking subjects to discourse, and that of discourse to the group, at least virtually, of speakers.

Finally, on a much broader scale, we have to recognise the great cleavages in what one might call the social appropriation of discourse. Education may well be, as of right, the instrument whereby every individual, in a society like our own, can gain access to any kind of discourse. But we well know that in its distribution, in what it permits and in what it prevents, it follows the well-trodden battle-lines of social conflict. Every educational system is a political means of maintaining or of modifying the appropriation of discourse, with the knowledge and the powers it carries with it.

I am well aware of the abstraction I am performing when I separate, as I have just done, verbal rituals, 'fellowships of discourse', doctrinal groups and social appropriation. Most of the time they are linked together, constituting great edifices that distribute speakers among the different types of discourse, and which appropriate those types of discourse to certain categories of subject. In a word, let us say that these are the main rules for the subjection of discourse. What is an educational system, after all, if not a ritualisation of the word; if not a qualification of some fixing of roles for speakers; if not the constitution of a (diffuse) doctrinal group; if not a distribution and an appropriation of discourse, with all its learning and its powers? What is 'writing' (that of 'writers') if not a similar form of subjection, perhaps taking rather different forms, but whose main stresses are nonetheless analogous? May we not also say that the judicial system, as well as institutionalised medicine, constitute similar systems for the subjection of discourse?

I wonder whether a certain number of philosophical themes have not come to conform to this activity of limitation and exclusion and perhaps even to reinforce it.

They conform, first of all, by proposing an ideal truth as a law of discourse, and an immanent rationality as the principle of their behaviour. They accompany, too, an ethic of knowledge, promising truth only to the desire for truth itself and the power to think it.

They then go on to reinforce this activity by denying the specific reality of discourse in general.

Ever since the exclusion of the activity and commerce of the Sophists, ever since their paradoxes were muzzled, more or less securely, it would seem that Western thought has seen to it that discourse be permitted as little room as possible between thought and words. It would appear to have ensured that *to discourse* should appear merely as a certain interjection between speaking and thinking; that it should constitute thought, clad in its signs and rendered visible by words or, conversely, that the structures of language themselves should be brought into play, producing a certain effect of meaning.

This very ancient elision of the reality of discourse in philosophical thought has taken many forms in the course of history. We have seen it quite recently in the guise of many themes now familiar to us.

It seems to me that the theme of the founding subject permits us to elide the reality of discourse. The task of the founding subject is to animate the empty forms of language with his objectives; through the thickness and inertia of empty things, he grasps intuitively the meanings lying within them. Beyond time, he indicates the field of meanings – leaving history to make them explicit – in which propositions, sciences, and deductive ensembles ultimately find their foundation. In this relationship with meaning, the founding subject has signs, marks, tracks, letters at his disposal. But he does not need to demonstrate these passing through the singular instance of discourse.

The opposing theme, that of originating experience, plays an analogous role. This asserts, in the case of experience, that even before it could be grasped in the form of a *cogito*, prior significations, in some ways already spoken, were circulating in the world, scattering it all about us, and from the outset made possible a sort of primitive recognition. Thus, a primary complicity with the world founds, for us, a possibility of speaking of experience, in it, to designate and name it, to judge it and, finally, to know it in the form of truth. If there is discourse, what could it legitimately be if not a discrete reading? Things murmur meanings our language has merely to extract; from its most primitive beginnings, this language was already whispering to us of a being of which it forms the skeleton.

The theme of universal mediation is, I believe, yet another manner of eliding the reality of discourse. And this despite appearances. At first sight it would seem that, to discover the movement of a logos everywhere elevating singularities into concepts, finally enabling immediate consciousness to deploy all the rationality in the world, is certainly to place discourse at the centre of speculation. But, in truth, this logos is really only another discourse already in operation, or rather, it is things and events themselves which *insensibly* become discourse in the unfolding of the essential secrets. Discourse is no longer much more than the shimmering of a truth about to be born in its own eyes; and when all things come eventually to take the form of discourse, when everything may be said and when anything becomes an excuse for pronouncing a discourse, it will be because all things having manifested and exchanged meanings, they will then all be able to return to the silent interiority of self-consciousness.

Whether it is the philosophy of a founding subject, a philosophy of originating experience or a philosophy of universal mediation, discourse is really only an activity, of writing in the first case, of reading in the second and exchange in the third. This exchange, this writing, this reading never involve anything but signs. Discourse thus nullifies itself, in reality, in placing itself at the disposal of the signifier.

What civilisation, in appearance, has shown more respect towards discourse than our own? Where has it been more and better honoured? Where have men depended more radically, apparently, upon its constraints and its universal character? But, it seems to me, a certain fear hides behind this apparent supremacy accorded, this apparent logophilia. It is as though these taboos, these barriers, thresholds and limits were deliberately disposed in order, at least partly, to master and control the great proliferation of discourse, in such a way as to relieve its richness of its most dangerous elements; to organise its disorder so as to skate round its most uncontrollable aspects. It is as though people had wanted to efface all trace of its irruption into the activity of our thought and language. There is undoubtedly in our society, and I would not be surprised to see it in others, though taking different forms and modes, a profound logophobia, a sort of dumb fear of these events, of this mass of spoken things, of everything that could possibly be violent, discontinuous, querulous, disordered even and perilous in it, of the incessant, disorderly buzzing of discourse.

If we wish – I will not say to efface this fear – but to analyse it in its conditions, its activity and its effects, I believe we must resolve ourselves to accept three decisions which our current thinking rather tends to resist, and which belong to the three groups of function I have just mentioned: to question our will to truth; to restore to discourse its character as an event; to abolish the sovereignty of the signifier.

These are the tasks, or rather, some of the themes which will govern my work in the years ahead. One can straight away distinguish some of the methodological demands they imply.

A principle of *reversal*, first of all. Where, according to tradition, we think we recognise the source of discourse, the principles behind its flourishing and continuity, in those factors which seem to play a positive role, such as the author discipline, will to truth, we must rather recognise the negative activity of the cutting-out and rarefaction of discourse.

But, once we have distinguished these principles of rarefaction, once we have ceased considering them as a fundamental and creative action, what do we discover behind them? Should we affirm that a world of uninterrupted discourse would be virtually complete? This is where we have to bring other methodological principles into play.

Next, then, the principle of *discontinuity*. The existence of systems of rarefaction does not imply that, over and beyond them lie great vistas of limitless discourse, continuous and silent, repressed and driven back by them, making it our task to abolish them and at last to restore it to speech. Whether talking in terms of speaking or thinking, we must not imagine some unsaid thing, or an unthought, floating about the world, interlacing with all its forms and events. Discourse must be treated as a discontinuous activity, its different manifestations sometimes coming together, but just as easily unaware of, or excluding each other.

The principle of *specificity* declares that a particular discourse cannot be resolved by a prior system of significations; that we should not imagine that the world presents us with a legible face, leaving us merely to decipher it; it does not work hand in glove with what we already know; there is no prediscursive fate disposing the word in our favour. We must conceive discourse as a violence that we do to things, or, at all events, as a practice we impose upon them; it is in this practice that the events of discourse find the principle of their regularity.

The fourth principle, that of *exteriority*, holds that we are not to burrow to the hidden core of discourse, to the heart of the thought or meaning manifested in it; instead, taking the discourse itself, its appearance and its regularity, that we should look for its external conditions of existence, for that which gives rise to the chance series of these events and fixes its limits.

As the regulatory principles of analysis, then, we have four notions: event series, regularity and the possible conditions of existence. Term for term we find the notion of event opposed to that of creation, the possible conditions of existence opposing signification. These four notions (signification, originality, unity, creation) have, in a fairly general way, dominated the traditional history of ideas; by general agreement one sought the point of creation, the unity of a work, of a period or a theme, one looked also for the mark of individual originality and the infinite wealth of hidden meanings.

I would like to add just two remarks, the first of which concerns history. We frequently credit contemporary history with having removed the individual event from its privileged position and with having revealed the more enduring structures of history. That is so. I am not sure, however, that historians have been working in this direction alone. Or, rather, I do not think one can oppose the identification of the individual event to the analysis of long term trends quite so neatly. On the contrary, it seems to me that it is in squeezing the individual event, in directing the resolving power of historical analysis onto official price-lists (*mercuriales*), title deeds, parish registers, to harbour archives analysed year by year and week by week, that we gradually perceive – beyond battles, decisions, dynasties and assemblies – the emergence of those massive phenomena of secular or multi-secular importance. History, as it is practised today, does not turn its back on events; on the contrary, it is continually enlarging the field of events, constantly discovering new layers – more superficial as well as more profound – incessantly isolating new ensembles – events, numerous, dense and interchangeable or rare and decisive: from daily price fluctuations to secular inflations. What is significant is that history does not consider an event without defining the series to which it belongs, without specifying the method of analysis used, without seeking out the regularity of phenomena and the probable limits of their occurrence, without enquiring about variations, inflexions and the slope of the curve, without desiring to know the conditions on which these depend. History has long since abandoned its attempts to understand events in terms of cause and effect in the formless unity of some great evolutionary process, whether vaguely homogeneous or rigidly hierarchised. It did not do this in order to seek out structures anterior to, alien or hostile to the event. It was rather in order to establish those diverse converging, and sometimes divergent, but never autonomous series that enable us to circumscribe the 'locus' of an event, the limits to its fluidity and the conditions of its emergence.

The fundamental notions now imposed upon us are no longer those of consciousness and continuity (with their correlative problems of liberty and causality), nor are they those of sign and structure. They are notions, rather, of events and of series, with the groups of notions linked to these; it is around such an ensemble that this analysis of discourse I am thinking of is articulated, certainly not upon those traditional themes which the philosophers of the past took for 'living' history, but on the effective work of historians.

But it is also here that this analysis poses some, probably awesome philosophical or theoretical problems. If discourses are to be treated first as ensembles of discursive events, what status are we to accord this notion of event, so rarely taken into consideration by philosophers? Of course, an event is neither substance, nor accident, nor quality nor process; events are not corporeal. And yet, an event is certainly not immaterial; it takes effect, becomes effect, always on the level of materiality. Events have their place; they consist in relation to, coexistence with, dispersion of, the cross-checking accumulation and the selection of material elements; it occurs as an effect of, and in, material dispersion. Let us say that the philosophy of event should advance in the direction, at first sight paradoxical, of an incorporeal materialism. If, on the other hand, discursive events are to be dealt with as homogeneous, but discontinuous series, what status are we to accord this discontinuity? Here we are not dealing with a succession of instants in time, nor with the plurality of thinking subjects; what is concerned are those caesurae breaking the instant and dispersing the subject in a multiplicity of possible positions and functions. Such a discontinuity strikes and invalidates the smallest units, traditionally recognised and the least readily contested: the instant and the subject. Beyond them, independent of them, we must conceive – between these discontinuous series of relations which are not in any order of succession (or simultaneity) within any (or several) consciousnesses – and we must elaborate – outside of philosophies of time and subject – a theory of discontinuous systematisation. Finally, if it is true that these discursive, discontinuous series have their regularity, within certain limits, it is clearly no longer possible to establish mechanically causal links or an ideal necessity among their constitutive elements. We must accept the introduction of chance as a category in the production of events. There again, we feel the absence of a theory enabling us to conceive the links between chance and thought.

In the sense that this slender wedge I intend to slip into the history of ideas consists in dealing not with meanings possibly lying behind this or that discourse, but with discourse as regular series and distinct events, I fear I recognise in this wedge a tiny (odious, too, perhaps) device permitting the introduction, into the very roots of thought, of notions of *chance, discontinuity* and *materiality*. This represents a triple peril which one particular form of history attempts to avert by recounting the continuous unfolding of some ideal necessity. But they are three notions which ought to permit us to link the history of systems of thought to the practical work of historians; three directions to be followed in the work of theoretical elaboration.

Following these principles, and referring to this overall view, the analyses I intend to undertake fall into two groups. On the one hand, the 'critical' group which sets the reversal principle to work. I shall attempt to distinguish the forms of exclusion, limitation and appropriation of which I was speaking earlier; I shall try to show how they are formed, in answer to which needs, how they are modified and displaced, which constraints they have effectively exercised, to what extent they have been worked on. On the other hand, the 'genealogical' group, which brings the three other principles into play: how series of discourse are formed, through, in spite of, or with the aid of these systems of constraint: what were the specific norms for each, and what were their conditions of appearance, growth and variation.

Taking the critical group first, a preliminary group of investigations could bear on what I have designated functions of exclusion. I have already examined one of these for a determinate period: the disjunction of reason and madness in the classical age. Later, we could attempt an investigation of a taboo system in language, that concerning sexuality from the sixteenth to the nineteenth century. In this, we would not be concerned with the manner in which this has progressively – and happily – disappeared, but with the way it has been altered and rearticulated, from the practice of confession, with its forbidden conduct, named, clarified, hierarchised down to the mallet detail, to the belated, timid appearance of the treatment of sexuality in nineteenth-century psychiatry and medicine. Of course, these only amount to somewhat symbolic guidelines, but one can already be pretty sure that the tree will not fall where we expect, and that taboos are not always to be found where we imagine them to be.

For the time being, I would like to address myself to the third system of exclusion. I will envisage it in two ways. Firstly, I would like to try to visualise the manner in which this truth within which we are caught, but which we constantly renew, was selected, but at the same time, was repeated, extended and displaced. I will take first of all the age of the Sophists and its beginning with Socrates, or at least with Platonic philosophy, and I shall try to see how effective, ritual discourse, charged with power and peril, gradually arranged itself into a disjunction between true and false discourse. I shall next take the turn of the sixteenth and seventeenth centuries and the age which, above all in England, saw the emergence of an observational, affirmative science, a certain natural philosophy inseparable, too, from religious ideology – for this certainly constituted a new form of the will to knowledge. In the third place, I shall turn to the beginning of the nineteenth century and the great founding acts of modern science, as well as the formation of industrial society and the accompanying positivist ideology. Three slices out of the morphology of our will to knowledge; three staging posts in our philistinism.

I would also like to consider the same question from quite another angle. I would like to measure the effect of a discourse claiming to be scientific – medical, psychiatric or sociological – on the ensemble of practices and prescriptive discourse of which the penal code consists. The study of psychiatric skills and their role in the penal system will serve as a point of departure and as basic material for this analysis.

It is within this critical perspective, but on a different level, that the analysis of the rules for the limitation of discourse should take place, of those among which I earlier designated the author principle, that of commentary and that of discipline. One can envisage a certain number of studies in this field. I am thinking, for example, of the history of medicine in the sixteenth to nineteenth centuries; not so much an account of discoveries made and concepts developed, but of grasping – from the construction of medical discourse, from all its supporting institutions, from its transmission and its reinforcement – how the principles of author, commentary and discipline worked in practice; of seeking to know how the great author principle, whether Hippocrates, Galen, Paracelsus and Sydenham, or Boerhaave, became a principle of limitation in medical discourse; how, even late into the nineteenth century, the practice of aphorism and commentary retained its currency and how it was gradually replaced by the emphasis on case histories and clinical training on actual cases; according to which model medicine sought to constitute itself as a discipline, basing itself at first on natural history and, later, on anatomy and biology.

One could also envisage the way in which eighteenth- and nineteenth-century literary criticism and history have constituted the character of the author and the form of the work, utilising, modifying and altering the procedures of religious exegesis, biblical criticism, hagiography, the 'lives' of historical or legendary figures, of autobiography and memoirs. One day, too, we must take a look at Freud's role in psychoanalytical knowledge, so different from that of Newton in physics, or from that an author might play in the field of philosophy (Kant, for example, who originated a totally new way of philosophising).

These, then, are some of the projects falling within the critical aspect of the task, for the analysis of instances of discursive control. The genealogical aspect concerns the effective formation of discourse, whether within the limits of control, or outside of them, or as is most frequent, on both sides of delimitation. Criticism analyses the processes of rarefaction, consolidation and unification in discourse; genealogy studies their formation, at once scattered, discontinuous and regular. To tell the truth, these two tasks are not always exactly complementary. We do not find, on the one hand, forms of rejection, exclusion, consolidation or attribution, and, on a more profound level, the spontaneous pouring forth of discourse, which immediately before or after its manifestation, finds itself submitted to selection and control. The regular formation of discourse may, in certain conditions and up to a certain point, integrate control procedures (this is what happens, for example, when a discipline takes on the form and status of scientific discourse). Conversely, modes of control may take on life within a discursive formation (such as literary criticism as the author's constitutive discourse) even though any critical task calling instances of control into play must, at the same time, analyse the discursive regularities through which these instances are formed. Any genealogical description must take into account the limits at play within real formations. The difference between the critical and genealogical enterprise is not one of object or field, but of point of attack, perspective and delimination.

Earlier on I mentioned one possible study, that of the taboos in discourse on sexuality. It would be difficult, and in any case abstract, to try to carry out this study, without at the same time analysing literary, religious and ethical, biological and medical, as well as juridical discursive ensembles: wherever sexuality is discussed, wherever it is named or described, metaphorised, explained or judged. We are a very long way from having constituted a unitary, regular discourse concerning sexuality; it may be that we never will, and that we are not even travelling in that direction. No matter. Taboos are homogeneous neither in their forms nor their behaviour whether in literary or medical discourse, in that of psychiatry or of the direction of consciousness. Conversely, these different discursive regularities do not divert or alter taboos in the same manner. It will only be possible to undertake this study, therefore, if we take into account the plurality of series within which the taboos, each one to some extent different from all the others, are at work.

We could also consider those series of discourse which, in the sixteenth and seventeenth centuries, dealt with wealth and poverty, money, production and trade. Here, we would be dealing with some pretty heterogeneous ensembles of enunciations, formulated by rich and poor, the wise and the ignorant, protestants and catholics, royal officials, merchants or moralists. Each one has its forms of regularity and, equally, its systems of constraint. None of them precisely prefigures that other form of regularity that was to acquire the momentum of a discipline and which was later to be known, first as 'the study of wealth' and, subsequently, 'political economy'. And yet, it was from the foregoing that a new regularity was formed, retrieving or excluding, justifying or rejecting, this or that utterance from these old forms.

One could also conceive a study of discourse concerning heredity, such as it can be gleaned, dispersed as it was until the beginning of the twentieth century, among a variety of disciplines, observations, techniques and formulae; we would be concerned to show the process whereby these series eventually became subsumed under the single system, now recognised as epistemologically coherent, known as genetics. This is the work François Jacob has just completed, with unequalled brilliance and scholarship.

It is thus that critical and genealogical descriptions are to alternate, support and complete each other. The critical side of the analysis deals with the systems enveloping discourse; attempting to mark out and distinguish the principles of ordering, exclusion and rarity in discourse. We might, to play with our words, say it practises a kind of studied casualness. The genealogical side of discourse, by way of contrast, deals with series of effective formation of discourse: it attempts to grasp it in its power of affirmation, by which I do not mean a power opposed to that of negation, but the power of constituting domains of objects, in relation to which one can affirm or deny true or false propositions. Let us call these domains of objects positivist and, to play on words yet again, let us say that, if the critical style is one of studied casualness, then the genealogical mood is one of felicitous positivism.

At all events, one thing must be emphasised here: that the analysis of discourse thus understood, does not reveal the universality of a meaning, but brings to light the action of imposed rarity, with a fundamental power of affirmation. Rarity and affirmation; rarity, in the last resort of affirmation – certainly not any continuous outpouring of meaning, and certainly not any monarchy of the signifier.

And now, let those who are weak on vocabulary, let those with little comprehension of theory call all this – if its appeal is stronger than its meaning for them – structuralism. . . .

23

Roland Barthes
(1915–1980)

The philosophical career of Roland Barthes was dedicated to a critique of culture carried out under the aegis of semiology. This 'science of signs', whose potential for extended analysis had first been suggested by Saussure, became the methodological tool Barthes deployed on a wide variety of cultural discourses. His semiological investigations covered such seemingly disparate domains as film, literature, wrestling, politics and popular media. As 'Director of the Sociology of Signs, Symbols, and Collective Representations' – a rubric which captured the breadth of his project – Barthes taught for many years at the Ecole Pratique des Hautes Etudes in Paris. We might more properly say that he turned his attention to all 'systems of signification', rather than language alone. For Barthes, the narrow focus of structural linguistics had to be exchanged for a semiology capable of analyzing gestures, images, sounds and complex combinations that surfaced in diverse public rituals.

It is interesting to note that Barthes' earliest work, *Writing Degree Zero* (1952), anticipated Derrida's focus on the *written* sign by at least a decade. In that text, Barthes redefined 'writing' (*écriture*) as a special locus that marked the junction of style and language. 'Zero-degree writing' no longer held 'communication' to be its primary function, but rather created its own world of surface effects and internal textual relations. For Barthes, the *nouveau roman* texts of Alain Robbe-Grillet epitomized this celebration of *écriture* over and against the tradition of fictional realism. Barthes thus took a stance in literary theory that privileged the formal role played by textuality itself.

With the publication of *Mythologies* (1957) and *Elements of Semiology* in 1964, Barthes formulated the link between his critical efforts and Saussure's linguistic theory, thereby clarifying his structuralist position. Semiology could now also be seen to operate on a 'translinguistic' level that recognized 'signs' structurally related to other 'signs' throughout the lifeworld. Barthes' social semiotics aspired to examine cultural discourses from the perspective of collective codes constantly working behind our backs to generate meaning. This hidden level of collective signification was defined as 'mythology' in so far as it camouflaged the ideological discourses underlying social reality as popular consciousness perceived it. Such 'myths' always relied on a second-level signification which added something undetected to a sign's apparent meaning. A certain ambiguity exists between the original meaning of a sign and its ideologically transformed variant. Quite commonly, the subliminal effects of advertising operate on this level. More worrisome to Barthes, however, was the invisible and seemingly depoliticized version of bourgeois ideology presenting itself as just another 'natural' fact in the world. He wished to reveal the necessary contrivances required to stifle social contradictions and tensions in the interests of legitimation. Barthes' attempts at 'semioclasm' – breaking through the sign to hidden levels of what is actually signified – exhibit an interesting combination of structuralist and hermeneutic activity that recognizes historical artifice over universal mind.

The later phase of Barthes' work, as exemplified by *Image/Music/Text* (1977) and the *Collège de France Inaugural Lecture* (1977), is more properly seen as 'poststructuralist' rather than 'structuralist'. In a sense, there is still great continuity with his earlier project, but the semioclastic strategy has changed. No longer can we rely on a site of origin to reveal fixed meaning; language and power interact to limit what is even sayable. Since Barthes believes we can find no place outside a language always infected by its own logocentricity, his semioclasm becomes a 'sarcasm' which subverts meaning from within by inviting displacement and plurality. The 'death of the author' gives rise to the birth of the reader, and every reader contributes to this revolutionary project of playfully refusing a single and ultimate meaning to the text. For 'the true place of writing is reading', the place where desire is finally unchained.

SELECT BIBLIOGRAPHY OF BARTHES' WORKS IN ENGLISH

Elements of Semiology, New York: Hill & Wang, 1968.
Writing Degree Zero, New York: Hill & Wang, 1968.
Critical Essays, Evanston, Ill.: Northwestern University Press, 1972.
Mythologies, London: Cape, 1972.
S/Z, New York: Hill & Wang, 1974.
The Pleasure of the Text, New York: Hill & Wang, 1975.
Barthes by Barthes, New York: Hill & Wang, 1977.
Image/Music/Text, London: Fontana, 1977.
A Lover's Discourse, London: Hill & Wang, 1978.
Camera Lucida, London: Fontana, 1979.
'Inaugural lecture at the *Collège de France* (1977)', *Oxford Literary Review*, vol. 4, no. 1, 1979.
Empire of Signs, London: Cape, 1983.
The Grain of the Voice (interviews), London: Cape, 1985.

The Responsibility of Forms, Oxford: Blackwell, 1986.
The Rustle of Language, Oxford: Blackwell, 1986.
Criticism and Truth, London: Athlone, 1987.
Sollers Writer, London: Athlone, 1987.
The Semiotic Challenge, Oxford: Blackwell, 1988.

ROLAND BARTHES

Inaugural Lecture at the Collège de France, 7 January 1977

I SHOULD PROBABLY begin with a consideration of the reasons which have led the Collège de France to receive a fellow of doubtful nature, whose every attribute is somehow challenged by its opposite. For though my career has been academic, I am without the usual qualifications for entrance into that career. And though it is true that I long wished to inscribe my work within the field of science – literary, lexicological, and sociological – I must admit that I have produced only essays, an ambiguous genre in which analysis vies with writing. And though it is also true that very early on I associated my investigations with the birth and development of semiotics, it is true as well that I have scarcely any claim as its representative, so inclined was I to shift its definition (almost as soon as I found it to be formed) and to draw upon the eccentric forces of modernism, located closer to the journal *Tel Quel* than to many other periodicals which testify to the vigour of semiological enquiry.

It is then a patently impure fellow whom you receive in an establishment where science, scholarship, rigour, and disciplined invention reign. In the interests of discretion, then, and out of a personal inclination to escape intellectual difficulty through the interrogation of my own pleasure, I shall turn from the reasons which have induced the Collège de France to welcome me – for they are uncertain, in my view – and address those which make my entry here more joyful than honorific; for an honour can be undeserved – joy never is. It is my joy to encounter in this place the memory or presence of authors dear to me and who teach or have taught at the Collège de France. First, of course, comes Michelet, through whom, at the start of my intellectual life, I discovered the sovereign place of History in the study of man, and the power of writing, once scholarship accepts that commitment. Then, closer to us, Jean Baruzi and Paul Valéry, whose lectures I attended as an adolescent in this very hall. Then, closer still, Maurice Merleau-Ponty and Emile Benveniste. As for the present, allow me to exempt from the discretion and silence incumbent upon friendship the affection, intellectual solidarity, and gratitude which bind me to Michel Foucault, for it is he who kindly undertook to present this Chair and its occupant to the Assembly of Professors.

Another kind of joy, more sober because more responsible, is mine today as well: that of entry into a place that we can strictly term *outside the bounds of power*. For if I may, in turn, interpret the Collège, I shall say that it is, as institutions go, one of History's last stratagems. Honour is usually a diminution of power; here it is a subtraction, power's untouched portion. A professor's sole activity here is research: to speak

From *Oxford Literary Review* 4(1), 1979.

– I shall even say to dream his research aloud – not to judge, to give preference, to promote, to submit to controlled scholarship. This is an enormous, almost an unjust, privilege at a time when the teaching of letters is strained to the point of exhaustion between the pressure of technocracy's demands and of revolutionary desire, the desire of its students. To teach or even to speak outside the limits of institutional sanction is certainly not to be rightfully and totally uncorrupted by power; power (the *libido dominandi*) is there, hidden in any discourse, even when uttered in a place outside the bounds of power. Therefore, the freer such teaching, the further we must enquire into the conditions and processes by which discourse can be disengaged from all will-to-possess. This enquiry constitutes, in my view, the ultimate project of the instruction inaugurated today.

Indeed, it is power with which we shall be concerned, indirectly but persistently. Our modern 'innocence' speaks of power as if it were a single thing: on one side those who have it, on the other those who do not. We have believed that power was an exemplarily political object; we believe now that power is also an ideological object, that it creeps in where we do not recognize it at first, into institutions, into teaching, but still that it is always one thing. And yet, what if power were plural, like demons? My name is Legion, it could say; everywhere, on all sides, leaders, massive or minute organizations, pressure groups or oppression groups, everywhere authorized voices which authorize themselves to utter the discourse of all power: the discourse of arrogance. We discover then that power is present in the most delicate mechanisms of social exchange: not only in the State, in classes, in groups, but even in fashion, public opinion, entertainment, sports, news, family and private relations, and even in the liberating impulses which attempt to counteract it. I call the discourse of power any discourse which engenders blame, hence guilt, in its recipient. Some expect of us as intellectuals that we take action on every occasion against Power, but our true battle is elsewhere, it is against *powers* in the plural, and this is no easy combat. For if it is plural in social space, power is, symmetrically, perpetual in historical time. Exhausted, defeated here, it reappears there; it never disappears. Make a revolution to destroy it, power will immediately revive and flourish again in the new state of affairs. The reason for this endurance and this ubiquity is that power is the parasite of a trans-social organism, linked to the whole of man's history and not only to his political, historical history. The object in which power is inscribed, for all human eternity, is language (*langage*), or to be more precise, its necessary expression: the language we speak and write (*langue*).

Language (*Langage*) is legislation, speech (*langue*) is its code. We do not see the power which is in speech (*langue*) because we forget that all speech is a classification, and that all classifications are oppressive: *ordo* means both distribution and commination. Jakobson has shown that a speech-system (*un idiome*) is defined less by what it permits us to say than by what it compels us to say. In French (I shall take obvious examples)

I am obliged to posit myself first as subject before starting the action which will henceforth be no more than my attribute: what I do is merely the consequence and consecution of what I am. In the same way, I must always choose between masculine and feminine, for the neuter and the dual are forbidden me. Further, I must indicate my relation to the other person by resorting to either *tu* or *vous*; social or affective suspension is denied me. Thus, by its very structure my language (*langue*) implies an inevitable relation of alienation. To speak, and, with even greater reason, to utter a discourse is not, as is too often repeated, to communicate; it is to subjugate: the whole language is a generalized *rection*. I am going to quote a remark of Renan's. 'French, ladies and gentlemen', he once said in a lecture, 'will never be the language of the absurd, nor will it ever be a reactionary language. I cannot imagine a serious reaction having French as its organ.' Well, Renan was, in his way, perspicacious. He realized that language (*langue*) is not exhausted by the message engendered by it. He saw that language (*langue*) can survive this message and make understood within it, with a frequently terrible resonance, something other than what it says, superimposing on the subject's conscious, reasonable voice the dominating, stubborn, implacable voice of structure, i.e. of the species inso-far as that species speaks. Renan's error was historical, not structural; he supposed that French – formed, as he believed, by reason – compelled the expression of a political reason which, to him, could only be democratic. But language – the performance of a language system (*la langue comme performance de tout langage*) – is neither reactionary nor progressive; it is quite simply fascist; for fascism does not prevent speech (*dire*), it compels speech.

Once uttered, even in the subject's deepest privacy, speech (*langue*) enters the service of power. In speech, inevitably, two categories appear: the authority of assertion, the gregariousness of repetition. On the one hand, speech (*langue*) is immediately assertive: negation, doubt, possibility, the suspension of judgment require special mechanisms which are them-selves caught up in a play of linguistic masks (*masques langagiers*); what linguists call modality is only the supplement of speech (*langue*) by which I try, as through petition, to sway its implacable power of verification. On the other hand, the signs composing speech (*langue*) exist only insofar as they are recognized, i.e. insofar as they are repeated. The sign is a follower, gregarious; in each sign sleeps that monster: a stereotype. I can speak (*parler*) only by picking up what *loiters* around in speech (*langue*). Once I speak, these two categories unite in me; I am both master and slave. I am not content to repeat what has been said, to settle comfort-ably in the servitude of signs: I speak, I affirm, I assert *tellingly* what I repeat.

In speech (*langue*), then, servility and power are inescapably inter-mingled. If we call freedom not only the capacity to escape power but also and especially the capacity to subjugate no one, then freedom can exist only outside language. Unfortunately, human language has no exterior: there is no exit. We can get out of it only at the price of the impossible: by mystical singularity, as described by Kierkegaard when he defines Abraham's sacrifice as an action unparalleled, void of speech (*parole*), even interior speech, performed against the generality, the gregariousness, the morality of language; or again by the Nietzschean 'yes to life', which is a kind of exultant shock administered to the servility of speech (*langue*), to what Deleuze calls its reactive guise. But for us, who are neither knights of faith nor supermen, the only remaining alternative is, if I may say so, to cheat with speech (*langue*), to cheat speech. This salutary trickery, this evasion, this grand imposture which allows us to understand speech (*langue*) *outside the bounds of power*, in the splendour of a permanent revolution of language, I for one call *literature*.

I mean by *literature* neither a body nor a series of works, nor even a branch of commerce or of teaching, but the complex graph of the traces of a practice, the practice of writing. Hence, it is essentially the text with which I am concerned – the fabric of signifiers which constitute the work. For the text is the very outcropping of speech (*langue*), and it is within speech that speech must be fought, led astray – not by the message of which it is the instrument, but by the play of words of which it is the theatre. Thus I can say without differentiation: literature, writing, or text. The forces of freedom which are in literature depend not on the writer's civil person, nor on his political commitment – for he is, after all, only a man among others – nor do they even depend on the doctrinal content of his work, but rather on the labour of displacement he brings to bear upon the language (*langue*). Seen in this light, Céline is quite as important as Hugo, and Chateaubriand as important as Zola. By this I am trying to address a responsibility of form; but this responsibility cannot be evaluated in ideological terms – which is why the sciences of ideology have always had so little hold over it. Of these forces of literature, I wish to indicate three, which I shall discuss in terms of three Greek concepts: *Mathesis, Mimesis, Semiosis.*

Literature accommodates many kinds of knowledge. In a novel like *Robinson Crusoe* there is a historical knowledge, a geographical, a social (colonial), a technological, a botanical, an anthropological knowledge (Robinson proceeds from nature to culture). If, by some unimaginable excess of socialism or barbarism, all but one of our disciplines were to be expelled from our education system, it is the discipline of literature which would have to be saved, for all knowledge, all the sciences are present in the literary monument. Whereby we can say that literature, whatever the school in whose name it declares itself, is absolutely, categorically *realist*: it is reality, i.e. the very spark of the real. Yet literature, in this truly encyclopaedic respect, displaces the various kinds of knowledge, does not fix or fetishize any of them; it gives them an indirect place, and this indirection is precious. On the one hand, it allows for the designation of possible areas of knowledge – unsuspected, unfulfilled. Literature works in the interstices of science. It is always behind or ahead of science, like the Bolognese stone which gives off by night what it has stored up by day, and by this indirect glow illuminates the new day which dawns. Science is crude, life is subtle, and it is for the correction of this disparity that literature matters to us. The knowledge it marshals is, on the other hand, never complete or final. Literature does not say that it knows something, but that it knows *of* something, or better, that it knows *about* something – that it knows about men. What it knows about men is what we might call the great *mess* of language, upon which men work and which works upon them. Literature can reproduce the diversity of sociolects, or, starting from this diversity, and suffering its laceration, literature may imagine and seek to elaborate a limit-language which would be its zero degree. Because it *stages* language instead of simply using it, literature feeds knowledge into the machinery of infinite reflexivity. Through writing, knowledge ceaselessly reflects on knowledge, in terms of a discourse which is no longer epistemological, but dramatic.

It is good form, today, to contest the opposition of sciences and letters, insofar as the number of relations, whether of model or method, uniting these two regions and often erasing their frontier is increasing, and it is possible that this opposition will appear one day to be a historical myth. But from the point of view of language, which is ours here, this opposition is pertinent; moreover it does not necessarily set up the opposition between the real and the fantastic, the objective and the subjective, the True and the Beautiful, but only the different loci of speech (*parole*). According to scientific discourse – or a certain discourse of science – knowledge is statement; in writing, it is an act of stating. The statement, the usual object of linguistics, is given as the product of the subject's absence. The act of stating, by exposing the subject's place and energy, even his deficiency (which is not his absence), focuses on the very reality of language, acknowledging that language is an immense halo of implications, of effects, of echoes, of turns, returns, and degrees. It assumes the burden of making understood a subject both insistent and ineffable, unknown and yet recognized by a disturbing familiarity. Words are no longer conceived illusively as simple instruments; they are cast as projections, explosions, vibrations, devices, flavours. Writing makes knowledge festive.

The paradigm I am proposing here does not follow the functional division: it is not aimed at putting scientists and researchers on one side, writers and essayists on the other. On the contrary, it suggests that writing is to be found wherever words have flavour (the French words for *flavour* (*saveur*) and *knowledge* (*savoir*) have the same Latin root). Curnonski used to say that in cooking 'things should have the taste of what they are'. Where knowledge is concerned, things must, if they are to become what they are, what they have been, have that ingredient, the salt of words. It is this taste of words which makes knowledge profound, fecund. I know for instance that Michelet proposes much that is denied by historical scholarship. Nonetheless Michelet founded something in the order of an ethnology of France, and each time a historian displaces historical knowledge, in the broadest sense of the term and whatever its object, we find, quite simply, writing.

Literature's second force is its force as representation. From ancient times to the efforts of our avant-garde, literature has been concerned to represent something. What? I will put it crudely: the real. The real is not representable, and it is because men ceaselessly try to represent it by words that there is a history of literature. That the real is not representable, but only demonstrable, can be said in several ways: either we can define it, with Lacan, as the *impossible*, that which is unattainable and escapes discourse, or in topological terms we observe that a pluri-dimensional order (the real) cannot be made to coincide with a unidimensional order (language). Now, it is precisely this topological impossibility that literature rejects and to which it never submits. Though there is no parallelism between language and the real, men will not take sides, and it is this refusal, perhaps as old as language itself, which produces, in an incessant commotion, literature. We can imagine a history of literature, or better, say, of productions of language, which would be the history of certain (often aberrant) verbal *expedients* men have used to reduce, tame, deny, or, on the contrary, to assume what is *always* a delirium, i.e., the fundamental inadequation of language and the real. I said a moment ago, apropos of knowledge, that literature is categorically realist, in that it never has anything but the real as its object of desire; and I shall say now, without contradicting myself – because I am here using the word in its familiar acceptation – that literature is quite as stubbornly unrealistic; it considers sane its desire for the impossible.

This function – perhaps perverse, therefore fitting – has a name: it is the utopian function. Here we come back to History. For it is in the second half of the nineteenth century, one of the grimmest periods of calamitous capitalism, that literature finds its exact figure, at least for us Frenchmen, in Mallarmé. Modernity – our modernity, which begins at this period – can be defined by this new phenomenon: that *utopias of language* are conceived in it. No 'history of literature' (if such is still to be written) could be legitimate which would be content, as in the past, to link the various schools together without indicating the gap which here reveals a new prophetic function, that of writing. 'To change language (*langue*)', that Mallarméan expression, is a concomitant of 'To change the world', that Marxian one. There is a *political* reception of Mallarmé, of those who have followed him and follow him still.

From this there follows a certain ethic of literary language, which must be affirmed, because it is contested. We often reproach the writer, the intellectual, for not writing 'everyone's' language (*langue*). But it is

good that men, within the same language (*idiome*) – for us, French
– should have several kinds of speech (*langues*). If I were a legislator
(an aberrant supposition for someone who, etymologically speaking, is an
'an-archist'), far from imposing a unification of French, whether
bourgeois or popular, I would instead encourage the simultaneous apprenticeship to several French forms of speech, of various function, promoted
to equality. Dante seriously debates which language he will use to write
the *Convivio*: Latin or Tuscan? Nor is it for political or polemical reasons
that he chooses the vulgar tongue (*langue*): it is by considering the appro-
priateness of either language to his subject. The two forms of speech
(*langues*) – as for us, classical French and modern French, written French
and spoken French – thus form a reservoir (*réserve*) from which he is free
to draw, *according to the truth of desire*. This freedom is a luxury which
every society should afford its citizens: as many languages as there are
desires – a utopian proposition in that no society is yet ready to admit
the plurality of desire. That a language (*langue*), whatever it be, not repress
another; that the subject may know without remorse, without repression,
the bliss of having at his disposal two kinds of language (*instances de
langage*); that he may speak this or that, according to his perversions, not
according to the Law.

Utopia, of course, does not save us from power. The utopia of
language (*langue*) is salvaged as the language (*langue*) of utopia – a genre
like the rest. We can say that no writer who began in a rather lonely
struggle against the power of language (*langue*) could or can avoid being
co-opted by it, either in the posthumous form of an inscription within
official culture, or in the present form of a mode which imposes its image
and forces him to conform to expectation. No way out for this author
than to shift ground – or to persist – or both at once.

To *persist* means to affirm the Irreducible of literature, that which
resists and survives the typified discourses, the philosophies, sciences,
psychologies which surround it, to act as if literature were incomparable
and immortal. A writer – by which I mean not the possessor of a function or the servant of an art, but the subject of a praxis – must have the
persistence of the watcher who stands at the crossroads of all other
discourses, in a position that is *trivial* in relation to purity of doctrine
(*trivialis* is the etymological attribute of the prostitute who waits at the
intersection of three roads). To persist means, in short, to maintain, over
and against everything, the force of drift and of expectation. And it is
precisely because it persists that writing is led to shift ground. For power
seizes upon the pleasure of writing as it seizes upon all pleasure, to manipulate it and to make of it a product that is gregarious, nonperverse, in
the same way that it seizes upon the genetic product of love's pleasure,
to turn it into soldiers and fighters to its own advantage. *To shift ground*,
then, can mean: to go where you are not expected, or, more radically, to
abjure what you have written (but not necessarily what you have thought),

when gregarious power uses and subjugates it. Pasolini was thus led to 'abjure' (as he said) his *Trilogy of Life* films because he realized that power was making use of them – yet without regretting the fact that he wrote them in the first place. 'I believe,' he said in a text published posthumously, 'that *before* action we must never in any case fear annexation by power and its culture. We must behave as if this dangerous eventuality did not exist ... But I also believe that *afterwards* we must be able to realize how much we may have been used by power. And then, if our sincerity or our necessity has been controlled or manipulated, I believe we must have the courage to abjure.'

To persist and, at the same time, to shift ground relates, in short, to a kind of acting. We must therefore not be surprised if on the impossible horizon of linguistic anarchy – at that point where language (*langue*) attempts to escape its own power, its own servility – we find something which relates to theatre. To designate the impossible in language (*l'impossible de la langue*), I have cited two authors: Kierkegaard and Nietzsche. Yet both have written. It was in each instance, however, in a reversal of identity, as a performance, as a frenzied gambling of proper names – one by incessant recourse to pseudonymity, the other by proceeding, at the end of his writing life, as Klossowski has shown, to the limits of the histrionic. We might say that literature's third force, its strictly semiotic force, is to *act* signs rather than to destroy them – to feed them into a machinery of language whose safety catches and emergency breaks have exploded; in short, to institute, at the very heart of servile language (*langue*), a veritable heteronymy of things.

Which brings us to semiology.

First of all we must repeat that the sciences (at least those in which I have done any reading at all) are not eternal; they are values which rise and fall on an Exchange – the Exchange of History. In this regard, it suffices to recall the exchange fate of Theology, now a diminished area of discourse, yet once so sovereign a science as to be placed outside and above the Septennium. The fragility of the so-called human sciences derives perhaps from this: that they are *unforeseeing* sciences (whence the disappointments and the taxonomic discomfort of Economics) – which immediately alters the notion of science. Even the science of desire, psychoanalysis, must die one of these days, though we all owe it a great deal, as we owe a great deal to Theology: for desire is stronger than its interpretation.

Semiology, which we can canonically define as the science of signs, of all signs, has emerged from linguistics through its operational concepts. But linguistics itself, somewhat like economics (and the comparison is perhaps not insignificant), is, I believe, in the process of splitting apart. On the one hand, linguistics tends toward the formal pole, and, like econometrics, it is thereby becoming more formalized; on the other hand, linguistics is assimilating contents that are more and more numerous and remote from its original field. Just as the object of economics today is every-where, in the political, the social, the cultural, so the object of linguistics is limitless. Speech (*langue*), according to an intuition of Benveniste's, is the social itself. In short, either due to excessive ascesis or excessive hunger, whether famished or replete, linguistics is deconstructing itself. It is this deconstruction of linguistics that I, for my part, call *semiology*.

You may have noticed that in the course of my presentation I have surreptitiously shifted from language (*langue*) to discourse, in order to return, sometimes without warning, from discourse to language, as if I were dealing with the same object. I believe, indeed, that today, within the pertinence chosen here, language and discourse are undivided, for they move along the same axis of power. Yet initially this originally Saussurian distinction (the pairing was *Langue/Parole*) was very useful. It gave semi-ology the courage to begin. By this opposition I could reduce discourse, miniaturize it into a grammatical example, and thereby hope to hold all human communication under my net, like Wotan and Loge securing Alberich transformed into a tiny toad. But the example is not 'the thing itself', and the matter of language (*la chose langagière*) cannot be held or contained in the limits of the sentence. It is not only the phonemes, the words, and the syntactical articulations which are subject to a system of controlled freedom, since we cannot combine them arbitrarily; it is the whole stratum of discourse which is fixed by a network of rules, constraints, oppressions, repressions, massive and blurred at the rhetor-ical level, subtle and acute at the grammatical level. Language flows out into discourse, discourse flows back into language; they persist one above the other like children topping each other's fists on a baseball bat. The distinction between language and discourse no longer appears except as a transitory operation – something, in short, to 'abjure'. There has come a time when, as though stricken with a gradually increasing deafness, I hear nothing but a single sound, that of language and discourse mixed. And linguistics now seems to me to be working on an enormous impos-ture, on an object it makes improperly clean and pure by wiping its fingers on the skein of discourse, like Trimalchio on his slaves' hair. Semiology would consequently be that labour which collects the impurity of language (*langue*), the waste of linguistics, the immediate corruption of the message: nothing less than the desires, the fears, the appearances, the intimidations, the advances, the blandishments, the protests, the excuses, the aggressions, the various kinds of music out of which active language (*langue*) is made.

I know how personal such a definition is. I know whereof it compels my silence: in one sense, and quite paradoxically, all of semiology, the semiology which is being studied and already acknowledged as the posi-tive science of signs, which is developing in periodicals, associations, universities, and study centres. Nevertheless, it seems to me that the inten-tion behind the establishment of a Chair at the Collège de France is not so much the consecration of a discipline as the allowing for the continuance of a certain individual labour, the adventure of a certain subject. Now, semiology, so far as I am concerned, started from a strictly emotional impulse. It seemed to me (around 1954) that a science of signs might stimulate social criticism, and that Sartre, Brecht, and Saussure could concur in this project. It was a question, in short, of understanding (or of describing) how a society produces stereotypes, i.e. triumphs of artifice, which it then consumes as innate meanings, i.e. triumphs of nature. Semiology (my semiology, at least) is generated by an intolerance of this mixture of bad faith and good conscience which characterizes the general morality, and which Brecht, in his attack upon it, called the Great Habit. *Language worked on by power*: that was the object of this first semiology.

Semiology then shifted ground, took on a different coloration, while retaining the same political object – for there is no other. This shift occurred because the intellectual community has changed, if only through the break of May '68. On the one hand, contemporary studies have modified and are modifying the critical image of the social subject and of the speaking subject. On the other hand, it has appeared that, insofar as the machinery of contestation was multiplying, power itself, as a discursive category, was dividing, spreading like a liquid leaking everywhere, each opposition group becoming in its turn and in its way a pressure group and intoning in its own name the very discourse of power, the universal discourse. Political bodies were seized with a kind of moral excitement, and even when claims were being made for pleasure, the tone was threatening. Thus we have seen most proposed liberations, those of society, of culture, of art, of sexuality, articulated in the forms of the discourse of power. We took credit for restoring what had been crushed, without seeing what else we crushed in the process.

If the semiology I am speaking of then returned to the Text, it is because, in this concert of minor dominations, the Text itself appeared as the very index of *nonpower*. The Text contains in itself the strength to elude gregarious speech (*parole*) (the speech which incorporates), even when that speech seeks to reconstitute itself in the Text. The Text always postpones – and it is this movement of *mirage* I have attempted to describe and to justify just now in speaking of literature. The Text procrastinates elsewhere, toward an unclassified, atopic site, so to speak, far from the *topoi* of politicized culture, 'that obligation to form concepts, species, forms, ends, laws . . . that world of identical cases', of which Nietzsche speaks. Gently, transitorily, the text raises that cope of generality, of morality, of in-difference (let us clearly separate this prefix from the root), which weighs on our collective discourse. Literature and semiology thereby combine to correct each other. On one side, the incessant return to the text, ancient or modern, the regular plunge into the most complex of signifying practices, i.e. writing (since writing operates with ready-made signs), forces semiology to work on differences, and keeps it from dogmatizing, from 'taking' – from taking itself for the universal discourse which it is not. And on the other side, semiotic scrutiny, focused on the text, forces us to reject the myth usually resorted to in order that literature may be saved from the gregarious speech surrounding and besetting it – from the myth of pure creativity. The sign must be thought – or rethought – the better to be deceived.

The semiology I speak of is both *negative* and *active*. Someone bedevilled throughout life, for better and for worse, by language, can only be fascinated by the forms of its void – as against its emptiness. The semiology proposed here is therefore negative – or better still, however heavy the term, *apophatic* – not in that it repudiates the sign, but in that it denies that it is possible to attribute to the sign traits that are positive, fixed, ahistoric, acorporeal, in short: scientific. This apophatic quality involves at least two consequences which directly concern the teaching of semiology.

The first is that semiology cannot itself be a metalanguage, though at its origin it was entirely so predisposed, since it is a language about languages. It is precisely in reflecting on the sign that semiology discovers that every relation of exteriority of one language to another is, *in the long run*, untenable. Time erodes my power of distance, mortifies it, turns this distance into sclerosis. I cannot function *outside* language, treating it as a target, and *within* language, treating it as a weapon. If it is true that the subject of science is that very subject which is not shown, and that it is ultimately this retention of the spectacle that we call 'metalanguage', then what I am led to assume, in speaking of signs with signs, is the very spectacle of this bizarre coincidence, of that strange squint which relates me to the Chinese shadow-casters when they show both their hands and the rabbit, the duck, and the wolf whose silhouettes they simulate. And to those who take advantage of this condition to deny that active semiology, the semiology which writes, has anything to do with science, we must reply that it is by an epistemological abuse, *which in fact is beginning to crumble*, that we identify metalanguage and science, as if one were the necessary condition of the other, whereas it is only its historical, hence challengeable, sign. It may be time to distinguish the metalinguistic, which is a label like any other, from the scientific, whose criteria are elsewhere (perhaps, let it be said in passing, what is strictly scientific is the destruction of the science which precedes).

Semiology has a relation to science, but it is not a discipline (this is the second consequence of its apophatic quality). What relation? An ancillary relation: it can help certain sciences, can be their fellow traveller for a while, offering an operational protocol starting from which each science must specify the difference of its corpus. Thus, the best-developed part of semiology, the analysis of narrative, can be useful for History, ethnology, textual criticism, exegesis, and iconology (every image is, in a way, a narrative). In other words, semiology is not a grid; it does not permit a direct apprehension of the real through the imposition of a general transparency which would render it intelligible. It seeks instead to elicit the real, in places and by moments, and it says that these efforts to elicit the real are possible without a grid. It is in fact precisely when semiology comes to be a grid that it elicits nothing at all. We can therefore say that semiology has no substitutive role with regard to any discipline. It is my hope that semiology will replace no other enquiry here, but will, on the contrary, help all the rest, that its chair will be a kind of wheelchair, the wild card of contemporary knowledge, as the sign itself is the wild card of all discourse.

This negative semiology is an active semiology: it functions outside death. I mean by this that it does not rest on a 'semiophysis', an inert naturalness of the sign, and that it is also not a 'semioclasty', a destruction of the sign. Rather, to continue the Greek paradigm, it is a *semiotropy*; turned towards the sign, this semiology is captivated by and receives the sign, treats and, if need be, imitates it as an imaginary spectacle. The semiologist is, in short, an artist (the word as I use it here neither glorifies nor disdains; it refers only to a typology). He plays with signs as with a conscious decoy, whose fascination he savours and wants to make others savour and understand. The sign – at least the sign he sees – is always immediate, subject to the kind of evidence that leaps to the eyes, like a trigger of the imagination, which is why this semiology (need I specify once more: the semiology of the speaker) is not a hermeneutics: it paints more than it digs, *via di porre* rather than *via de levare*. Its objects of predilection are texts of the Image-making process: narratives, images, portraits, expressions, idiolects, passions, structures which play simultaneously with an appearance of verisimilitude and with an uncertainty of truth. I should like to call 'semiology' the course of operations during which it is possible – even called for – to play with the sign as with a painted veil, or again, with a fiction.

This pleasure of the imaginary sign is conceivable now due to certain recent mutations, which affect culture more than society itself: the use we can make of the forces of literature I have mentioned is modified by a new situation. On one hand and first of all, the myth of the great French writer, the sacred depositary of all higher values, has crumbled since the Liberation; it has dwindled and died gradually with each of the last survivors of the *entre-deux-guerres*; a new *type* has appeared, and we no longer know – or do not yet know – what to call him: writer? intellectual? scribe? In any case, literary mastery is vanishing; the writer is no longer centre stage. On the other hand and subsequently, May '68 has revealed the crisis in our teaching. The old values are no longer transmitted, no longer circulate, no longer impress; literature is desacralized, institutions are impotent to defend and impose it as the implicit model of the human. It is not, if you like, that literature is destroyed; rather *it is no longer protected*, so that this is the moment to deal with it. Literary semiology is, as it were, that journey which lands us in a country free by default; angels and dragons are no longer there to defend it. Our gaze can fall, not without perversity, upon certain old and lovely things, whose signified is abstract, out of date. It is a moment at once decadent and prophetic, a moment of gentle apocalypse, a historical moment of the greatest possible pleasure.

If then, in this teaching which, given its very location, expects no sanction other than the loyalty of its auditors, if method intervenes as a systematic procedure, it cannot be a heuristic method meant to result in decoding. Method can bear only upon language itself, insofar as it struggles to baffle any discourse *which takes*, which is why we can justly claim that method, too, is a Fiction – a proposition already advanced by Mallarmé when he thought of preparing a thesis in linguistics: 'All method is a fiction. Language has appeared as the instrument of fiction; it will follow the method of language, language reflecting upon itself.' What I hope to be able to renew, each of the years it is given me to teach here, is the manner of presentation of the course or seminar, in short, of 'presenting' a discourse without imposing it: that would be the methodological stake, the *quaestio*, the point to be debated. For what can be oppressive in our teaching is not, finally, the knowledge or the culture it conveys, but the discursive forms through which we propose them. Since, as I have tried to suggest, this teaching has as its object discourse taken in the inevitability of power, method can really bear only on the means of loosening, baffling, or at the very least, of lightening this power. And I am increasingly convinced, both in writing and in teaching, that the fundamental operation of this loosening method is, if one writes, fragmentation, and, if one teaches, digression, or, to put it in a preciously ambiguous word, *excursion*. I should therefore like the speaking and the listening that will be interwoven here to resemble the comings and goings of a child playing beside his mother, leaving her, returning to bring her a pebble, a piece of string, and thereby tracing around a calm centre a whole locus of play within which the pebble, the string come to matter less than the enthusiastic giving of them.

When the child behaves in this way, he in fact describes the comings and goings of desire, which he endlessly presents and represents. I sincerely believe that at the origin of teaching such as this we must always locate a fantasy, which can vary from year to year. This, I know, may seem provocative: how, in the context of an institution, however free it may be, dare we speak of a phantasmic teaching? Yet if we consider for a moment the surest of human sciences, if we consider History, how can we help acknowledging that it has a continuous relation with fantasy? This is what Michelet understood: History is ultimately the history of the phantasmic site *par excellence*, that of the human body. It was by starting from this fantasy, linked for him with the lyric resurrection of past bodies, that Michelet could make History into an enormous anthropology. Science can thus be born of fantasy. It is to a fantasy, spoken or unspoken, that the professor must annually return, at the moment of determining the direction of his journey. He thereby turns from the place where he is expected, the place of the Father, who is always dead, as we know. For only the son has fantasies; only the son is alive.

The other day, I reread Thomas Mann's novel *The Magic Mountain*. This book deals with a disease I know well, tuberculosis. By my reading, I held in consciousness three moments of this disease: the moment of the story, which takes place before World War I; the moment of my own disease, around 1942; and the present moment, when this disease, vanquished by chemotherapy, has no longer the same aspect it once had. Now, the tuberculosis I experienced is, down to virtually the last detail, the tuberculosis of *The Magic Mountain*. The two moments were united, equally remote from my own present. I then realized with stupefaction (only the obvious can stupefy) that *my own body was historical*. In a sense my body is the contemporary of Hans Castorp, the novel's hero; my body, still unborn, was already twenty years old in 1907, the year when Hans entered and took up residence in 'the country up there'. My body is much older than I, as if we always kept the age of the social fears with which life has accidentally given us contact. Therefore, if I want to live, I must forget that my own body is historical. I must fling myself into the illusion that I am contemporary with the young bodies present before me, and not with my own body, my past body. In short, I must be periodically reborn. I must make myself younger than I am. At fifty-one, Michelet began his *vita nuova*, a new work, a new love. Older than he (you will understand that this parallel is out of fondness), I too am entering a *vita nuova*, marked today by this new place, this new hospitality. I undertake therefore to let myself be borne on the force of any living life, forgetfulness. There is an age at which we teach what we know. Then comes another age at which we teach what we do not know; this is called *research*. Now perhaps comes the age of another experience: that of *unlearning*, of yielding to the unforeseeable change which forgetting imposes on the sedimentation of the knowledges, cultures, and beliefs we have traversed. This experience has, I believe, an illustrious and outdated name, which I now simply venture to appropriate at the very crossroads of its etymology: *Sapientia*: no power, a little knowledge, a little wisdom, and as much flavour as possible.

24

Julia Kristeva

(b. 1941)

The versatility of Julia Kristeva's thought has generated a significant body of work that draws on such diverse fields as philosophy, psychoanalysis, linguistics, feminism and literature. Her interdisciplinary approach has proven particularly useful in exploring the problems of identity, which she develops and contextualizes in a critique of the Western philosophical tradition. While Kristeva's initial focus on structuralist semiotics was influenced by her mentor Roland Barthes, she quickly developed a poststructuralist perspective that acknowledged a potential for disruption and renewal linked to the 'subject-in-process'.

Kristeva was born and educated in Bulgaria, but left her native country to study in Paris in the mid-1960s, where she encountered Barthes, Lévi-Strauss, Lacan, Sollers and Derrida. Being already well-versed in Russian Formalism, particularly the work of Tzvetan Todorov, she quickly contributed to the structuralist debate with articles in *Critique* and *Tel Quel*, as well as producing a number of works on literary semiotics: *Semeiotikē* (1969), *Text of the Novel* (1970) and her doctoral thesis, *Revolution in Poetic Language* (1974). Although the work of Barthes and Lévi-Strauss served to highlight the constitutive role of language in culture, Kristeva did not fully embrace the autonomous model of structuralist linguistics. It was not enough for language to satisfy the requirement of internal coherence, i.e. *langue* as a total system, already constituted and impervious to change at the individual level of *parole*. Kristeva questioned this degree of closure, and sought to find an active site of change in language without invoking a Cartesian 'subject'. Her 'semanalysis' seeks to recognize the speaking subject, but as a 'subject-in-process'.

In order to carry out this project, Kristeva turned to the margins of discourse to examine poetic language and the potential for disruption and transgression it harbours. Kristeva was certainly influenced by Lacanian psychoanalysis in so far as Lacan rejected a simplistic Freudian biologism, prioritizing instead language and 'the symbolic order'. This change in the locus of identity formation suggested to Kristeva that, before the entry into language, pre-signifying forces in the infant that precondition all formal discourse are constitutive of the subject-in-process. And it is this resistance and otherness, whose undifferentiated locus Kristeva has called 'the semiotic', which emerges again to haunt the symbolic order in the guise of the avant-garde poet or the insane. This tension, between the pre-signifying otherness of the semiotic and the rational discourse of the symbolic, is responsible for the dynamic field she has designated as the subject-in-process.

Kristeva has also touched on issues that show potential for developing feminist critiques of identity as construed in the Western tradition. She has made a major contribution in the debate surrounding sexual difference through her critique of identity as a fixed, essentialist notion. She leaves room for manoeuvring and the potential for mobility and transformation in the 'subject-in-process' model she has advanced. Likewise, her 'semanalyses' and explorations of signifying relations have highlighted the constructed nature of meaning and sexuality, as well as stereotypical roles and signs active in identity formation. Kristeva reminds us in 'Women's Time', however, that it is equally dangerous to fall into the temptation of a dual-essentialism that a strongly divisive theory of sexual difference, such as Irigaray's, might risk. Indeed, for Kristeva, the 'maternal time' of repetition and cycle must be reconciled with the 'linear time' of history and politics. If anything, Kristeva ultimately maintains a dialectical stance on the issue of identity formation; neither the 'semiotic' nor the 'symbolic' offers permanent refuge. We are always in transit between the two.

SELECT BIBLIOGRAPHY OF KRISTEVA'S WORKS IN ENGLISH

About Chinese Women, London: Marion Boyars, 1977.
Desire in Language: A Semiotic Approach to Literature and Art, New York: Columbia University Press, 1980.
Powers of Horror, New York: Columbia University Press, 1982.
Revolution in Poetic Language, New York: Columbia University Press, 1984.
The Kristeva Reader, ed. Toril Moi, Oxford: Blackwell, 1986.
In the Beginning was Love: Psychoanalysis and Faith, New York: Columbia University Press, 1987.
Tales of Love, New York: Columbia University Press, 1987.
'On Melancholic Imagination' in Hugh Silverman and D. Welton (eds), *Postmodernity and Continental Philosophy*, Albany: SUNY, 1988.
The Black Sun, New York: Columbia University Press, 1989.
The Samurai, New York: Columbia University Press, 1991.
Strangers to Ourselves, London: Harvester Press, 1991.
Nations without Nationalism, New York: Columbia University Press, 1993.
Proust and the Sense of Time, London: Faber, 1993.

JULIA KRISTEVA

Women's Time

THE NATION – DREAM and reality of the nineteenth century – seems to
have reached both its apogee and its limits when the 1929 crash and the
National-Socialist apocalypse demolished the pillars that, according to
Marx, were its essence: economic homogeneity, historical tradition and
linguistic unity. It could indeed be demonstrated that the Second World
War, though fought in the name of national values (in the above sense of
the term), brought an end to the nation as a reality: it was turned into
a mere illusion which, from that point forward, would be preserved only
for ideological or strictly political purposes, its social and philosophical
coherence having collapsed. To move quickly towards the specific problematic that will occupy us in this article, let us say that the chimera of
economic *homogeneity* gave way to *interdependence* (when not submission to the economic superpowers), while *historical* tradition and *linguistic*
unity were recast as a broader and deeper determinant: what might be
called a *symbolic denominator*, defined as the cultural and religious
memory forged by the interweaving of history and geography. The
variants of this memory produce social territories which then redistribute
the cutting up into political parties which is still in use but losing strength.
At the same time, this memory or symbolic denominator, common to them
all, reveals beyond economic globalization and/or uniformization certain
characteristics transcending the nation that sometimes embrace an entire
continent. A new social ensemble superior to the nation has thus been
constituted, within which the nation, far from losing its own traits, rediscovers and accentuates them in a strange temporality, in a kind of 'future
perfect', where the most deeply repressed past gives a distinctive character
to a logical and sociological distribution of the most modern type. For
this memory or symbolic common denominator concerns the response that
human groupings, united in space and time, have given not to the problems of the *production* of material goods (i.e. the domain of the economy
and of the human relationships it implies, politics, etc.) but, rather, to
those of *reproduction*, survival of the species, life and death, the body,
sex and symbol. If it is true, for example, that Europe is representative
of such a socio-cultural ensemble, it seems to me that its existence is based
more on this 'symbolic denomination', which its art, philosophy and religions manifest, than on its economic profile, which is certainly interwoven
with collective memory but whose traits change rather rapidly under pressure from its partners.

It is clear that a social ensemble thus constituted possesses both a
solidity rooted in a particular mode of reproduction and its representations through which the biological species is connected to its humanity,

From *The Kristeva Reader*, ed. Toril Moi, Oxford: Blackwell 1986.

which is a tributary of time: as well as a certain *fragility* as a result of the fact that, through its universality, the symbolic common denominator is necessarily echoed in the corresponding symbolic denominator of another socio-cultural ensemble. Thus, barely constituted as such, Europe finds itself being asked to compare itself with, or even to recognize itself in, the cultural, artistic, philosophical and religious constructions belonging to other supra-national socio-cultural ensembles. This seems natural when the entities involved were linked by history (e.g. Europe and North America, or Europe and Latin America), but the phenomenon also occurs when the universality of this denominator we have called symbolic juxtaposes modes of production and reproduction apparently opposed in both the past and the present (e.g. Europe and India, or Europe and China). In short, with socio-cultural ensembles of the European type, we are constantly faced with a double problematic: that of their *identity* constituted by historical sedimentation, and that of their *loss of identity* which is produced by this connection of memories which escape from history only to encounter anthropology. In other words, we confront two temporal dimensions: the time of linear history, or *cursive time* (as Nietzsche called it), and the time of another history, thus another time, *monumental time* (again according to Nietzsche), which englobes these supra-national, socio-cultural ensembles within even larger entities.

I should like to draw attention to certain formations which seem to me to summarize the dynamics of a socio-cultural organism of this type. The question is one of socio-cultural groups, that is, groups defined according to their place in production, but especially according to their role in the mode of reproduction and its representations, which, while bearing the specific socio-cultural traits of the formation in question, are *diagonal* to it and connect it to other socio-cultural formations. I am thinking in particular of socio-cultural groups which are usually defined as age groups (e.g. 'young people in Europe'), as sexual divisions (e.g. 'European women'), and so forth. While it is obvious that 'young people' or 'women' in Europe have their own particularity, it is none the less just as obvious that what defines them as 'young people' or as 'women' places them in a diagonal relationship to their European 'origin' and links them to similar categories in North America or in China, among others. That is, in so far as they also belong to 'monumental history', they will not be only European 'young people' or 'women' of Europe but will echo in a most specific way the universal traits of their structural place in reproduction and its representations.

Consequently, the reader will find in the following pages, first, an attempt to situate the problematic of women in Europe within an inquiry on time: that time which the feminist movement both inherits and modifies. Secondly, I will attempt to distinguish two phases or two generations of women which, while immediately universalist and cosmopolitan in their demands, can none the less be differentiated by the fact that the first

generation is more determined by the implications of a national problematic (in the sense suggested above), while the second, more determined
by its place within the 'symbolic denominator', is European *and* trans-
European. Finally, I will try, both through the problems approached and
through the type of analysis I propose, to present what I consider a viable
stance for a European – or at least a European woman – within a domain
which is henceforth worldwide in scope.

WHICH TIME?

'Father's time, mother's species', as Joyce put it; and indeed, when evoking the name and destiny of women, one thinks more of the *space* generating and forming the human species than of *time*, becoming or history.
The modern sciences of subjectivity, of its genealogy and accidents, confirm in their own way this intuition, which is perhaps itself the result of
a socio-historical conjuncture. Freud, listening to the dreams and fantasies
of his patients, thought that 'hysteria was linked to place'.[1] Subsequent
studies on the acquisition of the symbolic function by children show that
the permanence and quality of maternal love condition the appearance
of the first spatial references which induce the child's laugh and then induce
the entire range of symbolic manifestations which lead eventually to sign
and syntax.[2] Moreover, anti-psychiatry and psychoanalysis as applied to
the treatment of psychoses, before attributing the capacity for transference
and communication to the patient, proceed to the arrangement of new
places, gratifying substitutes that repair old deficiencies in the maternal
space. I could go on giving examples. But they all converge on the
problematic of space, which innumerable religions of matriarchal (re)-
appearance attribute to 'woman', and which Plato, recapitulating in his
own system the atomists of antiquity, designated by the aporia of the *chora*,
matrix space, nourishing, unnameable, anterior to the One, to God and,
consequently, defying metaphysics.[3]

As for time, female[4] subjectivity would seem to provide a specific
measure that essentially retains *repetition* and *eternity* from among the
multiple modalities of time known through the history of civilizations.
On the one hand, there are cycles, gestation, the eternal recurrence of a
biological rhythm which conforms to that of nature and imposes a temporality whose stereotyping may shock, but whose regularity and unison
with what is experienced as extra-subjective time, cosmic time, occasion
vertiginous visions and unnameable *jouissance*.[5] On the other hand, and
perhaps as a consequence, there is the massive presence of a monumental
temporality, without cleavage or escape, which has so little to do with
linear time (which passes) that the very word 'temporality' hardly fits: all-
encompassing and infinite like imaginary space, this temporality reminds
one of Kronos in Hesiod's mythology, the incestuous son whose massive

presence covered all of Gea in order to separate her from Ouranos, the father.[6] Or one is reminded of the various myths of resurrection which, in all religious beliefs, perpetuate the vestige of an anterior or concomitant maternal cult, right up to its most recent elaboration, Christianity, in which the body of the Virgin Mother does not die but moves from one spatiality to another within the same time via dormition (according to the Orthodox faith) or via assumption (the Catholic faith).[7]

The fact that these two types of temporality (cyclical and monumental) are traditionally linked to female subjectivity in so far as the latter is thought of as necessarily maternal should not make us forget that this repetition and this eternity are found to be the fundamental, if not the sole, conceptions of time in numerous civilizations and experiences, particularly mystical ones.[8] The fact that certain currents of modern feminism recognize themselves here does not render them fundamentally incompatible with 'masculine' values.

In return, female subjectivity as it gives itself up to intuition becomes a problem with respect to a certain conception of time: time as project, teleology, linear and prospective unfolding: time as departure, progression and arrival – in other words, the time of history. It has already been abundantly demonstrated that this kind of temporality is inherent in the logical and ontological values of any given civilization, that this temporality renders explicit a rupture, an expectation or an anguish which other temporalities work to conceal. It might also be added that this linear time is that of language considered as the enunciation of sentences (noun + verb; topic–comment; beginning–ending), and that this time rests on its own stumbling block, which is also the stumbling block of that enunciation – death. A psychoanalyst would call this 'obsessional time', recognizing in the mastery of time the true structure of the slave. The hysteric (either male or female) who suffers from reminiscences would, rather, recognize his or her self in the anterior temporal modalities: cyclical or monumental. This antinomy, one perhaps embedded in psychic structures, becomes, none the less, within a given civilization, an antinomy among social groups and ideologies in which the radical positions of certain feminists would rejoin the discourse of marginal groups of spiritual or mystical inspiration and, strangely enough, rejoin recent scientific preoccupations. Is it not true that the problematic of a time indissociable from space, of a space-time in infinite expansion, or rhythmed by accidents or catastrophes, preoccupies both space science and genetics? And, at another level, is it not true that the contemporary media revolution, which is manifest in the storage and reproduction of information, implies an idea of time as frozen or exploding according to the vagaries of demand, returning to its source but uncontrollable, utterly bypassing its subject and leaving only two preoccupations to those who approve of it: Who is to have power over the origin (the programming) and over the end (the use)?

It is for two precise reasons, within the framework of this article, that I have allowed myself this rapid excursion into a problematic of unheard-of complexity. The reader will undoubtedly have been struck by a fluctuation in the term of reference: mother, woman, hysteric . . . I think that the apparent coherence which the term 'woman' assumes in contemporary ideology, apart from its 'mass' or 'shock' effect for activist purposes, essentially has the negative effect of effacing the differences among the diverse functions or structures which operate beneath this word. Indeed, the time has perhaps come to emphasize the multiplicity of female expressions and preoccupations so that from the intersection of these differences there might arise, more precisely, less commercially and more truthfully, the real *fundamental difference* between the two sexes: a difference that feminism has had the enormous merit of rendering painful, that is, productive of surprises and of symbolic life in a civilization which, outside the stock exchange and wars, is bored to death.

It is obvious, moreover, that one cannot speak of Europe or of 'women in Europe' without suggesting the time in which this socio-cultural distribution is situated. If it is true that a female sensibility emerged a century ago, the chances are great that by introducing *its own* notion of time, this sensibility is not in agreement with the idea of an 'eternal Europe' and perhaps not even with that of a 'modern Europe'. Rather, through and with the European past and present, as through and with the ensemble of 'Europe', which is the repository of memory, this sensibility seeks its own trans-European temporality. There are, in any case, three attitudes on the part of European feminist movements towards this conception of linear temporality, which is readily labelled masculine and which is at once both civilizational and obsessional.

TWO GENERATIONS

In its beginnings, the women's movement, as the struggle of suffragists and of existential feminists, aspired to gain a place in linear time as the time of project and history. In this sense, the movement, while immediately universalist, is also deeply rooted in the socio-political life of nations. The political demands of women; the struggles for equal pay for equal work, for taking power in social institutions on an equal footing with men; the rejection, when necessary, of the attributes traditionally considered feminine or maternal in so far as they are deemed incompatible with insertion in that history – all are part of the *logic of identification*[9] with certain values: not with the ideological (these are combated, and rightly so, as reactionary) but, rather, with the logical and ontological values of a rationality dominant in the nation-state. Here it is unnecessary to enumerate the benefits which this logic of identification and the ensuing struggle have achieved and continue to achieve for women (abortion, contraception, equal pay, professional recognition, etc.); these have already had or will soon have effects even more important than those of the Industrial Revolution. Universalist in its approach, this current in feminism *globalizes* the problems of women of different milieux, ages, civilizations or simply of varying psychic structures, under the label 'Universal Woman'. A consideration of *generations* of women can only be conceived of in this global way as a succession, as a progression in the accomplishment of the initial programme mapped out by its founders.

In a second phase, linked, on the one hand, to the younger women who came to feminism after May 1968 and, on the other, to women who had an aesthetic or psychoanalytic experience, linear temporality has been almost totally refused, and as a consequence there has arisen an exacerbated distrust of the entire political dimension. If it is true that this more recent current of feminism refers to its predecessors and that the struggle for socio-cultural recognition of women is necessarily its main concern, this current seems to think of itself as belonging to another generation – qualitatively different from the first one – in its conception of its own identity and, consequently, of temporality as such. Essentially interested in the specificity of female psychology and its symbolic real-izations, these women seek to give a language to the intra-subjective and corporeal experiences left mute by culture in the past. Either as artists or writers, they have undertaken a veritable exploration of the *dynamic of signs*, an exploration which relates this tendency, at least at the level of its aspirations, to all major projects of aesthetic and religious upheaval. Ascribing this experience to a new generation does not only mean that other, more subtle problems have been added to the demands for socio-political identification made in the beginning. It also means that, by demanding recognition of an irreducible identity, without equal in the opposite sex and, as such, exploded, plural, fluid, in a certain way non-identical, this feminism situates itself outside the linear time of identities which communicate through projection and revindication. Such a femi-nism rejoins, on the one hand, the archaic (mythical) memory and, on the other, the cyclical or monumental temporality of marginal movements. It is certainly not by chance that the European and trans-European problematic has been poised as such at the same time as this new phase of feminism.

Finally, it is the mixture of the two attitudes – *insertion* into history and the radical *refusal* of the subjective limitations imposed by this history's time on an experiment carried out in the name of the irreducible difference – that seems to have broken loose over the past few years in European feminist movements, particularly in France and in Italy.

If we accept this meaning of the expression 'a new generation of women', two kinds of questions might then be posed. What socio-political processes or events have provoked this mutation? What are its problems: its contributions as well as dangers?

SOCIALISM AND FREUDIANISM

One could hypothesize that if this new generation of women shows itself to be more diffuse and perhaps less conscious in the United States and more massive in Western Europe, this is because of a veritable split in social relations and mentalities, a split produced by socialism and Freudianism. I mean by *socialism* that egalitarian doctrine which is increasingly broadly disseminated and accepted as based on common sense, as well as that social practice adopted by governments and political parties in democratic regimes which are forced to extend the zone of egalitarianism to include the distribution of goods as well as access to culture. By *Freudianism* I mean that lever, inside this egalitarian and socializing field, which once again poses the question of sexual difference and of the difference among subjects who themselves are not reducible one to the other.

Western socialism, shaken in its very beginnings by the egalitarian or differential demands of its women (e.g. Flora Tristan), quickly got rid of those women who aspired to recognition of a specificity of the female role in society and culture, only retaining from them, in the egalitarian and universalistic spirit of Enlightenment Humanism, the idea of a necessary identification between the two sexes as the only and unique means for liberating the 'second sex'. I shall not develop here the fact that this 'ideal' is far from being applied in practice by these socialist-inspired movements and parties and that it was in part from the revolt against this situation that the new generation of women in Western Europe was born after May 1968. Let us just say that in theory, and as put into practice in Eastern Europe, socialist ideology, based on a conception of the human being as determined by its place in *production* and the *relations of production*, did not take into consideration this same human being according to its place in *reproduction*, on the one hand, or in the *symbolic order*, on the other. Consequently, the specific character of women could only appear as non-essential or even non-existent to the totalizing and even totalitarian spirit of this ideology.[10] We begin to see that this same egalitarian and in fact censuring treatment has been imposed, from Enlightenment Humanism through socialism, on religious specificities and, in particular, on Jews.[11]

What has been achieved by this attitude remains none the less of capital importance for women, and I shall take as an example the change in the destiny of women in the socialist countries of Eastern Europe. It could be said, with only slight exaggeration, that the demands of the suffragists and existential feminists have, to a great extent, been met in these countries, since three of the main egalitarian demands of early feminism have been or are now being implemented despite vagaries and blunders: economic, political and professional equality. The fourth, sexual equality, which implies permissiveness in sexual relations (including homosexual relations), abortions and contraception, remains stricken by taboo in Marxian ethics as well as for reasons of state. It is, then, this fourth equality which is the problem and which therefore appears *essential* in the struggle of a new generation. But simultaneously and as a consequence of these socialist accomplishments – which are in fact a total deception – the struggle is no longer concerned with the quest for equality but, rather, with difference and specificity. It is precisely at this point that the new generation encounters what might be called the *symbolic* question.[12] Sexual difference – which is at once biological, physiological and relative to reproduction – is translated by and translates a difference in the relationship of subjects to the symbolic contract which *is* the social contract: a difference, then, in the relationship to power, language and meaning. The sharpest and most subtle point of feminist subversion brought about by the new generation will henceforth be situated on the terrain of the inseparable conjunction of the sexual and the symbolic, in order to try to discover, first, the specificity of the female, and then, in the end, that of each individual woman.

A certain saturation of socialist ideology, a certain exhaustion of its potential as a programme for a new social contract (it is obvious that the effective realization of this programme is far from being accomplished, and I am here treating only its system of thought) makes way for . . . Freudianism. I am, of course, aware that this term and this practice are somewhat shocking to the American intellectual consciousness (which rightly reacts to a muddled and normatizing form of psychoanalysis) and, above all, to the feminist consciousness. To restrict my remarks to the latter: Is it not true that Freud has been seen only as a denigrator or even an exploiter of women? as an irritating phallocrat in a Vienna which was at once puritan and decadent – a man who fantasized women as sub-men, castrated men?

CASTRATED AND/OR SUBJECT TO LANGUAGE

Before going beyond Freud to propose a more just or more modern vision of women, let us try, first, to understand his notion of castration. It is, first of all, a question of an *anguish* or *fear* of castration, or of correlative penis *envy*; a question, therefore, of *imaginary* formations readily perceivable in the *discourse* of neurotics of both sexes, men and women. But, above all, a careful reading of Freud, going beyond his biologism and his mechanism, both characteristic of his time, brings out two things. First, as presupposition for the 'primal scene', the castration fantasy and its correlative (penis envy) are hypotheses, a priori suppositions intrinsic to the theory itself, in the sense that these are not the ideological fantasies of their inventor but, rather, logical necessities to be placed at the 'origin' in order to explain what unceasingly functions in neurotic discourse. In

JULIA KRISTEVA

other words, neurotic discourse in man and woman, can only be understood in terms of its own logic when its fundamental causes are admitted
as the fantasies of the primal scene and castration, even if (as may be the
case) nothing renders them present in reality itself. Stated in still other
terms, the reality of castration is no more real than the hypothesis of an
explosion which, according to modern astrophysics, is at the origin of the
universe: nothing proves it, in a sense it is an article of faith, the only
difference being that numerous phenomena of life in this 'big-bang'
universe are explicable only through this initial hypothesis. But one is
infinitely more jolted when this kind of intellectual method concerns
inanimate matter than when it is applied to our own subjectivity and
thus, perhaps, to the fundamental mechanism of our epistemophilic
thought.

Moreover, certain texts written by Freud (*The Interpretation of
Dreams*, but especially those of the second topology, in particular the
Metapsychology) and their recent extensions (notably by Lacan),[13] imply
that castration is, in sum, the imaginary construction of a radical operation which constitutes the symbolic field and all beings inscribed therein.
This operation constitutes signs and syntax; that is, language, as a *separation* from a presumed state of nature, of pleasure fused with nature so
that the introduction of an articulated network of differences, which refers
to objects henceforth and only in this way separated from a subject, may
constitute *meaning*. This logical operation of separation (confirmed by all
psycho-linguistic and child psychology) which preconditions the binding
of language which is already syntactical, is therefore the common destiny
of the two sexes, men and women. That certain biofamilial conditions
and relationships cause women (and notably hysterics) to deny this
separation and the language which ensues from it, whereas men (notably
obsessionals) magnify both and, terrified, attempt to master them – this
is what Freud's discovery has to tell us on this issue.

The analytic situation indeed shows that it is the penis which,
becoming the major referent in this operation of separation, gives full
meaning to the *lack* or to the *desire* which constitutes the subject during
his or her insertion into the order of language. I should only like to indicate here that, in order for this operation constitutive of the symbolic and
the social to appear in its full truth and for it to be understood by both
sexes, it would be just to emphasize its extension to all that is privation
of fulfilment and of totality; exclusion of a pleasing, natural and sound
state: in short, the break indispensable to the advent of the symbolic.

It can now be seen how women, starting with this theoretical apparatus, might try to understand their sexual and symbolic difference in the
framework of social, cultural and professional realization, in order to try,
by seeing their position therein, either to fulfil their own experience to a
maximum or – but always starting from this point – to go further and
call into question the very apparatus itself.

LIVING THE SACRIFICE

In any case, and for women in Europe today, whether or not they are conscious of the various mutations (socialist and Freudian) which have produced or simply accompanied their coming into their own, the urgent question on our agenda might be formulated as follows: *What can be our place in the symbolic contract?* If the social contract, far from being that of equal men, is based on an essentially sacrificial relationship of separation and articulation of differences which in this way produces communicable meaning, what is our place in this order of sacrifice and/or of language? No longer wishing to be excluded or no longer content with the function which has always been demanded of us (to maintain, arrange and perpetuate this socio-symbolic contract as mothers, wives, nurses, doctors, teachers . . .), how can we reveal our place, first as it is bequeathed to us by tradition, and then as we want to transform it?

It is difficult to evaluate what in the relationship of women to the symbolic as it reveals itself now arises from a socio-historical conjuncture (patriarchal ideology, whether Christian, humanist, socialist or so forth), and what arises from a structure. We can speak only about a structure observed in a socio-historical context, which is that of Christian, Western civilization and its lay ramifications. In this sense of psycho-symbolic structure, women, 'we' (is it necessary to recall the warnings we issued at the beginning of this article concerning the totalizing use of this plural?) seem to feel that they are the casualties, that they have been left out of the socio-symbolic contract, of language as the fundamental social bond. They find no affect there, no more than they find the fluid and infinitesimal significations of their relationships with the nature of their own bodies, that of the child, another woman or a man. This frustration, which to a certain extent belongs to men also, is being voiced today principally by women, to the point of becoming the essence of the new feminist ideology. A therefore difficult, if not impossible, identification with the sacrificial logic of separation and syntactical sequence at the foundation of language and the social code leads to the rejection of the symbolic – lived as the rejection of the paternal function and ultimately generating psychoses.

But this limit, rarely reached as such, produces two types of counter-investment of what we have termed the socio-symbolic contract. On the one hand, there are attempts to take hold of this contract, to possess it in order to enjoy it as such or to subvert it. How? The answer remains difficult to formulate (since, precisely, any formulation is deemed frustrating, mutilating, sacrificial) or else is in fact formulated using stereotypes taken from extremist and often deadly ideologies. On the other hand, another attitude is more lucid from the beginning, more self-analytical which – without refusing or sidestepping this socio-symbolic order – consists in trying to explore the constitution and functioning of this contract, starting less from the knowledge accumulated about it (anthropology, psychoanalysis, linguistics) than from the very personal affect experienced when facing it as subject and as a woman. This leads to the active research,[14] still rare, undoubtedly hesitant but always dissident, being carried out by women in the human sciences; particularly those attempts, in the wake of contemporary art, to break the code, to shatter language, to find a specific discourse closer to the body and emotions, to the unnameable repressed by the social contract. I am not speaking here of a 'woman's language', whose (at least syntactical) existence is highly problematical and whose apparent lexical specificity is perhaps more the product of a social marginality than of a sexual–symbolic difference.[15]

Nor am I speaking of the aesthetic quality of productions by women, most of which – with a few exceptions (but has this not always been the case with both sexes?) – are a reiteration of a more or less euphoric or depressed romanticism and always an explosion of an ego lacking narcissistic gratification.[16] What I should like to retain, none the less, as a mark of collective aspiration, as an undoubtedly vague and unimplemented intention, but one which is intense and which has been deeply revealing these past few years, is this: The new generation of women is showing that its major social concern has become the socio-symbolic contract as a sacrificial contract. If anthropologists and psychologists, for at least a century, have not stopped insisting on this in their attention to 'savage thought', wars, the discourse of dreams or writers, women are today affirming – and we consequently face a mass phenomenon – that they are forced to experience this sacrificial contract against their will.[17] Based on this, they are attempting a revolt which they see as a resurrection but which society as a whole understands as murder. This attempt can lead us to a not less and sometimes more deadly violence. Or to a cultural innovation. Probably to both at once. But that is precisely where the stakes are, and they are of epochal significance.

THE TERROR OF POWER OR THE POWER OF TERRORISM

First in socialist countries (such as the USSR and China) and increasingly in Western democracies, under pressure from feminist movements, women are being promoted to leadership positions in government, industry and culture. Inequalities, devalorizations, underestimations, even persecution of women at this level continue to hold sway in vain. The struggle against them is a struggle against archaisms. The cause has none the less been understood, the principle has been accepted.[18] What remains is to break down the resistance to change. In this sense, this struggle, while still one of the main concerns of the new generation, is not, strictly speaking, *its* problem. In relationship to *power*, its problem might rather be summarized as follows: What happens when, on the contrary, they refuse power and create a parallel society, a counter-power which then takes on aspects ranging from a club of ideas to a group of terrorist commandos?

The assumption by women of executive, industrial and cultural power has not, up to the present time, radically changed the nature of this power. This can be clearly seen in the East, where women promoted to decision-making positions suddenly obtain the economic as well as the narcissistic advantages refused them for thousands of years and become the pillars of the existing governments, guardians of the status quo, the most zealous protectors of the established order.[19] This identification by women with the very power structures previously considered as frustrating, oppressive or inaccessible has often been used in modern times by totalitarian regimes: the German National Socialists and the Chilean junta are examples of this.[20] The fact that this is a paranoid type of counter-investment in an initially denied symbolic order can perhaps explain this troubling phenomenon; but an explanation does not prevent its massive propagation around the globe, perhaps in less dramatic forms than the totalitarian ones mentioned above, but all moving towards levelling, stabilization, conformism, at the cost of crushing exceptions, experiments, chance occurrences.

Some will regret that the rise of a libertarian movement such as feminism ends, in some of its aspects, in the consolidation of conformism; others will rejoice and profit from this fact. Electoral campaigns, the very life of political parties, continue to bet on this latter tendency. Experience proves that too quickly even the protest or innovative initiatives on the part of women inhaled by power systems (when they do not submit to them right away) are soon credited to the system's account; and that the long-awaited democratization of institutions as a result of the entry of women most often comes down to fabricating a few 'chiefs' among them. The difficulty presented by this logic of integrating the second sex into a value-system experienced as foreign and therefore counter-invested is how to avoid the centralization of power, how to detach women from it and how then to proceed, through their critical, differential and autonomous interventions, to render decision-making institutions more flexible.

Then there are the more radical feminist currents which, refusing homologation to any role of identification with existing power no matter what the power may be, make of the second sex a *counter-society*. A 'female society' is then constituted as a sort of alter ego of the official society, in which all real or fantasized possibilities for *jouissance* take refuge. Against the socio-symbolic contract, both sacrificial and frustrating, this counter-society is imagined as harmonious, without prohibitions, free and fulfilling. In our modern societies which have no hereafter or, at least, which are caught up in a transcendency either reduced to this side of the world (protestantism) or crumbling (catholicism and its current challenges), the counter-society remains the only refuge for fulfilment since it is precisely an a-topia, a place outside the law, utopia's floodgate.

As with any society, the counter-society is based on the expulsion of an excluded element, a scapegoat charged with the evil of which the community duly constituted can then purge itself;[21] a purge which will finally exonerate that community of any future criticism. Modern protest movements have often reiterated this logic, locating the guilty one – in order to fend off criticism – in the foreign, in capital alone, in the other religion, in the other sex. Does not feminism become a kind of inverted sexism when this logic is followed to its conclusion? The various forms of marginalism – according to sex, age, religion or ideology – represent in the modern world this refuge for *jouissance*, a sort of laicized transcendence. But with women, and in so far as the number of those feeling concerned by this problem has increased, although in less spectacular forms than a few years ago, the problem of the counter-society is becoming massive: It occupies no more and no less than 'half of the sky'.

It has, therefore, become clear, because of the particular radicalization of the second generation, that these protest movements, including feminism, are not 'initially libertarian' movements which only later, through internal deviations or external chance manipulations, fall back into the old ruts of the initially combated archetypes. Rather, the very logic of counter-power and of counter-society necessarily generates, by its very structure, its essence as a simulacrum of the combated society or of power. In this sense and from a viewpoint undoubtedly too Hegelian, modern feminism has only been but a moment in the interminable process of coming to consciousness about the implacable violence (separation, castration, etc.) which constitutes any symbolic contract.

Thus the identification with power in order to consolidate it or the constitution of a fetishist counter-power – restorer of the crises of the self and provider of a *jouissance* which is always already a transgression – seem to be the two social forms which the face-off between the new generation of women and the social contract can take. That one also finds the problem of terrorism there is structurally related.

The large number of women in terrorist groups (Palestinian commandos, the Baader–Meinhoff Gang, Red Brigades, etc.) has already been pointed out, either violently or prudently according to the source of information. The exploitation of women is still too great and the traditional prejudices against them too violent for one to be able to envision this phenomenon with sufficient distance. It can, however, be said from now on that this is the inevitable product of what we have called a denial of the socio-symbolic contract and its counter-investment as the only means of self-defence in the struggle to safeguard an identity. This paranoid-type mechanism is at the base of any political involvement. It may produce different civilizing attitudes in the sense that these attitudes allow a more or less flexible reabsorption of violence and death. But when a subject is too brutally excluded from this socio-symbolic stratum; when, for example, a woman feels her affective life as a woman or her condition as a social being too brutally ignored by existing discourse or power (from her family to social institutions); she may, by counter-investing the violence she has endured, make of herself a 'possessed' agent of this violence in order to combat what was experienced as frustration – with arms which may seem disproportional, but which are not so in comparison with the subjective or more precisely narcissistic suffering from which they originate. Necessarily opposed to the bourgeois democratic regimes in power, this terrorist violence offers as a programme of liberation an order which is even more oppressive, more sacrificial than those it combats. Strangely enough, it is not against totalitarian regimes that these terrorist groups with women participants unleash themselves but, rather, against liberal systems, whose essence is, of course, exploitative, but whose expanding democratic legality guarantees relative tolerance. Each time, the mobilization takes place in the name of a nation, of an oppressed group, of a human essence imagined as good and sound; in the name, then, of a kind of fantasy of archaic fulfilment which an arbitrary, abstract and thus even bad and ultimately discriminatory order has come to disrupt. While that order is accused of being oppressive, is it not actually being reproached with being too weak, with not measuring up to this pure and good, but henceforth lost, substance? Anthropology has shown that the social order is sacrificial, but sacrifice orders violence, binds it, tames it. Refusal of the social order exposes one to the risk that the so-called good substance, once it is unchained, will explode, without curbs, without law or right, to become an absolute arbitrariness.

Following the crisis of monotheism, the revolutions of the past two centuries, and more recently Fascism and Stalinism, have tragically set in action this logic of the oppressed goodwill which leads to massacres. Are women more apt than other social categories, notably the exploited classes, to invest in this implacable machine of terrorism? No categorical response, either positive or negative, can currently be given to this question. It must be pointed out, however, that since the dawn of feminism, and certainly before, the political activity of exceptional women, and thus in a certain sense of liberated women, has taken the form of murder, conspiracy and crime. Finally, there is also the connivance of the young girl with her mother, her greater difficulty than the boy in detaching herself from the mother in order to accede to the order of signs as invested by the absence and separation constitutive of the paternal function. A girl will never be able to re-establish this contact with her mother – a contact which the boy may possibly rediscover through his relationship with the opposite sex – except by becoming a mother herself, through a child or through a homosexuality which is in itself extremely difficult and judged as suspect by society; and, what is more, why and in the name of what dubious symbolic benefit would she want to make this detachment so as to conform to a symbolic system which remains foreign to her? In sum, all of these considerations – her eternal debt to the woman-mother – make a woman more vulnerable within the symbolic order, more fragile when she suffers within it, more virulent when she protects herself from it. If the archetype of the belief in a good and pure substance, that of utopias, is the belief in the omnipotence of an archaic, full, total englobing mother with no frustration, no separation, with no break-producing symbolism (with no castration, in other words), then it becomes evident that we will never be able to defuse the violences mobilized through the counter-investment necessary to carrying out this phantasm, unless one challenges precisely this myth of the archaic mother. It is in this way that we can understand the warnings against the recent invasion of the women's movements by paranoia,[22] as in Lacan's scandalous sentence 'There is no such thing as Woman'.[23] Indeed, she does *not* exist with a capital 'W', possessor of some mythical unity – a supreme power, on which is based the terror of power and terrorism as the desire for power. But what an unbelievable force for subversion in the modern world! And, at the same time, what playing with fire!

CREATURES AND CREATRESSES

The desire to be a mother, considered alienating and even reactionary by the preceding generation of feminists, has obviously not become a standard for the present generation. But we have seen in the past few years an increasing number of women who not only consider their maternity compatible with their professional life or their feminist involvement (certain improvements in the quality of life are also at the origin of this: an increase in the number of daycare centres and nursery schools, more active participation of men in child care and domestic life, etc.), but also find it indispensable to their discovery, not of the plenitude, but of the complexity of the female experience, with all that this complexity comprises in joy and pain. This tendency has its extreme: in the refusal of the paternal function by lesbian and single mothers can be seen one of the most violent forms taken by the rejection of the symbolic outlined above, as well as one of the most fervent divinizations of maternal power – all of which cannot help but trouble an entire legal and moral order without, however, proposing an alternative to it. Let us remember here that Hegel distinguished between female right (familial and religious) and male law (civil and political). If our societies know well the uses and abuses of male law, it must also be recognized that female right is designated, for the moment, by a blank. And if these practices of maternity, among others, were to be generalized, women themselves would be responsible for elaborating the appropriate legislation to check the violence to which, otherwise, both their children and men would be subject. But are they capable of doing so? This is one of the important questions that the new generation of women encounters, especially when the members of this new generation refuse to ask those questions seized by the same rage with which the dominant order originally victimized them.

Faced with this situation, it seems obvious – and feminist groups become more aware of this when they attempt to broaden their audience – that the refusal of maternity cannot be a mass policy and that the majority of women today see the possibility for fulfilment, if not entirely at least to a large degree, in bringing a child into the world. What does this desire for motherhood correspond to? This is one of the new questions for the new generation, a question the preceding generation had foreclosed. For want of an answer to this question, feminist ideology leaves the door open to the return of religion, whose discourse, tried and proved over thousands of years, provides the necessary ingredients for satisfying the anguish, the suffering and the hopes of mothers. If Freud's affirmation – that the desire for a child is the desire for a penis and, in this sense, a substitute for phallic and symbolic dominion – can be only partially accepted, what modern women have to say about this experience should none the less be listened to attentively. Pregnancy seems to be experienced as the radical ordeal of the splitting of the subject:[24] redoubling up of the body, separation and coexistence of the self and of an other, of nature and consciousness, of physiology and speech. This fundamental challenge to identity is then accompanied by a fantasy of totality – narcissistic completeness – a sort of instituted, socialized, natural psychosis. The arrival of the child, on the other hand, leads the mother into the labyrinths of an experience that, without the child, she would only rarely encounter: love for an other. Not for herself, nor for an identical being, and still less for another person with whom 'I' fuse (love or sexual passion). But the slow, difficult and delightful apprenticeship in attentiveness, gentleness, forgetting oneself. The ability to succeed in this path without masochism and without annihilating one's affective, intellectual and professional personality – such would seem to be the stakes to be won through guiltless maternity. It then becomes a creation in the strong sense of the term. For this moment, utopian?

On the other hand, it is in the aspiration towards artistic and, in particular, literary creation that woman's desire for affirmation now manifests itself. Why literature?

Is it because, faced with social norms, literature reveals a certain knowledge and sometimes the truth itself about an otherwise repressed, nocturnal, secret and unconscious universe? Because it thus redoubles the social contract by exposing the unsaid, the uncanny? And because it makes a game, a space of fantasy and pleasure, out of the abstract and frustrating order of social signs, the words of everyday communication? Flaubert said, 'Madame Bovary, c'est moi'. Today many women imagine, 'Flaubert, c'est moi'. This identification with the potency of the imaginary is not only an identification, an imaginary potency (a fetish, a belief in the maternal penis maintained at all costs), as a far too normative view of the social and symbolic relationship would have it. This identification also bears witness to women's desire to lift the weight of what is sacrificial in the social contract from their shoulders, to nourish our societies with a more flexible and free discourse, one able to name what has thus far never been an object of circulation in the community: the enigmas of the body, the dreams, secret joys, shames, hatreds of the second sex.

It is understandable from this that women's writing has lately attracted the maximum attention of both 'specialists' and the media.[25] The pitfalls encountered along the way, however, are not to be minimized: for example, does one not read there a relentless belittling of male writers whose books, nevertheless, often serve as 'models' for countless productions by women? Thanks to the feminist label, does one not sell numerous works whose naïve whining or market-place romanticism would otherwise have been rejected as anachronistic? And does one not find the pen of many a female writer being devoted to phantasmic attacks against Language and Sign as the ultimate supports of phallocratic power, in the name of a semi-aphonic corporality whose truth can only be found in that which is 'gestural' or 'tonal'?

And yet, no matter how dubious the results of these recent productions by women, the symptom is there – women are writing, and the air is heavy with expectation: What will they write that is new?

IN THE NAME OF THE FATHER, THE SON ... AND THE WOMAN?

These few elements of the manifestations by the new generation of women in Europe seem to me to demonstrate that, beyond the socio-political level where it is generally inscribed (or inscribes itself), the women's movement – in its present stage, less aggressive but more artful – is situated within the very framework of the religious crisis of our civilization.

I call 'religion' this phantasmic necessity on the part of speaking beings to provide themselves with a *representation* (animal, female, male, parental, etc.) in place of what constitutes them as such, in other words, symbolization – the double articulation and syntactic sequence of language, as well as its preconditions or substitutes (thoughts, affects, etc.). The elements of the current practice of feminism that we have just brought to light seem precisely to constitute such a representation which makes up for the frustrations imposed on women by the anterior code (Christianity or its lay humanist variant). The fact that this new ideology has affinities, often revindicated by its creators, with so-called matriarchal beliefs (in other words, those beliefs characterizing matrilinear societies) should not overshadow its radical novelty. This ideology seems to me to be part of the broader anti-sacrificial current which is animating our culture and which, in its protest against the constraints of the socio-symbolic contract, is no less exposed to the risks of violence and terrorism. At this level of radicalism, it is the very principle of sociality which is challenged.

Certain contemporary thinkers consider, as is well known, that modernity is characterized as the first epoch in human history in which human beings attempt to live without religion. In its present form, is not feminism in the process of becoming one?

Or is it, on the contrary and as avant-garde feminists hope, that having started with the idea of difference, feminism will be able to break free of its belief in Woman, Her power, Her writing, so as to channel this demand for difference into each and every element of the female whole, and, finally, to bring out the singularity of each woman, and beyond this, her multiplicities, her plural languages, beyond the horizon, beyond sight, beyond faith itself?

A factor for ultimate mobilization? Or a factor for analysis?

Imaginary support in a technocratic era where all narcissism is frustrated? Or instruments fitted to these times in which the cosmos, atoms and cells – our true contemporaries – call for the constitution of a fluid and free subjectivity?

The question has been posed. Is to pose it already to answer it?

ANOTHER GENERATION IS ANOTHER SPACE

If the preceding can be *said* – the question whether all this is *true* belongs to a different register – it is undoubtedly because it is now possible to gain some distance on these two preceding generations of women. This implies, of course, that a *third* generation is now forming, at least in Europe. I am not speaking of a new group of young women (though its importance should not be underestimated) or of another 'mass feminist movement' taking the torch passed on from the second generation. My usage of the word 'generation' implies less a chronology than a *signifying space*, a both corporeal and desiring mental space. So it can be argued that as of now a third attitude is possible, thus a third generation, which does not exclude – quite to the contrary – the *parallel* existence of all three in the same historical time, or even that they be interwoven one with the other.

In this third attitude, which I strongly advocate – which I imagine? – the very dichotomy man/woman as an opposition between two rival entities may be understood as belonging to *metaphysics*. What can 'identity', even 'sexual identity', mean in a new theoretical and scientific space where the very notion of identity is challenged?[26] I am not simply suggesting a very hypothetical bisexuality which, even if it existed, would only, in fact, be the aspiration towards the totality of one of the sexes and thus an effacing of difference. What I mean is, first of all, the demassification of the problematic of *difference*, which would imply, in a first phase, an apparent de-dramatization of the 'fight to the death' between rival groups and thus between the sexes. And this not in the name of some reconciliation – feminism has at least had the merit of showing what is irreducible and even deadly in the social contract – but in order that the struggle, the implacable difference, the violence be conceived in the very place where it operates with the maximum intransigence, in other words, in personal and sexual identity itself, so as to make it disintegrate in its very nucleus.

It necessarily follows that this involves risks not only for what we understand today as 'personal equilibrium' but also for social equilibrium itself, made up as it now is of the counterbalancing of aggressive and murderous forces massed in social, national, religious and political groups. But is it not the insupportable situation of tension and explosive risk that the existing 'equilibrium' presupposes which leads some of those who suffer from it to divest it of its economy, to detach themselves from it and to seek another means of regulating difference?

To restrict myself here to a personal level, as related to the question of women, I see arising, under the cover of a relative indifference towards the militance of the first and second generations, an attitude of retreat from sexism (male as well as female) and, gradually, from any kind of anthropomorphism. The fact that this might quickly become another form of spiritualism turning its back on social problems, or else a form of repression[27] ready to support all status quos, should not hide the radicalness of the process. This process could be summarized as an *interiorization of the founding separation of the socio-symbolic contract*, as an introduction of its cutting edge into the very interior of every identity whether subjective, sexual, ideological, or so forth. This in such a way that the habitual and increasingly explicit attempt to fabricate a scapegoat victim as foundress of a society or a counter-society may be replaced by the analysis of the potentialities of *victim/executioner* which characterize each identity, each subject, each sex.

What discourse, if not that of a religion, would be able to support this adventure which surfaces as a real possibility, after both the achievements and the impasses of the present ideological reworkings, in which feminism has participated? It seems to me that the role of what is usually called 'aesthetic practices' must increase not only to counter-balance the storage and uniformity of information by present-day mass media, databank systems and, in particular, modern communications technology, but also to demystify the identity of the symbolic bond itself, to demystify, therefore, the *community* of language as a universal and unifying tool, one which totalizes and equalizes. In order to bring out – along with the *singularity* of each person and, even more, along with the multiplicity of every person's possible identifications (with atoms, e.g. stretching from the family to the stars) – *the relativity of his/her symbolic as well as biological existence*, according to the variation in his/her specific symbolic capacities. And in order to emphasize the *responsibility* which all will immediately face of putting this fluidity into play against the threats of death which are unavoidable whenever an inside and an outside, a self and an other, one group and another, are constituted. At this level of interiorization with its social as well as individual stakes, what I have called 'aesthetic practices' are undoubtedly nothing other than the modern reply to the eternal question of morality. At least, this is how we might understand an ethics which, conscious of the fact that its order is sacrificial, reserves part of the burden for each of its adherents, therefore declaring them guilty while immediately affording them the possibility for *jouissance*, for various productions, for a life made up of both challenges and differences.

Spinoza's question can be taken up again here: Are women subject to ethics? If not to that ethics defined by classical philosophy – in relationship to which the ups and downs of feminist generations seem dangerously precarious – are women not already participating in the rapid dismantling that our age is experiencing at various levels (from wars to drugs to artificial insemination) and which poses the *demand* for a new ethics? The answer to Spinoza's question can be affirmative only at the cost of considering feminism as but a *moment* in the thought of that anthropomorphic identity which currently blocks the horizon of the discursive and scientific adventure of our species.

NOTES

1   Sigmund Freud and Carl G. Jung, *Correspondance* (Paris: Gallimard, 1975), vol. I, p. 87.

2   R. Spitz, *La Première Année de la vie de l'enfant* [First year of life: a psychoanalytic study of normal and deviant development of object relations] (Paris: PUF, 1958); D. Winnicott, *Jeu et réalité* [Playing and reality] (Paris: Gallimard, 1975); Julia Kristeva, 'Noms de lieu', in *Polylogue* (Paris: Seuil, 1977), translated as 'Place names' in Julia Kristeva, *Desire in Language: a Semiotic Approach to Literature and Art*, ed. Leon S. Roudiez, tr. Thomas Gora, Alice Jardine and Leon Roudiez (New York: Columbia University Press, 1980).

3   Plato, *Timeus* 52: 'Indefinitely a place; it cannot be destroyed, but provides a ground for all that can come into being; itself being perceptible, outside of all sensation, by means of a sort of bastard reasoning; barely assuming credibility, it is precisely that which makes us dream when we perceive it, and affirm that all that exists must be somewhere, in a determined place . . .' (author's translation).

4   As most readers of recent French theory in translation know, *le féminin* does not have the same pejorative connotations it has come to have in English. It is a term used to speak about women in general, but, as used most often in this article, it probably comes closest to our 'female' as defined

by Elaine Showalter in *A Literature of Their Own* (Princeton, NJ: Princeton University Press, 1977). I have therefore used either 'women' or 'female' according to the context. – AJ (trans.).

5 I have retained *jouissance* – that word for pleasure which defies translation – as it is rapidly becoming a 'believable neologism' in English (see the glossary in *Desire in Language*). – AJ (trans.).

6 This particular mythology has important implications – equal only to those of the Oedipal myth – for current French thought. – AJ (trans.).

7 See Julia Kristeva, 'Stabat Mater', first published as 'Héréthique de l'amour', *Tel Quel*, 74 (1977), pp. 30–49.

8 See H. C. Puech, *La Gnose et le temps* (Paris: Gallimard, 1977).

9 The term 'identification' belongs to a wide semantic field ranging from everyday language to philosophy and psychoanalysis. While Kristeva is certainly referring in principle to its elaboration in Freudian and Lacanian psychoanalysis, it can be understood here as a logic, in its most general sense (see the entry on 'identification' in Jean Laplanche and J. B. Pontalis, *Vocabulaire de la psychanalyse* [The language of psychoanalysis], Paris: Presses Universitaires de France, 1967; rev. edn, 1976). – AJ (trans.).

10 See D. Desanti, 'L'autre sexe des bolcheviks', *Tel Quel*, 76 (1978); Julia Kristeva, *Des Chinoises* (Paris: des femmes, 1975), translated as *On Chinese Women*, tr. Anita Barrows (London: Marion Boyars, 1977).

11 See Arthur Hertzberg, *The French Enlightenment and the Jews* (New York: Columbia University Press, 1968); *Les Juifs et la révolution française*, ed. B. Blumenkranz and A. Seboul (Paris: Editions Privat, 1976).

12 Here, 'symbolic' is being more strictly used in terms of that function defined by Kristeva in opposition to the semiotic: 'it involves the thetic phase, the identification of subject and its distinction from objects, and the establishment of a sign system'. – AJ. (trans.).

13 See, in general, Jacques Lacan, *Ecrits* (Paris: Seuil, 1966) and in particular, Jacques Lacan, *Le Séminaire XX: Encore* (Paris: Seuil, 1975). – AJ (trans.).

14 This work is periodically published in various academic women's journals, one of the most prestigious being *Signs: Journal of Women in Culture and Society*, University of Chicago Press. Also of note are the special issues: 'Ecriture, féminité, féminisme', *La Revue des sciences humaines* (Lille III), no. 4 (1977); and 'Les femmes et la philosophie', *Le Doctrinal de sapience* (Editions Solin), no. 3 (1977).

15 See linguistic research on 'female language': Robin Lakoff, *Language and Women's Place* (New York: Harper & Row, 1974); Mary R. Key, *Male/Female Language* (Metuchen, NJ: Scarecrow Press, 1973); A. M. Houdebine, 'Les femmes et la langue', *Tel Quel*, 74 (1977), pp. 84–95. The contrast between these 'empirical' investigations of women's 'speech acts' and much of the research in France on the conceptual bases for a 'female language' must be emphasized here. It is somewhat helpful, if ultimately inaccurate, to think of the former as an 'external' study of language and the latter as an 'internal' exploration of the process of signification. For further contrast, see e.g. 'Part II: Contemporary Feminist Thought in France: Translating Difference', in *The Future of Difference*, ed. Hester Eisenstein and Alice Jardine (Boston: G. K. Hall, 1980); the 'Introductions' to *New French Feminisms*, ed. Elaine Marks and Isabelle de Courtivron (Amherst, Mass.: University of Massachusetts

Press, 1980); and for a very helpful overview of the problem of 'difference and language' in France, see Stephen Heath, 'Difference', in *Screen*, 19 no. 3 (autumn 1978), pp. 51–112. – AJ (trans.).

16 This is one of the more explicit references to the mass marketing of 'écriture féminine' in Paris over the last ten years. – AJ (trans.).

17 The expression *à leur corps défendant* translates as 'against their will', but here the emphasis is on women's bodies: literally, 'against their bodies'. I have retained the former expression in English, partly because of its obvious intertextuality with Susan Brownmiller's *Against Our Will* (New York: Simon & Schuster, 1975). Women are increasingly describing their experience of the violence of the symbolic contract as a form of rape. – AJ (trans.).

18 Many women in the West who are once again finding all doors closed to them above a certain level of employment, especially in the current economic chaos, may find this statement, even qualified, troubling, to say the least. It is accurate, however, *in principle*: whether that of infinite capitalist recuperation or increasing socialist expansion – within both economies, our integration functions as a kind of *operative* illusion. – AJ (trans.).

19 See *Des Chinoises*.

20 See M. A. Macciocchi, *Eléments pour une analyse du fascisme* (Paris: 10/18, 1976); Michèle Mattelart, 'Le coup d'état au féminin', *Les Temps Modernes* (January 1975).

21 The principles of a 'sacrificial anthropology' are developed by René Girard in *La Violence et le sacré* [Violence and the sacred] (Paris: Grasset, 1972) and esp. in *Des choses cachées depuis la fondation du monde* (Paris: Grasset, 1978).

22 Cf. Micheline Enriquez, 'Fantasmes paranoiaques: différences des sexes, homosexualité, loi du père', *Topiques*, 13 (1974).

23 See Jacques Lacan, 'Dieu et la jouissance de la femme', in *Encore* (Paris: Seuil, 1975), pp. 61–71, esp. p. 68. This seminar has remained a primary critical and polemical focus for multiple tendencies in the French women's movement. For a brief discussion of the seminar in English, see Heath (n. 15 above). – AJ (trans.).

24 The 'split subject' (from *Spaltung* as both 'splitting' and 'cleavage'), as used in Freudian psychoanalysis, here refers directly to Kristeva's 'subject in process/in question/on trial' as opposed to the unity of the transcendental ego. – AJ (trans.).

25 Again a reference to *écriture féminine* as generically labelled in France over the past few years and not to women's writing in general. – AJ (trans.).

26 See Seminar on *Identity* directed by Lévi-Strauss (Paris: Grasset & Fasquelle, 1977).

27 Repression (*le refoulement* or *Verdrängung*) as distinguished from the foreclosure (*la forclusion* or *Verwerfung*) evoked earlier in the article (see Laplanche and Pontalis). – AJ (trans.).

25

Gilles Deleuze
(b. 1925)

Although Gilles Deleuze has come to be chiefly associated with the 'post-structuralist' movement by anglophone readers of his work, he is a complex thinker who cannot be categorized so easily. In fact, much of his philosophical output has intrigued his French audience precisely because he has explored, in a highly original manner, such diverse philosophical paths as the thought of Spinoza, Hume, Kant, Bergson, Nietzsche, Freud and Marx. He was, to put it mildly, not exactly working in the Parisian mainstream of phenomenology, existentialism, or even budding structuralism in the 1950s and early 1960s.

A commitment that remains constant throughout Deleuze's work is the affirmation of philosophy as a 'critical enterprise of demystification'. He characterizes the thinking of traditional philosophy as 'sedentary', in that the uncritical acceptance of a 'first principle' (*archē*) categorizes and distributes entities far too rigidly. Such thinking privileges a philosophy of re-presentation and identity that forgets the gap, the difference, between particular manifestations or intuitions of the same concept. He acknowledges that Kant's *Transcendental Aesthetic* recognized the diversity of the sensible manifold, but suggests that Kant ultimately fell back on the *a priori* internal intuition of temporality to homogenize that diversity in a repetition of the same.

In other words, for Deleuze, what can be 'known' *a priori* about the conditions of all possible experience, can never satisfactorily account for the difference between conceptual intelligibility and sensory intuition. As an antidote to 'sedentary' thought, Deleuze proposes a 'nomadology' that resists the conceptual strait-jacket of identity thinking and extends the distributive range of attributes across an expanse of unified Being. Inspired by Nietzsche and Spinoza, Deleuze uses nomadic thought to maintain an anti-dialectical stance that refuses the Hegelian recuperation of negation and difference. Since thought is seen to be 'rhizomatic' rather than 'arboreal', the movement of differentiation and becoming is already imbued with its own positive trajectory.

In the wake of the upheavals of May 1968, Deleuze engaged in a project with Felix Guattari to develop a political analysis of desire (*Anti-Oedipus*) that presents a peculiar synthesis of Marx and Freud. By reconciling the Marxist opposition between production and ideology with the Freudian opposition between consciousness and desire, Deleuze and Guattari sought to introduce unconscious 'desire' as a productive feature of political economy. However, they also wished to point out that active and 'revolutionary' desire was always mingled with an opposing, 'reactive' desire for repression. In political and economic terms, 'paranoiac' investment has its own rewards under capitalism, in that the potential seduction of power, status and money encourages the repression of non-conforming, revolutionary desire. Thus, capitalism itself produces a norm of schizoid '*désirants*', desiring machines who acquiesce to their own slavery. A major target of this anti-Lacanian analysis was the alleged psychoanalytic 'priesthood' offering a 'mythical' Oedipal explanation of desire determined by lack, guilt and fear of castration confined to the family unit.

Deleuze's contributions to the discipline have generated much debate, and among some avid supporters, his philosophical project has almost acquired the status of a cult. Some of his works include *Empiricism and Subjectivity* (1953), *Nietzsche and Philosophy* (1962), *Kant's Critical Philosophy* (1963), *Difference and Repetition* (1968), *The Logic of Sense* (1969), *Spinoza* (1970), *Capitalism and Schizophrenia 1: Anti-Oedipus* (1972), *Capitalism and Schizophrenia 2: A Thousand Plateaus* (1980), *Cinema 1: The Movement Image* (1983) and *Cinema 2: The Time Image* (1985). Until his retirement in 1987, Deleuze was Professor of Philosophy at the University of Paris at Vincennes.

SELECT BIBLIOGRAPHY OF DELEUZE'S WORKS IN ENGLISH

Proust and Signs, London: Allen Lane, 1973.
Anti-Oedipus (with Guattari), New York: Viking, 1977.
Nietzsche and Philosophy, London: Athlone, 1983.
Kant's Critical Philosophy, Minneapolis: University of Minnesota Press, 1984.
Kafka: Toward a Minor Literature (with Guattari), Minneapolis: University of Minnesota Press, 1986.
Cinema 1: The Movement Image, London: Athlone, 1986.
A Thousand Plateaus (with Guattari), London: Athlone, 1988.
Foucault, London: Athlone, 1988.
Spinoza, Practical Philosophy, San Francisco: City Lights Books, 1988.
Cinema 2: The Time Image, London, Athlone, 1989.
The Logic of Sense, London: Athlone, 1989.

Introduction to *What is Philosophy?*

PERHAPS THE QUESTION 'What is philosophy?' can only be posed late in life, when old age has come, and with it the time to speak in concrete terms. It is a question one poses when one no longer has anything to ask for, but its consequences can be considerable. One was asking the question before, one never ceased asking it, but it was too artificial, too abstract; one expounded and dominated the question, more than being grabbed by it. There are cases in which old age bestows not an eternal youth, but on the contrary a sovereign freedom, a pure necessity where one enjoys a moment of grace between life and death, and where all the parts of the machine combine to dispatch into the future a trait that traverses the ages: Turner, Monet, Matisse. The elderly Turner acquired or conquered the right to lead painting down a deserted path from which there was no return, and that was no longer distinguishable from a final question. In the same way, in philosophy, Kant's *Critique of Judgment* is a work of old age, a wild work from which descendants will never cease to flow.

We cannot lay claim to such a status. The time has simply come for us to ask what philosophy is. And we have never ceased to do this in the past, and we already had the response, which has not varied: philosophy is the art of forming, inventing, and fabricating concepts. But it was not only necessary for the response to take note of the question; it also had to determine a time, an occasion, the circumstances, the landscapes and personae, the conditions and unknowns of the question. One had to be able to pose the question 'between friends' as a confidence or a trust, or else, faced with an enemy, as a challenge, and at the same time one had to reach that moment, between dog and wolf, when one mistrusts even the friend.

This is because concepts need conceptual personae that contribute to their definition. 'Friend' is one such persona, which is even said to attest to a Greek origin of philo-sophy: other civilizations had Wise Men, but the Greeks introduce these 'friends', who are not simply more modest wise men. It was the Greeks who confirmed the death of the Wise Man and replaced him with the philosophers, the friends of wisdom, those who search for wisdom, but do not formally possess it. Yet few thinkers have asked themselves what 'friend' means, even and especially the Greeks. Would 'friend' designate a certain competent intimacy, a kind of material affinity [*goût matériel*] or potentiality, like that of the carpenter with the wood: the good carpenter knows the potential of the wood, he is the friend of the wood? The question is an important one, since the friend, as it appears in philosophy, no longer designates either an extrinsic person,

From *Critical Inquiry* 17, Spring 1991.

an example, or an empirical circumstance, but rather a presence intrinsic to thought, a condition of possibility of thought itself – in short, a living category, a lived transcendental, a constitutive element of thought. And in fact, at the birth of philosophy, the Greeks made the friend submit to a power play [*coup de force*] that placed it in relation, no longer with another person, but with an Entity, an Objectivity, an Essence. This is what the oft-cited formula expresses, which must be translated, 'I am the friend of Peter, of Paul, or even of the philosopher Plato, but even more so, I am the friend of the True, of Wisdom, or of the Concept'. The philosopher knows a lot about concepts, and about the lack of concepts; he knows, in an instant, which are inviable, arbitrary, or inconsistent, and which, on the contrary, are well made and bear witness to a creation, even if it is a disturbing and dangerous one.

What does 'friend' mean when it becomes a conceptual persona, or a condition for the exercise of thought? Or even 'lover'; is it not rather the lover? And will not the friend reintroduce, within thought itself, a vital relation with the Other that one had believed excluded from pure thought? Or again, is it not a question of someone other than the friend or lover? For if the philosopher is the friend or lover of Wisdom, is it not because he lays a claim upon it, striving for it potentially rather than possessing it actually? Thus the friend would also be the claimant, and what he calls himself the friend of is the Thing on which the claim is made, but not the third party, who would become, on the contrary, a rival. Friendship would involve as much jealous distrust of the rival as it would amorous tension toward the object of desire. When friendship is turned toward essence, the two friends would be like the claimant and the rival (but who could distinguish them?). In this way, Greek philosophy would coincide with the formation of 'cities': relations of rivalry were promoted between and within cities, opposing claimants in all domains, in love, in the games, the tribunals, the magistratures, politics – and even in thought, which would find its condition, not only in the friend, but in the claimant and the rival (the dialectic that Plato defined by *amphisbētēsis*). A generalized athleticism. The friend, the lover, the claimant, and the rival are transcendental determinations which, for all that, do not lose their intense and animated existence, whether in a single persona or in several. And when, today, Maurice Blanchot, one of those rare thinkers to consider the meaning of the word 'friend' in *philosophy*, takes up this question internal to the conditions of thought as such, does he not again introduce new conceptual personae into the heart of the most pure Thought, personae that are now hardly Greek, but come from elsewhere, bringing in their wake new living relations raised to the status of *a priori* figures: a certain fatigue, a certain distress between friends that converts friendship itself to the thought of the concept, as an infinite sharing and patience. The list of conceptual personae is never closed, and for this reason plays an important role in the evolution or mutations of philosophy; their diversity must be understood without being reduced to the already complex unity of the philosopher.

The philosopher is the friend of the concept, he has the concept potentially. This means that philosophy is not a simple art of forming, inventing, or fabricating concepts, for concepts are not necessarily forms, discoveries, or products. Philosophy, more rigorously understood, is the discipline that consists of *creating concepts*. Would the friend then be the friend of his own creations? To create ever new concepts – this is the object of philosophy. It is because the concept must be created that it refers back to the philosopher as the one who has the concept potentially, or who has the potential and competence of the concept. One cannot object that creation is instead expressed through the sensible or through the arts, insofar as art brings spiritual entities into existence, and philosophical concepts are also 'sensibilia'. In fact, the sciences, arts, and philosophies are all equally creators, although it falls to philosophy alone to create concepts in the strict sense. Concepts do not wait for us readymade, like celestial bodies. There is no heaven for concepts. They must be invented, fabricated, or rather created, and would be nothing without the signature of those who create them. Nietzsche specified the task of philosophy when he wrote, 'Philosophers must no longer be content to accept the concepts that are given to them, so as merely to clean and polish them, *but must begin by fabricating and creating them, positing them and making them convincing to those who have recourse to them.* Hitherto they have generally trusted their concepts as if they were a miraculous gift from some sort of equally miraculous world', but this trust must be replaced by mistrust, and it is concepts that the philosopher must mistrust the most as long as he has not himself created them (Plato knew this well, though he taught the reverse . . .). What would be the worth of a philosopher of whom one could say: he did not create the concept? We at least see what philosophy is not: *it is neither contemplation, nor reflection, nor communication*, even if it can sometimes believe itself to be one or the other of these because of the capacity of every discipline to engender its own illusions, and to hide itself behind its own particular fog. It is not contemplation, for contemplations are things themselves, as viewed through the creation of their own concepts. It is not reflection, because no one needs philosophy in order to reflect on whatever one wants to reflect on: we believe that we are giving a great deal to philosophy by making it the art of reflection, but we take away everything from it, for mathematicians *per se* have never waited for philosophers in order to reflect on mathematics, nor artists, on painting or music; to say that they then become philosophers is a bad joke, as long as their reflection belongs to their respective creation. And philosophy finds no final refuge in communication, which works only with opinions, in order to create a 'consensus' and not a concept.

Philosophy does not contemplate, it does not reflect, nor does it communicate, although it has to create the concepts of these actions or passions. Contemplation, reflection, and communication are not disciplines, but machines that constitute Universals in all disciplines. The Universals of contemplation, then of reflection, are like the two illusions that philosophy has already traversed in its dream of dominating the other disciplines (objective idealism and subjective idealism), and philosophy does not honor itself by now falling back upon the universals of communication that would give it an imaginary mastery of the marketplace and the media (intersubjective idealism). Every creation is singular, and the concept, as the properly philosophical creation, is always a singularity. The first principle of philosophy is that Universals explain nothing, but must themselves be explained. *Knowledge through pure concepts* – we can consider this definition of philosophy as decisive. But the Nietzschean verdict falls: you will know nothing by concepts if you have not first created them. . . . To philosophize is to create concepts, and great philosophers are thus very rare.

To know oneself – to learn to think – to act as if nothing were self-evident – to wonder, 'to wonder why there is something . . .', these determinations of philosophy and many others form interesting though, in the long run, tiresome attitudes, but they do not constitute a well-defined occupation, a true activity, even from a pedagogical point of view. To create concepts, at least, is to do something. The question concerning the use or utility of philosophy, or even its harmfulness, must be changed accordingly.

Many problems crowd in upon the hallucinating eyes of an old man who would see himself confronting all sorts of philosophical concepts and conceptual personae. First of all, these concepts are and remain signs: Aristotle's *substance*, Descartes's *cogito*, Leibniz's *monad*, Kant's *condition*, Schelling's *potency*, Bergson's *durée*. . . . But, also, certain concepts demand an extraordinary word, sometimes barbarous or shocking, that must designate them, while others are content with a very ordinary word in current usage, which is swelled with such distant harmonics that they risk being imperceptible to a nonphilosophical ear. Some concepts call forth archaisms, others neologisms, through almost mad etymological exercises: etymology as a properly philosophical athleticism. In each case, there must be a strange necessity for these words and their choice, like an element of style. The baptism of the concept solicits a properly philosophical taste that proceeds with violence or with insinuation, and that constitutes, within language, a language of philosophy – not only a vocabulary, but a syntax that rises to the sublime or a great beauty. Now, although they are dated, signed, and baptized, concepts have their own way of not dying, and yet are submitted to constraints of renewal, replacement, and mutation that give philosophy a history and also a restless geography, of which each moment and each place are conserved, but within time, and pass away, but outside of time. If concepts never cease changing, it will be asked what unity remains for the philosophies. Is it the same unity as that of the sciences or the arts, which do not proceed by concepts? Where do their respective histories lie? If philosophy is this continuous creation of concepts, we will obviously want to ask not only what a concept is as a philosophical Idea, but also what the other creative Ideas consist of, which are not concepts and which belong to the sciences and the arts, and that have their own history and their own becoming, and their own variable relations among themselves and philosophy. The exclusivity of the creation of concepts assures philosophy a function, but gives it no preeminence, no privilege, insofar as there are other ways of thinking and creating, other modes of ideation that do not have to pass through concepts – beginning, for example, with scientific thought. And we will always come back to the question of knowing of what use is this activity of creating concepts, given that it is differentiated from scientific or artistic activity. Why is it necessary to create concepts, and ever new concepts; under what necessity, for what use? Create them for what? To respond that the greatness of philosophy would lie precisely in having no use at all is a stupid coquetry. In any case, we have never had any problem concerning the death of metaphysics or the overcoming of philosophy: this is useless and tiresome drivel. People today speak of the bankruptcy of systems, whereas it is only the concept of system that has changed. If there is a place and a time to create concepts, the operation that is carried out there will always be called philosophy, or would not even be distinguished from it even if one gave it another name. Philosophy would willingly yield its place to any other discipline that could better fulfill the function of creating concepts, but as long as that function subsists, it will still be called philosophy, always philosophy.

We know, however, that the friend or the lover, as claimants, are not without rivals. If philosophy has a Greek origin as we have so often been told, it is because the city, unlike empires or states, invents the *Agon* as the rule of a society of 'friends', the community of free men as rivals (citizens). This is the constant situation that Plato describes: if each citizen lays claim to something, he necessarily encounters rivals, so that it is necessary to be able to judge the well-foundedness of the claims. The carpenter claims the wood, but clashes with the forester, the lumberjack, and the joiner, who say, '*I* am the friend of the wood!' If it is a question of taking care of humans, there are many claimants who present themselves as the friend of humans – the peasant who nourishes them, the weaver who clothes them, the doctor who nurses them, the warrior who protects them. If in all these cases the selection is made, after all, from within a somewhat limited circle, it is no longer so in the case of politics, where, in the Athenian democracy as Plato sees it, anyone can claim anything. Hence the necessity for Plato to sort out these claims, to create instances according to which the well-foundedness of the claims can be judged: these are the Ideas as philosophical concepts. But even here, will we not encounter all sorts of claimants who say, '*I* am the true philosopher! I am the friend of Wisdom or of the Well-Founded'? The rivalry culminates with that of the philosopher and the sophist, who fight over the remains of the ancient sage. But how is one to distinguish the false friend from the true, and the concept from the simulacrum? The simulator and the friend: it is an entire Platonic theater that makes the conceptual personae proliferate by endowing them with the potential of the comic and the tragic.

Closer to us, philosophy has met with many new rivals. These were first of all the human sciences, and especially sociology, which wanted to replace it. But as philosophy had increasingly misunderstood its vocation of creating concepts, in order to take refuge in universals, it no longer knew very well what was at stake. Was it a matter of renouncing every creation of the concept in favor of a strict human science? Or, on the contrary, was it a matter of transforming the nature of concepts by making them either into collective representations, or into the conceptions of the world created by peoples, their vital, historical, and spiritual forces? Then it was the turn of epistemology, linguistics, or even psychoanalysis, and logical analysis. From test to test, philosophy confronted increasingly insolent and calamitous rivals, which Plato himself would not have imagined in his most comic moments. Finally, the deepest disgrace was reached when computer science, advertising, marketing, and design appropriated the word 'concept' itself, and said, 'This is our business, we are the *creative* ones, we are the "*conceptors*"! We are the friends of the concept, we put them into our computers.' Information and creativity, concept and enterprise: already an abundant bibliography. . . . The general movement that replaced *Critique* by commercial promotion has not left philosophy unaffected. The simulacrum, the simulation of a package of noodles, has become the true concept, and the person who packages the product, merchandise, or work of art has become the philosopher, the conceptual persona, or the artist. But how could philosophy, an old person, line up with smart young executives in a race for the universals of communication in order to determine a marketable form of the concept, *Merz*? The more philosophy clashes with impudent and silly rivals, the more it encounters them in its own heart, the more it feels itself driven to fulfill its task of creating concepts, which are meteorites [*aérolithes*] rather than merchandise. It has mad smiles that wipe away its tears. The question of philosophy is thus the singular point where the concept and creation are linked together.

Philosophers are not sufficiently concerned with the nature of the concept as a philosophical reality. They have preferred to consider it as a given representation or piece of knowledge, which would be explained by the faculties capable of forming it (abstraction, or generalization) or using it (judgement). But the concept is not given, it is created, it is to be created; and it is not formed, it posits itself in itself, a self-positing.

Each activity implies the other, since what is truly created, from the living being to the work of art, by that very fact enjoys a self-positing of itself, or a self-poetic character by which one recognizes it. The more the concept is created, the more it posits itself. What is dependent upon a free creative activity is also that which posits itself in itself, independently and necessarily: the most subjective will be the most objective. It is the post-Kantians, notably Schelling and Hegel, who paid the most attention, in this sense, to the concept as a philosophical reality. Hegel powerfully defined the concept by the Figures of its creation and the Moments of its self-positing: the Figures constitute the side under which the concept is created by and within consciousness, through the succession of minds, while the Moments make up the other side according to which the concept posits itself and brings together minds in the absolute of the Ego. Hegel thereby showed that the concept has nothing to do with a general or abstract idea that would not depend on philosophy itself. But he did so at the price of an indeterminate extension of philosophy that hardly allowed the independent movement of the sciences and arts to subsist, because it reconstituted universals with its own moments and no longer treated the personae of its own creation as anything but figuring phantoms. The post-Kantians circled around a universal *encyclopedia* of the concept that referred the creation of concepts to a pure subjectivity, instead of giving itself a more modest task, a *pedagogy* of the concept, that should analyze the conditions of creation as factors of moments that remain singular. If the three ages of the concept are the encyclopedia, pedagogy, and the professional commercial formation, only the second can prevent us from falling from the summits of the first into the absolute disaster of the third, an absolute disaster for thought, no matter what, of course, the social benefits from the point of view of universal capitalism.

26

Luce Irigaray
(b. 1930)

The philosophical project of Luce Irigaray is recognized as one of the most important, albeit controversial, interrogations of 'sexual difference' informing the discipline today. In stark contrast to Kristeva, Irigaray has maintained that female sexual identity should be understood as both 'specific' and 'autonomous' in its own right. This separatist orientation has thus resisted recuperation into any theoretical stance like Kristeva's that would posit a common genealogy for both male and female sexual identity. Irigaray's concerns have been explicated within an interdisciplinary matrix that draws on psychoanalysis and linguistics, as well as philosophy.

As a practising psychoanalyst, Irigaray has, on the one hand, acknowledged the importance of Freudian and Lacanian insights which emphasize the significance of repressed and hidden meanings. However, she has also criticized the exclusively masculine perspective of sexual identity dominated by the Oedipal model which theoretically grounds their discourse. Irigaray works to deconstruct the patriarchal assumptions that underlie this seemingly neutral account of sexual difference, a 'phallocentric' account, she claims, that remains 'isomorphic' with male sexuality. Thus, the ultimate aim and rationale of such psychoanalytic discourse is to eradicate difference, thereby conflating it with the 'sameness' of male representations. In patriarchal culture the feminine remains symptomatically repressed, as well as socio-economically oppressed, a situation that she maintains can only be remedied by 'jamming the theoretical machinery'.

Irigaray levels her critique at *all* forms of discourse that privilege sameness and repetition over difference and alterity. For her, the question of sexual identity cannot be extricated from the question of status within discourses that are constitutive of our active understanding and representation of 'reality'. As a result, discursive and political practices interact to reinforce patriarchal values that seem transparently 'natural'. In particular, she focuses on the '*logos*' of philosophical discourse 'that we have to challenge and disrupt'. As the 'master discourse' attempting to control every other discourse, philosophy is responsible for the 'phal-logocentrism' that buries the question of sexual *difference* beneath its monuments to sameness, identity and presence.

At this juncture, it is important to note that Irigaray participates in the kind of radical inquiry surfacing in French intellectual circles during the 1960s, especially synchronized with other thinkers like Derrida and Deleuze. Irigaray's work must, therefore, be understood in the context of evolving 'deconstructionist' strategies that highlighted the importance of '*différance*', as well as in the context of an emerging anti-Hegelianism that challenged the very notion of dialectical thought that could recuperate all differences into a higher synthesis (*Aufhebung*). Thus, the issue of sexual difference she interrogates has a positive value that cannot be reductively dismissed as another 'essentialist' project. Irigaray's stance repudiates the prioritizing of masculine structures of discourse and self-representation, demanding instead that they 'render up and give back what they owe the feminine'. Her work has stirred contemporary debate in philosophy that has been productive and often highly polemical. Nevertheless, she has raised some uncomfortable issues once carefully hidden in the labyrinth of philosophical discourse. By questioning the neutrality of this discourse, she invites us to remain vigilant and suspicious regarding the widespread historical exclusion of women from a discipline that ultimately constructs and interprets social reality.

SELECT BIBLIOGRAPHY OF IRIGARAY'S WORKS IN ENGLISH

Speculum of the Other Woman, Ithaca: Cornell University Press, 1985.
This Sex Which is Not One, Ithaca: Cornell University Press, 1985.
Marine Lover of Friedrich Nietzsche, New York: Columbia University Press, 1991.
Elemental Passions, London: Athlone, 1992.
The Irigaray Reader, ed. M. Whitford, Oxford: Blackwell, 1992.
An Ethics of Sexual Difference, London: Athlone, 1993.
Thinking the Difference, London: Routledge, 1994.

The Power of Discourse and the Subordination of the Feminine

INTERVIEW

Why do you begin your book with a critique of Freud?

STRICTLY SPEAKING, *SPECULUM*[1] has no beginning or end. The architectonics of the text, or texts, confounds the linearity of an outline, the teleology of discourse, within which there is no possible place for the 'feminine', except the traditional place of the repressed, the censured.

Furthermore, by 'beginning' with Freud and 'ending' with Plato we are already going at history 'backwards'. But it is a reversal 'within' which the question of the woman still cannot be articulated, so this reversal alone does not suffice. That is why, in the book's 'middle' texts – *Speculum*, once again – the reversal seemingly disappears. For what is important is to disconcert the staging of representation according to *exclusively* 'masculine' parameters, that is, according to a phallocratic order. It is not a matter of toppling that order so as to replace it – that amounts to the same thing in the end – but of disrupting and modifying it, starting from an 'outside' that is exempt, in part, from phallocratic law.

But to come back to your question. *Why this critique of Freud?*

Because in the process of elaborating a theory of sexuality, Freud brought to light something that had been operative all along though it remained implicit, hidden, unknown: *the sexual indifference that underlies the truth of any science, the logic of every discourse.* This is readily apparent in the way Freud defines female sexuality. In fact, this sexuality is never defined with respect to any sex but the masculine. Freud does not see *two sexes* whose differences are articulated in the act of intercourse, and, more generally speaking, in the imaginary and symbolic processes that regulate the workings of a society and a culture. The 'feminine' is always described in terms of deficiency or atrophy, as the other side of the sex that alone holds a monopoly on value: the male sex. Hence the all too well-known 'penis envy'. How can we accept the idea that woman's entire sexual development is governed by her lack of, and thus by her longing for, jealousy of, and demand for, the male organ? Does this mean that woman's sexual evolution can never be characterized with reference to the female sex itself? All Freud's statements describing feminine sexuality overlook the fact that the female sex might possibly have its own 'specificity'.

Must we go over this ground one more time? In the beginning, writes Freud, the little girl is nothing but a little boy; castration, for the girl,

From *This Sex Which is Not One*, Ithaca: Cornell University Press, 1985.

amounts to accepting the fact that she does not have a male organ; the girl turns away from her mother, 'hates' her, because she observes that her mother doesn't have the valorizing organ the daughter once thought she had; this rejection of the mother is accompanied by the rejection of all women, herself included, and for the same reason; the girl then turns toward her father to try to get what neither she nor any woman has: the phallus; the desire to have a child, for a woman, signifies the desire to possess at last the equivalent of the penis; the relationship among women is governed either by rivalry for the possession of the 'male organ' or, in homosexuality, by identification with the man; the interest that women may take in the affairs of society is dictated of course only by her longing to have powers equal to those of the male sex, and so on. Woman herself is never at issue in these statements: the feminine is defined as the necessary complement to the operation of male sexuality, and, more often, as a negative image that provides male sexuality with an unfailingly phallic self-representation.

Now Freud is describing an actual state of affairs. He does not invent female sexuality, nor male sexuality either for that matter. As a 'man of science', he merely accounts for them. The problem is that he fails to investigate the historical factors governing the data with which he is dealing. And, for example, that he takes female sexuality as he sees it and accepts it as a *norm*. That he interprets women's sufferings, their symptoms, their dissatisfactions, in terms of their individual histories, without questioning the relationship of their 'pathology' to a certain state of society, of culture. As a result, he generally ends up resubmitting women to the dominant discourse of the father, to the law of the father, while silencing their demands.

The fact that Freud himself is enmeshed in a power structure and an ideology of the patriarchal type leads, moreover, to some internal contradictions in his theory.

For example, woman, in order to correspond to man's desire, has to identify herself with his mother. This amounts to saying that the man becomes, as it were, his children's brother, since they have the same love object. How can the question of the Oedipus complex and its resolution be raised within such a configuration? And thus the question of sexual difference, which, according to Freud, is a corollary of the previous question?

Another 'symptom' of the fact that Freud's discourse belongs to an unanalyzed tradition lies in his tendency to fall back upon anatomy as an irrefutable criterion of truth. But no science is ever perfected; science too has its history. And besides, scientific data may be interpreted in many different ways. However, no such considerations keep Freud from justifying male aggressive activity and female passivity in terms of anatomical–physiological imperatives, especially those of reproduction. We now know that the ovum is not as passive as Freud claims, and that it chooses a spermatozoon for itself to at least as great an extent as it is chosen. Try transposing this to the psychic and social register. Freud claims, too, that the penis derives its value from its status as reproductive organ. And yet the female genital organs, which participate just as much in reproduction and if anything are even more indispensable to it, nevertheless fail to derive the same narcissistic benefit from that status. The anatomical references Freud uses to justify the development of sexuality are almost all tied, moreover, to the issue of reproduction. What happens when the sexual function can be separated from the reproductive function (a hypothesis obviously given little consideration by Freud)?

But Freud needs this support from anatomy in order to justify a theoretical position especially in his description of woman's sexual development. 'What can we do?' he writes in this connection, transposing Napoleon's phrase: 'Anatomy is destiny'. From this point on, in the name of that anatomical destiny, women are seen as less favored by nature from the point of view of libido; they are often frigid, nonaggressive, nonsadistic, nonpossessive, homosexual depending upon the degree to which their ovaries are hermaphroditic; they are outsiders where cultural values are concerned unless they participate in them through some sort of 'mixed heredity', and so on. In short, they are deprived of the worth of their sex. The important thing, of course, is that no one should know who has deprived them, or why, and that 'nature' be held accountable.

Does this critique of Freud go so far as to challenge psychoanalytic theory and practice?

Certainly not in order to return to a precritical attitude toward psychoanalysis, nor to claim that psychoanalysis has already exhausted its effectiveness. It is rather a matter of making explicit some implications of psychoanalysis that are inoperative at the moment. Saying that if Freudian theory indeed contributes what is needed to upset the philosophic order of discourse, the theory remains paradoxically subject to that discourse where the definition of sexual difference is concerned.

For example, Freud undermines a certain way of conceptualizing the 'present', 'presence', by stressing deferred action, overdetermination, the repetition compulsion, the death drive, and so on, or by indicating, in his theory or his practice, the impact of so-called unconscious mechanisms on the language of the 'subject'. But, himself a prisoner of a certain economy of the logos, he defines sexual difference by giving *a priori* value to Sameness, shoring up his demonstration by falling back upon time-honored devices such as analogy, comparison, symmetry, dichotomous oppositions, and so on. Heir to an 'ideology' that he does not call into question, Freud asserts that the 'masculine' is the sexual model, that no representation of desire can fail to take it as the standard, can fail to submit to it. In so doing, Freud makes manifest the presuppositions of the scene of representation: *the sexual indifference* that subtends it assures its coherence and its closure. Indirectly, then, he suggests how it might be analyzed. But he never carries out the potential articulation between the organization of the unconscious and the difference between the sexes. – Which is a theoretical and practical deficiency that may in turn constrict the scene of the unconscious. Or might it rather serve as the *interpretive lever* for its unfolding?

Thus we might wonder whether certain properties attributed to the unconscious may not, in part, be ascribed to the female sex, which is censured by the logic of consciousness. Whether the feminine *has* an unconscious or whether it *is* the unconscious. And so forth. Leaving these questions unanswered means that psychoanalyzing a woman is tantamount to adapting her to a society of a masculine type.

And of course it would be interesting to know what might become of psychoanalytic notions in a culture that did not repress the feminine. Since the recognition of a 'specific' female sexuality would challenge the monopoly on value held by the masculine sex alone, in the final analysis by the father, what meaning could the Oedipus complex have in a symbolic system other than patriarchy?

But that order is indeed the one that lays down the law today. To fail to recognize this would be as naive as to let it continue to rule without questioning the conditions that make its domination possible. So the fact that Freud – or psychoanalytic theory in general – takes sexuality as a theme, as a discursive object, has not led to an interpretation of the *sexualization of discourse* itself, certainly not to an interpretation of Freud's own discourse. His resolutely 'masculine' viewpoint on female sexuality attests to this as well as his very selective attention to the theoretical contributions of female analysts. Where sexual difference is in question, Freud does not fully analyze the presuppositions of the production of discourse. In other words, the questions that Freud's theory and practice address to the scene of representation do not include the question of the sexualized determination of that scene. Because it lacks that articulation, Freud's contribution remains, in part – and precisely where the difference between the sexes is concerned – caught up in metaphysical presuppositions.

All of which has led you to an interpretive rereading of the texts that define the history of philosophy?

Yes, for unless we limit ourselves naively – or perhaps strategically – to some kind of limited or marginal issue, it is indeed precisely philosophical discourse that we have to challenge, and *disrupt*, inasmuch as this discourse sets forth the law for all others, inasmuch as it constitutes the discourse on discourse.

Thus we have had to go back to it in order to try to find out what accounts for the power of its systematicity, the force of its cohesion, the resourcefulness of its strategies, the general applicability of its law and its value. That is, its *position of mastery*, and of potential reappropriation of the various productions of history.

Now, this domination of the philosophic logos stems in large part from its power to *reduce all others to the economy of the Same*. The teleologically constructive project it takes on is always also a project of diversion, deflection, reduction of the other in the Same. And, in its greatest generality perhaps, from its power to *eradicate the difference between the sexes* in systems that are self-representative of a 'masculine subject'.

Whence the necessity of 'reopening' the figures of philosophical discourse – idea, substance, subject, transcendental subjectivity, absolute knowledge – in order to pry out of them what they have borrowed that is feminine, from the feminine, to make them 'render up' and give back what they owe the feminine. This may be done in various ways, along various 'paths'; moreover, at minimum several of these must be pursued.

One way is to interrogate *the conditions under which systematicity itself is possible*: what the coherence of the discursive utterance conceals of the conditions under which it is produced, whatever it may say about these conditions in discourse. For example the 'matter' from which the speaking subject draws nourishment in order to produce itself, to reproduce itself; the *scenography* that makes representation feasible, representation as defined in philosophy, that is, the architectonics of its theatre, its framing in space-time, its geometric organization, its props, its actors, their respective positions, their dialogues, indeed their tragic relations, without overlooking the *mirror*, most often hidden, that allows the logos, the subject, to reduplicate itself, to reflect itself by itself. All these are interventions on the scene; they ensure its coherence so long as they remain uninterpreted. Thus they have to be reenacted, in each figure of discourse, in order to shake discourse away from its mooring in the value of 'presence'. For each philosopher, beginning with those whose names define some age in the history of philosophy, we have to point out how the break with material contiguity is made, how the system is put together, how the specular economy works.

This process of interpretive rereading has always been a *psychoanalytic undertaking* as well. That is why we need to pay attention to the way the unconscious works in each philosophy, and perhaps in philosophy in general. We need to listen (psycho)analytically to its procedures of repression, to the structuration of language that shores up its representations, separating the true from the false, the meaningful from the meaningless, and so forth. This does not mean that we have to give ourselves over to some kind of symbolic, point-by-point interpretation of philosophers' utterances. Moreover, even if we were to do so, we would still be leaving the mystery of 'the origin' intact. What is called for instead is an examination of the *operation of the 'grammar'* of each figure of discourse, its syntactic laws or requirements, its imaginary configurations, its metaphoric networks, and also, of course, what it does not articulate at the level of utterance: *its silences*.

But as we have already seen, even with the help of linguistics, psycho-analysis cannot solve the problem of the articulation of the female sex in discourse. Even though Freud's theory, through an effect of dress-rehearsal – at least as far as the relation between the sexes is concerned – shows clearly the function of the feminine in that scene. *What remains to be done, then, is to work at 'destroying' the discursive mechanism*. Which is not a simple undertaking . . . For how can we introduce ourselves into such a tightly-woven systematicity?

There is, in an initial phase, perhaps only one 'path', the one histor-ically assigned to the feminine: that of *mimicry*. One must assume the feminine role deliberately. Which means already to convert a form of subordination into an affirmation, and thus to begin to thwart it. Whereas a direct feminine challenge to this condition means demanding to speak as a (masculine) 'subject', that is, it means to postulate a relation to the intelligible that would maintain sexual indifference.

To play with mimesis is thus, for a woman, to try to recover the place of her exploitation by discourse, without allowing herself to be simply reduced to it. It means to resubmit herself – inasmuch as she is on the side of the 'perceptible', of 'matter' – to 'ideas', in particular to ideas about herself, that are elaborated in/by a masculine logic, but so as to make 'visible', by an effect of playful repetition, what was supposed to remain invisible: the cover-up of a possible operation of the feminine in language. It also means 'to unveil' the fact that, if women are such good mimics, it is because they are not simply resorbed in this function. *They also remain elsewhere*: another case of the persistence of 'matter', but also of 'sexual pleasure'.

Elsewhere of 'matter': if women can play with mimesis, it is because they are capable of bringing new nourishment to its operation. Because they have always nourished this operation? Is not the 'first' stake in mimesis that of re-producing (from) nature? Of giving it form in order to appropriate it for oneself? As guardians of 'nature', are not women the ones who maintain, thus who make possible, the resource of mimesis for men? For the logos?

It is here, of course, that the hypothesis of a reversal – within the phallic order – is always possible. Re-semblance cannot do without red blood. Mother-matter-nature must go on forever nourishing speculation. But this re-source is also rejected as the waste product of reflection, cast outside as what resists it: as madness. Besides the ambivalence that the nourishing phallic mother attracts to herself, this function leaves woman's sexual pleasure aside.

That *'elsewhere' of female pleasure* might rather be sought first in the place where it sustains ek-stasy in the transcendental. The place where it serves as security for a narcissism extrapolated into the 'God' of men. It can play this role only at the price of its ultimate withdrawal from prospection, of its 'virginity' unsuited for the representation of self. Feminine pleasure has to remain inarticulate in language, in its own language, if it is not to threaten the underpinnings of logical operations. And so what is most strictly forbidden to women today is that they should attempt to express their own pleasure.

That 'elsewhere' of feminine pleasure can be found only at the price of *crossing back through the mirror that subtends all speculation.* For this pleasure is not simply situated in a process of reflection or mimesis, nor on one side of this process or the other: neither on the near side, the empirical realm that is opaque to all language, nor on the far side, the self-sufficient infinite of the God of men. Instead, it refers all these categories and ruptures back to the necessities of the self-representation of phallic desire in discourse. A playful crossing, and an unsettling one, which would allow woman to rediscover the place of her 'self-affection'. Of her 'god', we might say. A god to which one can obviously not have recourse – unless its *duality* is granted – without leading the feminine right back into the phallocratic economy.

Does this retraversal of discourse in order to rediscover a 'feminine' place suppose a certain work on/of language?

It is surely not a matter of interpreting the operation of discourse while remaining within the same type of utterance as the one that guarantees discursive coherence. This is moreover the danger of every statement, every discussion, *about Speculum.* And, more generally speaking, of every discussion *about* the question of woman. For to speak *of* or *about* woman may always boil down to, or be understood as, a recuperation of the feminine within a logic that maintains it in repression, censorship, nonrecognition.

In other words, the issue is not one of elaborating a new theory of which woman would be the *subject* or the *object*, but of jamming the theoretical machinery itself, of suspending its pretension to the production of a truth and of a meaning that are excessively univocal. Which presupposes that women do not aspire simply to be men's equals in knowledge. That they do not claim to be rivaling men in constructing a logic of the feminine that would still take onto-theo-logic as its model, but that they are rather attempting to wrest this question away from the economy of the logos. They should not put it, then, in the form 'What is woman?' but rather, repeating/interpreting the way in which, within discourse, the feminine finds itself defined as lack, deficiency, or as imitation and negative image of the subject, they should signify that with respect to this logic a *disruptive excess* is possible on the feminine side.

An excess that exceeds common sense only on condition that the feminine not renounce its 'style'. Which, of course, is not a style at all, according to the traditional way of looking at things.

This 'style', or 'writing', of women tends to put the torch to fetish words, proper terms, well-constructed forms. This 'style' does not privilege sight; instead, it takes each figure back to its source, which is among other things *tactile*. It comes back in touch with itself in that origin without ever constituting in it, constituting itself in it, as some sort of unity. *Simultaneity* is its 'proper' aspect – a proper(ty) that is never fixed in the possible identity-to-self of some form or other. It is always *fluid*, without neglecting the characteristics of fluids that are difficult to idealize: those rubbings between two infinitely near neighbors that create a dynamics. Its 'style' resists and explodes every firmly established form, figure, idea or concept. Which does not mean that it lacks style, as we might be led to believe by a discursivity that cannot conceive of it. But its 'style' cannot be upheld as a thesis, cannot be the object of a position.

And even the motifs of 'self-touching', of 'proximity', isolated as such or reduced to utterances, could effectively pass for an attempt to appropriate the feminine to discourse. We would still have to ascertain whether 'touching oneself', that (self) touching, the desire for the proximate rather than for (the) proper(ty), and so on, might not imply a mode of exchange irreducible to any *centering*, any *centrism*, given the way the 'self-touching' of female 'self-affection' comes into play as a rebounding from one to the other without any possibility of interruption, and given that, in this interplay, proximity confounds any adequation, any appropriation.

But of course if these were only 'motifs' without any work on and/or with language, the discursive economy could remain intact. How, then, are we to try to redefine this language work that would leave space for the feminine? Let us say that every dichotomizing – and at the same time redoubling – break, including the one between enunciation and utterance, has to be disrupted. Nothing is ever to be *posited* that is not also reversed and caught up again in the *supplementarity of this reversal*. To put it another way: there would no longer be either a right side or a wrong side of discourse, or even of texts, but each passing from one to the other would make audible and comprehensible even what resists the recto-verso structure that shores up common sense. If this is to be practiced for every meaning posited – for every word, utterance, sentence, but also of course for every phoneme, every letter – we need to proceed in such a way that linear reading is no longer possible: that is, the retroactive impact of the end of each word, utterance, or sentence upon its beginning must be taken into consideration in order to undo the power of its teleological effect, including its deferred action. That would hold good also for the opposition between structures of horizontality and verticality that are at work in language.

What allows us to proceed in this way is that we interpret, at each 'moment', the *specular make-up* of discourse, that is, the self-reflecting (stratifiable) organization of the subject in that discourse. An organization that maintains, among other things, the break between what is perceptible and what is intelligible, and thus maintains the submission, subordination, and exploitation of the 'feminine'.

This language work would thus attempt to thwart any manipulation of discourse that would also leave discourse intact. Not, necessarily, in the utterance, but in its *autological presuppositions*. Its function would thus be to *cast phallocentrism, phallocratism*, loose from its moorings in order to return the masculine to its own language, leaving open the possibility of a different language. Which means that the masculine would no longer be 'everything'. That it could no longer, all by itself, define, circumvent, circumscribe, the properties of any thing and everything. That the right to define every value – including the abusive privilege of appropriation – would no longer belong to it.

Isn't there a political issue implicit in this interpretation of the philosophic order and this language work?

Every operation on and in philosophical language, by virtue of the very nature of that discourse – which is essentially political – possesses implications that, no matter how mediate they may be, are nonetheless politically determined.

The first question to ask is therefore the following: how can women analyze their own exploitation, inscribe their own demands, within an order prescribed by the masculine? *Is a women's politics possible within that order?* What transformation in the political process itself does it require?

In these terms, when women's movements challenge the forms and nature of political life, the contemporary play of powers and power relations, they are in fact working toward a modification of women's status. On the other hand, when these same movements aim simply for a change in the distribution of power, leaving intact the power structure itself, then they are resubjecting themselves, deliberately or not, to a phallocratic order. This latter gesture must of course be denounced, and with determination, since it may constitute a more subtly concealed exploitation of women. Indeed, that gesture plays on a certain naiveté that suggests one need only be a woman in order to remain outside phallic power.

But these questions are complex, all the more so in that women are obviously not to be expected to renounce equality in the sphere of civil rights. How can the double demand – for both equality and difference – be articulated?

Certainly not by acceptance of a choice between 'class struggle' and 'sexual warfare', an alternative that aims once again to minimize the question of the exploitation of women through a definition of power of the masculine type. More precisely, it implies putting off to an indefinite later date a women's 'politics', a politics that would be modeled rather too simplistically on men's struggles.

It seems, in this connection, that the *relation between the system of economic oppression among social classes and the system that can be labeled patriarchal* has been subjected to very little dialectical analysis, and has been once again reduced to a hierarchical structure.

A case in point: 'the first class opposition that appears in history coincides with the development of the antagonism between man and woman in monogamous marriage and the first class oppression coincides with that of the female sex by the male'.[2] Or again:

> With the division of labour, in which all these contradictions are implicit, and which in its turn is based on the natural division of labour in the family and on the separation of society into individual families opposed to one another, is given simultaneously the distribution, and indeed the unequal (both quantitative and qualitative) distribution, of labour and its products, hence property: the nucleus, the first form of which lies in the family, where wife and children are the slaves of the husband. This latent slavery in the family, though still very crude, is the first property, but even at this early stage it corresponds perfectly to the definition of modern economists who call it the power of disposing of the labour-power of others.[3]

Of this first antagonism, this first oppression, this first form, this first property, this nucleus . . ., we may indeed say that they never signify anything but a 'first moment' of history, even an elaboration – why not a mythical one? – of 'origins'. The fact remains that this earliest oppression is in effect even today, and the problem lies in determining how it is articulated with the other oppression, if it is necessary in the long run to dichotomize them in that way, to oppose them, to subordinate one to the other, according to processes that are still strangely inseparable from an idealist logic.

For the patriarchal order is indeed the one that functions as the *organization and monopolization of private property to the benefit of the head of the family*. It is his proper name, the name of the father, that determines ownership for the family, including the wife and children. And what is required of them – for the wife, monogamy; for the children, the precedence of the male line, and specifically of the eldest son who bears the name – is also required so as to ensure 'the concentration of considerable wealth in the hands of a single individual – a man' and to 'bequeath this wealth to the children of that man and of no other'; which, of course, does not 'in any way interfere with open or concealed polygamy on the part of the man'.[4] How, then, can the analysis of women's exploitation be dissociated from the analysis of modes of appropriation?

This question arises today out of a different necessity. For male–female relations are beginning to be less concealed behind the father–mother functions. Or, more precisely, man–father/mother: because the man, by virtue of his effective participation in public exchanges, has never been reduced to a simple reproductive function. The woman, for her part, owing to her seclusion in the 'home', the place of private property, has long been nothing but a mother. Today, not only her entrance into the circuits of production, but also – even more so? – the widespread availability of contraception and abortion are returning her to that impossible role: being a woman. And if contraception and abortion are spoken of most often as possible ways of controlling, or even 'mastering', the birth rate, of being a mother 'by choice', the fact remains that they imply the possibility of *modifying women's social status*, and thus of modifying the modes of social relations between men and women.

But to what reality would woman correspond, independently of her reproductive function? It seems that two possible roles are available to her, roles that are occasionally or frequently contradictory. Woman could be *man's equal*. In this case she would enjoy, in a more or less near future, the same economic, social, political rights as men. She would be a potential man. But on the exchange market – especially, or exemplarily, the market of sexual exchange – woman would also have to preserve and maintain what is called *femininity*. The value of a woman would accrue to her from her maternal role, and, in addition, from her 'femininity'. But in fact that 'femininity' is a role, an image, a value, imposed upon women by male systems of representation. In this masquerade of femininity, the woman loses herself, and loses herself by playing on her femininity. The fact remains that this masquerade requires an *effort* on her part for which she is not compensated. Unless her pleasure comes simply from being chosen as an object of consumption or of desire by masculine 'subjects'. And, moreover, how can she do otherwise without being 'out of circulation'?

In our social order, women are 'products' used and exchanged by men. Their status is that of merchandise, 'commodities'. How can such objects of use and transaction claim the right to speak and to participate in exchange in general? Commodities, as we all know, do not take themselves to market on their own; and if they could talk . . . So women have to remain an 'infrastructure' unrecognized as such by our society and our culture. The use, consumption, and circulation of their sexualized bodies underwrite the organization and the reproduction of the social order, in which they have never taken part as 'subjects'.

Women are thus in a situation of *specific exploitation* with respect to exchange operations: sexual exchanges, but also economic, social, and cultural exchanges in general. A woman 'enters into' these exchanges only as the object of a transaction, unless she agrees to renounce the specificity of her sex, whose 'identity' is imposed on her according to models that remain foreign to her. Women's social inferiority is reinforced and complicated by the fact that woman does not have access to language, except through recourse to 'masculine' systems of representation which disappropriate her from her relation to herself and to other women. The 'feminine' is never to be identified except by and for the masculine, the reciprocal proposition not being 'true'.

But this situation of specific oppression is perhaps what can allow women today to elaborate a 'critique of the political economy', inasmuch as they are in a position external to the laws of exchange, even though they are included in them as 'commodities'. A critique of the political economy that could not, this time, dispense with the critique of the discourse in which it is carried out, and in particular of the metaphysical presuppositions of that discourse. And one that would doubtless interpret in a different way *the impact of the economy of discourse on the analysis of relations of production.*

For, without the exploitation of the body-matter of women, what would become of the symbolic process that governs society? What modification would this process, this society, undergo, if women, who have been only objects of consumption or exchange, necessarily aphasic, were to become 'speaking subjects' as well? Not, of course, in compliance with the masculine, or more precisely the phallocratic, 'model'.

That would not fail to challenge the discourse that lays down the law today, that legislates on everything, including sexual difference, to such an extent that the existence of another sex, of an other, that would be woman, still seems, in its terms, unimaginable.

NOTES

1 *Speculum de l'autre femme* (Paris, 1974).
2 Frederick Engels, *The Origin of the Family, Private Property and the State*, trans. Alec West, rev. and ed. E. B. Leacock (New York, 1972), p. 129.
3 Karl Marx and Friedrich Engels, *The German Ideology*, parts 1 and 3, ed. R. Pascal (New York, 1939), pp. 21–2. (*Marxist Library*, Works of Marxism-Leninism, vol. 6.) Further references to this work are identified parenthetically by page number.
4 *The Origin of the Family*, p. 138.

27

Jean-François Lyotard

(b. 1924)

One of the leading figures in the 'postmodern' debate in philosophy, Jean-François Lyotard was born in Versailles in 1924. Lyotard studied phenomenology with Merleau-Ponty, and his first philosophical publication, *La Phénoménologie* (1954) dealt primarily with the work of this mentor. Other phenomenological thinkers, like Heidegger and Levinas, have also clearly influenced Lyotard's critical approach to the complex relations between the epistemological models of science and the lifeworld of culture and politics. The creative interdisciplinary approach which he brings to his project has affected not only the philosophical domain, but an entire spectrum of the human sciences as well.

Lyotard resisted certain aspects of the structuralist paradigm that was in the ascendancy when he began his philosophical career in the 1950s. There was for him always a 'gap' between our experience of the lifeworld and the language we use to speak about this experience. His treatment of this theme in *Discours, figure* (1971) makes explicit his discomfort with theoretical constructs that banish history in favour of timeless, universal, synchronic structures that remain self-regulating without reference to the extra-linguistic features of the lifeworld. Lyotard's association during the 1960s with a Marxist group, *Socialisme ou barbarie*, reinforced this distrust of any theory that ignored the critique of historical materialism and the freedom of political praxis. There have been, however, other developments in Lyotard's thought that have drawn on figures as diverse as Freud, Nietzsche, Kant and Wittgenstein. The Freudian influence to be found in his *Libidinal Economy* (1974) aligned him with *désirants* such as Deleuze and Guattari, while *Leçons sur l'analytique du sublime* drew on Kant's *Third Critique* as a critical influence in its treatment of the 'sublime'.

Lyotard himself has made his own highly original contributions to contemporary debates in philosophy, politics and art. In *The Differend* (1983), he expanded on this concept of a radical difference that cannot be recuperated by some appeal to universal consensus without doing violence to the interests of the weaker party. Clearly, in this sense he disagrees with

425

a thinker like Habermas, whose faith in the 'force of the better argument' leaves critically unquestioned the very *context* of argumentation, which is never ideal, but always marked by the effects of status, power, networking and influence. There is, for Lyotard, a danger in the presupposition that some 'Grand Narrative' of Western culture, like the Enlightenment's rationalistic bias, offers a solution that remains neutral and uncontaminated by the interests of domination. As he examines the collapse of such 'Grand Narratives' in *The Postmodern Condition* (1979), Lyotard suggests that these must give way to less ambitious *'petits récits'*, little narratives that resist closure and totality, stressing the singularity of every 'event' – whether ethical, political or aesthetic. There is no longer a final authority that can speak for all human beings from a universal perspective without already invoking some ideological formation. Only by means of repeated testimony as *petits récits* can we be reminded of the irreducibility and particularity of 'events' in our lives that resist global categorization.

Lyotard stresses that his use of the word *'postmodern'* does not merely imply a linear temporal sequence, i.e. 'modernity' followed by 'postmodernity', as if it were some kind of 'high modernity'. On the contrary, the postmodern is already implied by the modern because modernity, by its very nature, is continuously thrusting ahead of itself to become other than itself. There are obviously parallels and shared assumptions in other contemporary projects such as poststructuralism and deconstruction as set forth by Foucault, the later Barthes, Kristeva, Derrida and Deleuze. In the selection which follows from *The Postmodern Condition*, some of these similarities and connections emerge.

Lyotard has taught philosophy since 1952, first in Algeria, and for many years at the University of Paris. He is a former President of the Collège International de Philosophie in Paris. He has been a Visiting Professor at the universities of Wisconsin, California, Minnesota, Johns Hopkins, Montreal, Sao Paolo and Turin, among others. Most recently he has been a Henry Luce Scholar at Yale University and Robert Woodruff Visiting Professor at Emory University. His work continues to generate much excitement and interest both within and beyond the philosophical community.

SELECT BIBLIOGRAPHY OF LYOTARD'S WORKS IN ENGLISH

The Differend: Phrases in Dispute, Minneapolis: University of Minnesota Press, 1983.

Driftworks, New York: Semiotext(e), 1984.

The Postmodern Condition: A Report on Knowledge, Manchester: Manchester University Press, 1984.

Just Gaming (with Jean-Loup Thébaud), Manchester: Manchester University Press, 1985.

The Inhuman, Stanford: Stanford University Press, 1988.

Peregrinations: Law, Form, Event, New York: Columbia University Press, 1988.

The Lyotard Reader, ed. A. Benjamin, Oxford: Blackwell, 1989.

Heidegger and the Jews, Minneapolis: University of Minnesota Press, 1990.

The Postmodern Explained to Children, London: Turnaround Press, 1992.

Toward the Postmodern, eds R. Harvey and M. Roberts, Atlantic Highlands, NJ: Humanities Press, 1992.

Libidinal Economy, London: Athlone, 1993.

Political Writings of Lyotard, London: UCL Press, 1993.

Answering the Question: What is Postmodernism?

A DEMAND

THIS IS A period of slackening – I refer to the color of the times. From every direction we are being urged to put an end to experimentation, in the arts and elsewhere. I have read an art historian who extols realism and is militant for the advent of a new subjectivity. I have read an art critic who packages and sells 'Transavantgardism' in the marketplace of painting. I have read that under the name of postmodernism, architects are getting rid of the Bauhaus project, throwing out the baby of experimentation with the bathwater of functionalism. I have read that a new philosopher is discovering what he drolly calls Judaeo-Christianism, and intends by it to put an end to the impiety which we are supposed to have spread. I have read in a French weekly that some are displeased with *Mille Plateaux* [by Deleuze and Guattari] because they expect, especially when reading a work of philosophy, to be gratified with a little sense. I have read from the pen of a reputable historian that writers and thinkers of the 1960 and 1970 avant-gardes spread a reign of terror in the use of language, and that the conditions for a fruitful exchange must be restored by imposing on the intellectuals a common way of speaking, that of the historians. I have been reading a young philosopher of language who complains that Continental thinking, under the challenge of speaking machines, has surrendered to the machines the concern for reality, that it has substituted for the referential paradigm that of 'adlinguisticity' (one speaks about speech, writes about writing, intertextuality), and who thinks that the time has now come to restore a solid anchorage of language in the referent. I have read a talented theatrologist for whom postmodernism, with its games and fantasies, carries very little weight in front of political authority, especially when a worried public opinion encourages authority to a politics of totalitarian surveillance in the face of nuclear warfare threats.

I have read a thinker of repute who defends modernity against those he calls the neoconservatives. Under the banner of postmodernism, the latter would like, he believes, to get rid of the uncompleted project of modernism, that of the Enlightenment. Even the last advocates of *Aufklärung*, such as Popper or Adorno, were only able, according to him, to defend the project in a few particular spheres of life – that of politics for the author of *The Open Society*, and that of art for the author of *Ästhetische Theorie*. Jürgen Habermas (everyone had recognized him) thinks that if modernity has failed, it is in allowing the totality of

From *The Postmodern Condition: A Report on Knowledge*, Manchester: Manchester University Press, 1984.

life to be splintered into independent specialties which are left to the narrow competence of experts, while the concrete individual experiences 'desublimated meaning' and 'destructured form', not as a liberation but in the mode of that immense *ennui* which Baudelaire described over a century ago.

Following a prescription of Albrecht Wellmer, Habermas considers that the remedy for this splintering of culture and its separation from life can only come from 'changing the status of aesthetic experience when it is no longer primarily expressed in judgments of taste', but when it is 'used to explore a living historical situation', that is, when 'it is put in relation with problems of existence'. For this experience then 'becomes a part of a language game which is no longer that of aesthetic criticism'; it takes part 'in cognitive processes and normative expectations'; 'it alters the manner in which those different moments *refer* to one another'. What Habermas requires from the arts and the experiences they provide is, in short, to bridge the gap between cognitive, ethical, and political discourses, thus opening the way to a unity of experience.

My question is to determine what sort of unity Habermas has in mind. Is the aim of the project of modernity the constitution of socio-cultural unity within which all the elements of daily life and of thought would take their places as in an organic whole? Or does the passage that has to be charted between heterogeneous language games – those of cognition, of ethics, of politics – belong to a different order from that? And if so, would it be capable of effecting a real synthesis between them?

The first hypothesis, of a Hegelian inspiration, does not challenge the notion of a dialectically totalizing *experience*; the second is closer to the spirit of Kant's *Critique of Judgment*; but must be submitted, like the *Critique*, to that severe reexamination which postmodernity imposes on the thought of the Enlightenment, on the idea of a unitary end of history and of a subject. It is this critique which not only Wittgenstein and Adorno have initiated, but also a few other thinkers (French or other) who do not have the honor to be read by Professor Habermas – which at least saves them from getting a poor grade for their neoconservatism.

REALISM

The demands I began by citing are not all equivalent. They can even be contradictory. Some are made in the name of postmodernism, others in order to combat it. It is not necessarily the same thing to formulate a demand for some referent (and objective reality), for some sense (and credible transcendence), for an addressee (and audience), or an addressor (and subjective expressiveness) or for some communicational consensus (and a general code of exchanges, such as the genre of historical discourse). But in the diverse invitations to suspend artistic experimentation, there is an identical call for order, a desire for unity, for identity, for security, or popularity (in the sense of *Öffentlichkeit*, of 'finding a public'). Artists and writers must be brought back into the bosom of the community, or at least, if the latter is considered to be ill, they must be assigned the task of healing it.

There is an irrefutable sign of this common disposition: it is that for all those writers nothing is more urgent than to liquidate the heritage of the avant-gardes. Such is the case, in particular, of the so-called trans-avantgardism. The answers given by Achille Bonito Oliva to the questions asked by Bernard Lamarche-Vadel and Michel Enric leave no room for doubt about this. By putting the avant-gardes through a mixing process, the artist and critic feel more confident that they can suppress them than by launching a frontal attack. For they can pass off the most cynical eclecticism as a way of going beyond the fragmentary character of the preceding experiments; whereas if they openly turned their backs on them, they would run the risk of appearing ridiculously neoacademic. The *Salons* and the *Académies*, at the time when the bourgeoisie was establishing itself in history, were able to function as purgation and to grant awards for good plastic and literary conduct under the cover of realism. But capitalism inherently possesses the power to derealize familiar objects, social roles, and institutions to such a degree that the so-called realistic representations can no longer evoke reality except as nostalgia or mockery, as an occasion for suffering rather than for satisfaction. Classicism seems to be ruled out in a world in which reality is so destabilized that it offers no occasion for experience but one for ratings and experimentation.

This theme is familiar to all readers of Walter Benjamin. But it is necessary to assess its exact reach. Photography did not appear as a challenge to painting from the outside, any more than industrial cinema did to narrative literature. The former was only putting the final touch to the program of ordering the visible elaborated by the quattrocento; while the latter was the last step in rounding off diachronies as organic wholes, which had been the ideal of the great novels of education since the eighteenth century. That the mechanical and the industrial should appear as substitutes for hand or craft was not in itself a disaster – except if one believes that art is in its essence the expression of an individuality of genius assisted by an elite craftsmanship.

The challenge lay essentially in that photographic and cinematographic processes can accomplish better, faster, and with a circulation a hundred thousand times larger than narrative or pictorial realism, the task which academicism had assigned to realism: to preserve various consciousnesses from doubt. Industrial photography and cinema will be superior to painting and the novel whenever the objective is to stabilize the referent, to arrange it according to a point of view which endows it with a recognizable meaning, to reproduce the syntax and vocabulary which enable the addressee to decipher images and sequences quickly, and so to arrive easily at the consciousness of his own identity as well as the approval which he thereby receives from others – since such structures of images and sequences constitute a communication code among all of them. This is the way the effects of reality, or if one prefers, the fantasies of realism, multiply.

If they too do not wish to become supporters (of minor importance at that) of what exists, the painter and novelist must refuse to lend themselves to such therapeutic uses. They must question the rules of the art of painting or of narrative as they have learned and received them from their predecessors. Soon those rules must appear to them as a means to deceive, to seduce, and to reassure, which makes it impossible for them to be 'true'. Under the common name of painting and literature, an unprecedented split is taking place. Those who refuse to reexamine the rules of art pursue successful careers in mass conformism by communicating, by means of the 'correct rules', the endemic desire for reality with objects and situations capable of gratifying it. Pornography is the use of photography and film to such an end. It is becoming a general model for the visual or narrative arts which have not met the challenge of the mass media.

As for the artists and writers who question the rules of plastic and narrative arts and possibly share their suspicions by circulating their work, they are destined to have little credibility in the eyes of those concerned with 'reality' and 'identity'; they have no guarantee of an audience. Thus it is possible to ascribe the dialectics of the avant-gardes to the challenge posed by the realisms of industry and mass communication to painting and the narrative arts. Duchamp's 'ready made' does nothing but actively and parodistically signify this constant process of dispossession of the craft of painting or even of being an artist. As Thierry de Duve penetratingly observes, the modern aesthetic question is not 'What is beautiful?' but 'What can be said to be art (and literature)?'

Realism, whose only definition is that it intends to avoid the question of reality implicated in that of art, always stands somewhere between academicism and kitsch. When power assumes the name of a party, realism and its neoclassical complement triumph over the experimental avant-garde by slandering and banning it – that is, provided the 'correct' images, the 'correct' narratives, the 'correct' forms which the party requests, selects, and propagates can find a public to desire them as the appropriate remedy for the anxiety and depression that public experiences. The demand for reality – that is, for unity, simplicity, communicability, etc. – did not have the same intensity nor the same continuity in German society between the two world wars and in Russian society after the Revolution: this provides a basis for a distinction between Nazi and Stalinist realism.

What is clear, however, is that when it is launched by the political apparatus, the attack on artistic experimentation is specifically reactionary: aesthetic judgment would only be required to decide whether such or such work is in conformity with the established rules of the beautiful. Instead of the work of art having to investigate what makes it an art object and whether it will be able to find an audience, political academicism possesses and imposes *a priori* criteria of the beautiful, which designate some works and a public at a stroke and forever. The use of categories in aesthetic judgment would thus be of the same nature as in cognitive judgment. To speak like Kant, both would be determining judgments: the expression is 'well formed' first in the understanding, then the only cases retained in experience are those which can be subsumed under this expression.

When power is that of capital and not that of a party, the 'transa- vantgardist' or 'postmodern' (in Jencks's sense) solution proves to be better adapted than the antimodern solution. Eclecticism is the degree zero of contemporary general culture: one listens to reggae, watches a western, eats McDonald's food for lunch and local cuisine for dinner, wears Paris perfume in Tokyo and 'retro' clothes in Hong Kong; knowledge is a matter for TV games. It is easy to find a public for eclectic works. By becoming kitsch, art panders to the confusion which reigns in the 'taste' of the patrons. Artists, gallery owners, critics, and public wallow together in the 'anything goes', and the epoch is one of slackening. But this realism of the 'anything goes' is in fact that of money; in the absence of aesthetic criteria, it remains possible and useful to assess the value of works of art according to the profits they yield. Such realism accommodates all tendencies, just as capital accommodates all 'needs', providing that the tendencies and needs have purchasing power. As for taste, there is no need to be delicate when one speculates or entertains oneself.

Artistic and literary research is doubly threatened, once by the 'cultural policy' and once by the art and book market. What is advised, sometimes through one channel, sometimes through the other, is to offer works which, first, are relative to subjects which exist in the eyes of the public they address, and second, works so made ('well made') that the public will recognize what they are about, will understand what is signified, will be able to give or refuse its approval knowingly, and if possible, even to derive from such work a certain amount of comfort.

The interpretation which has just been given of the contact between the industrial and mechanical arts, and literature and the fine arts is correct in its outline, but it remains narrowly sociologizing and historicizing – in other words, one-sided. Stepping over Benjamin's and Adorno's reticences, it must be recalled that science and industry are no more free of the suspicion which concerns reality than are art and writing. To believe other- wise would be to entertain an excessively humanistic notion of the mephistophelian functionalism of sciences and technologies. There is no denying the dominant existence today of techno-science, that is, the massive subordination of cognitive statements to the finality of the best possible performance, which is, the technological criterion. But the mechanical and the industrial, especially when they enter fields traditionally reserved for artists, are carrying with them much more than power effects. The objects and the thoughts which originate in scientific knowledge and the capitalist economy convey with them one of the rules which supports their possibility: the rule that there is no reality unless testified by a consensus between partners over a certain knowledge and certain commitments.

This rule is of no little consequence. It is the imprint left on the politics of the scientist and the trustee of capital by a kind of flight of reality out of the metaphysical, religious, and political certainties that the mind believed it held. This withdrawal is absolutely necessary to the emergence of science and capitalism. No industry is possible without a suspicion of the Aristotelian theory of motion, no industry without a refutation of corporatism, of mercantilism, and of physiocracy. Modernity, in whatever age it appears, cannot exist without a shattering of belief and without discovery of the 'lack of reality' of reality, together with the invention of other realities.

What does this 'lack of reality' signify if one tries to free it from a narrowly historicized interpretation? The phrase is of course akin to what Nietzsche calls nihilism. But I see a much earlier modulation of Nietzschean perspectivism in the Kantian theme of the sublime. I think in particular that it is in the aesthetic of the sublime that modern art (including literature) finds its impetus and the logic of avant-gardes finds its axioms.

The sublime sentiment, which is also the sentiment of the sublime, is, according to Kant, a strong and equivocal emotion: it carries with it both pleasure and pain. Better still, in it pleasure derives from pain. Within the tradition of the subject, which comes from Augustine and Descartes and which Kant does not radically challenge, this contradiction, which some would call neurosis or masochism, develops as a conflict between the faculties of a subject, the faculty to conceive of something and the faculty to 'present' something. Knowledge exists if, first, the statement is intelligible, and second, if 'cases' can be derived from the experience which 'corresponds' to it. Beauty exists if a certain 'case' (the work of art), given first by the sensibility without any conceptual determination, the sentiment of pleasure independent of any interest the work may elicit, appeals to the principle of a universal consensus (which may never be attained).

Taste, therefore, testifies that between the capacity to conceive and the capacity to present an object corresponding to the concept, an undetermined agreement, without rules, giving rise to a judgment which Kant calls reflective, may be experienced as pleasure. The sublime is a different sentiment. It takes place, on the contrary, when the imagination fails to present an object which might, if only in principle, come to match a concept. We have the Idea of the world (the totality of what is), but we do not have the capacity to show an example of it. We have the Idea of the simple (that which cannot be broken down, decomposed), but we

433

cannot illustrate it with a sensible object which would be a 'case' of it. We can conceive the infinitely great, the infinitely powerful, but every presentation of an object destined to 'make visible' this absolute greatness or power appears to us painfully inadequate. Those are Ideas of which no presentation is possible. Therefore, they impart no knowledge about reality (experience); they also prevent the free union of the faculties which gives rise to the sentiment of the beautiful; and they prevent the formation and the stabilization of taste. They can be said to be unpresentable.

I shall call modern the art which devotes its 'little technical expertise' (son 'petit technique'), as Diderot used to say, to present the fact that the unpresentable exists. To make visible that there is something which can be conceived and which can neither be seen nor made visible: this is what is at stake in modern painting. But how to make visible that there is something which cannot be seen? Kant himself shows the way when he names 'formlessness, the absence of form', as a possible index to the unpresentable. He also says of the empty 'abstraction' which the imagination experiences when in search for a presentation of the infinite (another unpresentable): this abstraction itself is like a presentation of the infinite, its 'negative presentation'. He cites the commandment, 'Thou shalt not make graven images' (Exodus), as the most sublime passage in the Bible in that it forbids all presentation of the Absolute. Little needs to be added to those observations to outline an aesthetic of sublime paintings. As painting, it will of course 'present' something though negatively; it will therefore avoid figuration or representation. It will be 'white' like one of Malevitch's squares; it will enable us to see only by making it impossible to see; it will please only by causing pain. One recognizes in those instructions the axioms of avant-gardes in painting inasmuch as they devote themselves to making an allusion to the unpresentable by means of visible presentations. The systems in the name of which, or with which, this task has been able to support or to justify itself deserve the greatest attention; but they can originate only in the vocation of the sublime in order to legitimize it, that is, to conceal it. They remain inexplicable without the incommensurability of reality to concept which is implied in the Kantian philosophy of the sublime.

It is not my intention to analyze here in detail the manner in which the various avant-gardes have, so to speak, humbled and disqualified reality by examining the pictorial techniques which are so many devices to make us believe in it. Local tone, drawing, the mixing of colors, linear perspective, the nature of the support and that of the instrument, the treatment, the display, the museum: the avant-gardes are perpetually flushing out artifices of presentation which make it possible to subordinate thought to the gaze and to turn it away from the unpresentable. If Habermas, like Marcuse, understands this task of derealization as an aspect of the (repressive) 'desublimation' which characterizes the avant-garde, it is because he confuses the Kantian sublime with Freudian sublimation, and because aesthetics has remained for him that of the beautiful.

THE POSTMODERN

What, then, is the postmodern? What place does it or does it not occupy in the vertiginous work of the questions hurled at the rules of image and narration? It is undoubtedly a part of the modern. All that has been received, if only yesterday (*modo, modo*, Petronius used to say), must be suspected. What space does Cézanne challenge? The Impressionists'. What object do Picasso and Braque attack? Cézanne's. What presupposition does Duchamp break with in 1912? That which says one must make a painting, be it cubist. And Buren questions that other presupposition which he believes had survived untouched by the work of Duchamp: the place of presentation of the work. In an amazing acceleration, the generations precipitate themselves. A work can become modern only if it is first postmodern. Postmodernism thus understood is not modernism at its end but in the nascent state, and this state is constant.

Yet I would like not to remain with this slightly mechanistic meaning of the word. If it is true that modernity takes place in the withdrawal of the real and according to the sublime relation between the presentable and the conceivable, it is possible, within this relation, to distinguish two modes (to use the musician's language). The emphasis can be placed on the powerlessness of the faculty of presentation, on the nostalgia for presence felt by the human subject, on the obscure and futile will which inhabits him in spite of everything. The emphasis can be placed, rather, on the power of the faculty to conceive, on its 'inhumanity' so to speak (it was the quality Apollinaire demanded of modern artists), since it is not the business of our understanding whether or not human sensibility or imagination can match what it conceives. The emphasis can also be placed on the increase of being and the jubilation which result from the invention of new rules of the game, be it pictorial, artistic, or any other. What I have in mind will become clear if we dispose very schematically a few names on the chessboard of the history of avant-gardes: on the side of melancholia, the German Expressionists, and on the side of *novatio*, Braque and Picasso, on the former Malevitch and on the latter Lissitsky, on the one Chirico and on the other Duchamp. The nuance which distinguishes these two modes may be infinitesimal; they often coexist in the same piece, are almost indistinguishable; and yet they testify to a difference (*un différend*) on which the fate of thought depends and will depend for a long time, between regret and assay.

The work of Proust and that of Joyce both allude to something which does not allow itself to be made present. Allusion, to which Paolo Fabbri recently called my attention, is perhaps a form of expression indispensable to the works which belong to an aesthetic of the sublime. In Proust, what is being eluded as the price to pay for this allusion is the identity of consciousness, a victim to the excess of time (*au trop de temps*). But in Joyce, it is the identity of writing which is the victim of an excess of the book (*au trop de livre*) or of literature.

Proust calls forth the unpresentable by means of a language unaltered in its syntax and vocabulary and of a writing which in many of its operators still belongs to the genre of novelistic narration. The literary institution, as Proust inherits it from Balzac and Flaubert, is admittedly subverted in that the hero is no longer a character but the inner consciousness of time, and in that the diegetic diachrony, already damaged by Flaubert, is here put in question because of the narrative voice. Nevertheless, the unity of the book, the odyssey of that consciousness, even if it is deferred from chapter to chapter, is not seriously challenged: the identity of the writing with itself throughout the labyrinth of the interminable narration is enough to connote such unity, which has been compared to that of *The Phenomenology of Mind*.

Joyce allows the unpresentable to become perceptible in his writing itself, in the signifier. The whole range of available narrative and even stylistic operators is put into play without concern for the unity of the whole, and new operators are tried. The grammar and vocabulary of literary language are no longer accepted as given; rather, they appear as academic forms, as rituals originating in piety (as Nietzsche said) which prevent the unpresentable from being put forward.

Here, then, lies the difference: modern aesthetics is an aesthetic of the sublime, though a nostalgic one. It allows the unpresentable to be put forward only as the missing contents; but the form, because of its recognizable consistency, continues to offer to the reader or viewer matter for solace and pleasure. Yet these sentiments do not constitute the real sublime sentiment, which is in an intrinsic combination of pleasure and pain: the pleasure that reason should exceed all presentation, the pain that imagination or sensibility should not be equal to the concept.

The postmodern would be that which, in the modern, puts forward the unpresentable in presentation itself; that which denies itself the solace of good forms, the consensus of a taste which would make it possible to share collectively the nostalgia for the unattainable; that which searches for new presentations, not in order to enjoy them but in order to impart a stronger sense of the unpresentable. A postmodern artist or writer is in the position of a philosopher: the text he writes, the work he produces are not in principle governed by preestablished rules, and they cannot be judged according to a determining judgment, by applying familiar categories to the text or to the work. Those rules and categories are what the work of art itself is looking for. The artist and the writer, then, are working without rules in order to formulate the rules of what *will have been done*. Hence the fact that work and text have the characters of an *event*; hence also, they always come too late for their author, or, what amounts to the same thing, their being put into work, their realization (*mise en oeuvre*) always begin too soon. *Post modern* would have to be understood according to the paradox of the future (*post*) anterior (*modo*).

It seems to me that the essay (Montaigne) is postmodern, while the fragment (*The Athaeneum*) is modern.

Finally, it must be clear that it is our business not to supply reality but to invent allusions to the conceivable which cannot be presented. And it is not to be expected that this task will effect the last reconciliation between language games (which, under the name of faculties, Kant knew to be separated by a chasm), and that only the transcendental illusion (that of Hegel) can hope to totalize them into a real unity. But Kant also knew that the price to pay for such an illusion is terror. The nineteenth and twentieth centuries have given us as much terror as we can take. We have paid a high enough price for the nostalgia of the whole and the one, for the reconciliation of the concept and the sensible, of the transparent and the communicable experience. Under the general demand for slackening and for appeasement, we can hear the mutterings of the desire for a return of terror, for the realization of the fantasy to seize reality. The answer is: Let us wage a war on totality; let us be witnesses to the unpresentable; let us activate the differences and save the honor of the name.

28

Jacques Derrida

(b. 1931)

Widely acknowledged to be one of the most controversial philosophers of the twentieth century, Jacques Derrida has been both denounced as a charlatan and acclaimed as a supremely original thinker in our time. His rejection of what he calls the 'logocentric' bias of Western philosophy has generated the strategies of 'deconstruction' almost synonymous with his name.

Derrida was born in Algeria in 1931, but came to Paris in the 1950s to study phenomenology, particularly the work of Husserl and Heidegger, with Emmanuel Levinas and Paul Ricoeur. During the 1960s and early 1970s, Derrida published several revolutionary volumes in rapid succession: *Edmund Husserl's 'Origin of Geometry': An Introduction* (1962), *Speech and Phenomena* (1967), *Of Grammatology* (1967), *Writing and Difference* (1967), *Dissemination* (1972), *Margins of Philosophy* (1972) and *Glas* (1974). Since that time Derrida has remained equally prolific, as indicated by the extensive bibliography of his works which follows. He has taught at the Ecole Normale Supérieure in Paris, as well as at Johns Hopkins University and Yale University in the United States. Permeating many disciplines outside academic philosophy, his ideas have gained wide currency in fields such as literary theory, sociology, feminist studies, psychoanalysis and linguistics.

Like Heidegger, Derrida attacks the 'metaphysics of presence' that he claims has dominated Western philosophy from the time of the Greeks. Based on the logic of identity and non-contradiction, this 'logocentric' prejudice narrowly confines 'meaning' to an origin centred on presence, 'what is' rather than 'what is not'. Although an appreciative reader of Husserl, Derrida strongly criticizes him for insisting that signification in language is primarily linked to consciousness, intentionality and perception. Taking his cue from a more Saussurean view of language, Derrida privileges *'différance'*, coining a neologism to suggest not only that which is different, but also that which is deferred. Meaning only emerges in a field that has already excluded what is absent. For Derrida, this realization has radical consequences. No longer can one rely on the essential stability of signs. A radical 'undecidability' surrounds all signification; there can be no absolute origin or site of meaning.

Derrida also battles against the 'phonocentric' bias that privileges speech over writing in the Western philosophical tradition. Beginning as far back as Plato, writing has been viewed as a poor substitute for the spoken word because the speaker is no longer present to 'correct' misunderstandings. However, Derrida challenges this trust in phonocentricity, pointing out that 'différance' exists even when we speak to ourselves with the ideal of self-presence as soliloquy. Thus, in speech there is still 'archi-writing', i.e. an essential difference between distinct (and absent) acoustic signifiers allowing for possible meaning. By contrast, a text exhibits an autonomy that openly admits it requires neither the presence of a speaking subject nor the referential presence of the 'matter' of the text.

Indeed, there is a Derridean scepticism regarding almost all of the priorities which dominate the Western philosophical tradition: presence over absence, speech over writing, sameness over difference, and eternity over finite temporality. By implementing his programme of deconstruction, Derrida attempts to challenge these priorities and gain a critical perspective on the canonical texts of this tradition, interrogating them for what has been left out as well as for what has been explicitly inscribed. Yet, he knows that 'deconstruction' cannot become the dominant paradigm that replaces all others, or he will have succeeded only in exchanging one logocentric model for another.

SELECT BIBLIOGRAPHY OF DERRIDA'S WORKS IN ENGLISH

Speech and Phenomena and Other Essays on Husserl's Theory of Signs, Evanston, Ill.: Northwestern University Press, 1973.

Of Grammatology, Baltimore: Johns Hopkins University Press, 1975.

Writing and Difference, Chicago: University of Chicago Press, 1978.

Dissemination, Chicago: University of Chicago Press, 1981.

Margins of Philosophy, Chicago: University of Chicago Press, 1982.

Positions, Chicago: University of Chicago Press, 1982.

Signéponge/Signsponge, New York: Columbia University Press, 1984.

Glas, Lincoln: University of Nebraska Press, 1986.

'Shibboleth', in S. Budick and G. Hartman (eds), *Midrash and Literature*, New Haven: Yale University Press, 1986.

The Post Card: From Socrates to Freud and Beyond, Chicago: University of Chicago Press, 1987.

The Truth in Painting, Chicago: University of Chicago Press, 1987.

The Ear of the Other: Otobiography, Transference, Translation: Texts and Discussions with Jacques Derrida, Lincoln: University of Nebraska Press, 1988.

Limited Inc., ed. G. Graff, Evanston, Ill.: Northwestern University Press, 1988.

Edmund Husserl's Origin of Geometry: An Introduction, rev. edn, Lincoln: University of Nebraska Press, 1989.

Memoires for Paul de Man, New York: Columbia University Press, 1989.

Of Spirit: Heidegger and the Question, Chicago: University of Chicago Press, 1989.

Acts of Literature, London: Routledge, 1992.

The Other Heading: Reflections on Today's Europe, Bloomington: Indiana University Press, 1992.

Aporias, Stanford: Stanford University Press, 1993.

Given Time, Chicago: University of Chicago Press, 1993.

Memoirs of the Blind, Chicago: University of Chicago Press, 1993.

The Gift of Death, Chicago: University of Chicago Press, 1995.

Différance

THE VERB 'TO differ' [*différer*] seems to differ from itself. On the one hand, it indicates difference as distinction, inequality, or discernibility; on the other, it expresses the interposition of delay, the interval of a *spacing* and *temporalizing* that puts off until 'later' what is presently denied, the possible that is presently impossible. Sometimes the *different* and sometimes the *deferred* correspond [in French] to the verb 'to differ'. This correlation, however, is not simply one between act and object, cause and effect, or primordial and derived.

In the one case 'to differ' signifies nonidentity; in the other case it signifies the order of the *same*. Yet there must be a common, although entirely differant [*différante*], root within the sphere that relates the two movements of differing to one another. We provisionally give the name *differance* to this *sameness* which is not *identical*: by the silent writing of its *a*, it has the desired advantage of referring to differing, *both* as spacing/temporalizing and as the movement that structures every dissociation.

As distinct from difference, differance thus points out the irreducibility of temporalizing (which is also temporalization – in transcendental language which is no longer adequate here, this would be called the constitution of primordial temporality – just as the term 'spacing' also includes the constitution of primordial spatiality). Differance is not simply active (any more than it is a subjective accomplishment); it rather indicates the middle voice, it precedes and sets up the opposition between passivity and activity. With its *a*, differance more properly refers to what in classical language would be called the origin or production of differences and the differences between differences, the *play* [*jeu*] of differences. Its locus and operation will therefore be seen wherever speech appeals to difference.

Differance is neither a *word* nor a *concept*. In it, however, we shall see the juncture – rather than the summation – of what has been most decisively inscribed in the thought of what is conveniently called our 'epoch': the difference of forces in Nietzsche, Saussure's principle of semiological difference, differing as the possibility of [neurone] facilitation, impression and delayed effect in Freud, difference as the irreducibility of the trace of the other in Levinas, and the ontic-ontological difference in Heidegger.

Reflection on this last determination of difference will lead us to consider differance as the *strategic* note or connection – relatively or provisionally *privileged* – which indicates the closure of presence, together with the closure of the conceptual order and denomination, a closure that is effected in the functioning of traces.

I shall speak, then, of a letter – the first one, if we are to believe the

From *Speech and Phenomena, and Other Essays on Husserl's Theory of Signs*, Evanston, Ill.: Northwestern University Press, 1973.

alphabet and most of the speculations that have concerned themselves with it.

I shall speak then of the letter *a*, this first letter which it seemed necessary to introduce now and then in writing the word 'difference'. This seemed necessary in the course of writing about writing, and of writing within a writing whose different strokes all pass, in certain respects, through a gross spelling mistake, through a violation of the rules governing writing, violating the law that governs writing and regulates its conventions of propriety. In fact or theory we can always erase or lessen this spelling mistake, and, in each case, while these are analytically different from one another but for practical purposes the same, find it grave, unseemly, or, indeed, supposing the greatest ingenuousness, amusing. Whether or not we care to quietly overlook this infraction, the attention we give it beforehand will allow us to recognize, as though prescribed by some mute irony, the inaudible but displaced character of this literal permutation. We can always act as though this makes no difference. I must say from the start that my account serves less to justify this silent spelling mistake, or still less to excuse it, than to aggravate its obtrusive character.

On the other hand, I must be excused if I refer, at least implicitly, to one or another of the texts that I have ventured to publish. Precisely what I would like to attempt to some extent (although this is in principle and in its highest degree impossible, due to essential *de jure* reasons) is to bring together an *assemblage* of the different ways I have been able to utilize – or, rather, have allowed to be imposed on me – what I will provisionally call the word or concept of differance in its new spelling. It is literally neither a word nor a concept, as we shall see. I insist on the word 'assemblage' here for two reasons: on the one hand, it is not a matter of describing a history, of recounting the steps, text by text, context by context, each time showing which scheme has been able to impose this graphic disorder, although this could have been done as well; rather, we are concerned with the *general system of all these schemata*. On the other hand, the word 'assemblage' seems more apt for suggesting that the kind of bringing-together proposed here has the structure of an interlacing, a weaving, or a web, which would allow the different threads and different lines of sense or force to separate again, as well as being ready to bind others together.

In a quite preliminary way, we now recall that this particular graphic intervention was conceived in the writing-up of a question about writing; it was not made simply to shock the reader or grammarian. Now, in point of fact, it happens that this graphic difference (the *a* instead of the *e*), this marked difference between two apparently vocalic notations, between vowels, remains purely graphic: it is written or read, but it is not heard. It cannot be heard, and we shall see in what respects it is also beyond the order of understanding. It is put forward by a silent mark, by a tacit monument, or, one might even say, by a pyramid – keeping in mind not only the capital form of the printed letter but also that passage from Hegel's *Encyclopaedia* where he compares the body of the sign to an Egyptian pyramid. The *a* of differance, therefore, is not heard; it remains silent, secret, and discreet, like a tomb.

It is a tomb that (provided one knows how to decipher its legend) is not far from signaling the death of the king.

It is a tomb that cannot even be made to resonate. For I cannot even let you know, by my talk, now being spoken before the Société Française de Philosophie, which difference I am talking about at the very moment I speak of it. I can only talk about this graphic difference by keeping to a very indirect speech about writing, and on the condition that I specify each time that I am referring to difference with an *e* or differance with an *a*. All of which is not going to simplify matters today, and will give us all a great deal of trouble when we want to understand one another. In any event, when I do specify which difference I mean – when I say 'with an *e*' or 'with an *a*' – this will refer irreducibly to a *written text*, a text governing my talk, a text that I keep in front of me, that I will read, and toward which I shall have to try to lead your hands and eyes. We cannot refrain here from going by way of a written text, from ordering ourselves by the disorder that is produced therein – and this is what matters to me first of all.

Doubtless this pyramidal silence of the graphic difference between the *e* and the *a* can function only within the system of phonetic writing and within a language or grammar historically tied to phonetic writing and to the whole culture which is inseparable from it. But I will say that it is just this – this silence that functions only within what is called phonetic writing – that points out or reminds us in a very opportune way that, contrary to an enormous prejudice, there is no phonetic writing. There is no purely and strictly phonetic writing. What is called phonetic writing can only function – in principle and *de jure*, and not due to some factual and technical inadequacy – by incorporating nonphonetic 'signs' (punctuation, spacing, etc.); but when we examine their structure and necessity, we will quickly see that they are ill-described by the concept of signs. Saussure had only to remind us that the play of difference was the functional condition, the condition of possibility, for every sign; and it is itself silent. The difference between two phonemes, which enables them to exist and to operate, is inaudible. The inaudible opens the two present phonemes to hearing, as they present themselves. If, then, there is no purely phonetic writing, it is because there is no purely phonetic phone. The difference that brings out phonemes and lets them be heard and understood [*entendre*] itself remains inaudible.

It will perhaps be objected that, for the same reasons, the graphic difference itself sinks into darkness, that it never constitutes the fullness of a sensible term, but draws out an invisible connection, the mark of an inapparent relation between two spectacles. That is no doubt true. Indeed, since from this point of view the difference between the *e* and the *a* marked in 'differance' eludes vision and hearing, this happily suggests that we must here let ourselves be referred to an order that no longer refers to sensibility. But we are not referred to intelligibility either, to an ideality not fortuitously associated with the objectivity of *theōrein* or understanding. We must be referred to an order, then, that resists philosophy's founding opposition between the sensible and the intelligible. The order that resists this opposition, that resists it because it sustains it, is designated in a movement of differance (with an *a*) between two differences or between two letters. This differance belongs neither to the voice nor to writing in the ordinary sense, and it takes place, like the strange space that will assemble us here for the course of an hour, *between* speech and writing and beyond the tranquil familiarity that binds us to one and to the other, reassuring us sometimes in the illusion that they are two separate things.

Now, how am I to speak of the *a* of differance? It is clear that it cannot be *exposed*. We can expose only what, at a certain moment, can become *present*, manifest; what can be shown, presented as a present, a being-present in its truth, the truth of a present or the presence of a present. However, if differance is (I also cross out the 'is') what makes the presentation of being-present possible, it never presents itself as such. It is never given in the present or to anyone. Holding back and not exposing itself, it goes beyond the order of truth on this specific point and in this determined way, yet is not itself concealed, as if it were something, a mysterious being, in the occult zone of a nonknowing. Any exposition would expose it to disappearing as a disappearance. It would risk appearing, thus disappearing.

Thus, the detours, phrases, and syntax that I shall often have to resort to will resemble – will sometimes be practically indiscernible from – those of negative theology. Already we had to note *that* differance *is not*, does not exist, and is not any sort of being-present (*on*). And we will have to point out everything *that* it *is not*, and, consequently, that it has neither existence nor essence. It belongs to no category of being, present or absent. And yet what is thus denoted as differance is not theological, not even in the most negative order of negative theology. The latter, as we know, is always occupied with letting a supraessential reality go beyond the finite categories of essence and existence, that is, of presence, and always hastens to remind us that, if we deny the predicate of existence to God, it is in order to recognize him as a superior, inconceivable, and ineffable mode of being. Here there is no question of such a move, as will be confirmed as we go along. Not only is differance irreducible to every ontological or theological – onto-theological – reappropriation, but it opens up the very space in which onto-theology – philosophy – produces its system and its history. It thus encompasses and irrevocably surpasses onto-theology or philosophy.

For the same reason, I do not know where *to begin* to mark out this assemblage, this graph, of differance. Precisely what is in question here is the requirement that there be a *de jure* commencement, an absolute point of departure, a responsibility arising from a principle. The problem of writing opens by questioning the *archē*. Thus what I put forth here will not be developed simply as a philosophical discourse that operates on the basis of a principle, of postulates, axioms, and definitions and that moves according to the discursive line of a rational order. In marking out differance, everything is a matter of strategy and risk. It is a question of strategy because no transcendent truth present outside the sphere of writing can theologically command the totality of this field. It is hazardous because this strategy is not simply one in the sense that we say that strategy orients the tactics according to a final aim, a *telos* or the theme of a domination, a mastery or an ultimate reappropriation of movement and field. In the end, it is a strategy without finality. We might call it blind tactics or empirical errance, if the value of empiricism did not itself derive all its meaning from its opposition to philosophical responsibility. If there is a certain errance in the tracing-out of differance, it no longer follows the line of logico-philosophical speech or that of its integral and symmetrical opposite, logico-empirical speech. The concept of *play* [*jeu*] remains beyond this opposition; on the eve and aftermath of philosophy, it designates the unity of chance and necessity in an endless calculus.

By decision and, as it were, by the rules of the game, then, turning this thought around, let us introduce ourselves to the thought of differance by way of the theme of strategy or strategem. By this merely strategic justification, I want to emphasize that the efficacy of this thematics of differance very well may, and even one day must, be sublated, i.e. lend itself, if not to its own replacement, at least to its involvement in a series of events which in fact it never commanded. This also means that it is not a theological thematics.

I will say, first of all, that differance, which is neither a word nor a concept, seemed to me to be strategically the theme most proper to think out, if not master (thought being here, perhaps, held in a certain necessary relation with the structional limits of mastery), in what is most characteristic of our 'epoch'. I start off, then, strategically, from the place and time in which 'we' are, even though my opening is not justifiable in the final account, and though it is always on the basis of differance and its 'history' that we can claim to know who and where 'we' are and what the limits of an 'epoch' can be.

Although 'differance' is neither a word nor a concept, let us nonetheless attempt a simple and approximative semantic analysis which will bring us in view of what is at stake [*en vue de l'enjeu*].

We do know that the verb 'to differ' [*différer*] (the Latin verb *differre*) has two seemingly quite distinct meanings; in the *Littré* dictionary, for example, they are the subject of two separate articles. In this sense, the Latin *differre* is not the simple translation of the Greek *diapherein*; this fact will not be without consequence for us in tying our discussion to a particular language, one that passes for being less philosophical, less primordially philosophical, than the other. For the distribution of sense in the Greek *diapherein* does not carry one of the two themes of the Latin *differre*, namely, the action of postponing until later, of taking into account, the taking-account of time and forces in an operation that implies an economic reckoning, a detour, a respite, a delay, a reserve, a representation – all the concepts that I will sum up here in a word I have never used but which could be added to this series: *temporalizing*. 'To differ' in this sense is to temporalize, to resort, consciously or unconsciously, to the temporal and temporalizing mediation of a detour that suspends the accomplishment or fulfillment of 'desire' or 'will', or carries desire or will out in a way that annuls or tempers their effect. We shall see, later, in what respects this temporalizing is also a temporalization and spacing, is space's becoming-temporal and time's becoming-spatial, is 'primordial constitution' of space and time, as metaphysics or transcendental phenomenology would call it in the language that is here criticized and displaced.

The other sense of 'to differ' [*différer*] is the most common and most identifiable, the sense of not being identical, of being other, of being discernible, etc. And in 'differents', whether referring to the alterity of dissimilarity or the alterity of allergy or of polemics, it is necessary that interval, distance, *spacing* occur among the different elements and occur actively, dynamically, and with a certain perseverence in repetition.

But the word 'difference' (with an *e*) could never refer to differing as temporalizing or to difference as *polemos*. It is this loss of sense that the word differance (with an *a*) will have to schematically compensate for. Differance can refer to the whole complex of its meanings at once, for it is immediately and irreducibly multivalent, something which will be important for the discourse I am trying to develop. It refers to this whole complex of meanings not only when it is supported by a language or interpretive context (like any signification), but it already does so somehow of itself. Or at least it does so more easily by itself than does any other word: here the *a* comes more immediately from the present participle [*différant*] and brings us closer to the action of 'differing' that is in progress, even before it has produced the effect that is constituted as different or resulted in difference (with an *e*). Within a conceptual system and in terms of classical requirements, differance could be said to designate the productive and primordial constituting causality, the process of scission and division whose differings and differences would be the constituted products or effects. But while bringing us closer to the infinitive and active core of differing, 'differance' with an *a* neutralizes what the infinitive denotes as simply active, in the same way that 'parlance' does not signify the simple fact of speaking, of speaking to or being spoken to. Nor is resonance the act of resonating. Here in the usage of our language we must consider that the ending *-ance* is undecided between active and passive. And we shall see why what is designated by 'differance' is neither simply active nor simply passive, that it announces or rather recalls something like the middle voice, that it speaks of an operation which is not an operation, which cannot be thought of either as a passion or as an action of a subject upon an object, as starting from an agent or from a patient, or on the basis of, or in view of, any of these *terms*. But philosophy has perhaps commenced by distributing the middle voice, expressing a certain intransitiveness, into the active and the passive voice, and has itself been constituted in this repression.

How are differance as temporalizing and differance as spacing conjoined?

Let us begin with the problem of signs and writing – since we are already in the midst of it. We ordinarily say that a sign is put in place of the thing itself, the present thing – 'thing' holding here for the sense as well as the referent. Signs represent the present in its absence; they take the place of the present. When we cannot take hold of or show the thing, let us say the present, the being-present, when the present does not present itself, then we signify, we go through the detour of signs. We take up or give signs; we make signs. The sign would thus be a deferred presence. Whether it is a question of verbal or written signs, monetary signs, electoral delegates, or political representatives, the movement of signs defers the moment of encountering the thing itself, the moment at which we could lay hold of it, consume or expend it, touch it, see it, have a present intuition of it. What I am describing here is the structure of signs as classically determined, in order to define – through a commonplace characterization of its traits – signification as the differance of temporalizing. Now this classical determination presupposes that the sign (which defers presence) is conceivable only *on the basis of* the presence that it defers and *in view of* the deferred presence one intends to reappropriate. Following this classical semiology, the substitution of the sign for the thing itself is both *secondary* and *provisional*: it is second in order after an original and lost presence, a presence from which the sign would be derived. It is provisional with respect to this final and missing presence, in view of which the sign would serve as a movement of mediation.

In attempting to examine these secondary and provisional aspects of the substitute, we shall no doubt catch sight of something like a primordial differance. Yet we could no longer even call it primordial or final, inasmuch as the characteristics of origin, beginning, *telos, eschaton*, etc., have always denoted presence – *ousia, parousia*, etc. To question the secondary and provisional character of the sign, to oppose it to a 'primordial' differance, would thus have the following consequences:

1 Differance can no longer be understood according to the concept of 'sign', which has always been taken to mean the representation of a presence and has been constituted in a system (of thought or language) determined on the basis of and in view of presence.

2 In this way we question the authority of presence or its simple symmetrical contrary, absence or lack. We thus interrogate the limit that has always constrained us, that always constrains us – we who inhabit a language and a system of thought – to form the sense of being in general as presence or absence, in the categories of being or beingness (*ousia*). It already appears that the kind of questioning we are thus led back to is, let us say, the Heideggerian kind, and that differance *seems* to lead us back to the ontic-ontological difference. But permit me to postpone this reference. I shall only note that between differance as temporalizing-temporalization (which we can no longer conceive within the horizon of the present) and what Heidegger says about temporalization in *Sein und Zeit* (namely, that as the transcendental horizon of the question of being it must be freed from the traditional and metaphysical domination by the present or the now) – between these two there is a close, if not exhaustive and irreducibly necessary, interconnection.

But first of all, let us remain with the semiological aspects of the problem to see how differance as temporalizing is conjoined with differance as spacing. Most of the semiological or linguistic research currently dominating the field of thought (whether due to the results of its own investigations or due to its role as a generally recognized regulative model) traces its genealogy, rightly or wrongly, to Saussure as its common founder. It was Saussure who first of all set forth the *arbitrariness of signs* and the *differential character* of signs as principles of general semiology and particularly of linguistics. And, as we know, these two themes – the arbitrary and the differential – are in his view inseparable. Arbitrariness can occur only because the system of signs is constituted by the differences between the terms, and not by their fullness. The elements of signification function not by virtue of the compact force of their cores but by the network of oppositions that distinguish them and relate them to one another. 'Arbitrary and differential', says Saussure, 'are two correlative qualities'.

As the condition for signification, this principle of difference affects the *whole sign*, that is, both the signified and the signifying aspects. The signified aspect is the concept, the ideal sense. The signifying aspect is what Saussure calls the material or physical (e.g. acoustical) 'image'. We do not here have to enter into all the problems these definitions pose. Let us only cite Saussure where it interests us:

> The conceptual side of value is made up solely of relations and differences with respect to the other terms of language, and the same can be said of its material side. . . . Everything that has been said up to this point boils down to this: in language there are only differences. Even more important: a difference generally implies positive terms between which the difference is set up; but in language

448

there are only differences *without positive terms*. Whether we take the signified or the signifier, language has neither ideas nor sounds that existed before the linguistic system, but only conceptual and phonic differences that have issued from the system. The idea or phonic substance that a sign contains is of less importance than the other signs that surround it.[1]

The first consequence to be drawn from this is that the signified concept is never present in itself, in an adequate presence that would refer only to itself. Every concept is necessarily and essentially inscribed in a chain or a system, within which it refers to another and to other concepts, by the systematic play of differences. Such a play, then – differance – is no longer simply a concept, but the possibility of conceptuality, of the conceptual system and process in general. For the same reason, differance, which is not a concept, is not a mere word; that is, it is not what we represent to ourselves as the calm and present self-referential unity of a concept and sound [*phonie*]. We shall later discuss the consequences of this for the notion of a word.

The difference that Saussure speaks about, therefore, is neither itself a concept nor one word among others. We can say this *a fortiori* for differance. Thus we are brought to make the relation between the one and the other explicit.

Within a language, within the *system* of language, there are only differences. A taxonomic operation can accordingly undertake its systematic, statistical, and classificatory inventory. But, on the one hand, these differences *play a role* in language, in speech as well, and in the exchange between language and speech. On the other hand, these differences are themselves *effects*. They have not fallen from the sky ready made; they are no more inscribed in a *topos noētos* than they are prescribed in the wax of the brain. If the word 'history' did not carry with it the theme of a final repression of differance, we could say that differences alone could be 'historical' through and through and from the start.

What we note as *differance* will thus be the movement of play that 'produces' (and not by something that is simply an activity) these differences, these effects of difference. This does not mean that the differance which produces differences is before them in a simple and in itself unmodified and indifferent present. Differance is the nonfull, nonsimple 'origin'; it is the structured and differing origin of differences.

Since language (which Saussure says is a classification) has not fallen from the sky, it is clear that the differences have been produced; they are the effects produced, but effects that do not have as their cause a subject or substance, a thing in general, or a being that is somewhere present and itself escapes the play of difference. If such a presence were implied (quite classically) in the general concept of cause, we would therefore have to talk about an effect without a cause, something that would very quickly lead to no longer talking about effects. I have tried to indicate a way out of the closure imposed by this system, namely, by means of the 'trace'. No more an effect than a cause, the 'trace' cannot of itself, taken outside the context, suffice to bring about the required transgression.

As there is no presence before the semiological difference or outside it, we can extend what Saussure writes about language to signs in general: 'Language is necessary in order for speech to be intelligible and to produce all of its effects; but the latter is necessary in order for language to be established; historically, the fact of speech always comes first'.[2]

Retaining at least the schema, if not the content, of the demand formulated by Saussure, we shall designate by the term *differance* the movement by which language, or any code, any system of reference in general, becomes 'historically' constituted as a fabric of differences. Here, the terms 'constituted', 'produced', 'created', 'movement', 'historically', etc., with all they imply, are not to be understood only in terms of the language of metaphysics, from which they are taken. It would have to be shown why the concepts of production, like those of constitution and history, remain accessories in this respect to what is here being questioned; this, however, would draw us too far away today, toward the theory of the representation of the 'circle' in which we seem to be enclosed. I only use these terms here, like many other concepts, out of strategic convenience and in order to prepare the deconstruction of the system they form at the point which is now most decisive. In any event, we will have understood, by virtue of the very circle we appear to be caught up in, that differance, as it is written here, is no more static than genetic, no more structural than historical. Nor is it any less so. And it is completely to miss the point of this orthographical impropriety to want to object to it on the basis of the oldest of metaphysical oppositions – for example, by opposing some generative point of view to a structuralist–taxonomic point of view, or conversely. These oppositions do not pertain in the least to differance; and this, no doubt, is what makes thinking about it difficult and uncomfortable.

If we now consider the chain to which 'differance' gets subjected, according to the context, to a certain number of nonsynonymic substitutions, one will ask why we resorted to such concepts as 'reserve', 'protowriting', 'prototrace', 'spacing', indeed to 'supplement' or '*pharmakon*', and, before long, to 'hymen', etc.

Let us begin again. Differance is what makes the movement of signification possible only if each element that is said to be 'present', appearing on the stage of presence, is related to something other than itself but retains the mark of a past element and already lets itself be hollowed out by the mark of its relation to a future element. This trace relates no less to what is called the future than to what is called the past, and it constitutes what is called the present by this very relation to what it is not, to what it absolutely is not; that is, not even to a past or future considered as a modified present. In order for it to be, an interval must separate it from what it is not; but the interval that constitutes it in the present must also, and by the same token, divide the present in itself, thus dividing, along with the present, everything that can be conceived on its basis, that is, every being – in particular, for our metaphysical language, the substance or subject. Constituting itself, dynamically dividing itself, this interval is what could be called *spacing*; time's becoming-spatial or space's becoming-temporal (*temporalizing*). And it is this constitution of the present as a 'primordial' and irreducibly nonsimple, and, therefore, in the strict sense nonprimordial, synthesis of traces, retentions, and protentions (to reproduce here, analogically and provisionally, a phenomenological and transcendental language that will presently be revealed as inadequate) that I propose to call protowriting, prototrace, or difference. The latter (is) (both) spacing (and) temporalizing.

Given this (active) movement of the (production of) difference without origin, could we not, quite simply and without any neographism, call it *differentiation*? Among other confusions, such a word would suggest some organic unity, some primordial and homogeneous unity, that would eventually come to be divided up and take on difference as an event. Above all, formed on the verb 'to differentiate', this word would annul the economic signification of detour, temporalizing delay, 'deferring'. I owe a remark in passing to a recent reading of one of Koyré's texts entitled 'Hegel at Jena'.[3] In that text, Koyré cites long passages from the Jena *Logic* in German and gives his own translation. On two occasions in Hegel's text he encounters the expression 'differente Beziehung'. This word (*different*), whose root is Latin, is extremely rare in German and also, I believe, in Hegel, who instead uses *verschieden* or *ungleich*, calling difference *Unterschied* and qualitative variety *Verschiedenheit*. In the Jena *Logic*, he uses the word *different* precisely at the point where he deals with time and the present. Before coming to Koyré's valuable remark, here are some passages from Hegel, as rendered by Koyré:

> The infinite, in this simplicity is – as a moment opposed to the self-identical – the negative. In its moments, while the infinite presents the totality to (itself) and in itself, (it is) excluding in general, the point or limit; but in this, its own (action of) negating, it relates itself immediately to the other and negates itself. The limit or moment of the present (der Gegen-wart), the absolute 'this' of time or the now, is an absolutely negative simplicity, absolutely excluding all multiplicity from itself, and by this very fact is absolutely determined; it is not an extended whole or quantum within itself (and) which would in itself also have an undetermined aspect or qualitative variety, which of itself would be related, indifferently (gleichgültig) or externally to another, but on the contrary, this is an absolutely different relation of the simple.[4]

And Koyré specifies in a striking note: 'Different relation: *differente Beziehung*. We could say: differentiating relation.' And on the following page, from another text of Hegel, we can read: '*Diese Beziehung ist Gegenwart, als eine differente Beziehung*' (This relation is [the] present, as a different relation). There is another note by Koyré: 'The term "*different*" is taken here in an active sense.'

Writing 'differing' or 'differance' (with an *a*) would have had the utility of making it possible to translate Hegel on precisely this point with no further qualifications – and it is a quite decisive point in his text. The translation would be, as it always should be, the transformation of one language by another. Naturally, I maintain that the word 'differance' can be used in other ways, too; first of all, because it denotes not only the activity of primordial difference but also temporalizing detour of deferring. It has, however, an even more important usage. Despite the very profound affinities that differance thus written has with Hegelian speech (as it should be read), it can, at a certain point, not exactly break with it, but rather work a sort of displacement with regard to it. A definite rupture with Hegelian language would make no sense, nor would it be at all likely; but this displacement is both infinitesimal and radical. I have tried to indicate the extent of this displacement elsewhere; it would be difficult to talk about it with any brevity at this point.

Differences are thus 'produced' – differed – by differance. But *what* differs, or *who* differs? In other words, *what is* differance? With this question we attain another stage and another source of the problem.

What differs? Who differs? What is differance?

If we answered these questions even before examining them as questions, even before going back over them and questioning their form (even what seems to be most natural and necessary about them), we would fall below the level we have now reached. For if we accepted the form of the question in its own sense and syntax ('What?', 'What is?', 'Who is?'), we would have to admit that differance is derived, supervenient, controlled, and ordered from the starting point of a being-present, one capable of being something, a force, a state, or power in the world, to which we could give all kinds of names: a *what*, or being-present as a *subject*, a *who*. In the latter case, notably, we would implicitly admit that the being-present (for example, as a self-present being or consciousness) would eventually result in differing: in delaying or in diverting the fulfillment of a 'need' or 'desire', or in differing from itself. But in none of these cases would such a being-present be 'constituted' by this differance.

Now if we once again refer to the semiological difference, what was it that Saussure in particular reminded us of? That 'language [which consists only of differences] is not a function of the speaking subject.' This implies that the subject (self-identical or even conscious of self-identity, self-conscious) is inscribed in the language, that he is a 'function' of the language. He becomes a *speaking* subject only by conforming his speech – even in the aforesaid 'creation', even in the aforesaid 'transgression' – to the system of linguistic prescriptions taken as the system of differences, or at least to the general law of differance, by conforming to that law of language which Saussure calls 'language without speech'. 'Language is necessary for the spoken word to be intelligible and so that it can produce all of its effects.'[5]

If, by hypothesis, we maintain the strict opposition between speech and language, then differance will be not only the play of differences within the language but the relation of speech to language, the detour by which I must also pass in order to speak, the silent token I must give, which holds just as well for linguistics in the strict sense as it does for general semiology; it dictates all the relations between usage and the formal schema, between the message and the particular code, etc. Elsewhere I have tried to suggest that this differance within language, and in the relation between speech and language, forbids the essential dissociation between speech and writing that Saussure, in keeping with tradition, wanted to draw at another level of his presentation. The use of language or the employment of any code which implies a play of forms – with no determined or invariable substratum – also presupposes a retention and protention of differences, a spacing and temporalizing, a play of traces. This play must be a sort of inscription prior to writing, a protowriting without a present origin, without an *archē*. From this comes the systematic crossing-out of the *archē* and the transformation of general semiology into a grammatology, the latter performing a critical work upon everything within semiology – right down to its matrical concept of signs – that retains any metaphysical presuppositions incompatible with the theme of differance.

We might be tempted by an objection: to be sure, the subject becomes a *speaking* subject only by dealing with the system of linguistic differences; or again, he becomes a *signifying* subject (generally by speech or other signs) only by entering into the system of differences. In this sense, certainly, the speaking or signifying subject would not be self-present, insofar as he speaks or signifies, except for the play of linguistic or semiological differance. But can we not conceive of a presence and self-presence of the subject before speech or its signs, a subject's self-presence in a silent and intuitive consciousness?

Such a question therefore supposes that prior to signs and outside them, and excluding every trace and differance, something such as consciousness is possible. It supposes, moreover, that, even before the distribution of its signs in space and in the world, consciousness can gather itself up in its own presence. What then is consciousness? What does 'consciousness' mean? Most often in the very form of 'meaning' ['*vouloir-dire*'], consciousness in all its modifications is conceivable only as self-presence, a self-perception of presence. And what holds for consciousness also holds here for what is called subjective existence in general. Just as the category of subject is not and never has been conceivable without reference to presence as *hypokeimenon* or *ousia*, etc., so the subject as consciousness has never been able to be evinced otherwise than as self-presence. The privilege accorded to consciousness thus means a privilege accorded to the present; and even if the transcendental temporality of consciousness is described in depth, as Husserl described it, the power of synthesis and of the incessant gathering-up of traces is always accorded to the 'living present'.

This privilege is the ether of metaphysics, the very element of our thought insofar as it is caught up in the language of metaphysics. We can only de-limit such a closure today by evoking this import of presence, which Heidegger has shown to be the onto-theological determination of being. Therefore, in evoking this import of presence, by an examination which would have to be of a quite peculiar nature, we question the absolute privilege of this form or epoch of presence in general, that is, consciousness as meaning [*vouloir-dire*] in self-presence.

We thus come to posit presence – and, in particular, consciousness, the being-next-to-itself of consciousness – no longer as the absolutely matrical form of being but as a 'determination' and an 'effect'. Presence is a determination and effect within a system which is no longer that of presence but that of differance; it no more allows the opposition between activity and passivity than that between cause and effect or in-determination and determination, etc. This system is of such a kind that even to designate consciousness as an effect or determination – for strategic reasons, reasons that can be more or less clearly considered and systematically ascertained – is to continue to operate according to the vocabulary of that very thing to be de-limited.

Before being so radically and expressly Heideggerian, this was also Nietzsche's and Freud's move, both of whom, as we know, and often in a very similar way, questioned the self-assured certitude of consciousness. And is it not remarkable that both of them did this by starting out with the theme of differance?

This theme appears almost literally in their work, at the most crucial places. I shall not expand on this here; I shall only recall that for Nietzsche 'the important main activity is unconscious' and that consciousness is the effect of forces whose essence, ways, and modalities are not peculiar to it. Now force itself is never present; it is only a play of differences and quantities. There would be no force in general without the difference between forces; and here the difference in quantity counts more than the content of quantity, more than the absolute magnitude itself.

> Quantity itself therefore is not separable from the difference in quantity. The difference in quantity is the essence of force, the relation of force with force. To fancy two equal forces, even if we grant them opposing directions, is an approximate and crude illusion, a statistical dream in which life is immersed, but which chemistry dispels.[6]

Is not the whole thought of Nietzsche a critique of philosophy as active indifference to difference, as a system of reduction or adiaphoristic repression? Following the same logic – logic itself – this does not exclude the fact that philosophy lives *in* and *from* differance, that is thereby blinds itself to the *same*, which is not the identical. The same is precisely differance (with an *a*), as the diverted and equivocal passage from one difference to another, from one term of the opposition to the other. We could thus take up all the coupled oppositions on which philosophy is constructed, and from which our language lives, not in order to see opposition vanish but to see the emergence of a necessity such that one of the terms appears as the differance of the other, the other as 'differed' within the systematic ordering of the same (e.g. the intelligible as differing from the sensible, as sensible differed; the concept as differed-differing intuition, life as differing-differed matter; mind as differed-differing life; culture as differed-differing nature; and all the terms designating what is other than *physis* – *technē*, *nomos*, society, freedom, history, spirit, etc. – as *physis* differed or *physis* differing: *physis in differance*). It is out of the unfolding of this 'same' as differance that the sameness of difference and of repetition is presented in the eternal return.

In Nietzsche, these are so many themes that can be related with the kind of symptomatology that always serves to diagnose the evasions and ruses of anything disguised in its differance. Or again, these terms can be related with the entire thematics of active interpretation, which substitutes an incessant deciphering for the disclosure of truth as a presentation of the thing itself in its presence, etc. What results is a cipher without truth, or at least a system of ciphers that is not dominated by truth value, which only then becomes a function that is understood, inscribed, and circumscribed.

We shall therefore call differance this 'active' (in movement) discord of the different forces and of the differences between forces which Nietzsche opposes to the entire system of metaphysical grammar, wherever that system controls culture, philosophy, and science.

It is historically significant that this diaphoristics, understood as an energetics or an economy of forces, set up to question the primacy of presence *qua* consciousness, is also the major theme of Freud's thought; in his work we find another diaphoristics, both in the form of a theory of ciphers or traces and an energetics. The questioning of the authority of consciousness is first and always differential.

The two apparently different meanings of differance are tied together in Freudian theory: differing [*le différer*] as discernibility, distinction, deviation, diastem, *spacing*; and deferring [*le différer*] as detour, delay, relay, reserve, *temporalizing*. I shall recall only that:

1 The concept of trace (*Spur*), of facilitation (*Bahnung*), of forces of facilitation are, as early as the composition of the *Entwurf*, inseparable from the concept of difference. The origin of memory and of the psyche as a memory in general (conscious or unconscious) can only

be described by taking into account the difference between the facilitation thresholds, as Freud says explicitly. There is no facilitation [*Bahnung*] without difference and no difference without a trace.

2   All the differences involved in the production of unconscious traces and in the process of inscription (*Niederschrift*) can also be interpreted as moments of differance, in the sense of 'placing on reserve'. Following a schema that continually guides Freud's thinking, the movement of the trace is described as an effort of life to protect itself *by deferring* the dangerous investment, by constituting a reserve (*Vorrat*). And all the conceptual oppositions that furrow Freudian thought relate each concept to the other like movements of a detour, within the economy of differance. The one is only the other deferred, the one differing from the other. The one is the other in differance, the one is the differance from the other. Every apparently rigorous and irreducible opposition (for example, that between the secondary and primary) is thus said to be, at one time or another, a 'theoretical fiction'. In this way again, for example (but such an example covers everything or communicates with everything), the difference between the pleasure principle and the reality principle is only differance as detour (*Aufschieben, Aufschub*). In *Beyond the Pleasure Principle*, Freud writes:

> Under the influence of the ego's instincts of self-preservation, the pleasure principle is replaced by the reality principle. This latter principle does not abandon the intention of ultimately obtaining pleasure, but it nevertheless demands and carries into effect the postponement of satisfaction, the abandonment of a number of possibilities of gaining satisfaction and the temporary toleration of unpleasure as a step on the long indirect road (*Aufschub*) to pleasure.[7]

Here we touch on the point of greatest obscurity, on the very enigma of differance, on how the concept we have of it is divided by a strange separation. We must not hasten to make a decision too quickly. How can we conceive of differance as a systematic detour which, within the element of the same, always aims at either finding again the pleasure or the presence that had been deferred by (conscious or unconscious) calculation, and, *at the same time*, how can we, on the other hand, conceive of differance as the relation to an impossible presence, as an expenditure without reserve, as an irreparable loss of presence, an irreversible wearing-down of energy, or indeed as a death instinct and a relation to the absolutely other that apparently breaks up any economy? It is evident – it is evidence itself – that system and nonsystem, the same and the absolutely other, etc., cannot be conceived *together*.

If differance is this inconceivable factor, must we not perhaps hasten to make it evident, to bring it into the philosophical element of evidence, and thus quickly dissipate its mirage character and illogicality, dissipate it with the infallibility of the calculus we know well – since we have recognized its place, necessity, and function within the structure of differance? What would be accounted for philosophically here has already been taken into account in the system of differance as it is here being calculated. I have tried elsewhere, in a reading of Bataille,[8] to indicate what might be the establishment of a rigorous, and in a new sense 'scientific', *relating* of a 'restricted economy' – one having nothing to do with an unreserved expenditure, with death, with being exposed to nonsense, etc. – to a 'general economy' or system that, so to speak, *takes account of* what is unreserved. It is a relation between a differance that is accounted for and a differance that fails to be accounted for, where the establishment of a pure presence, without loss, is one with the occurrence of absolute loss, with death. By establishing this relation between a restricted and a general system, we shift and recommence the very project of philosophy under the privileged heading of Hegelianism.

The economic character of differance in no way implies that the deferred presence can always be recovered, that it simply amounts to an investment that only temporarily and without loss delays the presentation of presence, that is, the perception of gain or the gain of perception. Contrary to the metaphysical, dialectical, and 'Hegelian' interpretation of the economic movement of differance, we must admit a game where whoever loses wins and where one wins and loses each time. If the diverted presentation continues to be somehow definitively and irreducibly withheld, this is not because a particular present remains hidden or absent, but because differance holds us in a relation with what exceeds (though we necessarily fail to recognize this) the alternative of presence or absence. A certain alterity – Freud gives it a metaphysical name, the unconscious – is definitively taken away from every process of presentation in which we would demand for it to be shown forth in person. In this context and under this heading, the unconscious is not, as we know, a hidden, virtual, and potential self-presence. It is differed – which no doubt means that it is woven out of differences, but also that it sends out, that it delegates, representatives or proxies; but there is no chance that the mandating subject 'exists' somewhere, that it is present or is 'itself', and still less chance that it will become conscious. In this sense, contrary to the terms of an old debate, strongly symptomatic of the metaphysical investments it has always assumed, the 'unconscious' can no more be classed as a 'thing' than as anything else; it is no more of a thing than an implicit or masked consciousness. This radical alterity, removed from every possible mode of presence, is characterized by irreducible aftereffects, by delayed effects. In order to describe them, in order to read the traces of the 'unconscious' traces (there are no 'conscious' traces), the language of presence or absence, the metaphysical speech of phenomenology, is in principle inadequate.

The structure of delay (*retardement: Nachträglichkeit*) that Freud talks about indeed prohibits our taking temporalization (temporalizing) to be a simple dialectical complication of the present; rather, this is the style of transcendental phenomenology. It describes the living present as a primordial and incessant synthesis that is constantly led back upon itself, back upon its assembled and assembling self, by retentional traces and protentional openings. With the alterity of the 'unconscious', we have to deal not with the horizons of modified presents – past or future – but with a 'past' that has never been nor will ever be present, whose 'future' will never be produced or reproduced in the form of presence. The concept of trace is therefore incommensurate with that of retention, that of the becoming-past of what had been present. The trace cannot be conceived – nor, therefore, can differance – on the basis of either the present or the presence of the present.

A past that has never been present: with this formula Emmanuel Levinas designates (in ways that are, to be sure, not those of psycho-analysis) the trace and the enigma of absolute alterity, that is, the Other [autrui]. At least within these limits, and from this point of view, the thought of differance implies the whole critique of classical ontology undertaken by Levinas. And the concept of trace, like that of differance, forms – across these different traces and through these differences between traces, as understood by Nietzsche, Freud, and Levinas (these 'authors' names' serve only as indications) – the network that sums up and perme-ates our 'epoch' as the de-limitation of ontology (of presence).

The ontology of presence is the ontology of beings and beingness. Everywhere, the dominance of beings is solicited by differance – in the sense that *sollicitare* means, in old Latin, to shake all over, to make the whole tremble. What is questioned by the thought of differance, there-fore, is the determination of being in presence, or in beingness. Such a question could not arise and be understood without the difference between Being and beings opening up somewhere. The first consequence of this is that differance is not. It is not a being-present, however excellent, unique, principal, or transcendent one makes it. It commands nothing, rules over nothing, and nowhere does it exercise any authority. It is not marked by a capital letter. Not only is there no realm of differance, but differance is even the subversion of every realm. This is obviously what makes it threatening and necessarily dreaded by everything in us that desires a realm, the past or future presence of a realm. And it is always in the name of a realm that, believing one sees it ascend to the capital letter, one can reproach it for wanting to rule.

Does this mean, then, that differance finds its place within the spread of the ontic-ontological difference, as it is conceived as the 'epoch' conceives itself within it, and particularly 'across' the Heideggerian meditation, which cannot be gotten around?

There is no simple answer to such a question.

In one particular respect, differance is, to be sure, but the historical and epochal *deployment* of Being or of the ontological difference. The *a* of differance marks the *movement* of this deployment.

And yet, is not the thought that conceives the *sense* or *truth* of Being, the determination of differance as ontic-ontological difference – difference conceived within the horizon of the question of *Being* – still an intra-metaphysical effect of differance? Perhaps the deployment of differance is not only the truth or the epochality of Being. Perhaps we must try to think this *unheard-of* thought, this silent tracing, namely, that the history of Being (the thought of which is committed to the Greco-Western logos), as it is itself produced across the ontological difference, is only one epoch of the *diapherein.* Then we could no longer even call it an 'epoch', for the concept of epochality belongs within history understood as the history of Being. Being has always made 'sense,' has always been conceived or spoken of as such, only by dissimulating itself in beings; thus, in a particular and very strange way, differance (is) 'older' than the ontological difference or the truth of Being. In this age it can be called the play of traces. It is a trace that no longer belongs to the horizon of Being but one whose sense of Being is borne and bound by this play; it is a play of traces or differance that has no sense and is not, a play that does not belong. There is no support to be found and no depth to be had for this bottomless chessboard where being is set in play.

It is perhaps in this way that the Heraclitean play of the *hen diapheron heautōi*, of the one differing from itself, of what is in difference with itself, already becomes lost as a trace in determining the *diapherein* as ontological difference.

To think through the ontological difference doubtless remains a difficult task, a task whose statement has remained nearly inaudible. And to prepare ourselves for venturing beyond our own logos, that is, for a differance so violent that it refuses to be stopped and examined as the epochality of Being and ontological difference, is neither to give up this passage through the truth of Being, nor is it in any way to 'criticize', 'contest', or fail to recognize the incessant necessity for it. On the contrary, we must stay within the difficulty of this passage; we must repeat this passage in a rigorous reading of metaphysics, wherever metaphysics serves as the norm of Western speech, and not only in the texts of 'the history of philosophy'. Here we must allow the trace of whatever goes beyond the truth of Being to appear/disappear in its fully rigorous way. It is a trace of something that can never present itself; it is itself a trace that can never be presented, that is, can never appear and manifest itself as such in its phenomenon. It is a trace that lies beyond what profoundly ties fundamental ontology to phenomenology. Like differance, the trace is never presented as such. In presenting itself it becomes effaced; in being sounded it dies away, like the writing of the *a*, inscribing its pyramid in differance.

We can always reveal the precursive and secretive traces of this movement in metaphysical speech, especially in the contemporary talk about the closure of ontology, i.e. through the various attempts we have looked at (Nietzsche, Freud, Levinas) – and particularly in Heidegger's work.

The latter provokes us to question the essence of the present, the presence of the present.

What is the present? What is it to conceive the present in its presence?

Let us consider, for example, the 1946 text entitled 'Der Spruch des Anaximander'. Heidegger there recalls that the forgetting of Being forgets about the difference between Being and beings:

> But the point of Being (*die Sache des Seins*) is to be the Being *of* beings. The linguistic form of this enigmatic and multivalent genitive designates a genesis (*Genesis*), a provenance (*Herkunft*) of the pre*sent* from pre*sence* (*des Anwesenden aus dem Anwesen*). But with the unfolding of these two, the essence (*Wesen*) of this provenance remains hidden (*verborgen*). Not only is the essence of this provenance not thought out, but neither is the simple relation between pre*sence* and pre*sent* (*Anwesen und Anwesenden*). Since the dawn, it seems that pre*sence* and being-pre*sent* are each separately something. Imperceptibly, pre*sence* becomes itself a pre*sent*. . . . The essence of pre*sence* (*Das Wesen des Anwesens*), and thus the difference between pre*sence* and pre*sent*, is forgotten. *The forgetting of Being is the forgetting of the difference between Being and beings.*[9]

In recalling the difference between Being and beings (the ontological difference) as the difference between presence and present, Heidegger puts forward a proposition, indeed, a group of propositions; it is not our intention here to idly or hastily 'criticize' them but rather to convey them with all their provocative force.

Let us then proceed slowly. What Heidegger wants to point out is that the difference between Being and beings, forgotten by metaphysics, has disappeared without leaving a trace. The very trace of difference has sunk from sight. If we admit that differance (is) (itself) something other than presence and absence, if it *traces*, then we are dealing with the forgetting of the difference (between Being and beings), and we now have to talk about a disappearance of the trace's trace. This is certainly what this passage from 'Der Spruch des Anaximander' seems to imply:

> The forgetting of Being is a part of the very essence of Being, and is concealed by it. The forgetting belongs so essentially to the destination of Being that the dawn of this destination begins precisely as an unconcealment of the pre*sent* in its pre*sence*. This means: the history of Being begins by the forgetting of Being, in that Being retains its essence, its difference from beings. Difference is wanting; it remains forgotten. Only what is differentiated – the present and presence (*das Anwesende und das Anwesen*) – becomes uncovered, but not *insofar as* it is differentiated. On the contrary, the matinal trace (*die frühe Spur*) of difference effaces itself from the moment that presence

appears as a being-present (*das Anwesen wie ein Anwesendes erscheint*) and finds its provenance in a supreme (being)-present (*in einem höchsten Anwesenden*).[10]

The trace is not a presence but is rather the simulacrum of a presence that dislocates, displaces, and refers beyond itself. The trace has, properly speaking, no place, for effacement belongs to the very structure of the trace. Effacement must always be able to overtake the trace; otherwise it would not be a trace but an indestructible and monumental substance. In addition, and from the start, effacement constitutes it as a trace – effacement establishes the trace in a change of place and makes it disappear in its appearing, makes it issue forth from itself in its very position. The effacing of this early trace (*die frühe Spur*) of difference is therefore 'the same' as its tracing within the text of metaphysics. This metaphysical text must have retained a mark of what it lost or put in reserve, set aside. In the language of metaphysics the paradox of such a structure is the inversion of the metaphysical concept which produces the following effect: the present becomes the sign of signs, the trace of traces. It is no longer what every reference refers to in the last instance; it becomes a function in a generalized referential structure. It is a trace, and a trace of the effacement of a trace.

In this way the metaphysical text is *understood*; it is still readable, and remains to be read. It proposes *both* the monument and the mirage of the trace, the trace as simultaneously traced and effaced, simultaneously alive and dead, alive as always to stimulate even life in its preserved inscription; it is a pyramid.

Thus we think through, without contradiction, or at least without granting any pertinence to such contradiction, what is perceptible and imperceptible about the trace. The 'matinal trace' of difference is lost in an irretrievable invisibility, and yet even its loss is covered, preserved, regarded, and retarded. This happens in a text, in the form of presence.

Having spoken about the effacement of the matinal trace, Heidegger can thus, in this contradiction without contradiction, consign or countersign the sealing of the trace. We read on a little further:

> The difference between Being and beings, however, can in turn be experienced as something forgotten only if it is already discovered with the presence of the present (*mit dem Anwesen des Anwesenden*) and if it is thus sealed in a trace (*so eine Spur geprägt hat*) that remains preserved (*gewahrt bleibt*) in the language which Being appropriates.[11]

Further on still, while meditating upon Anaximander's τὸ χρεών, translated as *Brauch* (sustaining use), Heidegger writes the following:

> Dispensing accord and deference (*Fug und Ruch verfügend*), our sustaining use frees the pre*sent* (*das Anwesende*) in its sojourn and

sets it free every time for its sojourn. But by the same token the present is equally seen to be exposed to the constant danger of hardening in the insistence (*in das blosse Beharren verhärtet*) out of its sojourning duration. In this way sustaining use (*Brauch*) remains itself and at the same time an abandonment (*Aushändigung*: handing-over) of presence (*des Anwesens) in den Un-fug*, to discord (disjointedness). Sustaining use joins together the dis- (*Der Brauch fügt das Un-*).[12]

And it is at the point where Heidegger determines *sustaining use as trace* that the question must be asked: can we, and how far can we, think of this trace and the *dis* of differance as *Wesen des Seins*? Doesn't the *dis* of difference refer us beyond the history of Being, beyond our language as well, and beyond everything that can be named by it? Doesn't it call for – in the language of being – the necessarily violent transformation of this language by an entirely different language?

Let us be more precise here. In order to dislodge the 'trace' from its cover (and whoever believes that one tracks down some *thing*? – one tracks down tracks), let us continue reading this passage:

> The translation of τὸ χρεών by 'sustaining use' (*Brauch*) does not derive from cogitations of an etymologico-lexical nature. The choice of the word 'sustaining use' derives from an antecedent *trans*lation (*Über*setzen) of the thought that attempts to conceive difference in the deployment of Being (*im Wesen des Seins*) toward the historical beginning of the forgetting of Being. The word 'sustaining use' is dictated to thought in the apprehension (*Erfahrung*) of the forgetting of Being. Tὸ χρεών properly names a trace (*Spur*) of what remains to be conceived in the word 'sustaining use', a trace that quickly disappears (*alsbald verschwindet*) into the history of Being, in its world-historical unfolding as Western metaphysics.[13]

How do we conceive of the outside of a text? How, for example, do we conceive of what stands opposed to the text of Western metaphysics? To be sure, the 'trace that quickly disappears into the history of Being, . . . as Western metaphysics', escapes all the determinations, all the names it might receive in the metaphysical text. The trace is sheltered and thus dissimulated in these names; it does not appear in the text as the trace 'itself'. But this is because the trace itself could never itself appear as such. Heidegger also says that difference can never appear *as such*: 'Lichtung des Unterschiedes kann deshalb auch nicht bedeuten, dass der Unterschied als der Unterschied erscheint'. There is no essence of differance; not only can it not allow itself to be taken up into the *as such* of its name or its appearing, but it threatens the authority of the *as such* in general, the thing's presence in its essence. That there is no essence of difference at this point also implies that there is neither Being nor truth to the play of writing, *insofar* as it involves differance.

For us, differance remains a metaphysical name; and all the names that it receives from our language are still, so far as they are names, metaphysical. This is particularly so when they speak of determining differance as the difference between presence and present (*Anwesen/ Anwesend*), but already and especially so when, in the most general way, they speak of determining differance as the difference between Being and beings.

'Older' than Being itself, our language has no name for such a differance. But we 'already know' that if it is unnamable, this is not simply provisional; it is not because our language has still not found or received this *name*, or because we would have to look for it in another language, outside the finite system of our language. It is because there is no name for this, not even essence or Being – not even the name 'differance', which is not a name, which is not a pure nominal unity, and continually breaks up in a chain of different substitutions.

'There is no name for this': we read this as a truism. What is unnamable here is not some ineffable being that cannot be approached by a name; like God, for example. What is unnamable is the play that brings about the nominal effects, the relatively unitary or atomic structures we call names, or chains of substitutions for names. In these, for example, the nominal effect of 'differance' is itself involved, carried off, and reinscribed, just as the false beginning or end of a game is still part of the game, a function of the system.

What we do know, what we could know if it were simply a question of knowing, is that there never has been and never will be a unique word, a master name. This is why thinking about the letter *a* of differance is not the primary prescription, nor is it the prophetic announcement of some imminent and still unheard-of designation. There is nothing kerygmatic about this 'word' so long as we can perceive its reduction to a lower-case letter.

There will be no unique name, not even the name of Being. It must be conceived without *nostalgia*; that is, it must be conceived outside the myth of the purely maternal or paternal language belonging to the lost fatherland of thought. On the contrary, we must *affirm* it – in the sense that Nietzsche brings affirmation into play – with a certain laughter and with a certain dance.

After this laughter and dance, after this affirmation that is foreign to any dialectic, the question arises as to the other side of nostalgia, which I will call Heideggerian *hope*. I am not unaware that this term may be somewhat shocking. I venture it, all the same, without excluding any of its implications, and shall relate it to what seems to me to be retained of metaphysics in 'Der Spruch des Anaximander', namely, the quest for the proper word and the unique name. In talking about the 'first word of Being' (*das frühe Wort des Seins*: τὸ χρεών), Heidegger writes,

> The relation to the pre*sent*, unfolding its order in the very essence of pre*sence*, is unique (*ist eine einzige*). It is pre-eminently incomparable to any other relation; it belongs to the uniqueness of Being itself

(*Sie gehört zur Einzigkeit des Seins selbst*). Thus, in order to name what is deployed in Being (*das Wesende des Seins*), language will have to find a single word, the unique word (*ein einziges, das einzige Wort*). There we see how hazardous is every word of thought (every thoughtful word: *denkende Wort*) that addresses itself to Being (*das dem Sein zugesprochen wird*). What is hazarded here, however, is not something impossible, because Being speaks through every language; everywhere and always.[14]

Such is the question: the marriage between speech and Being in the unique word, in the finally proper name. Such is the question that enters into the affirmation put into play by differance. The question bears (upon) each of the words in this sentence: 'Being / speaks / through every language; / everywhere and always /.'

NOTE

1 Ferdinand de Saussure, *Cours de linguistique générale*, ed. C. Bally and A. Sechehaye (Paris: Payot, 1916); English translation by Wade Baskin, *Course in General Linguistics* (New York: Philosophical Library, 1959), pp. 117–18, 120.
2 *Course in General Linguistics*, p. 18.
3 Alexandre Koyré, 'Hegel à Iéna', *Revue d'histoire et de philosophie religieuse*, XIV (1934), 420–58; reprinted in Koyré, *Etudes d'histoire de la pensée philosophique* (Paris: Armand Colin, 1961), pp. 135–73.
4 Koyré, *Etudes d'histoire*, pp. 153–4.
5 De Saussure, *Course in General Linguistics*, p. 37.
6 G. Deleuze, *Nietzsche et la philosophie* (Paris: Presses Universitaires de France, 1970), p. 49.
7 Freud, *Complete Psychological Works*, XVIII, 10.
8 Derrida, *L'Ecriture et la différence*, pp. 369–407.
9 Martin Heidegger, *Holzwege* (Frankfurt: V. Klostermann, 1957), pp. 335–6.
10 Ibid., p. 336.
11 Ibid.
12 Ibid., pp. 339–40.
13 Ibid., p. 340.
14 Ibid., pp. 337–8.

Chronology

	Continental philosophy – Roots and dialogue	The arts, science and politics
1781	Kant, *Critique of Pure Reason*	Austria abolishes serfdom
1788	Kant, *Critique of Practical Reason*	First convicts shipped from Britain to Australia
1789		Storming of the Paris Bastille: the French Revolution begins
1790	Kant, *Critique of Judgment*	
1807	Hegel, *Phenomenology of Spirit*	British abolish slave trade throughout the Empire
1811		Luddite riots in England against mechanization in the textile industry
1814		Congress of Vienna (1814–15) restores Europe's crowned heads to power following Napoleon's defeat
1818	Schopenhauer, *The World as Will and Representation*	
1825	Saint-Simon, *The New Christianity*	
1843	Kierkegaard, *Fear and Trembling, Either/Or* and *Repetition*	
1844	Kierkegaard, *The Concept of Dread* Marx, *The Paris Manuscripts*	Heine, *Deutschland: Ein Wintermärchen*
1845	Marx, *Theses on Feuerbach* Marx and Engels, *The Holy Family*	
1848	Marx and Engels, *Communist Manifesto*	Revolutions throughout Europe

	Continental philosophy – Roots and dialogue	The arts, science and politics
1851	Proudhon, *General Idea of the Revolution in the 19th Century*	Verdi, *Rigoletto*
1862	Brentano, *On the Manifold Sense of Being in Aristotle*	Hugo, *Les Misérables* Gatling invents machine gun Bismarck becomes Prussian Prime Minister
1867	Marx, *Capital*	Scholes invents typewriter
1871	Darwin, *The Descent of Man*	Paris Commune crushed Wilhelm I declares German Empire
1873	Nietzsche, *Untimely Meditations* Stumpf, *On the Psychological Origin of the Idea of Space*	Rimbaud, *A Season in Hell*
1874	Brentano, *Psychology from an Empirical Standpoint*	
1876		Bell invents telephone
1879	Frege, *The Foundations of Arithmetic*	Ibsen, *A Doll's House*
1882	Nietzsche, *The Gay Science*	Wagner, *Parsifal*
1883	Dilthey, *Introduction to the Human Sciences* Mach, *The Science of Mechanics*	
1885		Cézanne, *Mont S. Victoire* Van Gogh, *The Potato-Eaters* and *The Sunflowers*
1887	Husserl, *On the Concept of Number* Nietzsche, *On the Genealogy of Morals*	Daimler and Benz develop car engine Italy and Ethiopia at war
1891	Husserl, *Philosophy of Arithmetic*	Edison patents the Kinetoscope and the Kinetograph
1893	Durkheim, *The Division of Labour in Society*	
1895	Freud, *Studies on Hysteria*	Roentgen discovers X-rays
1900	Freud, *The Interpretation of Dreams* Husserl, *Logical Investigations, I*	Mahler, *Fourth Symphony* Max Planck's quantum theory
1903		Wright Brothers' first aeroplane flight

466

	Continental philosophy – Roots and dialogue	The arts, science and politics
1903		Russian opposition splits into Bolsheviks and Mensheviks Emmeline Pankhurst forms Women's Social and Political Union
1905	Weber, *The Protestant Ethic and the Spirit of Capitalism*	Fauvism Einstein's Special Theory of Relativity St Petersburg 'Bloody Sunday': troops fire on crowd, triggering general strike and revolt
1907	Husserl, *The Idea of Phenomenology* W. James, *Pragmatism*	Picasso, *Les Demoiselles d'Avignon*
1909	Croce, *Pragmatic Philosophy*	Marinetti, *Futurist Manifesto* Henry Ford introduces assembly line production Peary reaches North Pole
1911	Bergson, 'Philosophical Intuition'	German expressionism Amundsen reaches South Pole
1913	Husserl, *Ideas: General Introduction to Pure Phenomenology* Jung, *Psychology of the Unconscious* Luxemburg, *The Accumulation of Capital*	Proust, *Remembrance of Things Past* Bohr's model of the atom
1914		First World War begins
1916	Saussure, *Course in General Linguistics*	Dada movement in Zurich German offensive on Western front
1917	Lenin, *State and Revolution*	October Revolution in Russia
1918		Malevich, *White Square on a White Background* Browning invents automatic rifle First World War ends
1919	Wittgenstein, *Tractatus Logico-Philosophicus*	Bauhaus architecture and design Treaty of Versailles Luxemburg murdered in Berlin League of Nations founded
1920	Freud, *Beyond the Pleasure Principle*	Weimar Republic in Germany Irish Civil War

	Continental philosophy – Roots and dialogue	The arts, science and politics
1922	Bergson, *Duration and Simultaneity*	Eliot, *The Waste Land* Joyce, *Ulysses* Mussolini's fascists march on Rome
1923	Cassirer, *The Philosophy of Symbolic Forms* (3 vols, 1923–9) Korsch, *Marxism and Philosophy* Lukács, *History and Class Consciousness*	Corbusier, *Vers une architecture* Hitler imprisoned after abortive Munich putsch
1924		Breton, *Surrealist Manifesto* Schoenberg, 12-tone *Suite for Piano* Stalin succeeds Lenin
1927	Heidegger, *Being and Time*	Woolf, *To the Lighthouse* Heisenberg's 'Uncertainty Principle' First transatlantic flight by Lindbergh
1929	Heidegger, *What is Metaphysics?* and *Kant and the Problem of Metaphysics* Husserl, *Formal and Transcendental Logic* Mannheim, *Ideology and Utopia* Piaget, *The Child's Concept of the World*	Moravia, *Gli indifferenti* Bakhtin, *Problems of Dostoyevsky's Poetics* Wall Street crash leads to worldwide economic crisis
1930	Freud, *Civilization and Its Discontents* Ortega y Gasset, *The Revolt of the Masses*	Buñuel and Dali, *L'Age d'or* Whittle develops jet engine
1931	Husserl, *Cartesian Meditations* Jaspers, *Man in the Modern Age*	
1933	Kojève's seminars on Hegel's *Phenomenology* (1933–9)	Malraux, *The Human Condition* Hitler appointed German Chancellor
1935		Watson-Watt discovers radar Mao Tse-tung's communists begin their 'Long March'
1936	Benjamin, 'The Work of Art in the Age of Mechanical Reproduction'	Spanish civil war (1936–9) Moscow show trials

	Continental philosophy – Roots and dialogue	The arts, science and politics
1936	Husserl, *The Crisis of European Sciences and Transcendental Phenomenology*	
1937		Picasso, *Guernica*
1938	Bachelard, *The Psychoanalysis of Fire*	Sartre, *Nausea* Hitler annexes Austria (*Anschluß*)
1939	Sartre, *Sketch for a Theory of Emotions*	Germany invades Poland: the Second World War begins
1940		Seaborg discovers plutonium Nazis occupy Paris Japan joins Axis Powers Trotsky assassinated in Mexico
1941	Marcuse, *Reason and Revolution* Whorf, *Language, Thought and Reality* (1941–56)	Germany invades Soviet Union Japan bombs Pearl Harbour: USA enters Second World War
1942	Merleau-Ponty, *The Structure of Comportment*	Camus, *The Outsider* German troops defeated at Stalingrad and in North Africa
1943	Sartre, *Being and Nothingness*	Musil, *The Man Without Qualities* Italian government surrenders
1944	Adorno and Horkheimer, *Dialectic of Enlightenment*	Allied forces land in Normandy Paris and Brussels liberated

1945	Bataille, *On Nietzsche*
	Merleau-Ponty, *Phenomenology of Perception*
		USA drops atomic bombs on
		  Hiroshima and Nagasaki
		Partisans assassinate Mussolini
		Hitler commits suicide
		Allies agree on spheres of
		  influence at Yalta conference

1946	Sartre, *Existentialism and Humanism*	Rossellini, *Rome Open City* Eckert and Mauchly develop electronic computer UN replaces League of Nations Nuremburg trials French Indo-China War begins
1947	de Beauvoir, *Ethics of Ambiguity* Gramsci, *Letters from Prison* Heidegger, 'Letter on Humanism' Horkheimer, *Eclipse of Reason* Levinas, *Existence and Existents*	Pollock, *Full Fathom Five*

	Continental philosophy – Roots and dialogue	The arts, science and politics
1948	Adorno, *Philosophy of Modern Music* Gramsci, *Prison Notebooks* (6 vols, 1948–51) Merleau-Ponty, *Sense and Non-Sense*	Orwell, *1984* De Sica, *Bicycle Thieves* Carlson invents xerography, Goldmark the long-playing record and Bardeen, Brattain and Schockley the transistor Soviet blockage of West Berlin State of Israel declared
1949	de Beauvoir, *The Second Sex* Weil, *The Need for Roots*	Germany is divided into the Federal Republic and the German Democratic Republic
1950	Austin, *How to Do Things with Words* Marcel, *The Mystery of Being*	Blanchot, *The Space of Literature* Ionesco, *The Bald Soprano* Korean War begins
1951	Adorno, *Minima Moralia* Arendt, *The Origins of Totalitarianism* Camus, *The Rebel*	Beckett, *Molloy* and *Malone Dies* Dali, *Christ of St John of the Cross*
1952		Buñuel, *El* European Coal and Steel Community implemented
1953	Barthes, *Writing Degree Zero* Heidegger, *Introduction to Metaphysics* Lacan, 'The Function of Language in Psychoanalysis' ('Rome Discourse') and *Seminar I* (26 seminars, 1953–78) Wittgenstein, *Philosophical Investigations*	Beckett, *Waiting for Godot* Crick and Watson establish molecular structure of DNA Stalin dies
1954	Heidegger, *Discourse on Thinking*	French defeat at Dien Bien Phu
1955	Lévi-Strauss, *Tristes Tropiques* Marcuse, *Eros and Civilization*	Pincus invents contraceptive pill
1956		Soviet troops crush Hungarian uprising
1957	Barthes, *Mythologies* Bataille, *Eroticism* Chomsky, *Syntactic Structures*	Stockhausen, *Gruppen* USSR launch first Sputnik Treaty of Rome establishes common European market (EEC)

Continental philosophy – Roots and dialogue	The arts, science and politics
1958 Arendt, *The Human Condition* Lévi-Strauss, *Structural Anthropology*	Primo Levi, *If This Is a Man*
1959 Bloch, *The Principle of Hope*	Godard, *Breathless* Truffaut, *The 400 Blows* Duras and Resnais, *Hiroshima Mon Amour* Fidel Castro overthrows Batista's government in Cuba
1960 Gadamer, *Truth and Method* Merleau-Ponty, *Signs* Ricoeur, *The Symbolism of Evil*	Fellini, *La Dolce Vita* Maiman invents laser
1961 Fanon, *The Wretched of the Earth* Heidegger, *Nietzsche* (2 vols) Levinas, *Totality and Infinity*	Robbe-Grillet and Resnais, *Last Year in Marienbad* Berlin Wall divides East from West
1962 Deleuze, *Nietzsche and Philosophy* Derrida, *Husserl's 'Origin of Geometry'*	Warhol, *Campbell's Soup Cans 200* Algeria gains independence from France Cuban missile crisis
1963 Arendt, *On Revolution* Habermas, *Theory and Praxis*	Celan, *Die Niemandsrose* J. F. Kennedy assassinated
1964 Barthes, *Elements of Semiology* Lévi-Strauss, *The Raw and the Cooked* Marcuse, *One-dimensional Man*	USA openly enters Vietnam War in support of South Vietnam
1965 Althusser, *For Marx* Bachelard, *The Poetics of Space* Foucault, *Madness and Civilization* and *Discipline and Punish* Ricoeur, *Freud and Philosophy: An Essay on Interpretation*	Venturi and Jencks inaugurate postmodernist architecture Malcolm X assassinated
1966 Adorno, *Negative Dialectics* Chomsky, *Cartesian Linguistics* Foucault, *The Order of Things* Greimas, *Structural Semantics* Lacan, *Ecrits*	Chinese government launches 'cultural revolution' UN imposes economic sanctions on Rhodesia
1967 Derrida, *Speech and Phenomena*, *Of Grammatology* and *Writing and Difference*	France vetoes British application to join EEC Arab–Israeli Six-day War

	Continental philosophy – Roots and dialogue	The arts, science and politics
1967	Horkheimer, *Critique of Instrumental Reason*	
1968	Althusser and Balibar, *Reading Capital* Habermas, *Knowledge and Human Interests*	Martin Luther King assassinated Riots and strikes in Paris spark student revolts throughout Europe Soviet troops invade Czechoslovakia to halt 'Prague Spring' reforms
1969	Blanchot, *Infinite Conversation* Foucault, *The Archaeology of Knowledge* Kristeva, *Semeiotiké*	US astronauts land on moon
1970	Barthes, *S/Z* Kuhn, *The Structure of Scientific Revolutions*	
1971	de Man, *Blindness and Insight* Habermas, *Legitimation Crisis* Hassan, *The Postmodern Turn* Rawls, *A Theory of Justice*	Communist China joins UN, and Taiwan is expelled
1972	Baudrillard, *For a Critique of the Political Economy of the Sign* Bourdieu, *Outline of a Theory of Practice* Deleuze and Guattari, *Anti-Oedipus* Derrida, *Dissemination* Marcuse, *Counter-Revolution and Revolt*	Bertolucci, *Last Tango in Paris*
1973	Bataille, *Inner Experiences* Bloom, *The Anxiety of Influence* Geertz, *The Interpretation of Cultures*	Britain, Ireland and Denmark join European Community Paris peace settlement ends US involvement in Vietnam OPEC countries restrict oil supplies, causing the first oil crisis
1974	Derrida, *Glas* Irigaray, *Speculum of the Other Woman* Kristeva, *Revolution in Poetic Language*	Watergate scandal

	Continental philosophy – Roots and dialogue	The arts, science and politics
1975	Barthes, *The Pleasure of the Text* Castoriadis, *The Social Imaginary* Cixous and Clement, *The Newly Born Woman* Feyerabend, *Against Method*	General Franco dies in Spain

1976	Eco, *A Theory of Semiotics*
	Foucault, *The History of Sexuality*
	    (3 vols, 1976–84)
	Gadamer, *Philosophical
	    Hermeneutics*
		Mao Tse-tung dies

1977	Derrida, *Limited, Inc.*
	Irigaray, *This Sex Which Is Not
	    One*
		French *nouveaux philosophes*
		    movement (Levy, Benoist,
		    Glucksmann)
		Czech Charta 77 movement

1978	Castoriadis, *Crossroads in the Labyrinth* Derrida, *Truth in Painting* Marcuse, *The Aesthetic Dimension*	

1979	Baudrillard, *Seduction*
	de Man, *Allegories of Reading*
	Lyotard, *The Postmodern Condition*
	    and *Just Gaming (Au Juste)*
		Fassbinder, *Lili Marlene*
		First direct elections for European
		    Parliament

1980	Kristeva, *Powers of Horror*
	Le Doeuff, *The Philosophical
	    Imaginary*
	Rorty, *Philosophy and the Mirror
	    of Nature*
	Vattimo, *The Adventure of
	    Difference*
	Williams, *Problems in Culture
	    and Materialism*
		Eco, *The Name of the Rose*
		Solidarity movement confronts
		    Polish government

1981	Baudrillard, *Simulations*
	Habermas, *Theory of
	    Communicative Action* (2 vols)
	Jameson, *The Political Unconscious*
		Rushdie, *Midnight's Children*
		Greece joins EEC as tenth
		    member state
		First US space shuttle mission

1983	Habermas, *Moral Consciousness
	    and Communicative Action*
	Lyotard, *The Differend*
	Said, *The World, the Text, and the
	    Critic*
		Indira Ghandi assassinated

	Continental philosophy – Roots and dialogue	The arts, science and politics
1984	Eco, *Semiotics and the Philosophy of Language* Giddens, *The Constitution of Society: Outline of a Theory of Structuration*	Kundera, *The Unbearable Lightness of Being*
1985	Benhabib, *Critique, Norm and Utopia* Habermas, *The Philosophical Discourse of Modernity* Taminiaux, *Dialectic and Difference* Vattimo, *The End of Modernity*	Gorbachev becomes leader of Soviet Communist Party
1986		'Challenger' space shuttle explodes on take-off Chernobyl nuclear disaster in USSR
1987	Derrida, *Psyché: Inventions of the Other, The Post Card* and *Schibboleth*	Calvino, *The Literature Machine* USSR and USA agree to reduce nuclear weapons
1988	Habermas, *Postmetaphysical Thinking* Lyotard, *The Inhuman* Vattimo, *The Transparent Society*	Anderson and Rosenfeld investigate neurocomputing
1989		Fall of the Berlin Wall
1990		Santa Fe Institute studies chaos, entropy and complexity Nelson Mandela freed after 27 years' imprisonment in South Africa Iraqi forces invade Kuwait
1991	Derrida, *Given Time* Jameson, *Postmodernism, or the Cultural Logic of Late Capitalism* Kristeva, *Strangers to Ourselves* Rorty, *Philosophical Papers* Said, *Musical Elaborations*	Enzensberger, *Europe in Ruins* Soviet Union dissolved UN forces drive Iraq from Kuwait
1992	Benhabib, *Situating the Self* Habermas, *Facticity and Validity* Honneth, *The Struggle for Recognition* Ricoeur, *Lectures I and II* (1991–2)	Break-up of Yugoslavia: Croats, Serbs and Bosnians at war

	Continental philosophy – Roots and dialogue	The arts, science and politics
1993	Derrida, *Specters of Marx* Kofman, *Explosion 2* Lyotard, *The Postmodern Contradiction* Levinas, *God, Death and Time*	Ratification of Maastricht Treaty on European Union
1994		Civil war in Rwanda: government forces kill an estimated 500,000 in indiscriminate massacres
1995	Derrida, *The Gift of Death*	France resumes nuclear tests programme

Index